BATTLES OVER FREE TRADE

CONTENTS OF THE EDITION

VOLUME 1
General Introduction
By Mark Duckenfield

The Advent of Free Trade, 1776–1846
Edited by Gordon Bannerman and Cheryl Schonhardt-Bailey

VOLUME 2
The Consolidation of Free Trade, 1847–1878
Edited by Gordon Bannerman and Anthony Howe

VOLUME 3
The Challenge of Economic Nationalism, 1879–1939
Edited by Anthony Howe and Mark Duckenfield

VOLUME 4
The Emergence of Multilateral Trade, 1940–2006
Edited by Mark Duckenfield

Index

BATTLES OVER FREE TRADE

General Editor: Mark Duckenfield

Volume 1
The Advent of Free Trade, 1776–1846

EDITED BY
Gordon Bannerman and Cheryl Schonhardt-Bailey

LONDON AND NEW YORK

First published 2008 by Pickering & Chatto (Publishers) Limited

Published 2016 by Routledge
2 Park Square, Milton Park, Abingdon, Oxfordshire OX14 4RN
711 Third Avenue, New York, NY 10017, USA

First issued in paperback 2015

Routledge is an imprint of the Taylor & Francis Group, an informa business

Copyright © Taylor & Francis 2008
Copyright © Editorial material Gordon Bannerman and Cheryl Schonhardt-Bailey

All rights reserved, including those of translation into foreign languages.
No part of this book may be reprinted or reproduced or utilised in any form or
by any electronic, mechanical, or other means, now known or hereafter
invented, including photocopying and recording, or in any information storage
or retrieval system, without permission in writing from the publishers.

Notice:
Product or corporate names may be trademarks or registered trademarks, and
are used only for identification and explanation without intent to infringe.

BRITISH LIBRARY CATALOGUING IN PUBLICATION DATA

Battles over free trade: Anglo-American experiences with international trade,
1776–2006
1. Free trade – History
I. Duckenfield, Mark
382.7'1'09

ISBN-13: 978-1-138-66049-6 (pbk)
ISBN-13: 978-1-1387-5032-6 (hbk)
ISBN-13: 978-1-85196-935-7 (set)

Typeset by Pickering & Chatto (Publishers) Limited

CONTENTS

General Introduction	xi
Abbreviations	xxiii
Introduction	xxv

Tentative Moves towards Free Trade, 1778–86   1

Anglo-Irish Relations and Irish Free Trade Agitation of 1779–85

Motion respecting Trade in Ireland, 19 January 1779, *Cobbett's Parliamentary Debates* (1778–80)	7
'Debate in the Commons on the State of the Trade and Commerce of Ireland', 15 February 1779, *Cobbett's Parliamentary Debates* (1778–80)	9
Sir James Caldwell to Lord George Germain, 28 September 1779, in *Report on the Manuscripts of Mrs. Stopford-Sackville* (1904–10)	12
Speech of the Lord Lieutenant to the Irish Parliament, Dublin Castle, 12 October 1779, *Annual Register* (1780)	13
'Debate in the Commons on Lord North's Propositions for the Relief of the Trade of Ireland', 13 December 1779, *Cobbett's Parliamentary Debates* (1778–80)	14
John Hely Hutchinson, *The Commercial Restraints of Ireland, Considered in a Series of Letters to a Noble Lord* (1779)	23
William Eden, *A Letter to the Earl of Carlisle from William Eden Esq. on the Representation of Ireland respecting a Free Trade* (1779)	33

Anglo-French Commercial Treaty of 1786

'Commerce with France. Observations on, Office' ([*c.* late 1785])	44
Minutes of the Committee of Trade, 14 March 1786	50
William Eden to Lord Carmarthen, 6 June 1786, in *The Journal and Correspondence of William, Lord Auckland*, ed. G. Hogge (1861–2)	52
William Pitt to William Eden, 12 September 1786 (extract), in *The Journal and Correspondence of William, Lord Auckland*, ed. G. Hogge (1861–2)	53

William Pitt to the Marquis of Stafford, 27 August 1786, in *The Diaries and Correspondence of the Right Hon. George Rose*, ed. L. V. Harcourt (1860)   55

William Eden to Robert Liston, 27 September 1786   56

Ralph Woodford to Robert Liston, 24 October 1786   57

Daniel Hailes to the Marquis of Carmarthen, 25 October 1786   58

Ralph Woodford to Robert Liston, 29 December 1786, Liston Papers, National Library of Scotland, MS 5545, fols 151–2.   64

A Letter from a Manchester Manufacturer to the Right Honourable Charles James Fox, on his Political Opposition to the Commercial Treaty with France (1787)   65

Trade as an Instrument of War, 1793–1812   69

The Continental System

'Abstract of the Treaty between Great Britain and the United States of America', *Annual Register* (1795)   75

'Southwark Petition', *Annual Register* (1795)   79

George Sinclair to Henry Dundas, 9 November 1796   81

On the Continental System, following the Berlin Decree, 20 November 1806, *Annual Register* (1806)   82

The British Response: Orders in Council

James Stephen to Spencer Perceval, 5 December 1807   85

'Orders in Council; or, An Examination of the Justice, Legality, and Policy of the New System of Commercial Regulations', *Edinburgh Review* (1808)   88

James Stephen to Spencer Perceval, 23 May 1808   101

'Financial Situation of England and France', *Examiner* (1810)   102

Prince Regent in Council, Orders in Council and War with America, enclosed in Castlereagh to Mr Russell, 23 June 1812, *Parliamentary Papers* (1812–13)   104

Mr Foster to Viscount Castlereagh, 20 June 1812, enclosing Madison's Declaration of War on Britain, 18 June 1812, *Parliamentary Papers* (1812–13)   105

[James Stephen], *A Key to the Orders in Council* (1812)   106

Madame de Stael Holstein, *An Appeal to the Nations of Europe Against the Continental System* (1813)   121

Divergent Paths: Britain and America, 1812–30   129

Post-War Protection and the United States

H. U. Addington to George Canning, Washington, 30 May 1824 (extract), in 'Papers relative to American Tariffs', *Parliamentary Papers* (1828) — 137

Report of the Committee on Commerce, 22 May 1824, in 'Papers relative to American Tariffs', *Parliamentary Papers* (1828) — 140

Address of the Committee on Behalf of the General Convention of Agriculturists and Manufacturers, and Others Friendly to the Encouragement of the Domestic Industry of the United States, Assembled at Harrisburg, 30 July 1827, in 'Papers relative to American Tariffs', *Parliamentary Papers* (1828) — 141

Charles Richard Vaughan to the Earl of Dudley, 27 April 1828, in 'Papers relative to American Tariffs', *Parliamentary Papers* (1828) — 143

'The American Tariff', *Edinburgh Review* (1828) — 144

Britain and Cautious Reciprocity

'Merchants' Petition of 1820 in Favour of Free Trade', in *Revised Report of the Proceedings at the Dinner of 31st May, 1876, Held in Celebration of the Hundredth Year of the Publication of the 'Wealth of Nations'* (1876) — 162

Edinburgh Petition for Free Trade, 20 April 1820, *Caledonian Mercury*, 29 April 1820 — 166

William Huskisson, Speech on the 'Foreign Commerce of the Country', 25 March 1825, *Hansard* (1825) — 168

Vote of Thanks from Manchester Chamber of Commerce to Huskisson, 16 July 1828; and Huskisson to Manchester Chamber of Commerce, 20 July 1828, in *The Speeches of the Right Honourable William Huskisson, with a Biographical Memoir* (1831) — 188

Solomon Atkinson, *The Effects of the New System of Free Trade upon our Shipping, Colonies and Commerce, Exposed* (1827) — 190

Henry Stephens, *A Letter Addressed to the Landowners and Tenantry of the County of Forfar* (1827) — 202

The Mechanic in his Own Defence; or Word About with Henry Stephens, Esq. of Balmadies (1827) — 222

A Movement Halted: International Perspective 1830–42 — 237

Anglo-French Commercial Relations

John Bowring, First Report on the Commercial Relations between France and Britain, *Parliamentary Papers* (1834) — 243

Chamber of Commerce of Boulogne-sur-Mer to the Minister of Commerce ([c. 1834]), in John Bowring, Second Report on the Commercial Relations between France and Britain, *Parliamentary Papers* (1835) — 246

Correspondence between Havre Chamber of Commerce and the Minister of Commerce, 14 and 18 October 1834, *Parliamentary Papers* (1835) 252

'First Report of Messrs. Villiers and Bowring', *Westminster Review* (1834) 254

Britain and the Zollverein

Minute of the Board of Trade, 17 January 1826, relative to the Commercial Relations between Great Britain and Prussia, December 1825–January 1826, *Parliamentary Papers* (1839) 260

Lord Palmerston to the Earl of Minto, 17 January 1834 266

'The Prussian League', *British and Foreign Review* (1842) 268

The Corn Laws: The Evolution of British Commercial Policy, 1832–46 281

Elite Debate on the Corn Laws in the 1830s

Ebenezer Elliott, 'An Address to the People of England, on the Corn Laws', *Tait's Edinburgh Magazine* (1834) 289

'Anti Corn-Law Association', *Dundee, Perth, and Cupar Advertiser*, 16 May 1834 297

'The Corn Laws', *British and Foreign Review* (1836) 299

Richard Cobden, 'Modern History of the Corn Laws', *Anti Corn-Law Circular* (1839) 319

From the Politicians to the Populace: Civil Society and Repeal of the Corn Laws, 1838–46

Petition of the President, Vice President and Directors of the Chamber of Commerce and Manufactures of Manchester, 20 January 1838, in *Appendix to the Report of the Select Committee on Public Petitions* (1837–8) 331

Richard Cobden to John Norton, 23 August 1838 333

'Dilemmas on the Corn Law Question', *Blackwood's Magazine* (1839) 334

'Petitions' and 'Our Weapons of War', *Anti Corn-Law Circular* (1840) 344

'Support of the Anti Corn-Law League by the Working Classes', *Anti Corn-Law Circular* (1840) 346

'Address of the Metropolitan Anti Corn-Law Association', *Anti Corn-Law Circular* (1840) 349

'Manifestation of Public Feeling on the Bread Tax', *Anti Corn-Law Circular* (1840) 353

'Corn-Law Agitation Humbug', *Chartist Circular* (1840) 355

'The Bread-Taxing Bishops and the Bible-Reading People', *Anti Corn-Law Circular* (1840) 356

'Petition! Petition! Petition!', *Anti Corn-Law Circular* (1840) 359

'Mr. John Gladstone's Remedy for the Distress of the Working Classes', *Liverpool Mercury*, 21 May 1841 — 361

Protectionist Editorial, *Chelmsford Chronicle*, 28 May 1841 — 364

H. N. Burroughes and E. Wodehouse, Joint Election Address to the Electors of East Norfolk, *Norfolk Chronicle and Norwich Gazette*, 12 June 1841 — 366

John Bowring, Election Address, *Bolton Chronicle*, 26 June 1841 — 367

Richard Cobden to George Wilson, 25 September 1841 — 369

'America and the British Corn Law. Compiled from the Work of Mr. John Curtis of Ohio', *The Anti-Bread-Tax Almanack* (1842) — 370

'Corn Laws are Potato Laws', *The Anti-Bread-Tax Almanack* (1842) — 373

Petition of Inhabitants of Manchester, *Manchester Times, and Lancashire and Cheshire Gazette*, 11 March 1843 — 375

First Annual Meeting of the Agricultural Protection Society for Great Britain and Ireland, *Morning Herald*, 14 December 1844 — 376

Lord Palmerston to the Earl of Minto, 27 December 1845 — 380

P. Bennet, Speech to Central Suffolk Agricultural Protection Association, *Bury and Suffolk Herald*, 21 January 1846 — 381

'The Corn Laws as a Buttress for the Aristocracy', *Economist* (1846) — 383

Richard Cobden to William Rathbone, 2 February 1846 — 386

French Reaction to the Reduction of British Duties on Brandy and Silk, *Kentish Gazette*, 10 February 1846 — 387

House of Lords Protest against the Corn Bill, 25 June 1846, *Hansard* (1846) — 388

'The Ghost of a Dead Monopoly!', *Economist* (1846) — 391

Copyrights and Permissions — 395

GENERAL INTRODUCTION

Debates over economic policy have long been a staple of nations' foreign economic policy and battles over free trade have formed a crucial part in linking domestic political and economic conflicts to the international arena. 'Free trade' poses an intriguing historical case as its fluctuations over the past two centuries are in many ways a mirror on the ebbs and flows of the world economy and the spread of the Industrial Revolution from Europe to the rest of the world. At its heart, globalization is the increased exposure of domestic societies to international economic, political and social forces. Along with the rapidity of foreign direct investment, lower barriers to trade are one of the most prominent features of this aspect of globalization. Since the Second World War, the growth in international trade has been steadily out-pacing growth in world output and the share of most countries' economies exposed to international competition is now quite considerable – even in the relatively large economies of the G-8 countries.

We use 1776 as our start date, not to imply that this year was somehow the 'birth-date' of free trade or ideas about free trade, but rather because it provides a useful point of convergence between the intellectual history of economic thought in the publication of Adam Smith's *An Inquiry into the Nature and Causes of the Wealth of Nations* and the political crisis triggered by the North American separatist group known as the Continental Congress. Although Smith's ideas had been around for some time, 1776 marked their widespread dissemination. Likewise, the American colonies had been in a state of unrest for the better part of a decade over the economic restrictions of mercantilist legislation and the lack of political representation in Britain's governing institutions. The year 1776 marked the crisis point when they made the collective decision to sever all political ties with the mother country and pursue political independence. Britain did not immediately adopt free trade policies in 1776, nor did the United States pursue trade liberalization, but domestic debates and international battles over free trade began to increasingly characterize debates over economic policy in the United Kingdom and elsewhere. By the middle of the nineteenth century, trade and tariff policies were among the central features of national economic strategy in most major countries in Europe, a position they have retained

– xi –

– with allowance for the political development of the European Union – until the present day.

Ideas

Ideas provide the basic conceptual framework for how people see the relationship between cause and effect, weigh different values and assess how different actions and policies will affect their interests. The concept that 'free trade' would enhance the division of labour, promote greater efficiency and lead to increased aggregate welfare was not an isolated intellectual exercise. The ideas underpinning free trade were part of a broad, interconnected liberal programme that included economic, social and political components that were mutually supporting and hard to disentangle. Smith's assault was not simply on the extensive system of regulations that controlled British commerce in the eighteenth century, but with the whole myriad of restrictions that fettered Britain's economy: the various taxes, the limits on inheritance and land sales, the support for monopolies, the prevalence of guilds and all the other state-sanctioned restrictive practices that limited economic activity. These prescriptions for reform were accompanied by a critique of the ruling elite and its privileges. Smith was not the first, and he was not the last, liberal thinker to condemn state interference in individual liberty.

For Victorian thinkers, free trade was the commercial counterpart to the gold standard and the international partner of laissez-faire domestic economic policies. All three were viewed as self-regulating mechanisms for harnessing the self-interest of individuals at home and abroad to maximum efficiency. Governments that deviated from orthodoxy would be automatically punished through deteriorating market conditions that would undo any short-term advantages they had sought to gain. Major proponents such as Richard Cobden and John Bright also saw free trade as a contributor to international cosmopolitanism and a force for world peace.[1] This strand of liberalism found its most prominent – and ill-timed – expression in Norman Angell's *The Great Illusion*, where he argued that extensive trading ties and economic interdependence between Britain and the other European economies made a major war impossible. Within five years of its publication in 1909, Europe had descended into the First World War.[2]

Smith's and David Ricardo's ideas had resonance outside the United Kingdom, but they also met with resistance and reaction. In some of Britain's major trading partners – especially France, Germany and the United States – free trade doctrines were often seen as a British ideology suited to British economic realities rather than those of later developers. Thinkers outside Britain were not so quick to accept the economic merits of free trade or its purported pacific tendencies. American, German and French intellectuals and policymakers were very suspicious of free trade, viewing it as the ideology of the dominant economic and political power

General Introduction xiii

of the era. While free trade might be the most appropriate policy for the world's first industrialized nation, it seemed to promise a perpetuation of second-class economic status to any less-developed economy that accepted it. This was especially true in the development of more capital-intensive industries such as coal and steel with high start-up costs. New firms in Britain's rival economies would not only have to create new industries, but they would also have to compete on equal terms against Britain's already established producers. For many, doctrinaire free trade did not seem like a recipe for successful industrialization.[3]

After Jean-Baptiste Colbert's tenure as finance minister (1665–83), French policymakers remained protectionist with only sporadic liberalization in periods of good relations with Britain. France returned decisively to the pursuit of policies of import prohibition and heavy customs duties after the Napoleonic Wars as part of a strategy of national industrial development. It was not until 1860, under Emperor Louis-Napoléon, that Britain and France signed a commercial treaty, the Cobden-Chevalier Treaty, liberalizing trade between the two countries.

In the United States, Alexander Hamilton's and the German-born Friedrich List's theories of national economy provided an alternative to Smith's and Ricardo's liberalism that emphasized the primacy of the nation and the strengthening of the state as appropriate priorities for a national economic strategy. Hamilton's *Essay on Manufactures* placed high tariffs as an integral part of a nation-building, industry-enhancing strategy of national development. Hamilton's work influenced List's own *National System of Political Economy*, which, in its advocacy of protection to support 'infant industries', was highly influential in the political and economic development of the German states.[4]

More influential was the work of Gustav Schmoller and the school of historical economics which linked the division of labour to the rising tide of inequality in Germany. Schmoller and his *Verein für Sozialpolitik* actively debated fundamental economic questions with an eye to promoting social reform while resisting both laissez-faire liberalism and socialism. Schmoller did not hold a principled view of either free trade or protection, taking a pragmatic view based on what benefits might accrue to workers in the form of cheaper food under free trade versus those that would fall to industry in the form of greater efficiencies in the organization of production in a protected market.[5]

The rapid pace of industrial development in the United States and Germany – behind high tariff walls in both countries – placed British industry under intense competitive pressure. As new rivals emerged, the traditional intellectual and political support for free trade began to wane. From the turn of the twentieth century until the Second World War, the Conservative Party repeatedly raised the issue of 'imperial preference' as a counter-policy to free trade. Initially handed a stinging rebuke in the 1906 elections, the Conservatives returned to their protectionist theme again (unsuccessfully) after the First World War during the 1920 general election and then again in the national elections held in 1931 in the midst of the Great Depression. With unemployment rising to historic heights, the gold standard abandoned and tariffs rising around the world, ideas such as Joseph Chamberlain's old dream of an imperial economic and political bloc were revived at Ottawa in 1932.[6] While not entirely successful, the Ottawa agreements did lay the foundation for a system of imperial preference, one that Britain sought to adhere to even after the Second World War.

While the British believed that restrictive economic policies and limiting trade had helped stabilize their economy in the Great Depression, the Americans believed that government tariff policies, especially the Smoot-Hawley tariff, had contributed to a deepening of the Depression. After the Second World War, the Americans were able to use their dominant economic and political position to promote their ideas for the proper functioning of the world economy. American economic advisors assisted in the reformulation of European economic policies and served as a conduit for Keynesian ideas for management of the domestic economy.[7] American economists and the politicians they influenced were also supportive of international institutions that would complement domestic Keynesianism, thus 'embedding' liberalism into the fabric of the international system.[8]

Support for economic cooperation and management of the economy also became wedded to ideas of the European movement and provided an impetus to the European project that had previously been lacking. Trade and how it could be managed both internally and externally formed one of the fundamental activities of the European Economic Community and later the European Union. The creation of regional institutions in Europe with binding authority over member states in certain policy areas created the legal framework for the common internal market based around the unimpeded exchange of goods. This paved the way for the Single Europe Act and later culminated in the adoption of the euro as a common currency for most members of the European Union.

The unrivalled position of the United States after the end of the Cold War led to a brief period of institutional flux and policy convergence around the American model.[9] The World Trade Organization was established and neo-liberal economic policies became the International Monetary Fund's doctrinaire response to economic emergencies around the world. A rash of economic crises in developing countries that could be linked to the sudden introduction of more market-oriented policies undermined the newly enthroned 'Washington consensus', as confidence in the precepts of the new system quickly faded and commitment to free trade and unfettered financial liberalization waned. Trade unions, environmentalists, students and even Nobel Prize-winning economists joined the critics of the free trade and investment regime. Vaguely defined but alternative models of international exchange, falling under the old banner of 'fair trade', became more prominent in pubic debates and demonstrations.[10]

General Introduction xv

Interests

Evolving economic ideas provided a prism for government officials, politicians and economic actors to evaluate the likely effects of changes to national trade policies. However, even when there is an agreement about the underlying theoretical arguments, differences of interests can result – an import-competer and exporter can both accept that free trade increases aggregate welfare but still find themselves on opposite sides of the trade argument. Looking through this prism, different groups in society could anticipate that different policies would impose different costs and benefits on their members. These groups would then often mobilize their members to lobby the government to support their economic interests. The 'production profile' of a group influenced how it saw its interests.[11] Groups that expected an influx of imports to undercut prices for their products tended to support protection. We examine the influence of groups through two primary avenues – lobbying by economic interests and the partisan activities of political parties.

The movement to repeal the Corn Laws in Britain was the centrepiece of the Manchester school's campaign for economic rationalization. Cobden, Bright and their followers were able to create the Anti-Corn Law League and recruit middle-class and labour supporters, organize rallies, circulate pamphlets and sponsor public meetings, all designed to exert pressure on Parliament to repeal the obnoxious duties and restrictions on the import of food. As political campaigns go, the League was remarkably well funded, with a budget of £250,000 in 1845, the year prior to repeal.[12] As a point of comparison, this corresponds to a budget of approximately £25 million in today's currency (2007).[13] While Peel and his rump Tory faction were ultimately responsible for the repeal of the Corn Laws, it was the nascent Liberal Party which took free trade as one of its founding principles. Thus, the ideas of free trade became part of the dominant ideology of one of Britain's leading parties of the nineteenth and early twentieth centuries.

The role of a dominant political party and economic coalition, but in opposition to free trade, can be seen in both the United States and Germany in the latter part of the nineteenth century. During the first fifty years of the United States' existence, until 1846, a predominantly protectionist coalition with support from manufacturers in the north-east and farmers in the north-west controlled tariff policy. With the splintering of the free trade Democrats in 1860, the Republican Party was elected on a protectionist platform and promptly raised tariffs substantially.[14] American tariffs were used to provide revenue for the government as well as protection for industry.

In the United States there were few alternative sources of revenue to the tariff for the federal government and it needed to fund a series of wars (War of 1812, the Mexican War, Civil War) and pay off debts, not to mention programmes of internal improvements.[15] Protection and government land grants provided the glue xvi

that preserved the Republican's political coalition in the face of free trade pressures from the Democrats as the nineteenth century wore on. Despite being out of power for most of the period between the American Civil War and the Great Depression, the Democrats remained staunch supporters of free trade. The passage of federal income tax legislation during one of their brief periods in office in this period created the fiscal prospects for reducing reliance on the tariff for revenue. The Democrats' political hegemony during and after the New Deal enabled them both to translate their free trade preferences into national policy and to embed them in international institutions in the wake of the Second World War.

In Germany, an internal customs union, the Zollverein, was used to encourage national integration, although most members continued to pursue particularist policies.[16] Only after German unification did a protectionist alliance, this time between Prussian agrarians and German heavy industry, provide Germany with a ruling coalition and the funds for a welfare state under Otto von Bismarck.[17] In France, economic interest groups in the nineteenth century were both powerful and usually protectionist. A few deviations from the norm – such as French wine producers – proved unable to overcome the deep-rooted political resistance of protectionist majorities in the Chamber of Deputies. Importantly, the Cobden-Chevalier Treaty was implemented through imperial decree rather than obtaining approval in the French National Assembly.

International security interests can also play a role in setting a country's trade policies. Contrary to Smith, mercantilists like Colbert certainly did not reject the acquisition of wealth as a means of expanding the potential power and resources available to the state.[18] However, they did seek to harness the power of commerce to enhance the strength of their own country and reduce the capacity of their rivals. More than a century after Colbert's death, the Napoleonic Wars marked a period of sustained economic warfare between Britain and France aimed at limiting each other's economic capacity to wage war. Britain's blockade and interference with neutral vessels bound for France soon brought Britain into conflict with the United States. Napoleon's Continental System had all the characteristics of a rigorous mercantilist system of exclusion.[19]

The First World War again brought economic warfare to the fore as Britain and her allies discussed whether or not to create an Allied economic cartel to wage economic war on the Central Powers both during times of hostilities and times of peace.[20] Similar ideas were percolating in Germany, where Friedrich Naumann was proposing a series of strong centralizing institutions to provide the backbone to a Central European confederation, *Mitteleuropa*, with a common economic 'general staff' and movement towards a single currency.[21] The United States opposed the Allied cartel, and as Germany lost the war its economic plans remained unfulfilled ambitions rather than reality.

The attempt to reconstruct the world economy after the war had mixed outcomes. The Allies' economic dependence on the United States created serious problems of financing. Germany required export markets for its products to earn the foreign exchange to pay reparations and the Allies needed both German reparations and foreign markets to repay their loans to the Americans. In practice, this meant that European countries needed to be able to sell goods in the enormous American market. During the 1920s, the booming American economy had little difficulty absorbing foreign and domestically-produced goods; however, as the economy began to slow down near the end of the decade, farmers and business clamoured for higher tariffs to stimulate domestic production and preserve American corporate profits and jobs. While the Americans were not alone in placing restrictions on trade, the high tariffs imposed by the Smoot-Hawley Act closed off a potentially lucrative market to overseas producers, triggered extensive retaliation and contributed to the collapse of world trade in the 1930s.

American policymakers after the Second World War were keen to avoid a repetition of the disastrous international economic experience of the interwar period. In this regard, they were strengthened by the support of internationally-oriented banks, industry and labour. The Democratic Party, too, was solidly behind the Roosevelt and Truman administrations' programme of creating international economic institutions such as the International Monetary Fund and the World Bank. It was only when there was solid Republican opposition and the absence of support from internationally-oriented businesses and labour, as was the case with the failed ratification of the International Trade Organization, that the expansion of international economic institutions was hindered.

However, partisan positions have not necessarily been constant over time. For more than 150 years, the Democratic Party in the United States was a bastion of free trade sentiment and support. However, as the twentieth century drew to a close, this historic attachment to free trade began to unwind as the United States began to shed industrial jobs. American labour unions came to see foreign trade less as an opportunity to sell goods abroad and more as a threat to domestic employment. With the defection of this important constituency, the Democratic Party increasingly became a home for protectionist sentiment in the twenty-first century. The Republican Party, in contrast, was traditionally the party of protection, a position that it has all but repudiated as its support from the business community and especially from multinational corporations has expanded.[22]

Institutions

National trade policies since 1776 have moved from the domestic arena, where their fate was determined by a combination of ideas and interests represented within domestic institutions, to one where multilateral institutions serve as venues for national negotiations over an extensive range of issues affecting not only trade in goods but also intellectual property and trade in services. This new arena provides a binding system for resolving disputes between members (the World Trade Organization), although some countries have given up their own ability to negotiate trade deals and other international agreements (the European Union).

The 1860 Cobden-Chevalier Treaty contained a most-favoured-nation clause that, when combined with other bilateral treaties that Britain and France had with other countries throughout the world, contributed to the creation of an international network of reciprocal trading agreements. In a real sense, this created the first system of multilateral trade.[23] The worldwide depression of 1873–96 and the French turn back to protection in the wake of their military defeat at the hands of Prussia in 1870–1 spelt the end of this first multilateral system of free trade. Britain remained at the centre of a network that was increasingly protectionist (at Britain's expense) and tended to be less reciprocal than its predecessor.

The end of the First World War led to an attempt to reconstruct the world economy along the lines that had existed prior to the war, including a general absence of international economic institutions. During this period, international economic issues were dealt with in ad hoc conferences rather than free-standing international institutions. It was not until 1930 that the first major international economic institution, the Bank for International Settlements, was created to facilitate the repayment of German war reparations. The rise of more far-reaching international economic institutions with a wide remit came about in the immediate aftermath of the Second World War. Unlike monetary affairs, the primary international institution designed to deal with trade, the International Trade Organization, fell foul of American domestic politics and the General Agreement on Tariffs and Trade (GATT), which was originally designed as a temporary institution, became the primary forum for managing and negotiating international trade agreements. Like with other aspects of globalization, the increased ease of international travel, especially by aeroplane, and more rapid and sophisticated international communications made it easier to operate standing international institutions with expert staff rather than relying solely on extraordinary conferences of national delegations. National delegations, especially in trade, continued the ongoing negotiations that lasted many years in multiple rounds, but the immediate supervision of existing agreements could be carried out by the GATT and its international secretariat.[24]

The development of closer regional economic ties also accompanied the post-war movement towards increased internationalization of economic policies. In this regard, Europe was clearly in the forefront, first with cooperative economic proposals for distributing American Marshall Plan aid, then with joint management of the coal and steel industries around the Rhine.[25] The Treaty of Rome created the European Economic Community and began a

General Introduction xix

fitful process that has seen the group grow over the past half century from the original six members to twenty-seven in 2008, and expand its competencies from coal and steel to include the management of a single currency and a common commercial policy with common external tariffs.[26] Other regions have followed suit to a lesser degree, with cooperative endeavours among the countries of East Asia (Asia-Pacific Economic Cooperation and Association of South East Asian Nations), South America (the Andean Pact and Mercosur), the Persian Gulf (Gulf Cooperation Council) and North America (North American Free Trage Agreement) being the most prominent.

The United States' promotion and pursuit of regional free trade agreements (FTA) since the mid-1980s stands out as a dramatic change in political strategy. While other countries, especially the European Union, had been extremely active before this time in taking advantage of the GATT's exception for regional free trade agreements outside the standard system of multilateral trade negotiation, the United States had consistently focused its efforts solely on the expansion of the GATT. This changed in the mid-1980s, first with the fairly innocuous United States–Israeli FTA in 1985. More substantial was the United States–Canada FTA of 1988 and the even more dramatic North American FTA with Canada and Mexico. American trade negotiators continued to pursue FTAs, primarily in Latin America and the Middle East.[27] By the end of 2007, in addition to the global World Trade Organization agreement, the United States was party to six regional trade agreements and fifteen bilateral FTAs. The European Union is party to over thirty preferential trade agreements.

Texts Selected and Sources

The texts selected for inclusion in the four volumes of this edition were chosen first to draw out the major themes of the debate over ideas, the role of interest group politics and the functioning of different institutions at the national and international levels. These documents illustrate many of the specific debates over free trade and the appropriate relationship between government, politics and economic activity. Issues of national economic development, industrialization and sovereignty are intertwined in the documents as politicians and activists discuss issues of the appropriate response to foreign competition, the consequences of trade agreements and whether to enter into bilateral or multilateral treaties. The material we have collected is typically rare and difficult to access and has been drawn from primary texts from national government archives, periodicals from the era, the records of economic interest groups and private letters between key individuals. Much of the material has not been published before, including previously unpublished letters by Richard Cobden, the driving force behind the Anti-Corn Law League, from the Cobden Letters Project. Other sources include the archives of the British Liberal Party, the United Kingdom National Archives, the British Library, the National Archives of Scotland and several Presidential libraries in the United States.

The first two volumes have a strong Anglo-centric bias as most of the theorizing and political disputes over free trade were concentrated in the United Kingdom at the time. Documents include letters between officials, copies of speeches, Napoleon's trade edicts, pamphlets, petitions, selections from treaties and newspaper commentaries. The third volume begins more thoroughly to explore counter-theories of national economy and the documents covered include increasing numbers of foreign sources, such as letters between Cobden and his Continental correspondents, meetings with ambassadors and press accounts of trade disputes and negotiations. The final volume primarily addresses itself to the development of multilateral trade institutions. These include both international (International Trade Organization, World Trade Organization) and regional (European Union, Association of South East Asian Nations, North American Free Trade Agreement) institutions and each section contains appropriate sources from the coverage of topics in local and international press to ambassadorial accounts, parliamentary and presidential debates, television transcripts, judicial opinions and internal briefing documents. As the venues of battles over free trade have expanded, so too have the range of sources.

Mark Duckenfield
London School of Economics

Notes

1. O. MacDonagh, 'The Anti-Imperialism of Free Trade', *Economic History Review*, new series, 14:3 (1962), pp. 489–501.
2. N. Angell, *The Great Illusion* (1909; Harmondsworth: Penguin, 1938).
3. A. Gerschenkron, *Economic Backwardness in Historical Perspective* (Cambridge, MA: Harvard University Press, 1962).
4. F. List, *National System of Political Economy, Volume 3: The Systems and the Politics* (1841; London: Cosimo, 2005).
5. E. Grimmer-Solem, *The Rise of Historical Economics and Social Reform in Germany, 1864–1894* (Oxford: Oxford University Press, 2003), p. 200.
6. A. Howe, *Free Trade and Liberal England, 1846–1946* (Oxford: Oxford University Press, 1997).
7. A. O. Hirschmann, 'How the Keynesian Revolution was Exported from the United States, and Other Comments', in P. Hall (ed.), *The Political Power of Economic Ideas: Keynesianism across Nations* (Princeton, NJ: Princeton University Press, 1989), pp. 347–59.
8. J. G. Ruggie, 'International Regimes, Transactions and Change: Embedded Liberalism in the Postwar Economic Order', *International Organization*, 36:2 (1982), pp. 379–415.
9. For an extreme example of this phenomena, see T. Friedman, *The World is Flat: The Globalized World in the Twenty-First Century*, 2nd edn (London: Penguin, 2007).

10. J. Stiglitz, *Making Globalization Work* (New York: W. W. Norton, 2006), pp. 61–102; J. Stiglitz, *Globalization and Its Discontents* (London: Penguin, 2002), pp. 166–79.

11. R. Rogowski, *Commerce and Coalitions* (Princeton, NJ: Princeton University Press, 1991); P. A. Gourevitch, *Politics in Hard Times* (Ithaca, NY: Cornell University Press, 1986).

12. C. Schonhardt-Bailey, *From the Corn Laws to Free Trade: Interests, Ideas and Institutions in Historical Perspective* (Cambridge, MA: MIT Press, 2006), p. 13.

13. L. H. Officer, 'Purchasing Power of British Pounds from 1264 to 2007' (2008), MeasuringWorth.com, http://www.measuringworth.com/ppoweruk/.

14. F. W. Taussig, *The Tariff History of the United States* (New York: G. P. Putnam's Sons, 1931).

15. J. Atack, S. P. Lee and P Passell, *A New Economic View of American History*, 2nd edn (New York: W. W. Norton, 1994).

16. W. O. Henderson, *The Zollverein* (New York: Frank Cass, 1984).

17. C. Schonhardt-Bailey, 'Parties and Interests in the "Marriage of Iron and Rye"', *British Journal of Political Science*, 28 (1998), pp. 291–330.

18. J. Viner, 'Power Versus Plenty as Objectives of Foreign Policy in the Seventeenth and Eighteenth Centuries', *World Politics*, 1:1 (1948), pp. 1–29.

19. See On the Continental System, following the Berlin Decree, 20 November 1806, *Annual Register* (1806), in this volume, pp. 82–4.

20. See 'The Paris Economic Conference, 1916', in Volume 3, pp. 183–259.

21. F. Naumann, *Central Europe* (New York: Alfred A. Knopf, 1917), pp. 248–83.

22. I. M. Destler, *American Trade Politics* (Washington, DC: Institute for International Economics, 2005).

23. A. Brown, *Reluctant Partners: A History of Multilateral Trade Cooperation, 1850–2000* (Ann Arbor, MI: University of Michigan Press, 2003), pp. 54–7.

24. B. M. Hoekman and M. M. Kostecki, *The Political Economy of the World Trading System: From GATT to WTO* (Oxford: Oxford University Press, 1995).

25. F. B. Tipton and R. Aldrich, *An Economic and Social History of Europe from 1939 to the Present* (London: Macmillan Education, 1987), pp. 57–64.

26. D. Dinan, *Europe Recast* (Basingstoke: Palgrave, 2004); A. Moravcsik, *The Choice for Europe* (Ithaca, NY: Cornell University Press, 1998).

27. D. W. Drezner, *U.S. Trade Strategy: Free Versus Fair* (New York: Council on Foreign Relations, 2006).

ABBREVIATIONS

BL   British Library, London
  Add. MS Additional Manuscripts

PRO   Public Record Office, National Archives, Kew, Surrey
  BT   Board of Trade
  CAB   Cabinet Office Papers
  DO   Dominion Office
  FCO   Foreign and Commonwealth Office Papers
  FO   Foreign Office Papers
  PREM   Prime Minister's Office
  T   Treasury

INTRODUCTION

In an incisive and prophetic comment on Adam Smith's *An Inquiry into the Nature and Causes of the Wealth of Nations*, Hugh Blair informed Smith 'Your work ought to be, and I am perswaded [*sic*] will in some degree become, the Commercial Code of Nations'.[1] If the qualification retains contemporary resonance, it possessed particular force in the immediate aftermath of Smith's publication. Nevertheless, Blair was correct in assigning great influence to the doctrine contained within the *Wealth of Nations*. The idea that mercantilist regulations and protective duties restricted commerce and prevented the benefits that flowed from free commercial intercourse between nations gained adherents in the following years, although Smith himself considered the practical attainment of free trade to be utopian.[2] The period covered in this volume begins with the publication of Smith's work in 1776 and ends with repeal of the Corn Laws in Britain in 1846. Thus presented, the success of commercial liberalism in underpinning the commercial policy of the world's leading nation appears remarkable.[3] Nevertheless, in this period protection remained popular throughout Europe, and received renewed vibrancy in the New World.[4] Amidst a multitude of kingdoms and nation states, with varying levels of economic development and divergent political cultures, the ideological contours and practical application of commercial liberalism varied considerably. In many ways, with the ideological development of free trade doctrines occurring alongside rapid global industrial and technological development, this period merely constitutes the first in a series of 'battles' over free trade.

Whilst historians and political scientists have become accustomed to assessing policymaking and policy choices as heavily influenced by economic interest groups, it was seldom the case that economic interests solely determined national commercial policy options. A form of economic determinism which identifies 'Free Trade' and 'protection' as policies dependent on national export and import orientation should be resisted, for assessment of commercial policy by governments was conditioned by considerations of state revenue, national security, self-sufficiency, political alliances and ideology, as well as national economic composition and interest groups. Tariffs served a number of functions, including the provision of revenue and protection of domestic industries. In terms of the latter, self-suffi-

– xxv –

ciency, national security and independence entered into the equation, particularly in relation to agriculture. No state wished to be dependent on food imports. This was a powerful argument justifying agricultural protection, prominently displayed during debates on the 1815 Corn Law, but commonly debated long afterwards.[5] Similar arguments could be adduced for industrial protection. The harnessing of industrial resources was viewed as highly important to national strength and independence, and domestic employment. Anticipating nineteenth-century advocates of protection, Tucker had earlier outlined the theoretical justification for protection by reference to the demarcation and economic divergence of countries at different stages of development.[6] Within this framework, theories of comparative advantage outlined by Smith and Ricardo appeared cosmopolitan and anti-national, and were anathema to those with a mercantilist mindset.

Whilst it has been shown that the growth of protection owed little to economic theory or long-term conceptions of commercial policy, but rather emanated from the fiscal needs of governments, it was also the case that the protective effects of these policies were perceived as vital to the commercial activity of nations.[7] Over time, they became inextricably linked with the interests and economic well-being of nations. One example of this process was France, where the theory of national economic interests inherited from Jean-Baptiste Colbert resulted in systematic protectionism, with prohibitions and high tariffs on imported manufactures, and tariffs on exports of raw materials. With the original objective of enhancing domestic production and strengthening the Bourbon monarchy, France's comparative self-sufficiency and reliance on native resources led to an economy highly sensitive to internal political and social factors, and a political culture deeply suspicious of external economic theories.[8] Whilst the 'productive profile' of nations always influenced the shaping of commercial policy, it was never the only consideration. In 1846, no less than in 1776, other, weightier considerations were perceived to be at stake. The battle over the Corn Laws in 1846 was perceived by its protagonists in no lesser terms than a struggle for control of the state apparatus.[9] Intellectually, the case for free trade, at least in Britain, emerged from disparate currents of thought, which merged with technological and industrial development to forge a powerful movement which, in common with mercantilism and protectionism, was multi-faceted and encompassed a world view.

This volume documents incidents in the commercial policy of nations between 1776 and 1846 that illuminate the contours and content of global commercial policy debates. In each case there is analysis of policy development, and the influences which impinged on the policymaking process, keeping in mind relative economic development and variations in national economic composition. Little justification is required for the Euro-centric, indeed almost Anglo-centric, nature of the volume. Britain was the leading protagonist in commercial policy disputes in this period, and the most innovative in reforming the form and substance of commercial policy. For Continental European states, free trade as a policy could rarely be dissociated from British commercial and manufacturing pre-eminence. For this reason, the commercial policies of other nations were often informed primarily by the nature of their relationship with Britain.

France and Ireland

In the aftermath of the American Revolution, Britain attempted to reconstruct, and to some extent redefine her commercial and imperial connections. The loss of America was a blow to national prestige and military power, but military defeat did not mean that Britain ceased to be a formidable commercial and manufacturing power. The peace treaty between Britain and France stipulated that commercial negotiations should take place, and that a commercial treaty should be signed before 1 January 1786.[10] A treaty was successfully completed which, whilst it did not represent a fundamental readjustment of the principles underpinning the commercial policy of either nation, at least represented a significant advance in Anglo-French commercial and political relations.

The controversy between Britain and Ireland offers further evidence of the limits to reform. The mercantilist framework of British commercial policy was fundamentally imperialist rather than national, for the Empire was treated as an economic bloc, although this did not imply equality between its constituent parts.[11] Commercial legislation sought to protect British shipping and trade, whilst giving trading preferences to Britain's colonial possessions. On the basis of geography, strategic importance, and less tangible factors such as language and culture, Ireland was a constitutional anomaly. Anglo-Irish commercial relations were complicated by political and constitutional issues, and the free trade controversy referred not to tariff reductions and commercial liberalism, but to Ireland's right to share in the benefits of Britain's imperial trading system. These two episodes indicate that the framework of mercantilism and protectionism remained firmly established features of British commercial policy, and that emerging doctrines of free trade had very limited contemporary applicability.

Trade as an Instrument of War

The limited progress towards commercial liberalism was undermined by war with Revolutionary and Napoleonic France (1793–1815). Commerce was utilized as an instrument of war, with extreme measures adopted by both sides. The complex web of regulations issued during the conflict all pointed towards recognition of the intricate relationship between strategy, commerce and military capability. As Henry Dundas argued in 1801: 'It is therefore as much the duty of those entrusted with the conduct of a British war to cut off the colonial resources of our enemy as it would be that of a general of a great army to destroy or intercept the magazines of his opponent'.[12] France reciprocated, and a barrage of measures and counter-measures were enacted, testifying to the belief on both sides that commerce was an effective instrument of war.

Commerce was central to the struggle for, as an island and trading nation, Britain's prosperity, and hence her ability to wage war, was based upon her maritime supremacy. The domination of the European land mass by Napoleon posed a challenge to British maritime and commercial supremacy. After Nelson's victory at Trafalgar in 1805 effectively removed the possibility of invading Britain, Napoleon turned to economic warfare and attempted to defeat Britain by removing her main source of strength and power. With Europe blockaded by Napoleon's Continental System, commerce sought other avenues, and towards the end of the war the importance of extra-European markets was indicated by the abolition of the East India Company's monopoly of the China trade.[13] The interference with commerce which the war entailed resulted in the United States declaring war on Britain in 1812 over violation of neutral rights, a particularly difficult problem in wartime, especially with commerce such a prominent factor in the struggle.

The execution of legislation prohibiting commerce required the active participation of a multitude of local port and customs officials, and effective monitoring, and was never completely achieved. Smuggling was extensive, and resistance to the Continental System appeared across Europe. For European consumers, the Continental System meant denial of necessities and luxuries, for British manufactures had improved to such an extent that many countries found it impossible to dispense with them completely.[14] Napoleon thus alienated many different elements within the commercial classes, and the Continental System was undermined by officially-sanctioned measures, such as licensing, and non-official measures, such as privateering and smuggling.[15]

With Napoleon's defeat in 1815, it remained to be seen whether the commercial components of a reconstructed world order would encompass a return to normal commercial intercourse. Theories of commercial policy which emerged during the war, such as Alexander Hamilton's justification for protection of American domestic industries, and Johann Fichte's proposals for an autarkic, self-sufficient state, made this appear unlikely.[16]

Britain and America Post-1815

In the aftermath of the war, the protectionist inclinations of European nations appeared unshaken. France, Spain and Russia returned to high protection and prohibitions.[17] In Britain, the income tax was abolished by the landed interest in Parliament, and a highly protectionist Corn Law enacted, which served fiscal, social and economic purposes.[18] The United States drifted towards protection as a national policy suitable for her position as an emerging industrial power. The formidable obstacles in the way of promoting a liberalized commercial system were already becoming apparent to contemporary observers.[19] Nevertheless, Britain paved the way, with a series of reciprocal agreements relating to shipping and navigation which promoted a partial liberalization of trade.

The famous merchants' petition of 1820 calling for free trade elicited the qualified approval of Lord Liverpool, who warned the advocates of free trade that a more liberal policy was unlikely to be reciprocated by foreign nations.[20] This proved to be a shrewd analysis, for reciprocity remained the hallmark of commercial policy, with tariff bargaining and negotiations indicative of the national basis of commercial policy. Despite increasingly favourable rhetoric, a broad range of factors complicated national responses towards tariff liberalization. Amongst the most important was distrust of Britain. Having secured a lead in manufacturing, Britain was suspected of promoting freer trade as a means to choke foreign industrialization and promote British hegemony.[21] With manufacturing increasingly viewed as an important element of state power, foreign nations supported protection as a means to promote native industries. Self-sufficiency, state revenue and domestic employment were all cited as important factors justifying such a policy stance. The post-1815 period thus witnessed something of a bifurcation between Britain and the rest of the world, most pronounced in the case of the United States, where a powerful protectionist critique which married 'nation-building' and national and economic independence emerged under Hamilton and Clay, and provided an important theoretical underpinning to American policy choices and objectives in the nineteenth century.[22]

Germany and France in the 1830s

The emergence of a body of protectionist thought that justified protection in national terms was also apparent in Europe, particularly in France and Germany. The failure of British commercial diplomacy to promote a liberal system of commerce in Europe was most apparent in the failed negotiations of the 1830s. In both countries, there was much support for the 'infant industry' argument, propagated by the German economist Friedrich List and later grudgingly accepted by John Stuart Mill.[23] Clearly influenced by Hamilton, List viewed protection as justifiable when emergent industries were faced with more highly developed competitors who could afford to produce cheaper and better products. Such views commanded much support in France and Germany, where emerging manufacturing industries faced British competition.

Whilst demonstrating the inherent protectionism of countries such as France and Germany, the negotiations were also important in indicating the limits to which Britain was willing to go in pursuing tariff liberalization. In Britain's trade relations with both countries, the legacy of the Napoleonic wars and the commercial legislation it provoked caused difficulties. Preferential duties Britain granted to Canadian timber caused difficulties with Prussia, and in France the protectionist legacy of the war was carried over into the post-war period. The difficulties in promoting commercial reform were readily apparent amidst the prevalence of ideas of self-sufficiency, and the pervasive fear of British competition and suspicion of British motives.

On the evidence presented in this volume, the theory that Britain pursued an open global trading system suited to British purposes, or a system of 'hegemonic stability', appears inapplicable before 1846.[24] The main demand made by the German states organized in the Zollverein was for Britain to reduce the duties on corn. This Britain refused to do. The Corn Laws were viewed in terms of national self-sufficiency and safety, but also as an essential prop of the Constitution in maintaining the predominance of the landed interest. Successive commercial missions indicated that foreign states would not engage in serious commercial discussions until Britain was prepared to alter the Corn Laws. These missions were vitally important in providing moral and material evidence for the sustained attack on the Corn Laws which began with the formation of the Manchester Anti-Corn Law Association in 1838.[25]

Corn Laws

Perhaps the most famous event in global commercial history in the nineteenth century occurred with repeal of the Corn Laws in Britain in 1846. The historical debate on the rationale for and implications of repeal continues to interest historians and political scientists.[26] Whilst the domestic political implications of repeal were clearly cataclysmic, in terms of the international trading system the policy was one that signalled an end to lengthy and mainly futile tariff bargaining with foreign nations. Repeal was also the most potent symbol of the triumph in Britain of doctrines of commercial liberalism. It was hoped that its unilateral adoption of free trade measures[27] would inaugurate a free international trading system.[28] Richard Cobden was fortified in this belief by the constant complaints of foreign nations that the Corn Laws were the main obstacle to tariff reductions across Europe. Cobden was to be disappointed, for it was always the case that tariffs served a number of functions, and the idea that foreign nations were inhibited from adopting a liberal system of commerce merely by the existence of the Corn Laws proved far too simplistic.

The battle over Corn Law repeal gave rise to a torrent of debate on the nature of commercial policy which engaged a large proportion of the British population. Much of the responsibility for the agitation resides with the Anti-Corn Law League, which aimed to exert sufficient pressure to force repeal through Parliament. League agitation was notable not only for the scale of operations, and the commitment required from its advocates, but also on account of its multi-faceted nature. Moral and religious elements supplemented the economic case for repeal. League propaganda indicated that the enlightened self-interest of the manufacturing and commercial classes promoted the good of the entire community. This was contrasted with the inherent exploitation of the aristocratic 'feudal oligarchy'.[29]

Local political mobilization, through public meetings, and the transmission of memorials and petitions to Parliament was a vital component of a nationwide campaign, with the provincial press an important vehicle of opinion and information. On a lesser scale, this was also true of the League's opponents, with protectionists organizing themselves in response to League agitation. Whilst Parliament was the 'decisive theatre'[30] for the final resolution of the question, the constellation of economic sectors and interest groups throughout the country presented a remarkable mosaic, and testified to national recognition of the importance of the question. In terms of the scale of the struggle, it is difficult to find parallels in other countries. Corn Law repeal reaffirmed the course of events in the post-1815 period, by identifying Britain as the most innovative nation in reformulating commercial policy.[31] Yet, during the course of the parliamentary debates there was a widespread fear, confidently predicted by protectionists, that foreign nations would not follow Britain in tariff liberalization, and that a new era of commercial relations had not yet arrived.[32]

Sources

The material published in this volume is at once relevant to its themes, and comparatively rare. No single type of source has been preferred, for over-reliance on a particular source type might present a partial and narrow view. Such a danger most obviously emanates from 'official' documentation from government departments. Exclusive use of such material would essentially lead to a diplomatic history of commercial policy, and a particular view of policy formation and opinion based on an inner circle of officials and politicians. Manuscript material is therefore supplemented by press and parliamentary reports, petitions from local organizations and pamphlets. In these terms, the material presented here seeks to be broad-ranging and representative of the views of different social groups and economic sectors. Yet for each episode a particular type of source is appropriate and indeed necessary. It would indeed be unusual to examine the Orders in Council without reference to the correspondence of James Stephen and Spencer Perceval.[33] Similarly, whilst the material on the Corn Laws attempts to portray civic and extra-parliamentary opinion, a few sources are included that throw particular light on events at Westminster. Palmerston's letter to the Earl of Minto illustrates an important contemporary perception of Prime Minister

Sir Robert Peel's position, and the Lords protest is an important, concise, and hitherto neglected statement of protectionist opposition to repeal.[34]

The documentation of the volume illustrates that commercial policy controversies were far more extensive by the early 1840s than during any previous period. This was partly the work of the Anti-Corn Law League, but was also attributable to free traders in governmental positions such as John Bowring and Charles Poulett Thomson.[35] One could argue that in the eighteenth century officials such as William Eden used their position to advance their own particular philosophy. Whilst this may be true, the later period incorporated a much more systematic agitation, orchestrated by a powerful combination of officials and manufacturers. This was certainly not the case in the eighteenth century, where economic interests and policy proscriptions were far less uniform, and when a popular movement did not exist.

More widely, heightened agitation reflected the growth and popularity of political economy as a mode of public discourse. Indeed, it has been convincingly claimed it was the 'favoured mode of analysing, debating, or justifying the significance of British policies, institutions, and ideas'.[36] The great diffusion of tracts and evangelical and secular didactic literature is solid testimony of this intellectual preoccupation.[37] By 1815, free trade was a very complex doctrine, encompassing theological, anti-aristocratic and purely economic strands. Smith remained influential, especially to legislators such as Huskisson who saw the necessity of gradual reform, but the influence of evangelicalism and Malthusian and Ricardian political economy were far from negligible.[38] The 'two models' of free trade, those of evangelical political economy and professional economists, emanated from different sources but were effectively merged by those such as Cobden who argued that Providence designed commerce to unify and moralize mankind, and that free trade was the international law of God, to spread Christianity through commerce across the world.[39]

If the pattern of British economic development and industrialization facilitated the forging of a powerful coalition in favour of free trade, it is also true that support for free trade or protection was something of a proxy for opinion on the extent to which Britain should become an industrial society.[40] As a descriptive term reflecting a body of beliefs on the nature of commerce and exchange free trade became far more prominent in the first half of the nineteenth century, on account of a firmer union between the theoretical basis of commercial liberalism and the practical application of free trade policies.

Yet the success of free trade was not easily achieved, and the fundamental aim of the documents included in this volume is to illustrate the contested nature of commercial policy, and, more widely, to illustrate the complexities behind the formation of national commercial policy in the eighteenth and nineteenth centuries.

Notes

1. 3 April 1776, in E. C. Mossner and I. S. Ross, *The Correspondence of Adam Smith*, 2nd edn (Oxford: Clarendon Press, 1987), pp. 187–90.

2. B. Semmel, 'The Hume-Tucker Debate and Pitt's Trade Proposals', *Economic Journal*, 75:300 (1965), pp. 759–70, on pp. 762–3; J. Ehrman, *The British Government and Commercial Negotiations in Europe, 1783–1793* (Cambridge: Cambridge University Press, 1962), p. 29.

3. For repeal as the fulfilment of Smith's doctrine, see 'Death of Mr. Cobden', *Times*, 3 April 1865, p. 9c; Smith, of course, was not the first to advocate commercial liberalism; Arthur Young and Josiah Tucker were more often cited as promoters of free trade, see J. E. Crowley, 'Neo-Mercantilism and the Wealth of Nations: British Commercial Policy after the American Revolution', *Historical Journal*, 33:2 (1990), pp. 339–60; discussing Chartered Companies, even the 1771 *Encyclopaedia Britannica* argued 'all restrictions of trade are found to be hurtful', *Encyclopaedia Britannica*, 3 vols (Edinburgh: A. Bell and C. Macfarquhar, 1771), vol. 2, p. 243.

4. For example, Spain and Austria became more protectionist from the 1780s, J. B. Williams, *British Commercial Policy and Trade Expansion, 1750–1850* (Oxford: Clarendon Press 1972), pp. 156–7, 209.

5. 'Without some efficient protection it was impossible that our farmers, surrounded by difficulties, could be successful in the struggle against foreign agriculturists. There was also much of political consideration in the question; as it was by no means fitting that this country should depend for its subsistence on the caprice or on the hostility of other countries'. Sir John Newport, 23 February 1815, *Hansard* (1814–15), xxix, c. 1011; cf. dependence on foreign agriculture as harmful to national welfare 'if not fatal to our existence', M. Gore, *Thoughts on the Corn Laws*, 2nd edn (London: Saunders and Otley, 1840), p. 9.

6. Semmel, 'The Hume-Tucker Debate', p. 762; B. Semmel, *The Rise of Free Trade Imperialism: Classical Political Economy: The Empire of Free Trade and Imperialism, 1750–1850* (London: Cambridge University Press, 1970), p. 180.

7. R. Davis, 'The Rise of Protection in England, 1689–1786', *Economic History Review*, 19:2 (1966), pp. 306–17, on pp. 306, 313.

8. See S. B. Clough, *France: A History of National Economics, 1789–1939* (New York: C. Scribner's Sons, 1939).

9. See 'The Corn Laws as a Buttress for the Aristocracy', *Economist* (1846), below, pp. 383–5; 'That measure could be considered in no other light than as a stepping-stone to ulterior measures', Duke of Cleveland, 25 May 1846, *Hansard* (1846), lxxxvi, c. 1123.

10. W. Bowden, 'The English Manufacturers and the Commercial Treaty of 1786 with France', *American Historical Review*, 25:1 (1919), pp. 18–35.

11. R. L. Schuyler, *The Fall of the Old Colonial System: A Study in British Free Trade, 1770–1870* (New York: Oxford University Press, 1945), p. 62.

12. Cited in P. Kennedy, *The Rise and Fall of British Naval Mastery*, 3rd edn (London: Fontana, 1991), p. 151; see George Sinclair to Henry Dundas, 9 November 1796, below, p. 81, for a proposal to prohibit Russian naval supplies reaching France.

13. 'East India Charter', *Times*, 20 January 1813, p. 1e; Minutes of Committee of Court of Directors, *Times*, 20 July 1813, p. 2c.

14. W. Cunningham, *The Growth of English Industry and Commerce in Modern Times: Laissez Faire* (Cambridge: Cambridge University Press, 1925), p. 677; Williams, *British Commercial Policy*, p. 348 ff.

15. R. Ruppenthal, 'Denmark and the Continental System', *Journal of Modern History*, 15:1 (1943), pp. 7–23, on p. 16.

16. Alexander Hamilton's *Report of the Secretary of the Treasury of the United States, on the Subject of Manufactures* ([Philadelphia], 1791) was a strong argument in favour of protection as a national policy; German philosopher Johann Fichte outlined state autarky in *The Closed Commercial State* (1801), see B. F. Hoselitz, 'Socialism, Communism, and International Trade', *Journal of Political Economy*, 57:3 (1949) pp. 227–41, on pp. 228–9.

17. For Spain, see Williams, *British Commercial Policy*, p. 391; Russia, under Finance Minister Count Egor Frantsevich Kankrin, raised tariffs several times between 1823 and 1844; Kankrin was influenced by Fichte's doctrine of an autarkic national economy, but revenue was also a consideration, see W. McKenzie Pintner, *Russian Economic Policy Under Nicholas I* (Ithaca, NY: Cornell University Press, 1967), pp. 44–7.

18. H. Jephson, *The Platform: Its Rise and Progress*, 2 vols (London: Macmillan and Co., 1892), vol. 1, pp. 370–1.

19. During the Corn Law debates, Mr Philips stated: 'Foreign nations mistaking, like the advocates of the regulations before the committee, the circumstances which have operated against our wealth for the causes of it, are now following our example. They are protecting or imposing restraints on the import of our fabrics, in order to encourage their own manufactures, from which they will receive inferior fabrics at higher prices', 17 February 1815, *Hansard* (1814–15), xxix, c. 818.

20. Williams, *British Commercial Policy*, pp. 449–50.

21. For British hegemony and its supposed objectives, see T. J. McKeown, 'Hegemonic Stability Theory and 19th Century Tariff Levels in Europe', *International Organization*, 37:1 (1983), pp. 73–91; A. A. Stein, 'The Hegemon's Dilemma: Great Britain, the United States, and the International Economic Order', *International Organization*, 38:2 (1984), p. 355–86; S. C. James and D. A. Lake, 'The Second Face of Hegemony: Britain's Repeal of the Corn Laws and the American Walker Tariff of 1846', *International Organization*, 43:1 (1989), pp. 1–29.

22. United States Congressman Henry Clay's 'American System' comprised protection of domestic manufacturing and agriculture as bulwarks of national strength and power.

23. The infant industry argument was included in Mill's *Principles of Political Economy* (London: Parker, 1848), paving the way for its 'formal acceptance into international trade theory', D. A. Irwin, 'Retrospectives: Challenges to Free Trade', *Journal of Economic Perspectives*, 5:2 (1991), pp. 201–8, on p. 202.

24. McKeown, 'Hegemonic Stability Theory', p. 88.

25. This group transformed into the Anti-Corn Law League in 1839. An Anti-Corn Law Association was formed in London in 1836, but by 1838 the initiative had passed to Manchester. See N. McCord, *The Anti-Corn Law League, 1838–1846* (London: George Allen & Unwin, 1958), p. 16.

26. A. Gambles, *Protection and Politics: Conservative Economic Discourse, 1815–1852* (London: Royal Historical Society, 1999); C. Schonhardt-Bailey, *From the Corn Laws to Free Trade: Interests, Ideas, and Institutions in Historical Perspective* (Cambridge, MA: MIT Press, 2006).

27. Repeal was accompanied by a raft of other tariff reductions.

28. 'Anti-Corn Law League at Covent-Garden Theatre', *Times*, 29 September 1843, p. 5e.

29. Thus acting as what Karl Marx termed a 'universal class', see G. R. Searle, *Entrepreneurial Politics in Mid-Victorian Britain* (New York: Oxford University Press, 1993), p. 319.

30. McCord, *The Anti-Corn Law League*, pp. 188–207.

Introduction

xxxv

31. In 1848, Benjamin Disraeli claimed the commercial policy of 1846 violated William Pitt and William Huskisson's legacy of regulated competition and reciprocal commercial relations, Gambles, *Protection and Politics*, p. 210.
32. Speeches of Colonel Conolly and Sir Howard Douglas, 13 and 24 February 1846, in A. S. O'Brien (ed.), *The Battle for Native Industry: The Debate Upon the Corn Laws, the Corn Importation and Customs' Duties Bills, and the Other Financial Measures of the Government, in Session 1846*, 2 vols (London: Society for the Protection of Agriculture, 1846), vol. 1, pp. 273–4, 483.
33. See James Stephen to Spencer Perceval, 5 December 1807, and James Stephen to Spencer Perceval, 23 May 1808, below, pp. 85–7, 101.
34. See Lord Palmerston to the Earl of Minto, 27 December 1845; and House of Lords Protest against the Corn Bill, *Hansard* (1846), both below, pp. 380, 388–9.
35. For the crucial role of the Board of Trade, see L. Brown, *The Board of Trade and the Free-Trade Movement 1830–42* (Oxford: Clarendon Press, 1958).
36. D. Winch, 'Introduction', in D. Winch and P. K. O'Brien (eds), *The Political Economy of British Historical Experience, 1688–1914* (Oxford: Oxford University Press, 2002), p. 2.
37. A. Howe, 'Restoring Free Trade: The British Experience, 1776–1873', in Winch and O'Brien (eds), *The Political Economy of British Historical Experience*, pp. 193–213, on p. 200.
38. Ibid., pp. 194–7.
39. B. Hilton, *The Age of Atonement: The Impact of Evangelicalism on Social and Economic Thought, 1785–1865* (Oxford: Clarendon Press, 1988), pp. 69–70, 246.
40. Howe, 'Restoring Free Trade', p. 199; Hilton, *The Age of Atonement*, p. 68.

TENTATIVE MOVES TOWARDS FREE TRADE, 1778–86

If Adam Smith's theories almost immediately found a receptive audience, it remains equally true that there were limits to how far his theories would be systematically applied. Attempts to promote freer trade in the 1770s and 1780s were hampered by the protectionist inclinations of foreign nations and the vested interests of protected domestic industries. Two significant controversies of this period, reconstruction of the Anglo-Irish commercial relationship and the 1786 Anglo-French commercial treaty, contained both elements. Both episodes indicated the limited applicability of Smith's ideas, whilst illustrating the multi-faceted nature of commercial policy and the non-commercial influences which impinged on it.

It would be difficult to assign changing perceptions of commercial policies and relationships purely to the work of Smith.[1] Whilst Smith provided the theoretical justification and conceptual framework for commercial reformers, other influences were at work. Many viewed the commercial restraints imposed on Ireland as a major cause of the distress which enveloped the country in the 1770s and 1780s.[2] Here, free trade agitation was an attempt to participate in the imperial trading system, and predominantly concerned reforming mercantilist regulations rather than reducing tariff rates. It was understandable that the agitation should assume an imperial form. Ireland was a dependency of the British Crown, and was thus excluded from the benefits of the imperial trading system by the provisions of the Navigation Acts, and restraints on manufacturing and agricultural exports. The rationale for such restrictions emanated from the desire to protect British agriculture and manufacturing industries from ruinous competition.[3] In 1663 Ireland was forbidden to ship goods directly to the colonies, except horses, servants and provisions. In 1667, Irish cattle imports to England were forbidden and, most notably, in 1699, Irish woollen exports to foreign countries were banned.[4] Within the mercantilist structure of restriction and exclusion, it is nevertheless true that certain industries were encouraged. Irish linen imports were exempt from duty after 1696, and in 1742 a bounty was granted to Irish and Scottish linen exported from England.[5]

– 1 –

In 1779, the agitation of the Irish Volunteers for 'Free Trade' led to Lord North making sweeping concessions, permitting Ireland to export and import goods directly with the British colonies, and henceforth 'upon equal conditions with Great Britain'.[6] The propositions were recognized as important in encouraging Irish commerce and manufacturing and met with little opposition.[7] The readiness of British politicians to reform mercantilist regulations arose from concerns over wartime stability and domestic security. Yet the commercial relationship was merely a facet of the wider problem of the ambiguous constitutional position of Ireland, and this problem was not resolved by commercial concessions.[8]

In 1785, a further attempt to remove constraints on Irish trade was promoted by William Pitt's proposals to revise the Navigation Acts, define Ireland's position within the Empire in terms of treaties with foreign powers, and equalize many customs duties. This package of reforms raised a storm of opposition from British manufacturers, with the General Chamber of Manufactures of Great Britain raising concerns over Irish competition.[9] Interestingly, these fears were earlier dismissed by Smith in terms of the underdeveloped nature of the Irish economy.[10]

Such a broad view did not convince British manufacturers, with Matthew Boulton, James Watt and Josiah Wedgwood prominent in the agitation. The manufacturers received parliamentary support from Charles James Fox, and more surprisingly, William Eden and Lord Sheffield, both promoters of trade liberalization. Eden and Sheffield believed Britain was conceding too much. In itself, such a response was indicative of the limits to which even progressive eighteenth-century minds were supportive of free trade. Yet, it was the Irish Parliament rather than British manufacturers who defeated Pitt's proposals. The issue became entangled with the question of Irish legislative independence, a sensitive political issue since the new Constitution of 1782. Pitt's clumsy proposal that Ireland enact the British Navigation Laws was construed as attempted dictation and an attack on Irish legislative independence. That most of the measures were accepted by 1787, crucially, at the request of the Irish, merely illustrates that it was the affront to legislative independence rather than the commercial measures which aborted Pitt's original plan.[11]

If the Irish campaign revealed the strength of mercantilist structures and mindsets, events surrounding the Anglo-French commercial treaty indicated that any reform would be achieved in a piecemeal fashion. In the eighteenth century there was very little legitimate trade between Britain and France.[12] From the late seventeenth century, commercial, military and economic rivalry dominated, with England responding to the challenge of Louis XIV with a raft of measures, including at times complete prohibition of trade, but more commonly very high tariffs on French products.[13] Sheltered by prohibitions and high tariff walls, similar industries emerged in both countries, thus making it more difficult to make any agreement which would not in some way damage industrial and commercial interests in both countries.[14]

In 1785, frustrated at British reticence to lower duties, France issued a series of *arrêts* which raised duties and excluded foreign cottons, muslins, gauzes and linens from France itself. An *arrêt* of 21 October forbade the importation of foreign iron, steel and cutlery.[15] These measures had the desired effect and Britain began preparing for negotiations at the end of 1785. Many in Britain considered that the disruption to commerce caused by the American War of Independence made such a treaty a necessity.[16] France's reasons for making the treaty were attributed by many to increasing revenue receipts, and mitigating the worst effects of the chronic financial position of the Ancien Régime.[17]

There was considerable opposition to the Treaty in Britain, in and out of Parliament. Fox led Whig parliamentary opposition to the measure, on the basis of loyalty towards the 1703 Methuen Treaty with Portugal. Having earlier supported manufacturers in their opposition to concessions to Ireland his stance now dismayed those same manufacturers, who saw advantages arising from the treaty.[18] Outside Parliament, opposition predictably arose from industries fearful of French competition. Another strand of opposition, encompassing the Foxite critique, expressed general distrust towards France and objected to making any treaty.[19] A related strand married these two elements in viewing the aggrandizement of French commerce as the precursor of enhanced French naval power.[20]

Support for the treaty came from export industries which viewed lower duties and abolition of prohibitions as a positive boon. The theoretical commitment to economic liberalism of manufacturers who supported trade liberalization with France must however be questioned, for many of the same men used 'all their lobbying resources to wreck a commercial treaty with Ireland'.[21] The support of manufacturers and ironmasters should not be taken as a precursor of a free trade supporting manufacturing interest.[22] The manufacturers of 1786 were not a precursor of the Anti-Corn Law League, for, as Ehrman has convincingly argued, 'it was no consistent economic theory or enlightened social ideal that dictated the attitude of Wedgwood, Garbett, the Ironmasters, and the Manchester manufacturers'. As befitted larger industries with less to fear from foreign competition, self-interest and expediency fuelled their support for a more liberal system of commerce.[23]

Philosophical support for the treaty was perhaps best expressed by politicians, particularly Pitt, whose language anticipated Richard Cobden in linking commerce and peace.[24] For Pitt, the treaty signified the changing nature of the Anglo-French relationship, based on 'friendly intercourse, cemented by mutual benevolence'.[25] William Eden, the British negotiator, displayed a similar enlightened view.[26] Nevertheless, Pitt was realistic enough to consider the power of old enmities, in arguing 'though in the commercial business I think there are reasons for believing the French may be sincere, I cannot listen without suspicion to their professions of political friendship'.[27]

More serious opposition to the treaty, largely dictated by economic geography, existed in France. The treaty was welcomed by southern wine growers and manufacturers in central and western France whose manufactures did not compete directly with Britain, but it was highly unpopular with northern commercial and industrial interests.[28] With Britain far advanced in the application of machinery in manufacturing, she was able to translate this advantage into cheaper manufactured goods.[29] Such opposition was viewed by many in Britain as positive proof that the treaty was favourable to Britain.[30]

In the long-term, the Anglo-French Commercial Treaty represented an important step towards the acceptance of reciprocal tariff negotiations and reductions, and represented a diplomatic model for the future. Reciprocal commercial relationships appeared to offer a guarantee that commercial policy would be conducted with national commercial and industrial interests in mind. Mercantilist restrictions, import prohibitions and protective duties remained central to the commercial portfolio of nations, in terms of protecting national industries and raising revenue. Moreover, the limited success of commercial diplomacy, notably in Spain, indicated the vibrancy of mercantilist mindsets, fear of British competition and the power of national industries.[31] Even amidst the successful accomplishment of the treaty, Minister Plenipotentiary Daniel Hailes warned that as soon as one country felt disadvantaged, they would 'cut the knot' that bound them.[32] This hardly bespoke a new era of commercial cooperation and recognition of mutual advantage amongst nations.[33] Commercial policy remained set within a mercantilist framework, which identified and linked national power and wealth with commercial advantages. Negotiations for reciprocal tariff reductions were underpinned by such notions. The idea that the comparative advantage of nations should be the prime determinant of policy was anathema to mercantilist mindsets equating self-sufficiency with economic power. French dissatisfaction with the treaty had always been more marked than in Britain, and the treaty proved to be short-lived. Revolution and war further undermined the liberalization of commercial policy in the following years.

Notes

1. It has been convincingly argued that the liberalism of commercial policy symbolized by the commercial treaty gave currency to Smith, not the reverse, J. E. Crowley, 'Neo-Mercantilism and the Wealth of Nations: British Commercial Policy after the American Revolution', *Historical Journal*, 33:2 (1990), pp. 339–60, on p. 340.

2. See John Hely Hutchinson, *The Commercial Restraints of Ireland* (1779), below, pp. 23–32; G. O'Brien, 'The Irish Free Trade Agitation of 1779', *English Historical Review*, 38:152 (1923), pp. 564–81, and 39:153 (1924), pp. 95–109.
3. R. Davis, 'English Foreign Trade, 1700–1774', *Economic History Review*, 15:2 (1962), pp. 285–303, on pp. 290–1
4. See Sir James Caldwell to Lord George Germain, 28 September 1779, below, p. 12; F. G. James, 'Irish Colonial Trade in the Eighteenth Century', *William and Mary Quarterly*, 3rd series, 20:4 (1963), pp. 574–84; W. Cunningham, 'The Repression of the Woollen Manufacture in Ireland', *English Historical Review*, 1:2 (1886), pp. 277–94, on p. 285.
5. R. Davis, 'The Rise of Protection in England, 1689–1786', *Economic History Review*, 19:2 (1966), pp. 306–17, on p. 307; Davis, 'English Foreign Trade', pp. 287–8.
6. See Motion respecting Trade in Ireland, 19 January 1779, *Cobbett's Parliamentary Debates* (1778–80); 'Debate in the Commons on the State of the Trade and Commerce of Ireland', 15 February 1779, *Cobbett's Parliamentary Debates* (1778–80); Speech of the Lord Lieutenant to the Irish Parliament, 12 October 1779, *Annual Register* (1779); and 'Debate in the Commons on Lord North's Propositions for the Relief of the Trade of Ireland', 13 December 1779, *Cobbett's Parliamentary Debates* (1778–80), all below, pp. 7–8, 9–11, 13, 14–22. See also T. Bartlett, '"This Famous Island set in a Virginian Sea": Ireland in the British Empire, 1690–1801', in N. Canny, P. J. Marshall et al. (eds), *The Oxford History of the British Empire*, 5 vols (Oxford: Oxford University Press, 1998–9), vol. 2, pp. 253–75, on p. 266.
7. See William Eden, *A Letter to the Earl of Carlisle on the Representation of Ireland respecting a Free Trade* (1779), below, pp. 33–43; John Hely Hutchinson's speech to Cork electors, 18 December 1779, in *Historical Manuscripts Commission, Twelfth Report: Manuscripts of the Duke of Beaufort* (London: HMSO, 1891), p. 295; cf. Welbore Ellis to Hutchinson, 16 December 1779, in ibid. pp. 293–4.
8. Lord Hertford to Hutchinson, 22 January 1780, on English concerns that despite commercial concessions 'Constitutional points as may unhinge the whole and divide the interests of the two kingdoms' were being agitated in Ireland, in *Manuscripts of the Duke of Beaufort*, p. 295.
9. W. Bowden, 'The Influence of the Manufacturers on Some of the Early Policies of William Pitt', *American Historical Review*, 29:4 (1924), pp. 655–74.
10. Adam Smith to Henry Dundas, 1 November 1779, in 'Adam Smith and Free Trade for Ireland', *English Historical Review*, 1:2 (1886), pp. 308–11, on p. 309.
11. P. Kelly, 'British and Irish Politics in 1785', *English Historical Review*, 90:356 (1975), pp. 536–63, on p. 562.
12. See 'Commerce with France' ([*c.* late 1785]), below, pp. 44–9.
13. J. B. Williams, *British Commercial Policy and Trade Expansion, 1750–1850* (Oxford: Clarendon Press 1972), p. 186; J. Ehrman, *The British Government and Commercial Negotiations in Europe, 1783–1793* (Cambridge: Cambridge University Press, 1962), p. 28.
14. The silk and linen industries in Britain and Ireland constitute 'fairly clear examples of infant industries reared to maturity under protection', Davis, 'The Rise of Protection in England', p. 316.
15. Ehrman, *The British Government and Commercial Negotiations*, pp. 31–2.
16. For example, Anglicanus, *The Necessity and Policy of the Commercial Treaty with France, &c. Considered* (London: William Richardson, 1787), p. 41.

17. See Daniel Hailes to the Marquis of Carmarthen, 25 October 1786, below, pp. 58–63; 'The French government will improve their revenue by it, which probably was the principal motive with them for making it', Viscount Barrington to Earl of Huntingdon, 8 December 1786, in *Historical Manuscripts Commission: Report on the Manuscripts of the Late Reginald Rawson Hastings*, 3 vols (London: HMSO, 1928–34), vol. 3, p. 200.
18. See *A Letter from a Manchester Manufacturer to the Right Honourable Charles James Fox, on his Political Opposition to the Commercial Treaty with France* (1787), below, pp. 65–7.
19. For a contrast between French militarism and commercial Britain, see *A Series of Letters, on the Commercial Treaty with France Published in the Kentish Gazette, in the Year MDCCLXXVII by a Country Gentleman* (London: G. & T. Wilkie, 1787), pp. iv–v.
20. Anon., *Observations on the Agricultural and Political Tendency of the Commercial Treaty* (London: J. Debrett, 1787), p. 19; 'A nation of manufacturers may be more rich, but less powerful', p. 21.
21. A. V. Judges, 'The Idea of a Mercantile State', in D. C. Coleman (ed.), *Revisions in Mercantilism* (London: Methuen & Co., 1969), pp. 35–60, on p. 41.
22. See Minutes of the Committee of Trade, 14 March 1786, below, pp. 50–1.
23. Ehrman, *The British Government and Commercial Negotiations*, p. 48; the impact on particular sectors rather than wider conceptions of commercial policy still predominated, Williams, *British Commercial Policy*, p. 186.
24. See William Pitt to the Marquis of Stafford, 27 August 1786, below, p. 55.
25. H. B. Wheatley (ed.), *The Historical and the Posthumous Memoirs of Sir Nathaniel William Wraxall, 1772–1784*, 5 vols (London: Bickers & Son, 1884), vol. 1, p. 380.
26. See William Eden to Robert Liston, 27 September 1786, below, p. 56.
27. Pitt to Eden, 10 June 1786, in G. Hogge (ed.), *The Journal and Correspondence of William, Lord Auckland*, 4 vols (London: Richard Bentley, 1861–2), vol. 1, p. 127; see William Eden to Lord Carmarthen, 6 June 1786, and William Pitt to William Eden, 12 September 1786, both below, pp. 52, 53–4.
28. W. M. Sloane, 'The Continental System of Napoleon', *Political Science Quarterly*, 13:2 (1898), pp. 213–31, on p. 214.
29. H. See, 'The Normandy Chamber of Commerce and the Commercial Treaty of 1786', *Economic History Review*, 2:2 (1930), pp. 308–13, on p. 308.
30. The *Times* viewed the treaty as 'more beneficial than could possibly have been expected', and argued the 7s. duty per gallon on French brandies would countervail internal duties on British distillers, securing them from that 'dangerous competition which at first was apprehended', 5 October 1786, p. 2a; Anglicanus, *The Necessity and Policy of the Commercial Treaty with France*, pp. 41–2.
31. See Ralph Woodford to Robert Liston, 24 October 1786, and Ralph Woodford to Robert Liston, 29 December 1786, both below, pp. 57, 64.
32. See Daniel Hailes to the Marquis of Carmarthen, 25 October 1786, below, pp. 58–63. On Hailes, see D. B. Horn (ed.), *British Diplomatic Representatives, 1689–1789*, Camden society, 3rd series, vol. 46 (1932), pp. 26–7.
33. Ehrman, *The British Government and Commercial Negotiations*, pp. 48–9.

TENTATIVE MOVES TOWARDS FREE TRADE, 1778–86

Anglo-Irish Relations and Irish Free Trade Agitation of 1779–85

Motion respecting Trade in Ireland, 19 January 1779, *Cobbett's Parliamentary Debates*, vols 13–30 (1743–94) (London: R. Bagshaw; Longman & Co., 1812–20), vol. 20 (1778–80), c. 111.

Jan. 19. Earl *Nugent* moved, 'That there be laid before this House, an Account of the quantity and value of goods exported from Great Britain to Ireland, and imported from Ireland into Great Britain, from the 1st of January 1768,' which was agreed to. His lordship said, that this motion was preparatory to one for leave to bring in a Bill for granting further relief to the trade of Ireland. He represented the inhabitants of Ireland as being in a famishing condition, and appealed to two noble lords in administration for the truth of his assertion. He said that a secretary of the viceroy was just come over, expressly to lay before government the deplorable state of Ireland: he referred to a letter he had received from Dr. Woodward, dean of Clogher, mentioning that all had been done that could be effected by contribution to relieve the starving poor, but in vain; employment alone could remedy the evil. He appealed to the noble lord at the head of the Treasury for the truth of another observation; that the revenue of Ireland was so diminished, that it now yielded little more than the expences of its civil establishment. These facts pointed the necessity, as we had lost our trade with our American colonies, of taking care we did not lose Ireland next, by a separation or invasion. If our impolitic restraints were not removed from the trade of that country, we should lose our best customers for many articles of merchandize. Good estates in Ireland were offered to sale at 16 and 14 years purchase, yet no buyers appeared even at that low price. He expected to be opposed by those who had particular interests to support against the national welfare intended by his Bill; but he remembered many similar oppositions to Bills which, after they had

–7–

passed, and the good effects had been experienced, had been highly applauded. For instance, the Bill for importing bar iron from America was strongly opposed by the parties concerned in mines and iron-works at home; yet it was found that Great Britain did not produce a tenth part of the iron wanted for consumption. He declared himself as warm a friend to England as any man; and if he did not think it was promoting the interest of this country to grant Ireland relief to her trade, he would not move it. He concluded with a kind of prophecy, that if Ireland was not assisted in her commerce, it might become a question in that House, to vote a sum for the support of that country, from the insufficiency of its own revenue. The establishment of a cotton manufactory, and leave to export the manufacture to Great Britain, with leave to export and import to and from America, the West Indies, and Africa, were the points he had in contemplation. He concluded with saying, if all he wished could not be obtained, he must be satisfied with a part.

Mr. *Stanley* requested the noble lord would give as long notice as possible of the day he should bring in his Bill, that his constituents might be early apprised of it, as not only the town of Manchester, but all the manufacturing towns in the country, concerned in the cotton branches, were alarmed.

Sir *George Yonge* intreated the noble earl not to hurry on a Bill of such consequence, but wait for better information. He could not consider the state of Ireland in the melancholy light it had been described; but if the people really were famishing, it was not owing to the trade laws of this country, but to mismanagement in their own internal police.

Mr. *T. Townshend* reminded the House, that by a narrow policy America had been lost, and bid them beware of losing Ireland. He declared himself impartial, not having any property in Ireland; yet he considered his property in England as dependent in a great measure on the prosperity of Ireland; and as a member of the community, he wished to remove those partial restraints on her trade, which certainly are the cause of her distresses.

'Debate in the Commons on the State of the Trade and Commerce of Ireland', 15 February 1779, *Cobbett's Parliamentary Debates*, vols 13–30 (1743–94) (London: R. Bagshaw; Longman & Co., 1812–20), vol. 20 (1778–80), cc. 136–8.

Debate in the Commons on the State of the Trade and Commerce of Ireland.]

Feb. 15. Lord *Newhaven* addressed the House in a very pathetic manner, in favour of Ireland. He painted her distressed situation with much sensibility, and hoped gentlemen would consider the obligations this country were under, to take off those burthensome restrictions that lay upon her trade. He stated, that the imports for which Glasgow, Bristol, Liverpool, and the other seaport towns so loudly called, were not more than 9,000*l.* and a fraction in their favour, and for this sum they laboured and stretched all their interest to distress that unhappy country. He gave as an instance of that distress, an account of a man, who, when his cattle had been seized to satisfy his landlord, had prayed for leave to bleed them, that his perishing family might subsist for some days longer on the blood. The export Bill granted in favour of Ireland last session, he said, would be of no avail, if parliament did not also grant them an import trade, since, if they could not take commodities in return at the West India markets, their trade would be nugatory. He therefore wished to bring in a Bill granting Ireland a free import trade from the West India islands. But in the mean time, and as a preparatory measure, he would move, That the House do form themselves into a committee of the whole House, to consider of the best means of granting Ireland an import trade.

Sir *Thomas Egerton* objected to this motion. He said that the distresses of Britain were equal to those of Ireland, and that in granting them favours we must not forget ourselves. This was no time to create disturbances at home, by giving up the trade of the country, and he was sensible that an import trade could not be granted to Ireland without awakening clamours of a very alarming nature. The people did not even now sit easy under their misfortunes. Edinburgh had been, for some days, in the possession of a mob. London had been offended by one, and the whole people felt and loudly lamented their distresses. The county which he had the honour to represent, was in a very lamentable situation with respect to trade, and he was sensible that if it was permitted to the Irish to import cotton, which was the staple manufacture of Manchester and its environs, the trade of the county would be totally annihilated. He therefore moved that the consideration of this business be postponed for six months.

Sir *George Yonge* seconded this motion, and was warm in his opposition to the motion of the noble lord. He said, he conceived it had been the sense of parliament last year, that nothing more was to be granted to Ireland than was granted, and he thought they were very well satisfied, at least the worthy gentleman who was their ambassador, sir Lucius O'Brien, had expressed the utmost satisfaction, and the greatest gratitude for what had been done. He declared, he wished to give every reasonable indulgence to Ireland, and if a mode could be found out to do so without injuring Britain, no man would be more happy or more earnest than himself in doing it. But this was no time, nor was the mode proposed the most eligible, for doing services to Ireland. He conceived the greatest part of her misfortunes arose, not from the restrictions of trade, but from the fault of her internal policy. So shameful a waste of their treasure in the support of pensioners and placemen, was the great source of their calamities, and before they came imploring the assistance of Britain, they should do all they could to extricate themselves. He would not dare to say what would be the consequences of going upon this business at this time. When we had nothing left to bestow, burdened with taxes, involved in a war, and sinking under every calamity, this was no time to throw away the little remnant we had left of trade and manufacture.

Lord *North* expressed his astonishment, that further relief should be asked for Ireland, before time had been taken to observe how far the indulgences granted had operated towards it. No one had a greater desire to serve Ireland than he had: but the commercial situation of this country was by no means to be thought able to give way in favour of the trade of that country, who had, it must be admitted, every indulgence granted to her last session that the circumstances of the times would allow of; and as for further privileges in trade, his lordship was clearly of opinion, they could not be granted without materially affecting the interest of this kingdom.

Mr. *Burke* exploded the arguments against the motion, with keenness and satire. He wanted words to express his amazement at the ostensible reasons given for the opposition to the motion. It had been pronounced dangerous for us to consider the laws relating to the trade of Ireland. And what was the reason given against our relieving Ireland? Why, truly, that we ought to do nothing, because if we did grant her one thing, she might ask another. Such horrid reasoning was too gross to dwell upon! It was such narrow and illiberal policy as this that had lost us America for ever, and would in all probability prove the destruction one day or another of the British empire.

Mr. *Stanley* reprobated the idea of relieving Ireland, on account of our own distresses, remarking that England ought to enjoy a more beneficial trade than Ireland, as the taxes she paid were much higher, and the whole of the navy by which the latter was protected, entirely paid by the former.

Lord *Nugent* supported the cause of Ireland. The distresses of the Irish, he affirmed, could not be suffered to go unrelieved much longer, without endangering the safety of this country; for however depressed it might be in itself, it was for our own interest to put the commerce of Ireland upon a better footing. Upon the whole, a relief, and the most speedy one that could be given, was the only thing that could be done to prevent rebellion in Ireland.

Lord *Beauchamp* was of the same opinion, and hinted that the Irish were so reduced, that they had not been able to pay for the militia they were empowered to call out, remarking at the same time the independent companies that had been raised to the amount of 20,000 men, as a subject of enquiry highly worthy the attention of the House.

Sir Harry Hoghton, Mr. Grenville, and several other members, spoke on the same side.

General *Conway*, lamenting that the question could not be granted in the manner it stood, and willing at the same time that something should be done for Ireland, moved, 'That this House will, upon the 25th instant, resolve itself into a committee of the whole House, to take into consideration the several acts of parliament relating to the trade and commerce of Ireland.'

This motion brought on some little conversation, when Mr. Bamber Gascoyne moved for the order of the day to be read, which being put, was agreed to without a division, and the House adjourned.

Sir James Caldwell to Lord George Germain, 28 September 1779, in *Historical Manuscripts Commission: Report on the Manuscripts of Mrs. Stopford-Sackville*, 2 vols (London: HMSO, 1904–10), vol. 1, pp. 257–8.

1779, September 28. Sidmouth, Devon. – A long letter upon the woollen trade of Ireland; combating the objections of the monopolist English merchants to a free trade in Irish wool. The Yorkshire merchants seem not unwilling to grant it, but those of Norfolk, Devon and Manchester object, first, that the Irish would undersell them, and secondly, that they would be deprived of the Irish wool, so essential to their manufacture. The difference in expense is certainly very considerable. In England a wool-comber must be employed, who earns from 9s. to 10s. a week; the wool is prepared with oil costing 7½d. to 8d. a pound or more, and the woman that spins it would think 6d. a day small wages. In Ireland the spinner would be content to earn 3d. a day herself goes through the whole process, from the sheep's back until the worsted is ready for the loom, preparing it with the worst butter at 2d. or 3d. a pound, mixed with a mucilaginous juice got from fern roots. The spinning can be done by girls of six or seven years old, and the weaving is also done very cheaply, as 'the women of every peasant manufactures clothing and blankets for the family.'

'The confined notions of the selfish monopoliser will always induce him to be averse to the encouragement of competitors' but England has more interest in the prosperity of Ireland than they imagine, and by the preventing of smuggling, and the better chance of making these kingdoms the great centre of the woollen trade, the prosperity of the traders would probably be greatly increased. 'Plenty, variety and cheapness must always draw an extensive trade; a person that wants goods would sooner go to a town where there were ten shops that manufactured and sold them, than to a town where there was only one.'

Enclosing, letters from the Right Hon. Owen Wynne, M.P., Mr. Armour Lowry Corry, M.P. for co. Tyrone, Sir Fitzgerald Aylmer, Bart., M.P. for Kildare, Mr. George Rochfort and Mr. Patrick Cullen, on the bad condition of trade in Ireland, and on the dangers that may arise from the martial spirit stirred up in the people by the rumoured prospect of invasion.

Speech of the Lord Lieutenant to the Irish Parliament (1779)

Speech of the Lord Lieutenant to the Irish Parliament, Dublin Castle, 12 October 1779, *Annual Register* (1780), pp. 352–3.

Dublin Castle, October 12.

THIS day the parliament having met according to the last prorogation, his Excellency the Lord Lieutenant went in state to the House of Peers, and the Commons being sent for and come thither accordingly, his Excellency made the following speech to both Houses:

My Lords and Gentlemen,

AT a time when the trade and commerce of this kingdom are, to a more particular manner, the objects of public attention, it was to be wished that the general tranquillity, ever desirable, had been restored, so as to have left you entirely at leisure to deliberate on those great and important subjects. But I am persuaded you will not permit any interests, however dear to you, to impede your efforts, or disturb your unanimity at this most important period: and I am have it expressly in command from his Majesty to assure you, that the cares and solicitudes inseparable from a state of hostility, have not prevented him from turning his royal mind to the interests and distresses of this kingdom with the most affectionate concern; of which the money remitted to this country for its defence, when England has every reason to apprehend a most formidable and immediate attack, affords a convincing proof. Anxious for the happiness of his people his Majesty will most cheerfully co-operate with his Parliament in such measures as may promote the common interests of all his subjects.

'Debate in the Commons on Lord North's Propositions for the Relief of the Trade of Ireland', 13 December 1779, *Cobbett's Parliamentary Debates*, vols 13–30 (1743–94) (London: R. Bagshaw; Longman & Co., 1812–20), vol. 20 (1778–80), cc. 1272–85.

Debate in the Commons on Lord North's Propositions for the Relief of the Trade of Ireland.]

Dec. 13. The House went into a committee on the Affairs of Ireland, the earl of Drogheda in the chair.

Lord *North* opened his three propositions relative to the allowing Ireland a free export of her wool, woollens, and wool flocks; a free exportation of glass, and all kinds of glass manufactures; and a freedom of trade with the British plantations on certain conditions, the basis of which was to be an equality of taxes and customs, upon an equal and unrestrained trade. To demonstrate the matter of right, as well as favour, he stated the two following propositions: first, that Ireland had a free and unlimited right to trade with the whole world: secondly, that Ireland did not, nor could not, pretend to claim any right, directly or co-relatively, with any part of the British colonies or plantations. Every person in both kingdoms must instantly give an universal assent to the latter proposition. It was not his wish on the present occasion, to enter into the discussion of the former, or debate points merely speculative: so much, however, he could hazard, that mixing the broad claim of a free and unrestrained trade, and qualifying it with the advantage derivable from a connection with Great Britain, it would not be too much to say, that although the claim was with Ireland, the option of a connection with this country, and a participation of commercial interests was clearly in favour of the latter, in preference to any ideal or remote benefits, which might be drawn in future from what by some was understood, perhaps very erroneously, to be included in the undefined terms of a free trade. He would even go further, and affirm from every thing he could learn, that the people of the first rank and consequence in that kingdom perfectly met his opinion on the subject, and that their own good sense led them to make the estimate, and wisely determine on the choice.

He said, it was both the interest and inclination of Ireland to stand well with England; that on the idea of such a natural and political connection, they had been rather harshly and impolitically treated, Before the Restoration they enjoyed every commercial advantage and benefit in common with England. The commerce, import and export, was held in common by both kingdoms, till the reign of Charles the 2nd. Even the Act of Navigation, the great foundation of our plantation laws, put England and Ireland upon exact terms of equality; nor was it till two years after that the first commercial restriction was laid on Ireland, and that not directly, but by a side wind, and by deductive interpretation. When the Act first passed, there was a general governing clause, for giving bonds to perform the conditions of the Act; but when the Act was amended, in the 15th Charles 2, the word Ireland was omitted, whence a conclusion was drawn, that the Acts of the two preceding parliaments, 12th, 13th, and 14th Charles 2, were thereby repealed, though it was as clearly expressed in those Acts as it was possible for words in convey, that ships built in Ireland, navigated with the people thereof, were deemed British, and qualified to trade to and from the British plantations, and that ships built in Ireland, and navigated with his Majesty's subjects of Ireland, were entitled to the same abatements and privileges to which importers and exporters of goods in British built ships were entitled by the book of rates. Ireland was, however, omitted in the manner he had already mentioned. The giving bond being omitted in the Act of the 15th of the same king, the very condition which was to give it a general operation, namely, confining the liberty to trade only with Great Britain and Ireland, and vesting the power in Ireland to trade with the colonies on the same footing as England, having been left out, Ireland was thereby as much excluded from trading with the British colonies as France, Spain, or any other strange nation, in the way of a direct export or import trade, except in a few instances, which were by subsequent Acts declared exceptions to the general rule, such as the export of servants, horses, and victual; and in the reign of king William, of linen, and some few enumerated articles since that period.

There were anecdotes still extant, relative to the real causes of those harsh and restrictive laws. They were supposed to have originated in a dislike or jealousy of the growing power of the then duke of Ormond, who, from his great estate and possessions in Ireland, was supposed to have a personal interest in the prosperity of that kingdom. Indeed, so far was this spirit carried, whether from personal enmity to the duke of Ormond, from narrow prejudices, or a blind policy, that the parliament of England passed a law to prohibit the importation of Irish lean cattle.

The wool export and woollen manufacture still remained in the possession of Ireland to restore, which was the object of his present motion. In 1692, from jealousy, or some other motive, the two Houses of the English parliament addressed the crown, recommending a kind of compact between both kingdoms; the terms of which were, that England should enjoy the woollen manufacture exclusively, and Ireland the linen. Yet however solemnly this compact was observed by the latter kingdom, the truth was, that England carried on the linen manufacture to full as great an extent as Ireland, while the monopoly of the woollens remained totally with England. The first step Ireland took in consequence of this compact, was to lay an export duty upon wool and woollens of all kinds equal to a prohibition; and when the Act expired, for it was but a temporary one by way of experiment, the British parliament, without consulting that of Ireland, by the 10th and 11th William 3, passed a similar Act, and made it perpetual. That was the Act that at once put an end to the woollen trade of Ireland. The next Act was a law of the 5th Geo. 1; the next the 5th and the 12th of the late king, which last went so far even as to prohibit the export of a kind of woollen manufacture called waddings, and one or two other articles excepted out of the 10th and 11th of William; but these three last Acts swept every thing before them.

His lordship next proceeded to state some facts relative to the trade of that country. He said, upon an average of the six years from 1766 to 1772, the export to Ireland was somewhat more than two millions; and in the succeeding six years, ending in 1778, about as much more, one half nearly British manufacture or produce, the other half certificated articles, of which this country was the medium of conveyance. Out of the native produce, which was something more than 900,000*l.* per annum, on the average, only 200,000*l.* were woollens; so that in this light, supposing every thing that any man could wish to conclude from the fact, he submitted, whether it would be sound policy to risk a million export of native produce for a woollen export of 200,000*l.*

Another consideration was, that Ireland, when restored to good humour, joined with motives of common interest, as she had always hitherto proved, would continue to be the best customer this country has. The woollen manufacture must for a very long time indeed continue in a state of infancy; and though cloths had been manufactured sufficient to answer a considerable part of the home consumption, yet it could be hardly expected, that Ireland would be able to rival Great Britain at the foreign markets, when, after the expence of land-carriage, freight, insurance, factorage, &c. she was able to under-sell Ireland in her own markets on the very spot, though aided by the advantage of low wages and taxes.

He then turned to reconsider the state of the linen trade, which, however prosperous it might appear, was still capable of great improvement. It was a pamphlet written by the celebrated sir William Temple, that first suggested the idea of extending and improving the linen manufacture of Ireland, and gave rise to the compact which he had alluded to. It was an opinion which prevailed with many, he believed, that as the compact was now to be dissolved, should the Irish be permitted to enjoy a free export of woollens, that the bounties paid on the importation into England of certain species of fabrics of Irish linens, ought to be discontinued. In this he should differ greatly from gentlemen who might reason in that manner, and he would support his difference of opinion by the following authentic documents which he had in his hand. From hence it appeared, the number of yards of linen manufactured for foreign consumption, or exported in 1751, was twelve millions; the next year the British bounty was discontinued, and it fell to ten millions; in 1756 it was no higher than eleven millions; and in the next year, 1757, when the bounties were again granted, the number of yards

'Debate in the Commons on Lord North's Propositions' (1779)

entered for exportation suddenly rose to fifteen millions; and so continued to increase for several years so high, he believed, within a period of fifteen years (1771) as to twenty-five millions of yards. This was sufficient ground for him to conclude, that the British bounty operated as a great encouragement. It was not a large sum that was appropriated for this purpose, the whole not being, in the highest year, above 13,000*l.* or thereabouts ...

After making a number of miscellaneous observations, to shew that Ireland had relinquished her woollen trade and woollen manufacture, upon the conditions of a compact made *boná fide* between both kingdoms; that the compact had been, broken, if not had at least been strictly adhered to by the parliament of Great Britain, that Ireland would never be able to rival England in the fine woollen fabrics; that Ireland manufacturing her own wool would prevent the contraband export of the raw material to France; that the woollen export, laying it down on the largest scale, was not more than the fifth of the native produce of this kingdom exported annually to Ireland; that a manufacture of the ordinary woollen fabrics of Ireland would not affect that of Great Britain; that whatever was a benefit to Ireland must, sooner or later, be of singular advantage to Great Britain. He concluded this part of his speech by moving the following Resolution: 'That it is expedient to repeal so much of any of the laws of Great Britain, as prohibit the exportation from the kingdom of Ireland, of all woollen manufactures whatsoever, or manufactures made up, or mixed with, wool or wool flocks.'

His lordship said, should the committee agree to the resolution, and the House on the report confirm the sense of the committee, he meant to move for leave to bring in a Bill pursuant to the said resolution, and likewise for the repeal of such parts of the several acts of the British parliament, as laid any restriction on the export of wool, woollen goods, flocks, &c. When this Bill should pass into a law, there would of course be an end of the compact between England and Ireland, respecting the woollen and linen manufactures; but he trusted, as a more liberal spirit had manifested itself on both sides of the water, that both kingdoms would be perfectly contented. He was satisfied, that the measure would be productive of mutual advantage; the commercial interest would be put upon a more equitable and solid footing, and as an act of policy as well as benefit, he had no doubt, but the individual advantage accruing to either, would terminate in the wished for point of union, the good of the whole.[1]

Respecting his third proposition, that of allowing a free trade, or what he understood the words to import, an equal trade to the British colonies and plantations in America and the West Indies; the case was very different from the two he had mentioned. Ireland gave up her woollen trade by compact. The compact was an exclusive linen trade, rather a fair competion [*sic*] with England: Ireland, of her own accord, gave up the woollen trade, by an act of her

1 [Ed.: There follows a detailed examination of glass manufacturing, which has been deleted.]

own legislature, which, when it expired, was made perpetual, by an act of the British parliament. But this compact was no sooner made, than it was violated by England; for instead of prohibiting foreign linens, duties were laid on and necessarily collected; so far from amounting to a prohibition on the import of the Dutch, German, and East-country linen manufactures, those manufactures have been able, after having the duties imposed upon them by the British parliament, to meet, and, in some instances, to undersell Ireland both in Great Britain, the West Indies, and several other parts of the British empire. Neither did his third proposition partake of the nature of the second: the materials used in the composition of glass were of native produce, and, if having the liberty to export, they could have arrived at an excellence in the manufacture, or to import it upon terms much lower than it could be procured from Great Britain, it had every appearance of severity, as glass was not a commodity which called for commercial regulation, so far as it became a commodity of internal consumption.

He would therefore repeat, that his third proposition was very different from the two preceding; a trade with our colonies of any kind, or of any extent from Ireland, must be considered as a matter of favour to that kingdom. Considering her even as an independent state, she could set up no claim to a commercial intercourse with the British colonies. These colonies had been settled, established and raised to their present opulence by the blood, treasure and industry of Great Britain. By every principle of justice, of the law of nations; and the custom of the other powers of Europe who had settlements and distant dependencies, the mother country had an exclusive right to trade with, and to forbid all others from having any intercourse with them. Such an exclusive right was of the very essence of colonization, for what nation under the sun would spend their blood and treasure in establishing a colony and protecting and defending it in its infant state, if other nations were to reap the advantages derivable from their labour, hazard and expence?

The colony trade laws, so far as they related to Ireland, were full of restrictions, though the colony trade was open before the 15th, 22d and 23d Charles 2, in which the word Ireland was omitted: after that period several statutes were passed, some general, others particular, to restrain and in many cases to prohibit the trade of Ireland with America and the West Indies. By the Act last mentioned of Cha. 2, 7th and 8th Wm. 3, 3d and 4th Anne, ch. 5 and 10, 8th Geo. 1, 4th Geo. 2, and 4th Geo. 3. By these several Acts, the following articles, being the growth, product or manufacture of any British plantation in Africa, Asia, or America, cannot be imported into or landed in Ireland, except they are first landed in Great Britain: viz. sugar, tobacco, cotton wool, indigo, ginger, fustic, or other dying woods, specle or Jamaica wood; rice, molasses, tar, pitch, turpentine, masts, yards and bow-sprits, beaver-skins, and other furs: copper-ore, coffee, pimento, cocoa-nuts, whale-fins, raw silk, hides and skins; pot and pearl-ashes, and gum senega. But by the Acts of the 4th Geo. 2, and 7th Geo. 3,

'Debate in the Commons on Lord North's Propositions' (1779)

all other goods (except hops) of the growth, product or manufacture of the plantations, may be imported from thence into Ireland, in British shipping, whereof the master and three fourths of the mariners are British. By the 15th Cha. 2, and 7th Wm. 3, his lordship observed, that goods the product of Europe, cannot be imported into any British plantation unless shipped in Great Britain, and carried directly from thence in British built shipping, except salt for the fisheries, horses, and victual and linen cloth from Ireland, provisions and implements for the fisheries, clothing and accoutrements for the army, and other articles of manufacture, permitted to be exported from thence into the British plantations, by 3d and 4th Anne, 3d Geo. 1st, 15th and 18th of Geo. 3d.

His lordship enumerated several other Acts of the same tenor, directed to particular articles of import and export, all framed upon the same principle. Having laid down these premises, as the foundation on which he was to rest his intended proposition, he declared that in his opinion, it was the interest and consequently the duty of Great Britain, to do every thing in her power which might promise to advance, promote and extend the interest and commerce of Ireland, upon the broadest ground and firmest basis; and one of the most certain means of rendering that country useful to herself and truly valuable to this, would be to open new sources of commerce to her, and such as it would be impossible for Ireland to obtain without the liberality and indulgence of this country, though she had been totally an independent nation. This, he said, would prove the only wise and prudent means to afford our sister kingdom relief, and that species of relief, too, that would serve more to convince her of the sincere and affectionate desire we have to render her happy, rich, and prosperous. It would be an unequivocal proof of the candour and sincerity of Great Britain, and he made no doubt but Ireland would receive it as such, and that the whole have an happy termination.

This he acknowledged was but a rough outline of the general plan, on the idea of an equal trade. It would demand much consideration, and require much modelling. It was a matter of infinite delicacy, would call for a great deal of detail and enquiry. Esteeming it so, he meant to throw out his proposition as a matter worthy of the attention of the Irish parliament. It might be proper to communicate with that body on the subject; and as such it would be proper to postpone any further proceeding on the proposition until after the Christmas recess, as probably by the time the resolution he meant to move, should reach Ireland, the parliament of that kingdom would be on the eve of an adjournment.

His lordship stated the comparative advantages and disadvantages that Ireland would experience, should the idea now intended to be stated be brought to maturity. If we did not open this source of commerce to Ireland, we should act unkindly towards her; on the other hand, should it be thought proper to throw open our colony trade to Ireland without accompanying the enjoyment of it with similar burthens to those which we submitted to ourselves, it would be an act of the highest injustice to Great Britain, and the rankest folly in those who should advise such a measure. He therefore was of opinion, that an equal trade in the sense he had already explained it, including an equality of taxes and duties both upon the export and import, was the only equitable ground on which the advantages to be held out by his intended resolution, could be granted or expected. The equalizing the duties, and every consequence whether relative to manufacture, trade or commerce, must necessarily lie with the Irish parliament, who from the nature of their constitution, could only lay on those taxes and duties which would bring the British and Irish commodities, upon equal terms to market.

His lordship frequently repeated, that the last of his three propositions, would call for great attention, modification and deliberation. There was one particular, which he begged to state, and which for aught he could perceive, would still be imported into Ireland, in the same circuitous manner it was wont to be, that was sugar. This article paid a duty of six shillings on importation into England; and at present, it could not be directly imported into Ireland from the place of growth, but was obliged by one of the acts he had recited, to be landed in Great Britain, and relanded in Ireland. When entered for Ireland the whole of the duty was drawn back: now supposing, which was the great principle of this plan, that an equal duty was to be laid upon every commodity of the growth or produce of America, the West Indies, &c. on its importation into Ireland, the sugars brought circuitously *viá* Great Britain, in which the whole or the greatest part of the duty was to be drawn back on its being entered upon bond, for the Irish market would come to the refiner, and consequently to the consumer, much dearer if imported directly from the place of growth, than if imported circuitously from Great Britain. He condemned local prejudices and national partialities very warmly: though under different legislatures, he maintained that Great Britain and Ireland had but one conjugal inerest, and were, in the genuine sense of the phrase, but one people. He acknowledged that Great Britain ought to be no sufferer by her bounty to Ireland. The latter would, it was certain, gain much, but this country would be no loser. But even if the sister kingdom should be enabled to rival us at foreign markets, in a few commodities of native growth, cheapness of labour, and other incidental circumstances, we should not forget that Ireland formed a part of the British empire, and the only part, too, out of this island to which we could look for assistance in the moment of peril. He wished that every person who turned his thoughts to the subject, would look at it fairly, and consider it without partiality or prejudice, not upon a narrow or contracted, but upon a liberal and extensive scale. It was a duty every man owed his country, to look attentively and gravely to our present situation, and to reflect that the surplus commerce of Ireland, let it arise from the profit of which branch of trade it might, would necessarily center in the seat of empire; if not the whole, at least much the greatest part; and might be well estimated as forming a part of the accumulating wealth of Great Britain. He hoped Ireland would learn to put the proper estimate upon what was offered to her. He, indeed, had little doubt but she would; he had heard the sentiments of several persons of weight and consequence from that country, or nearly connected with it, and he had every rational ground to hope, that the present propositions would not prove unacceptable ... His lordship enumerated several matters of favour which the present parliament had conferred on Ireland, but observed, that however well intended, they had failed in their expected effect, and by no means came up to the point of substantial relief. The restrictions on the trade of Ireland formed the great grievance, and was the source of all the national calamities which she now felt; to that point her attention was solely fixed. Whatever opinions some persons in that country might hold respecting the defects in her constitution, or internal government, the voice of the people pointed out another object; an object more pressing in its nature, and, of course what preoccupied their minds in preference to matters merely speculative. There was no need of many proofs of the real sentiments of the Irish, they had declared them frequently, and publicly; they had been collected in the only constitutional mode, in which they could be heard and attended to, namely, by the address from the legislature of that kingdom to the crown. What these sentiments were was upon record. Nothing, they tell the crown, short of a free trade will administer relief; and what he understood by a free trade, he hoped he had sufficiently explained in the course of the evening; namely, a free and equal trade, upon condition of an equality of taxes. His lordship then moved the third Resolution: 'That it is expedient to allow the trade between Ireland and the British colonies in America, and the West Indies, and the British settlements on the coast of Africa, to be carried on in like manner, and subject to the same regulations and restrictions, as it is now carried on between Great Britain and the said colonies and settlements; provided all goods and commodities of the growth, product, or manufacture of such colonies and settlements shall be made liable, by laws to be made in Ireland, to the same duties as the like goods are or may be liable to upon importation into Great Britain.'

Mr. *Fox* said, he did not mean to enter into the discussion of the question, till the sentiments of Ireland were first known; nor should he assign his reasons, as every thing he could offer must be deemed premature, till the matter came to be considered by the Irish parliament. The particular situation of affairs had rendered it absolutely necessary to trust ministers on the present occasion; and all he could with propriety add on the subject of the noble lord's propositions, was, that the silence of the gentlemen with whom he had the honour to act, would not be understood to be founded in active approbation. He would for his part consider the resolutions, not as matters discussed, deliberated, and determined upon in parliament, but solely as composing a measure of state, for which ministers were and would accordingly be responsible. He thought it therefore an act of candour to give this early intimation to the noble lord of the real motives for his silence; he sincerely wished, however, that Ireland might, as the noble lord had so confidently asserted, be satisfied by these concessions. His friends and he had openly given their thoughts on the subject, on a motion made by a noble friend of his (lord Ossory): that motion expressed very fully the sentiments of those with whom he had the honour to act.

The Resolutions were agreed to.

John Hely Hutchinson, *The Commercial Restraints of Ireland, Considered in a Series of Letters to a Noble Lord, Containing an Historical Account of the Affairs of that Kingdom, so far as they Relate to this Subject* (Dublin: William Halhead, 1779), pp. 130–53.

Dublin, 6th September, 1779.

My Lord,

Between the 23rd of October, 1641, and the same day in the year 1652, five hundred and four thousand of the inhabitants of Ireland are said to have perished and been wasted by the sword, plague, famine, hardship, and banishment.[1] If it had not been for the numbers of British which those wars had brought over,[2] and such who, either as adventurers or soldiers, seated themselves here on account of the satisfaction made to them in lands, the country had been, by the rebellion of 1641 and the plague that followed it, nearly desolate. At the restoration almost the whole property of the kingdom was in a state of the utmost anarchy and confusion. To satisfy the clashing interests of the numerous claimants, and to determine the various and intricate disputes that arose relative to titles, required a considerable length of time. Peace and settlement, or, to use the words of one of the Acts of Parliament[3] of that time, the repairing the ruins and desolation of the kingdom were the great objects of this period.

The English law[4] of 1663, restraining the exportation from Ireland to America, was at that time, and for some years after, scarcely felt in this kingdom, which had then little to export except live cattle, not proper for so distant a market.

The Act of Settlement, passed in Ireland the year before this restrictive law, and the explanatory statute for the settlement of this kingdom, was not enacted until two years after. The country continued for a considerable time in a state of litigation, which is never favourable to industry. In 1661, the people must have been poor; the number of them of all degrees who paid poll money in that year was about 360,000.[5] In 1672, when the country had greatly improved, the manufacture bestowed upon a year's exportation from Ireland did not exceed eight thousand pounds,[6] and the clothing trade had not then arrived to what it had been before the last rebellion. But still the kingdom had much increased in wealth, though not in manufactured exports. The customs which set in 1656 for £12,000 yearly were, in 1672, worth £80,000[7] yearly, and the improvement in domestic wealth, that is

---

1 Sir William Petty's 'Political Survey of Ireland.' p. 19
2 Sir William Temple, vol. iii., p. 7
3 The Act of Explanation
4 15 Ch. II.
5 Sir William Petty, p. 9
6 Ib. pp. 9 and 110
7 Sir William Petty, p. 89

24 *Battles over Free Trade, Volume 1*

to say, in building, planting, furniture, coaches, &c., is said to have advanced from 1652 to 1673 in a proportion of from one to four. Sir William Petty, in the year 1672, complains not of the restraints on the exportation from Ireland to America,[1] but of the prohibition of exporting our cattle to England, and of our being obliged to unlade in that kingdom the ships bound from America to Ireland, the latter regulation he considers as highly prejudicial to this country.[2]

The immediate object of Ireland at this time seems to have been to get materials to employ her people at home, without thinking of foreign exportations. When we advanced in the export of our woollen goods the law of 1663,[3] which excluded them from the American markets, must have been a great loss to this kingdom; and after we were allowed to export our linens to the British colonies in America, the restraints imposed by the law of 1670 upon our importations from thence became more prejudicial, and will be much more so if ever the late extension of our exports to America should under those restraints have any effect. For it is certainly a great discouragement to the carrying on trade with any country where we are allowed only to sell our manufactures and produce, but are not permitted to carry from them directly to our own country their principal manufactures or produce. The people to whom we are thus permitted to sell want the principal inducement for dealing with us, and the great spring of commerce, which is mutual exchange, is wanting between us.

As the British legislature has thought it reasonable to extend, to a very considerable degree, our exportation to their colonies, and has, doubtless, intended that this favour should be useful to Ireland, it is hoped that those restraints on the importation from thence, which must render that favour of little effect, will be no longer continued.

From those considerations it is evident that many strong reasons respecting Ireland are now to be found against the continuance of those restrictive laws of 1663 and 1670, that did not exist at the time of making them.

The prohibition of 1699 was immediately and universally felt in this country; but in the course of human events various and powerful reasons have arisen against the continuance of that statute, which did not exist, and could not have been foreseen when it was enacted.

At the Restoration the inhabitants of Ireland consisted of three different nations – English, Scotch, and Irish – divided by political and religious principles, exasperated against each other by former animosities, and by present contests for property. When the settlement of the country was completed, the people became industrious, manufactures greatly increased, and the kingdom began to flourish. The prohibition of exporting cattle to England, and perhaps

1   Ib., pp. 9 and 10
2   Ib., pp. 34, 71, 125
3   15 Ch. II., ch. 7.

that of importing directly from America the materials of other manufactures, obliged the Irish to increase and to manufacture their own material. They made so great a progress in both, from 1672 to 1687, that in the latter year the exports of the woollen manufacture alone amounted in value to £70,521 14s. 0d.

But the religious and civil animosities continued. The papists objected to the settlement of property made after the Restoration,[1] wished to reverse the outlawries, and to rescind the laws on which that settlement was founded, hoped to establish their own as the national religion, to get the power of the kingdom into their own hands, and to effect all those purposes by a king of their own religion. They endeavoured to attain all those objects by laws[2] passed at a meeting which they called a parliament, held under this prince after his abdication; and by their conduct at this period, as well as in the year 1642,[3] showed dispositions unfavourable to the subordination of Ireland to the Crown of England. They could not be supposed to be well affected to that great prince who defeated all their purposes.

At the time of the revolution the numbers of our people were again very much reduced; but a great majority of the remaining inhabitants consisted of papists. Those, notwithstanding their disappointment at that era, were thought to entertain expectations of the restoration of their Popish king, and designs unfavourable to the established constituton [sic] in Church and State. It is not to the present purpose to inquire how long this disposition prevailed. It cannot be doubted but that this was the opinion conceived of their views and principles at the time of passing this law in the year 1699.

England could not then consider a country under such unfortunate circumstances as any great additional strength to it. Foreign Protestants were invited to settle in it, and the emigration of papists in great numbers to other countries was allowed, if not encouraged. Though at this period a regard to liberty as well as to economy, occasioned the disbanding of all the army in England, except 7,000, it was thought necessary for the security of Ireland that an army of 12,000 men should be kept there; and for many years afterwards it was not allowed that this army should be recruited in this kingdom. This distinction of parties in Ireland was in those times the mainspring in every movement relative to that kingdom, and affected not only political but commercial regulations. The reason assigned by the English statute, allowing the exportation of Irish linen cloth to the plantations, is, after reciting the restrictive law of 1663,[4] 'yet, forasmuch as

1   Carte, vol. ii., pp. 425 to 428, 465.

2   Archb. Bishop King's State, 209. James II., in his speech from the throne in Ireland, recommended the repeal of the Act of Settlement.

3   Their demands in 1642 were the restitution of all the plantation lands to the old inhabitants, repeal of Poyning's Act, &c. – Macaulay's Hist., vol. iii, p. 222. In the meeting called a parliament, held by James in Ireland, they repealed the Acts of Settlement and Explanation, passed a law that the Parliament of England cannot bind Ireland, and against writs of error and appeal to England.

4   3rd and 4th Anne, ch. 8

the Protestant interest of Ireland ought to be supported, by giving the utmost encouragement to the linen manufactures of that kingdom, in tender regard to her Majesty's good Protestant subjects of her said kingdom, be it enacted,' &c.

The papists, then disabled from acquiring permanent property in lands, had not the same interest with Protestants in the defence of their country and in the prosperity of the British Empire. But those seeds of disunion and diffidence no longer remain. No man looks now for the return of the exiled family any more than for that of Perken Warbec; and the repeal of Magna Charta is as much expected as of the Act of Settlement. The papists, indulged with the exercise of their religious worship, and now at liberty to acquire permanent property in lands, are interested as well as Protestants in the security and prosperity of this country; and sensible of the benign influence of our Sovereign, and of the protection and happiness which they enjoy under his reign, seem to be as well affected to the King and to the constitution of the State as any other class of subjects, and at this most dangerous crisis have contributed their money to raise men for his Majesty's service, and declared their readiness, had the laws permitted, to have taken arms for the defence of their country. They owe much to the favour and protection of the Crown, and to the liberal and benevolent spirit of the British legislature which led the way to their relief, and they are peculiarly interested to cultivate the good opinion of their Sovereign, and of their fellow-subjects in Great Britain.

The numbers of our people, since the year 1698, are more than doubled; but in point of real strength to the British Empire are increased in a proportion of above eight to one. In the year 1698 the numbers of our people did not much, if at all, exceed one million. Of these 300,000 are thought to be a liberal allowance for Protestants of all denominations. It is now supposed that there are not less in this kingdom than 2,500,000 loyal and affectionate subjects to his Majesty, and well affected to the constitution and happiness of their country.

A political and commercial constitution, if it could have been considered as wisely framed for the years 1663, 1670, and 1698, ought to be reconsidered in the year 1779; what might have been good and necessary policy in the government of one million of men disunited among themselves, and a majority of them not to be relied upon in support of their king and of the laws and constitution of their country, is bad policy in the government of two millions and a-half of men now united among themselves, and all interested in the support of the Crown, the laws, and the constitution.

What might have been sufficient employment, and the means of acquiring a competent subsistence for one million of people, when a man, by working two days in the week, might have earned a sufficient support for him and his family, will never answer for two millions and a-half of people,[1] when the hard labour of six days in the week can scarcely supply a scanty subsistence. Nor can

1 Sir W. Petty's 'Survey.'

Hutchinson, The Commercial Restraints of Ireland (1779)

the resources which enabled us in the last century to remit £200,000 yearly to England[1] support remittances to the amount of more than six times that sum.

Let the reasons for this restrictive system at the time of its formation be examined, and let us judge impartially whether any one of the purposes then intended has been answered. The reasons respecting America were to confine the Plantation trade to England, and to make that country a storehouse of all commodities for its colonies. But the commercial jealousy that has prevailed among the different states of Europe has made it difficult for any nation to keep great markets to herself in exclusion of the rest of the world. It was not foreseen at those periods that the colonies, whilst they all continued dependent, should have traded with foreign nations, notwithstanding the utmost efforts of Great Britain to prevent it. It was not foreseen that those colonies would have refused to have taken any commodities whatever from their parent country, that they should afterwards have separated themselves from her empire, declared themselves independent, resisted her fleets and armies, obtained the most powerful alliances, and occasioned the most dangerous and destructive war in which Great Britain was ever engaged. Nor could it have been foreseen that Ireland, excluded from almost all direct intercourse with them, should have been nearly undone by the contest. The reasons then respecting America no longer exist, and whatever may be the event of the conflict, will never exist to the extent expected when this system of restraints and penalties was adopted.

The reasons relating to Ireland have failed also. The circumstances of this country relative to the woollen manufacture are totally changed since the year 1699. The Lords and Commons of England appear to have founded the law of that year on the proportion which they supposed that the charge of the woollen manufacture in England then bore to the charge of that manufacture in Ireland. In the representation from the Commissioners of Trade, laid before both houses,[2] they think it a reasonable conjecture to take the difference between both wool and labour in the two countries to be one- third; and estimating on that supposition, they find that 43-⅞ per cent. may be laid on broadcloth exported out of Ireland, more than on the like cloth exported out of England, to bring them both to an equality. This must have been an alarming representation to England.

But if those calculations were just at the time, which is very doubtful, the supposed facts on which they were founded do certainly no longer exist. Wool is now generally at a higher price in Ireland than in England, and the trifling difference in the price of labour is more than overbalanced by this and the other circumstances in favour of England, which have been before stated; and that those facts supposed in 1698, and the inferences drawn from them, have no foundation in the

---

1   Ib., p. 117

2   Order 14th March, 1698, Lords' Journ., vol. xvi. Eng. Com. Journs., 18th Jan., 1698, vol. xii., p. 440.

present state of this country is plain from the experience every day, which shows that instead of our underselling the English, they undersell us in our own markets.

Besides our exclusion from foreign markets, England had two objects in the discouragement of our woollen trade.

It was intended that Ireland should send her wool to England, and take from that country her woollen manufactures.[1] It has been already shown that the first object has not been attained, the second has been carried so far as, for the future, to defeat its own purpose. Whilst our own manufacturers were starving for want of employment, and our wool sold for less than one-half its usual price, we have imported from England, in the years 1777 and 1778, woollen goods to the enormous amount of £715,740 13s. 0d., as valued at our Custom House, and of the manufactures of linen, cotton, and silk mixed, to the amount of £98,086 1s. 11d., making in the whole in those two years of distress, £813,826 14s. 11d.[2] Between 20 and 30,000 of our manufacturers in those branches were in those two years supported by public charity. From this fact it is hoped that every reasonable man will allow the necessity of our using our own manufactures. Agreements among our people for this purpose are not, as it has been supposed, a new idea in this country. It was never so universal as at present, but has been frequently resorted to in times of distress. In the sessions of 1703, 1705, and 1707,[3] the House of Commons resolved unanimously, that it would greatly conduce to the relief of the poor and the good of the kingdom, that the inhabitants thereof should use none other but the manufactures of this kingdom in their apparel and the furniture of their houses; and in the last of those sessions the members engaged their honours to each other, that they would conform to the said resolution. The not importing goods from England is one of the remedies recommended by the council of trade in 1676, for alleviating some distress that was felt at that time;[4] and Sir William Temple, a zealous friend to the trade and manufactures of England, recommends to Lord Essex, then Lord Lieutenant, 'to introduce, as far as can be, a vein of parsimony throughout the country in all things that are not perfectly the native growths and manufactures.'[5]

1   The Commissioners of Trade, in their representation dated 11th November, 1697, relating to the trade between England and Ireland, advise a duty to be laid upon the importation of oil, upon teasles, whether imported or *growing* there, and upon *all the utensils* employed in the making any woollen manufactures, on the utensils of worsted combers, and particularly a duty by the yard upon all cloth and woollen stuffs, except friezes, before they are taken off the loom. Eng. Com. Journ., vol. x., p. 428.

2   See in the Appendix an account of those articles imported from England into Ireland for ten years, commencing in 1769, and ending in 1778.

3   Com. Jour., vol. iii., pp. 348, 548.

4   Sir W. Petty's 'Political Survey,' p. 123.

5   Sir W. Temple, vol. iii., p. 11.

Hutchinson, The Commercial Restraints of Ireland (1779) 29

The people of England cannot reasonably object to a conduct of which they have given a memorable example.[1] In 1697 the English House of Lords presented an address to King William to discourage the use and wearing of all sorts of furniture and cloths, not of the growth or manufacture of that kingdom; and beseech him by his royal example effectually to encourage the use and wearing of all sorts of furniture and wearing cloths that are the growth of that kingdom, or manufactured there; and King William assures them that he would give the example to his subjects,[2] and would endeavour to make it effectually followed. The reason assigned by the Lords for this address was that the trade of the nation had suffered by the late long and expensive war. But it does not appear that there was any pressing necessity at the time, or that their manufacturers were starving for want of employment.

Common sense must discover to every man that, where foreign trade is restrained, discouraged, or prevented in any country, and where that country has the materials of manufactures, a fruitful soil, and numerous inhabitants, the home-trade is its best resource. If this is thought, by men of great knowledge, to be the most valuable of all trades,[3] because it makes the speediest and the surest returns, and because it increases at the same time two capitals in the same country, there is no nation on the globe whose wealth, population, strength, and happiness would be promoted by such a trade in a greater degree than ours.[4]

Two other reasons were assigned for this prohibition: that the Irish had shown themselves unwilling to promote the linen manufacture,[5] and that there were great quantities of wool in Ireland. But they have since cultivated the linen trade with great success, and great numbers of their people are employed in it. Of late years by the operation of the land-carriage bounty, agriculture has increased in a degree never before known in this country; extensive tracts of lands, formerly sheep-pasture, are now under tillage, and much greater rents are given for that purpose than can be paid by stocking with sheep; the quantity of wool is greatly diminished from what it was in the year 1699, supposing it to have been then equal to the quantity in 1687,[6] it has been for several years lessening, and is not likely to be increased. In those two important circumstances the grounds

1   Lord's Journ., 16th Feb., 1697.
2   Lord's Journ, 19th Feb., 1697.
3   See Dr. Smith's 'Wealth of Nations.'
4   The consumption of our own people is the best and greatest market for the product and manufactures of our own country. Foreign trade is but a part of the benefit arising from the woollen manufacture, and the least part; it is a small article in respect to the benefit arising to the community, and Dr. Smith affirms that all the foreign markets of England cannot be equal to one-twentieth part of her own. – Dr. Smith's 'Memoirs of Wool,' vol. ii., pp. 113, 529, 530, and 556, from the *British Merchant* and Dr. Davenant.
5   Address of Eng. Commons, *ante*.
6   King's Stat., pp. 160, 161.

of the apprehensions of England have ceased, and the state of Ireland has been materially altered since the year 1699.

Another reason respecting England and foreign States, particularly France, has failed. England was, in 1698, in possession of the woollen trade in most of the foreign markets, and expected still to continue to supply them, as appears by the preamble of her Statute passed in that year.

She at that time expected to keep this manufacture to herself. The people of Leeds, Halifax, and Newberry,[1] petition the House of Commons 'that by some means the woollen manufacture may be prevented from being set up in foreign countries;' and the Commons, in their address, mention the keeping it as much as possible *entire* to themselves. But experience has proved the vanity of those expectations; several other countries cultivate this trade with success. France now undersells her. England has lost some of those markets, and it is thought probable that Ireland, if admitted to them, might have preserved and may now recover the trade that England has lost.

A perseverance in this restrictive policy will be ruinous to the trade of Great Britain. Whatever may be the state of America, great numbers of the inhabitants of Ireland, if the circumstances of this country shall continue to be the same as at present in respect of trade, will emigrate there; this will give strength to that part of the empire on which Great Britain can least, and take it from that part on which at present she may most securely depend. But this is not all the mischief; those emigrants will be mostly manufacturers, and will transfer to America the woollen and linen manufactures, to the great prejudice of those trades in England, Scotland, and Ireland; and then one of the means used to keep the colonies dependent by introducing this country into a system of colonisation, will be the occasion of lessening, if not dissolving, the connection between them and their parent State.

Great Britain, weakened in her extremities, should fortify the heart of her empire; Great Britain, with powerful foreign enemies united in lasting bonds against her, and with scarcely any foreign alliance to sustain her, should exert every possible effort to strengthen herself at home. The number of people in Ireland have more than doubled in fourscore years. How much more rapid would be the increase if the growth of the human race was cherished by finding sufficient employment and food for this prolific nation! it would probably double again in half a century. What a vast accession of strength such numbers of brave and active men, living almost within the sound of a trumpet, must bring to Great Britain, now said to be decreasing considerably in population! – a greater certainty than double those numbers dispersed in distant parts of the globe, the expense of defending and governing of which must at all times be great. Sir W. Temple,[2] in 1673, takes notice of the circumstances prejudicial to the trade and

---

1   Eng. Com. Journ., vol. xii., pp. 514, 523, 528.

2   Vol. iii., p. 8.

riches of Ireland, which had hitherto, he says, made it of more loss than value to England. They have already been mentioned. The course of time has removed some of them, and the wisdom and philanthropy of Britain may remove the rest. 'Without these circumstances (says that honest and able statesman), the native fertility of the soils and seas, in so many rich commodities, improved by multitudes of people and industry, with the advantage of so many excellent havens, and a situation so commodious for all sorts of foreign trade, must needs have rendered this kingdom one of the richest in Europe, and made a mighty increase both of strength and revenue to the crown of England.'[1]

During this century, Ireland has been, without exaggeration, a mine of wealth to England, far beyond what any calculation has yet made it. When poor and thinly inhabited she was an expense and a burden to England; when she had acquired some proportion of riches and grew more numerous, she was one of the principal sources of her wealth. When she becomes poor again, those advantages are greatly diminished. The exports from Great Britain to Ireland, in 1778,[2] were less than the medium value of the four preceding years in a sum of £634,444 3s. 0d; and in the year 1779, Great Britain is obliged, partly at her own expense, to defend this country, and for that purpose has generously bestowed out of her own exchequer a large sum of money. Those facts demonstrate that the poverty of Ireland ever has been a drain, and her riches an influx of wealth to England, to which the greater part of it will ever flow, and it imports not to that country through what channel; but the source must be cleared from obstructions, or the stream cannot continue to flow.

Such a liberal system would increase the wealth of this kingdom by means that would strengthen the hands of government, and promote the happiness of the people. Ireland would be then able to contribute largely to the support of the British Empire, not only from the increase of her wealth, but from the more equal distribution of it into a greater number of hands among the various orders of the community. The present inability of Ireland arises principally from this circumstance, that her lower and middle classes have little or no property, and are not able, to any considerable amount, either to pay taxes or consume those commodities that are the usual subjects of them; and this has been the consequence of the laws which prevent trade and discourage manufactures. The same quantity of property distributed through the different classes of the people would supply resources much superior to those which can be found in the present state of Ireland.[3] The increase of people there under its present restraints makes but a small

1 See Sir John Davis's 'Discourses,' pp. 5, 6, 194.

2 Summary of Imports and Exports to and from Ireland, laid before the British House of Commons in 1779.

3 Those states are least able to pay great charges for public disbursements whose wealth resteth chiefly in the hands of the nobility and gentry. – Bac., vol. i., p. 10; Smith's 'Wealth of Nations,' vol. ii., p. 22.

addition to the resources of the State in respect of taxes.[1] In 1685, the amount of the inland excise in Ireland was £75,169. In 1762, it increased only to £92,842. Those years are taken as periods of a considerable degree of prosperity in Ireland. The people had increased, from 1685 to 1762, in a proportion of nearly 7 to 4,[2] which appears from this circumstance, that in 1685 hearth-money amounted to £32,659, and in 1762 to £56,611. At the former period the law made to restrain and discourage the principal trade and manufacture of Ireland had not been made. There were then vast numbers of sheep in Ireland, and the woollen manufacture was probably in a flourishing state. At the former of those periods the lower classes of the people were able to consume excisable commodities; in the latter they lived for the most part on the immediate produce of the soil. The numbers of people in a state, like those of a private family, if the individuals have the means of acquiring, add to the wealth, and if they have not those means, to the poverty of the community. Population is not always a proof of the prosperity of a nation; the people may be very numerous and very poor and wretched. A temperate climate, fruitful soil, bays and rivers well stocked with fish, the habits of life among the lower classes, and a long peace, are sufficient to increase the numbers of people: these are the true wealth of every state that has wisdom to encourage the industry of its inhabitants, and a country which supplies in abundance the materials for that industry. If the state or the family should discourage industry, and not allow one of the family to work, because another is of the same trade, the consequences to the great or the little community must be equally fatal.

Is there not business enough in this great world for the people of two adjoining islands, without depressing the inhabitants of one of them? Let the magnanimity and philanthropy of Great Britain address her poor sister kingdom in the same language which the good-natured Uncle Toby uses to the fly in setting it at liberty: – 'Poor fly; there's room enough for thee and me.'

I have the honour to be,

My Lord, &c.

---

1   A very judicious friend of mine has, with great pains and attention, made a calculation of the numbers of people in Ireland in the year 1774, and he makes the numbers of people to amount to 2,325,041; but supposes his calculation to be under the real number. I have, therefore, followed the calculation commonly received, which makes their number amount to 2,500,000. He computes, as has been before mentioned, the persons who reside in houses of one hearth, to be 1,877,220. Those find it very difficult to pay hearth money, and are thought to be unable to pay any other taxes. If this is so, according to this calculation, there are but 447,821 people in Ireland able to pay taxes.

2   Ireland was much more numerous in 1685 than at any time, after the Revolution, during that century, there having been a great waste of people in the rebellion at that era.

William Eden, *A Letter to the Earl of Carlisle from William Eden Esq. on the Representation of Ireland respecting a Free Trade* (Dublin: R. Marchbank, 1779).

Greenwich, Nov. 4, 1779.

MY LORD,

HAVING had leisure to advert to the printed accounts of some occurrences which have lately engaged the public attention; I should think that I had very imperfectly executed my first proposition, of stating to your Lordship 'the sincere sentiments of a plain mind upon things as they are,' if I were to keep back the first and genuine ideas which occur to me respecting the recent applications of the Irish Parliament for a free trade. I proceed, however, in this new task, more destitute of competent information, if possible, than your Lordship has thus far found me; but my pen will at least be guided by a similar anxiety to promote candid recollection, and fair enquiry.

And here too we must divest ourselves of all prejudices contracted from the popular altercations of the day; we must endeavour to enter upon the subject before us with as much benevolence, and as little partiality, as may be compatible with the just interests of the society to which we belong. – The wish, indeed, of all good and prudent men, both in Great Britain and in Ireland, must be, to shun with abhorrence all the contagious delirium incident to national questions, and to promote only that constitutional warmth, which may act kindly, and with an invigorating influence, in both kingdoms.

It is not the strict policy of a former century, or the accidental distress of the present hour; it is not the supposed procrastination of a reasonable hope, or the harsh tone of a precipitate demand; it is not an imaginary neglect on the one hand, or an urgent eagerness on the other, which should call forth between two countries connected together by the ties of sovereignty, language, law, blood, interests, and situation, any unbecoming expression, or any ungenerous sentiment. – A kind and manly confidence in the equity and wisdom of Great Britain should regulate the expectations of Ireland; a due persuasion that Ireland is incapable of unworthy motives, or unreasonable wishes, should preside over the deliberations of Great Britain. – Hasty inferences, and decisive assertions, are fit only for disputants who do not seek fair discussion, and cannot or will not understand each other: – The respective interests of Great Britain and Ireland should be considered in a very different tone and temper; without passion, but with earnestness; without precipitation, but with all practicable dispatch. The distress of Ireland (by whatever circumstances occasioned) exists and operates; Great Britain cannot hesitate to give relief; the principle wing of her buildings is in danger; it is for the safety and strength of the great center-edifice, that every part should be diligently examined, and sufficiently repaired.

It is an indisputable and undisputed fact, that there has prevailed through the times in which we live, a voluntary and warm-hearted anxiety in this country, to express her sense of the affectionate conduct of Ireland. It would be superfluous to refer your Lordship to the various acts of parliament, made in this disposition, during the last five years; they were numerous, but have not had the beneficial effects which were meant: –

Nam neque chorda sonum reddit, quem vult manus et mens,

Poscentique gravem persaepe remittit acutum.

The growing distresses of Ireland have over-powered the endeavours of Great Britain to avert them; and we are now told that 'nothing short of a free trade' can give relief!

It was wisdom in the Irish Parliament to chuse an undefined expression upon a subject so complicated and extensive in all its connections and consequences. The whole consideration is now opened to both kingdoms, and it is the interest of both to come to an early, kind, and efficient conclusion.

It is possible that there may be many individuals in both kingdoms, who know as little of this subject as I do; and I freely own that the doubts and difficulties which the first view of it suggests to my mind, are such as preclude all farther reasonings without fuller information. The questions to be asked are indeed numerous, nice, and intricate. Theoretical deductions will not assist us; trading establishments, regulations of commerce, and the whole system of revenue, are involved in the proposition. A principal spring or wheel of a complicated clock-work may be deranged; but to turn the key round upon the instant with violence, would tend only to demolish all the component parts; if we value the machine, we should previously examine it. – When I state my reasonings to your Lordship, I shall be better understood.

I do not wish to carry back your attention to the days of Prince Fitz-Murchard or Earl Strongbow. It would give me little concern if the histories left by Giraldus Cambrensis, Hoveden, and even Matthew Paris, had been buried with the historians; – nor do I feel anxious to bring to light the ancient statutes and ordinances of Henry the Third, Edward the First, and other early reigns, supposed to be made for the purpose of binding Ireland. The antiquated discussions upon the fact of conquest; at what particular point the rights of the conqueror are restricted by the laws of nature and reason; whether the principle of subjugation can extend to any exorbitancy of power; and whether implied acquiescence constitutes a positive acceptance; are questions little calculated at any period of our history to promote any good purpose to either kingdom.

It is a political truth more material to be known, that happiness and strength should be extended through the constituent parts of an empire, as far as wise

Eden, A Letter to the Earl of Carlisle from William Eden (1779)

and beneficent laws can operate to that effect. It would next be easy to shew, that public happiness and strength are diffused in proportion to the plenty and convenience with which not only the natural wants of a people are supplied, but such adventitious ones as are superinduced by universal habit and industry; when this end is not attained to a certain degree, an empire may indeed exist, and may increase in numbers, but it will grow, like an unwieldy body, liable to dangerous and acute humours.

Whatever may have been the system of government adopted or accepted by Ireland, the recent and most interesting fact is, that she now complains of some distresses which she conceives to result from that system. Those distresses are possibly no more than may have resulted from temporary causes; – from the late rebellion within the colonies, or from the calamities incident to war; but we know perfectly, that the complaint is founded in real sufferings. The first inference which would arise from this fact in any mind reasoning kindly towards a part of the empire, and discreetly in respect to the whole, is, that the Irish, as fellow-subjects, are entitled to every relief compatible with the general interests. Still, however, we decide without precision, and must draw the circumstances of the two countries to a nearer comparison, if we mean to form any useful conclusion.

The most obvious remark which presents itself is, that Ireland, possessing, on a smaller scale, nearly all the natural advantages of Great Britain, and having, besides, in point of commerce, some others peculiar to her situation towards the prevailing winds, has yet in all ages been comparatively poor and distressed.

The reasons why this phænomenon has so long existed, and why Ireland has not hitherto availed herself of the blessings which God and nature seem to hold forth with a liberal hand, are variously assigned; and as they have generally received some colour from popular and occasional appearances, there is cause to suspect that they do not reach the origin of the evil.

I have seen it somewhere remarked, that the madness of Ajax, who took a flock of sheep for his enemies, would be the wisdom of Ireland; and that a principal cause of the poverty of the latter was the system of her landlords, who, in defiance of the practice and prudence of all other nations, had preferred pasturage to tillage, and, by restraining the industry of the tenants, had reduced numberless families to the alternative of either leaving the kingdom or strolling about in beggary. Sir William Temple attributed the poverty and distress of Ireland to her plenty and superabundance. In another part of his works he takes notice, that the Dutch had turned over to the Danes the patriarchal trade of cow-keeping, for supplying them with lean cattle, and to the Polanders that of plowmen, for growing corn for their use, in order to reserve their own lands and their own people for better and more useful employments. Such, in fact, may be the situation of the nations alluded to, but perhaps it is less the work of policy than of local circumstances. At the same time, if we even should admit that a country which addicts itself chiefly to grazing, or even to grazing and agriculture, will generally be poor, we do not describe the case of Ireland: it has not been the system of the Irish merely to support herdsmen and shepherds by grazing, nor to raise cattle to be sent in flocks to distant countries; but they employ many useful citizens in a variety of manufactures, to which the simple occupations first alluded to furnish only the materials. It is still, however, to be remembered, that the mere necessaries of life are raised by the labour of a very small proportion of people; artificial wants and habitual luxuries must be introduced, to occupy those in manufactures who are not engaged in agriculture, and to promote a general industry, interchange, and circulation through the state.

Dean Swift, who ascribed the poverty of his country to a multiplicity of causes, and amongst others, to a radical error in the whole system of Irish leases, to the avarice of landlords in drawing severe rents, and to the undue encouragement of grazing, admitted also that there was a want of an industrious disposition among the people; but he attributed that want to the restraints laid upon their commerce, and to the discouragement of manufactures, which had made them mere hewers of wood, and drawers of water, to their neighbours. Under this impression, he was wont to quote a verse from the book of Exodus: – 'Ye are idle, ye are idle, cried Pharaoh unto the children of Israel; go therefore now and work; for there shall no straw be given you, yet shall ye deliver the tale of bricks.'

It is a similar reasoning which has produced the application now before us. And if in our own days we were to state to an Irish gentleman the long continued poverty and idleness which have prevailed over so large a proportion of his countrymen, he would probably answer,

'All this may be true; but the monopolizing spirit of our Sister Kingdom is the cause of it. That spirit exercising itself upon Ireland in a very early state of her civilization, nipped her disposition to industry, and indeed made it impossible for her to become industrious. In the very infancy of our country, and whilst we were contenting ourselves with the exportations and sale of our cattle, you made an act[1] to prohibit those exportations. We next gave our attention to the increase of our sheep, in order to export wool; but you forthwith[2] prohibited the exportation of wool, and made it subject to forfeiture. We then endeavoured to employ and support ourselves by salting provisions for sale; but you immediately[3] refused them admittance into England, in order to increase the rents of your lands, though you thereby increased the wages of your labourers. We next began a woollen manufacture; but it was no sooner established than destroyed; for you prohibited[4] the exportation of manufactured woollens to any other place

1   8 Eliz. chap. 3.
2   13 and 14 Car. II. c. 18.
3   18 Car. II. cap. 2.
4   10 and 11 William III. cap. 10.

than England and Wales: and this prohibition alone is reported to have forced 20,000 manufacturers out of the kingdom.

'The navigation Act[1] had unwittingly but kindly permitted all commodities to be imported into Ireland, upon the same terms as into England: but by an act[2] passed three years afterwards, the exportation of any goods from Ireland into any of the Plantations was prohibited: and as if that had not sufficiently crippled the benefits given by the Navigation Act, we were soon[3] afterwards forbid to import any of the enumerated commodities from the Plantations into Ireland. This restriction too was much enforced by subsequent acts, and the list of enumerated goods was much increased. – I say nothing of your regulations respecting glass, hops, sail-cloth, &c. and other inferior barriers, and obstructions to our commerce: we subsisted under all this, and under a drain also, which has gradually increased upon us, by remittances to our own absentees, English mortgagees, government annuitants, and other extra-commercial purposes, to the amount of half a million sterling annually. And though we retained no trade but in linen and provisions, the latter has been under a three years prohibition, during which period we lost the principal market for our own beef, though three-fourths of our people were graziers. Many of us indeed carried on a clandestine trade, and it was essential to our support; but that too has been lately checked, first by the revolt of the Colonies, and now by the war with France and Spain.

'Our annual remittances and debts to Great Britain now increase with our distresses; our subscriptions for loans have been lately filled from Great Britain; our estates, when sold, are purchased by Englishmen; our leases, when they expire, are raised by absentees; the drain is become greater than all our means can supply; our manufacturers find little demand for their work, the farmers sell their produce with difficulty; our land rents indeed are estimated at near three millions sterling, but our land-holders will soon be obliged to reduce them. We allow that several of your restrictions upon us have lately been much softened or modified, but the want of an annual profit in our intercourse with Great Britain equal to our remittances still prevails, and is every hour more felt. By the unfortunate situation of the Colonies, we have lost even our old refuge in emigrations. – After having for many years taken British manufactures, to the annual amount of perhaps two millions sterling, we are for the present reduced to non-importation agreements, as a measure, not of expediency, but of necessity. It would have suited the generosity of our feelings, and the affection which we bear towards you, to have made our representations in better and more peaceable times; but you see that our circumstances are urgent, and that your recent indulgencies are insufficient. We desire therefore a free trade, otherwise our distresses must, if

1   12 Car. II. cap. 18
2   15 Car. II. cap. 7
3   2 Car. II. cap. 26

possible, increase, and the conveniency of our ports will continue of no more use to us, than a beautiful prospect to a man shut up in a dungeon.'

There is nothing in the imaginary detail here offered to your Lordship, which has not been stated to you in better words, as often as you have had occasion to converse with friends who wish warmly towards Ireland, and are moderately acquainted with the principal features in her situation; and as every complaint of human hardship is entitled either to a refutation, or to some redress, we are next to consider what answer might be given to the allegations now before us.

Believing, as I do, that in these days of general science and liberal disquisition, the respectable and leading men in this kingdom (of which description there is a large proportion), are unlikely to inclose themselves within the rusty and rugged armour of Monopoly, I think it possible that their first impressions might be to the following effect:

'Many of the regulations here complained of relate to England's internal commerce, and may be matters of regret to Ireland, but cannot afford any just cause of complaint: – other circumstances may be admitted, to the extent stated; but we should hesitate before we admit the causes to which they are ascribed: we might examine, for instance, merely as a question of commerce, whether before and during the late embargo on the usual exports of provisions to France and Spain in time of peace, more extensive, safe, and profitable markets were not opened and encouraged; by which the price of the commodity, and freight, and the quantity of specie were increased. – The emigrations too which are alluded to, as well as some other effects of national distress, were occasioned, perhaps, by the increase and injudicious modes of land-rents, which were thought grievous sixty years ago, and have been generally advanced near one-third since. – With respect to the larger question; we will neither criminate nor justify the system of our ancestors. The fact is, that, aided by their general system and progressive industry, the commerce of Great Britain has flourished, and continues to flourish. We are sorry that her Sister Kingdom has not kept pace with her. That she has not done so, is perhaps owing chiefly to the frequent interference of civil distractions, and to other causes so forcibly described by Dean Swift, as bearing hard on the industry of the middle and lower classes of the people. We have already given proofs of our conviction, that our interests are in a great degree mutual. We wish that Ireland may be assisted, but we desire, that before proceedings are adopted to reverse all the system pursued by wise statesmen during two centuries, due information may be obtained, and due discretion exercised. In the general anxiety to assist Ireland, it must appear to be as little her interest as ours, to give any sudden shock or precipitate revulsion to the course of British trade, commerce, and revenue. Let the legislatures of the two countries act with dispatch, but let that dispatch be guided by a previous and competent knowledge of all the operative and interesting circumstances!

Eden, A Letter to the Earl of Carlisle from William Eden (1779) 39

'It is not possible, in the nature of commerce, to decide, without a full investigation of the subject, what can be meant, or ought to be meant, by a free trade; and till the proposition has been discussed and ascertained, between well informed and well intentioned men of the respective countries, it must vary in every point of view that we can place it.

'1. Do the people of Ireland understand, by what they ask, the power of exporting their own produce to any foreign country, wherever they can find the best market, except only the countries which may at any time be at war with their Sovereign?

'2. Do they imply the power of drawing such goods and consumable commodities as they may want, from any country where they may best purchase them?

'3. Do they wish to be allowed a commerce to North America, the West Indies, and Africa, free from the restraints to which it was left subject when the 18th of his present Majesty extended their power of exportation?

'4. Do they mean to ask a free trade to Great Britain, their manufactures and produce, when imported into this country, being subject to no other duties than the like manufactures and produce of our own?

'5. Do they mean a repeal of particular restrictions, which the relative circumstances of the two countries may, in their opinion, no longer make requisite?

'Under all or any of these propositions, there are many points of nice and difficult consideration. What regulations or burdens are meant to be proposed, analogous to what now prevail, in regard to the manufactures, imports, and exports of Great Britain? What prohibitions respecting the export of certain raw materials? What arrangements in respect to our distant possessions and factories? Other subjects of discussion will arise, and some upon nice and intricate points of commerce, involved as it happens to be, in considerations of revenue, and in the maintenance of the public expense. We do not know, that emulation among manufacturers and merchants is mischievous either to them or to the state: We do not know that the enterprising industry and increasing wealth of Lancashire have tended to obstruct, instead of promoting, those of Yorkshire: We do not know that the flourishing of Glasgow in her commerce, is any detriment either to Liverpool or Bristol: We do not know that the prosperity of the staple manufacture of Ireland has lessened the advantages of a similar manufacture in Scotland. We admit at least that such competitions furnish employment, produce riches, and encourage population for the general happiness and strength of the empire; and we trust that there will be demand and trade enough in the world for the industry of us all: But we must repeat, that if unadvised measures are adopted, they are likely to affect the prosperity of the British commerce, without promoting that of Ireland.'

If it should be the disposition of the respectable and leading men of Great Britain to feel such sentiments and to hold such language, it is beyond a doubt that much farther information might be collected from them; and it seems impracticable to advance without their aid and advice.

There are many theorems of trade which are plausible on paper, yet it may be impossible for trading nations to adopt them. Maxims being too narrow to embrace all the combinations of human events, political operations must often be influenced by circumstances.

It is an old, but not the less fallible principle of state-policy, that whoever is the cause of another's advancement, contributes to his own diminution. The opposite position is oftner applicable to the respective situations of merchants and mercantile bodies, or of commercial nations. It is now well understood that the flourishing of neighbouring nations in their trade is to our advantage, and that if we could extinguish their industry and manufactures, our own would languish from the want of emulation and interchange. This reasoning is, or ought to be, still better understood with respect to different parts of the same empire.

If we are capable of looking beyond the extent of a single shop-board, we cannot consider the Irish as rivals in interest, even though they should become our associates in lucrative pursuits. Mr. Davenant, who had some jealousies respecting their progress in particular branches of trade, and who, in the close of the last century, recommended the bill to prevent the export of their woollen manufactures, was still extremely doubtful as to his own reasonings, and appears to have admitted a position current in the speculations of those days, 'that the *lucrum cessans* of Ireland is the *damnum emergens* of England.' Sir M. Decker, who wrote in a subsequent period, and upon some points with singular ability, was clearly of opinion, that the restraints on the Irish woollens contributed, in their effect, to diminish the foreign trade of Great Britain. He describes monopolies as a species of trade-tyranny, whereby the many are oppressed for the gain and good pleasure of a few: – 'Never yet (he observes) was a monopolized trade extended to the degree of a free one.' – 'We, in our abundant wisdom, pay nearly all the charges of Government, whilst large classes of our fellow-subjects are made unable to contribute more than a trifle to the general support.' – 'They exist, indeed, under the protection of fleets which cost them not a doit; we contrive to starve them without expence, and ourselves with expence; we drive one part of our people out of trade by monopolies, and the other by taxes. We bleed ourselves almost to death, and think to recruit our spirits by devouring millions of famished fellow-subjects: thus, by excess of cunning, we make the ruin general.'

There is a modern anecdote of a Dutchman, who was employed to settle the woollen manufacture at Abbeville, and stipulated that no work of the same kind should be carried on within thirty leagues. This might help to introduce and give stability to an useful and expensive manufacture, such as in the event that of Abbev-

Eden, A Letter to the Earl of Carlisle from William Eden (1779)   41

ille has proved. When, however, the advantages are once settled, and the art in question generally known, such a monopoly may indeed give a personal advantage, but it must operate to the detriment of the whole circle which is swept by its radius. Particular merchants or manufacturers, as well as particular districts, may, as in the instance just mentioned, derive a reasonable advantage from the exclusive possession of new branches of trade; but when those branches have fairly taken root, such advantages bear hard on other merchants, manufacturers, and districts, and operate powerfully against general emulation, and the interests both of commerce and of the state. It seems demonstrable, that the export of native manufactured commodities from any one part of the King's dominions, must be advantageous to the whole, whenever the burdens and duties are so regulated as to leave no exclusive advantage; for that again would operate as a monopoly.

Subject to the last remark, it is farther demonstrable, that Great Britain loses whenever Ireland is deprived of any reasonable gain. – And with respect to the situation of the latter for the western navigation, we know that it is the interest of a dominion to carry on her commerce, from whatever corner she can conduct it to the best advantage; and it would be thought a gross absurdity in the City of London, if because Bristol is so situated as to have an advantage in the Irish trade, the former should desire to have the port of the latter shut up.

In all these reasonings, the commercial and political interests are inseparably blended. When the liberty of commerce is unequally enjoyed, one part of an empire may be in danger of becoming a burden to the other. An increase of support in aid of the common exertions, might in course of time result to Ireland from the advancement of her trade, and from the produce of duties, analagous to those of Great Britain.

It is sometimes found, that a liberty to export manufactures, increases the produce of raw materials beyond the demand of the particular manufacture; and from the experience of the linen trade, it might be doubted whether less woollen yarn would be exported to Great Britain by Ireland, if the export of manufactured woollens were less restrained; in which case the smuggling of raw wool to the continent of Europe might be checked. It is said that, the wool of the southern nations being tender, and that of the northern countries being harsh, it is of great importance to both to obtain British or Irish wool, which, like a middle quality, unites equally with the two extremes, and produces an excellent cloth, that rivals our own. – It is the computation of many disinterested writers on this subject, that one pack of Irish wool works up two packs of French wool, which would not otherwise be saleable; and Sir M. Decker labours much to shew that the benefit resulting to England, by every pack of wool manufactured in Ireland, instead of being run to France, amounts to fifty-six pounds sterling; which indeed he founds upon an estimate, that one-third of what Ireland gets centers at last in Great Britain. It must still be observed, that no extent of the woollen manufacture can be expected to prevent entirely the exportation of the raw materials, the demand for which is such as to elude all the contrivances of law, and all the vigilance of coast-officers even in Great Britain; and this is analogous to a remark of Mr. Locke's, that 'it is death in Spain to export money, and yet they who furnish all the world with gold and silver, have least of it among themselves; trade fetches it away from that lazy and indigent people, notwithstanding all their artificial and forced contrivances to keep it there; it follows trade against the rigour of their laws, and their want of foreign commodities makes it openly be carried out at noon day.'

I must however again observe to your Lordship, that all these theorems of trade, however plausible they may appear on paper, must be received subject to much previous examination, and a diligent discussion of all collateral circumstances. We are not to proced with that short-sighted wisdom which may enable us to shun the mere difficulty of a day; still less are we, upon a sudden outcry, which like other commercial complaints may be fallacious or ill-founded, to make a sudden revolution in all the practical system of our trade; and upon the spur of a moment to overturn a plan of commerce and revenue which has been the work of ages.

We are to proceed upon the principle, that what we are to give shall be for the good of the whole: Ireland is a jewel to our crown, and not a thorn in our side. The point is, to know what solid assistance can be given, and in what form it can best be given. When men talk of an union to be completed between two great nations, as the cure of all their ills, they talk rashly, and like the state empiric described to your Lordship in my first letter. The case of Scotland was different in every point of view, and the benefits resulting to her by the act of union do not apply to the present consideration. There can be little doubt, that, in the present instance, the separate legislatures of the two countries are fully equal to all the difficulty: – we shall sufficiently know, from a cordial and temperate communication with Ireland herself, what specific measures will be of service to her: we shall know too, from the information to be collected at home, what measures may be adopted with a due regard to the general interests of commerce. We are not to subject ourselves to the remark left by Dean Swift, who says, that in his time, when any thing kind had been intended towards Ireland, she was invariably treated like a sick lady, who has physic sent by doctors at a distance, strangers to her constitution and the nature of her disease.

It may even deserve enquiry, whether the unqualified grant of every thing that human ingenuity can bring within the description of a free trade, would have the effects expected, or convey the relief which is wanted and intended. It was once supposed, that because the importation of Irish cattle into England had been prohibited, with a view to advance the rents of English landlords, and the interests of the feeding countries, the suspension of that measure might be of use to Ireland: this was accordingly tried (and nearly within our memory); but it was a matter of great offence to many of the Irish inhabitants, who resisted the exportation; few cattle, therefore, were brought to Great Britain, and those were chiefly lean.

We should recollect, that though Ireland has at all times had full liberty to manufacture goods for her own consumption, the consumers have hitherto found it easier to purchase from England many articles both of luxury and convenience, than to make them at home. That jealousy must be very lively indeed, which, contemplating this circumstance, can derive disquietude from such reasonings, as that a people should suddenly run away with an extensive commerce, because they are admitted to a participation of its advantages.

The change is more difficult from indolence to industry, than it is from labour to ease; and it is forcibly observed by Mr. Hume, that 'when one nation has got the start of another in a trade, it is very difficult for the latter to gain the ground which she has lost, because of the superior industry and skill of the former, and the greater stock of which its merchants are possessed, and which enables them to trade for so much smaller profits.'

Amidst the difficulties which time, and the fostering attention of this country, alone can enable Ireland to overcome, it deserves remark, that she has little coal, is ill provided with wood, and is also without inland navigations. – In short, the constitution and establishment of a flourishing commerce imply a well-regulated order through the nation, a steady and effective police, habits of docility and industry, skill in manufactures, and large capitals in trade; all which can be the result only of a continued and gradual progress, aided by a combination of other favouring circumstances.

No prudent man, however sure of his principles, will venture to issue, prophecies upon the course of human events; but I see much solid ground to hope that an amicable discussion between the two kingdoms, promoted with activity, moderated by temper, and guided by discretion, may tend to convey essential benefits to Ireland, without any permanent disadvantage to Great Britain. I am unwilling to think, for a moment, that the salutary effects of such a discussion may be frustrated by popular impatience and precipitation.

I shall subjoin[1] to this Letter a Table of English Acts, respecting the trade to and from Ireland; and also an account of some particulars respecting the Course of Exchange between Dublin and London, the estates of absentees, and the revenue and expences of the Irish Government. I happen to have these papers in my possession, and they seem at least sufficiently accurate to be of some assistance to your Lordship in the consideration now before you.

I am my dear LORD,
Respectfully and affectionately, &c.
W. EDEN.

---

1 [Ed.: Appendices have not been included.]

Anglo-French Commercial Treaty of 1786

'Commerce with France. Observations on, Office' ([*c.* late 1785]), PRO BT 6/111/4.

1ˢᵗ Question.

In forming a Commercial arrangement with France, how far it may be consistent with the Interest of our Foreign Commerce, and of our own Manufactures, to agree, that Articles, the produce or Manufacture of either Country, shall be admitted into the other, upon the same Terms on those of the most favored Nation?

In answer to this Question it may be proper to observe,

First – That if a Commercial Arrangement with France should be formed on this principle, We should obtain Terms less advantageous that those agreed to by France, in the Treaty of Commerce of 1713; for tho' by that Treaty, France was to be put with respect to England, on the footing of the most favored Nation, Great Britain was to be put, with respect to France on a still more advantageous Footing, by being allowed to import into Kingdom, not only Goods the produce and Manufacture of Great Britain, but also all Foreign Goods, on the Footing of the Tarif [*sic*] of 1664, four species of Goods only excepted, & which were to be placed on the Footing of the Tarif of 1699 – both which Tarifs imposed duties on Goods imported into France, lower than the Duties then existing, and yet the parliament of Great <Britain> at that Time, rejected these proposals, as disadvantageous to the Commerce of this Country – It appears also that by the Treaty of Commerce recommended by the Board of Trade, upon the Advice of the most eminent Merchants then consulted to be offer's at the Conferences of Gertruydenburgh in the Year 1709, it was therein required that all Articles without any exception imported into France from the British Dominions should be made subject to no higher Duties than those of the Tarif of 1664.

Secondly – That a Treaty founded on the before mentioned principle could not be of the least benefit to the Manufactures of Great Britain; for, if at any Time France in order to prevent the Importation of any Species of British Manufactures should impose prohibitions, or high Duties on the importation of the like Goods into that Kingdom from all other Countries

– 44 –

she would be able without infringing a Treaty formed on such a principle totally to prevent, or very much obstruct the importation of any species of British Manufactures into France – On the other hand, by adopting this principle, France would obtain the Advantage of importing her Wines and Linens into this Country upon the same footing with any other Foreign Country contrary to the present Laws and subsisting Treaties – for these Articles Great Britain is under a necessity of taking from some Foreign Country or other. And with respect to Our Commerce with other Foreign Countries Great Britain might by adopting such a principle indispose many of those Nations whose Trade she at present favors more than that of France, without obtaining any advantage for her own.

Thirdly – By the 24[th.] & 25[th.] Articles of the Family Compact in the Year 1761, France has it not in her power to make a Treaty of Commerce with any other power upon the Footing of the most favored Nation – For it is therein stipulated that the Treatment of Spaniards in France, shall in such case be excepted and ought not to be quoted or serve as an Example – Before We Treat therefore with France upon this principle, she ought either to declare that she no longer considers these Articles of the Family Compact to be in force; or that she is ready to make such a Declaration upon the forming a Treaty.

Question – 2nd. – Whether there be any other principle, on which it appears more proper, that the Arrangement should be concluded? That the Committee may be enabled to form an opinion upon this Question it will be proper to consider

First. – What advantages can safely be offered to France, to induce her to admit any of the Manufactures of Great Britain on advantageous Terms: and under this Head: Great Britain may, in the first place offer to reduce the Duties on French Wines, so that they shall be imported in future upon a Duty not more than One Third higher than what is now paid on <the> Wines of Portugal: – This Reduction will take from the present Duties on French Wines more than One Third – And yet the condition of the Methuen Treaty will still be fully complied with – The Court of Lisbon cannot justly complain of this alteration; for her Conduct has been such with respect to Great Britain as not to entitle her to any favors beyond those she can strictly claim under the Terms of subsisting Treaties.[1]

1 'The Portugal Merchants should however be consulted on this Subject, and it should be enquired whether Portugal can find a market place for her Wines in any other Country but Great Britain.'

Secondly – Great Britain may offer to take off the prohibition upon Cambricks and to reduce the Duties on that Article and other French Linens to the same Amount as are now payable on the Linens of other Foreign Countries – This would certainly introduce into this Country from France a great Quantity of Cambricks and Linens to the Advantage of that Kingdom; but on the other hand it might operate to the detriment of the Commerce of this Country, with Flanders, Holland, Germany and Russia; by diminishing the sale of British Manufactures taken in return for Linen now imported from those Countries;[1] on this head therefore it will be proper to consult the Russia and Hamburgh Merchants.

If it can be supposed, that under such Duties the French will be able to import their Linnens into Great Britain, Cheaper than the before mentioned Countries at present import Linnens of the like sort, such a Measure may prove detrimental to the Linnen Manufactures of Great Britain, and Ireland: It is necessary therefore that this point should be clearly ascertained and on this Subject it may be proper to Consult in some way or other some Capital traders in Linnen and the Manufacturers of that Article in England, Scotland and Ireland.

In return for these Concessions so to be made to France, it may be proper next to consider what are the Manufactures of this Country which it may be expedient for us to propose that they should admit under such Duties as will Open a Market for them, in that Kingdom – The Objects that first occur under this head are Cottons, mixed Goods, & Hardware. Our Superiority in these Manufactures is so great, that we never can expect France will admit them to her Markets unless in return for some Advantage to be granted to her – In order to ascertain what the Duties on these Articles should be, it will be necessary to consult in some mode or other the Manufacturers in these two Branches, and to Learn what is the highest Duty under which they can find their way into the Markets of France.

It must always be understood however, that French Manufactures of the like Sorts must be admitted into this Country under the like Duties to which there is no Doubt but we safely accede.

In the next place it may be worth considering, whether we may not safely propose, that the Leather Manufactures and earthen Ware of the two Countries be admitted into Each Kingdom upon equal Duties; And in such Case, what these Articles <Duties> should be; attention being in that respect paid to the Excise Duties imposed in this Kingdom upon the first of these two Branches; but upon these Heads it may be proper to Consult the Manufacturers in both Articles.

---

1 'Since writing this paper a representation has been received from the Norwich Manufacturers imputing the present great decline of their Trade to the high duties on German Linnens [sic]'.

It is apprehended that no Commercial Intercourse can be held between the two Countries either in Woollens or Silks or any other Manufactures.[1]

It may be proper likewise to consider whether we cannot treat for the admission into France of some Article the Produce or Manufacture of Ireland, as that Kingdom will certainly be jealous of the Admission of French Linnen here.

Quest 3^d.

How far the Interests of this Country would suffer, if the present subsisting treaties of Commerce should be considered by France, as no longer in Force, and no new Treaty should be concluded between the two Countries?

In forming an Opinion upon this Question, it is to be presumed that the Comparison is meant to be drawn between the Non Existence of any Commercial Treaty with France and the Terms of the Treaty of Utrecht of 1713, for we cannot yet know to what other Terms France may be inclined to accede –

And on this Head it is proper first to observe that the Treaty of Utrecht consists of three parts

1st Of Articles respecting the Navigation of the two Countries

2^{ndly} Of Articles conferring personal Privileges on Merchants of each Country trading in the other.

3^{rdly} Of Articles purely Commercial. With respect to the Articles which relate to the Navigation of the two Countries, it is hardly to be supposed that France will wish to abrogate these, and if She does Great Britain will not suffer by it; the only Law by which both Countries will be guided in future must be that of Nations, and if France should ever be engaged in a Maritime War in which Great Britain takes no part and we could in such Case be able to Establish the principles adopted by the Armed Neutrality in the Course of the last War the Navigation of this Country would derive great Advantages from it. –

With respect to the personal Privileges which that Treaty confers upon the Merchants of each Country the French Minister has, in his Declaration annexed to the last Treaty of Peace, declared that it was not meant to abrogate or diminish them. –

With respect to the Articles purely Commercial, there are but two points in which the French Ministers can expect to derive any advantage <by the abrogation> of the Treaty of Utrecht –

1 'Beer & Glass[.] The representation of the Norwich Manufacturers makes it very necessary that some stipulation in their favour should be obtained in a Commercial Treaty with France, if by the admission of French Linnens, the Importation of those from Germany, & consequently our Trade with that country should be further diminished.'

48   *Battles over Free Trade, Volume 1*

1st. They might again impose the Duty of Sous p ton on all British shipping but in such case the Duty of 5^s/ p ton would by the Laws now in force in this Kingdom become payable on all French Shipping – In the Intercourse therefore between the ports of one Kingdom and the Other, matters would still remain precisely on the same footing, and France could derive no benefit from such a Measure unless it can be supposed that British Ships are now allowed by the Laws of France to import into that Kingdom Merchandize from any other Foreign Country or to Trade from one French port to another which is not probably the Case.

2^{ndly} The other privilege of which we should be deprived by the Abrogation of the Treaty of Utrecht, is the suspension of the Droit Daubaine. This is merely a personal Right, and if we are to Trust to the before mentioned Declaration of Monsr. de Vergennes, France has no Intention to anull [*sic*] it – If they do many Reasons may be assigned to shew, that their Commerce is more likly [*sic*] to suffer by such a Measure than that of Great Britain, And that it would not be wise in this Country to retaliate. –

Upon the whole It appears by the following Accounts that the lawful Commerce between this Country & France has been for many Years very inconsiderable and consequently that Great Britain would suffer very little by the total loss of it.

NB The Accounts since the last War are called for – Those that relate to England are brought in, but not those from Scotland, so that the whole of that Trade, particularly the Exportation of Tobacco, cannot be fully Stated as in the foregoing Accounts, but it appears evidently that the Trade between the two Countries in every other Article, but Tobacco and other American Produce is much the same as before the War. –

There is reason to believe that British Manufactures in great quantities now find their way into France, not by any Direct Importation, but by other Channels, and from Causes which will equally subsist whether the Treaty of Utrecht, or any other Treaty of Commerce is in force or not – The principal Articles of the produce of this Country which we import openly into France, are Lead Tin, Allom and Coals – This last Article France will probably grow more in want of, every Year, and France is indeed under a necessity of taking from us all the articles before mentioned, – while on the other hand, Great Britain is not under the necessity of taking from France any one article, for Wines and Linnens we can import with equal advantage from other Countries –

The only Foreign Articles we exported to France before the War in any quantity, were pepper and East India Goods, Rice, Indigo and Tobacco, as appears by the above Accounts, and of the average of £524,000, the three last articles amounted to £502,000 and of this large proportion the Tobacco alone £476,000 – It is impossible to suppose that any Treaty of Commerce can secure to us in future these Branches of Foreign Trade –

The Great Commerce we carried on in these articles before the War, was owing to their being produced in countries, then under our Dominion, and to the monopoly secured to us by the operation of the Laws of Trade, – that being no longer the Case <Our situation in these respects being alter'd> The Share we now have or may hereafter have in that Trade will <must> depend <not on the stipulations of any Commercial Treaty but> on Circumstances which may enable us to furnish France with them more Conveniently, or at an easier Rate than they can be procured from the Countries where they are produced –

Minutes of the Committee of Trade, 14 March 1786, Liverpool Papers, BL, Add. MS 38389, fols 271–5.

Letter of an unknown correspondent delivered by Richard Crawshay, Alexander Raby and Joseph Stanley, London iron merchants, to the Committee of Trade, 14 March 1786

Havre de Grace 19th February 1786

Dear Sirs

I am extremely happy to find there is a real and most sincere design of concluding a commercial Treaty between the two unrivalled Countries: God sent it soon may take place, as it can't fail to connect them in Friendship and a long lasting peace, as the consequences will convince both Nations of the great benefit it will bless the Inhabitants with of both Countries; and that Benefit will be reciprocal and the more agreable [sic] to both parties, as it will give a mortal blow to other Countries who only enrich themselves by the rivalry and badly calculated Laws passed in Opposition to each other of our Countries. – It would need a volume to explain the advantages that Manufacturers on both sides will derive, tho' in my opinion that class of people in England will have the advantage over this Country. Industry and bright Talents pierce faster in England, because infinitely more money is employed in Manufactories than here; a poor Man who by Invention or Talents can be of Use, applies to a busy Minister who knows nothing about the matter, and asks advice of people who frequently know less; he is trifled with for a long time, spends what money he may have obtained from a friend for to make applications, in attendances, and seldom succeeds but by a powerful protection. – In your Country it is to Rich Manufacturers or people who glory to promote the good of their Country in encouraging Industry, even at the Expence of their Fortunes, that a Scheme is proposed, and if approved of by Men of Judgment, instantly put in execution. This will also be the case here whenever we have lost the prejudices of Education that are common to all our Gentry, and even rich people who look on Trade as below their dignity, and when we are convinced Trade is the Soul of the Welfare of a Country.

The chief Manufactory in England that will draw a benefit, is the Iron; that Branch will be furnished here to an immense amount, and will come cheaper than any we can get from other Foreign Countries; Cast Iron and all Utensils for cultivating the Sugar plantations and Mills of all kinds, will be exported to our West India Islands; Cutlery, which was smuggled, will go out in abundance with one word: Bar Iron and every other sort that formerly was not admitted, will be imported, and I don't doubt but similar Manufactories to that of Carron in Scotland will be wanted for the demand; this you'll be convinced of when I tell you

Minutes of the Committee of Trade (1786) 51

that Ship's Anchors costs us here 50 a 52.10. p Cent – Whereas I can have them in London at 28 a 30 p.g. equal to 35 a 37, judge of the rest by this Article.

Copper and Brass Manufacturers will also reap great advantages from the Treaty – Sweden and Germany cannot manufacture neither as well nor as cheap as England. Add to this, we are neighbours, and the foregoing Countries subject to long detentions, owing to the Winter and distance by Sea on the part of Sweden, and as to Germany, Land Carriage burthens their Manufactory; this Branch will materially affect the Northern Countries that furnish Copper.

Both Copper and Iron ware of all kinds are liable now to seizure if proved to be English, even if they came via Neutral ports, without the proofs can be regularly traced, in which case tho' the Manufactory shews itself, yet Government would not admit of presumptions: however these prohibitive Laws, have frightened people from giving Orders for Iron Wares & c. and I dont doubt but what Iron Tinplate Manufacturers have felt the Consequence – At foot you have a List of the objects imported from England, and that may and will be imported if the Treaty takes place. (NB: The list includes anchors, cutlery, and railings)

Earthenware in profusion will arrive; what is for the West Indies will enrich your Manufacturers; all those are smuggled into this Country in small quantities, and at larger Expences in some parts than others: 15 to 20 p Cent for incumbrant [*sic*] Goods: 10 p. Cent for those of value, I am informed are the premiums, – Manchester also will benefit, supposing their Goods importable the same as other Foreign Countries.

France will also find her account by paying less for the Manufactured Goods which she can't do without at any rate; and the Intercourse of the two Countries being opened will enlighten the commercial part greatly; but the chief advantage is the disposing of her wines, Brandies and produce of the Kingdom, which will enrich the owners and Farmers of the Lands; – some manufacturers also will benefit, such as Modes of all kinds, perfumeries, Snuff Boxes, Gloves, Cambricks, certain qualities of Hats, Silks, & c. It is impossible without judging all our Goods to say the whole; a convincing proof of its being for the Countries' welfare, is the wish of the whole of the Inhabitants to see the Treaty hastily concluded; even the most invetrate [*sic*] Enemies of the English say highly that why not sell to the English the benefit of our Trade, by enjoying an augmentation in our own with them whilst we give gratis to other Nations what we may benefit by. The Swedes, Danes and Dutch, who have this benefit does nothing for us and Exports every Thing to us, even English Manufactures, which is a fact.

These few reflections which I have taken the liberty to send you, might be useful if taken into Consideration, which if you can convey to those that may treat the matter you render service to both Countries. –

I am Sincerely
Dear Sir & c.

William Eden to Lord Carmarthen, 6 June 1786, in *The Journal and Correspondence of William, Lord Auckland*, ed. G. Hogge, 4 vols (London: Richard Bentley, 1861–2), vol. 1, p. 123.

William Eden to Lord Carmarthen, 6 June 1786

The Journal and Correspondence of William, Lord Auckland, ed. G. Hogge, 4 vols (London: Richard Bentley, 1861-2), vol. 1, p. 123

My Lord, – My principal motive for re-dispatching the messenger so soon, with the concurrence of the Duke of Dorset, is to submit to your lordship how far His Majesty may think it expedient to avail himself of the apparent disposition of this Court to concur in any further measures for adding stability to the pacific system which at present prevails in the world. It is a consideration of infinite importance, and if any measure should be desired respecting it, I could much wish to be apprised of it before the Duke of Dorset avails himself of his leave of absence, for the purpose of arranging some family affairs in England. It would rest with His Grace to mention the business, and to carry it into effect.

I mention it only because it is in some degree connected with the line of my situation, and many occasions arise in my conferences with the French ministers which necessarily lead to it in all its parts. In truth, from many circumstances attending the commercial discussions, it is impossible for me not to feel that my ostensible negotiation is a secondary object in the view of this government.

It is difficult to feel confident in the sincerity of any foreign Court, but there are strong appearances here of a disposition to believe that Great Britain and France ought to unite in some solid plan of permanent peace, and many of the most considerable and efficient people talk with little reserve of the dangers to be apprehended from the revolted colonies if they should be encouraged to gain commercial strength and consistency of government.

I cannot presume to conjecture the sentiments of His Majesty and his confidential minister on this great subject; but from what I see here, I should think myself culpable if I omitted to suggest it for consideration.

I have the honour to be, with the utmost respect, my Lord, your Lordship's most obedient servant,

WM. EDEN

William Pitt to William Eden, 12 September 1786 (extract), in *The Journal and Correspondence of William, Lord Auckland*, ed. G. Hogge, 4 vols (London: Richard Bentley, 1861–2), vol. 1, pp. 160–1.

(Private.)

My dear Sir, – Your dispatches reached me this morning in the country. I allow fully for your impatience, which is natural, and arises from considerations which I feel in common with you; – but I wish to remove one impression. We never thought of confining you so closely as you seem to imagine to the amended draught of the articles, but coupled them with the instructions, pursuant to which I think you would have been warranted, if you had signed the Treaty in the shape last transmitted to us, with the exception only of the addition at the end of the first article, which is too dangerous to be admitted, at least in its present extent. I persuade myself nothing can now prevent or retard the happy completion of the business.

The new idea of fifteen per cent in general, or on the essential article of cottons, cannot be listened to, and I hope will not be proposed, though pressing it would in fact be breaking off the Treaty. – Silk gauzes are, for very good reasons, too important to us to be given up. The glass which we now give (a little adventurously, as you see by the enclosed evidence) will, I hope, assist you in carrying this point.

The liberty to import *into all ports*, or at least into most of them, is really necessary to the objects of the Treaty. And lastly, the reduction we again ask on the heavy articles of iron, seems so well justified by the state of the present duties from other countries, that the French can hardly refuse some satisfaction on that head. But this last point, though very material, should not be made a sine quâ non.[1]

You may venture to assure M. de Rayneval, that we are in earnest endeavouring to make it practicable to reduce the duty on brandy a good deal below the specified rate, though it is quite impossible yet to speak positively, as you know the interests we have to deal with. We are also making good progress in the idea of classing the duties on linens, so as to put every other country on as favourable terms as Germany in the same species.

I am now more and more satisfied every hour with every part of this business, but still I cannot flatter myself that it is to be all triumph here without any discontent or opposition; and I am persuaded your presence here will be materially beneficial, both with a view to satisfying many of the manufacturers, and also when the point comes before Parliament.

I should be particularly glad if you would come over, if it were only for a week, soon after the signature of these articles. That time might be usefully spent

---

1 [Ed.: An indispensable condition.]

for the business itself, – and I should be glad of the opportunity of talking on many other points on which I would rather talk than write. Among them is the suggestion of your having the appointment of Ambassador to ratify the Treaty. There may be some difficulty in it, but if you wish it upon the whole, I shall be much inclined to settle it so. At all events, it will certainly come best after the preliminaries are known to be signed.

William Pitt to the Marquis of Stafford, 27 August 1786, in *The Diaries and Correspondence of the Right Hon. George Rose*, ed. L. V. Harcourt, 2 vols (London: Richard Bentley, 1860), vol. 1, pp. 63–4.

MR. PITT TO THE MARQUIS OF STAFFORD.

'Hollwood, Sunday, Aug. 27th, 1786.

'MY DEAR LORD,

'The papers which accompany this letter will show your Lordship the state of the French negotiation; and, as it seems drawing to a point, I am anxious to know your Lordship's sentiments upon it. On the different occasions in which this has been under consideration, I think we have been all agreed that the concessions in favour of France were such as we might very safely make; and we certainly shall procure a most ample equivalent by the admission of our manufactures on the terms proposed. I flatter myself, therefore, that there will be no objection to empowering Mr. Eden to sign, if he and the French Ministers agree in the manner we may expect from his last dispatch. Indeed the advantage to be gained by this country seems to me so great that I cannot help feeling impatient to secure it.

'Colonel Cathcart has arrived from the Mauritius to which place he had been deputed by the Government of Bengal, and has brought with him a provisional treaty concluded with the French Governor-General on the point of dispute which had arisen in India. It seems to be a subject which will still require much discussion, but, in the mean time, everything bears the appearance of its being amicably settled.

'I am, with the greatest respect and esteem,
'My dear Lord,
'Your Lordship's most obedient and faithful servant,
'W. PITT.'

William Eden to Robert Liston, 27 September 1786, Liston Papers, National Library of Scotland, MS 5545, fols 84–5.

Paris 27 – Septem[r.] 1786

Dear Sir

I have the Honor to inform You that Yesterday I signed at Versailles a Treaty of Navigation & Commerce between the King Our Master and His Most Christian Majesty.

This Treaty consists of 47 articles: It's [*sic*] duration is for Twelve Years – It is founded on Principles of reciprocity in the mutual Interchange of Produce & Manufacture and gives Concessions of mutual advantage much more extensive than have hitherto been attempted in the Commercial System of the World – You will concur sincerely with me in the Hope that this new Connection of Interests between these two great Neighbouring Nations may not only promote their mutual Prosperity & Harmony but may tend to consolidate & preserve the general Peace of Mankind – I have the Honor to be with great Truth and regard,

Dear Sir, Your most obedient | humble servant | W[m.] Eden

Ralph Woodford to Robert Liston, 24 October 1786, Liston Papers, National Library of Scotland, MS 5545, fols 118–19.

New Norfolk Street 24th Oct 1786

Private

My Dear Sir,

I have not held any conference with Campo since Major's Arrival. He has sent me Word that he redispatches today his Monthly <Messenger> and as the Consideration of the Letters will take up some Time He will be ready to send away another soon if We do not. – I feel a good deal disapointed, [*sic*] but still hope that when You & Count Floridablanca come to sit down coolly together and weigh considerably all Lord Carmarthen's Arguments, He will approach much nearer to Our Point. –

France You see prefers filling Her Coffers by Duties, to letting the Profits escape to Smuglers, [*sic*] and to the ruining Her Finances for a set of Soi-disant Manufacturers, whom if a Countervailing Duty cannot protect, had better turn their Hands to Something else, as I am sure Many <of Them> had better to do in Spain, in cultivating Their Vineyards & Barilla –

I have not had Time to have the Letters from the Consuls copied, so must return Them another Time.

Believe me to be with great Regard & Esteem,

My Dear Sir,
Your most faithfull hble Serv.
R. Woodford

Daniel Hailes to the Marquis of Carmarthen, Fontainebleau, 25 October 1786, PRO, FO 27/18, no. 20.

Fontainebleau, Octr 25 1786

My Lord

A Residence of between two and three years in this Kingdom, where I have not been inattentive to the course of public events, has considerably lessen'd the diffidence I felt at the beginning of submitting to your Lordship such accounts as I received from others, unconfirmed by my own observation. Being more emboldn'd now, I have to entreat your indulgence for the freedom which I shall venture to use in the delivery of my sentiments upon those matters which may appear to require you Lordship's full information.

According to Monsr Necker's Calculation, the public debts of England and France by great singularity of accident, at the end of the War, amounted to nearly the same Sum. France had been, taking all circumstances together, full as great a Sufferer as Great Britain by the War, and she had nothing to console herself with but the unproductive gratification of seeing America politically separated from her parent Country, without any increase of Commercial advantage to herself: – and that for reasons evidently existing in her inability to furnish those Articles of first necessity of which America stands in need, either so good, so cheap, or at so long credit as England. Disappointed then in those hopes (if she really had entertained any) of securing the Trade of the United States to herself it might have been expected that she would have turned her eyes inward upon her own domestic condition, and, after having seen the mischief which she had brought upon herself in Common with the enemy, that she would have taken some effectual Steps towards the contracting her expenditure, and have applied to her wounds the only medicament from which she could expect relief, that of Oeconomy. Great Britain, by setting that example, made such a conduct doubly necessary, each Country being accustomed, and with reason, to measure its own wants and distress, by the advantages and resources of its rival. But France, at the present moment, seems to have lost entirely Sight of that policy; and your Lordship will have observed that I have particularly dwelt, in the course of my Correspondence, upon those operations of finance which I have thought most likely to throw light upon a conduct so opposite to what might have been expected. Although I have always been in the perfect persuasion that the systems of reform proposed, and begun indeed, in this Reign, by Monsr Turgot and Monsr Necker, are as impracticable as they are inapplicable to the Government of this Monarchy, and altho' it be evidently necessary that that powerful class which stands between the Throne and the people should be supported by a part of the Revenues of the Country, Yet (if I may be allow'd the expression) the wise management of venality, and the oeconomy of corruption and favor, by not heaping, as is the case in the present day, too many honors and Emoluments on the same persons, offer such great resources as to constitute, perhaps, the only essential and practicable superiority of a good over a bad administration of the Finances. It is to the Court, My Lord, that you must look for the source of the present evil.

The Queen, not only during the latter years of the reign of the late King, but even till after the birth of the Dauphin, by which event the succession seem'd in some measure, Secured, was very far from enjoying that degree of power and influence which she is possessed of at present; – but that event decided all the Courtiers, and they hasten'd with precipitation to the Standard of favor, whilst those who before had constituted her Majesty's entourage and circumscribed society, were soon consolidated into a formidable party in the State. The Strong propensity of this Princess to every kind of pleasure and expence has been improved into great advantage, by all those who have considered only their own elevation and advancement. Her pretended Friends by administering to her pleasures are become the intimate participators of her Secrets, and having once got possession of them they may, in fact, be said to be the Master of their Mistress, and to have secured, by that Means, the permanence of that power which, otherwise, the changeableness of her disposition render'd extremely precarious.

Although a Spirit of intrigue may be said to be woven into the Characters of almost all French men, and particularly of those brought up in a Court, the Duke and Dutchess of Polignac can neither of them be supposed, from the narrowness of their capacities, to have laid, of themselves, any concerted plan whatever for the purpose of securing to themselves the direction of that favor which accidently [*sic*] shone upon them. M. de Vaudreuil and M. D'Adhemar both consummately ambitious and intriguing, and both attached, at first from motives of gallantry to the Dutchess, are those who have had the chief direction of her conduct. All their own little talents <of society> were successfully employed in a Court where pleasure was the principal concern.

But in order that the Source, from whence the Streams of liberality were to flow, might be well supplied, it was become an essential object with the party to have a Comptroller General at their disposal. M. de Calonne, formerly Intendant of Metz, and afterwards of Lille, a man of wit, and parts, and infinite pliability, was fixed upon by M. de Vaudreuil for the place. M. de Vaudreuil has been justified in his choice for no one was ever truer to the trust reposed in him than the present Minister of France. I mean to that of supplying with unbounded profusion every one that could in any shape be considered to be of his party. No man was ever more Systematical in his Corruption. No Minister was ever more Studious to increase the jealousy of the Court with respect to the privileges of the Parlements: The voice of people is now and then faintly heard <indeed> in their remonstrances, but as the avenues to the throne are all secured by the profusion of the Minister to all who are in credit and power, it has little or no effect, and dies away for want of being seconded.

I know it has been said that the extent of the influence of the Queen's party goes no farther than to the dispersal of certain places and pensions, without interfering with the great line of public business, and particularly that of Foreign Affairs; but it ought surely to be observed, that, when any set of them can command the person who holds the purse of the State, they must necessarily have the greatest direct influence in all internal, and a considerable indirect share in all Foreign Affairs.

Your Lordship might expect with reason some particular proofs in support of these general assertions of the prodigality of the Department of Finance, were I not to repeat what I have already had the honor of observing to you, and which is, that, at the moment that this Country is in the profoundest State of Tranquillity that it can at any period expect to enjoy, it is obliged every year to have recourse to new Loans – I know that the pretext for borrowing is the paying off the Debt contracted during the War, but Government borrows this year near Two Millions of Levies, and the amount of the Reimboursent is no more than seventy five; and that too when the sovereign is in possession of an annual income of upwards of Six hundred Millions.

With respect to the Loan of Thirty Millions, to which the City of Paris was lately induced to set it's name, the distress of the Government may be measured by the grossness of the Artifice it employ'd to get possession of so small a Sum. The Money was said to be raised for the purpose of the buildings and improvements of Paris; but it was no sooner raised than it was paid into the Royal Treasury; the Government out of it's pretended care, having promised to issue annually for those public purposes the Sum of three or Four Millions, as the Works proceeded. This plain question might have been asked. What occasion can the City have to raise more at any one time than three of four Millions, according as the expences incurred, and why should it burthen itself with so large a Sum as Thirty Millions raised all at once, and which it could not employ all at once?

But as if the derangement of the Finances were not yet great enough, and as if Cherbourg were not sufficient to swallow up all the unemployed treasure of France, immense works are carrying on or intended to be carry'd on, in all the Royal Houses. The additions to Sᵗ Cloud are estimated at eleven Millions; fifteen hundred Workmen have been employed for some months past at Fontainebleau – Compiegne, Darmboilles and other places have been improved in the greatest Style of magnificence, and it is said the Versailles is very shortly to undergo a thorough repair, the expence of which can hardly be calculated. I will not trouble your Lordship with a detail of the establishments of His Majesty's Brothers, which are equal perhaps to those of some of the most independent princes in Europe – The inconsiderable people of the Capital are however constantly boasting the immense resources of the Kingdom, without reflecting that those resources are found in the most wretched and oppressed Class of Mankind!

If it be a wise Maxim that every Government should endeavor to preserve it's Customs and manners as distinct as possible from those of it's neighbours, and to keep alive those patriotic prejudices which are the source of persevering Courage in War, and a steady attachment to internal produce and manufacture sin time of peace; None has so much to reproach itself with for an opposite conduct as that of France. The Strong characteristic features that formerly marked the subjects of this Monarchy, are so much alter'd, that the French appear to be a different people to what they were before the beginning of the late War. Different Circumstances have concurred to produce this effect, and Men of a Speculative turn of mind do not fail to discern it, tho' at a distance, the most important revolutions. The intercourse of the French with the Americans, whose Manners and opinions could not but have influence, have brought them nearer to the English than they had ever been before. The almost unrestrained introduction of our daily publications (tolerated indeed by the Government from the conviction of the improbability of preventing it) having attracted the attention of the people more towards the freedom and advantages of our Constitution, has also infused into them a spirit of discussion of public matters which did not exist before. But amongst the most disadvantageous effects of this intercourse, may certainly be reckoned an almost universal taste for the Elegances and Luxuries of British Manufacture, a taste which since the War has turned the scale of Trade entirely against this Nation.

Whatever may be the views of France with respect to other Nations in acceding so readily to the commercial propositions made by England, they must be such as will take time to discover; in the mean while, by considering the Nature of the French Government, and the present state of it's finances, trade and Manufactures, I am much inclined to think that it will appear probable to Your Lordship that motives more domestic, and more immediately pressing, have had their weight.

When Your Lordship did me the honor to instruct me about this time twelve month to see M. de Vergennes upon the Subject of the Commercial Treaty, and to assure him that it was sincerely the wish of England to bring that business to a conclusion, upon the footing of reciprocal advantage, I informed you of the temper in which I found him, and of the very warm, I may say indeed angry language which he held upon that occasion. This Conversation had been preceded by several Arrets de Conseil, establishing such duties upon British manufacture as amounted almost to an absolute prohibition. The French had, at that time, certainly the fullest right to lay on these duties, but after having done so, they could have none to express any dissatisfaction towards any prohibition having been answer'd by prohibition, and instead of reciprocal advantages, mutual disadvantages having taken place.

As far therefore as the Acts of the two Governments went, there could be no just ground of reproach. Whatever there might be for ill-humor on the part of France; the Conduct of both being the same – The ill-humor, it must be confessed, was not without cause, and it spoke loudly their inferiority in their Commercial intercourse with us.

The French before, and ever since the peace, had been endeavoring to establish Manufactures to rival ours for which the most decided taste prevailed amongst them, and as much encouragement as the Government could give, it gave: but it was soon seen that tho ingenuity and industrious imitation might go a good way, equal perfection & equal cheapness were not easily attainable.

The Ministers of this Government cannot be so ignorant of the manner in which it is constituted not to know how difficult it is to give force to all laws, but particularly to those of a prohibitory nature, where great credit and power are interested in the infringement of them. In Great Britain, His Majesty's Ministers, with uncommon wisdom, Vigilance and perseverance have, at last, found means to carry into effect the revenue laws which had been so long eluded; but they had been only eluded; – they had not been suspended in favor of individuals, – whereas in France they are both the one and the other. – The extent of the first mischief is known and can be appreciate, but that of the latter is out of all calculation. – The cause is not difficult to assign. – The Ministers, at least those of the present day, are all activated by one invariable principle, that of attachment to their places, and whoever is a little attentive of their conduct, must see that to ward off intrigues, and to conciliate and gratify the powerful, are the chief means they employ for securing themselves. I will beg leave to suppose, for the sake of example, that the Visites Domiciliares, which, before any progress had been made in the Treaty, had been idly threaten'd to be established, had taken place; without entering into the consideration of the long train of mischiefs attendant on that Species of inquisition, it may be asked what would have been the probable Consequence? – That every one having Credit enough with the great, or the Mistresses of the great, to procure an exemption, would not have failed to apply for it in favor of some dependant of other. – The fatal effects of such partiality are too evident to require any comment.

It seems therefore probable that the French Government felt it's own inability to give effect to it's prohibitory Laws against the importation of British Manufactures, and in that respect, at all events, they may be said to have been Gainers by the Treaty.

But I think I can take upon me to assure your Lordship that there exists another, and a no less principal Cause, of the eagerness of France to conclude the Commercial arrangements. – I mean that of the immediate relief of the Tresor Royal by the increase of the Revenue; an increase which, it may be presumed, will prove immense from the sudden influx of all sorts of British Merchandize paying the legal duties, as soon as the Treaty shall take effect. If this opinion should prove to be well grounded, and from the attention I have paid to the late Conduct of the Comptroller General, I am much inclined to think it is, it will be a strong part of the Corruption of that Minister, who sacrifices to an immediate & temporary resource the dearest interests of his Country.

In defence however to the public of the Concessions which appear to have been made to Great Britain, it is said by the Minister that France looks forward to future Advantages: – but that language is too speculative to satisfy people in general, and, as far as the substance of the Treaty is known, it seems to be condemned. An Argument which I have met with in the World, and which I have found to be adopted by some Men of Sense, whose opinions have weight, has I think made a considerable impression: – on that account I have always endeavored to controvert it.

England, say they, has the immense advantage of supplying a Country that reckons Twenty six Millions of Inhabitants, with her Manufactures: whilst France cannot expect to supply half that immense population in her Trade with us. My answer to this has been, that tho' it be true that there is that great difference between the population of the two Countries, yet, it ought also to be observed that there is a very great difference between the conditions of the two Countries, and that there is diffused thro' Great Britain a degree of affluence that does not pervade this kingdom; on which account, taking all things together, it may be presumed that there exists in England full as many people who are able to afford themselves foreign Luxuries, as there are in France.

Altho', when your Lordship did me the honor to direct me to speak to the Minister upon the Subject of the Treaty, I made use of such conciliatory language as I judged most expedient for the purpose of putting him into good humor, and spoke of the projected Treaty as likely to ensure the duration of the peace, yet (without entering into the consideration of great political objects) I confess I did not understand then, nor do I now, in what manner that arrangement can essentially contribute to produce such an effect. If, as your Lordship seems inclined to think, the French have shewn great facility and have granted us more than we had reason to expect, may it not be asked where is the present reciprocity which is spoken of as the Cement of union between us both? But even supposing that reciprocity to exist at this moment, it seems to be a task beyond the reach of human reason, to compute how long the balance can be kept in the equal poise of mutual advantage, without inclining in favor of one or the other: That it should always remain in the same State seems both physically and morally impossible, and whenever it shall come to weigh down in any considerable degree either on one side or the other, will not the probable policy of the disadvantaged Country be (if, I may be allow'd the expression) to cut the knot which it finds itself unable to untie?

Ralph Woodford to Robert Liston, 29 December 1786, Liston Papers, National Library of Scotland, MS 5545, fols 151–2.

New Norfolk Street 29th. Decr. 1786 –

Dear Sir,

I take the Opportunity of this Messenger to send You Copies of Mine of the 17th. & 24th. Nov^{r.} – And I add a short Paper of Observations that I shewed [sic] in an amicable Manner to Campo One Day: – After reading your Letter of 13th. With great Attention, I do not dislike it's complexion: What I can assure You <is> that if They <(Sp^{sh.} M^{rs.})> persist in not lowering The Duties and taking off the Prohibitions, Our Manufactures will find Their way thro' France, and the Contraband then will be carried on upon safe Ground, as the Manufactures will not be confined any longer to the precuring [sic] Hand of the <unknown> Smugler, [sic] but to rich Capital Houses in France, therefore We must have Patience if Spain will not yield, – and will refuse to open a new Market for her Manufactures, and to bring here herself her own W.I. Produce and Industry –

I am ever Your's [sic] sincerely R. Woodford

A Letter from a Manchester Manufacturer to the Right Honourable Charles James Fox, on his Political Opposition to the Commercial Treaty with France (Manchester: J. Stockdale, 1787).

SIR,

I FEEL little hesitation in addressing a Letter to you upon a subject of the highest importance to the manufacturers of Lancashire; especially when I call to mind the permission you have allowed us, of writing to you freely upon our commercial concerns.

Your late parliamentary language on the Treaty with France has spread an alarm through every trading town in this quarter: for we little expected, after your promises of constant attention to our manufacturing interests, that you would have opposed a measure which we had previously advised, from a thorough conviction of its beneficial consequences to this nation; far less did we apprehend that you would have raised objections from an affected regard for the *political, rather than the commercial consequence of the empire*, by unseasonably reviving national jealousies, that ought never to be mentioned, if the advantages of trade have the least weight with you.

Under this impression, I cannot help telling you how little your Lancashire friends (whose very existence depends on the extensive sale of their goods) expected to be sneeringly told, *that their speculations are their own concerns*.

These speculations, however lightly you may treat them, have cleared our warehouses of goods, which had lain long on hand for want of markets. In the ultimate success of these speculations, allow me to assure you, we have still a considerable interest.

But have we merited this disregard, not to say disdain, from you, Sir, who once made popularity with us an object of your closest pursuit?

The Irish Propositions, we conceived, had a tendency injurious to our trade; you opposed them, and gained the thanks of a grateful people. But the present Treaty is replete with advantages to us and to the nation at large. – You cannot be uninformed of these circumstances; – yet you have derided our judgments, and opposed our interests. – You will not therefore be surprised that every one here begins to observe that opposition is your darling object; that it is not at the measures, but at the Minister, your attacks are levelled.

I wish not, Sir, to be considered in the light of a mere individual throughout this Address: I speak the sentiments of this county, if not of every trading town in the kingdom. I am sorry to say, your determined purpose to reject our favourite Treaty has not been confined within the walls of Parliament: – Pamphlets have been circulated with no common industry, in order to instruct us in our particular business, and to inflame the passions of those, who have no interest in the success or rejection of this Treaty.

Among other treatises, which have been sent us on this subject, I observe one, intituled, '*A Compleat Investigation of Mr. Eden's Treaty:*' a production conceived in faction, and prosecuted with prejudice.

I cannot adduce a stronger instance of the intentions of its author, or a more powerful support in favour of the present Treaty, than by borrowing his own argument: We are not, he says, to open a trade with France at this time, because a treaty failed in 1713.

I will not suppose the author capable of entertaining so contemptible an opinion of his readers, as to imagine them inadequate to the distinction between those times and the present.

If I am to regard him as acquainted with the relative situation of the then commercial interests of the two countries, his intentions have been grossly to mislead us: If he is so uninformed, I must tell him, that the very cause of the treaty's failing at that time, is an indisputable proof of the expediency of adopting a Treaty, which has been framed in concert with the manufacturers themselves. Need I mention the complete change this country has undergone in every branch of manufactures, commerce, and navigation, during the last hundred years? Need I mention the infant state of our manufactures, and the acknowledged superiority of those of France, during the last century?

We have now before us a quite different prospect; our manufactures are reared to maturity, and brought to a degree of perfection, that dreads no competition.

It is not my intention, Sir, to intrench myself in figures, or to support my opinions by minute calculations, or tedious detail. I will even view the subject in your own favourite light: – Let me ask you what advantages we are to gain by alarming the apprehensions, and exciting the jealousies of our countrymen? I will even appeal to you, and submit to your decision, whether war has not invariably obstructed our industry and commerce: whether peace has not given energy to both: – whether conquest ever yielded any thing but additional taxes and accumulating debts.

I may be biassed by my own employments, and my own interests; but I cannot refrain from submitting to your calmer reflection, whether the encouragement of industry, the extension of trade and navigation, by opening new markets, be not the most effectual mode to render us capable of repelling the insults even of the most formidable powers. By thus improving the opportunities of peace, we shall be the better able to sustain the calamities of war.

The American war (if you will allow me to quote it) is a proof of the justice of the sentiments I am anxious to impress on your mind. A great association of powers attempted to annihilate the commerce, and to depress the faculties of this country: – But, how much soever those powers were aided by the mismanagement of the minister, and the violence of party, three years of peace, assisted

A Letter from a Manchester Manufacturer (1787)   67

by salutary regulations, and owing to the skill, the industry, and the enterprizes of individuals, have brightened the gloomiest prospect that ever presented itself to a desponding people.

Before I take leave of you, allow me to apologize for this interruption: I dare not presume to expect that the plain stile of a mercantile man can be possessed of any very attractive qualities; – but, as I write at the instigation of my best neighbours, and my brother manufacturers, I trust that this freedom will in a great degree plead its own excuse.

At this time, perhaps, Mr. Fox could dispense with the opinions even of a commercial man; yet the time has been, and very lately too, when he did not consider himself degraded, or his time misapplied, in listening to our suggestions, however inconsiderable; need I say, too, that the time has also been, when it was the pride of Mr. Fox to speak the sentiments of

A BRITISH MANUFACTURER.

Manchester,
5th Feb, 1787.

TRADE AS AN INSTRUMENT OF WAR, 1793–1812

Whilst it may be an exaggeration to posit a link between the unpopularity of the 1786 commercial treaty and the Revolution of 1789, approximately seventy *cahiers*, mostly from large towns in northern France, denounced the treaty; none explicitly approved it.[1] Indeed, France claimed British violation of the treaty, in terminating corn exports to France whilst continuing them to other countries, as a casus belli.[2] The Revolutionary and Napoleonic Wars spanned the years 1793–1815. Instead of forging reciprocal trade links, the commercial policies of combatants became instruments of war, Pitt's 'mutual benevolence' was savagely undermined, and the moderate progress of commercial liberalization halted.[3] Commerce was recognized as an important weapon in warfare, and the status of the commerce of combatants and non-combatants was steadily developed.[4] The Declaration of the League of Armed Neutrality in 1780 asserted the right of neutral vessels to trade with belligerents except in contraband, and established the requirement that a blockade must be effective to be recognized. Although of little consequence in military terms, this declaration was important diplomatically, and was supported by the United States on the basis of freedom for neutral commerce.

Napoleon's method of defeating Britain by the economic warfare of a blockade of the Continent became known as the 'Continental System'. Yet, commercial warfare characterized the war from the beginning. The disruption to commerce was intended to cause distress and ultimately ruin.[5] France forbade the importation of British manufactures in September 1793, with Bertrand Barére informing the Convention that strict measures were necessary to combat the maritime supremacy of a hostile Britain: 'Those proud Islanders have long since aspired to the exclusive empire of the seas ... The English have fathomed all kinds of crimes to destroy us. CATO said in the Senate of Rome, Let proud Carthage perish. Exactly such is the sentence which the French Senate ought to pronounce upon Modern Carthage.'[6] The Navigation decree of 21 September 1795 followed, which decreed all shipping was to be in French bottoms.[7] In 1796, foreign goods carried in British ships were also classified as British. An act to this effect (Loi de Brumaire, An V, 31 October) forbade importation of all manufactured articles made in England or those that passed through channels of English trade by land or sea, except under

– 69 –

stringent regulations.[8] In presenting a bill for extending the treason laws in 1793, the British government aimed 'to prevent the enemy, during the war, from being supplied by subjects of this country, in the way of commerce, with any articles useful and important to them in carrying on the war against us, or from deriving any resources, through the medium of this country, which might afford them the means of prosecuting the war'.[9] In 1796 when Spain declared war, British ships were seized and manufactured imports prohibited.[10]

One can see the effects of commercial warfare in contemporary literature, with the emergence of theories of commercial restriction and autarky, representing something of a reaction against Smith's internationalism but also practical expressions of contemporary political and strategic considerations. Johann Fichte's *The Closed Commercial State* of 1801 or Comte de Montgaillard's memorial presented to Napoleon in 1805 have been cited as formative influences underpinning the Continental System. Equally, James Stephen's *War in Disguise: or, Frauds of the Neutral Flags* of 1805 proved extremely influential in high political circles in arguing for the destruction of French commerce.[11] Yet if commerce was always intrinsically important in warfare, it became much more so during the Napoleonic Wars. Neutral shipping was the central issue, for by these means combatants could be supplied under 'the frauds of the neutral flags'.[12] It was this issue that prompted Britain to declare a blockade of the Channel from Brest to the Elbe in May 1806.

This action allowed Napoleon to pose as the defender of national rights against British economic and commercial tyranny, with the Berlin Decree of 21 November 1806, which declared the British action an infraction of the recognized principles of international law. Claiming the right of retaliation, he declared Britain to be in a state of blockade, and forbade his allies and conquests from trading with Britain.[13] The British response, the Order in Council of 7 January 1807, declared that neutral vessels were not to trade from port to port on the French coasts, or with allies of France.[14] This was followed by another Order, on 11 November, which declared that neutrals could only trade with a hostile port after touching at a British port, and paying duties imposed by the British government.[15] Napoleon responded with the Milan Decree of 17 December, declaring that all neutral shipping using British ports or paying British tariffs was to be regarded as British and would be seized.[16] After the Tilsit treaties with Russia and Prussia in July 1807 and totally dominant in Europe, Napoleon again declared Britain to be in a state of blockade.[17] In theory, this meant that all foreign ports were closed to Britain, but in practice there was considerable smuggling with the connivance of local officials. France was even obliged to depend on Britain for cotton yarns, twist and white fabrics for printing.[18]

Despite the failure of the Continental System to achieve its objectives, the attempt was sufficiently bold to cause alarm, and provided an impetus for merchants to search for new markets free from Napoleonic dominion. British exclusion from the Continent was temporary, for the Continental System was over-ambitious, and created resentment in many parts of occupied Europe.[19] With French annexation of the Netherlands and north-west Germany in 1810, Napoleon was able to exert stricter controls. Across Europe, British goods were confiscated and burnt, and draconian decrees passed such as the Trianou tariff (August 1810) and the Fontainbleau Decree (October 1810). From 1807, it became increasingly difficult to smuggle British goods into Europe, although licensing and bargaining mitigated suffering on both sides.[20] Yet the denial of British goods caused alienation and dissatisfaction, and the system was never wholly operational. In broad terms, the Continental System failed from not being applied consistently or for a sufficiently long period.[21]

Commercial reprisals were a notable feature of the war, but by their actions Britain and France violated the accustomed principles of maritime warfare and infringed neutral rights. In a sense this was unavoidable, for any attempt to damage the enemy by such comprehensive measures would inevitably result in neutral powers being affected, the most important of which was the United States. During the war, Anglo-American relations were volatile and tense. At the end of the War of Independence, special privileges proposed for American shipping were abandoned in the face of a hostile British shipping lobby: a signal defeat for advocates of commercial liberalism. The American tariff of 1789 was moderate, although American shipping enjoyed advantages in discriminating duties.[22] Disputes over seizure of American ships with goods for France or the French colonies strained the relationship, but a treaty of commerce and navigation of 1794 temporarily improved relations, by allowing America access to Britain's East and West Indian ports.[23]

The treaty was useful for Britain since warfare closed Continental markets, and exports to America recovered dramatically by the end of the century. Despite benefits for both sides, the demands of war intruded, as Britain sought to curtail America's right to ship Spanish and French West Indian produce to the United States before re-shipment to Europe. Complete prohibition of neutral trade with colonies was now sought, and hostility heightened by an Order in Council of 21 November 1804 decreeing termination of Anglo-American West Indian trade after six months. Influenced by Stephen's view that nothing less would suffice, the British government tightened regulations on neutral commerce to the point of complete prohibition, thus dividing mercantile opinion and prompting American retaliation.[24] As Chancellor of the Exchequer in the Duke of Portland's ministry, Spencer Perceval framed the commercial restrictions in the Orders in Council, which were based heavily on Stephen's 1805 pamphlet *War in Disguise*.[25]

In drafting the Orders, British politicians and sympathetic observers were concerned with the reaction of the United States towards neutrals.[26] William Wilberforce accurately predicted in 1808 that the legislation on neutral trade would produce a war with America.[27] The United States quickly retaliated with the Embargo Act of 8 January 1808, prohibiting the sailing of any vessel from any American port to any foreign port, except public ships and foreign merchant vessels in ballast.[28] This was followed by the Non-Intercourse Act, 15 March 1809, prohibiting all commercial intercourse with Britain and France, although collusion and smuggling inhibited its practical effectiveness. Anglo-American relations worsened, largely on account of resentment of the Orders in Council. British criticism mainly focused on counterposing war and commerce as distinct entities, and on the extent to which the Orders contributed to the decline of British trade. In political circles, Alexander Baring presented the most coherent opposition.[29] Baring's views reflected those of many, though not all, merchants trading with America.[30] Repeal of the Orders by the government occasioned some surprise, not least by their acceptance of Brougham's claim that Napoleon had withdrawn his decrees, a claim which was widely known to be false and based on forged documentation.[31] Charged with this evidence, Castlereagh replied 'one does not like to own that we are forced to give way to our manufacturers'.[32] The repeal was unknown in America when she declared war on Britain in 1812, although there was knowledge of Perceval's death and the ongoing parliamentary inquiry.[33]

Success against Napoleon was not achieved without a struggle. British seapower was essential in reducing the value of French commerce by 1800 with Asia, Africa and America to less than $356,000. British merchants successfully found new markets, and overseas trade with the United States, Asia and the West Indies soared, whereas Dutch, French and Spanish industries were damaged by the loss of colonial markets and the naval blockade of European waters. The evolution of an effective convoy system, including Convoy Acts of 1793, 1798 and 1803, protected trade routes, reduced shipping losses, and tightened the naval/commercial nexus central to British war strategy.[34] Nevertheless, there were serious slumps in 1808 and 1812, the latter of which was attributed by Gladstone's father, a Liverpool ship-owner and merchant, to the exclusion of British trade from Europe and the reduced volume of manufacturing exports to America.[35] Commercial restrictions also promoted middle-class radicalism, expressed in commercial terms by calls for an end to the East India Company's monopoly of the India and China trade. The wars damaged the progress of commercial liberalization by making it unlikely the combatants would agree to tariff reductions in the post-war world. Dependence on foreign countries for supplies continued to be viewed as dangerous.[36] Given recent events, there was some justification for the adoption of quasi-autarkic policies by the leading powers. The disruption to commerce also encouraged the development of hitherto negligible industrial economies, most notably the United States. Fuelled by the necessity to check the drain of specie and maximize revenue, she followed the path of seeking protection from foreign competition.[37] Indeed, the gradual popularity and advocacy of protection for

Trade as an Instrument of War 73

American industries was a new factor in the international state system in the post-1815 period. Thus, the progress of commercial liberalization which many hoped had been inaugurated in 1786 was not only halted by war, but reversed.

Notes

1. B. F. Hyslop, 'French Gild Opinion in 1789', *American Historical Review*, 44:2 (1939), pp. 252–71, on p. 269, n. 85.
2. Debate in National Convention, 1 February 1793, *Annual Register for the Year 1793*, pp. 153–4; 'Declaration of War on the Part of the French against Great Britain and Holland', *Times*, 11 February 1793, p. 2c.
3. See George Sinclair to Henry Dundas, 9 November 1796, below, p. 81.
4. J. B. Williams, *British Commercial Policy and Trade Expansion, 1750–1850* (Oxford: Clarendon Press 1972), p. 230.
5. See 'Southwark Petition', *Annual Register* (1795), below, pp. 79–80.
6. 21 September 1793, in *The Times*, 5 October 1793, p. 3a.
7. S. B. Clough, *France: A History of National Economics, 1789–1939* (New York: C. Scribner's Sons, 1939), p. 46.
8. W. M. Sloane, 'The Continental System of Napoleon', *Political Science Quarterly*, 13:2 (1898), pp. 213–31, on pp. 214–15; the value of British manufacturing exports to France fell from £743,280 in 1792 to £66,677 in 1793 to zero in 1795, Williams, *British Commercial Policy*, p. 396.
9. Lord Grenville, 15 April 1793, *Annual Register* (1793), 'Public Papers', p. 96.
10. Williams, *British Commercial Policy*, p. 158.
11. Sloane, 'The Continental System of Napoleon', pp. 216, 223.
12. In 1805, James Stephen published his *War in Disguise, or the Frauds of the Neutral Flags*, a work which dealt with the vexed question of the commercial rights of neutrals, and which provided the theoretical underpinning of the Orders of Council; see Sloane, 'The Continental System of Napoleon', pp. 219–20.
13. See On the Continental System, following the Berlin Decree, 20 November 1806, *Annual Register* (1806), below, pp. 82–4.
14. *Times*, 12 January 1807, p. 4a.
15. Williams, *British Commercial Policy*, p. 232, n. 6; B. Perkins, 'George Canning, Great Britain, and the United States, 1807–1809', *American Historical Review*, 63:1 (1957), p. 1–22, on pp. 8–11.
16. W. Cunningham, *The Growth of English Industry and Commerce in Modern Times: Laissez Faire* (Cambridge: Cambridge University Press, 1925), pp. 682–3.
17. R. Ruppenthal, 'Denmark and the Continental System', *Journal of Modern History*, 15:1 (1943), pp. 7–23, on p. 10; Tilsit resulted in Russia's short-lived participation in the Continental System, and attendant exclusion of British ships and seizure of property, Williams, *British Commercial Policy*, p. 172.
18. Ibid., pp. 347–8.
19. See Madame de Stael Holstein, *An Appeal to the Nations of Europe Against the Continental System* (1813), below, pp. 121–8.
20. Williams, *British Commercial Policy*, pp. 197, 349–50.

74 *Battles over Free Trade, Volume 1*

21. P. Kennedy, *The Rise and Fall of British Naval Mastery*, 3rd edn (London: Fontana, 1991), pp. 169–70.
22. Williams, *British Commercial Policy*, pp. 219–20, 225, 232.
23. See 'Abstract of the Treaty between Great Britain and the United States of America', *Annual Register* (1795), below, pp. 75–8.
24. Cunningham, *The Growth of English Industry and Commerce*, pp. 681–2; Williams, *British Commercial Policy*, p. 227–32.
25. See Stael Holstein, *An Appeal to the Nations of Europe Against the Continental System*, below, pp. 121–8; 'He [Stephen] agrees with Perceval passim, and with the government as to their grand scheme of policy – Order in Council; indeed it is his measure', R. I. Wilberforce and S. Wilberforce, *The Life of William Wilberforce*, 5 vols (London: John Murray, 1838), vol. 3, p. 358.
26. See James Stephen to Spencer Perceval, 5 December 1807, below, pp. 85–7; cf. Bartholomew Huber to Huskisson, 7 December 1806, Huskisson Papers, BL, Add. MS 38737, fols 169–70.
27. *The Life of William Wilberforce*, vol. 3, p. 357.
28. Despite some losses, this was beneficial to Britain in virtually ending neutral trading with France and conferred on Britain a near monopoly of trade with the few remaining neutrals. Perkins, 'George Canning', p. 11; Napoleon responded with the Bayonne decree, 17 April 1808, ordering sequestration of American vessels entering European ports.
29. See Orders in Council, *Edinburgh Review* (1808); and James Stephen to Spencer Perceval, 23 May 1808, both below, pp. 88–100, 101; Williams, *British Commercial Policy*, pp. 232–4, 394.
30. Minutes of Evidence Taken at the Bar of the House of Commons on Considering Petitions of Merchants and Manufacturers, Respecting Orders in Council, 1808, *Parliamentary Papers* (1808), 119, x.[81], pp. 10–11, 16; John Gladstone considered the Orders successful, in forcing Napoleon to permit trade with Britain by licence, thus effectively abandoning the Continental System, 27 May 1812, Minutes of Evidence before the Committee of the Whole House of Commons relating to Orders in Council, *Parliamentary Papers* (1812), 210, iii.[1], p. 502.
31. See Prince Regent in Council, Orders in Council and War with America, 23 June 1812, *Parliamentary Papers* (1812–13), below, p. 104.
32. *The Life of William Wilberforce*, vol. 4, p. 35.
33. See Prince Regent in Council, Orders in Council and War with America; and Mr Foster to Viscount Castlereagh, 20 June 1812, both below, pp. 104, 105.
34. Kennedy, *The Rise and Fall of British Naval Mastery*, pp. 155, 158–71; for an argument in favour of convoys, see London merchant John Inglis to Henry Dundas, 14 November 1797, Melville Papers, National Archives of Scotland, GD51/1/399/1.
35. See 'Financial Situation of England and France', *Examiner* (1810), below, pp. 102–3; Minutes of Evidence, *Parliamentary Papers* (1812), 210, iii.[1], p. 488.
36. Although war was at an end, 'even in peace, the habitual dependence on foreign supply is dangerous', *A Letter on the Corn Laws, by the Right Hon. W. Huskisson, to One of His Constituents, in 1814* (London: James Ridgway, 1827), p. 8.
37. Williams, *British Commercial Policy*, pp. 223 ff.

TRADE AS AN INSTRUMENT OF WAR, 1793–1812

The Continental System

'Abstract of the Treaty between Great Britain and the United States of America', *Annual Register* (1795), pp. 294–7.

Abstract of the Treaty between Great Britain and the United States of America.

THIS Treaty consists of twenty-eight articles:

The first article establishes peace and friendship between his Britannic majesty and the United States.

In the second, his majesty consents to withdraw all his troops and garrisons from all posts and places within the boundary lines assigned by the treaty of peace to the United States. The evacuation is to take place on or before the 1st of June 1796.

The third article allows to his majesty's subjects and the citizens of the United States, and to the Indians dwelling on either side of the said boundary line, freely in pass and repass by land or inland navigation into the respective territories of the two parties. The country within the limits of the Hudson's Bay Company is excepted. Vessels belonging to the United States are not to be admitted into the ports of his majesty's said territories, nor British vessels from the sea into the rivers of the United States beyond the highest ports of entry for foreign vessels from the sea. The navigation of Mississippi, however is to be entirely free. Goods and merchandise shall be conveyed into the territories of his Britannic majesty by American citizens, and into the territories of the United States by British subjects, subject to the regulations established by both parties.

The fourth article relates to the ascertaining of the extent of the Mississippi to the northward.

The fifth article alludes to the doubts that have arisen relative to the river St. Croix, and agrees to refer these doubts to commissioners.

– 75 –

The sixth article allows British subjects the power of recovering debts due to them by American citizens previously to the peace: which debts have not been recovered hitherto, on account of some legal impediments. The United States agree to make full and complete compensation to the creditors who have suffered by those impediments. The amount of the losses and damages is to be ascertained by five commissioners – two to be appointed by Great Britain, two by the president of the United States, and one by the other four.

When the five commissioners appointed shall first meet, they shall, before they proceed to act, respectively take the following oath or affirmation, in the presence of each other, which oath or affirmation being so taken, and duly attested shall be entered on the record of their proceedings, viz. I, A.B. one of the commissioners appointed in pursuance of the sixth article of the treaty of amity, commerce, and 'navigation, between his Britannic majesty and the United States of America, do solemnly swear, or affirm, that I will honestly, diligently, impartially, and carefully examine, and to the best of my judgment, according to justice and equity, decide all such complaints, as under the said article shall be referred to the said commissioners; and that I will forbear to act as a commissioner in any case in which I may be personally interested.

Three of the said commissioners shall constitute a board, and shall have power to do any act appertaining to the said commission, provided that one of the commissioners named on each side, and the fifth commissioner shall be present, and all decisions shall be made by the majority of the voices of the commissioners then present; eighteen months from the day on which the said commissioners shall form a board, and be ready to proceed to business, are assigned for receiving complaints and applications; but they are nevertheless, authorized, in any particular cases, in which it shall appear to them to be reasonable and just, to extend the said term of eighteen months for any term not exceeding six months after the expiration thereof. The said commissioners shall first meet at Philadelphia, but they shall have power to adjourn from place to place as they shall see cause.

The award of the said commissioners, or any three of them as aforesaid, shall in all cases be final and conclusive.

The seventh article allows indemnification, by the British Government, to such of the citizens of the United States as have suffered, during the late war, by irregular and illegal captures. The United States also agree to indemnify British subjects for irregular illegal captures taken by American ships during the war.

For the purpose of ascertaining the amount of any such losses and damages, five commissioners shall be appointed and authorised to act in London, exactly in the manner directed with respect to those mentioned in the preceding article, and after having taken the same oath or affirmation (*mutatis mutandis*) the same term of eighteen months is also assigned for the reception of claims, and they are in like manner authorised to extend the same in particular places. They shall receive

'Abstract of the Treaty between Great Britain and the United States of America' (1795)   77

testimony, books, papers, and evidence in the same latitude, and exercise the like discretion and powers respecting that subject; and shall decide the claims in question according to the merits of the several cases, and to justice, equity, and the laws of nations. The award of the commissioners, or any such three of them as aforesaid, shall in all cases be final and conclusive, both as to the justice of the claim, and the amount of the sum to be paid to the claimant; and his Britannic majesty undertakes to cause the same to be paid to such claimants in specie, without any deduction, at such place or places, and at such time or times, as shall be awarded by the same commissioners, and on condition of such releases or assignments to be given by the claimants, as by the said commissioners may be directed.

The eighth article refers to the two former, and settles the mode of paying the amount of the losses.

The ninth article permits the subjects of each country to hold lands in either country, and to sell and devise them in the same manner as if they were natives.

In the tenth article it is agreed, that in case of a war, no money belonging to individuals shall be sequestered or confiscated.

The eleventh article establishes a perfect liberty of navigation and commerce between the two countries.

The twelfth article allows the citizens of the United States to carry the produce of the United States to the West Indies, in vessels of not more than seventy tons burthen. The citizens are also allowed to carry away the produce of the islands to the territories of the United States alone. – This article is to continue in force for two years after the present war, when further regulations are to be made.

In the thirteenth article his Britannic Majesty consents to admit American vessels into the British ports in the East Indies. This consent, however, is not to extend to the carrying on of the coasting trade in the East Indies.

The citizens of the United States are not to reside or go into the interior parts of the East India settlements. They are not to export, in time of war, stores or rice from the East-Indies; they may touch at St. Helena for refreshment.

The fourteenth article relates to liberty of commerce and navigation between the dominions of his majesty in Europe, and the territories of the United States in America.

The fifteenth article states, that no higher duties shall be paid by the ships or merchandize of the one party in the ports of the other, than the duties paid by other nations. No higher duties shall be paid upon importation or exportation than the duties paid on the importation or exportation of similar articles the produce of other nations.

The sixteenth article relates to the appointment of consuls for the protection of trade.

The seventeenth article relates to vessels being captured or detained, on suspicion of having the enemy's property on board. Such property alone is to be

78 *Battles over Free Trade, Volume 1*

taken out; the vessels are to be permitted to proceed to sea with the remainder of their cargo.

The eighteenth article decides what articles the term contraband is to be applied to.

The nineteenth article provides for the security of the respective subjects and citizens, and for the preventing of injuries by men of war.

The twentieth article relates to the refusal of the repective [*sic*] parties to receive pirates into any harbours or towns, and to the seizure of goods and merchandize taken by pirates.

The twenty-first article provides, for the subjects and citizens of the two nations shall not do any acts of hostility against each other, and shall not accept commissions from foreign states or princes, to commit hostilities.

The twenty-second article prevents acts of reprisal, without due notice.

The twenty-third relates to the treatment of ships, officers, and crews, in the respective ports of the two powers.

The twenty-fourth article provides, that privateers of nations at enmity with either of the two powers, shall not arm their ships in the respective ports of the two powers, or sell what they have taken.

The twenty fifth allows the ships of war belonging to the said parties, to carry the ships and goods, taken from their enemies, whithersoever they please.

In case of war between the two nations, the twenty-sixth article permits the merchants and others, of each of the two nations, to reside in the dominions of the other, and to continue their trade.

The twenty-seventh article agrees that the two powers shall respectively deliver up persons charged with murder and forgery.

The twenty-eighth, alluding to the preceding articles, states, that the first ten articles shall be permanent, and that the subsequent articles (the twelfth excepted) shall be limited in their duration to twelve years. The treaty is to be binding and obligatory as soon as it is ratified.

The treaty is signed

GRENVILLE,
JOHN JAY.

'Southwark Petition', *Annual Register* (1795), pp. 106–7.

Southwark Petition.

To the Honourable the House of Commons of Great Britain in Parliament assembled.

The humble Petition of the Inhabitants of the Town and Borough of Southwark, convened by public Advertisement of the High Bailiff of the said Borough.

Sheweth,

THAT your petitioners, sincerely and awfully affected by a due sense of the trying and momentous circumstances, under which they now appeal to the wisdom and to the feelings of their constitutional representatives, the commons of Great Britain, in parliament assembled, find it their bounden duty to give their opinion upon the present alarming state of public affairs, with all the frankness and explicitness which the crisis demands.

And, first, your petitioners freely and zealously declare their true and unshaken attachment to the monarch on the throne, and to his royal family; and their firm determination to support the genuine principles of this most excellent constitution, should any attempt, from whatever quarter, whether foreign or domestic, be made to subvert it.

In revolving, however, the events of the present war with France, your petitioners, with the deepest concern, have observed that the uniform bravery, manifested by the British fleets and armies, has in no respect, advanced the presumed object of the war, and now less than ever, appears likely to attain it.

The consideration of the disasters and defeats which have lately attended the unsupported efforts of the British arms on the continent, is, in the minds of your petitioners, bitterly aggravated by the reflection that those allies, whose councils and resentments first engaged us in the contest, have wrung, from the credulity and confidence of the generous and industrious people of Great Britain, large sums of money, for which, in violation of all faith, no adequate service appears to have been performed, or attempted.

In the events of a campaign, so unparalleled in calamity, your petitioners, among other fatal consequences, perceive a large addition in the existing national debt, the speedy diminution of which has been long held forth to your petitioners, and to the country, as a measure indispensably necessary to the maintenance of the constitution, as well as to the credit of Great Britain.

Under the increasing pressure of such burthens, your petitioners are convinced, however highly they are disposed to estimate the fortitude and loyalty of all descriptions of their countrymen, and however readily they admit the temporary advantages which both the general commerce and the public funds of this country may have derived from the terrors and calamities of other nations, that the consequences of persevering in the present destructive war must tend rapidly to depress and ruin the occupations of useful labour, and profitable industry; and ultimately to destroy the only true sources of the nation's power, our trade, our commerce, and our manufactures.

Under this impression, your petitioners are compelled to turn their thoughts most seriously, and eagerly, to the only real remedy for, the evils they apprehend, peace; – for in the tranquillity, the civilized intercourse, and the commercial prosperity of the surrounding nations of Europe, your petitioners conceive the commercial interests of Great Britain can alone find their interest and support. In the pursuits of vengeance or ambition, in wars and camps, in desolation and bloodshed, even were the contest attended with temporary success, the result to a country, circumstanced as this is, must be national bankruptcy, and ultimate ruin.

On these grounds your petitioners humbly, but distinctly, pray, that your honourable house, disclaiming every pretence of right, on the part of Great Britain, to create or correct a government for France, and disregarding whatever is or may be the title or construction of the ruling power, which either does, or may exist in that country, will earnestly adopt the most effectual means for recommending an immediate negotiation for peace, on terms consistent with the honour and security of the British empire. And your petitioners further assure your honourable house, that if, contrary to the hopes of your petitioners, motives of inordinate ambition, or of implacable resentment, however rashly and improvidently excited, in the mind of the enemy, should render it impossible to obtain a termination of hostilities upon safe and honourable terms, your petitioners will be found, among the readiest of his majesty's loyal subjects, to stand forward to the last means of exertion, in defence of their country, or to perish with its fall.

And your petitioners will ever pray.

George Sinclair to Henry Dundas, 9 November 1796, Melville Papers, National Archives of Scotland, GD51/1/393.

Leith 9 November 1796

Sir

My zeal for the public welfare, is the only apology which I shall offer, for presuming to encroach on Your Time, at present.

For the consideration of a Subject which I may hereafter lay before You a few Ideas have occurred to me, which I have conceived may be of such public utility, as to induce my venturing to communicate them to You.

In case his Majesty may find it expedient, to continue the war with the present Rulers of France I beg leave to suggest, as a means of annoying them & all our other enemies, that his majesties Ministers endeavor, to prevail on the Empress of Russia, to prohibit the French Dutch & all other powers, except such as are engaged in the war against them, from the supply of Hemp Flax, Tar & all other naval Stores produced in her dominions.

As our Distilleries will soon consume all the grain which we spare from alimentary food, I would induce the Empress to this Scheme; by taking from her Subjects a given quantity of Barley Rye & perhaps Wheat to be applied to the purpose of Distilling.

To finish, I would further humbly suggest to exclude the importation into this Country of all kind of Malt Spirits and raise an additional Tax on distilling to the amount of what that revenue has been found to produce, which may revert a beneficial Trade from the Dutch & become an immense <permanent> saving to Great Britain.

I have the honor to be with sincere Respect

Sir,

Your most obedient & most devoted servant

Geo Sinclair

82   *Battles over Free Trade, Volume 1*

On the Continental System, following the Berlin Decree, 20 November 1806, *Annual Register* (1806), pp. 200–2.

From Hesse and Hanover Mortier proceeded to Hamburgh, which he entered without opposition on the 19th of November, and next day he issued an order for the sequestration of all English produce and manufactures found in the city, whether belonging to English subjects or to other persons. Statements were demanded from the merchants and bankers, of the English manufactures or funds arising from the sale of English manufactures in their possession; domiciliary visits were threatened to enforce compliance; and those who gave false returns, were menaced with summary punishment by martial law. To strike greater terror, the English merchants at Hamburgh were put under arrest, and though afterwards released on their parole, they were placed under a guard of soldiers, and threatened to be sent to Verdun. These acts of violence brought less profit to the French, than they did harm to the Hamburghers. The trade of Hamburgh was annihilated, while the amount of English property manufactures confiscated was inconsiderable. Before the armed force sent to Cuxhaven to stop the English vessels at the mouth of the river, arrived at that place, the merchantmen apprised of the danger had made their escape. The seizure of Hamburgh had been less foreseen, and though the French minister in that city persisted to the last in his declarations that its neutrality would be respected, little credit had been given to his assurances. The fate of Leipzig had been a warning to the merchants of Hamburgh. No exertions had been spared by the factors and commercial agents of the English in disposing of their goods and winding up their concerns before the arrival of Mortier and his army; so that, after all, the most valuable prize from this expedition proved to be the corn found in the magazines of Hamburgh, great quantities of which were sent to Berlin, where apprehensions of famine began to be entertained.

But the order for confiscating English property at Hamburgh, and the rigorous though ineffectual measures taken to enforce it, were not insulated acts of violence and rapacity, but parts of an extensive plan for excluding the produce of English industry from the continent, which the French emperor in his present intoxication of success, vainly imagined he had power to accomplish. This new system of warfare he promulgated at Berlin on the 20th of November in a decree interdicting all commerce and correspondence, direct or indirect, between the British dominions and the countries subject to his controul. By this decree the British islands were declared to be in a state of blockade: all subjects of England found in countries occupied by French troops were declared prisoners of war, and all English property was declared lawful prize; all letters addressed to Englishmen or written in the English language were ordered to be stopped; all commerce in English produce and manufactures was prohibited; and all vessels touching at England or any English colony, were excluded from every harbour under the controul of France. The pretext for these infringements of the law and practice of civilized nations was founded, partly, on the extension given by England to the right of blockade, and partly on the difference in the laws of war by sea and by land. By land the property of an enemy is not considered lawful prize, unless it belongs to the hostile state. By sea the property of unarmed, peaceable merchants is liable to capture and confiscation. By land no one is considered prisoner of war who is not taken with arms in his hands. By sea the crews of merchantmen are considered prisoners of war equally with the crews of armed vessels. For these reasons the French emperor declared, that the regulations of the decree, which he now promulgated, 'should be regarded as a fundamental law of the French empire, till England recognized the law of war to be one and the same by sea and by land, and in so case applicable to private property or to individuals not bearing arms; and till she consented to restrict the right of blockade to fortified places actually invested by a sufficient force.'

On these reasons we shall merely observe, that the superiority of England by sea being at that time as great and undisputed as the superiority of France was by land, the difference between the laws of war by sea and by land was entirely to the advantage of England and to the disadvantage of France; and in these circumstances it was not unnatural for the French emperor to attempt either to confine hostilities at sea within the same limits to which they were restricted by land, or to extend to a war by land all the rights claimed and exercised by belligerents at sea. But, though it was the interest of France to attempt such an innovation in public law, the decree was not less an innovation of the most pernicious kind, on account of its tendency to revive the ancient laws of war, which the progress of civilization had gradually softened. Nor was the assertion in the preamble of the decree less a falsehood, that the conduct of England is not conformable to the law followed by other civilized states, and laid down and approved of as the law of nations; for the law of England with respect to blockade and capture at sea is the same, which all writers on public law have held, and all nations, France not excepted, have followed. That part of the decree, which declared the British islands to be in a state of blockade, at a time when the fleets of France and her allies were confined within their ports by the naval forces of England, was an empty menace, which the French government had no power to enforce, nor as it afterwards appeared, any intention to act upon. But those parts of the decree which prohibited all commerce in English produce or manufactures, filled the commercial cities of the continent with dismay, as a measure fatal to their prosperity. Deputations were sent to Bonaparte from Hamburgh, and from Nantes, Bourdeaux, and other cities of France, to solicit, upon this head, some relaxation of a decree, not less injurious to his own subjects than to the English. But his answers were stern and uncomplying. When told by the merchants of Hamburgh, that 'these measures would involve them in universal bankruptcy, and banish commerce from the continent,' his reply is said to have been, 'so much the better; the bankruptcies in England will be more numerous, and you will be less able to trade with her. England must be humbled, though the fourth century should be revived, commerce extinguished, and no interchange of commodities left but by barter.' But notwithstanding these alarming appearances, this decree soon became perfectly harmless and inoperative. Some slight and temporary embarassments [*sic*] in commerce were experienced from it at first; but, in a short time, though formally extended to Holland and other countries under the controul of France, its existence was only known by the bribes given to generals of division and custom-house officers for omitting to enforce it, and by the occasional confiscation of some unfortunate vessel, which had neglected that necessary precaution.

The British Response: Orders in Council

James Stephen to Spencer Perceval, 5 December 1807, Perceval Papers, BL, Add. MS 49183, fols 25–8

Serjeants Inn Decr. 5 – '7

Dear Sir

You desired me to make such remarks as might occur to me on the further Orders of the 25th Ulto but I have been too much hurried since I saw them to do so sooner – The new Instrons are but just sent to me from Doctors Commons –

Thinking as I do, that it is an essential part of the new system to lift our manufacturers over the enemy's blockading wall by the aid of his own subjects, or subjects of the blockading countries, of course I must approve of every thing that tends that way[.]

To prevent their being freely carried to the foot of that wall in all directions, is to aid his system & to counteract the remedy you apply. I like therefore the provisions in regard to Gibraltar & Malta as far as they go; & I like the clause at the top of p. 6 in the new printed Instrons still better. But I submit that to give both their due effect, the utmost publicity is necessary, & I believe that Instrons have not usually appeared in the Gazette – They find their way to our Cruisers in general long before they are known even to the British public, whereas this important information ought to be given immediately to the embarrassed Merchants of the hostile & blockaded countries, through every channel that the enemy has left open, & especially sho^d be blazoned in our own prints.

The Orders respecting Prussia Lubeck & Portugal may be founded on causes to which I am incompetent – What you told me confidentially respecting the latter may have made something of the kind in her favour unavoidable. To my poor judgement however it seems inconsistent with the practical purpose, & still more with the justificatory principle of our new system, not to make the retaliation equal in its local extent to be wrong. At all events these new Orders seem to be motive'd improperly.

Our new system should not be represented as vindicatory but remedial – If regarded as the former it would be difficult to refuse more & wider exceptions, or even to justify the retaliation itself at the expence of Neutrals. It seems to me too that in going so far <& no farther> in respect of Countries not hostile, but forced into the blockading system of France, you open a very specious ground of complaint to Neutrals, in other words to Americans, trading to those countries or their Colonies. The Orders taken collectively create a fourth & new species of belligerent relation – To enemies, allies & neutrals, they have added blockading Countries not hostile'. But the two Orders on which I am remarking, add a fifth Viz blockading Countries not hostile which have been forced into the system of France

Now you deliver these from the effect of your own retaliation on a principle of which Neutrals trading with those countries are clearly as much intitled to the benefit as those countries themselves, & yet you give a greater range to the trade of these semi-blockaded Countries with yourselves, & even with Neutrals, than to the trade of Neutrals with them e.g. a Portuguese Ship may not only trade to Brazil or to New York but from New York to Charlestown, but an American Ship if I understand the Order aright, cannot lawfully trade from Lisbon to Brazil, or vice versa, nor from Oporto to Lisbon.

My chief objection however to these Orders, is that they are expressly placed on a principle incompatible with that on which we must rely for the justice of our whole system as far as friends or neutrals are exposed by it to inconvenience or loss <perhaps also for our treatment of Denmark> If retaliation were not necessary to prevent our own ruin, if it were merely a matter of revenge, our defence would be as difficult as it appears to me now to be easy, simple & decisive.

When I say that this is my chief objection to the discrimination made in favour of Portugal & Prussia, it is on the presumption that, on some ground or other, there must for reasons of State have been such a practical distinction. As far as the case is before the Public, I should certainly think such a distinction, however made, impolitic. Neither can I at all enter into the views upon which in the original Order the retaliation <on blockading Countries not hostile> is confined to Europe. Indeed to my views, the operation of this remedial measure will be more important & more extensively beneficial, as well as more certain, in the Colonies than in the Mother Countries.

It seems to me demonstrable that you have it in your power to give to British Manufacturers a speedy monopoly of every market in the New World, whatever may become of those in the Old. But I cannot answer for the effects of leaving open to foreign rivals such a market & such a thoroughfare, & such a colourable place of destination, as Brazil.

I am Dear Sir

Very sincerely & respectfully Yours

Jas. Stephen

Turn over

As the complexity of these Orders & Instructions will form a great drawback on their utility (I find Merchants who generally applaud the system complaining that they are puzzled & perplexed with its apparent intricacy) would it not be advisable on that ground to make one consolidated Order, in which any defects found in the present Orders & Instrons might be easily & without express notice be remedied, and a few simple rules with exceptions annexed, clearly indicate all that is or is not competent for our Merchants & Cruizers <& for> foreign Merchants to do. It is a case in which the clearness of the law is hardly less important than the law itself.

88   *Battles over Free Trade, Volume 1*

'Orders in Council; or, An Examination of the Justice, Legality, and Policy of the New System of Commercial Regulations', *Edinburgh Review*, 11 (January 1808), pp. 484–98.

> ART. XIV. *Orders in Council; or, an Examination of the Justice,*
> *Legality, and Policy of the New System of Commercial Regulations.*
> *With an Appendix of State Papers, Statutes and Authorities.* pp. 114.
> Longman & Co. and J. Ridgway, London, 1808.

WE have received this interesting and very able little publication, just as we were preparing to close our labours for the present quarter; and have been so much struck with the importance and novelty of the disquisitions which it contains, that we cannot resist the temptation of laying a hasty account of it before our readers.

As a considerable part of the argument is applicable to the question in the precise shape which it will assume before Parliament, and regards, therefore, the particular form of the measures lately adopted by the English government, rather than the general views of belligerent, or commercial policy, from which those measures took their rise, we shall pass over this branch of the subject very rapidly; and referring our readers to the work itself for satisfaction on it, shall bestow our chief attention upon the latter portion of the discussion, in itself quite general, and applicable to the prevalent notions of trade and war, as a system.

The tract is divided into three parts. The first, discusses the question, whether the late Orders in Council are consistent with the law of nations; and endeavours to show, from various considerations, that they are wholly repugnant to it: That they are measures of pretended retaliation against our enemy, whom no one ever considered as a party in the cause; but are in reality directed against neutral nations, whom we have no possible right to injure, merely because our enemy has done so, unless they have first acquiesced in the wrong, and thus made themselves parties to his quarrel: That no time was given for even asking the neutrals, whether they were disposed to yield or to resist, – the French decree of blockade having been explained by the French government in a manner quite consistent with the law of nations, and acted upon accordingly, up almost to the date of our Orders in Council: That even admitting the general plea of retaliation, the act of our Government is not in the nature of a retaliating or reciprocal proceeding;– it is not preventing neutrals from direct trade with France, because she would prevent them from direct trade with England, but forcing them to trade with France in a particular way profitable to ourselves, because France would blockade England altogether: That the regulations respecting certificates of origin, are still less like retaliation; and that, in truth, whatever may be the enemy's intention as to

'Orders in Council' (1808)

his decree, his power of executing it is confined to the part which is strictly justifiable by the law of nations, viz. the shutting of his ports to certain ships, – all the rest being empty threat and insult, and forming no excuse whatever for our aggressions on neutrals, whether they resent them or put up with them.

To every one of these arguments we are ready to subscribe; and they appear to us quite decisive of the question, touching the law of nations. But we could have wished that the defence of the Order issued by the late Administration, on January 7, 1807, had been less broadly stated. The arguments by which it is supported, are many of them just; and, viewing it as an application only (for it is in truth scarcely an extension) of the rule of the war 1756, we must admit, that it rests on the same grounds with this rule. The preamble, too, when it mentions retaliation as the plea for issuing it, very possibly means only to state the motive for using a just right, and not to defend the justice of that right. Moreover, this Order, even as a retaliation, is not without its favourable circumstances; for there were several neutrals at that time beside America; and the measures may have been taken with a view to the majority of cases, leaving to America her exceptions, founded on time not having been given her for acquiescing in, or resisting the French decree; which exceptions, it may be said, were competent before our prize courts. After making all these concessions, we shall not be accused of too much rigour towards the defenders of the Order 7. January, if we add, that they should state more explicitly their avowal, and their defence, too, of the Rule 1756, on which it ultimately, and by their own showing, rests. It is a good argument against the author of 'War in Disguise,' and his adherents, to quote the Rule 1756, when they attack the Order January 1807, which they certainly never will do, unless to accuse it of not going far enough. But what defence of the Order is it to those who deny that Rule? If the rule is fairly avowed, then we are at issue with the supporters of the Orders upon the Rule; – if it is not avowed, or if they fail in maintaining it, then we are at issue with them upon the whole of their Order. Unhappily, such *argumenta ad hominem*, are too commonly introduced in discussing great state questions in this debating and eloquent country. Is a great measure to be defended? Its friends never think what are its merits, but who are its opponents; and instead of justifying their conduct to the world, or to the people whose interests it affects, think they do enough, if they throw a sop to the barking animals who are attacking it. *You* did so yourselves;' or, '*You* did worse;' – or, 'What would *you* have said had we not done this?' These, alas, are the arguments by which our great statesmen but too often vindicate to their country the very questionable policy which they are pursuing! – To all such topics *we* make one answer. 'It may be your adversaries have done as bad or worse; but what is that to the country? *We* appear for the country, and require, not that you shall *estop* your opponents, by proving them to be worse than yourselves; – this is no comfort to the people; – but that you shall defend your cause on its own merits.' The misery of the system we have alluded to is just this; – that from *defend-*

ing measures on the ground of their being justified by former example, or because the adversary's mouth is stopped by his own conduct, the transition is too easy to *adopting* measures with a view to such wretched considerations; or, at any rate, without the salutary dread of an opposition, controlling the executive upon broad, statesmanlike principles. Are we quite sure that no compromise is made upon the public welfare, in the cabinet as well as in the senate; that measures are never taken, merely lest such a party would cry out on such a false pretence were they neglected; that resolutions are never adopted hastily, and without due consideration of their own merits, because the former conduct of the adversary having disarmed him, no danger of rigid scrutiny in public is apprehended? In a word, is not the country in some risk of slipping through between the two bodies of men appointed to sustain her, while they are busied with their mutual contentions? These reflections, amounting to somewhat more than matters of suspicion, are naturally suggested by the conduct of the argument upon the Orders of January 7th in the tract before us; and though they are connected with the vulgar clamour against all public men, lately too prevalent in this country, we are convinced that they have at least thus much of solidity, that they will either receive the attention of the higher class of statesmen to whom we allude, or they will raise up a third and powerful party in the nation, to the exclusion of all the rest.

Whatever countenance these remarks may seem to afford to the popular doctrines held by certain ignorant and thoughtless persons in the present crisis, we are confident that the next remark, suggested by the branch of the subject now under review, will not be liable to any such misconstruction.

In arguing the question of public law, it would have been advisable in the writer before us, to recollect that there are unhappily many people who have lately been seduced into a contempt of the whole idea of rights of states, and to whom a measure is rather recommended by any proof of its repugnance to the law of nations. While such wild and profligate doctrines were only circulated among the ignorant multitude, we were disposed to disregard them altogether; and, accordingly, we argued the neutral question in our last Number upon the old established grounds, satisfied with proving any pretension to be against the public law, in order to prove that it should instantly be abandoned. But since that period, a melancholy change has taken place; and these shallow and pernicious fancies have, unhappily for all Europe as well as this country, rapidly crept upwards in the state, until they have actually reached the very highest places, – are acted upon by our fleets and armies, proclaimed in royal speeches, and openly avowed in national manifestoes. The doctrine which denies that nations have any common laws, and assets that *Right* should now be read as *Might*, is therefore by no means so contemptible a political heresy as we once thought it; and we regret that the present tract did not undertake a refutation of it, as preliminary to the argument on the justice of the new measures.

The second part of this work is devoted to an exposition of the illegality of the new system, or an examination of the question, Are the late Orders in Council consistent with the municipal laws of the realm? It is proved very satisfactorily, that they are contrary to the whole spirit and practice of the Constitution; that they violate the laws most firmly established for the protection of trade, from the Great Charter down to the present times; and that they, moreover, directly infringe a fundamental branch of the Navigation Act. For the proofs of these propositions, we must refer to the Tract itself, and the numerous authorities and statutory enactments which it cites. We shall only extract the concluding passage of this part of the discussion, where the general tendency of such measures in a constitutional view is pointed out.

'If a temporary pressure of circumstances had rendered some deviation from a particular law, or even some infringement upon the general spirit of the Constitution absolutely necessary, and Government had, *for the mean while*, and as if sensible of the illegality of their proceedings, issued orders upon the face of them temporary like the emergency; the Parliament in its justice might have granted them that indemnity which they respectfully asked. But here is a new system of Royal enactment – of Executive legislation – a Privy Council Code promulgated by some half dozen individuals (for as such only the law knows them) upon principles utterly repugnant to the whole theory and practice of the Constitution – a full grown Cabinet Statute book, not authorizing any single and temporary proceeding, but prescribing general rules for a length of time; dispensing with the laws of the land in some points; adding to them in others; in not a few instances annulling them. It is an entire new Law-merchant for England during war, proclaimed by the court, not of Parliament, but of St James's, with as much regard to the competent authorities, or to the rightful laws of the realm, as the Rescripts of the latter Roman Emperor. It is not such a daring attempt as this that should be sanctioned by the Parliament, against whose authority it is levelled.

'But the Ministers, should they obtain an Indemnity, may now come forward, and propose to carry their new system into effect by a regular act of the legislature. It will then be for Parliament to consider whether they can by one deed of theirs overthrow the most ancient and best established principles of the British Constitution. The statute may indeed have all the formalities of law – it may supply the solemnity which the illegal orders now want. But repugnant as it must be to the genuine spirit of our Government, men may perhaps look for the substance of the English law rather in those fundamental maxims of our jurisprudence which it will have supplanted. All the proofs formerly adduced to illustrate the unconstitutional nature of the late Orders, form, in truth, insurmountable objections to any measure which may be proposed for erecting them into laws, unless indeed some paramount and permanent reasons of expediency can be urged, for enterprizing so mighty an innovation upon the constitution of the state.' p. 34–36

It is not inconsistent with the plan of a literary Journal to give a place among its extracts to remarks upon the general theory and the history of our laws. We transcribe, therefore, one more passage from this division of the argument.

'Thus, from the earliest times, the tenderness of the English Constitution for the trading interests of this country, is remarkably exemplified. They are regarded with more peculiar favour than almost any other subject of legislation. Even in ages when their magnitude was but inconsiderable, every measure appears to have been taken which might promise to cherish or promote them. To say that these endeavours were often fruitless, and very hurtful in their effects, is only to make in this instance an observation suggested by the history of all public transactions; and to regret that, as governments often display less virtue than prudence, so their intentions are sometimes better than their abilities. The efforts of our ancestors may frequently have been injudicious, but their desire was always the same – to promote the commerce of these realms. In pursuing this object, they seem not to have cared how much they encroached upon the power of the Crown, or how little they humoured the prejudices of the people. It is not unworthy of our observation, that, in many respects, their anxiety for encouraging at once both trade and civil liberty, led them to more liberal views of policy than have always marked the commercial legislation of later times. Even in the present day, a man might incur the fashionable imputations of '*not being truly British*,' or of '*indulging in modern philosophy*,' who should inculcate the very maxims handed down from the Barons of King John and his successor. And persons whose knowledge of the English history goes no further back than the French Revolution, or who have only studied the Constitution in the war of words which it has excited, would probably make an outcry about '*the wisdom of our ancestors*,' if one were disposed to repeat some liberal doctrines, antient even at the date of Magna Charta. If by some of the laws already cited, traders are placed on the footing with nobles, and the great baron's independence of the king's prerogative, shared with the merchant; if by a multitude of others, foreigners at amity with the realm are protected and highly favoured; if within the period of our written laws certain rights and privileges are secured to alien enemies themselves, and they are in some degree secured from the absolute controul of the Crown – what will the thoughtless persons alluded to think, should it appear that, in the remotest times to which the history of our law reaches, and before the men were born who obtained the great charter of our liberties, all the warlike spirit of the day – all the inveterate hatreds of a military people towards the enemy, and their contempt for peaceful industry, did not prevent them from extending to the persons of hostile merchants the same protection, in the midst of warlike operations, which the sanctity of their functions secured to the priests? It was in those remote times held to be a duty incumbent on all warriors to spare the persons of enemies within the realm, if they happened to be

'Orders in Council' (1808)

either priests, husbandmen, or merchants; or as their rude verses expressed it (in a style which some of our wise and classical statesmen may now a days deride)

Clericus, Agricola, Mercatus, tempora belli
Ut overque, colat, commutet pace fruantur

'Nor let it be thought mere matter of curious reflection to indulge, upon the present occasion, in such restrospects as these. The remarkable facts which have been stated deserve our most serious attention, as descriptive of the liberal and politic spirit of the Constitution from its most antient times. They prove that at least a prescriptive title cannot be shown for the narrow-minded views which the little men of this day entertain. They show that our ancestors held the rights of the people so sacred, and, as intimately connected with those rights, the great interests of trade, that they would in nowise compromise them, either to gratify a spirit of national rivalry, or to exalt the powers of the Crown, or to humour the caprice of the aristocracy. For it is a mere epigram to say, as Montesquieu hath done, in allusion to Magna Charta, 'that the English alone have made the rights of foreign merchants a condition of national freedom.' Our ancestors favoured and protected foreign merchants, out of respect to the interests and liberties of England. They knew that no more deadly blow could be aimed at the merchants and people of these realms, than by allowing them an exclusive possession of freedom, while their foreign customers should be placed at the disposal of the Prince. They saw the impossibility of long preserving any such limited system of popular rights; and they saw too, that commerce being in its nature a mutual benefit, the power of the Crown would triumph over the prosperity of the people, as well as over their liberties, the moment that the protection of the Constitution was withdrawn from the merchant-stranger. For this reason it was, that the wise laws which we have cited were continually passed and acted upon in a long, uninterrupted series, from the time when they arose out of those early traditional maxims of our Norman ancestors, down to the reign of Philip and Mary, when the judges, according to their true spirit, declared that the *rights of English subjects* were attacked by injuries offered to *foreign merchants*.' p. 18–22

We now come to the third question discussed in the work, – the Policy of the new system. In the present temper of men's minds, this is perhaps the ground upon which it will be most willingly put by both parties; and many, whom every view of its repugnance to the law of nations, and to the municipal law of the land, might fail to move, or even dispose in its favour, will probably listen with some attention to proofs of its being absolutely detrimental to the country. When they find that we have been violating the rights of foreign states, and breaking through our own constitution, for *nothing* – nay, to our great and manifest injury in point of profit; – that we have been breaking all laws public and municipal, and gained nothing – nay, lost a great deal by it; – they may be disposed to review their

94   *Battles over Free Trade, Volume 1*

former contemptuous judgment upon the value of those sacred principles which bind nations and individuals together; and to reprobate as unjust and unlawful, that conduct which they find to be ungainful.

This *third* part of the dissertation begins with clearing the way towards a correct understanding of the new system, by some preliminary remarks upon the confused, and in many particulars contradictory, regulations laid down in the Orders of Council. A general statement in then given of their substance, – a sketch of the sum of the changes which they are intended to produce upon the commercial intercourse of the world. This general view is illustrated by the following statement of the case, and the summary to which it leads of the principal points that touch the question of policy.

'To illustrate the operation of this new system, let us take the example of an American vessel, and observe what she is allowed and forbidden to do. She may sail with an American cargo to England, and from thence to France, without landing her cargo, if it consists not of cotton or manufactured goods. From France she may return with a French or other restricted cargo, which she must land before she can carry it back to America. The chief exports of America are raw produce; therefore, almost her whole trade with the restricted countries is limited by the necessity of touching at an English port twice, and landing the cargo once: if the American cargo consist of cotton, it must be landed in the outward voyage also, and can only proceed by license. The American may trade directly to and from the enemy's West India islands; but cannot (on account of the former law) bring their produce to this country; nor, by the Orders, can she carry it to the restricted European ports. She cannot pursue her voyage to and from the north of Europe, by touching at Man, Guernsey or Jersey, either going or coming. But, besides touching there, she must touch at a British or Irish port. It is evident then, that unless for convenience of smuggling, and evading the French decrees, no American will trade to Europe, through Man, Guernsey and Jersey. The American cannot pursue her voyage to or from the south of Europe, by touching at Malta and Gibraltar; but must go first to a British or Irish port, and afterwards return thither.

'This illustration comprehends the only material features of the new system, viz. its forcing all the neutral commerce to run through the ports of the United kingdom; its giving the English government a command of the supply of cotton, and some smaller articles, as brandies, wines, European snuff and tobacco; and its stopping the exportation of all enemy's West India produce, except cotton, cochineal and indigo, either to this country or to any restricted part of Europe. It is upon these points that the policy of the measure must be tried.' p. 41, 42

The substance of the new regulations being obtained in a sufficiently simple and comprehensive form for examining the expediency of the system, and the ground, as it were, cleared for the discussion, the consequences of the intended changes to our commerce, and the commerce of our enemies and allies, are investigated at considerable length, upon the supposition that the whole of our edicts are quietly acquiesced in by neutrals; and then their tendency to irritate those neutrals is separately pointed out. Instead of following the plan of the work, and analyzing its contents minutely, we shall, according to our practice, endeavour to exhibit a view of its substance, after our own way of considering it, and shall intersperse such additional remarks as suggest themselves to us, although they may have been omitted in the work under review. The subject is of infinite importance, not merely to this country at the present moment, but to the whole science of politics, in which, views, of a tendency the most novel, are now industriously propagated, and a great, and, in our opinion, not merely perilous, but fatal, experiment is attempted, by persons under the guidance of the most blind and extravagant passions with which the rulers of an enlightened people were ever stricken.

France having attempted, or rather threatened to blockade this country, and cut off all intercourse between us and our foreign customers, a prudent statesman would naturally have considered, in the first place, the probable consequences of such a resolution on the enemy's part being enforced. He would immediately have perceived, that the most rigorous execution of this measure could only have cut off our direct intercourse with the parts of the Continent where French influence prevails, leaving us all our trade with neutrals; that is, our trade with America, and with those parts of Europe not overrun by French troops; consequently, he would have concluded, that the utmost exertions of the French government, admitting them to prevail over the proverbial ingenuity of neutral traders, and to prevent our goods from getting in their bottoms directly over to the Continent, could have gone not one step further; and that our direct trade with those neutrals, and, consequently, through their countries, with the countries most subject to the enemy's influence, would still have remained to us. Thus, it would have appeared, that even if France had succeeded in preventing Americans (for example) from carrying over our goods direct to the Continent, she never could prevent them from carrying those same goods from hence to their own ports, and from their own ports to France. No certificates of origin, nor any other conceivable regulation, could have prevented a British cargo from finding its way over by such a route. Nothing but the resolution to give up her whole trade at once, or the possession of fleets sufficient to invest our coasts, and cut off our direct trade with America, could have destroyed our roundabout trade with France. She neither has shown this resolution, nor does she possess those fleets.

The prudent statesman (whose *existence* we are assuming as a bare possibility) would next have inquired by what means he could diminish most effectually the total amount of the restrictions which the enemy was thus enabled to impose on our commerce. As the roundabout trade was of all others the surest means of defeating those restrictions, he would, at all events, have left that untouched – encouraged it

– relied upon it – satisfied that nothing but the destruction of it could ever carry the threats of France into execution. *This* would have struck him at any rate, and he would have laid it down as a matter of course. As little would it have been a question, whether the direct trade, which the enemy prohibited between us and himself, should be encouraged in spite of him, and prohibited on our side, as a measure of retaliation. Whether we should say to neutrals, 'You shall not enter here from enemy's ports, because he won't allow you to land from our ports;' or, 'Come here freely, and depart freely; endeavour, by all means, to evade his restrictions; and we shall afford you every facility for this purpose.' This question would not have detained our statesman long; for he would immediately perceive that, by adopting the former alternative, he was just playing into the enemy's hand – confirming his decree – carrying into execution parts of it which he himself could not have enforced – and guarding against evasions of it, which must have rendered it almost nugatory without our assistance. To have encouraged the trade between the enemy's country and our own, direct by neutrals, would therefore be the next resolution of the reasoning which we are supposing. By leaving the roundabout trade with France untouched, we should have left open a channel of communication with the Continent in spite of her; and, by promoting all evasions of her decrees against the direct trade, we should have done our best to prevent her from blocking up another channel, much more within her power.

What do the *statesmen*, whose system we are examining, propose to themselves? They resolve at once to shut up the channel of the roundabout trade, which the enemy could least of all have effected himself; and they try to encourage the direct channel, which is the most under his controul. They do his business for him, where he most wants their aid, and can the least do without them. Where he is powerful, and may do something in spite of their teeth, they attempt to counteract his regulations. There are two gates in our field through which we wish to drive our sheep; one of them we can open and shut at pleasure; it leads into the highway, and we have the key in our pockets: the other belongs, half to us, and half to a malicious neighbour, who wishes to prevent us from driving out our sheep at all. What shall we do? The great counsellors of the time tell us to shut up our own gate by all means – to make it as fast as we can with bolts and bars, so that not a lambkin may get out; and then to go struggle with our neighbour at the other gate, and try to drive our flocks through that passage. It is related, that the Chancellor Oxenstiern said to his son, when he sent him to a congress of statesmen, and the young man was struck with awe at the solemnity of the occasion, 'Go, my child, and see how little wisdom it takes to govern the world.'

But supposing the prudent statesman, above imagined, had a mind to consider the question of retaliating upon the enemy, let us see how he would reason. He would certainly, in the first place, ask himself, whether, by any conceivable mode of retaliation, he could avoid doing, in great part at least, the very thing which

'Orders in Council' (1808)

the enemy wishes? Whether, commerce being essentially, and in its own nature, a mutual benefit, he could stop the trade of France, without either immediately or ultimately stinting the trade of England? He would then inquire, which party is likely to suffer most in the contest of self-destruction, in the rivalry of privations and losses? And as it is clear that this must be the party which has most trade – whose trade is most extensive in proportion to his whole resources – whose commerce, in a word, is most essential to his general prosperity – so would it likewise be manifest, that any injury we might inflict on the enemy would be trifling, compared with its expense to ourselves; and that we should damage our own interests so much more than we could injure his, that the utmost we could gain by such a bargain would not be worth the price we must pay.

If, however, retaliation must be resorted to, and if we are resolved to hurt the enemy, cost what it will to ourselves, our statesman would take especial care to see that his measures were really those of retaliation; and if he had the sense of a child, he would be cautious how he mistook *cooperation* for *retaliation*. Our new system makes exactly this mistake. We attack the commerce of neutrals and allies; and we favour the trade of the enemy. One of the greatest markets, if not the greatest market for American commerce, is France, and the rest of the restricted country. We at once obstruct all direct communication between America and this market. One of the best markets of France and the restricted country is England. We not only facilitate, by every means in our power, the access to this market; but we actually compel all neutrals to drive the traffic of France with her best customers in the shortest and easiest way. American commerce, we say, shall be all confined, roundabout and indirect. Hostile commerce – French commerce, shall be easy, direct and open!

In truth it now depends on our enemy, by means of our assistance, whether any, and what commerce, shall be carried on between himself and England. And this we call a blockade of France, which is in truth much like a blockade of England. In truth, a general and rigorous blockade of France, liable though it be to many of the objections already stated, is at least an intelligible and consistent measure.

'It cuts off his foreign trade entirely, although it deprives us of trade our trade with him; and if commercial distress can ruin him, such a proceeding gives us some chance of effecting his downfall. But the new system is only a blockade of the enemy, if the enemy himself chuses that it shall be so. It can never, by possibility, ruin him, or even materially injure his commerce: for the moment he is pinched, he can relieve himself. He can allow neutrals to enter his own ports, from those of Great Britain; and thus obtain as large a share of foreign commerce as she desires.[1] These neutral carriers, it is true, must land and reship in England certain cargoes; and many (but by no means all) of these voyages will be somewhat more circuitous

---

1 'It is confidently reported that some relaxation of the French Decree has already been allowed in Holland, though this does not appear very likely.'

than formerly. An American bound to Bordeaux, must touch at Cork, Falmouth, & c. which is somewhat out of her course; if bound to Dunkirk, Amsterdam, & c. she would probably touch at Cowes from choice, to receive advices respecting the market from London correspondents. Admitting that some considerable inconvenience arises from hence, in all cases, on an average; the whole effect is to raise the prices of the neutral goods a little to the enemy, and to lower somewhat the profits of the neutral, without any gain whatever to ourselves. Our friends and our enemies lose each a little, and we gain nothing at all. The obligation to land certain cargoes can do us no more real good. It increases somewhat the loss of the neutral and the enemy, and may enable us to keep a few more customhouse officers. If, indeed, the Orders in Council are followed up by an act of Parliament imposing duties on the goods so landed, then we clearly shall propose to ourselves, not certainly to distress the enemy's trade, but to profit both by his commerce and that of our friends. Would it not be a much simpler expedient, and answer the very same purpose, to propose that America should pay us a yearly tribute, and to raise it as she best can, either upon her own citizens, or her French customers? If the duty which we mean to lay on is not the merest trifle, we may be well assured that America will not submit to it.' p. 44–46

Upon the probable consequences of a colonial blockade, (the only thing like a blockade in the new system), as it applies to the enemy's designs in Europe, the following remarks are quite conclusive.

'This measure is much more plain and consistent with belligerent views than the rest of the plan; but, when examined, it appears equally shortsighted and unwise. The blockade of the enemy's colonies can only have two objects – to deprive the enemy of certain articles of consumption – and to increase the demand for those articles in our own market. These objects are, in a considerable degree, incompatible; for our West India produce commonly finds a vent on the Continent, by supplying the wants of the enemy. But supposing, for argument sake, that both the two ends may be gained at once, let us examine the consequences.

'The French have borne every species of public and private calamity for nearly eighteen years; they have passed through all the vicissitudes of revolution, from anarchy to despotism; they have tasted only of war, with its whole train of evils, of which privations have been the smallest; they have suffered the most unsparing conscription, augmented in rigour as the service of the army became more irksome and dangerous: to all this they have submitted in quiet, with rallying points for emigration in the neighboring nations, and for rebellion in the heart of their own country. No dangers, no calamities, no private distresses, not even the conscription itself, has ever extorted a murmur of discontent – and we now expect insurrections to break out as soon as coffee and sugar shall become scarce at Paris, or the army shall find tobacco growing dear! The conscription is at an end, or is become only holiday work; the armies go out, not to fight, but to revel in triumph, and to amuse themselves with foreign travel: But grocery and snuff are advancing in price, and let Bonaparte look to it! If he does not speedily make peace on our terms, restore the Bourbons, and give up Belgium, his earthly course is run! – This is the argument.

'But if it be not a waste of time to give such positions as these a serious refutation, let us only consider how little chance any commercial blockade has of being effectually enforced. Every successful attempt of this kind which we make, augments incalculably the temptations to elude our vigilance. If certain drugs, for example, were almost excluded from France by the activity of our cruizers, their price would rise so enormously, that a neutral merchant would find his account in attempting to land a cargo of bark, (necessarily lowered in price elsewhere), though he should lose three fourths in the attempt: so that we shall in vain continue to wage war against the wretched hospital of our enemy. To a certain degree the same remark applies in all the other cases. In one way or another the goods will find their way from the places of glut, to those of demand. Their prices may be somewhat enhanced; and the use of such as are not essentially necessary, will be diminished.

'All the changes of this sort, however, which we attempt to make, and to a certain degree successfully, will take place gradually. The stock in hand will be economized in proportion as the further supplies are obstructed, and, instead of producing lasting discontents, or even disgust with the war, among our enemies, we cannot help furnishing the very remedy along with the evil, by teaching them gradually to alter certain habits, in themselves indifferent. It would not be so irrational for their rulers to expect that some hatred of England should arise out of this policy; but for us, who have not once excited the least disposition to throw off the French yoke by all our hostilities – who see the French people themselves, not merely unsubdued, but even flourishing after all our victories over their trade – for us to think of conquering, by the scarcity of two or three wares, the people whom our greatest captains and innumerable ships have never humbled during years of the most successful naval warfare – surely exceeds the bounds even of popular or party delusion.' p. 47–51.

The only remaining part of the subject, the effects of the blockade in relieving our own planters, we have already, in treating of West Indian affairs, had occasion to anticipate. Referring our readers to last Number for the discussion, it may be proper merely to add in this place, that such relief is confessedly temporary; – it is bounded by the war; and the produce which it must cause to be accumulated in the hostile colonies, coming over suddenly and in enormous quantities the moment peace is restored, will give even those planters, who have been relieved in the mean while, abundant reason to lament so shortsighted a policy, and to wish that they had wisely had recourse to the only radical cure for the evils complained of – a diminished cultivation of the great staples.

Convinced, as we are, that the general view which we have now taken, is sufficient to expose the monstrous errors of the new system; and considering, that the arguments now offered apply to the case of the neutrals yielding implicit obedience, as well as to the more probable supposition of their quarrelling with us, we are the less anxious about examining the last branch of the work before us, which exposes the dangers of the system to our relations with America. One of the most striking parts of the whole folly is, the peculiar time chosen for proclaiming it. The Americans, then the only neutrals, were on bad terms with France; – a month's delay might have induced them to join us heartily in our hostilities; – and we preclude the possibility of this event by our own act and deed. It is, however, justly remarked in the tract before us, that they are shortsighted politicians indeed, who would prefer the cooperation to the neutrality of America. Our commerce could only be more injured by one event, than by America quarrelling with France; and that event is, – her quarrelling with England.

It is impossible to close these remarks, without alluding to the topics touched upon at the conclusion of this tract, – the gloomy prospects of the country in the present awful crisis. Destined to fight the battles of Europe, with an enemy always upbraided for his want of principle, and his utter contempt of the rights of nations, England has chosen, for the first time, to abandon the high ground on which she has hitherto stood, and to strive with that enemy in the pernicious, as well as despicable race of injustice to unoffending and unprotected states. It is this which forms the worst feature in our present case – this avowal of profligacy, first in our actions, and since, even in our state papers – this regret, which we have now seen expressed in declarations under the Sovereign's name, that we have so long abstained from deeds of violence, and stuck so long to the wreck of public principle; – this it is which may justly terrify us, now that we are preparing for new battles, whether we view it as the sure symptom of approaching downfall, or as a no less certain cause of diffidence in our own courage, and exultation to the enemy.

This nation has always been too fond of war; and has usually gone on fighting, as Mr Hume has observed, for a year or two after the objects were attained, or finally lost, for which it had entered into hostilities. The rancour which has been generated during our present contest with France, and the tone of boastful defiance which has been encouraged in its later periods, have strengthened this national propensity to a degree, which seems to us to border on insanity. But the love of war, we trust, is not, even at the present moment, so strong in the body of the nation, as the love of justice and the dread of dishonour; – and, when they find under what form, and with what consequences, our future hostilities are to be carried on, they may look with less aversion to the cessation of a contest, that threatens, in its progress, to undo the civilization of the world.

Stephen to Perceval (1808) 101

James Stephen to Spencer Perceval, 23 May 1808, Perceval Papers, BL, Add. MS 49183, fols 58–9.

Serjeants Inn

May 23^d 1808

My dear Sir

If you have time enough it may be worth your while to look at an Article in the last No. of the Edinburgh Review (which came out last week) on the Orders in Council.

The strange & audacious misrepresentations there, like those in the Morng Chronicle, & c, shew clearly what the plan of the Party is – They know, like their teacher Buonaparte, that the effrontery of incessant false assertions before the public, tho opposed by notoriety & evidence, will in a great degree make its way, & that they have the advantage of being read by thousands who neither know the mercantile case, nor will ever see the Parliamentary evidence.

They therefore proclaim still as Baring you know had the assurance <in effect> lately to do in the H^o of Com., that the trade of the Country flourished till destroyed by the Orders of Council, & they even dare to add that the rates of Insurance were not raised!!!

What is to be done? for these vile arts may do you much mischief – I tho^t that from the society of the public & of Parl^t on that subject, it was better to let it drop – but I now doubt – Pray think of it. What say you to moving some distinct resolutions of fact as deductions from the evidence. Viz. The total stop of our trade with the Continent from Sep^t the facts as to insurance, & c, and perhaps a general resolution of the House as to the injustice & expediency & necessity of the O. in Council.

If you think this advisable & wish me to do it, I am of course at your service. – In that case Tierney should not be allowed to prepare the examons longer <than you can prevent>. This perhaps is part of their plan.

I am Dear Sir

Very sincerely & respectfully Yours

J. Stephen

P.S. Turn over

If you approve that plan, I will not only make a speech as carefully as I can but print it with notes containing extracts of the evidence, & c.

You may rely on it that notwithstanding the salvo artfully thrown in, implying that they knew nothing of the evidence <u>on your side</u> when this Review was written, the contrary was the fact. There can indeed be no doubt that the article was written either by Brougham himself or under his inspection. It is by no means in this case only that they trample shamefully & willfully on the truth & fair dealing to serve their purposes.

102   *Battles over Free Trade, Volume 1*

'Financial Situation of England and France', from the *Journal de l'Empire, Examiner*, 144 (30 September 1810), pp. 611–12.

The *Journal de l'Empire* contains the following article:–

FINANCIAL SITUATION OF ENGLAND AND FRANCE.

ENGLAND. – England cannot have more than 300 million of revenue: she has, however, 1500 millions: but 300 million represent her actual wealth, 1200 millions the revenue of he[r] monopoly; whence it results, that when England is ever so little cramped in her commerce, the exchange becomes unfavourable to her: she can no longer support herself, and she require a paper-money. Paper-money is a natural and indispensable consequence of the situation of a nation which, like England has created a factitious revenue. England pays 600 millions of interest for debt; that is, twice her real and reasonable revenue

FRANCE – France has 800 millions of revenue in time of peace. This is only two-thirds of what she can raise in time of war. By adding 30 *centimes* to her rates of imports, her revenue is raised to 1200 millions. This revenue is wholly derived from her own territory. She has 50 millions of debt, that is to say, 1-16th of her ordinary income. It is obvious from this, that France has not, and ought not, to have a paper-money. France may be considered as a rich farmer, who finds every thing on his farm. She has no need of commerce, but as an agent for selling her productions. Germany, Italy, are open to her speculations; and even England is glad to receive, when she chooses to send, the surplus of her produce. The bank discounts twice as much as the *Caisse de compte* discounted in 1780. It has 120 millions of notes in circulation. These are the bank notes, convertible into specie at pleasure, and not forced. The coinage of France is the best in Europe. Money is there abundant, and the rate of interest is from 4 to 5 percent. Her manufactures are in such a state of prosperity, that they supply not only her own consumption, but that of Italy and Germany. The manufactures of France never before prospered so much.

COMMERCIAL SITUATION OF ENGLAND AND FRANCE.

ENGLAND. – As the power of England rests upon her commerce, that commerce consists in the circulation of the produce of the New World. We have proved that four-fifths of her revenue arose from brokerage; it is the coffee, therefore, the sugar, the indigo, the dye-woods, the muslins of India, which constitute her

'Financial Situation of England and France' (1810)

fortune; all her prosperity consists in drawing these productions from both the Indies, and promoting their introduction into Europe.

FRANCE. – France has an interest wholly continental; her revenue arises from the produce of her fields, of her vines, her olives, her tobacco, her fabrics of silk and linen, and from the cotton of her southern provinces. Like the Continent, she has an interest in rejecting the merchandize of the Indies, and in profiting by the bounty of nature, which has placed within the Old Continent what may enable it to dispense with the New. Thus the shackles which she has thrown upon English brokerage are such, that the consumption of sugar, of coffee, and colonial produce, has within three years decreased one-half in Europe. The discoveries which she has made enable her even to replace the productions of the Continent. The sugar from grapes is sold cheaper than the cane-sugar ever was, even at the period of the greatest communication with the colonies. The cottons of Naples and of Rome are superior to those of America. The kermes, the wood, and the madder, thanks to the aids of chemistry, compensate for the want of colonial dyes. Already soda is made every where. When the New World was discovered the arts of chemistry were in their infancy.

The Continental system has produced a real, a prodigious revolution. It will oppose an insurmountable obstacle to the brokerage of England; and in proportion as the Continental Powers feel, and they have felt it for a long time, that it is their interest to tax the importation of colonial produce, they will have sugar, coffee, cotton, and indigo, from the Continent itself. The result is not chimerical. The actual prosperity of France, the aid which she derives from the Arts to procure that which she wants, from that this revolution has advanced 5-6ths of its course. It has been silently working, it will burst forth; and at a general Continental Peace, England will be astonished at the progress of the arts of chemistry in Europe, of the naturalization of the culture of the plants of America on the Continent, and of the repugnance of the Continent to give her its gold and impoverish itself when it finds an equivalent within itself. These are the great causes of the diminution of English commerce; these effects will be more efficacious than the Decrees of Milan and Berlin. Let these decrees continue in force a few years longer, and they will make themselves be felt a century after they have been revoked.

104   *Battles over Free Trade, Volume 1*

Prince Regent in Council, Orders in Council and War with America, enclosed in Castlereagh to Mr Russell, 23 June 1812, *Parliamentary Papers* (1812–13), xiv.1, pp. 10–11.

At the Court of Carlton-House, the 23d of June 1812, present, His Royal Highness the Prince Regent in Council

'That if at any time hereafter the Berlin and Milan Decrees shall, by some authentic act of the French Government, publicly promulgated, be absolutely and unconditionally repealed, then and from thenceforth the Order in Council of the 7th of January 1807, and the Order in Council of the 26th of April 1809, shall, without any further Order, be, and the same are hereby declared from thenceforth to be, wholly and absolutely revoked.

And whereas the Chargé des Affaires of the United States of America, resident at this Court, did, on the 20th day of May last, transmit to Lord Viscount Castlereagh, one of His Majesty's principal Secretaries of State, a copy of a certain instrument, then for the first time communicated to this Court, purporting to be a Decree passed by the Government of France, on the 28th day of April 1811, by which the Decrees of Berlin and Milan are declared to be definitively no longer in force, in regard to American vessels.

And whereas His Royal Highness the Prince Regent, although He cannot consider the tenor of the said instrument as satisfying the conditions set forth in the said Order of the 21st of April last, upon which the said Orders were to cease and determine; is nevertheless disposed on His part to take such measures as may tend to re-establish the intercourse between neutral and belligerent nations, upon its accustomed principles – His Royal Highness the Prince Regent, in the name and on the behalf of His Majesty, is therefore pleased, by and with the advice of His Majesty's Privy Council, to order and declare, and it is hereby ordered and declared, that the Order in Council bearing date the 7th day of January 1807, and the Order in Council bearing date the 26th day of April 1809, be revoked, so far as may regard American vessels and their cargoes, being American property, from the 1st day of August next.

But whereas by certain Acts of the Government of the United States of America, all British armed vessels are excluded from the harbours and waters of the said United States, the armed vessels of France being permitted to enter therein; and the commercial intercourse between France and the said United States having been restored; His Royal Highness the Prince Regent is pleased hereby further to declare, in the name and on behalf of His Majesty, that if the government of the said United States shall not, as soon as may be, after this Order shall have been duly notified by His Majesty's Minister in America to the said Government, revoke, or cause to be revoked, the said Acts, this present Order shall in that case, after due notice signified by His Majesty's Minister in America to the said Government, be thenceforth null and of no effect.'

Mr Foster to Viscount Castlereagh, 20 June 1812, enclosing Madison's Declaration of War on Britain, 18 June 1812, *Parliamentary Papers* (1812–13), xiv.1, p. 301.

I have the honour to transmit to your Lordship, the inclosed printed copy of the Act of Congress, declaring war to exist between the United States and Great Britain, and authorizing the President to carry it on by land and sea ... I have to remark on this extraordinary measure, that it seems to have been unexpected by nearly the whole nation; and to have been carried in opposition to the declared sentiments of many of those who voted for it, in the House of Representatives, as well as in the Senate, in which latter body, there was known to have been at one time, a decided majority against it

106 *Battles over Free Trade, Volume 1*

[James Stephen], *A Key to the Orders in Council*, 6th edn (London: John Murray, 1812).

THE French Decrees and our Orders in Council are at this moment objects of great interest and general discussion; yet it is to be apprehended that very few persons have been able to make themselves acquainted with the true progress and real state of these affairs. No publication exists which presents the whole series of French, British, and American proceedings in one view; and it is for the purpose of supplying this desideratum, and explaining and simplifying this complex subject, that I have endeavoured to draw up an impartial, compendious, and chronological statement of the several official documents which it has produced, interspersing and subjoining such observations as may tend to exhibit the whole case in the clearest and truest point of view.

I.

The first[1] of these documents is the Berlin Decree, so called because it was issued from the camp near that city on the 21st Nov. 1806.

It consists of two parts:

1st. A statement of the wrongs done by England.

2nd. Of the measures which these wrongs have obliged him to adopt.

The first part states: – *that England has ceased to observe the laws of civilized nations – that she considers the individuals of a hostile nation as enemies – that she seizes as prize the property of such individuals – that she blockades commercial ports, bays, and mouths of rivers, and other places not fortified – that she declares places to be in a state of blockade where she has no actual force to enforce the blockade – that this abuse is intended to aggrandize the commerce and industry of England by means of the commerce and industry of the continent – that those who traffic in English commodities on the continent second her views and render themselves her accomplices – that this conduct of England is worthy the age of barbarism, and is advantageous to her at the expence of every other nation – that it is just to attack her with the same weapons which she employs.*

And in pursuance of this assertion the second part proceeds to decree:

---

1   It may be here proper to observe, that, at a subsequent period of the discussion, France asserted, and America seemed willing to admit, that the first departure from the laws of nations was, *not* this Berlin Decree, but Mr. Fox's order for blockading the ports from Brest to the Elbe in May 1806. But this pretence could not stand; Mr. Fox's blockade was a military measure intended to be maintained by actual force, and rendered expedient by the military operations in which the enemy was then engaged in the north of Germany. This was therefore a strictly legal blockade; but the French have since explained that they do not consider as legal, blockade of a river or harbour that is not fortified, nor a fortified place unless it is invested by sea and land. This, to be sure, makes all maritime blockade illegal; but no man alive will maintain this doctrine except a Frenchman, who will maintain any thing.

[Stephen], *A Key to the Orders in Council (1812)*

–   *that the British Islands are in a state of blockade.*

–   *that all commerce and correspondence with the British Isles are prohibited.*

–   *that letters and packets addressed to England or to Englishmen, or written in English, shall be intercepted.*

–   *that every British individual whom the troops of France or those of her allies can lay hold of, shall be a prisoner of war.*

–   *that every warehouse, any commodity, every article of commerce which may belong to a British subject is good prize.*

–   *that the trade in English goods is prohibited, and every article that belongs to England or is the produce of her manufactories or colonies is good prize.*

–   *that no ship from England or her colonies, or which shall have touched there, shall be admitted into any harbour.*

–   *that this decree shall be communicated to all our allies whose subjects as well as those of France have been victims of the injustice and barbarity of the English maritime code.*

–   *and this decree is further stated to be in force, and considered as a fixed and fundamental law of the French Empire as long as England shall adhere to the* PRINCIPLES *herein complained of.*

The sum of this decree is, that England shall be erased from the list of commercial and even civilized nations, until she abandons her maritime code which has raised her to her present pitch of superiority over other nations, and that France and her allies and dependants are pledged and required invariably to maintain this which has been since called the continental system, till England shall have been reduced to make these concessions.

II.

On the 24th November, 1806, the above decree was recapitulated in a proclamation from the French minister to the senate of Hamburgh, which states:

– *that as several of the citizens of Hamburgh were notoriously engaged in trade with England, the Emperor of the French was obliged to take possession of the city in order to execute his decree.*

This threat was the same day executed by Marshal Mortier at the head of a division of the French army.

This proclamation and occupation of Hambro' is particularly important, as being the first act of that principle on which France has ever since, as we shall see, proceeded, of not only extending her continental system to all places within her reach, but actually seizing upon neutral countries, that she might extend the continental system to them; so that the original violence and injustice against England became the source and pretence of more violence and injustice against

108   *Battles over Free Trade, Volume 1*

all rights and laws of nations, and an excuse for the most outrageous usurpation and hostile seisure of neutral territory that has ever been attempted.

III.

These proceedings of the government of France produced, on the part of England, the measure which is called Lord Grey's Order in Council, because his lordship was secretary of state at the time it was issued: 7th January, 1807.

This order states:

–   *that the decrees issued by the French government to prohibit the commerce of neutral nations with the British dominions, or in their produce or manufactures, are in violation of the usages of war.*

–   *that such attempts on the part of the enemy would give His Majesty an unquestionable right of retaliation, and would warrant His Majesty in enforcing against all commerce with France, the same prohibition which she vainly hopes to effect against us.*

–   *that His Majesty, though unwilling to proceed to these extremities, yet feels himself bound not to suffer such measures to be taken by the enemy, without some step on his part to restrain this violence, and to retort upon them the evils of their own injustice.*

–   *–and that therefore it is ordered that no vessel shall be permitted to trade from one part to another belonging to France or her allies, or so far under her controul that British vessels may not freely trade thereat.*

This was, as it expresses itself to be, a mitigated measure of retaliation, one intended rather to call France to a sense of her injustice and the neutrals to a sense of their own duty, than to inflict a vengeance on the enemy adequate to his aggression; but it very properly states the *right* in Great Britain to go the *whole length* of complete *retaliation;* and it strongly intimates that if this moderate proceeding should fail of its effect, more effective, but equally justifiable modes of retaliation would be adopted.

Shortly after the publication of this order, Lord Grenville's and Lord Grey's ministry went out of power, and that of the Duke of Portland, which included Mr. Perceval and Mr. Canning, came in. Their first proceeding in this matter was on the 11th November, 1807; when finding the measures of further retaliation, threatened in Lord Grey's order of January preceding, were become absolutely necessary from the increasing violence of the French, and the continued supineness of the neutrals, they published an Order in Council which is the next document that I present to my readers.

IV.

On the 11th of Nov. 1807, The Duke of Portland's administration issued two Orders in Council; the first of which states:

– *that the Order of the 7th January has not effected the desired purpose either of compelling the enemy to recall his Orders, or of inducing Neutral nations to interpose against them; but, on the contrary, that they have been recently enforced with increased rigour.*

– *that His Majesty is therefore obliged to take further measures for vindicating the just rights and maritime powers of His People, which are not more essential to our own safety, than to the independence and general happiness of mankind; and in pursuance of these principles of retaliation* (already asserted in the first Order) *all the ports of France, and her Allies, and all other ports or places in Europe from which the British flag is excluded, shall be considered in a state of blockade; and all their goods and manufactures shall be considered as lawful prize, thus retaliating upon France, and her Allies, their own violence.*

– *that His Majesty would of course be justified in making this retaliation, as unqualified and without limit, as the original offence; but that unwilling to subject Neutrals to more inconvenience than is necessary, he will permit to Neutrals such trade with the enemy's ports, as may be carried on directly with the ports of His Majesty's dominions, under several specifications and conditions which are set forth as favourable exceptions to the general rules of blockade.*

The second Order in Council of this date sets forth:

– *that articles of the growth or manufacture of foreign countries cannot be by law (namely the Navigation Act), imported into Great Britain, except in British Ships, or the native shipping of the country itself which produces the goods.*

– *that in consequence of the former order of this date, which says, that all neutral trade with France must touch at a British port, it is expedient to relax, in some degree, this law, and to permit the shipping of any friendly or neutral country to import into Great Britain the produce or manufactures of countries at war with her.*

– *that all goods so imported shall be liable to the same duties, and under the same warehousing regulation as if imported according to the Navigation Act.*

The sum of these Orders in Council is, that France having declared that there shall be no trade in communication with England, His Majesty resolves that the ports of France, and every port from which, by the controul of France, the British flag is excluded, shall have no trade except to or from a British port; but that His Majesty is still desirous to encourage and protect Neutral Commerce, as far as is consistent with such an opposition to the enemy's measures, as is essential to the safety and prosperity of the British dominions.

V.

Next comes the Decree, dated *Milan*, December 17, and published in Paris the 26th of December, 1807, reciting:

110   *Battles over Free Trade, Volume 1*

   –   *that the ships of Neutral and Friendly Powers are, by the English[1] Orders in Council of the 11th of November, made liable not only to be searched, but to be detained in England, and to pay a tax rateable per centum on the cargo.*

   –   *that, by these Acts, the British Government denationalizes ships of every nation; and that it is not competent to any Sovereign or country to submit to this degradation of the Neutral flag, as England would construe such submission into an acquiescence in her right to do so, as she has already availed herself of the tolerance of other Governments, to establish the infamous principle that free ships do not make free goods, and to give the right of blockade an arbitrary extension, which infringes on the sovereignty of every State, and it is therefore decreed,*

   –   *that every ship, to whatever nation it may belong, which shall have submitted to be searched by an English ship, or to a voyage to England, or shall have paid any English tax, is, for that alone, declared to be denationalized, to have forfeited the protection of its own Sovereign, and to have become English property.*

   –   *that all such ships, whether entering the ports of France, or her Allies, or met at sea, are good prizes.*

   –   *that the British Islands are in a state of blockade, both by sea and land, and that all vessels sailing from England, or any of her colonies, or the port of any of her Allies to England, or her colonies, or the port of an ally, are declared good and lawful prize.*

   –   *that these measures (which are resorted to only in just retaliation of the barbarous system adopted by England, which assimilates its legislation to that of Algiers,) shall cease to have effect with respect to all nations who shall have the firmness to compel the English Government to respect their flag. They shall continue to be rigorously enforced as long as that Government does not return to the principle of the law of nations, which regulates the relation of civilized states in a state of war. The provisions of the present decree shall be abrogated and null, in fact, as soon as the English abide again by the principles of the law of nations, which are also the principles of justice and honour.*

On the whole of this decree I cannot offer any more appropriate observations than those which were contained in the MORNING CHRONICLE of the 4th of January 1808, which I therefore extract.

'The Orders in Council of the 11th of November have produced from the Emperor of the French the decree (just inserted). Totally overlooking the *first* violence offered by himself to the Neutral Commerce, which the law of nations had sanctioned as the means of softening the calamities of war, he imputes to the measure of our government all the blame of this his last most furious denunciation against the trade of the world. Without at all entering into the question of

---

1   Though this decree recites the Orders of the 11th November, it has been said, that these orders were not known at Milan when the decree was made; and that this preface was subsequently affixed in Paris, when the decree came to be published there.

whether our ministers were prudent or the contrary, in imitating the act of the enemy, we must say that nothing can be more impudent, or more false, than the allegation that the British were the original aggressors against the freedom of commerce. The late ministers (Lords Grenville and Grey) in the firm and temperate notice which they took of the French Decree which put the British Isles in a state of blockade, DISTINCTLY STATED TO THE UNITED STATES OF AMERICA, THAT THEIR ACQUIESCENCE IN A CODE WHICH VIOLATED THE RIGHTS OF INDEPENDENT STATES, WOULD COMPEL THIS COUNTRY TO TAKE MEASURES FOR ITS OWN PROTECTION.

'As to the origin of the violence there is nothing more clear, and Buonaparte cannot, by any pomp of words, disguise from his own people, or from America, to whom indeed the whole basis of the present decree is addressed, the fact of his being the author of the hardships which France and its dependencies are doomed to suffer.

'The decree, indeed, is entirely directed to America: it is a menace to her – she must chuse her party – and we suspect the result will be that she will abstain from all intercourse with both.

'The 4th paragraph in which he professes to hold himself in readiness 'to abrogate and annul the provisions of the decree as soon as the English shall again abide by the principles of the law of nations,' was yesterday interpreted, we know not why, into an offer of pacification. It is obvious that his meaning in the above quotation is, that if we shall yield to 'his law of nations,' we may have peace. HIS LAW OF NATIONS IS NOT THE LAW AS WRITTEN, SETTLED, AND ACTED UPON BY THE CIVILIZED WORLD, BUT A NEW CODE, BY WHICH ALL THE ADVANTAGES OF OUR MARITIME RIGHTS ARE TO BE SACRIFICED, AND FREE BOTTOMS ARE TO MAKE EVERY THING THEY CARRY FREE, EVEN ARTICLES WHICH ARE CONTRABAND OF WAR. TO THIS LAW OF NATIONS WE TRUST GREAT BRITAIN WILL NEVER SUBMIT.'

VI.

A good deal of discussion arose with America about the operation of these Decrees and Orders upon the American Trade; and in order to simplify the construction of the latter, and to apply the principle of retaliation more directly against France herself, and with less injury to Neutrals, the Orders of November 1807 were superseded by that of 26th of April 1809; which declares *the whole coast of France and her Dominions, as far northward as the river Ems, and southward to Pesaro and Orbitello in Italy, to be under blockade, and all vessels coming from any port whatever to any French port, liable to capture and condemnation;* the effect of this order was to open all ports, not actually ports of France, even though the British flag should be excluded therefrom, to neutral commerce, and

112   *Battles over Free Trade, Volume 1*

to place France and France only, in the precise situation in which, by her decrees, she endeavours to place Great Britain.

VII.

By a decree of the French government, issued at Fontainbleau on the 19th of October, 1810, it was expressly declared, *that in pursuance of the 4th and 5th articles of the Berlin decrees, all kinds of British merchandize and manufactures which may be discovered in the custom-houses, or other places of France, Holland, the Grand Duchy of Berg, the Hans Towns, (from the Mayne to the sea), the kingdom of Italy, the Illyrian Provinces, the kingdom of Naples, and in such towns of Spain and their vicinities as may be occupied by French troops, shall be confiscated and* BURNED.

Thus the matter at present stands; on the side of France the decrees of Berlin and Milan are in force, and to them are opposed the British order of 26 April, 1809; and as long as the blockade of England by France remains unrepealed, so long must England possess an undoubted right to persist in her system of *retaliation*.

It now becomes necessary to explain shortly the CONDUCT OF AMERICA towards England and France respectively: – from which we shall judge whether America has always acted with a strict impartiality towards the two belligerents, and whether she really has any fair ground of complaint against Great Britain.

VIII.

A very short time before France began to act upon these new principles, A TREATY OF COMMERCE had been, in 1806, negotiated at London (between Lords Holland and Auckland on the part of England, and Messrs. Munroe and Pinckney on that of America), and sent over to America to be ratified: but the Berlin Decree having appeared almost at the moment of the signature of this treaty, it was accompanied by a Declaration by Lords Holland and Auckland on the part of England:

– '*That in consequence of the new and extraordinary measures of hostility on the part of France, as stated in the Berlin Decree, Great Britain reserved to herself (if the threats should be executed, and that Neutrals should acquiesce in such usurpations) the right of retaliating on the enemy in such manner as circumstances might require.*'

IX.

This treaty, the President of the United States refused to ratify; principally *because the question of impressing seamen was not definitively settled.* The British Government replied, that *this was a subject of much detail, and of considerable difficulty, arising out of the almost impossibility of distinguishing British subjects from Americans:* and, it added, *that it would be highly inexpedient that the gen-*

[Stephen], *A Key to the Orders in Council (1812)*

eral treaty should be lost, or even delayed on this account; that Great Britain was ready immediately to proceed in a separate negociation in this point; and that in the meantime, her officers should be ordered to exercise the right of search and impressment, with the greatest possible forbearance.

These arguments and this proposition did not, however, induce the American President to ratify the treaty. He would settle *all* or nothing; and thus, not only this point remains undecided, but many others (of much greater importance), which the treaty had concluded, have been set adrift again, and all the relations between the two countries rendered precarious, and almost hostile.

It unfortunately happened, that June, 1807, the commanding officer of His majesty's ship Leopard having understood that some deserters from his ship had been received on board the American frigate Chesapeake, and having in vain required their release from the American captain, attacked the Chesapeake at sea, and obliged her to strike; but he then contented himself with taking out of her his own men, and restored the ship to the American commander. An event of this nature called for, and received the immediate disavowal of His Majesty's government; the captain was tried, and his admiral superseded; and Mr. Rose was sent without loss of time to America *to offer reparation*, and to state to the American government, *that Great Britain did not pretend to a right to demand by force any sailors whatever from the national ship of a power with which she was on terms of peace and amity.* In the mean time the President had issued a proclamation, excluding all English ships of war from the American harbours. Mr. Rose was instructed to require the recall of this proclamation, previous to his official offer of reparation. This was refused on the part of America; and of course the negotiation was not concluded. The proclamation continued to be executed against England, while the ships of the other belligerents were freely admitted.

X.

Exclusive of this affair of the Chesapeake, America appeared, in the spring of 1808, to have considered herself equally aggrieved by the acts of both countries, and (unwilling to side with England in order to oblige France to withdraw from her system of violence against neutral rights, which had obliged England to have recourse to her retaliatory acts) the United States determined to draw within their shell, and have nothing to do with either. In this view they laid a GENERAL EMBARGO upon all the shipping in their ports, and denied themselves all commercial intercourse whatever with any European state.

XI.

This act of the American government was very unpopular throughout the Union, and on the first of March, 1809, THE NON-INTERCOURSE LAW was substituted in its place, *by which the commerce of America was opened to all the world except*

114   *Battles over Free Trade, Volume 1*

to England and France, and British and French ships of war were equally excluded prospectively from the American ports.

XII.

In the interval, Mr. Canning had instructed Mr. Erskine His Majesty's Minister to offer to America *a reciprocal repeal of the prohibitive laws on both sides upon certain terms; namely, 1st. The enforcement of the non-intercourse and non-importation acts against France. 2dly, The renunciation on the part of America of all trade with the enemies colonies, from which she was excluded during peace. 3dly, Great Britain to enforce the American embargo against trade with France, or powers acting under her decrees.*

Mr. Erskine did indeed on the 18th and 19th April, 1809, conclude an arrangement with the American government, but in terms by no means conformable to the spirit or letter of his instructions; and Mr. Erskine having frankly communicated those instructions to the American government, it was aware how unlikely it was that such an arrangement should be ratisfied [*sic*] at home. It was therefore no matter of surprise either here or in America that this negociation again failed.

XIII.

In the mean time the French government, (affecting to be indignant at certain pretended advantages given by America to the British trade, in passing the non-intercourse act) in a decree dated from Rambouillet, 23d March, 1810, declared, *that from the 20th May, 1809, all American vessels which should enter the French ports, or ports occupied by French troops, should be sold and sequestered.* This act however was not made known till the 14th May, 1810.

XIV.

Notwithstanding these acts of violence on the part of France, America could not be persuaded that her honour and interests demanded some immediate act of retaliation, and nothing was done till the non-intercourse act expired, when an act of the congress was passed, eventually renewing certain parts of the non-intercourse act in certain events. By this act it was decreed, *that in case either of the belligerents should cease to violate the neutral rights of America before the 2d of February, 1811, the non-importation articles of the non-intercourse act should be revived against the other.* By this act, America still contemplated France and England as EQUALLY injuring her commerce; and contented herself with merely complaining through her minister, of the operation of the Rambouillet decree, though it was, at the same time, characterised by America *as a signal aggression on the principles of justice and good faith.*

XV.

The condition thus offered by America, France determined speciously to accept; but in accepting it to act in such a manner as still to reap the advantages accruing from her decrees, without relieving England from her part of the pressure occasioned by them; and in this she was but too well seconded by the disposition of America, who proposed to her *that whilst she suspended the operation of her decrees against the American trade* AT SEA, (which indeed, had she been inclined, she had not the means to enforce), *she might in effect do the same thing by giving to the enforcement of her decrees the character of* MUNICIPAL REGULATIONS; and accordingly on the 5th of August, 1810, the Duke of Cadore intimated to General Armstrong, *that the decrees would not be executed upon the citizens of America, after the 1st of November following, if either England recalled her Orders, or America should cause her flag to be respected.*

XVI.

As England could not, upon this insidious offer, accept the first part of the alternative, offered by France, America in her turn accepted the second, and declared that she would cause her flag to be respected: but as there would be some inconvenience in demanding from England the abandonment of her most sacred maritime rights, such as the right of visiting and searching a neutral ship for enemy's property – the right of blockading, by actual force, the ports and harbours and rivers of the enemy's coast – the right of precluding a neutral from carrying on, in time of war, the trade of a belligerent, to which she is not admitted in time of peace – (*all* of which and *more* indeed is demanded by France, and apparently acceded to by America) the Government and Congress of the United States deemed it to be sufficiently conformable to the demands of France, *that they should exclude British ships of war from their ports, and prohibit all importation of British produce;* and France seems to consent to consider *these restrictions as tantamount to causing the American flag to be respected, and as rescuing the American ships from the imputation of being denationalized.* Upon this principle the President proclaimed the renewal of the non-importation articles of the NON-INTERCOURSE ACT against Great Britain on the 2d of November, 1810; and the Congress enacted the same by law on the 28th February, 1811. When this act passed, the relations of peace and commercial intercourse were restored between France and America, and French ships were allowed to enter into American ports, at a time when *France still retained many millions of American property seized under the Rambouillet Decree*, which had had a retrospective effect for the space of twelve months, and when the operation of the burning decree was carried into effect without any regard whether or not the produce of British industry, so destroyed, had legally become, by purchase or barter, the *bonâ fide property of neutral merchants.*

With respect to England, who by the act of the 28th Feb. 1811, was put upon the footing of an enemy, the *only* source of complaint which America possessed, was that the blockade of the *French* coast was still persisted in and enforced, as

116 *Battles over Free Trade, Volume 1*

the only effectual means of retaliating upon the violent and unjust decrees of the enemy.

XVII.

On the 1st Nov. 1811, Mr. Foster, His Majesty's Minister in America, was at length enabled to bring to a conclusion the differences which had arisen on the Chesapeake affair without sacrificing the rights of Great Britain, or derogating from the honour of His Majesty's Crown; but it cannot be said that the American Government accepted the concession and atonement with either dignity or grace.

XVIII.

During the last year (1811) little else has passed between the British and American governments, than assertions on the part of America; *that, as the French Decrees have ceased to violate the neutral rights of the United States, they must claim from Great Britain an equally favourable exemption from the operation of her Orders in Council.* The reply of Great Britain is, *that the fact is not so; that France continually and formally declares upon all occasions, that her Decrees* ARE STILL IN EXISTENCE; *that they are, and must remain, the* FUNDAMENTAL *laws of the French empire; that they are to lead the way to the destruction of the maritime power of Great Britain, the enemy, as France will have it, and the only enemy of the liberty of the seas.* From the alleged necessity of continuing these Decrees in operation, and of enforcing their efficiency in countries which still pretend even to national independence, Bonaparte endeavours to convince Europe, that she ought to submit quietly to his usurpations; and he is extending the line of the French frontier from the mouths of the Rhine to those of the Niemen, for the express purpose of excluding the British trade from all the ports of Holland and the Baltic, and of enabling himself to ensure a punctual execution on the part of his allies of his continental system.

XIX.

While America was thus asserting that the French decrees were repealed, the minister of foreign relations at Paris put an end to all doubt on the subject, by an official report to the Emperor, dated the 10th March, 1812, which sets forth; first, an explanation of the maritime laws of the nations; viz.

The flag covers merchandise; the goods of an enemy under a neutral flag are neutral, and the goods of a neutral under an enemy's flag are enemy's goods – the only goods not covered by the flag, is contraband of war; and the only contraband of war are arms and ammunition – In visiting neutrals, a belligerent must send only a few men in a boat, but the belligerent ship must keep out of cannon shot. – Neutrals may trade between one enemy's port to another, and between enemy's and neutral ports – The only ports excepted, are those really blockaded; and ports really blockaded, are those only which are actually invested, besieged, and in danger of being taken – such are the duties of belligerents and the rights of neutrals. The report then proceeds to state, that the Berlin and Milan decrees *have rendered the manufacturing towns of Great Britain deserts – distress has succeeded prosperity; and the disappearance of money and the want of employment endangers the public tranquillity;* and then it denounces that, *until Great Britain recalls her Orders in Council,* AND SUBMITS TO THE PRINCIPLES OF MARITIME LAW ABOVEMENTIONED, *the French decrees must subsist against Great Britain, and such neutrals as should allow their flags to be denationalized*; and finally, the report avows that *nothing will divert the French emperor from the objects of these decrees, – that he has already, for this purpose, annexed to France, Holland, the Hans Towns, and the coasts from the Zuyder Zee to the Baltic; that no ports of the continent must remain open, either to English trade or denationalized neutrals; and that all the disposeable force of the French empire shall be directed to* EVERY PART OF THE CONTINENT, *where British and denationalized flags still find admittance; and finally, this system shall be persevered in, till England, banished from the continent and separated from all other countries, shall return to the laws of nations recognized by the treaty of Utrecht.*

The sum of this report is, that the Berlin and Milan decrees are in full force, and must continue to be so, until England shall, *not only* recall her Orders in Council, but, shall also abandon all her great maritime rights; and that these decrees subsist against not England alone, but America, and all other countries which shall not unite in an endeavour to overthrow the ancient system of maritime law; and further, that France considers herself authorized to invade and seize any neutral territory whatsoever, for the sole object of excluding all British trade from the continent, and that all his violent and outrageous usurpations in Holland, Germany, and the shores of the Baltic, have been prompted, and are attempted to be justified by this motive. Will, or can America submit to this?

XX.

In order to bring to a distinct issue the verbal discussion between England and America, and to place the relative measures of England and France clearly before the neutrals; the British government on the 21st April 1812, put forth to the public a Declaration and Order in Council, detailing *the present state of the contest between the two belligerents* – and stating *that as soon as the Berlin and Milan decrees are revoked, the Orders in Council are abrogated – and engaging beforehand that a proof of the absolute repeal of the French Decrees produced in an Admiralty court shall be held, in fact, to be a satisfactory proof of the absolute revocation of the British Orders in Council.*

XXI.

Since this declaration, but before it reached America, an embargo was laid on by act of Congress for ninety days, for the 4th day of April, 1812.

CONCLUSION.

Thus the matter now stands; and I think it must be clear that until France repeals her decrees, it is impossible that Great Britain can relinquish the PRINCIPLE *of retaliation*. Great Britain, who is herself the main spring of the commerce of the world, must more than any other country regret and suffer, from the interruptions of trade; but will trade revive, if she should recede? Will commerce thrive, if she abandons her ancient maritime rights? For it is nothing less than this, that France demands, and America endeavours *collaterally* to enforce.

If America admits that France, under the pretence of *municipal regulations*, has a right to prohibit *all* commerce with Great Britain; and that British produce and manufactures (to whomsoever belonging or whenever found, not only in France itself, but in countries under her control, or in territories adjoining to France, and subject to invasion from her *on this very pretence*,) are to be seised, confiscated, and burned; if, I say, America suffers all these infractions of neutral rights, without remonstrance or complaint, it is plain, that, as far as she is concerned, she plays into the hands of France, and lends her assistance to the ruin of England.

But what effects would the repeal of the Orders in Council actually have? I will enumerate them.

1. It would restore the American trade; and that portion of manufactures which are usually consumed in America itself would immediately revive.

2. It would open to England no other market for any branch of manufacture whatsoever than the *home market of America* – for France having a right by municipal regulations to exclude British articles from her territory, and to extend for this purpose her territory over the whole face of Europe; any article of British produce and manufacture imported by an American, would be as liable to be confiscated or burned as it is at this moment.

3. France would be relieved from all the pressure she now feels. America would supply her with all kinds of raw materials, as well as of colonial produce, and would convey to her from the distant parts of Europe all kinds of stores and timber, and the various materials of naval strength. France would have just what trade she pleased to have; she would continue the prohibition, all over Europe, of British manufactures, with a double view, first to encourage her own, and next to ruin ours. And all inconvenience and pressure being thus removed from her, there would no longer exist any means or hopes of forcing her to a system more equitable towards Great Britain.

4. America would become the carrier of the world. – She and France would divide the trade of the globe; and Great Britain, with all her command of the sea, would have the mortification to see the ocean covered with the commerce of France, protected under the American flag.

5. The British shipping interest would be *annihilated*, and that of America would rise up in its stead. – The East and West Indies and the home coasting trade would alone remain to us: and the two former we should not long possess, in competition with a rival whose means of ship-building are inexhaustible; whose flag would be the *only* neutral flag in the world; whose ships *alone* could trade at the ports of the continent of Europe; whose rates of freight and insurance would be proportionably small; in short, who would have all possible advantages, while Great Britain would have to labour with every possible disadvantage.

6. All British produce and manufacture would decline and expire, except only those for American or home consumption; because America, which would bring the produce of all other countries to France, would return with the manufacture of France to all other countries. It may be said, that England would undersell France: and so she certainly would in a fair state of trade; but; excluded from Europe and rivalled by America, there would remain to us neither the means nor motives of commercial enterprize.

7. Nor would the American market itself be of the advantage to Great Britain that at first appears; much of the ironwork, and all the linens of Germany would soon undersell the similar articles of English or Irish manufacture; and the increased intercourse between America and France, would inevitably oblige the merchants of the former to take returns in the produce of France or the continent of Europe; and by degrees, we should find that the natural result of such an intercourse would be, the advancement of manufactures and the influence of France, and the decline of those of Great Britain.

Much more might be added on this subject; but these are the principal topics that occur to me. I do not say that the Orders in Council may not be advantageously modified. I only insist upon it, that if the PRINCIPLE on which they are built be abandoned, we shall find that our commercial and political prosperity, so far from being improved, will be vitally impaired by such a concession. Gold may be bought too dearly; and the immediate loss of all our European trade, and the eventual diminution of that which we should have with her, is rather too much to pay for a temporary accommodation with America.

When we shall have so far conceded, the *other* demands of France will be pressed upon us; then will be extorted from us the renunciation of our maritime rights, which Bonaparte candidly allows are the source of all our prosperity.

We live in perilous times: let us see that we are not driven *step by step* to the edge of a precipice, from which we shall not be afterwards able to recede, and let us not be induced, by temporary or local embarrassments in this or that branch of trade, to risk the ruin of all. Let us remember that every great public character of our days has assented, in its different stages, to the principle of the Orders in Council; let us pause well before we abandon a system which has had the concurrence of Mr. Fox, Lords Greenville, Grey, and Holland; of the Duke of Portland, the Marquis Wellesley, Mr. Canning, and Mr. Perceval.

Let *us beware*, lest the course we pursue be that of the savage, who cuts down the tree to get at the fruit, and who sacrifices the means of future existence to the gratification of an immediate and temporary want. – Let America too beware, for the danger is common; let her candidly and dispassionately review all her discussions with both parties, and she will find but too much reason to lament the keenness of her government to discover cause of complaint against England, and its almost miraculous deafness and blindness to the insults of France. There are now but two free nations on the face of the globe, Great Britain and America – let the latter beware how she raises her parricidal hand against the parent country; her trade and liberty cannot long survive the downfall of British commerce and British freedom. If the citadel which now encloses and protects all that remains of European liberty be stormed, what shall defend the American union from the inroads of the despot?

But it is not to be believed; America is too wise, is too honest, is too strong, to suffer herself to be dragged by any internal faction, or external force, into such a warfare; her causes of complaint against England are *trivial* when compared with the dangers with which the insatiable ambition and gigantic despotism of France threaten the civilized world.

Devoutly then I pray, and confidently even do I hope, that America, true to her own individual interest, and to the general and future welfare of mankind, will consent to establish with Great Britain the sincerest relations of amity, and to oppose to the outrageous aggressions of France, in the first instance, a firm tone of remonstrance, and, if that should fail, a bold and active spirit of hostile retaliation.

Madame de Stael Holstein, *An Appeal to the Nations of Europe Against the Continental System, Published at Stockholm, by Authority of Bernadotte* (London: J. M. Richardson, 1813), pp. 56–74.

Thrice had Russia engaged in coalitions against France, and always in a disinterested and generous manner. Paul I. was disarmed by the flatteries of the Chief Consul; it required a deeper hypocrisy to fascinate Alexander, a sovereign equally humane and magnanimous, who, since 1805, has been hailed by Germany as her future deliverer. Napoleon succeeded in persuading him that the obstinacy of the English in maintaining their maritime preponderance was the sole cause of all the misfortunes of the civilized world; that France, having lost her colonies, her navigation, and the greatest part of her commerce, had been driven, in spite of her wishes, to aggrandisements; that the sovereignty of the seas must be wrested from England, by vigorously excluding her ships and merchandize from the ports of Europe; that, in this event, whatever was burdensome in the Continental System would cease of itself, and that all the branches of industry would take a new turn, while the general peace would be guaranteed by the union of the two preponderating powers.

For many years the declaimers and wagerers against Buonaparte had foretold, as the result of his prohibitory measures against England, the stagnation of his commerce, the ruin of his manufactures, the misery of his people, public bankruptcy, insurrection, and the overthrow of his states. But all these predictions were not exactly verified. Buonaparte had of himself not a little damped these exaggerated hopes, by putting off this catastrophe for thirty years. However closely the coasts were watched by clouds of douaniers, it was discovered that a great quantity of English merchandize had slipped into the Continent and even into France. Domiciliary visits were made every where, colonial produce was confiscated, and the English manufactures were burnt. While these commercial *auto da fe's* were celebrated with ridiculous pomp, Buonaparte, in order to cover the deficiency of his finances, caused by the inactivity of the douaniers, opened his ports himself by giving licenses to English vessels; i.e. he seized upon all contraband trade as an imperial monopoly. Russia had therefore a right to complain that France was the first to break her engagements: she might have complained of a thousand other vexations: she contented herself with re-establishing under a neutral flag a feeble portion of her antient [*sic*] commercial relations after having for several years continued the enormous and fruitless sacrifice of her foreign commerce. To conclude, she awaited, in a calm and dignified attitude, the most impudent and atrocious aggression.

Buonaparte published no manifesto on the subject of this war: he relied too much on his good fortune to appeal to justice. Nevertheless, by his own confession, his only motive was the admission of English vessels and English merchandize into the ports of Russia. This dreadful conflict between the Russians, single-handed on the one hand and a multitude of nations on the other, such as had not been seen for ages united under one flag; of Germans and Italians of all denominations; Dutchmen and Croats, already become French subjects; Swiss, Portuguese, and Spaniards, torn from their country; this devastaing [*sic*] war, which dragged the youths of Western Europe to the confines of Asia; this holy league – Will posterity believe it? – was announced to the world as a crusade against sugar and coffee, and against muslins and laces! Is the human race to be thus trifled with? And how long will the most enlightened people sacrifice themselves, patiently, to charm away the ennui, flatter the vanity, and allay the thirst for dominion, of a single man!

But, perhaps, it may be objected to all that we have developed, that, if the policy of France be oppressive, that of England is not less so, and that her maritime despotism is equally contrary to the welfare of other nations as is the spirit of of [*sic*] conquest which animates the French government. Assertions, the most devoid of truth, incessantly repeated with assurance and inculcated with due emphasis, end in making an impression upon unthinking minds, whose idleness reposes amidst vague ideas. We shall, therefore, examine what is signified by this cry of the *liberty of the seas;* we shall prove that it has no direct meaning; and, that if it is possible to tyrannise upon the ocean, it is not England, but France, which attempted it, so far as her maritime force will permit.

England, at present, possesses the greatest naval force which has ever been known; in short, the navies of all other powers put together would not equal it. If this be an evil, it is one of those which have been brought upon Europe during the last twenty years; for, in the American war, the united navies of France, Holland, and Spain, gave England abundance of trouble, and she respected the armed neutrality of the three maritime powers of the north, although it was extremely contrary to her interests. The equilibrium could only be restored by a long peace, during which England disarmed, while trading-vessels alone composed the navy of other nations.

Supposing that there was an universal peace. No person ever accused the English, to my knowledge, of harassing, in time of peace, the navition [*sic*] of other powers, however feeble; no person has reproached them with not observing, towards their enemies, the laws of war, sanctioned among civilized nations. It is, therefore, upon their conduct towards neutrals alone that the question hinges.

In order to probe this matter to the bottom, we must not lose sight of the nature of a maritime war. It is undertaken chiefly for the interests of commerce; it would become completely illusory, if it was not allowed to attack in all ways the commercial navigation of the enemy. It is this principle which has authorised the practice of seizing upon all the property of subject enemies, exposed upon the high seas, or even to destroy them, which, in wars upon *terra firma*, is deprecated as barbarous.

Of the two belligerents by sea, the weakest will always naturally favour neutrals, who can render them the most important services. Are her merchant-vessels confined in port for want of a squadron to protect them? the neutrals become her carriers; they transport merchandize between the mother-country and her colonies; and if they are requested, even between the two hostile countries; and, after all, the subjects of the power which has recourse to them, only lose by this expedient the profits of the freight, retaining those of the trade itself.

There could not be a more lucrative situation than that of a neutral in a maritime war, if the belligerents were dupes to these pretended rights of neutrality, and put no restrictions upon them. Their ships would be wasted in fruitless cruises, if they did not now and then humble an enemy for the honour of the flag, and all the profits of the war would accrue to the states which had borne no share in the risk.

It is useless, in order to elucidate this subject, to go back to the principles of the law of nature, the decisions of which are often vague, without the concurrence of positive laws founded upon treaties; but more particularly insufficient for relations of so complicated a nature as those of the commerce of civilized nations. The rights of neutrality can only be limited, therefore, by the conflict between the disadvantages of reciprocal negotiations, and those consequent upon a rupture. It will be necessary for the belligerents, for instance, to ascertain if they ought to prefer the war in disguise which neutrals wage against them to open war; whereas, neutral states must consider whether it is their interest to subject their navigation to some constraint or to expose it entirely.

To maritime belligerents the right is generally granted of preventing the importation of goods contraband of war into an enemy's port and the rights of blockading one or more of his ports, which in cases of contravention justifies the confiscation of neutral vessels. No dispute has arisen as to the right to seize the property of an enemy in neutral vessels, and consequently to visit them and to blockade their coasts.

During the war with America, *armed neutrality* proclaimed the principle that 'the flag covered the merchandize.' England never recognized this principle, for good reasons. This claim, if pushed to extremities, would not only place belligerents at the mercy of the neutral powers, so far as goods contraband of war are concerned, but would admit of troops being conveyed in neutral vessels for the invasion of an enemy's territory.

The blockade of a coast differs from that of a particular port only in the extent of the measure. If a power has the means of effecting it, why has she not the right also? If it is difficult to blockade a whole coast as vigorously as a single port, neutral vessels will enter and depart at their own peril.

Finding his shores blockaded, Buonaparte, by the Berlin decree, declared the British isles themselves in a state of blockade; as, in a quarrel, an insult is retorted on the person offering it. The English government may well despise this stupid menace, since it would require immense naval resources to realise it; and those which France possesses are almost useless. If it were an act of reprisal, it would only fall upon neutrals; and it was a violation of their rights, infinitely more atrocious than any thing that England had ever done. Buonaparte declared to all maritime states: 'I have not a single ship of war at sea to prevent your vessels from visiting England; but, I forbid you to send them there. I cannot hinder English vessels from freely navigating the seas; but, I order you to exclude them from your ports. If you do not prohibit all intercourse with England, all is over with you: I shall attack you, nor shall I lay aside my arms until your coasts are guarded by my own douaniers.'

This is not all. As there were maritime states which Bounaparte could not attack by land, – among others, America, – he made, expressly on their account, an ordinance, which bears: that 'After any neutral vessel shall have been visited by any English ships of war, and shall have touched, by their orders, at any English port, and paid duties there, her flag is *denationalized*; and, wherever she is seized, she shall be declared a lawful prize.'

In this way Buonaparte punishes neutrals, for the weakness which puts it out of their power to oppose the claims of the British government. As a motive for this outrage, he says that it behoves every state to maintain its own independence. Granted: – but it is a duty which she owes to *herself*, and not to *you*: Who gave you the right to call her to account? Besides, no obligation is binding beyond a possibility.

From all that has been said, it results, that, if England sometimes handle neutrals roughly, Buonaparte never tolerates any whatever, and destroys, as far as in his power, even to the shadow of the rights of neutrality. The violence of his proceedings being such, while his ships are blockaded in port, what would his conduct be if he were powerful at sea?

The French minister incessantly proclaims the liberty of the seas as the sublime object of the continental system; it is the watchword for every new war. Nevertheless, in all the negotiations with England, this same minister has never paid neutrals the compliment of proposing any stipulation in their favour for the future.

For twenty years Europe has been deluged with declamations and calumnies against the British government: for ten years and more the journals and other political writings, published in England, have been contraband in France and in all the countries under her influence. Facts are disfigured by mutilated extracts from the opposition newspapers. If the new French catechism were to contain a lecture on the sacred rights of the Napoleon dynasty, one of the articles of their creed would be '*the English are the tyrants of the Ocean and the eternal enemies of the Continent.'* We have already refuted the first of these imputations; the second will disappear upon examining the true relations of England with Europe.

The English are described as a nation of shopkeepers. This may be said in as much as commerce is one of the principal bases of their riches and their power; and, consequently, in public transactions, their government ought never to lose sight of commercial advantages: but it is an arrant falsehood to say that commerce is their sole occupation, their only resource, and that no other materials enter into the admirable structure of their national prosperity.

The occupation of a merchant, on a limited scale, from incapacity or aversion to other pursuits, with a desire for gain disproportioned to the means of acquiring it, produces that mercantile spirit which is justly condemned as selfish, and contrary to a noble and disinterested nature. But, when commerce is conducted on a large scale, by a great and enlightened nation, whose social institutions are chefs d'œuvres of reason and experience, among whom the sciences and learning, the mechanical arts, and agriculture, far from being neglected, are brought to perfection, in proportion as mercantile speculations become extended; then commerce necessarily leads to liberal views and renders every citizen a cosmopolite. Not only in order to be flourishing do they require peace and liberty; but a commercial people, as a matter of necessity, are interested that others should enjoy the same benefits. War takes off hands from the manufactories, while it consumes a quantity of production: it impoverishes, therefore, in general, the two belligerents, at least one of them. Liberty, and the reign of equitable laws, to the exclusion of every arbitrary act, guarantee property; and it is upon this security that public and private credit rest. Can we for a moment suppose that a commercial nation will rejoice in the oppression and ruin of those with whom they carry on trade? They could no longer find any markets, for a poor country has nothing to sell and has no money with which to purchase. Petty merchants may be jealous of each other, wish to seize upon a monopoly, or grasp at merchandize, and use all means to succeed; and the politics of some states have frequently resembled these vices of tradesmen. But such artifices cannot be profitable in the main: in commercial affairs of states, as of individuals, nothing is durable but that which is voluntary in every sense of the word, and founded upon mutual advantages. When a nation has acquired a superiority in most branches of human industry, when their navigation intrepidly visits every portion of the globe, and traverses the ocean as securely as the waters of a canal; when the most valuable luxuries of all countries pour into their harbours as well as the first objects of necessity: when it possesses the art of multiplying one hundred fold the value of the latter, by fashioning them with durability, elegance, and perfection; and when the perfection of mechanics, sparing manual labour, admits of their commanding for the productions of their manufactures a superior market; then the whole progress of civilization, whether in extent or in rapidity, are so many augmentations of their capital. It is with the surplusage of productive labour over the consumption of the interior, that a nation procures foreign merchandize: and the more numerous the productions it has to receive, the more will it be able and willing to buy. A taste for the conveniences of life, the enjoyments of luxury, and of all the external embellishments of life, may be diffused among all classes, multiplied and varied *ad infinitum*. A nation which knows how to satisfy this taste in a thousand ways must add to the comforts of its own population and to the luxuries of others.

The experience of several years seems to have proved that England can subsist her population although shut out from the Continent, but not without submitting to privations. The other three quarters of the globe are more open than ever to her mercantile speculations, to her colonial establishments, and even to her conquests, if such were necessary to maintain her prosperity. We do not mean to say that European connections are not very important to England, but they are not so much so as formerly: a wonderful focus of moral and intellectual excellence has concentrated, within a space comparatively small, and little favoured by nature, a population the most numerous, the most active, and the most powerful, by the ascendancy of the human mind. But if, by this frightful levelling, with which all states are threatened, the genius of the national character is sunk into a mechanical uniformity, if the most insolent and illiberal despotism should plunge Europe into misery and into barbarism, there would only be a single corner of the globe from which it could be excluded: and England, remaining like the ark afloat in the midst of the universal deluge, will find ample compensation, in directing all her efforts towards those vast and rich countries of Asia, where civilization has become stationary from its antiquity: and towards others still unexplored in Africa, America, and the Pacific Ocean, where prodigal nature only wants the finishing hand of man. Let us not forget that there already exists an Europe beyond the seas: our languages, our manners, and our arts have been carried there: this American Europe is only in its infancy, because it has been neglected or badly administered: that part which has become independent has sprung up with astonishing rapidity. If there be not some happy change in store for our old world, the vigorous youth of the new, may speedily put to shame the aged decrepitude of the mother-country. In several countries confederated with France, projects of emigration towards the other hemisphere are treated as state offences, while the English government, by the wisdom of its laws, has in a few years transformed a place of transportation for criminals into a flourishing colony. Can we mistake the revolutions which are announced by those symptoms?

So far from England finding it her interest to ferment the troubles, and to perpetuate the dissensions of the Continent, she is interested that Europe, after twenty years convulsion, should finally enjoy peace, – a peace which shall be guaranteed by the stability of her governments, and the re-establishment of the barriers of the independence of every state. Let it not be said, that the English minister pursues a line of policy separate from the interests of the nation: that is rendered impossible by the British constitution, by virtue of which the government ought always to give way to the wishes of the enlightened majority. England continues the war at the expense of immense sacrifices; she may purchase peace with the stroke of a pen, by subscribing to the new system of the oppression of the public law of Europe. The greatest disappointment would be suffered by those powers which are still in the field, and by those nations which their own princes have been forcibly chained to the chariot-wheels of the usurper. England continued adverse to every project of conquest in Europe, notwithstanding the allurements which presented themselves: she has been always faithful to her engagements, and always zealous in succouring such of her allies as remained true to themselves. As she ought to have done, she has, in the first place, fought for her own safety: but it must be at the same time admitted, that she has fought with a noble enthusiasm for the common cause.

The ministers of Buonaparte, like official defenders of the general anathema against English commerce, maintain, that he ought to take advantage of his internal commerce, and improve his agriculture and manufactures; they say that England herself has prohibitory laws against the importation of foreign commodities. It must be in the first place remarked, that exportation is also annihilated by the Continental System, since that of England is interdicted by the decrees of blockade, and there is no navy to protect the remains of the navigation of those countries which are in a state of hostility against her. The carriage by land of goods to great distances is so expensive, that it amounts to a prohibition of many productions; and the canals, which ought to supply the want of external navigation, as yet are only magnificent projects. Measures prohibitory of importation, adopted under proper modifications and regulations, may have a good effect, when there is a progressive advance of industry and prosperity in a country. For, it is clear, that there must be disposable, or at least spare, capitals, in order to ameliorate agriculture, and for the cultivation of natural productions; but there is nothing of this kind in France. But when the maritime cities, formerly so opulent, are ruined by the shutting up of their harbours; when every kind of industry is crushed by the weight of imposts; when wars, less sparing of human lives than ever, make continual drafts upon the population, and annually carry off a great proportion of their young men from useful labours; then the sudden and general prohibition of the usual importations must lead to disagreeable results. The indigenous manufactories, freed from all rivalship, will produce goods of a high price and bad quality; an artificial high price will be laid upon goods of all descriptions; but, being able to attain their customary enjoyments, all the world will consent to privations; the deficiences [*sic*] in the consumption will diminish the receipts of the indirect imposts, and force the government to raise the tarif, [*sic*] or, if possible, to invent new ones; misery and depopulation will increase in a frightful manner. Thus France, and all the countries under her regime, will be impoverished in a twinkling. Let us compare Holland, at the present day, with what it was previous to 1795! After all which it has suffered, its junction with France has given it the last blow of a public bankruptcy; for this is the true name of the reduction of the national debt to one-third, not of the capital, but of interest. Eighteen years have been sufficient to dissipate the riches, accumulated by the wisdom and political energy, by economy and commercial activity, during upwards of two centuries. The north of Germany, in general more distinguished for a careful cultivation than for fertility, had acquired a high degree of improvement, as the consequence of enlightened administrations and a long peace. For forty years this country had not been the theatre of any war; it remained tranquil even during those of the revolution, to 1806. The Hanseatic cities were more flourishing than ever, because commerce, expelled from Holland, took refuge there. Within the space of six years, reckoning from the Prussian war, or nine since the occupation of Hanover, the whole of the north of Germany has been turned topsy-turvy. A precise calculator has exerted himself to prove, that, in spite of the pretended prosperity of the finances, of which Napoleon's ministers make an ostentatious parade, there is a deficit in his receipts, which he is constantly obliged to make good by military enterprizes; not daring to diminish his military power, and not being able to keep it up with his own resources. Be the case as it may, it is certain that not only has he brought to the highest points of perfection the art of subsisting his troops at the expense of the enemy; but, even in the intervals of peace, he scarcely permits them to return to France. The most fortunate of his allies are those through whose states his numerous armies have only occasion to pass; other countries have the burden of providing for all their wants during a long residence. He is at all times particular in having some country in reserve to be given up to plunder until its fate be definitively settled; when there is absolutely nothing more to extort, he then re-unites it to the Grand Empire, or generously gives it to some ally. The fortunate inhabitants of Sweden, who have never seen one of Buonaparte's armies inundate their country, cannot conceive how expensive his friendships have been; every petty district of Germany can furnish melancholy details on this subject.

DIVERGENT PATHS: BRITAIN AND AMERICA, 1812–30

A legacy of bitterness and distrust characterized Anglo-American relations in the aftermath of the Napoleonic Wars. The war of 1812 and the hostile commercial regulations of the war played a part in forging divergent notions of commercial policy. Whilst Britain, guided by William Huskisson, moved towards 'freer trade', the United States acted as a high-tariff nation determined to protect its emerging domestic industries against foreign competition. These contradictory trends reflected disparate rates of industrial and economic development, and divergences in the 'productive profile' of the nations, notably the prominence of export-dependent industries within the respective national economies. These were fundamental factors which determined the trajectory of different political ideas concerning the nature and objectives of commercial policy.

Britain emerged from the war as the dominant global power, whose dominance was so marked that the phrase 'Pax Britannica' has been used to signify her economic superiority. Yet Britain did not act, at least immediately, according to the dictates of 'hegemonic stability' theory in creating a stable international order, not least because she actually became more protectionist after 1815, with the abolition of income tax, and a highly protectionist Corn Law.[1] However, by the 1820s a shift towards freer trade had occurred which represented more than administrative efficiency or institutional rationalization. The nature of the measures indicates they were underpinned by a vision of Britain's future as a manufacturing economy dependent on international trade expansion.

Commercial policy reform in the 1820s owed much to the leading Liberal Tory William Huskisson. As President of the Board of Trade, Huskisson instigated reform in a cautious but convincing manner.[2] Committed to reform of the Corn Laws although opposing repeal, Huskisson accepted David Ricardo's law of diminishing returns. To this effect, the 1828 Corn Law implicitly acknowledged Britain's future dependence on foreign corn to feed her growing population.[3] In overhauling the British tariff, Huskisson equalized British and Irish duties, substituted moderately protective duties for prohibitions, lowered import duties on raw materials, and abolished many export duties and bounties. In the same vein,

– 129 –

he promoted the Spitalfields Act, abolishing wage regulation in the silk industry. The free export of gold, free emigration of artisans, and the licensed export of machinery were further moves in establishing freer trade.[4] There was mercantile support, most notably from the petitions of leading merchants in London and Edinburgh in 1820, thus tempting many writers to date the origins of the modern free trade movement to that date.[5] Although providing a framework for the establishment of a liberal commercial system, the temptation to view Huskisson's reforms as a precursor to the dramatic denouement of 1846 should be resisted.

The policy areas with which Huskisson is most often associated indicate the persistence of protectionism within the British body politic. In reforming the Navigation Acts, Huskisson revealed that reciprocity and retaliation were central to his commercial policy strategy. The Reciprocity of Duties Act (1823) granted equality of duties on goods and shipping to any country agreeing to grant the same to Britain, although reserving the right of retaliation against those retaining discriminatory duties. The policy resulted in twenty-seven reciprocity treaties by 1844. Nevertheless, France exposed the limits to British concessions by requesting equalization of wine duties as the price of a reciprocal agreement, which Britain refused on the basis of the long-established preference to Portugal.[6] Further concessions that made a breach in the Navigation Laws included regulations permitting the United States to trade directly with the West Indies, and the permission granted to the new Latin American states to trade directly to Britain. Nevertheless, in many areas, the mercantilist/protectionist structure was maintained, even extended. Not only was Canadian timber granted preference, a legacy of the closure of the Baltic during the war, but attempts by Prussia to reduce the differential were rejected, and Canadian corn was granted a similar privilege in 1825. Huskisson therefore extended imperial preference.[7]

In tampering with the complex, interest-laden body of commercial regulations, Huskisson polarized opinion. Many commercial bodies such as the Manchester Chamber of Commerce viewed them as the product of enlightened statesmanship.[8] However, opposition was voiced in terms of the sacrifice of traditional interests of agriculture, empire and shipping to the nefarious manufacturing interest.[9] These fears were heightened by pending reform of the Corn Law and fears that free trade principles would now be applied to agriculture.[10] Yet the actual extent of liberality in the British tariff regime was questioned by many. Protective duties on corn were held to inhibit commerce with foreign nations, including the United States, where the emergence of a highly protectionist woollen goods sector was claimed to be a response to the exclusion of American corn from British markets.[11]

This was a line of argument which became much more prominent amongst supporters of free trade in the following decade with reference to European industries. Clearly, there were practical limits to what could be done, and duties on corn were, in Huskisson's time, non-negotiable. For Huskisson, free trade consisted of balanced commercial growth, expansion of manufacturing employment, and imperial union.[12] He was not a unilateralist but rather sought to extend commercial intercourse by negotiation and reciprocal commercial arrangements, and supported differential duties and preferences. Different in nature and extent from unilateral free trade, in revising traditional notions of the practical application of commercial policy, Huskisson's reforms represented a significant advance within the context of Britain's highly protective polity.

It was perhaps more difficult to convince foreign nations that freer trade was in their own interest and, a related point, that it was not merely a policy ensuring Britain was the main beneficiary. France was not alone in denouncing perfidious Albion. In the post-1815 United States, many elements coalesced to form a powerful protectionist movement. The strength of protectionist sentiment was not merely a reflection of the power of economic interests within the country. The theoretical arguments of American protectionists were accepted as appropriate for a country which was 'nation-building' and striving for national and economic independence and power.

The intellectual force behind American commercial policy was Alexander Hamilton, whose influential *Report on Manufactures* in 1791 provided the rationale for American protectionism for generations, and formed the central component of Clay's 'American System' in the nineteenth century. Hamilton outlined a comprehensive philosophy which located protection as a central strand in the transformation of the United States into a first-rate manufacturing power. In viewing protection of national economic resources as integral to national development, Hamilton was heavily influenced by Colbert and mercantilism. His views found a receptive audience in the post-1815 United States, where economic conditions were favourable. After 1815, the United States lost many foreign markets it had supplied during wartime, resulting in a fall in the prices of land and agricultural products. The simultaneous development of manufacturing industries seeking protection from foreign competition produced a powerful movement, the duality of which became apparent from its advocating a sweeping programme of agricultural and industrial protection.[13]

During the war interests had emerged favourable to free trade, particularly amongst New England importers. Although duties on raw materials would raise costs for a number of manufacturing industries, it was the southern states who were the most ardent opponents of protection. In opposing the 1820 Tariff Bill, it was clear that the south grasped the fact that the existence of slavery made the prospect of southern manufacturing industry unlikely, and underlined their reliance on imports from Europe and the north. Protection would only make their goods more expensive, whilst they feared British retaliation or exclusion of American cotton. Yet domestic manufacturing industries which had flourished during the war were now a powerful interest at the core of the protectionist movement, and represented something of a new factor in American politics.[14] On 16 April 1824, a further Tariff Bill raised protective duties to American manufacturing industries such as cotton, wool, lead, iron and hemp.[15] The eastern States were particularly prominent in agitating for an increase in iron duties. The tariff revealed a pattern followed in later years, with shipping and commercial interests of the New England states and the Atlantic coast opposed, and manufacturing industries of Pennsylvania, New York, New Jersey, and the eastern and western states strongly in favour.[16] Agriculture was the sector which balanced these interests. Yet, agricultural interests were divided between growers of produce such as tobacco, cotton and rice, based in Maryland, Virginia and Louisiana, who opposed the tariff, and the grain growers of Pennsylvania, New York, the western states and parts of New England, who supported it.

The crucial part played by the agricultural states in passing the tariff was attributed largely to the existence of the Corn Laws in Britain.[17] With a broad coalition supporting protection, it proved possible to make significant increases in tariff rates, with that on wool raised to 33⅓ per cent, whilst cotton was raised to 25 per cent.[18] After 1824, the protectionist movement made further progress. The woollen industry suffered from British competition, and the agitation began in Massachusetts, the base of the industry, with the state legislature requesting protection. Prompted by the Philadelphia Society for the Promotion of Domestic Industry, founded by Alexander Hamilton, a National Convention was called.[19] Held at Harrisburg, the Convention was attended by ninety-seven delegates, with thirteen of the twenty-four states represented, and resulted in a recommendation to Congress for higher protection for woollens, iron, hemp, flax, cotton and spirits.[20] It was correctly adduced from the proceedings that the United States wished to be independent of imported manufactured goods, especially from Britain.[21]

Whilst the southern states opposed the encouragement of woollen manufactures as this must increase the price of articles previously supplied by Britain, the protectionist movement proved its strength by its geographical and sectoral diversity.[22] By their insistence on protection for American manufacturing industries, the Convention laid particular emphasis on the illiberal, hypocritical nature of British commercial policy.[23] These sentiments were echoed by the Treasury report of 1827 outlining the unequal terms of Anglo-American trade. With the value of British cotton and woollen goods imports exceeding $100 million, and iron and iron manufactured goods exceeding $17 million in the six years ending in 1826, the United States' means of exchange were limited by British restrictions on wheat and tobacco. Only cotton was accepted freely, and this only as a means of enriching the British cotton manufacturing sector. In stating 'Commerce upon the terms attested by such facts, cannot be pronounced just, as between the two parties', the report recommended increases in woollen goods, foreign wool, fine cotton goods, bar iron and hemp, with these industries described as 'of very high moment to the nation'.[24]

The so-called 'Tariff of Abominations' of 1828 was highly protectionist. There were increases in almost all raw materials, with a particularly steep rise in wool duties. With the south and two-thirds of New England members voting against it, it was the western and middle states, combined with New England protectionists, which carried the Act.[25] The popularity of protection was apparent from the support it received from both presidential candidates of that year, John Quincy Adams and Andrew Jackson.[26] The almost prohibitive duties provoked anger in Britain, with even Huskisson threatening retaliation.[27] In Britain, the anti-liberal principles of such legislation were particularly contrasted with Huskisson's enlightened liberalism.[28] After 1828 the desire for highly protective tariffs was satiated.[29] Indeed, the period 1833–42 was a liberal period when the excesses of 1828 were moderated. The compromise tariff of 1833 reduced tariff rates to those of 1824, and provided for continual, gradual reduction of duties. On reaching the planned level in July 1842, the period of 'liberalization' ended and a new tariff of September 1842 marked a return to protection.[30]

American tariff policy before 1846 was remarkably consistent. Not only was it highly protectionist, but it was made with little reference to the policies of other nations. It was the internal dynamics of the American economy, and the economic and industrial composition of states, which largely determined policy. Highly influenced by Henry Clay's vision of a semi-autarkic commercial strategy, American policy remained wedded to the concept of independent development of national manufacturing industries, and a vibrant agricultural sector. Yet, in such a complex economy, opposition to this policy had always existed. Prior to 1846, the agricultural western states largely held the balance between the twin poles of the protectionist north and the free-trade south, and had backed the former as more appropriate to their interests. In 1846, they shifted allegiance, thus facilitating the commercial liberalism of the Walker tariff.[31]

Notes

1. A. A. Stein, 'The Hegemon's Dilemma: Great Britain, the United States, and the International Economic Order', *International Organization*, 38:2 (1984), pp. 355–86, on p. 360.

2. For Huskisson's reforms, see C. R. Fay, *Great Britain from Adam Smith to the Present Day: An Economic and Social Study* (London: Longmans, Green and Co. Ltd., 1928), pp. 48–58.

3. A. C. Howe, 'William Huskisson (1770–1830)', in H. C. G. Matthew and B. Harrison (eds), *Oxford Dictionary of National Biography*, 61 vols (Oxford: Oxford University Press, 2004), vol. 28, pp. 974–80.

134   *Battles over Free Trade, Volume 1*

4. Stein, 'The Hegemon's Dilemma', p. 361.
5. See Merchants Petition of 1820 in Favour of Free Trade, in *Revised Report of the ... Celebration of the Hundredth Year of the Publication of the 'Wealth of Nations'* (1876), and Edinburgh Petition for Free Trade, *Caledonian Mercury*, 29 April 1820, both below, pp. 162–5, 166–7; see also, typically, Fay, *Great Britain from Adam Smith to the Present Day*, p. 44.
6. T. J. McKeown, 'Hegemonic Stability Theory and 19th Century Tariff Levels in Europe', *International Organization*, 37:1 (1983), pp. 73–91, on p. 82.
7. See William Huskisson, Speech on the 'Foreign Commerce of the Country', 25 March 1825, in *Hansard* (1825), below, pp. 168–87.
8. See Vote of Thanks from Manchester Chamber of Commerce to Huskisson, 16 July 1828; and Huskisson to Manchester Chamber of Commerce, 20 July 1828, in *The Speeches of the Right Honourable William Huskisson* (1831), below, pp. 188–9.
9. See Solomon Atkinson, *The Effects of the New System of Free Trade upon our Shipping, Colonies and Commerce, Exposed* (1827), below, pp. 190–201.
10. See Henry Stephens, *A Letter Addressed to the Landowners and Tenantry of the County of Forfar* (1827), below, pp. 202–21.
11. See *The Mechanic in his Own Defence; or Word About with Henry Stephens* (1827), below, pp. 222–35.
12. A. Howe, 'Restoring Free Trade: The British Experience, 1776–1873', in D. Winch and P. K. O'Brien (eds), *The Political Economy of British Historical Experience, 1688–1914* (Oxford: Oxford University Press, 2002), pp. 193–213, on pp. 199–200.
13. F. W. Taussig, 'The Early Protective Movement and the Tariff of 1828', *Political Science Quarterly*, 3:1 (1888), pp. 17–45, on p. 18.
14. J. B. Williams, *British Commercial Policy and Trade Expansion, 1750–1850* (Oxford: Clarendon Press, 1972), pp. 236–8.
15. See H. U. Addington to George Canning, 30 May 1824, below, pp. 137–9.
16. H. U. Addington to George Canning, 2 February 1824, in 'Papers relative to American Tariffs', *Parliamentary Papers* (1828), xix.[578], p. 3; Williams, *British Commercial Policy*, p. 240.
17. See Addington to Canning, 30 May 1824, below, pp. 137–9.
18. Tariff Schedule, in 'Papers relative to American Tariffs', pp. 6–9.
19. Taussig, 'The Early Protective Movement', p. 27; Williams, *British Commercial Policy*, pp. 240–1.
20. See Report of the Committee on Commerce, 22 May 1824, *Parliamentary Papers* (1828); Address of the Committee on Behalf of the General Convention of Agriculturists and Manufacturers, *Parliamentary Papers* (1828); and Charles Richard Vaughan to the Earl of Dudley, 27 April 1828, *Parliamentary Papers* (1828), all below, pp. 140, 141–2, 143.
21. Taussig, 'The Early Protective Movement', p. 22.
22. Anthony St. John Baker to Earl of Dudley, 9 November 1827, in 'Papers relative to American Tariffs', pp. 23–5.
23. See Report of the Committee on Commerce, 22 May 1824, *Parliamentary Papers* (1828); and Address of the Committee on Behalf of the General Convention of Agriculturists and Manufacturers, *Parliamentary Papers* (1828), both below, pp. 140, 141–2.
24. Report of Secretary of the Treasury [extract], in Vaughan to Dudley, 18 December 1827, in 'Papers relative to American Tariffs', pp. 128–36, on pp. 130–1.

Divergent Paths

25. P. Ashley, *Modern Tariff History: Germany – United States – France* (London: John Murray, 1904), p. 162; for widespread dissatisfaction, see Baker to Dudley, 11 June 1828, in 'Papers relative to American Tariffs', p. 247.
26. R. V. Remini, 'Martin Van Buren and the Tariff of Abominations', *American Historical Review*, 63:4 (1958), pp. 903–17.
27. Taussig, 'The Early Protective Movement', pp. 27–8; Williams, *British Commercial Policy*, p. 241–2.
28. See 'The American Tariff', *Edinburgh Review* (1828), below, pp. 144–61.
29. Taussig, 'The Early Protective Movement', p. 41.
30. S. C. James and D. A. Lake, 'The Second Face of Hegemony: Britain's Repeal of the Corn Laws and the American Walker Tariff of 1846', *International Organization*, 43:1 (1989), pp. 1–29, on pp. 9–11; Ashley, *Modern Tariff History*, pp. 168–9, 182–3.
31. Ibid., p. 187; James and Lake, 'The Second Face of Hegemony', p. 9.

DIVERGENT PATHS: BRITAIN AND AMERICA 1812–30

Post War Protection and the United States

H. U. Addington to George Canning, Washington, 30 May 1824 (extract), in 'Papers relative to American Tariffs', *Parliamentary Papers* (1828), xix.[578], pp. 4–6.

Sir,

The new Tariff of Duties on goods imported into the United States from Foreign Countries, having now passed both Houses of Congress, the Lower on the 16th ult., and the Upper on the 18th inst., after having engaged their attention above three months, I have the honour to inclose a copy of that document as it has been published by authority in the National Intelligencer; and I now proceed to give you some account of its progress through those assemblies, as well as to present you with as clear a view as I am able of its bearing and operation on the various component parts of this Republic.

The interests of this country relatively to this Bill, may be broadly classed under three heads: the Shipping and Commercial, the Manufacturing, and the Agricultural.

Of these, the former is almost altogether opposed to it; the second is equally decided in its favour, and the third decided [*sic*] in sentiment; the growers of produce adapted to the foreign market being hostile, and those of articles calculated for internal consumption friendly, to it.

The first, or shipping and commercial interest, comprises a considerable portion of the New England States and the Atlantic coast.

The second, or manufacturing interest, embraces parts of Pennsylvania, New York, New Jersey, and the Eastern and Western States.

That portion of the third, or agricultural interest, which is opposed to the Tariff, comprises parts of Maryland, Virginia, the Carolinas, Georgia and Louisiana,

– 137 –

being the principal growers of produce, such as cotton, rice, tobacco, &c, calculated for the foreign market. On the other hand, the measure is supported by a very powerful branch of this interest, especially the grain growers, comprehending Pennsylvania, New York, the Western States, and parts of New England.

Of these conflicting interests, those opposed to the Tariff appear greatly to overbalance their adversaries in numbers and substance; but the advocates of it have the advantage in point of activity and the energy of feeling conferred by present distress. This is more especially the case with the Western States, a considerable portion of whose principal proprietors, having heretofore engaged largely in losing speculations in the purchase, mostly on credit, of national lands, find themselves at the present moment involved in a state of serious embarrassment; and being also deprived of the war market for their produce, which they once enjoyed, as well as of the forced circulation of specie resulting from the government expenditure in their country, they are disposed to catch at any chance which offers for the amelioration of their condition.

This chance they consider to be held out to them in what they call the encouragement of the home market, by the imposition of heavy duties on articles of importation from abroad; and, under this impression, they have been induced to advocate and press with the utmost eagerness and energy for, the adoption of that system.

It has been opposed with no less warmth by the Southern States, who see in the establishment of it the immediate diminution, and possibly eventual annihilation of the market for their staple product, cotton. Virginia and Maryland are also affected in the same way, though to a less extent, in the market for their tobacco. In addition to these grounds of opposition, the general increase in many articles of consumption, more particularly affecting the Southern States (especially woollen and cotton goods, as furnishing clothing for their slaves) which must necessarily result from the additional duties imposed under the new Tariff, forms also a sufficient motive for resistance to a scheme, by which the ease and affluence of the proprietors will be materially disturbed.

The opposition offered by the shipping interest is bottomed on broader and more public grounds. They contend, that as an export trade cannot exist alone, the general interests of the Republic must in time suffer irretrievable injury from the death-blow thus inflicted on the main, though indirect, arm of her defence, and the principal support of her national honour, her mercantile navy.

The opponents of the bill in its original shape maintained also that the principal portion of the public revenue being derived from the Customs, the measure proposed, by diminishing most, and annihilating a part, of those sources of receipt, would irrecoverably embarrass the national finances, and compel a recourse to a system of internal taxation, or excise, to the very name of which the citizens of this Republic have in general an insuperable aversion.

Addington to Canning (1824)

The arguments used by the advocates of the Bill, it is unnecessary that I should recapitulate in detail. Independence of foreigners, eventual increase of the revenue, an extended internal market proportional to the extension of population resulting from the encouragement of internal industry, whether agricultural or manufacturing, consolidation of the public credit, and prosperity accruing from a reliance on internal resources, have been the principal topics insisted on in the debates.

The example of Great Britain has been adduced as the main support of the arguments used on either side, both parties admitting with equal zeal and admiration the fact of her unrivalled prosperity, but each ascribing it to those grounds which best suited their own line of reasoning. The recent measures adopted by her for the liberalization of her external commercial system, and her emancipation from her ancient system of restriction, are pretty generally ascribed by the advocates of the Tariff to a desire to inveigle other nations into an imitation of her example, with the intention, as soon as they shall have embarked sufficiently deeply in her scheme of turning short round upon them, and resuming, to their detriment, her old system of protection and prohibition. This scheme, they affirm, Great Britain will, by her superior means, be enabled to execute without hazard to herself ... I have only to add, that had no restrictions on the importation of foreign grain existed in Europe generally, and especially in Great Britain, I have little doubt that the Tariff would never have passed through either House of Congress, since the great agricultural states, and Pensylvania [*sic*] especially, the main mover of the question, would have been indifferent, if not opposed, to its enactment.

140   *Battles over Free Trade, Volume 1*

Report of the Committee on Commerce, 22 May 1824, in 'Papers relative to American Tariffs', *Parliamentary Papers* (1828), xix.[578], pp. 12–14.

The Committee on Commerce, to which has been referred a resolution, 'Instructing them to report to this House whether any law exists, in contravention of the provisions of the convention of the 3d of July 1815, made between this country and Great Britain; also, to inquire into the expediency of countervailing, by law, any duties or port charges on American commerce and tonnage, which Great Britain may lay thereon, in her colonies or elsewhere,' respectfully submit the following REPORT:

That, having bestowed on the first part of the resolution the consideration due to its importance, take leave to state to the House, that no law has been passed by Congress which contravenes or violates any provision of the convention subsisting between the United States and Great Britain. They regret, however, to find, that an opinion is entertained by the British Government that the Act of Congress, passed the 27th of April 1816, entitled 'An Act to regulate the Duties on Imports and Tonnage,' in imposing a higher duty on iron manufactured by rolling than on hammered iron, contravenes the provisions of that convention, on the ground that the duty operates exclusively on iron manufactured by that mode in Great Britain ... The ports of the United States have been open, generally, to the introduction of British manufactures, before and since the convention, on principles of amity and liberality; and the Committee are not a little surprised to find that the Government of the United States should be charged with giving to the convention an astuteness of construction incompatible with its provisions, especially when the ports of His Britannic Majesty in Europe are closed against the introduction of the staple article of the Eastern and Middle States. Will the Government of Great Britain allow the importation into Great Britain of cotton and wool cards, and cut nails, manufactures of the United States, on the ground that those articles are manufactured exclusively in the United States, by machines, the invention of ingenious citizens? or [*sic*] does it allow, on any terms, the importation of those articles into Great Britain? The statutes of that kingdom will give the answer and the commentary. In short, on which side soever the Committee look, they see the industry and enterprize of the citizens of the United States subjected, by British policy, to prohibitions or restrictions, that are not retorted by the Government of the United States, on the industry and enterprize of British subjects. From the views which the Committee have taken of this subject, they cannot recommend to the House any alteration or modification of the Act of Congress, imposing a higher duty on iron, manufactured by rolling, than on that prepared by the hammer.

Address of the Committee on Behalf of the General Convention of Agriculturists and Manufacturers, and Others Friendly to the Encouragement of the Domestic Industry of the United States, Assembled at Harrisburg, 30 July 1827, in 'Papers relative to American Tariffs', *Parliamentary Papers* (1828), xix.[578], pp. 40, 48.

It was the great united and allied interest of agriculture and manufactures, in their *actual* effect upon the state of society, that the convention was charged to consider – with more immediate regard, however, to the growth and manufacture of wool; and for the purpose of really obtaining that degree of protection which is seemingly extended by existing laws, but actually denied, or rendered only partially effective, by the counteraction of foreigners, and in the ingenuity and ability with which they violate the principle supposed to be established, for the protection of American farmers, manufacturers, and merchants.

It is believed that more than eighty millions of dollars are embarked in the wool business at the present time; and many millions more would have been invested, but for the rapid and ruinous depreciation of value in the capital so employed. We think that there is no other country in which so great an interest as this would have been so much neglected. But this neglect arises in part from an ill-founded spirit of jealousy, built upon sectional feelings, and in part from peculiar opinions, some of which are antiquated, some very new, and others having more regard to things as they should be than to things as they exist. Great mistakes have been caused by the last, and they are defended, because European writers on political economy, like other manufacturers, have sent forth their products for *foreign* use. Adam Smith, for example, presents many sound propositions and matters of deep interest, though not, perhaps, always defensible; and his countrymen, with the peculiar adroitness of merchants, recommend his doctrines for *our* adoption, but will not permit them to influence their *own* actions. They restrict trade in every way that it will bear; their whole legislation is directed to their own peculiar advantage, and we do not blame them for that; but they desire others to open their ports unreservedly, and practise the principle 'free trade,' alleging that commerce is best left to its own regulation! and supplies of foreign *bread* are refused to their own people, though often half-starved *because of the unnatural price of provisions* ... The protection of domestic industry has notably built up the commerce and navigation of the United States, but continues to increase both; it adds to the public revenue, by furnishing the means of purchasing taxed commodities; it has reduced the cost of articles by exciting the domestic competition; it has probably added 50 per cent to the internal and coasting trade within the last five years; it has opened *new* markets for flour and grain, equal to the whole foreign export of these articles; it has caused greatly increased supplies of mineral substances and of coal; it has countervailed, in part, the restrictions and prohibitions of Europe, and will place us on an equality with all nations in matters of trade, if persevered in and extended: in short, it has subsisted a large part of the people of the United States, giving employment to millions on millions of active capital, and become indispensable to the well being of the republic. Without its aids, we should be poor and miserable as the Portuguese, whose workshops are in their ally, Great Britain. It is incorporated with all that we enjoy in the comforts of private life, or possess in national reputation or power. These are broad, but, we think not, bold assertions – and capable of fullest demonstration and undeniable proof.

Charles Richard Vaughan to the Earl of Dudley, 27 April 1828, in 'Papers relative to American Tariffs', *Parliamentary Papers* (1828), xix.[578], pp. 151–2.

My Lord,

The Bill, imposing additional duties upon the importation of goods of foreign manufacture into the United States, passed in the House of Representatives on the 22d instant, on a division of 105 to 94 ... The 'Tariff Bill,' as it is called, does not differ essentially from the Bill reported to the House of Representatives by the committee to which was referred, at the commencement of the session, all the papers presented to Congress in favour of and against an increase of duties on foreign manufactures.

The committee was appointed by the speaker, and composed of a majority of members opposed to the present executive government, and when their Bill was presented to the House, it was considered by the supporters of the manufacturing interests in the United States, as contrary to the recommendations of the Harrisburg convention (to which I had the honour of calling your Lordship's attention in my despatches of the 13th August and 21st October of the last year (and a mockery of the wants and demands of the manufacturers.) In order to render it more palatable to the latter, several amendments of the Bill were moved, during the long discussion which it underwent, but they were rejected.

The repeated divisions upon those amendments showed that the majority against them was composed of representatives of the southern states, a majority of those from the western states, of eighteen to five of the representatives of Pennsylvania, and of an equal division of those of New York.

The representatives of the southern states consider the Bill as calculated to oppress and to tax the south, for the benefit of certain manufacturers established in the north-eastern states; and Major Hamilton, of South Carolina, went so far as to threaten a dissolution of the Union, should the Bill finally pass into a law ... I have the honour to inclose a copy of the minutes of evidence taken before the committee which will explain the state of the rising manufactures in this country which the government is anxious to promote, and which, it appears, are not in a state to compete in their own market with British manufactures, but by the imposition of duties upon imported articles, amounting to a prohibition.

144 *Battles over Free Trade, Volume 1*

'The American Tariff', *Edinburgh Review*, 48 (December 1828), pp. 390–410.

Art. IV. – 1. *An Act in Alteration of the several Acts Imposing Duties on Imports into the United States, subscribed by the President, 19th May, 1828.*
2. *Papers relative to American Tariffs. Printed by order of the House of Commons, 25th July, 1828.*
3. *Report of a Committee of the Citizens of Boston and its Vicinity, opposed to a farther Increase of Duties on Importations.* Pp. 196. Boston, 1827.

WE are truly sorry to observe the illiberal and narrow views which seem to characterise the proceedings of the United States, with respect to the commercial intercourse between them and other countries. It is a mistake, we find, to suppose that our House of Lords is the only depositary of the prejudices that pervaded the commercial legislation of Europe during the sixteenth and seventeenth centuries, and gave a peculiar and not very enviable distinction to the administration of Mr Vansittart, and Mr George Rose. The United States do not merely hold out an asylum for the proscribed liberties and virtues of the Old World; but have kindly taken the superannuated and exploded errors of the mercantile system under their protection. Were his Grace of Newcastle, and my Lords Malmesbury, Kenyon, &c. transplanted to the United States, though they might have to lament the want of close boroughs, the admission of Catholics to places of trust and emolument, and the non-existence of tithes, they might still console themselves on having escaped from the sphere of the free-trade system, of having got to a country in whose councils neither a Huskisson nor a Grant was to be found; and whose legislators held the science of Political Economy in as much contempt, and were as ignorant of its principles, as themselves. But if this be, on the one hand, matter of rejoicing to a few individuals amongst us, it is, on the other, a source of regret to all – and fortunately they form the great majority of the British public – who take a juster view of national interests, and who are anxious for the diffusion of liberal principles, and for the advancement of every nation that forms a part of the great commercial commonwealth. – We entertain no jealousy of America: If we did, we should hail the enactment of the late Tariff with unmingled satisfaction. But we disclaim any such feeling; and are convinced that none such is entertained towards her by any considerable portion of our countrymen. For our own part we are truly anxious for her prosperity; and being so, we cannot help lamenting the blindness of her statesmen, and regretting that they should have become so desperately enamoured of a system of commercial policy unfavourable to the general interests of nations, and which cannot fail to entail the most pernicious consequences on those by whom it is adopted.

The restrictions on industry and the freedom of commerce that still exist in this and other European countries, had their origin in a comparatively dark and unenlightened age. That they have, in the majority of instances, been supported with a blind and bigoted obstinacy, is most true: but, at the same time, it must be conceded, that after an exclusive system has been long acted upon, and has, in consequence, become interwoven with the national institutions and the various interests of society, and given an artificial bias and direction to a large amount of capital and industry, its abolition becomes a work of no common difficulty; and a government may well be excused for pausing, before it proceeds to involve a considerable proportion of its subjects in distress and difficulties, even for the sake of a greater ultimate public advantage. But notwithstanding the formidable obstacles that thus oppose the return from a long-continued, artificial, and exclusive, to a natural and liberal system, it cannot be denied that, in Great Britain, at least, a very great progress has recently been made in this desirable course. The Apprentice laws and the Combination laws have been repealed; the Navigation laws and the old Colonial system have been greatly relaxed; moderate *ad valorem* duties have been laid on the importation of foreign Silks, and various other articles that were formerly prohibited; the Usury laws will hardly outlive next session; and the most oppressive of all our restrictions – that on the importation of foreign Corn – is now left without any one to defend it whose opinion is entitled to the least attention, and is supported only by the miscalculating rapacity and powerful influence of a majority of the landlords. That changes so extensive, and immediately affecting the interests of a large body of people, should have been effected with so little inconvenience, clamour, and opposition, as have been experienced, must be ascribed partly to the more general diffusion of sounder opinions, and partly to the discretion that has been displayed in the introduction of the new system. Mr Huskisson has not been more distinguished as a bold and extensive, than as a prudent and cautious reformer of our commercial code. It was not, indeed, to be expected that he could be the principal agent in such various and important changes without exasperating many individuals, and rendering himself the object of much calumny and abuse. But we arrogate very little of the prophetical character when we venture to predict, that when the factious brawls and wrangles of the day have been forgotten, it will be universally allowed that the glory is due to Mr Huskisson, of being the first British Minister, whose whole system of commercial policy was founded on sound, liberal, and enlarged principles; and who laboured earnestly and successfully to promote the power, happiness, and glory of his own country, not by seeking to exalt her at the expense of others, but by opening her ports to the ships and goods of all countries, and making her the centre and animating principle of a vast commerce, founded on the gratification of the reciprocal wants and desires that subsist among nations.

The American Ministers had no such difficult task to perform. When *their* country achieved her independence, she was encumbered with none of those antiquated and vicious systems which had taken root in Europe during the

Dark Ages. Her industry was perfectly free and unfettered – Her citizens were at liberty to pursue their own interest in their own way without any bias from government. They were in the very state which the researches of Dr Smith and other ingenious writers had shown was best calculated to forward the progress of a nation in the career of improvement. The real sources of national power and prosperity had been laid open – the exclusive system had been proved to be contradictory in its principles, and injurious in its results. It had been shown that England and France had not become rich and powerful in consequence, but in despite, of its operation; and the governments of both, under the guidance of their most celebrated ministers, Mr Pitt and M. Turgot, had begun to retrace their steps, to abandon the restrictive system, and to adopt one more in accordance with the spread of knowledge and the spirit of the age. In addition to all this extrinsic and foreign experience of the pernicious effect of monopolies and restrictions, the unprecedentedly rapid progress of America herself afforded the most satisfactory and convincing proof of the immeasurable superiority of a free system. She had advanced with giant steps in the career of improvement. The few ragged and needy adventurers who, little more than a century and a half before, had established themselves on the margin of a vast continent, overspread with almost impenetrable forests, and occupied only by a few miserable savages, three thousand miles distant from the dwellings of civilized man, had grown into a mighty people, possessed of strength sufficient to wrest, by force of arms, their independence from the warlike and powerful nation from whom they had sprung! All this had been achieved without the miserable aid of custom-house regulations and protecting duties; and it might have been supposed that so extraordinary a career would have satisfied even the most ambitious.

There were plainly, therefore, two conclusive and unanswerable reasons, why the Legislature of the United States should have abstained from the introduction of the restrictive system: In the *first* place, the researches of the philosophers, the concessions of the statesmen, and the experience of other nations, had proved that it was decidedly inimical to the advancement of mankind in opulence and population; and, in the *second* place, the Americans were not entangled in the web of existing restrictions and prohibitions, but had, under a free system, made an advance that had no parallel in the history of nations; and had therefore every motive to continue in the course on which they had fortunately entered.

But strange as it may seem, the best established scientific conclusions, the experience of all ages and nations, and their own progress, failed to convince the legislators of America of the expediency of pursuing that liberal line of policy, from the adoption of which they had already reaped so many advantages. Not satisfied with the progress they had already made, with the enjoyment of free and liberal institutions, and a boundless extent of fertile and unoccupied land, they resolved to call custom-house regulations to their aid! Mistaking the effusions of a few miserable pamphleteers, and the speeches of the Newcastles and Kenyons of the day, for the wisdom of the British nation, they persuaded themselves, that those very restrictions which had clogged and impeded our progress, had been the main causes of our advancement. Instead of dwelling on the advantages of free competition, their statesmen deemed it productive only of poverty and ruin. Mr Vansittart himself could not have descanted more eloquently on the advantages resulting from the adoption of protecting duties, bounties, and drawbacks; and those who doubted whether the prohibitive system would be so productive, in a pecuniary point of view, as had been represented, appear to have generally supported it, on the ground of its being necessary to the *independence* of the republic, that she should not have to rely on foreigners for supplies of necessary articles. Selfishness, patriotism, and ignorance, each lent its aid to the introduction of what has been pompously designated by its more ardent supporters, as the 'American system;' and, by a singular contradiction, the *regime* of prohibitions and restrictions seems now to be firmly established under republican auspices.

Among the supporters of the restrictive system in America, the first place is due to the late General Hamilton. His celebrated Report on the subject of manufactures was presented to the House of Representatives towards the close of 1791. It had a very great effect. It is written with considerable talent, and is well calculated to make an impression on those who have not analyzed the real sources of wealth. A very slight examination is, however, sufficient to show the fallacy of the principles on which it is founded. General Hamilton dwells at great length on the advantages resulting from the establishment of manufactures – on the stimulus which they give to industry and invention, the ample field which they lay open for enterprise, and the great scope which they furnish for the exercise of the various talents and dispositions with which men are endowed. That all this, and much more, may be truly said in praise of manufactures, no one, with perhaps the exception of the Laureate, will presume to deny. But the point which General Hamilton had to consider, was not, whether the prosecution of manufacturing industry was, abstractly considered, advantageous, but whether it was for the advantage of the United States to *force* the establishment of manufactures, by imposing duties and prohibitions on the importation of manufactured goods from abroad? He has not, indeed, wholly overlooked this part of the question; but, as was to be expected, he has entirely failed to make good his view of the case.

That the great principle of the division of labour ought to be respected by states, as well as by individuals, is a doctrine too well established, to require us to say one word in its defence. The circumstances, too, under which America is placed, render it peculiarly incumbent on her not to lose sight of this principle. It is not easy to say what species of industry is best suited for most of the old settled and densely peopled countries of Europe, or which they may prosecute with the greatest advantage. Industry is, amongst them, in a state of perpetual oscil-

148   *Battles over Free Trade, Volume 1*

lation; every new discovery in the arts attracting capital to manufactures, and every improvement in agriculture again drawing it back to the land. But this is not the case in America. There neither is nor can be any doubt about the species of industry which it is most for *her* advantage to prosecute. And it is admitted by General Hamilton, and has been admitted by all the subsequent advocates of duties and prohibitions, that were government to abstain from interfering to protect manufactures, none but the coarser and bulkier sorts could maintain themselves, and that agriculture would draw to itself most of the capital and industry of the nation. Nor is it difficult to perceive why this should be so. The most fertile lands of England, France, and most other European countries, have been long since exhausted; and we are now compelled to resort to soils of very inferior fertility, to obtain a part of our supplies of food. But America is in a totally different situation. She is still possessed of an almost unlimited extent of fertile and unappropriated land; and it is as obviously her interest to apply herself in preference to its cultivation, and to obtain supplies of the finer sorts of manufactured goods from nations less favourably situated for the prosecution of agricultural industry, as it is the interest of the West Indians to apply themselves to the raising of sugar and coffee. The growth of raw produce *must*, for a long series of years, be the most profitable species of employment in which the citizens of America can engage. There can be no doubt, indeed, that those branches of manufacture, naturally adapted to her peculiar situation, will gradually grow up and flourish in America, according as her population becomes denser, and as the advantage which now exists on the side of agriculture becomes less obvious and decided. But to encourage, by means of duties and prohibitions, the *premature* growth of manufactures, is plainly to force a portion of the industry and capital of the nation into channels into which it would not otherwise have flowed, because it would, but for these duties and prohibitions, be less productively employed in them, than in those in which it was already invested.

Whatever, therefore, may be said with respect to the restrictive system in other countries, in America it seems to be destitute even of the shadow of an excuse. The advantages on the side of agricultural industry are there so very signal and obvious, that to attempt forcibly to draw capital from it to manufactures, is really to adopt that precise line of conduct which is best fitted to check the progress of wealth and population. But though the advantages on the side of agriculture were less obvious than they are, the policy of the American Legislature would yet be wholly indefensible. Let it be supposed, in illustration of the effect of prohibitions, that American has been accustomed annually to import a million's worth of woollens, or some other manufactured product, from Great Britain, France, or any other foreign country; and let it be farther supposed, that in order to encourage the manufacture of a similar article at home, she prohibits its importation. Now, in this case – and what is true of this case is true of all restrictions whatever – it is, in the *first* place, plain, that to whatever extent the home demand for the produce of American industry may be increased by the prohibition, the foreign demand for that produce will be equally diminished. Commerce is merely an exchange of equivalents; and those who refuse to import, really, by so doing, refuse to export. If America cease to *buy* a million's worth of produce from foreigners, she *must*, at the same time, cease *selling* to them a million's worth of some other species of produce; that is, she must cease sending to the foreigner the articles she had previously been accustomed to export, to pay the articles obtained from him, that are in future, through the agency of the prohibition, to be raised at home. All, therefore, that she will accomplish by this measure, will be the transference of capital from one branch of industry to another. That equality of protection, to which all the citizens of the Union are justly entitled, will be encroached upon; the increase of one employment will be brought about by the depression of some other employment, which, to say the very least, was equally advantageous. But it is obviously false to affirm that such a measure can make the smallest addition to the capital and industry of the republic, or to the facilities for employing them with security and advantage.

This, however, is to look at the measure in the most favourable point of view. It is necessary, in the *second* place, to advert to the *price* at which the prohibited article will henceforth be sold. If the American manufacturers could have produced it as cheaply as the foreigners, the prohibition would not have been thought of, as the article would not have been imported. The price must, therefore, rise when its importation is prohibited. Instead of being obtainable as before for a million, it will henceforth cost, perhaps, a million and a half, or two millions. Now, it is obvious, that the effect of this artificial increase is precisely the same, as to its operation on the consumers, as if a direct and peculiar tax had, under a free system, been laid upon them of L.500,000, or L.1,000,000 a-year. But it will be observed, that had such a tax been laid on the consumers, its produce would have come into the hands of government, and would have formed a portion of the national income; whereas, the increased cost of the article is, under the circumstances supposed, *occasioned by an increased difficulty of production*, and is, therefore, of no advantage to any individual.

It consequently results, that, even in those rare cases in which a restrictive regulation has no tendency to raise the price of commodities, it is injurious by changing the natural distribution of capital, and lessening the foreign demand for the produce of industry to the same extent that it increases the home demand. But in that infinitely more numerous class of cases, in which a restriction is the cause of a rise in the price of the article which it affects, it is incomparably more injurious. Besides the injuries arising from varying the natural distribution of capital, and circumscribing the foreign trade of the country, such restriction has the effect of imposing a heavy burden on the people, for no purpose of general

150   *Battles over Free Trade, Volume 1*

or public utility, but to produce a certain and grievous mischief, by tempting individuals to withdraw from really advantageous businesses, to engage in one that cannot be prosecuted without great national loss.

The truth of what has now been stated is very strikingly exemplified by what has actually occurred in America. The manufacture of Woollen goods is one which Congress seems to have been most anxious to promote. In 1790, an *ad valorem* duty of 5 *per cent* was laid, for the sake of revenue, on all woollen cloths imported into the republic. In 1798, after the restrictive mania had begun to gather strength, the duty was raised from 5 to 12½ per cent; in 1804, it was raised to 15 per cent; in 1812, during the war with England, it was increased to 27 per cent; in 1816, after peace had been restored, it was reduced to 25 per cent; and in 1824, it was nominally raised to 33-⅓, but really to 38 per cent! This was pretty well; but it fell far short of what has since been effected: By the tariff recently passed, it is enacted, that all goods which have cost 50 cents, (2s. 1½d.) a yard, *or under*, shall be deemed to have cost 50 cents, and shall be charged with a duty of 45 per cent *ad valorem*; and it is farther enacted, that all goods which cost above 50 cents the yard, and not more than 100 cents, *shall be considered as costing* 100 *cents, or* 4s. 3d., *and shall pay a duty of* 45 *per cent on that sum*; so that every yard of cloth shall pay a duty of 45 per cent, and that which costs 51 cents, will be valued at 100, and will consequently pay a duty of 45 cents, or nearly 90 per cent! The whole iniquity of this regulation is not apparent at first sight: – For it is so devised as to press far more heavily on the lower and middle than on the upper classes. The price of by much the largest proportion of the cloth which the former make use of varies from 50 to 100 cents a yard; and while this is loaded with a duty varying from 90 to 45 per cent, or 67½ per cent at an average, superfine cloth, costing four dollars the yard, is only loaded with a duty of 50 per cent! The encouragement of smuggling and fraud seems also to have been a favourite object with the framers of this regulation; for they have so contrived it, that if an importer can, by falsifying his papers or otherwise, succeed in sinking the price of his goods from 51 to 50 cents, he will save 45 per cent of duty! This is out-heroding old George Rose, and would, we are inclined to think, satisfy even Lord Malmsbury himself. Whether, indeed, there be any regulation equally iniquitous and absurd in the commercial code of Austria or Spain, is what we very much doubt; but, objectionable and vexatious as many of our custom-house regulations certainly are, still it is satisfactory to know that the very worst amongst them is fair and reasonable compared with the above.

The population of the United States is estimated, in a very able and detailed examination of the new tariff bill by a committee of the citizens of Boston and its vicinity, at 12 millions; and the value of the annual consumption of woollen goods is supposed to amount, at an average, to 6 dollars, or 25s. 6d. a-head, giving a total sum of about 72,000,000 dollars for the entire value of the woollens consumed in the Union. But if the duties were reduced, the cost of the woollens would also be reduced. It is estimated that, under the tariff of 1824, the various charges, including the duty of 38 per cent, the expense of freight and insurance, the profits of the importing and exporting merchants, &c. attending the importation of foreign woollens into the United States, amounted to full 57 per cent of their entire value. But referring for the present only to the operation of the duty, it is plain that it *must* have been paid before the woollens could be brought to market; and as they were imported in considerable quantities, notwithstanding its imposition, it is further plain, as has been previously remarked, that if it had been lowered or repealed, their price would have been proportionally diminished. But this is not the only fall that would have been occasioned by the reduction of the duties. The woollens manufactured in the United States sold in the market along with the foreign woollens charged with the duty of 38 per cent; and it is certain that they did not, quality for quality, sell cheaper; for had they done so, the foreign woollens would neither have been bought nor imported. On the whole, therefore, it is undeniable that the duty under the late tariff added 38 per cent to the cost of the whole woollens consumed in the republic, or made 27,360,000 of the 72,000,000 of dollars, which their aggregate value was supposed to amount to.

The value of the annual imports of woollens amounted, under the tariff of 1824, to about 9,000,000 of dollars. The gross amount of duty on this importation amounted to 3,420,000 dollars; by deducting this sum from the 27,360,000 dollars, which the duty added to the cost of the woollens consumed in the United States, the balance of 23,940,000 dollars is the net amount of the bounty, or *bonus*, which the American public were obliged to pay to their countrymen engaged in the woollen manufacture, to enable them to prosecute their business. (Report, p. 19.) And yet it appears, by the confession of the manufacturers themselves, that this immense *bonus* has been quite inadequate for their support. In any country not blessed with a legislature thoroughly embued with a love of all the contradictions and absurdities of the mercantile system, such a confession would have been reckoned equivalent to a declaration, that the prospect of engaging, on any thing like equal terms, in a successful competition with foreigners, in the woollen manufacture, was as yet altogether visionary, and that the protection that had already been so unwisely given to the manufacturers ought to be gradually withdrawn. But Congress thought differently. They determined that the manufacture should be supported, whatever might be the cost. There was more, however, of apparent than of real generosity in this conduct: For, as we have already seen, the members of Congress thought proper to throw the additional expense of supporting the manufacturers principally on the lower and middle classes, having considerately discriminated the duties laid on the articles consumed by their own *caste*.

152 *Battles over Free Trade, Volume 1*

Besides the statements in the Report of the Boston Committee, on which the previous remarks are chiefly founded, we may observe, that a precisely similar view of the question is taken in the Report of a Committee of the House of Representatives, appointed to inquire into the state of the finances. The policy of the new tariff, then under consideration, was fully and ably discussed, and strongly condemned by this Committee. They state, that, in their apprehension, the effect of the proposed (now enacted) tariff, will be, to take millions from the income of the planting, agricultural, commercial, and shipping interests, to add hundreds of thousands to the income of the manufacturers and wool-growers – 'In a word, that *the contemplated prohibitory duties will* DESTROY TEN TIMES AS MUCH WEALTH AS THEY WILL CREATE.'[1]

But the American legislature have not been satisfied with attempting to bolster up the Woollen manufacture. They have made equally strenuous efforts to establish the Cotton manufacture, which have been crowned with about equal success. On the coarser description of cotton fabrics, costing from 8 to 15 cents a yard, the duty under the tariff of 1824 was as high as 7½ cents, being from about 50 to 90 per cent *ad valorem;* on other fabrics, costing from 15 to 20 cents, the duty varied from 38 to 50 per cent; and on the more costly fabrics it amounted to 38 per cent. Such an extraordinary degree of protection could not fail to divert a considerable quantity of capital and labour to the manufacture of cottons; but instead of being of any advantage, every cotton-mill that has been built under this system, is an evidence of the folly of government, and of the misemployment of so much capital. Withdraw the protection – that is, prevent the public from being taxed for the sake of tempting cotton-spinners and manufacturers to embark in a disadvantageous business, and the utter annihilation of these establishments would follow as a matter of course. The manufacturers derive no part of their subsistence from their own industry or ingenuity; they derive it wholly from the monopoly which they possess of the home market, and which enables them to put their hands into the pockets of their neighbours. This is what the 'American system' really amounts to; and we can truly say, that we do not envy our Transatlantic friends the advantages of which it can be productive.

It appears from the Report of the Boston Committee, that notwithstanding the imposition of the exorbitant duties now alluded to, cottons, which sold for about 18 millions of dollars, were imported into the United States in 1826. (Page 24.) And yet, in the teeth of these facts, it is said by the advocates of the restrictive system, that 'America is not only supplied, but over-flowing with cotton manufactures, the produce of her own labour.' – 'The goods made by our own mills,' it is stated in a paper published by the Harrisburg Convention,[2] 'are the

1 Papers relative to American Tariffs, printed by order of the House of Commons, p. 233.

2 Consisting of delegates from all parts of the Union friendly to the encouragement of domestic industry; they met at Harrisburg, 30th July, 1827.

CHEAPEST AND BEST IN THE WORLD. They have driven like British goods out of every market accessible to us as to them, though our great rival has attempted to *counterfeit* our goods in numerous instances, to deceive the people of Mexico and South America. Some small parcels of our goods were *smuggled into England, and sold with a good profit!!!* American cottons would drive the like British or India goods out of Calcutta, were their importation thereat liberally allowed. There is nothing but *sober truth* in these statements; but how wonderful (wonderful truly!) are the changes that have taken place.'[1]

In our ignorance, we long imagined that John Bull had been the most gullible of animals; but if Jonathan can swallow such assertions as these, John has not the vestige of a claim to that distinction. *Smuggle* American cottons into Great Britain! What an opinion must the Harrisburg delegates have formed of their countrymen, when they could presume to call such a statement a 'sober truth'! Is there a merchant in the United States so profoundly ignorant, as not to know that American, and all other foreign cottons, may be freely imported into our markets on paying an *ad valorem* duty of TEN per cent? Let us now see how they are driving our cottons out of foreign markets. In 1826, the estimated official value of the whole exports from the United States amounted to 77,595,322 dollars, of which coarse cotton goods of *domestic* manufacture amounted to 1,138,125 dollars; and of these, 711,959 dollars worth were sent to Mexico, and South America. Now, it appears from the official accounts of our customhouse, that the value of *our* exports of cotton goods only, in 1825, amounted to L.30,795,000, or about 150,000,000 dollars; and there are good grounds for thinking, that the value of those exported to Mexico and South America exceeded 25,000,000 dollars; so that the American exports to those countries, some of which are their immediate neighbours, amount to about *two-thirds of a per cent* of our own; a marvellous progress, certainly, towards '*supplanting the British in all foreign markets!*'

But the truth is, that this is setting the progress made by the Americans in a much too favourable point of view. 'It is well known,' says the Boston Committee, which, it will be observed, consisted wholly of merchants and practical men, 'that in such a various and extensive trade as we carry on, there are many markets where *assorted* cargoes are required, and they must be made up of both foreign and domestic goods, even though they may cost more than in the country where these, or similar articles, are produced. As evidence of this, we re-exported, in 1825, of European linens, imported at a cost of from 15 to 20 per cent, to the amount of 2,433,625 dollars; yet no one acquainted with trade would infer from that, our ability to undersell the same articles going direct from the places where they are made, to the markets to which we export them. This is now the case, and always has been, with many of the articles which we import from all quarters of the world. But our

---

1 Papers relative to the American Tariffs, printed by order of the House of Commons, p. 107.

154   *Battles over Free Trade, Volume 1*

re-exportation of cotton goods will be more to the point. From the custom-house returns the committee find, that the export of foreign cotton goods, principally or all British, for 1825, amounted to 1,810,591 dollars, of which 1,106,214 dollars went to Mexico, and different ports in South America; and that in 1826, the export was 1,714,788 dollars, of which 901, 849 dollars went to the same places, besides the shipments that went direct from Europe to those countries. We think this is a just view of the case, and such as will convince every reasonable man, that no satisfactory evidence has been furnished to show that we can undersell the British in *any* market; indeed, nothing can be more absurd than to pretend that we can, while we levy a duty of from 50 to 90 per cent on those very goods in which we most excel, in order to keep British cottons out of our markets, and which is still to be increased, if the manufacturers prevail.' Page 26.

The same system of forcing has been applied to almost every sort of manufacture; and it would seem that *coute qui coute* it is to be persevered in. Its advocates have proclaimed, that 'the principle of the tariff is to enable each article manufactured at home to sustain a competition with the same article when imported.' – 'We,' it was said in Congress, 'want protection; and *it matters not whether it be* 50 *or* 150 *per cent*, so long as it is protection.' Entertaining such views, we think Congress would do well to prohibit foreign commerce altogether; to make it, as the Spaniards did in South America, a capital offence to carry on any sort of intercourse with foreigners. If their system of prohibitions and restrictions could take effect, it would destroy the foreign trade of the republic as effectually as if her territories were surrounded by Bishop Berkeley's wall of brass.

We observe that very great stress is generally laid by the speakers in Congress, and the writers out of doors, favourable to the 'American system,' on the alleged indisposition of the European powers, and particularly of Great Britain, to import the staple productions of America. We are accused of acting with inconceivable rapacity, illiberality, and so forth. We are said to have excluded almost every sort of Transatlantic produce from our markets. The injury done the Union by our corn laws is particularly dwelt upon; and they are triumphantly referred to as showing that we are still zealously attached to the prohibitive system. It is alleged, that the recent changes in some departments of our commercial legislation have been of no material consequence, and that they were really intended only to deceive foreigners, and make them enter into ruinous commercial treaties with us.

There is, however, a great deal of falsehood and exaggeration in these statements. With respect, indeed, to the corn laws, it is perhaps unnecessary for us to say that we are quite as hostile to them as any foreigner, whether an American or a Pole, can possibly be. We look upon them as decidedly opposed to all our best interests; as occasioning the misemployment of a large amount of capital and industry; as multiplying, at one and the same time, the chances, not only of famine, but also of gluts; and as tending, by raising the average price of food, and, consequently, the rate of wages, to an artificial elevation, to depress the rate of profit, and cause the transference of capital to other countries. All, therefore, that can be said even by the Harrisburg delegates, in vituperation of the corn laws, will be assented to by us. We are enemies of prohibitions and restrictions, not because they have been enacted by aristocrats, autocrats, or democrats – by England, Austria, or America, but because we are thoroughly convinced that they are in the last degree inimical to the real wealth and permanent improvement of every nation by whom they are adopted. It is needless, therefore, to tell us that England has acted, and is, in this instance, still acting, upon that very system of policy, which we condemn. We admit, and lament the fact. At the same time, however, we are gratified in thinking that a very great progress indeed has been already made, notwithstanding the statements to the contrary by the American writers and speakers, in the way to a better system.

But why should Jonathan, who is so very sharp-sighted in other plain practical questions, be so very blind in this? He sees clearly enough that the corn laws operate as a heavy tax on the consumers of corn in this country, of which a small part only finds its way into the pockets of the landlords, the rest being wasted in the heavy expenses attending the tillage of the poor soils, which we are, through the agency of these laws, compelled to cultivate. Jonathan has the most perfect comprehension of all this, and can descant, in good set phrases, on its impolicy and absurdity – And yet, with an Irish sort of consistency, he sets about doing the very same thing himself that he so loudly condemns in us! He sees that the English might import corn from abroad for a half, or perhaps a third, of what it takes to raise it on the worst lands now in tillage; and not to be behind us in wisdom, he hastens to lay prohibitory duties on foreign woollens, cottons, hardware, glass, sugar, &c., that he may have the pleasure of paying twice as much for these articles as he might otherwise obtain them for, and thus be on a level with the English! After this, who will presume to say that John Bull is the greatest goose in the world? Had he been in Jonathan's place, and no longer kept in leading strings by the Newcastles, Kenyons, &c, we believe he would have said, that the line of conduct followed by the British government, with respect to the trade in corn, ought to be avoided, not followed; and that it was clearly for his interest to buy his woollens, cottons, and hardware, wherever he could get them cheapest, whatever the English might do.

It is quite a mistake to affirm, as Mr Otis and other advocates of the tariff have done, that we import almost nothing that the Americans produce. It appears from the American customhouse report, that the estimated value of the *domestic* produce exported from the United States amounted, in 1825, to 66,944,745 dollars; and of this *no less than 40,372,987 dollars worth was sent to Great Britain and her colonies; 35,043,466 dollars worth being exported direct to Great Britain.* Well and truly, therefore, might the merchants of Boston say in their Report,

156   *Battles over Free Trade, Volume 1*

that 'Whatever view we take of the trade with Great Britain, it will be found to be *equal in value to TWO THIRDS OF ALL THE COMMERCE which we carry on with the remaining parts of the whole world*; but it will be impossible for us to retain more than a small portion of what we now enjoy, if the system we are opposing should prevail.' – p. 127.[1]

There cannot be a question, indeed, that the commerce with Great Britain is of the utmost consequence to the Americans, and that we deal with them on infinitely more liberal terms than they deal with us. We annually import more than 125 millions of pounds weight of American cotton, charging it only with a duty of *six* per cent. Our supplies of tobacco are principally imported from America; and though it is charged with a heavy duty of 3s. a pound, that duty is imposed solely for the sake of revenue, and certainly with no view to check the consumption of an American product, in order to encourage the use of one raised at home. With the exception, indeed, of ashes and rice, no articles brought from America pay a protecting duty; and on the majority of the American articles we import, the duties do not, at an average, exceed *eight* per cent *ad valorem*. But there is not, as we have already seen, any reciprocity in the proceedings of the Americans. They charge our woollen goods with a duty of from 45 to 90 per cent, cottons with a duty of from 30 to 100 per cent, iron bolts and bar-iron with a duty of L.7, 17s. per ton, and so on. It would be well, therefore, if in future discussions of this matter, the advocates and eulogists of the 'American system' were to lay somewhat less stress on our 'cupidity' and 'illiberality.' Whatever may be our defects in that way, it does not really seem that the Americans have any very peculiar right to reproach us with them.

It is true, that it is our own interest we have in view in admitting American raw cotton, and other products, at comparatively low duties. Nor do we object to the Americans that they act on this principle; for no nation ever acts on any other. What we object to in their conduct is, that they mistake wherein their own interest really lies; and that their prohibitions and restrictions, by narrowing the field of commercial enterprise, are a public and general nuisance; though it is certain that they are infinitely more injurious to themselves than to any other people.

On hearing the terms in which some of the leading American orators talk about the mischiefs arising from the *balance of trade* being unfavourable to the republic, and the consequent exportation of specie, one is almost tempted to believe in the doctrine of the metempsychosis, and to conclude that the Roses, the Kenyons, and the Lauderdales of a former age, are again revived in the Baldwins, the Lawrences, and the Everetts of the present. It is difficult to argue with those who, at this time of day, can talk seriously about the balance of trade. To

1   In 1827 the value of the exports from the United States to Great Britain and her dependencies amounted to 32,870,465 dollars, of which 28,297,692 dollars worth went direct to Great Britain.

say that the old doctrine with respect to it has been a thousand times shown to be false, contradictory, and absurd, is not enough. The fact is, that the very reverse of it is true; and that every nation carrying on an advantageous foreign commerce must import *more* than she exports, and must therefore, according to the Transatlantic illuminati, have the balance against her. But in despite of the speeches of honourable gentlemen, and the innumerable essays of Mr Carey, we apprehend that Jonathan is not quite so simple as to export any commodity, except in the view of importing a more valuable one in its stead. It is this greater value that constitutes the profits of the merchants engaged in the foreign trade; and to affirm that it is large, is to affirm, what is not reckoned a very serious evil on this side the Atlantic, whatever it may be on the other, that the external trade of the country is very lucrative.

It would, however, be unjust to individual members of the American Legislature to represent them as all approving the exploded and absurd notions with regard to the balance of trade. Mr Cambreleng, in an able pamphlet, entitled an Examination of the Tariff proposed in 1821, forcibly exposed the fallacy of the opinion of those who believe, or affect to believe, in the pernicious effect of what is called an unfavourable balance. Mr Webster, too, in an admirable speech on the tariff bill of 1824, set the real nature of commerce, and the true doctrine as to the balance, in the clearest point of view. Mr Webster illustrated his statement by a case which, although it failed to make any impression on the majority of his auditors, is so very conclusive, that we believe it will carry conviction to every one who may happen to throw his eye over these pages. 'Some time since,' said Mr Webster, 'a ship left one of the towns of New England, having on board 70,000 dollars in specie. She proceeded to Mocha, on the Red Sea, and there laid out these dollars on coffee, drugs, spices, &c. With this new cargo she proceeded to Europe; two thirds of it were sold in Holland for 130,000 dollars, which the ship brought back and placed in the vaults of the same bank whence she had taken her original outfit; the other third was sent to the ports of the Mediterranean, and produced a return of 25,000 dollars in specie, and 15,000 dollars in Italian merchandise. These sums together make 170,000 dollars imported, which is 100,000 dollars more than were exported; and forms, therefore, according to the doctrine of honorable gentlemen on the other side, an *unfavourable balance* to that amount.' But honourable gentlemen were proof against this *reduction ad absurdum* – They continued firm in their belief, that the doctrine of the balance was no chimera, and that the adventure described by Mr Webster was a losing one!

Some members of the American Legislature, who advocate the protecting system, and of the purity of whose motives no doubt can be entertained, seem to lay a great deal of stress on the assumed principle, that no people can truly be said to be *independent*, if they are indebted to foreigners for supplies of any commodity of very great utility. There is some apparent, but no real foundation for this opinion. The fallacy lies in attaching an erroneous meaning to the term independent. No one would reckon a private gentleman, who had his clothes, hats, shoes, &c. made in his own house, as in any respect more independent than one who had money enough to buy them of the tailors, hatters, shoemakers, and other tradesmen. The same is the case with nations. Each, by applying itself in preference to those pursuits for which it has some peculiar aptitude, will be able to obtain a greater command over the necessaries and conveniences of life, through the intervention of an exchange, and will, consequently, be *richer*, and consequently more truly *independent*, than if it had directly produced the various articles for which it has a demand. In commerce, equivalents are always given for equivalents; so that there can be no dependence, in the vulgar acceptation of the term. The Americans, it is true, have on one or two occasions experienced a scarcity of foreign manufactured goods; but this was a consequence of *their own policy*, of their non-importation acts, and not of the prohibitive regulations of any foreign power. They may rest assured, that *no manufacturing nation will ever refuse to sell*. No such circumstance has ever yet occurred; and it may be safely affirmed that it never will. The danger that the American statesmen would provide against is therefore altogether imaginary. The independence at which they aspire, is the independence of those who swim across the river that they may owe nothing to the bridge.

We have hitherto argued this question, on the assumption that the provisions of the tariff might be carried into effect; but this seems to be quite out of the question. The great corrector of vicious commercial and financial legislation, the Smuggler, will prove too powerful for the utmost vigilance of the custom-house officers. The vast extent of the American frontier, and the facilities it affords for the clandestine importation of foreign goods, present insuperable obstacles to the success of the mad attempt in which the government has embarked. We have no idea, indeed, that our exports to the United States will be very materially diminished by the new Tariff. Free access to Canada will afford our merchants so many facilities for smuggling, that unless the Americans place a custom-house officer in every bush, and station a gun-boat in every creek, it will not be in their power to prevent the introduction of our products. The American Legislature will not, therefore, be able, do what it will, to establish the finer branches of manufacture within the Union. It may carry the protecting duties from 100 to 500 or 1000 per cent; it will only be so much additional premium to the clandestine trader. The injury will fall heavy on the Americans themselves; but will be comparatively little felt by the foreigner. Instead of reaping a large revenue from moderate custom duties, they will empty the public coffers of the state to fill the pockets of the smuggler; instead of having the population on their frontier engaged in the clearing of land, and in extending the empire of civilization, they will imbue them with predatory and ferocious habits, and teach them to defy the laws, and to place their hopes of rising in the world, not in the laborious occupations of agriculture, but in schemes to defraud the public revenue. Commerce will be diverted from its natural and wholesome channels; and instead of being one of the most productive sources of wealth and civilization, it will become, under the operation of the 'American system,' a prolific source of every sort of disorder.

But it is alleged by some, that, whatever may be the merits or demerits of the 'system,' Congress has now gone too far in its support to be able to recede. It is alleged that a vast amount of capital has been expended in the erection of woollen and cotton mills, and other manufacturing establishments, in the belief that the protecting system would be continued, and that the Legislature cannot now abandon that system, and revert to the sound principle of moderate duties, imposed for the sake of revenue only. But the sophistry of this sort of reasoning is apparent. Were it admitted to be sound, it would be virtually admitting that no system of legislation, however vicious, in the support of which some individuals have an interest, could ever be changed or amended! Error and abuse would be perpetuated for ever, and every sort of improvement would be at an end. Had the American Legislature declared that any particular duty was to continue for a given number of years, then, certainly, it could not have modified that duty within the period mentioned, without making full compensation to those who might suffer by it. But we believe we are correct in saying, that, how absurdly soever it may have acted in many respects, it has not done this. It has imposed no duties for definite periods; it has reserved to itself full power to increase or diminish them when it thinks proper; and it might, without laying itself under a charge of acting with bad faith towards any one, repeal the duties, and throw the ports open to-morrow. Of course, we do not say that it would be expedient to make any such sudden change, even from a supremely bad to a good system. But if the Americans be wise, they will set about retracing their steps, and will continue gradually to reduce the duties on imports, till they have brought them to, at most, the rates they were fixed at in 1818.

That the present tariff can be allowed to regulate the commerce of America for any very lengthened period, is what we do not believe. It was carried by extremely narrow majorities both in the House of Representatives and the Senate; and has excited, more especially in the Southern States, an extreme degree of dissatisfaction. Its opponents contend, that in imposing heavy duties, not for the sake of revenue but of *protection*, Congress has exceeded its powers, and violated one of the fundamental principles of the constitution. Whether this be really the case, it would be presumptuous in us to attempt to decide. We may however observe, that Mr Jefferson took this view of the matter; and, in a letter to Mr Giles, written after the passing of the Tariff of 1824, has expressed himself very strongly indeed on the subject – 'Under the power,' said this truly distinguished patriot and statesman, 'to regulate commerce, they (Congress) assume indefinitely that also over agriculture and manufactures; and call it regulation, too, to *take the earnings of one of these branches of industry, and that too the most depressed, and put them into the pockets of the others, the most flourishing of all.'* And after briefly noticing some of the objectionable proceedings of Congress, Mr Jefferson adds – 'Are we then to stand at arms? No! that must be the last resource, not to be thought of until much longer and greater sufferings. If every infraction of a compact of so many parties is to be resisted at once as a dissolution of it, none can ever be formed which would last one year. We must have patience and long endurance then with our brethren *while under delusion.* Give them time for reflection and experience of consequences; keep ourselves (Virginia and the Southern States) in a situation to profit by the chapter of accidents, and separate from our companions only when the sole alternatives left, are the dissolution of our union with them, or submission to a government without limitation of powers. *Between these two evils when we must make choice, THERE CAN BE NO HESITATION:* but in the mean time, the States should be careful to note every material usurpation on their rights, to denounce them as they occur in the most peremptory terms, to protest against them, as wrongs to which our present submission shall be considered, not as acknowledgment or precedent of right, but as temporary yielding to the lesser evil, *until their accumulation shall outweigh that of separation.'*

This, if any thing can, ought to make Congress pause in the hazardous and desperate career on which it has entered. Strong indeed must have been the conviction of the impolicy of the 'American system,' that could have induced Mr Jefferson to declare that a dissolution of that confederation, in the formation of which he had borne so distinguished a part, would be a preferable alternative to a toleration of the evils that must spring from it. So solemn and impressive a denunciation will not surely be disregarded by Congress; and must, at any rate, have the greatest public influence. It cannot be said of Mr Jefferson that he was actuated by selfish or factious motives. He was one of the founders of his country's constitution, understood her interests, and was anxious only for her welfare. The letter containing this truly important passage was not a public one; it was a confidential communication to an intimate friend, disclosing the undisguised sentiments of the writer on a vitally important question; nor had Mr Jefferson the least idea that it would ever see the light. It is idle, therefore, to consider, as some individuals here have done, the vituperations of the tariff at public meetings in America, and the vehement attacks made upon it by a large part of the public press, as the mere exasperation of the moment. The terms in which Mr Jefferson speaks of it show the deep and profound impression that the policy on which it is founded had made on the soberest and ablest individuals. That the coldness, or rather jealousy, which formerly existed between the Southern and Northern divisions of the Union, has been vastly increased by the enactment of the present tariff, is a fact of which no one at all conversant with American affairs can be ignorant. It has irritated where conciliation was of the utmost importance; and has inflamed the violence of parties, already too much incensed against each other. As sincere friends to America, we deeply regret the infatuation that has produced such baleful results. But we trust that the good sense of the people will prevent her rulers, even if they be so disposed, from carrying matters to extremities; and compel them to recede from a system of policy, which, at the same time that it is destructive of the public wealth, threatens to put in peril the very existence of the Union.

It has been asked, what ought England to do in this emergency? The commerce of no other nation will be so much affected as ours by the proceedings of the Americans; and it is contended that we ought either to remonstrate or retaliate. We believe, however, that it will be infinitely better to do neither. The proceedings of the Americans ought rather to excite pity than anger. They cannot injure us without injuring themselves to a tenfold greater extent. But if we were to retaliate, by excluding American produce from our markets, we should not only aggravate, in a very great degree, whatever inconvenience we may already experience from the proceedings of Congress, but would enable them to give effect to their measures. So long as we allow the produce of America to enter our markets, it will not be possible for her to exclude ours. The smuggler, provided we allow him to bring back equivalents, will take care of our interests. Cheap goods will in this, as in all other instances, make their way through every barrier; and British manufactures will be displayed in the halls of Congress, and the drawing-rooms of Washington, in mockery of the impotent legislation that would seek to exclude them. At the same time, however, it is quite clear, that the less dependence we now place on the trade with America, so much the better. She cannot, indeed, inflict any material injury on us by refusing to *buy* our products, but at present she might injure us by refusing to *sell*; and after what we have seen of Congress, it could excite no surprise though some attempt of that sort were made. We are not, therefore, sure, that it might not be good policy to endeavour to encourage the importation of cotton from India, Egypt, South America, &c. by reducing or wholly repealing the existing duty on all cotton not imported from the United States. We would not increase the present duties on any commodity brought from America; but when she is every year making fresh efforts, by means of oppressive duties, to exclude our produce from her markets, she cannot blame us if we begin to look about us for means, and they may easily be had, of making ourselves wholly independent of any intercourse with her.

Britain and Cautious Reciprocity

'Merchants' Petition of 1820 in Favour of Free Trade', in *Revised Report of the Proceedings at the Dinner of 31st May, 1876, Held in Celebration of the Hundredth Year of the Publication of the 'Wealth of Nations'* (London: Longmans, Green, Reader and Dyer, 1876), pp. 57–60.

Merchants' Petition of 1820 in favour of Free Trade – Members of the Club at its formation in 1821.

THE Political Economy Club was founded in London in the year 1821, chiefly by the exertions of the late Thomas Tooke, F.R.S., (who died February 1858, aged 84) and as a consequence of the discussions which arose out of the interest excited by the presentation on 8th May, 1820, in the House of Commons, by Mr. Alexander Baring (afterwards Lord Ashburnham), one of the members for the City, of the famous Petition of the Merchants of London in favour of Free Trade – a document of which Mr. Tooke was the author.

As the presentation of this Petition marks a distinct era of the progress of Political Economy in this country, and the Petition itself is not readily accessible, it is here reprinted as an appendix not inappropriate to the Centenary of the 'Wealth of Nations': –

May 8, 1820.

To the Honourable the House of Commons of the United Kingdom of Great Britain and Ireland.

'The Humble Petition of the undersigned Merchants of the City of London, showeth,

That Foreign Commerce is eminently conducive to the wealth and prosperity of a country, by enabling it to Import the Commodities for the production of which the soil, climate, capital, and industry of other countries are best calculated; and to Export, in payment, those articles for which its own situation is better adapted.

That Freedom from Restraint is calculated to give the utmost extension to Foreign Trade, and the best direction to the Capital and Industry of the country

– 162 –

That the maxim of buying in the Cheapest Market, and selling in the Dearest, which regulates every merchant in his individual dealings, is strictly applicable as the best rule for the trade of the whole Nation.

That a policy founded on these principles would render the Commerce of the World an interchange of mutual advantages, and diffuse an increase of wealth and enjoyments among the inhabitants of each State.

That, unfortunately, a policy the very reverse of this has been, and is, more or less, adopted and acted upon by the Government of this and of every other country, each trying to exclude the productions of other countries, with the specious and well-meant design of encouraging its own productions; thus inflicting on the bulk of its subjects, who are Consumers, the necessity of submitting to privations in the quantity or quality of commodities, and thus rendering what ought to be the source of mutual benefit and of harmony among States, a constantly recurring occasion of jealousy and hostility.

That the prevailing prejudices in favour of the Protective or Restrictive System may be traced to the erroneous supposition that every importation of foreign commodities occasions a diminution or discouragement of our own productions to the same extent: whereas it may be clearly shown that although the particular description of production which could not stand against unrestrained foreign competition would be discouraged, yet as no importation could be continued for any length of time without a corresponding Exportation, direct or indirect, there would be an encouragement, for the purpose of that exportation, of some other production to which our situation might be better suited; thus affording at least an equal, and probably a greater, and certainly a more beneficial, employment to our own Capital and Labour.

That of the numerous Protective and Prohibitory Duties of our commercial codes, it may be proved, that while all operate as a very heavy tax on the community at large, very few are of any ultimate benefit to the classes in whose favour they were originally instituted; and none to the extent of the loss occasioned by them to other classes.

That, among the other evils of the Restrictive or Protective System, not the least is, that the artificial protection of one branch of industry, or source of production, against foreign competition, is set up as a ground of claim by other branches for similar protection; so that, if the reasoning upon which these restrictive or prohibitory regulations are founded were followed out consistently, it would not stop short of excluding us from all foreign commerce whatsoever. And the same train of argument, which with corresponding prohibitions and protective duties should exclude us from Foreign Trade, might be brought forward to justify the re-enactment of restrictions upon the interchange of productions (unconnected with public revenue) among the kingdoms composing the Union, or among the counties of the same kingdom.

That an investigation of the effects of the Restrictive System, at this time, is peculiarly called for, as it may, in the opinion of your Petitioners, lead to a strong presumption that the distress which now so generally prevails is considerably aggravated by that system; and that some relief may be obtained by the earliest practicable removal of such of the restraints as may be shown to be most injurious to the capital and industry of the community, and to be attended with no compensating benefit to the public revenue.

That a declaration against the anti-commercial principles of our Restrictive System is of the more importance at the present juncture, inasmuch as, in several instances of recent occurrence, the merchants and manufacturers in foreign States have assailed their respective governments with applications for further protective or prohibitory duties and regulations, urging the example and authority of this country, against which they are almost exclusively directed, as a sanction for the policy of such measures. And certainly, if the reasoning upon which our restrictions have been defended is worth anything, it will apply in behalf of the regulations of foreign States against us. They insist upon our superiority in capital and machinery; as we do upon their comparative exemption from taxation; and with equal foundation.

That nothing would more tend to counteract the commercial hostility of foreign States than the adoption of a more enlightened and more conciliatory policy on the part of this country.

That although, as a matter of mere Diplomacy, it may sometimes answer to hold out the removal of particular prohibitions, or high duties, as depending upon corresponding concessions by other States in our favour, it does not follow that we should maintain our restrictions in cases where the desired concessions on their part cannot be obtained. Our restrictions would not be the less prejudicial to our own capital and industry, because other Governments persisted in preserving impolitic regulations.

That, upon the whole, the most liberal would prove to be the most politic course on such occasions.

That, independent of the direct benefit to be derived by this country on every occasion of such concession or relaxation, a great incidental object would be gained by the recognition of a sound principle or standard, to which all subsequent arrangements might be referred, and by the salutary influence which a promulgation of such just views by the Legislature, and by the Nation at large, could not fail to have on the policy of other States,

That in thus declaring, as your Petitioners do, their conviction of the impolicy and injustice of the Restrictive System, and in desiring every practicable relaxation of it, they have in view only such parts of it as are not connected, or are only subordinately so, with the Public Revenue. As long as the necessity for the present amount of Revenue subsists, your Petitioners cannot expect so important a branch of it as the Customs to be given up, nor to be materially diminished, unless some substitute less objectionable be suggested. But it is against every Restrictive Regulation of trade, not essential to the Revenue – against all duties merely Protective from Foreign competition – and against the excess of such duties as are partly for the purpose of revenue, and partly for that of protection – that the prayer of the present Petition is respectfully submitted to the wisdom of Parliament.

Your Petitioners therefore humbly pray that your Honourable House will be pleased to take the subject into consideration, and to adopt such measures as may be calculated to give greater freedom to Foreign Commerce, and thereby to increase the resources of the State.'

Edinburgh Petition for Free Trade, 20 April 1820, *Caledonian Mercury*, 29 April 1820.

AT a GENERAL MEETING of the MEMBERS of the CHAMBER OF COMMERCE and MANUFACTURES of EDINBURGH, on the 20th April 1820, the following Petition was unanimously agreed to and ordered to be forwarded to Mr. Baring, M. P. to be by him presented to the House of Commons.

Unto the Honourable the House of Commons of the United Kingdom of Great Britain and Ireland,

The Humble PETITION of the CHAMBER OF COMMERCE and MANUFACTURES of the CITY OF EDINBURGH: –

SHEWETH,

That this Chamber having been instituted by Royal Charter, for the express purpose of watching over the commercial interests of this part of the United Kingdom, they humbly conceive it a duty highly incumbent on them, at a period of unprecedented pressure on every branch of mercantile industry, most respectfully to call the attention of the House to the depressed state of foreign commerce, and to offer their opinion of the causes that in a great measure contribute to this depression, whereby the general industry of this kingdom is checked, its manufactures consequently deeply injured, and its revenue in danger of being soon most seriously diminished.

It appears to your Petitioners, that the system so long persevered in, of laying on heavy duties on imports from foreign countries, tends directly to lessen the demand in these countries for the produce of the industry of our own nation.

That this doctrine maintained by many Statesmen, that in order to accumulate wealth by trade, a nation must export more than it imports, is most erroneous.

That upon this erroneous doctrine is founded the present commercial policy of this country.

It appears to your Petitioners, that the profits derived from the exportation of the produce of our manufactures, agriculture, fisheries, and mines, can in no other shape be realized, or made effective to the increase of the national wealth, but in the form of imports.

That it appears to your Petitioners, that the sure way to increase foreign commerce, is to encourage the industry of other nations with whom we trade; or, in other words, to enable them to become our customers.

That, to that end, we should admit on low duties, the raw produce of other countries, and such articles of commerce as we are precluded from producing, by climate or other circumstances.

That your Petitioners consider, that the high duties on Baltic wood and iron, on wines, and more particularly on French wines, on raw silk, and on many other articles of trade, the produce of foreign countries, have directly and indirectly lessened the demand in those countries for the productions of this realm; for by checking the industry of those foreign nations, we disable them from being our customers, and we hold out an example to their Governments to lay on heavy duties on the manufactures and other exports from this country.

That it appears to your Petitioners, that this system of restrictive commerce has been followed since the peace, by the Government of almost every nation with which we trade, in strict conformity with the system adopted by Great Britain.

That whatever may be the perseverance of other nations in this system, the British Government should begin a more liberal and wise commercial policy, without regard to reciprocity of benefit between us and any particular nation, because, by encouraging an increased import from one nation, we are certain of gaining an increased export directly to that nation, or intermediately to some other nation.

That it appears to your Petitioners, that such a liberal system of commercial policy, which is thus humbly submitted to the consideration of the Honourable House, would produce a greater revenue, from the increased quantity of imports, although subject only to low rates of duties; and at the same time would promote national industry, as a consequence of a proportional increase of exports.

May it therefore please your Honourable House to permit this petition to be taken into the consideration of a Committee of the House, and to adopt such measures as, in the wisdom of your Honourable House, may be deemed most prudent and efficacious:

And your Petitioners will ever pray.

Signed in the name, and on the behalf of the Chamber of Commerce and Manufactures of the City of Edinburgh, and the Seal of the Corporation affixed thereto, the 20th day of April, in the year 1820.

(Signed) ALEXANDER HENDERSON, CHAIRMAN

Published by order of the Meeting,
DAVID STEUART
ALEX. WIGHT, Secretaries.

168   *Battles over Free Trade, Volume 1*

William Huskisson, Speech on the 'Foreign Commerce of the Country', 25 March 1825, *Hansard* (1825), xii, cc. 1196–222.

FOREIGN COMMERCE OF THE COUNTRY.

The House having resolved itself into a committee to consider of the consolidated Custom Duties, Mr. *Huskisson* rose and spoke, in substance, as follows:[1]–

Sir; – In requesting the attention of the committee, whilst I state (in continuation of the subject which I had the honour to open on Monday last) the alterations which I propose to recommend in the duties levied upon the importation of materials employed in some of our principal manufactures, and also in the prohibitory duties now imposed upon the manufactured productions of other countries, I need scarcely bespeak the disposition of the committee to countenance the principle of these proposals, so far as they shall be found not inconsistent with the protection of our own industry. I feel the more assured of this general disposition in the committee, not only as it was manifested on the former evening, but also from the experience, which the House and the country now have of the benefits to be derived from the removal of vexatious restraints, and meddling interference, in the concerns of internal industry, or foreign commerce.

However confident either my right hon. friend the chancellor of the Exchequer, or, I myself, may have been, that the changes which, since the restoration of peace, it has been our duty to propose in our commercial policy, would be attended with the most salutary consequences, it was impossible for us – at least it was impossible for me – not to feel that, in the application of the soundest principles, the result, from unforeseen causes, may sometimes disappoint our expectations. It became us, therefore, to watch the issue of each experiment, and not to attempt too much at once, until we had felt our way, and until the public were prepared to accompany us in our further progress. But I think I am not too bold in stating that, in every instance, as far as we have hitherto gone, not only have the fears and forebodings of the particular interests by which we were opposed proved to be visionary and unfounded, but the expectations of our most sanguine supporters have been more than realized. In these advantages, therefore, the opponents of the measures by which they were produced, must, on the one hand, find a matter of consolation, that their admonitions did not persuade – that their arguments did not convince – that their predictions did not intimidate: and, on the other hand, past success is, to the supporters of those measures, a source of encouragement to follow up the same path, as likely to lead us still further in the career of public prosperity.

The committee will recollect that, when the change was made last year in the system of our Silk trade, one great alteration was the substitution of an ad

1   From the original edition, printed for J. Hatchard and Son, Piccadilly.

valorem duty of 30*l.* per cent instead of an absolute prohibition of all articles manufactured of silk. A doubt was suggested at the time, and in that doubt I participated, whether 30*l.* per cent was not too high a duty; – not too high, indeed, according to the apprehensions of the British manufacturer, (for he stated it would be quite inadequate to his protection) but whether its amount would not still leave some latitude to the smuggler. This latter ground of doubt still remains – the former, I believe is already pretty well removed. If alarm now exist any where, and I know it does exist, it is transferred to the other side of the channel, and is to be found only among the manufacturers of France, in consequence of the great progress and improvement, since made in this country, in every branch of the silk trade.

Having thus ruled that 30*l.* per cent is the highest duty which could be maintained for the protection of a manufacture, in every part of which we were most behind foreign countries – the only extensive manufacture, which, on the score of general inferiority, stood in need of special protection – surely it was time to inquire in what degree our other great manufactures were protected, and to consider if there be no inconvenience, no unfitness, no positive injury caused to ourselves, no suspicion and odium excited in foreign countries, by duties which are either absolutely prohibitory – or, if the articles to which they attach admit of being smuggled, which have no other effect than to throw the business of importing them into the hands of the smuggler.

To bring this subject more particularly before the House, I will begin with our greatest manufacture, that of cotton. It will not be denied that, in this manufacture, we are superior to all other countries: and that, by the cheapness and quality of our goods, we undersell our competitors in all the markets of the world, which are open alike to us and to them. I do not except the market of the East Indies (the first seat of manufactures), of which it may be said to be the staple, where the raw material is grown, where labour is cheaper than in any other country, and from which England and Europe were, for a long time, supplied with cotton goods. Now, however, large quantities of British cottons are sold in India at prices lower than they can be produced by the native manufacturers. If any possible doubt could remain that this manufacture has nothing to apprehend from competition any where, and, least of all, from a competition in our own home market, it must vanish when I state to the committee, that the official value of cotton goods, exported last year, amounted to the astonishing sum of 30,795,000*l.* : and yet such have been the extravagant fears of a jealous monopoly, and such is the influence of old prejudices, that in our book of rates, the duties, will the committee believe it? – stand at this moment as follows:–on certain descriptions of cotton goods, 75*l.* per cent, on others 67*l.* 10*s.* per cent, on a third class 50*l.* per cent.

It is impossible not to smile at the discriminating shrewdness which made these distinctions, and which could discover that, with a protection of 67*l.* per cent, ten shillings more were wanting, to make the balance incline on the side of the British manufacturer, in the market of his own country. These absurd duties, and equally absurd distinctions, attach alike upon the productions of our own subjects in the East Indies, as upon those of foreign countries; whilst our manufactures are admitted, almost duty free, into all the territories of the East-India Company. Instead of this graduated, but monstrous scale, I propose to admit all foreign articles manufactured wholly of cotton, whether from the East Indies or elsewhere, at one uniform duty of 10*l.* per cent, which, I conceive, is sufficient to countervail the small duty levied upon the importation of the raw material into this country, and the duty upon any other articles used in the manufacture. Any protection, beyond this, I hold to be not only unnecessary but mischievous.

From cotton, I proceed to woollens, one of our oldest manufactures – that which has been most nursed and dandled by the legislature – a favourite child, which like other favourites, has, I suspect, suffered, rather than profited, by being spoilt and petted in rearing; whilst its younger brother of cotton, coming into the world much later, has thriven better by being much more left to rough it, and make its own way in life. Some detailed and authentic history of the paternal and zealous solicitude with which our ancestors in this House interposed to protect the woollen manufacture (should such a history ever be written), will alone preserve future generations from incredulity, in respect to the extent to which legislative interference was once carried in this branch of internal industry. Within my own time, regulating acts, dealing with every minute process of the manufacture, have been repealed by the score; as have also heaps of other laws, equally salutary and wise, prescribing the mode of clipping wool, its package, the time to be allowed, and the forms to be observed, in removing it from one place to another – laws, the violation of which, in some instances, amounted to felony, but which now no longer disgrace the Statute-book. Fortunately for the cotton manufacture, it was never favoured with this species of protection, so abundantly lavished upon woollen, and which was only withdrawn last year from silk, by the repeal of the Spitalfields acts.

I am well aware that this retrospect to former systems may be wearisome to the committee, but it is not without its importance, if it were only to strengthen us against falling again into erroneous courses. I trust, therefore, that I may be allowed to state, from official documents, what has been the relative progress of our cotton and woollen manufactures, since the year 1765, being a period of sixty years:–

The quantity of cotton wool imported into Great Britain, in the year ended the 5th of January, 1765, was about 3,360,000 *lbs.* The value of cotton goods exported 200,000*l.*

The quantity of cotton wool imported in the year ended the 5th of January, 1825, was 147,174,000 *lbs*. The value of cotton goods exported 30,795,000*l*.

The quantity of lamb and sheeps' wool imported in the year 1765, was 1,926,000*lbs*. The value of woollen goods exported 5,159,000*l*.

The quantity of lamb and sheeps' wool imported in the year 1825, was 23,858,000*lbs*. The value of woollen goods exported 6,926,000*l*.

Perhaps I may just add, that the quantity of raw silk imported in 1765, was 418,000*lbs*; and in 1825 3,047,000*lbs*.

In submitting these satisfactory statements, I cannot refrain from calling the attention of the committee to one observation which they suggest to my mind. It must, I think, be admitted, that, in the year 1765, the whole quantity of sheeps' wool grown in this country could not be nearly so great as at present, when, owing to the many improvements in husbandry, and particularly in the art of raising winter food for the flocks, the number of sheep must be greatly increased; and yet the, quantity of wool imported in that year, was not one-twelfth of the quantity imported in 1825. Out of this aggregate supply from home growth, and foreign import, the whole wants of our own population were supplied in 1765, leaving to the amount of 5,159,000*l*. of manufactured woollens for exportation. In the year 1825, out of the aggregate of the home growth, and of an import of wool so greatly exceeding that of 1765, the whole manufactured export is 6,926,000*l*, being an increase over that of 1765, of only 1,765,000*l*. Now, let me ask the committee, how often, in these sixty years, has the increase of consumption in cotton and silk clothing been contemplated with alarm and jealousy, by the wool-grower, and the woollen manufacturer; by the descendants of those who passed laws, (repealed only within these last ten years), compelling us to be buried in woollens? – And yet what was our consumption of cotton – that other great article of clothing? – in 1765, next to nothing; and what is it now? – greater probably than the whole amount of our woollens, to say nothing of the consumption of silk, which has also increased eight-fold. Can any statement show more decidedly the wonderful increase in the power of consumption by this country? Can any thing more forcibly illustrate that general position to which I have already adverted, and which cannot be too strongly impressed on those who legislate for the interests of commerce and industry – that the means which lead to increased consumption, and which are the foundation, as that consumption is the proof, of our prosperity, will be most effectually promoted by an unrestrained competition, not only between the capital and industry, of different classes in the same country, but also by extending that competition, as much as possible to all other countries.

The present rates of duty on foreign woolens vary from 50*l*. to 67*l*. 10*s*. per cent. I am satisfied that 15*l*. per cent will answer every purpose of reasonable and fair protection; and this is the reduction, therefore, which I intend to submit to the committee.

The next great branch of manufacture is that of linens: – this also has been the object of more nursing and interference than were good for its healthy and vigorous growth. But not to weary the committee with details, I will proceed at once to state, that the present duties, which are very complicated, fluctuate from 40*l.* to 180*l.* per cent, and that I propose to simplify and reduce them, by putting them all at 25*l.* per cent.

In like manner, the duties on paper, which are now altogether prohibitory, I propose to reduce, so that they shall not exceed double the amount of the excise duty payable upon that article manufactured in this country. This reduction will extend to printed books, which now pay, if in any way bound, 6*l.* 10*s.* and, if unbound, 5*l.* the cwt. The amount of these duties is sufficient, as I have been assured, to lead to the smuggling of books printed abroad; and I am sure that, for the character of this country – for the interests of science and literature – the importation of foreign works, which do not interfere with any copyright in England, ought not to be discouraged. I should, therefore, propose to lower these duties regard being had to copyrights, which may require specific provisions, to 3*l.* 10*s.* and 3*l.* respectively.

Upon glass, the present duty, which is 80*l.*, I propose to lower to 20*l.* per cent; and, instead of the heavy duty, so justly complained of, upon common glass bottles, amounting to 16*s.* 2*d.* a dozen (which, now that wine is reduced in price, amounts in many cases to more than half its value), I intend to recommend a duty of three shillings only.

Upon all descriptions of foreign earthenware, an article with which we supply so many other countries, the present duty is 75*l.* per cent; the effect of which is, that ornamented porcelain is abundantly smuggled from the continent. I propose to reduce the duty on earthenware, and plain porcelain goods to 15*l.*, and upon porcelain, gilt, or ornamented, to 30*l.* per cent; which is quite as much as can be demanded, without throwing this branch of import into the hands of the smuggler.

To foreign gloves, another manufacture, now altogether prohibited, but which are to be bought in every shop, I apply the same observation, and the same measure of duty, 30*l.* per cent.

I now come to the metallic substances. – The amount of the reduction which I propose upon Iron, from 6*l.* 10*s.* to 1*l.* 10*s.* a ton, has already been stated by my right hon. friend the chancellor of the Exchequer. It afforded me great satisfaction, on that occasion, to hear the liberal sentiments avowed by a worthy alderman (Thompson), who is very extensively concerned in the iron works of this country. His unqualified approbation of this important change, I had flattered myself, would have been echoed by all the other iron masters: but in this expectation I have been disappointed. Deputations from the mining districts have since been at the Board of Trade. I have heard their representations – but I have not been convinced by them. I am bound to say, that they fully partake of the character of nearly all the communications (and they are many) which I have received from those whose interests in manufacture or trade are affected, or likely, in their apprehensions, to be affected, by the changes which I am now submitting to the committee. They are all great advocates for free trade generally, all alike forward in their approbation of the principles on which the government is now acting; but each has some reason to assign, quite conclusive, I have no doubt, in his own mind, why his peculiar calling should be made an exception. All these special reasons, I own, have only satisfied me, that the general rule of free competition is the best for all trades, as it is certainly the best for the public; though I can quite understand, that a privilege or monopoly given to any one branch, whilst it is denied to all others, might be an advantage to that particular trade. But is it fit that in an article like iron, of universal use in all our manufactures, in all the arts and conveniences of life, in agriculture, in houses, in ships, we should now be suffering from a scarcity of that metal? That we should submit to have every article, in which it is used, greatly increased in price, as well as deteriorated, perhaps, in quality, on account of the enormous duty imposed upon foreign iron, not for the purpose of revenue, but for that of protection – a duty which amounts nearly to a monopoly in favour of the British iron masters? Has not the price of British iron, of late, been almost doubled? Have not all the iron masters demands for iron beyond what they can supply? Is there no risk or danger to our hardware manufactures at Birmingham and Sheffield, from this state of things? Can they execute the orders which they receive from abroad, if iron continues at its present price, or is to rise still higher? How many thousand workmen will be thrown out of employ, if this branch of trade be lost to this country? Is there no reason to apprehend its being transferred to Germany, the Netherlands, and other parts of the continent? I have been assured, upon authority not likely to mislead me, that very extensive orders, which have lately been received at Birmingham from the United States, and other parts, have been refused, because the great rise in the price of iron does not admit of the articles being made within the limits specified in those orders. And what is the consequence? They are transferred to the continent; and the share of this country in their execution, is confined to making the models and drawings, which are prepared here, for the guidance of the foreign artificers. It is, therefore, of the greatest importance, that the duties on foreign iron should be reduced, in reference, not only to the interests of the consumer in this country, but also to the well-being of those numerous classes who are employed in all the manufactures of this metal for foreign countries. The necessity of this reduction becomes the more urgent, from the fact, that, at this time, the whole produce of the British mines is not adequate to supply the present demand. But, quite independent of this evil, which may be temporary, I own it appears to me, that it would be of great advantage to the manufactures of this country to be able to procure foreign iron, particularly that of Sweden, on easy terms. Swedish iron is known to be superior to our own; its admixture with British iron would improve the quality of our manufactures; they would be held in higher estimation, and not only be able to command a more decided preference in foreign markets, but become more valuable for all the purposes to which iron is applied in our domestic consumption. – Take, for instance, the important article of iron cables now so generally used by our shipping; it will not be denied that, by a due proportion of Swedish iron in their composition, their strength and tenacity would be improved. Here, then, an important advantage to our naval interests, connected too with the safety of every ship using iron cables, is directly counteracted by the present high duties on foreign iron. The result of its more free admission, I am persuaded, will be, not only to check those extreme fluctuations, which, of late years, we have witnessed in the price of iron – at one time so low as to be ruinous to the producer, at another so high, as to be greatly distressing to all the other interests of the country – but also by the improvements to which it will lead, to extend the use and consumption of manufactured iron (the bulk of which will always be our own) both at home and abroad. This increased demand, joined to a more steady price, will, ere long, more than compensate to the British iron masters the temporary inconvenience, if any, which some of them apprehend from the extent to which it is proposed to carry the reduction of this duty.

The next metal upon which I have to propose a reduction, is copper. The duty, which in 1790 did not exceed 10*l.*, now amounts to 54*l.* a ton. This high duty is not less injurious to the manufacturer than the high duty on iron. Now, if the price of our copper manufactures is to exceed that of the like articles of foreign manufacture, in any thing like a proportion to this enormous duty, it is evident, that, even assuming some superiority in the skill of our workmen, we must ultimately be driven from the markets of other countries. The quantity of copper produced by the English mines amounts to about 10,000 tons annually, of which something less than one-half suffices for the home consumption. This being the proportion, do not the owners of copper mines see, that if, by the high price at which the manufacturer buys copper, he should lose his hold upon the foreign market, they must be injured by the effects of their own monopoly? The annual supply required would then be diminished to less than 5,000 tons; and they would, therefore, run the risk of losing more by the continuance of the present high duties, than by the repeal of them. These prohibitory duties have already, in my judgment, been attended with serious injury. They have prevented copper, not only in an unmanufactured, but in an imperfectly smelted state, from coming into this country. This metal exists in great abundance, not only in several parts of Europe, but also in some of the new States of America. It would have been sent here, as it used to be, in an imperfect state, in payment for British manufactures. Here is would have undergone the process of purifying, of rolling, or of being otherwise prepared for consumption, by the means of our superior machinery, had it not been kept away by impolitic restrictions. They operated as a bounty upon the transfer of our capital to other countries, and as a premium to encourage the inhabitants of those countries to do for themselves that which, greatly to our advantage, we should otherwise have continued to do for them. At the same time I am aware, that considerable capitals have been invested in our copper mines, under the encouragement given by the present monopoly, and how difficult it is to do all that the public interest would require, without injury to those particular interests. This, in almost every instance, is the most arduous part of the task which a sense of public duty has imposed upon me. In the present case, however, I believe that I may safely, and I hope with advantage to both parties, propose to reduce the duty on copper from 54*l.* to 27*l.* a ton; without committing myself, not to recommend, at a future period, even a further reduction, if it should appear that the present limit is not sufficient to enable our manufacturers to preserve their foreign market, and that, at a lower rate of duty, no great or sudden check would be given to the British mines.

There is another metallic substance, in some degree connected with the copper manufacture, the duty upon which ought to be considerably lowered. – I mean zinc, commonly known in trade under the name of spelter. This semi-metal enters, in the proportion of about one-third, I understand, into the composition of brass. The selling price of spelter, on the continent, is about 20*l.* a ton, here about 45*l.*, and the duty is 28*l.* Now, with a duty upon copper of 54*l.* a ton, and upon spelter of 28*l.*, what chance can we have of maintaining a footing in the foreign market for any description of brass wares? None: – and accordingly I am assured that, at this moment, our briskest demand in this trade is in the preparation of moulds and patterns for the foreign manufacturer. Upon spelter, I shall propose to reduce the duty full one half. I feel that I ought to go still lower, and perhaps I shall, after making further inquiry, in some future stage; for I am convinced that the mines of this country cannot successfully compete with those of Silesia, in which spelter is principally produced.

Upon tin, the present duty is excessive. It is an article of which we have more the command, and is of less extensive consumption. I propose, however, to reduce the duty more than one half – from 5*l.* 9*s.* 3*d.* to 2*l.* 10*s.* the cwt.

The duty on lead is now 20*l.* per cent ad valorem; this I propose to lower to 15*l.*, which, I hope, will be sufficient to admit of a foreign import, and to check the present exorbitant price of that metal. If I shall find, upon further investigation, that this is not likely to be the case, I shall reserve to myself to suggest, on some future stage, a further reduction in this duty also.

There are several other enumerated articles in the Book of Rates, upon which I propose to reduce the duties upon the same principle. I should only weary the committee by going through the detail of these alterations – they will be found in the schedule annexed to one of the resolutions which I shall submit for their consideration. Perhaps, however, I ought to state that, although every thing which can, by any accident, be considered as an object of jealousy to any of our manufactures, is enumerated by name in the Book of Rates, there are other things not directly connected with trade or merchandize, but with art, science, and literature, and deriving their value solely from such connexion, which, whenever they are brought into this country, cost the person who imports them 50*l.* per cent on their estimated value, under a sweeping clause, at the end of that book, which provides, that upon all goods, wares, and merchandize, being, either in part or wholly, manufactured, and not enumerated, a duty of 50*l.* per cent shall be payable, and a duty of 20*l.* per cent upon all non-enumerated goods, not being either in part or wholly manufactured. Now this duty of 50*l.* per cent, of little value to the Exchequer, and attaching principally upon such objects as I have adverted to, is, I am sure, one which the committee will concur with me in thinking ought to be reduced. The instances, in which this high duty attaches on articles of curiosity and interest, are not very numerous; they are sometimes ludicrous, perhaps, but not very creditable to the good taste and character of this country. One instance, which I recollect to have heard, I will mention. A gentleman imported a mummy from Egypt. The officers of the customs were not a little puzzled by this non-enumerated article. These remains of mortality, muscles and sinews, pickled and preserved three thousand years ago, could not be deemed a raw material; and therefore, upon deliberation, it was determined to tax them as a manufactured article. The importer, anxious that his mummy should not be seized, stated its value at 400*l.* The declaration cost him 200*l.*, being at the rate of 50*l.* per cent on the manufactured merchandize which he was about to import. I propose to reduce the duty on manufactured articles, not enumerated, from 50*l.* to 20*l.*, and on articles unmanufactured, from 20*l.* to 10*l.* per cent.

The result of the alterations, which I have now stated to the committee, will be this – that upon foreign manufactured articles generally, where the duty is imposed to protect our own manufactures, and not for the purpose of collecting revenue, that duty will, in no instance, exceed 30*l.* per cent. If the article be not manufactured much cheaper or much better abroad than at home, such a duty is ample for protection. If it be manufactured so much cheaper, or so much better abroad, as to render 30*l.* per cent. insufficient, my answer is, first, that a greater protection is only a premium to the smuggler; and, secondly, that there is no wisdom in attempting to bolster up a competition, which this degree of protection will not sustain. Let the state have the tax, which is now the reward of the smuggler, and let the consumer have the better and cheaper article, without the painful consciousness that he is consulting his own convenience at the expense of daily violating the laws of his country. When my right hon. friend, the chancellor of the Exchequer, is labouring to put an end, as fast as he can, to the evils of smuggling, by lowering the duties, increased during the pressure of the war, and for the purposes of revenue, upon articles of consumption, the last thing which we ought to countenance, is the continuance of high duties, not for the benefit of the Exchequer, but for the supposed protection of certain branches of manufacture. Is the illicit importation of foreign spirits to be checked, merely to give fresh life to the smuggling of cambrics and lace from Flanders, or of gloves and porcelain from France? I cannot think that gentlemen are aware to what an extent all the moral evils of smuggling are encouraged by the prohibition of these comparatively petty articles. Let any one go down to Brighton, and wander on the coast from thence to Hastings; I will undertake to say, that he shall most easily find, at every place he comes to, persons who will engage to deliver to him, within ten days or a fortnight, any prohibited article of manufacture, which he can name, and almost in any quantity, upon an advance of 30*l.* per cent beyond the prime cost at Paris. What is the consequence of such a system? A number of families, that would otherwise be valuable and industrious members of society, exist, and train up their children, in a state of perpetual warfare with the law, till they insensibly acquire the habits and feelings of outlaws, standing rather in the relation of pirates, than of fellow-subjects, to the rest of the community. And is this abominable system to be tolerated, not from any over-ruling necessity of upholding the revenue, nay, possibly, to the injury of the Exchequer, but merely because, in a few secondary branches of manufacture, we do not posses the same natural advantages, or the same degree of skill, as our neighbours? If cambrics are made better at Valenciennes, is that a sufficient reason for imposing a prohibitory duty on all linens; a duty from which the revenue gets next to nothing, whilst the country is full of the proscribed article? If certain descriptions of paper for engraving are made more perfect in France, are we always to be condemned to the use of an inferior and dearer article of home manufacture? The time has been, when it was found quite a sufficient reason for imposing a prohibitory duty upon a foreign article, that it was better than we could make at home; but, I trust, when such calls are made upon this House hereafter, our first answer at least will be, let us see what can be done by competition; first try to imitate, and by and by, perhaps, you will surpass your foreign rival. This is the feeling, this is the hope and the emulation which we have now created in the silk trade; and, I believe, with a very reasonable prospect of the most complete success. But this feeling would never have been called forth under the old and helpless system of prohibitory protection. Prohibitions, in fact, are a premium to mediocrity. They destroy the best incentive to excellence, the best stimulus to invention and improvement. They condemn the community to suffer, both in price and quality, all the evils of monopoly, except in so far as a remedy can be found in the baneful arts of the smuggler. They have also another of the great evils of monopoly, that of exposing the consumer, as well as the dealer, to rapid and inconvenient fluctuations in price.

With the knowledge of this fact, that we furnish, in a proportion far exceeding the supply from any other country, the general markets of the world, with all the leading articles of manufacture, upon which I have now proposed greatly to lower the duties, I own that I am not afraid of this country being overwhelmed with foreign goods. Some, I know, will come in, which are now excluded; I shall be glad of it. In various ways, their admission will be beneficial to the general interests of the country. That it cannot be extensively injurious to any of those interests, may be inferred, not only from the arguments with which I have already troubled the committee, but from actual experience. In the year 1786, we entered into a commercial treaty with France. Under the stipulations of that treaty, the cottons and woollens of France were admitted into this country, upon a duty of 12*l.* per cent. – I now propose for the latter 15*l.* Hardware, cutlery, turnery, &c. upon a duty of 10*l.*, I now propose 20*l.* per cent. Pottery, and glass, &c. under a duty of 12*l.* – I now propose 15*l.* upon the former, and 20*l.* upon the latter. What was the result of this treaty? We sent goods of various descriptions to the French market, and England was supplied with other goods of French production; but no injury accrued – no check was given to any particular branch of our staple manufactures, in consequence of this interchange. One advantage arising from it was, to create a spirit of emulation, an instance of which occurred in the woollen trade. Soon after the opening of the intercourse between the two countries, French cloths of a fine quality were imported in considerable quantity. – They were preferred to our own. No fashionable man was to be seen without a coat of French cloth. What followed? In less than two years, the cloth of our own manufactures became equal to that imported from France; the one could not be distinguished from the other; and coats of French cloth were still the fashion, whilst the cloth of which they were made was manufactured in this country. In like manner, we shall now, in all probability, import some printed cottons from Alsace and Switzerland, of richer and brighter colours than our own; some fancy muslins from India; some silk stuffs, some porcelain from France, objects for which curiosity or fashion may create a demand in this metropolis; but they will not interfere with those articles of more side and universal consumption, which our own manufactures supply cheaper and better; whilst they will excite the ingenuity of our artists and workmen, to attempt improvements, which may enable them to enter the lists with the foreigner, in those very articles in which he has now an acknowledged superiority.

I know it may be objected, that a great change has taken place, in the situation of the British manufactures, since the French treaty of 1786, that we have been engaged in a long and expensive war, and that we have now to support the weight of a great many new and heavy taxes. I admit that such is the case: other countries, however, have not been exempted from the calamities of war; their taxes, too, have been increased; their burthens made to press more heavily. What is still more mischievous, in most of those countries, their commercial and manufacturing establishments have felt more directly the ravages and interruption of war; many of them have been violently swept away; whilst the capitals which they had called forth, if not confiscated, have been impaired or diminished, by the exactions of military power. In this country no such calamity has been experienced. The trading capital of England remains entire; even during the war, it continued constantly increasing; and in respect to the comparative cheapness of labour in foreign countries, although by no means an immaterial part of the present consideration, it is not alone sufficient, as experience has shown, to make the balance preponderate in their favour. Since the invention of the steam engine, coupled with the application of so many other discoveries, both in mechanical and chemical science, to all the arts of life, the mere estimate of manual labour is lost sight of in comparison with that of the creative powers of mind. It is the union of those powers, and of the great capitals which call them into action, which distinguishes British industry, and has placed it in the commanding situation which it now holds in the world. To these advantages, are joined that energy and continuity of enterprise, that perseverance and steadiness of exertion, which, even by our rivals, are admitted to belong to the English character. It is upon these qualities, and these advantages, much more than upon any system of bounties and protecting duties, that I rely with confidence, for the maintenance and improvement of the station which we now occupy, among the trading communities of the world.

I expect further to be told, as a general objection to the course which I now recommend – Indeed I have already been told, in the correspondence which I have felt it right to hold with some of our most intelligent and accomplished merchants and manufacturers on this subject, before I brought it before this committee – that in 1786, we had insured from France, by treaty, a reciprocity of commercial advantages; but that, at present, we have made no such arrangement. This objection, I admit, in one respect, deserves consideration. I mean in its relation to the foreign market – with regard to the danger of our being undersold in our own market, it does not hold at all. Now, in respect to our deferring any improvement in our own commercial system, until we can persuade foreign States to view it as a concession to them, which we are ready to make in return for similar concessions on their part, I cannot, I own, discover much wisdom in such a line of policy; but, as I have already stated that I had corresponded with others on this part of the subject, I am sure it will be an acceptable relief to the committee (wearied as they must be with hearing me), if I substitute, for

180   *Battles over Free Trade, Volume 1*

my own arguments, the more forcible reasoning of one of my correspondents, a gentleman deeply concerned as a manufacturer and a merchant, who unites to great practical knowledge a vigorous understanding, of which he has formerly given proofs in this House, which must make us all regret that he is no longer a member of it; I mean Mr. Kirkman Finlay. I received from him a letter, dated the 18th of February, of which the following is an extract:

'Subscribing, as I do, to every one of the advantages stated in your letter, I will not occupy your time by going further into the subject; at the same time, I must not lead you to suppose that such a measure is likely to be adopted, without some opposition from manufacturers, who have all their old prejudices to remove before they can subscribe, in their own case, to the sound principles of free commercial intercourse, which you are, so much to the public advantage, endeavouring to establish. Believe me, that no one takes a deeper interest than I do in the success of all such measures; and I am certain that the adoption of such a plan as we are now talking of, will go far in its consequences, to satisfy persons both at home and abroad, of the benefits that will arise to all countries from the general establishment of such measures. It is no doubt true, that it will be argued that such concessions ought not to be granted to foreign States, without being accompanied by some stipulation for the admission into their consumption of some of our produce or manufactures, on the payment of a moderate duty. But in my view of the case, we ought not to suffer ourselves to be influenced by such reasoning, since our whole object being to benefit ourselves, our inquiry is naturally confined to the consideration of whether such a mode of acting be really advantageous, independent altogether of what may be done by the governments of other countries. Now, if the measure be really beneficial to us, why shall we withhold from ourselves an advantage, because other States are not yet advanced so far as we are in the knowledge of their own interests, or have not attained the power of carrying their own views into practice?'

In the last sentence of this letter, the writer has, I believe, stated the real grounds which may still, for some time, prevent foreign States from following our example, namely, 'their ignorance of their own true interests, or their incompetence to carry their own views into effect.' But let my right hon. friend, the chancellor of the Exchequer, continue his good practice of coming down to this House, session after session, to accumulate fresh proofs, that the removal of restrictive impositions and excessive duties is not diminution, but, frequently, increase of revenue:–Let foreign countries see him, year after year (and I hope he will long be able to do so), largely remitting public burthens, and at the same time exhibiting a prosperous Exchequer, still flowing to the same perennial level; and, I have no doubt, when the governments of the continent shall have contemplated, for a few years longer, the happy consequences of the system in which we are now proceeding, that their eyes will be opened. They will, then, believe – but, at present they do not – that we are sincere and consistent in our principles; and, for their own advantage, they will, then, imitate us in our present course, as they have, of late, been adopting our cast-off system of restrictions and prohibitions. That they have, hitherto, suspected our sincerity, and looked upon our professions as lures to ensnare them, is not very surprising, when they compared those professions with that code of prohibition which I am now endeavouring to pare down and modify to a scale of moderate duties. At the same time, as a stimulus to other countries to adopt principles of reciprocity, I shall think it right, to reserve a power of making an addition of one-fifth to the proposed duties, upon the productions of those countries which may refuse, upon a tender by us of the like advantages, to place our commerce and navigation upon the footing of the most favoured nation. I need scarcely add, that no part of these arrangements will interfere with the power of the Crown, to enter into specific treaties of commerce with the particular States, by which treaties, the duties now proposed may be still further varied or modified, subject always to the approbation of parliament.

Having now stated the alterations which I intend to propose, with regard to the protecting and prohibitory duties, I have only to add that, with a view to give the British manufacturer every fair advantage in the competition with which he has to contend in the foreign market, it is desirable to consider how far this object can be promoted, by a reduction of some of the duties now levied upon the raw materials, which he is obliged to use in his manufacture.

During the exigencies of the late war, duties were laid, or increased, upon various articles used in dyeing. The revenue derived from these duties is not considerable: but in proportion to the amount of the charge, must be the increased price of the manufactured commodity. Be that charge, upon our woollen cloths, for instance, only 1 or 2 per cent, even this small addition in the present open competition of the foreign market, may turn the scale against us, and ought therefore, to be withdrawn. On most of the articles in question, I shall propose a large reduction in the existing rate of duty. They are so numerous that I shall not weary the patience of the committee, by mentioning them specifically: they will all be found in the schedule, which will form part of the intended resolutions. To one or two articles, however, not included under the class of dyeing drugs, I must beg leave shortly to refer. Olive oil is very much used in the manufacture of the finer woollen cloths. – The duty upon it was somewhat more than doubled during the war. I propose to reduce it to a rate rather below that of the year 1790; from 15*l.* 13*s.* the present duty, to 7*l.* a ton. This will be a great relief to the manufacturer. There is another species of oil, extracted from rape seed, largely used in the preparation of the coarse woollens, upon which I also propose to give relief. The committee may, perhaps, recollect that a few years ago, when the panic of agricultural distress was in full force – when fears were openly expressed in this House, that England must cease to grow corn, (and fear it is said, is seldom a wise counsellor) it was suggested, that the raising of rape seed might become a profitable substitute; and, upon this suggestion, a duty, almost prohibitory, was laid on foreign seed, which till then had been imported free from any charge. This measure, of which the benefit, if beneficial at all, was confined to a very few districts of the kingdom, has certainly contributed nothing to the revival of our agriculture, but it has, in various ways, been attended with detriment to our manufactures. It has greatly injured the manufacture of rape oil and rape cake in this country, and it has increased the price of the former to the woollen trade. The cake, indeed, being wanted for agricultural purposes, is allowed to come in from abroad nearly duty free; so that, in this instance, and to this extent, our recent policy has been, to prohibit the raw material and to encourage its importation in a manufactured state. I propose to revert to our ancient policy in respect to this article; and, after giving a certain time to the dealers to get rid of their stock in hand, to allow the free importation of rape seed, upon a duty which will be merely nominal. The only other article, which I think it necessary to mention, is Wool. The duty is now one penny a pound upon all foreign wool. It has been stated to me, that even this rate of duty presses severely upon the manufacturers of coarse woollens, in which we have most to fear from foreign competition, and that considerable relief would be afforded by reducing it to one half, upon all wool, not exceeding the value of one shilling a pound. I therefore propose to make this alteration, by which, I am assured, the quantity of coarse wool imported into this country, to be mixed in the manufacture with our own long wool, is likely to be greatly increased.

All these reductions I consider to be right and proper in principle; but, as measures calculated to afford encouragement and assistance to our manufactures, I am particularly anxious to propose them at the same time when I am bringing forward other measures not unlikely, till better understood, to excite alarm in particular quarters. Some of the duties which I am now dealing with, I am aware, were imposed for the purposes of revenue; it may, therefore, be thought, that in repealing them, I am travelling out of my own department, and encroaching, in some degree, upon that of the chancellor of the Exchequer. But my right hon. friend, I have no doubt, will forgive me where the pecuniary sacrifice is trifling, and the relief to our manufactures the more important consideration. He, I am sure, will allow me to consider myself, however humble, as a fellow-labourer with him in the same vineyard. Whilst I am pruning away the useless and unsound branches, which bear at best, but a scanty and bad crop, my object is to draw forth new and vigorous shoots, likely to afford better and more abundant fruit; the harvest of which, I trust, it will be his lot hereafter to present, to his applauding country, in the shape of further relief from taxation.

I now come to the last of the three heads, into which I have divided the subject, to be submitted to the committee – the means of affording some further

Huskisson, Speech on the 'Foreign Commerce of the Country' (1825)

encouragement to the shipping and navigation of the empire. There is already a bill on the table which will contribute very essentially to the relief of that important interest. I mean the bill which repeals all the quarantine duties. They operated as a very considerable burthen, unfairly placed on the particular ships and goods which were compelled to perform quarantine. This was a precaution adopted, not for the special advantage of those engaged in any particular trade – on the contrary, to them the detention and loss of time were great inconveniences however unavoidable – but for the general protection and safety of the community. The committee of Foreign Trade was, therefore, perfectly justified in recommending that the expense of quarantine should be borne by the country at large, and not by any particular class in it; and a bill has been brought in, accordingly by my right hon. friend, the vice president of the Board of Trade. Another measure of substantial relief, now in contemplation, I have already mentioned to the House, but I am convinced, from the communications which I have since received, that I, then, underrated its importance. That measure is the abolition of fees upon shipping and trade in our colonies. Besides the vexation and liability to abuse, inseparable from the present system, I know that in many instances, the fees alone, upon a ship and cargo, amount to much more than all the public duties collected upon the same.

The next measure, which I have to propose, is the repeal of the Stamp duty now payable upon the transfer of a whole ship, or of any share in a ship, from one person to another. A ship, I believe, is the only chattel upon which a duty of this sort attaches, as often as it changes hands. I can trace no reason for this anomaly, except one, which ought rather to be a plea for exemption. From motives of state policy, we compel the owner, or part owner of any ship, to register his interest or share therein. From this registry the ship-owner derives no advantage – on the contrary, however improved the forms and regulations now observed, it is at best to him troublesome, and more or less obnoxious to litigation. By consolidating and amending the registry laws, I have done every thing in my power to mitigate these inconveniences, but still every transfer must be registered. Now, to take advantage of a law, which compels the names of all owners to be registered, in order to attach a heavy stamp duty on every transfer that may be made in the owner-ship, is an unnecessary aggravation of a necessary inconvenience, and in itself a great injustice. I shall, therefore, submit a resolution for abolishing the whole of this transfer duty upon shipping, by which I shall, at once, relieve the owners of this description of property from a partial tax, and from some degree of annoyance.

There is also another stamp duty, in respect to which I am anxious to afford relief. I mean the duty on debentures for the payment of drawbacks, and on bonds, given by the merchants, for the due delivery of the goods which they have declared for exportation. I propose this relief, partly upon the same principle as that which I have stated in respect to the transfer of ships. These bonds are not entered into

184 *Battles over Free Trade, Volume 1*

for the benefit of the merchant, but for the security of the revenue; besides, from their being ad valorem stamps, they frequently lead to great abuses and perjury. I will not trouble the committee with details upon this subject. I propose to reduce these stamps to a fixed duty of only 5s. upon each instrument.

As connected with the same subject – the relief of our commerce and shipping from direct pecuniary charges – I beg leave now to call the attention of the committee to the change which I shall propose in the system of our consular establishments in foreign ports. These establishments are regulated by no fixed principle, in respect to the mode of remunerating the individuals employed in this branch of the public service. In one port, the consul receives a salary – in another he is paid exclusively by fees – in a third, he receives both a salary and fees. There is no general rule in this respect, applicable even to the whole of the same country. The consuls at Havre and Marseilles have no salaries. The consul at Bourdeaux has a salary, and is allowed fees. The consul at Antwerp has a salary. The consul at Rotterdam has none. The consul at Stettin has a salary. The consul at Danzig none. At Madeira the consul has a salary – at the Azores none. The scale of fees, the principle upon which they are levied, the authority for enforcing their payment, and the mode of levying them, appear to be quite as various and unsettled as the mode of remuneration. In some ports, the fees attach upon the vessel – in others, upon the merchandize. In some ports, vessels pay all alike, without regard to their tonnage – in others, the fees are rated in proportion to the size of the vessel. In some ports, again, the fees are an ad valorem charge upon the cargo – in others, so much per ton upon the freight, without regard to its value. Now not only all this discrepancy in the details of the same establishment cannot be right, and would require revision; but I am of opinion, that the whole principle of providing for our consuls, by authorising them to levy a tax upon the shipping and commerce of the country is wrong. In the first place, the foreign trade of the country is one of its great public interests, and as much entitled to be protected at the public expense, as far as it wants protection in foreign countries, as any other great interest. In the next place, in the performance of many of the duties for which consuls are appointed, the ship-owner and merchant have no direct or exclusive interest. The navigation laws, the quarantine laws, instead of being advantageous, are inconveniently restrictive to trade; yet to these it is the peculiar duty of the consuls to attend. They have other essential duties to discharge, in which the merchant and the ship-owner have no interest distinct from that of the whole community. It therefore appears to me, that it would be just as reasonable to tax English travellers in foreign countries, for the support of our political missions, by which they are protected, as it is to tax the shipping or the trade for the payment of our consular establishments. My object is, to grant to all our consuls fixed and moderate salaries, to be paid out of the public purse; such salaries to vary, of course, according to the importance and responsibility of the station, to the country in which the consul may reside, and to other circumstances, which must, from time to time, come under the consideration of the government. In the civil list, which is granted for the life of the sovereign, a sum of 40,000*l.* is allotted for the payment of consular expenses. A considerable part of this sum is required for the salaries of certain officers, designated as consuls, but who are, at the same time, diplomatic agents: I mean our residents at Algiers, and the other courts on the coast of Africa, in the Mediterranean. As the remainder of this sum will fall far short of what will be necessary for the payment of the whole consular charge, I propose that the difference should be voted annually by this House, upon estimates to be laid before us by the proper department.

If this change should be approved of by the House, the effect will be the abolition, generally, of all the present fees payable to our consuls, either upon ships or goods, in foreign ports. Certain small fees would still remain for personal acts that a consul may be called upon to perform, such as notarial instruments, and other documents to which his attestation or signature may be required. Those fees will be specified in the bill, and will be reduced to the most moderate amount. In regard to another expense, provided for, in certain ports, by a tax upon shipping – I mean the maintenance of a place of worship, the payment of a chaplain, and other charges of that description – I trust that the British merchants and inhabitants residing at, or resorting to, those ports, will find no difficulty in raising, by a small voluntary rate among themselves, a sufficient sum for these purposes. But, as an encouragement to them to provide the means of performing the important duties of religion, I shall propose, in the bill, to give a power to the government, to advance a sum equal to the amount of any subscription which may be so raised, either for erecting a place of worship, providing a burial ground, or allotting a suitable salary to a chaplain, in any foreign port, where a British consul may reside.

Having now stated the outlines of the plan, which I have to propose, for the improvement of our consular system, it only remains for me to mention one other subject, in immediate connexion with it, and certainly of great importance to a very valuable branch of our foreign trade – I mean, our trade to those countries, which are known under the name of the Levant. This trade was placed under the direction of a chartered company, so far back as the reign of James 1st. Great privileges were conferred upon that company; and they had also important duties to perform. Among their privileges, they were allowed to appoint all the consuls to the Levant, and to levy considerable duties on all British ships resorting to those countries, for the maintenance of those consuls, and the other expenses of their establishment. They also obtained, partly by acts of parliament, and partly by treaty and concession from the Porte, the right of exercising, by their agents and consuls, a very extensive jurisdiction over all British subjects in the Turkish dominions. These powers and trusts have been exercised by the serv-

186   *Battles over Free Trade, Volume 1*

ants of the company, for two centuries, often under very difficult circumstances; and, generally speaking, with great correctness, fidelity, and discretion. In the present state, however, of a great part of the countries in which these consuls reside, and looking, moreover, to our relations with Turkey as well as with other powers, to the delicate and important questions of international law, which must constantly arise out of the intercourse of commerce with a country in a state of civil war – questions involving discussions, not only with the contending parties in that country, but with other trading and neutral powers – it is impossible not to feel that, upon political considerations alone, it is highly expedient that the public servants of this country, in Turkey, should hold their appointments from the Crown. It is to the Crown that foreign powers will naturally look for regulating and controlling the conduct of those officers in the exercise of their authority; and it is certainly most fit, not only on this account, but for the due maintenance of that authority, that they should be named, not by a trading company, however respectable, but, like other consuls, directly by the Crown, advised, as it must be in their selection, by its responsible servants.

If this change in the mode of appointing the consuls in the Levant, be called for upon political grounds, it would be highly absurd not to take advantage of the occasion to bring them, in all other respects, under the regulations of the new consular establishment. It becomes the more important not to neglect this opportunity of affording relief to the Levant trade, as the dues, which the company is authorized to levy, are very considerable, amounting to a tax not much short of two per cent upon the whole of that trade; a charge quite sufficient, in these times, to divert a considerable part of it from the shipping of this country to that of other states. It is due to the noble lord (lord Grenville), who is at the head of the Levant company, to state, that, as soon as this subject was brought under his consideration, he manifested the greatest readiness to assist the views of government in respect to the proposed changes. Nothing less was to be expected from this distinguished individual, who, in his dignified retirement, still interests himself, with the feelings of a statesman, and the wisdom of a philosopher, in the progress of those sound commercial principles, which, in their application, have already conferred so much benefit upon this country. This noble lord called together the company over which he presides, and proposed to them a voluntary surrender of the charter which they had enjoyed for two hundred years. In the most praiseworthy manner, the company acquiesced in this suggestion. His majesty will be advised to accept the surrender so tendered; but it cannot be carried into effect without an act of parliament. Among other requisite arrangements to be provided for by the bill, will be the transfer of a fund which the company has accumulated out of their revenue, and the abolition of the taxes by which that revenue was produced.

I have now travelled over the wide field of the alterations, which I undertook to submit to the committee, in the commercial concerns of this country. I wish that my statement, to many members of this House comparatively uninteresting, had been more perspicuous, for the sake of those who have paid attention to this subject. I was desirous to bring it under consideration, before the recess, in order that the details might be dispassionately and generally considered by the several interests, throughout the country, which are likely to be affected by the measures which I have now proposed. They are open to alterations, and to amendment. I shall be happy to pay every attention in my power, to whatever suggestions may be transmitted to me, from any quarter, for this purpose. All I ask now of the committee is, to take under their protection the comprehensive principle of the system which I have ventured to recommend, and that, so far, they will look upon it as a state measure, connected with the public prosperity. If, to this extent, it shall receive their steady countenance and support, this session will not close without our having proved to this, as well as to other countries, that we have not lost sight of the recommendation from the throne – to remove as much, and as fast, as possible, all unnecessary restrictions upon trade. – The right hon. gentleman concluded, amidst loud cheers, with moving his first Resolution.

188   *Battles over Free Trade, Volume 1*

Vote of Thanks from Manchester Chamber of Commerce to Huskisson, 16 July 1828; and Huskisson to Manchester Chamber of Commerce, 20 July 1828, in *The Speeches of the Right Honourable William Huskisson, with a Biographical Memoir*, 3 vols (London: John Murray, 1831), vol. 1, pp. 174–7.

'Manchester Chamber of Commerce and Manufactures,
'SIR:

'July 16th, 1828.

'I have the honour to transmit a Vote of Thanks, from the Directors of this Chamber, expressive of the obligations which they feel that the country is under for the services you have rendered to it, in the important offices of state which you have been successively called upon to fill.

'Of some of the measures of policy brought forward under your sanction, the Board of Directors has before expressed its favourable opinion; and although, with respect to others, its members may occasionally have entertained some degree of doubt, they are desirous, on your retirement from office, of conveying to you their honest belief, that the general scope and tendency of those measures, as a whole, have been eminently conducive to the welfare of the community at large, and demand from them the expression of their respect and gratitude.

'I feel particularly happy in being the organ of this communication, and in the opportunity thus afforded me of declaring, individually, my hearty concurrence in the sentiments of my colleagues.

'I have the honour to be, &c.
(Signed) 'GEO. WM. WOOD,
'President.'

'The Right Hon.
'Wm. Huskisson.'

'At a Meeting of the Board of Directors of the Manchester Chamber of Commerce and Manufactures, held 16th July 1828,

'GEORGE WILLIAM WOOD, Esq. President, in the Chair,

'It was resolved unanimously,

'That the Thanks of this Board be communicated to the Right Hon. William Huskisson, late Secretary of State for the Colonies, for the enlightened, judicious and valuable services which, whilst a Minister of the Crown, he has rendered to the commerce of the country – services which have had for their object the permanent prosperity of the State, and which, it is the sincere and deliberate opinion of this Board, will, in their general character and consequences, materially promote the true and lasting welfare of all classes of his Majesty's subjects.

'GEO. WM. WOOD,
'President.'

Vote of Thanks from Manchester Chamber of Commerce to Huskisson (1828) 189

To this flattering mark of approbation Mr. Huskisson returned the following answer:

'Eartham, Petworth,
'20th July 1828.

'Sir:

'Your letter of the 16th instant, transmitting to me an unanimous resolution of the Board of Directors of the Manchester Chamber of Commerce and Manufactures, was received by me yesterday.

'The unexpected honour conferred upon me by this distinguished mark of their approbation, is to me personally most gratifying.

'Greatly, however, as I value so flattering a reward of my endeavours to promote the interests and prosperity of our country, I should very inadequately convey all that I feel on this occasion, were I to confine myself to the expression of my individual thanks.

'In one sense, indeed, except to myself, it may be matter of little moment, that my labours, as a late servant of the Crown, are viewed so favourably by the Board over which you preside. But, in another sense, looking to that Board as representing the sentiments of the largest manufacturing community in the kingdom, it is, I conceive, highly important, upon public grounds, that the system of Commercial and Colonial Policy, which it has been my official duty to carry into effect, should be stamped with their deliberate sanction and concurrence, as tending, in its 'general character and consequences, materially to promote the true and lasting welfare of all classes of his Majesty's subjects.'

'In thanking you, Sir, for the very handsome manner in which you have conveyed to me the Resolution of the Board, I have to request that you will take a proper opportunity of tendering to the Directors my grateful acknowledgment of the sense which they have been pleased to express of my public conduct, and the assurance that, as a private member of Parliament, I shall, at all times, be ready to receive from them any suggestions which they may consider calculated to assist the Industry, and promote the Commerce of this country.

'I have the honour to be, &c.
(Signed) 'W. Huskisson.'

'Geo. Wm. Wood, Esq. &c. &c. &c.'

190   *Battles over Free Trade, Volume 1*

Solomon Atkinson, *The Effects of the New System of Free Trade upon our Shipping, Colonies and Commerce, Exposed, in a Letter to the Right Hon. W. Huskisson, President of the Board of Trade* (London: James Ridgway, 1827), extracts, pp. 3–8, 10–11, 13, 28–9, 39–40, 47, 50–4, 60–3.

TO THE
RIGHT HON. W. HUSKISSON.

SIR,

THE progress of knowledge in the recent commercial revolution of this country, like the progress of liberty in France during her political revolution, has been an apology for the adoption of the wildest theories. In one instance, all the excesses of the populace, and all the atrocities of factious leaders, were hailed as the elements of a state of political perfection; in the other, every change has been characterized as the march of liberality, and the triumph of intellect over the prejudices of a barbarous age.

From whatever source these commercial theories originally sprang, – whoever may claim the credit of having discovered them, – their adoption into the commercial code of this country, is, no doubt, mainly to be ascribed to your own exertions. I have observed with much anxiety, the progress of your new system; and have felt, from its commencement, that it was a most hazardous innovation on the policy of our ancestors; I have watched with the most painful interest the course of calamity, which has been evolved from its operation, and have been long convinced that the new principles you have introduced into our navigation and colonial laws, must, sooner or later, be repealed by direct or annulled by indirect legislation. But for circumstances which have recently occurred, it was not my intention to have addressed you till I was in possession of all the official returns for the year 1826, by which any illustration could have been thrown on the character and tendency of your measures; for to this year, I have always looked as the period which would practically shew whether the measures you have recommended, did contain within themselves the elements of future wealth and prosperity – or whether, as I have always believed, they were only the harbingers of distress to all, and of ruin to many, of the most important interests of the empire. Whatever merit or demerit may finally be found to belong to these changes, you will unquestionably be entitled to a considerable share of the praise or dispraise which may attach to them. If they should be found to have materially promoted our country's welfare, you will merit, and will doubtless obtain the sincere and lasting gratitude of the country, and your name will pass down to posterity in association with Burleigh, and Chatham, and Pitt. If, on the other hand, they should be found to be a series of rash experiments, undertaken without forecast, and followed up without moderation – if, in the mean time, they should produce nothing but unmingled evil; and, in the end, should lay the foundation of the decadence of the national power and the national prosperity, you must be content to be placed amongst those ministers who, meaning well to their country, had the rashness and perseverance of enthusiasm, without the practical sagacity and penetration, which alone can render it useful.

The Order in Council, prohibiting the direct trade between the United States and our West Indies, and the general tone of the negotiation which has since followed, indicate, as I am willing to hope, the return of better principles to the councils of the State. It appears to me to be just possible, that at the present moment his Majesty's Ministers may be hesitating as to whether or no they should any farther pursue that policy which they have recently adopted, and which has already produced so much mischief. At all events, it is quite certain that the present Session of Parliament will determine whether the liberal principles, so called, shall triumph over the ancient policy by which this country was governed, and under which it has risen to an unexampled degree of greatness and power.

In this state of hesitation and uncertainty, before you have completed your system by the overthrow of the landowners – while there is a possibility that the carrying trade with the West Indies, which the obstinacy of a party in the United States has opened to our shipowners, may be permanently secured to them – before the ruin of some of the most important branches of our carrying trade be fully accomplished – while there is still an opportunity, if not of retracing your measures, at all events of modifying their operation; and before the Legislature fairly sits down to confirm or abrogate your new commercial system, I have determined, at the hazard of impairing the force of my argument, to endeavour to draw your attention, and that of Parliament, to the operation of the recent changes in our colonial and navigation system, and more particularly to their effect on the carrying trade of Great Britain.

Those changes you have defended in a speech, admirable, I was going to say, for its eloquence; but undoubtedly, for its specious and cunning argument not surpassed in the whole history of parliamentary debating. As the exposition of a statesman, I have no hesitation in stating it to be in the highest degree imperfect and unsatisfactory – but as the harangue of a sophist, I would readily concede to it the most distinguished praise.

Probably no subject of paramount interest, much more one involving the existence of the British navy, ever excited so little attention within the walls of Parliament, as the alterations in our navigation laws. Posterity will scarcely believe the fact, that only eleven Members were in the House of Commons when you stood up to reply to the loud and unanimous remonstrances of the shipown-

192   *Battles over Free Trade, Volume 1*

ers of Great Britain, to rebut the charges and the facts which they adduced, and to show to the country that our navy was not, as they asserted, falling headlong into ruin, but, that it was in a state of the highest prosperity, and daily progressing in its greatness and its might.

When you denounce a system out of which has grown the grandeur of England – when you propose a new policy which rests on no better foundation than the theories of men who have no knowledge of the world; whose writings teem with error; who condemn the work of all past ages, and dream about some future state of political perfectibility to spring up when all mankind shall adopt their dogmas – when you pass from a system about which the prosperity of our country is entwined, and venture on an ocean of untried speculation – when it is manifest, from the whole course of your career, that your mind leads you to a bold, enterprising spirit of reform, rather than to that deliberate and cautious consideration, so essential to the character of a British legislator – it becomes the duty of Parliament to sift your measures with vigilance, and to receive your changes with distrust. Giving to you, Sir, the most ample credit for sincerity of purpose, I, for one, hesitate not to declare my conviction, that such is the tendency of your mind, – whether that tendency may have sprung from the early events of your life, or whether from any subsequent acquaintance with the writings of the economists, – that the nation ought to regard with the keenest jealousy any amendments which you may propose in the ancient policy of the kingdom. It has unfortunately happened, that many of your most important changes have passed as it were *sub silentio*. I need not remind you, that the new Navigation Act was hurried through the House at the close of the Session, and almost without a debate; and that the amendments it introduced were taken rather upon your authority, than on any deliberate discussion on the effects they might produce on our carrying trade and naval power, or their collateral effects on other branches of our complicated commercial relations.

That your views have met with much opposition among your colleagues in the Ministry, is, I believe, more than surmised by the public. That there are great differences of opinion amongst his Majesty's Ministers as to the policy of the measures you have recommended, and which claim their origin more immediately from yourself, I can state as a fact; and I speak from the very best authority, when I say that these differences have been matter of deep regret to yourself. I can name the individual – an individual to whom you have been much indebted for information in support of your views of commercial policy – to whom you have more than once declared how keenly you felt, and how sincerely you deplored, the opposition you had experienced in the Cabinet.

In former times, when England was governed by men who had English feelings and English prepossessions, before the cant of philosophy, and the leaven of the French revolution had infected the councils of the State, it was always a leading object with the British Government to keep up, in time of peace, a large body of able seamen. With this view, the inhabitants of the metropolis were compelled to import, coast-wise, from Newcastle, the coals which they could have been supplied with at a much cheaper rate from the inland counties. With the same view, Parliament gave bounties to the ships trading to the fisheries, which you, Sir, and your colleagues, have thought fit to put an end to, in deference to that notion of our Political Economists, that all bounties are bad. With the same object in view, bounties were formerly given on the importation of masts, timber, deals, &c., from the British Colonies in North America; and subsequently, in the same spirit, that trade was encouraged by imposing protecting duties on timber imported from the Baltic.

The *Fisheries* and the *Coal* and *Timber Trade* have always furnished the great nursery for our seamen. These branches of our navigation have been cultivated and protected as a means of national defence, and the mere question of cheapness has merged in considerations of national security. The Ministers of former times held all these great interests sacred: they regarded them as the ark of our safety, and guarded and protected them with unceasing vigilance.

If we estimate the relative value of these three great branches of the carrying-trade by the amount of tonnage they severally employ, the most important is, doubtless, the timber trade; and to that, therefore, I shall first call your attention. A series of legislative measures, beginning with the act for the alteration of the timber duties, and terminating with the 'Reciprocity of Duties Act,' have laid the foundation for the speedy annihilation of the British carrying-trade in timber ...

From whatever country we obtain our timber, it is of the very last importance that we should ourselves have the conveyance of it. If we import it from Canada, we can assure ourselves of three things – first, the exclusive conveyance of it to British shipping; second, that it will be paid for in British manufactures; and third, that this trade will very greatly add to the prosperity of these Colonies. If we import our timber from the Baltic, we may be quite as sure of the following facts: – that a very great part of it must be paid for in specie; that by far the greatest part of it will be imported in foreign ships; and that Canada will be deprived of all encouragement in its staple produce. So long as your reciprocity treaties are in force, and the present duty on Canada timber is continued, it is quite clear that the greatest part of our timber will be imported from the Baltic in foreign bottoms. Is it wise, is it consistent with the permanence of our naval power, that such a state of things should exist?

I will venture to predict, however, that this is a state of things which cannot long continue. There is, I verily believe, enough of patriotism in the country, in despite of modern fashions, to cling to our ancient means of defence, and to enforce the measures by which these means shall be preserved in their original vigour. We need no longer look to the Baltic; that source of employment is melting away like snow before a mid-day sun. But, thank God, we have yet a resource unfettered by treaty. Repeal, abrogate the duty on Canada timber; cast off that odious, that impolitic burthen, and the equilibrium will be restored. Employment will be furnished for British shipowners, a nursery will be found for British seamen, encouragement will be given to the industry and prosperity of our North American possessions, and a due check will be thrown in the way of the growth of the shipping of Northern Europe.

The rapid falling off of British shipping, and the rapid increase of foreign in the Baltic trade, is not matter of inference merely – it is matter of plain indisputable fact – of which you were, or ought to have been in possession, when you made your *exposé* to the House – which it was a great derilection [*sic*] of duty to withhold from the country ...

The more minute, Sir, and extensive our inquiries are, the more strongly and unequivocally do they lead to the conclusion, that British shipping is falling off with a rapidity that cannot fail to inspire the utmost alarm. It is quite manifest, that unless the most prompt and decided remedies be resorted to, the whole of the Baltic carrying trade, except part of our trade with Russia, will be lost to us. A great and powerful navy will rise up among our rivals, familiar with our own shores, while we ourselves shall become strangers to the navigation of the German and Baltic seas. Has the mania of universal citizenship so seized possession of your mind as to induce a belief, that we shall be at perpetual peace with these warlike nations of the north? Can you be so blind to all past history as to harbour an opinion so inconsistent with it? Do you believe that by benefits, conferred at the expense of national sacrifices we shall ever be able to smother their hostility, or conciliate their permanent friendship? Sir, you may believe it, the disciples of Bentham may believe it; the disciples of M'Culloch may believe it; the Society of Political Economists may believe it; but I never will, nor will any Englishman who entertains a just view of the means which are necessary for the defence of the Empire. I know, Sir, and so does every one who is acquainted with mankind and the world, that England can secure peace from her neighbours only when she can command it. Our green fields, our gardens, our palaces spread over the land, our cities, our harbours, our bays, have been and always will be the prey at which the national cupidity of Europe will aim, when it dares to lift a finger against us ...

If you be able to contemplate the effects, which I have been tracing, with satisfaction or indifference, I honestly confess that I cannot. I candidly own that my sympathies are more warmly excited for my own country, and my fellow citizens, than for any other country, or any other part of mankind. I do not wish to see the crust of bread taken from the mouth of the English labourer, or the English seaman, and put into the hands of a foreigner. I do not wish to see the flag of the foreigner floating proudly in our harbours, while our own ships are rotting, and our own seamen strolling idly among the wreck of our own mercantile navy. I am too much of an Englishman, and too little of a general citizen, to look either with satisfaction or apathy on this decay of the ancient and peculiar resources of the country. I have no objection to other nations becoming wealthy and industrious, like ourselves, but I cannot calmly see them come into our fields, and gather the harvest that we have sown at so much cost and toil.

Had there been any paramount irresistible necessity for this change of situation – had it been forced upon us by events which we could neither control nor oppose – had we by some vast revolution been hurled from our lofty rank among living empires, why then it would have been our duty to submit patiently to a change which we could not prevent.

Unless some means be devised whereby employment may be found for British shipping, it is clear as daylight that British ship-owners will become Prussian and American ship-owners. If they cannot employ their capital in navigating British ships, manned by British seamen, they will employ it in navigating foreign ships, manned by foreign seamen. No greater evil, I think you yourself will admit, could befall the interests of our navigation. To see our rivers and basins covered by foreign ships, put in motion by British capital, is a spectacle which could be gratifying to no one, except, perhaps, the political economists and the advocates of universal brotherhood.

Hitherto it has been the pride and the boast of Englishmen, that the mercantile navies which reposed within our harbours, or floated in our rivers, were owned by Englishmen, navigated by Englishmen, and employed in carrying the produce of English industry. Woe betide us, when this picture shall be reversed, when England shall be converted into a workshop, and her manufactures shall be carried by the foreigner!

For my own part, I am free to state that I think England is already too much of a workshop. I think we have already enough of those vast prisons, called factories, with the half-starved, and half-naked population that they feed. I should be glad to see the extension of our manufactures somewhat less an object of the exclusive care of Government. Hitherto they have helped no doubt, on the one hand, to swell the revenue largely, and to accumulate a small number of immense private fortunes; but on the other they have been the means of placing the country, several times within a few years, on the very verge of rebellion and civil war. The misery that they create, even in times of their prosperity, is immense; but during their depression it is incalculable. I could wish to see a part of these people turned to other pursuits. Our fisheries, both foreign and domestic, under due management and protection, would afford an immense field of employment – emigration to our Colonies, and the healthy pursuits of agriculture, would afford another still more exhaustless. In a word, I could wish to see our population more employed in tilling the earth, and bringing forth the riches of the ocean, and less in whisking about a shuttle, and converting cotton gossamer into cloth; I could wish to see the bulk of the population more employed in getting at the means which support and less in the arts which merely decorate the body. In short, Sir, I do not wish to see every interest in the empire made subservient to the promotion of our foreign commerce ...

I have adverted, incidentally, to the growing manufactures of the United States. Permit me, for one moment, more distinctly to call your attention to them. It is a fact – a fact of which the country is not aware, and which the government either does not or professes not to believe – a fact which ought to be impressed on the country, and forced on the attention of ministers, – that the manufactures of the United States are making the most rapid strides, – that they are most vigilantly protected and encouraged, both as well by the legislatures of the several northern states, as by the general government, – that in the course of a few years they will entirely supersede ours among themselves, – that even now, they interfere with ours in Upper Canada and South America, materially, and that they have already reached the Mediterranean, to one port of which, within the last few months 1,500 bales of American cotton goods have been sent from Boston.

Nothing can be more idle and ignorant than to talk of young countries not manufacturing for themselves. I know very well what is the philosophical cant of the day on the subject, and I feel also that it could never have been promulgated by any man who had looked into the actual business, habits and feelings of nations.

I dont [*sic*] know whether you be aware of the fact, but I can tell you that in all the northern and midland states of the American Union, shows are periodically held for exhibiting the best specimens of national manufactures, and these specimens of national ingenuity and skill are rewarded not always by a prize, but by selling these productions to some patriotic citizen at a price which abundantly gratifies both the pride and the cupidity of the manufacturer. I have been present on these occasions and have been utterly astonished at the skill and variety which have been displayed. Finer or more substantial fabrics of woolen or cotton goods, I have never seen even in England; and nothing can be more ingenious than their various specimens of cutlery and glass-work. Then again, there were models and plans, and specimens of all kinds of farming implements and household utensils, many of them admirable for facilitating the operations for which they were designed. Then again, we all know that many of the most curious inventions connected with our staple manufactures have originated in the United States. I need not go into any details on this subject; you are of course perfectly familiar with them.

I think then that the time for considering the United States as a non-manufacturing country has passed away. It behoves us to watch the progress of this branch of their industry with at least the same degree of jealousy with which they regard ours, and to meet the imposts of their tariff by corresponding regulations ...

These Northern States of Europe, whose interests and whose trade you seem so anxiously to encourage, by an act of unprecedented perfidy and ill faith, gave the first great impulse to the industry and the enterprise of our American colonies. When Bonaparte issued his Milan and Berlin decrees, our intercourse with these States was nominally put an end to. The trade was, however, carried on for some time longer by means of licences, till the year 1811, when at the command of their great master, by a sudden and simultaneous movement, they confiscated every vessel in their ports that came from this country, together with their cargoes, to the value of not less than seven millions sterling. Believing us to be dependent on them for wood and naval stores, they thought that by cutting off all communication with this country, they at once destroyed the main pillar of our strength, and that we should be compelled to make peace on any terms they should propose. The ports of the Baltic closed against us, their supplies of timber, hemp, flax, &c. suddenly suspended, what could England have done, had she not possessed colonies, from whence she could obtain the supplies which had thus been withdrawn? England must have succumbed to her enemy.

We turned to our possessions in North America, and there we found forests exhaustless, and a country boundless in extent, rich in all the facilities for producing what we wanted. These fine countries took a sudden spring in the career of industry, enterprise, and wealth. – Hitherto neglected and abandoned, we resorted to them only in the hour of need and peril; and well have they paid us for an encouragement, bestowed only from self-interest, – from motives of self-preservation ...

What call or necessity was there to interfere at all with the Colonial policy of former times? Suppose that the Americans from some peculiarity of circumstances, had wrung from us the concession of a direct intercourse with our West Indies – did the same peculiarity of situation compel you to open out to them a direct trade with the East Indies, and thus grant to a most dangerous and encroaching rival, a privilege which was not possessed by the British merchants? Was not this a boon to America given without the shadow of a necessity, and without any show of an equivalent? Again, admitting that it was expedient or necessary to grant either or both of these privileges to America, was there the same necessity or expediency for extending them to Prussia and the other powers of Europe? If from any cause whatever you had been compelled or entrapped into a deviation from the strict spirit of our Colonial system, was that any reason, could that induce any necessity, for destroying it altogether? Were we unable to supply such manufactured or raw materials as were necessary to the well-being and prosperity of our Colonies? – Were our shipowners unable to carry these materials whether raw or manufactured? I presume you cannot answer either of these questions in the negative. – Well, then, what were your motives for a course of policy which could only abstract from our wealth and means of employment, and which could not in any way add to them?

You will reply to this, I have no doubt, by stating, that by enriching foreigners we shall finally enrich ourselves; that by letting them participate in the benefit of our trade, they will acquire wealth, the superabundance of which will in the end return upon us, and water and feed the sources of our own industry – that is, the manufactures and the shipping of these powers must first be encouraged at the expense of our own, and then some fifty or a hundred years hence, we shall again be enriched by their overflowing commerce. In plain words, we give away the loaf of bread for a doubtful chance, that we shall be permitted to pick up the crumbs that may fall under the table.

You will say in the next place, that our system created a spirit of discontent and hostility against us on the Continent. And what did their hostility or discontent matter to us, so long as we were able to bid them defiance? Do you suppose, Sir, that their hostility is the less, because you are suffering them to destroy the very elements of our strength? No; but their contempt is immeasurably increased. In all former times they have hated and feared us – I hope I shall never live to see the time when they will hate and despise us. Sir, they have always looked up to us with a spirit of hostility – in that spirit they always will look up to us, so long as we cover the ocean with our ships, and gird the world with our possessions, colonies, and forts.

As men do not commonly make large concessions without exacting some equivalent, I would fain know what consideration you received for the privileges and immunities which you have wantonly bestowed on the rivals of Great Britain. – When you put into the hands of Prussia, and the other Northern states of Europe, nearly the whole of our carrying-trade with those countries, and threw open to them our West India Colonies and our possessions in the East, what did they give in return? What present compensation, what remote contingency, did you obtain from their crafty and firm diplomatists?

I will not be so disingenuous as to disguise what I believe to have been the *ignis fatuus*, the will-o'-the-whisp, that lured you on to concessions discreditable to the resolute and commanding spirit which once guided the councils of the British empire. You were willing to flatter yourself that these concessions would extend our manufactures and commerce. This was the pretext on which you founded these measures; this was the justification which you offered to your opponents.

Such being the fact, let me ask you, why, among the returns you moved for, you did not move for the number of Baltic ships which, during the last five years, left our ports with cargoes, and for the value of those cargoes? Such a return would have shewn at once how far our trade with the German states had realized your expectations. This, Sir, would have shewn what disposition there was in them to compensate the privileges which we had granted; this, Sir, would have shown whether they came into our ports to carry back in return our cottons, woollens, and hardware; or whether they sought only for our gold to buy their manufactures in some other market, and convert the very means we gave them to encourage, not the manufactures of Great Britain, but those of Prussia, Denmark, and Sweden.

When you proposed your system of reciprocity, you of course expected, that it was finally to go into operation with all the great Powers of Europe and America; and you expected also, that these Powers should not merely conform to the letter of these treaties, but that they would, in fact, be ready and anxious to reciprocate those benefits which we had spontaneously held out to them; and that a spirit of conciliation and amity would pervade the whole of their intercourse with us. If we are to take the past as any earnest of the future, these expectations have been totally overthrown. France and the United States, notwithstanding all our truckling and all our solicitation, have refused to accept your proffered boon. Sweden accepted it, with a large exception in favour of herself. Prussia accepted it, because thereby we did, in fact, concede to her every thing which the most rapacious policy, on her part, could have desired. But has Prussia manifested in return, any kindly disposition toward this country? Has she shown any spirit of conciliation – anything at all approximating to concession? I think, Sir, on examination, it would be found that she was determined to take advantage of every circumstance from which she can wring a farthing out of us. Why, Sir, even so trifling a matter as the surplus stores of a British merchant vessel cannot be admitted into that country, without being subject to a heavy duty. She cannot even permit us to load our own ships at her ports, with her produce. We are absolutely obliged to submit to have our vessels loaded by Prussian labourers, while our seamen, though fully competent to the work, are standing idly by, and looking on at this insult on our country – this injustice to our merchants and shipowners. This, Sir, is the present condition of things; this is the return which the reciprocity system has met with. Yes, Sir, the official authorities in Prussian ports actually send Prussian labourers on board our own ships, and we are compelled to receive their services!! ...

In all commercial regulations, it ought to be borne in mind, that the preservation of our naval supremacy is the most vital point in the whole of our political system. Every question of cheapness or extended commerce and manufactures, must be subservient to this. The Minister who in this matter betrays his trust, is a traitor to his country, and deserves, as he will doubtless obtain, the curses of all posterity. However, Sir, our naval power may be neglected – however our naval glories may be despised, amid the more recent recollections of military triumph – to our navy we must be finally indebted for the protection of our land from the pollution of a foreign enemy.

To carry into effect your system of free trade, wages and prices must be equalized throughout the world. Our high prices must be reduced to the level of foreign countries, which in our present state of things is impossible, – or those of other countries must be raised to the level of our own, which would be just as possible as to raise the ocean to the level of the New River by a cut from the River-head at Islington to the coast, – or your system of reciprocity and free trade must be abandoned. You cannot stop where you are; you must either revise and modify your measures, or you must pursue them to their full extent. The former of these I am convinced is essential to the welfare of the nation – the latter I am as thoroughly convinced would lead to its ruin.

The question of the Corn Trade comes before Parliament in the course of a few days. On the settlement of that question the fate of your system will in some degree depend. It is not necessary for me on the present occasion to state what are my opinions on that important subject, neither would it be expedient so to do, unless I went into all the details on which it is founded. But if, as I think there is strong reason to apprehend, Parliament should decide for the importation of foreign corn on the payment of a duty, I would at least wish to enforce on you the necessity of our securing the carrying of it to ourselves. This is a boon which has always been held out as an inducement to a free trade in corn; without some specific regulation, however, it is quite clear in the present state of our relations with the north of Europe, that the whole of it will be imported in foreign vessels. Whatever may be done on this subject, there is one view of the question which appears to me to deserve the most serious consideration; and that is, if we must become a corn-importing country, the expediency of encouraging importation from our North American Provinces.

I have adverted to the possibility of British merchants becoming Prussian shipowners: I now state, on the authority of information on which I can place the utmost reliance, that this is no longer a possibility, but a fact. I can name an eminent British merchant and a member of the British legislature, who possesses a timber-yard within the dominions of Prussia, and who is the owner of more than one Prussian vessel. The considerations that arise on this fact, its immediate effects, and remote consequences, I leave to your own meditation.

In taking up the line of argument which I have endeavoured to explain, I know that I have arrayed myself against many of the most liberal and enlightened spirits of the age; against the whole body of political economists; against a very large portion of the most respectable part of the public press; but I know, also, that I have been maintaining the opinions of a very numerous and weighty body of sound-judging practical men – men whose lives have been spent in business, and who are intimately acquainted with the details and the reciprocal operation of our complex commercial system. I have, however, placed myself on a pedestal of facts, and rested my shoulders against a rock of truth. I have stood forward to maintain the principles and the policy under which England has grown to her present magnitude; or if you will not allow me this mode of language – cotemporaneously, [sic] and side by side with which, England has progressed in commerce, in wealth, in arts, in arms. I have concealed nothing

– I have misrepresented nothing – I have disguised nothing – I have exaggerated nothing. I have come forward in defence of what I conceive to be the best interests of the empire. I have thrown down the gauntlet, in what I verily believe to be the cause of my country. If the policy you have been the main instrument of recommending should be persevered in – if Parliament shall not arrest its progress, annul, or abrogate it – when that ruin comes, which I anticipate with the most perfect assurance, I shall at least have the satisfaction of knowing, that I had raised my humble voice to denounce the system from whence it sprung.

I have the honour to be, Sir,
Your very obedient Servant,

S. ATKINSON.

London, Feb. 8, 1827.

Henry Stephens, *A Letter Addressed to the Landowners and Tenantry of the County of Forfar* (Dundee: D. Hill, 1827).

LETTER ADDRESSED TO THE LANDOWNERS AND TENANTRY OF THE COUNTY OF FORFAR. BY HENRY STEPHENS, Esq. OF BALMADIES.

TO THE LANDOWNERS AND TENANTRY OF THE COUNTY OF FORFAR.

GENTLEMEN,

WHATSOEVER be the nature of the alteration which is to be effected in the present Corn Law, we are certain it will be an important one; and whenever an important change is to be made in the protection to our agriculture, it is but right that we, as agriculturists, should examine its probable effects upon our future prospects. The importance of such examination will apologise for my troubling you at this time, and in this manner; and although I could wish the subject had engaged the attention of an abler advocate – yet, having already had a little trouble in the matter, I am willing to take a little more, though it were for no better reason than to maintain the consistency of the proverb which is applied to our profession – 'that he that puts his hand to the plough must not look back.' But I *have* a better reason for attracting your attention to the subject at this time. There is a clamour, and a spirit of denouncement against us abroad in the land. I would therefore wish to point out to you the sentiments of many of the petitions which are drawn up by that lynx-eyed class of the community, who always look sharply after their own interest, but who pray that you may be left without protection. I would guard you against the dangers which threaten your future prospects. I would wish to instil into you some *zeal* for our own cause; for, without it, any thing great or good cannot be effected in this world. I may fail to accomplish my object, but I hope you feel that interest in the subject which will urge you to bestow some attention on the following paragraphs.

There are only two ways of altering the present Corn Law – in its details, or in its principle. Its mode of operation is, that it permits foreign corn to be imported into this country, only when the home corn has reached in price eighty shillings per quarter, at a duty of seventeen shillings. In order to ascertain whether the price has attained that height, quarterly averages are taken in the twelve principal maritime counties in England; the average prices in which, for six weeks prior to the fifteenths of November, February, May, and August, regulate the admission or prohibition of foreign grain into our *markets* for the succeeding three months respectively; but foreign corn may be imported and warehoused at all times in this country.

There have been several objections urged against this state of things. I confess there is an apparent clumsiness in the machinery employed for the purpose; but, as far as I can learn, the system has worked well, and at no great expense, and therefore it ought to be meddled with with great caution. British agriculture must have protection – but it does not follow that simplicity of operation in a corn law is indispensably [*sic*] necessary to bestow that protection. On the contrary, this country is in an artificial state, and has been brought to that by artificial means long employed. Would it be safe or prudent to abandon this artificial system hastily – to leap at once from restriction to freedom? Would any man, who had a regard for the life of his horse, first groom, physic, feed, and train him, to high mettle and high wind for the race, and then *suddenly* allow him to deluge himself, at will, with water and cut grass? But the striking of the averages, it is said, has been often attended with fraud. This has always been a fruitful source of clamour against the bill. The imperfections always inseparable from the inventions and actions of man, must no doubt cling to the operations of this law, as well as to that of every other; but of all the classes of the community, the commercial have the least to complain of on that score, as it is the agriculturists themselves who suffer from the effects of those frauds, which are perpetrated by the interested motives of dealers, to get quit of their warehoused grain. Frauds, after all, can only be attempted with any prospect of success when the price reaches nearly to the amount of the import duty. Another objection which has been stated against the present law is, that it keeps up the price of corn to an exorbitant extent. The object, certainly, of establishing the corn law in 1815 was to give protection, ample protection, to agriculture, but not to maintain exorbitant prices – by which must be meant, that it maintains the price of corn beyond the relative value of other things. This I can safely deny, and not only that, but contend, that corn is, and has been, comparatively cheap. The average price of wheat for the last ten years, has not exceeded much above its average price in 1792, when the national debt was only a fourth part of its present amount; and every one who has paid the least attention to the rates of wages in that period, must know that they have risen much above the relative value of corn. I refer, in particular, to the year 1792, as that appears to be the period which the Ministry wish to take as a pattern, and to which they apparently think the nation should retrograde, after having been subjected for thirty years to better living, higher wages, and increasing taxation. During the discussion on the corn bill in 1815, it was maintained in the House of Commons, and reiterated out of its doors by its opponents, that if eighty shillings per quarter were allowed as a protecting duty, the price of wheat would never fall below that amount; and that the quartern loaf would never be less than one shilling and sixpence. The price of wheat was for some time in 1816, and again in 1817, owing to two consecutive bad crops, far above eighty shillings; but the loaf did not then rise above one shilling and threepence in price. The advocates of the bill always denied that prices would *necessarily* be kept up to the protecting duty; and time, that handmaid of truth, has since clearly declared who have been the true, and who the false prophets on the subject.

A third objection has been started against the bill, that under it prices of corn have fluctuated very much. This has been the ground of a general hue and cry in the country, and the Edinburgh Review has lately thought proper to re-echo the vulgar error. It is demonstrable by reference to facts, and the Caledonian Mercury newspaper has given those proofs in a most satisfactory manner, that the price of corn has fluctuated *less* since the existence of the present bill, than at any period previous to that of the same length of time. Indeed, common sense would conclude so, for good encouragement of home growth, will always produce abundance of corn in this country. But no legislative enactment whatever *can prevent* a fluctuation in the price of corn. A manufacturer can supply the market with goods according to the demand in it, but, it is in the power of Providence alone to give us more or less corn, and the supply in this case cannot altogether be regulated by the demand. Good and bad seasons will cause fluctuations in the prices of grain, though the trade in it were as 'free as the air we breathe.'

It thus appears, that the present bill affords us protection but no more, as the profits of the farmer have been very small for the last ten years. It also appears, that even with protection, the price of corn has been, on an average of years, moderately high, nor has fraud exhibited itself so frequently, and so odiously, as to justify the clamour which has been raised against the operation of the bill. What necessity then exists for a change? But even the professed friends of agriculture cry aloud for a change, and Mr Whitmore, not only joins the cry, but proposes a plan of his own, which is to remedy the defects of the present measure. What is his remedy, is it to alter the present bill in its principle, or only in its details? Only in its details! He proposes a graduating scale of duty for the admission of foreign corn: but how is this graduating scale to be applied but through the instrumentality of the *average system* – that system which is said to be replete with all the fraud and duplicity imaginable, and which it is a disgrace to see tolerated in such a country as this? Where then is the superiority of Mr Whitmore's plan? His main object, after all, is to depress still farther the average price of grain in this country.

These appear to me to be the chief objections which have been urged against a continuance of the present bill. If the arguments in favour of it be weak, it is because those against it are themselves weak; indeed, the latter are not arguments at all, but mere assertions, which a simple reference to facts, as they have been developed by the operation of the bill for years past, can amply confute. It is remarkable, and you may have remarked it in all that has been spoken and written against the present bill, not a single case has been made out, not a fact adduced, which can in the least invalidate the design of the original promoters of the measure. If it could be pointed out, by a reference to facts, wherein it has belied those sentiments which urged its adoption at first, there might be cause for the outcry which at present deafens our ears. But no – it has only given to the farmer protection against the inroads of the Continental vassals – it has only secured to him such prices for his grain as he could expect to receive from a plentiful supply produced by an ample encouragement to home growth. It never promised him exorbitant prices and immense profits, for these were never in its power to bestow. In short, it has performed all that its originators intended it should perform, yet it must be demolished – it must be scattered to the winds. Surely nothing but a love of change – a spirit of innovation – could desire to abandon that, the only fault of which is fidelity to its original principle, and adherence to its appointed work.

If some of the professed friends to agriculture wish to get rid of the present corn law, because they say it is inimical to the interest of the farmer, there are other people who scruple not to ascribe all the distress which this country has suffered, and is still suffering, to its existence. If there be a spark of truth in this assertion, let that law, like the riches of the land already, take to itself wings and fly away. Let no Pandora's box be suffered to remain open in this fair land, to paralyze, by its pestilential influence, the vital energy of its inhabitants. Rather let some cordial be administered to the country which shall restore her wonted strength, and by which she shall not only re-establish her own glory and supremacy, but shall impart wealth and power to the sinking states of the Continent. Let some good Samaritan be invited to pour the balm of health into the wounds of the country, and affect such a cure in all her interests, as will enable them to renew their activity and vigour like the eagle. Happily for her prospective benefit this panacea is discovered. This can be no other than Free Trade, whose power is talismanic!

We are now arrived on the debateable [*sic*] land – the arena upon which the fate of the agriculturist must soon be decided. According to the ability with which we advocate our cause, so will our success be; and we will be obliged to muster all our strength, for we have 'the powers that be' to contend with – we have the clamorous vociferations of thousands to listen to and argue with. But we have also the interest of half the population of the land to maintain – we have the strength and power of Britain to support. Break but Britania's [*sic*] 'right arm,' by which she wields the lance, and the left will soon be unable to use the shield for her own defence. In plain terms, remove protection from British agriculture, and it will be ruined. Mr Whitmore's plan would affect the present corn bill only in its *details;* but the measure which his Majesty's Ministers are about to propose to Parliament will subvert its very *principle*. The present bill will, I believe, be abolished altogether, and another, differing quite from it in principle, is to be substituted. The principle of the present bill is prohibitory: it admits foreign corn into our markets only when it is wanted; but the new measure will

206 *Battles over Free Trade, Volume 1*

allow it to come in at all times, whether it be wanted or no. The present bill says – 'I will protect the agriculture of my country to the utmost of my power; for I know that by that protection the farmers will be enabled to raise as much corn as her inhabitants can consume; but should Providence in his decrees see fit to shorten man's means of subsistence, then I will, to avert such a calamity, allow as much corn as can come in to supply the deficiency.' On the other hand the new bill would say – 'Protection to our agriculture is necessary and proper to a certain extent; but the present one must be reduced, for the farmers are getting too high prices for their grain, and I am not bound to give them profits when the other interests of the state are not getting any. I will therefore allow foreign corn to be imported at all times and seasons, that the price of corn may be kept low in the country; for I wish foreigners to be induced to barter with us their corn for our manufactures.' Thus, you observe, the very *spirit* of our law would be entirely changed; and that being the case, is it not natural for us to apprehend danger in such a measure – the operation of which we cannot estimate from experience, nor indeed can exactly anticipate? Our present apprehensions may afterwards be proved to have been too great; but they are certainly founded in reason, and spring from a conviction derived from the dictates of common sense, and are therefore entitled to respect. That under the *present* circumstances of the country such a change would be inimical to the agricultural interest, I have not a shadow of doubt; and, influenced by such a conviction, I shall endeavour, by the following objections, with the reasonings thereon, to impress such of your minds as maintain the negative of the above sentiment, to think well beforehand, for fear you give your sanction with temerity to such a subverting measure.

Britain consumes a certain quantity of corn every year. It is an indisputable fact, that she has raised as much corn as her inhabitants could consume for some years past. The simple fact of the ports having continued shut against importation for that length of time, corroborates the assertion. What use, then, is there for foreign corn? – What use can we make of *two* watches at the same time, even though the one were made *abroad* and the other at home? If there was an actual deficiency in the quantity of corn raised to supply the wants of the country in any year, common sense and prudence would doubtless suggest to get that deficiency supplied from abroad for that year. The new bill, however, would allow foreign corn to be imported freely at all times. The evident consequence of this free importation would be, either the foreign corn must remain unused in this country, or an equal quantity of our own be unused to make way for the foreign. *If the price of both in the market were exactly alike,* it is probable the foreign corn would be rejected; as, in general, it is neither so fine in quality, so cleanly handled, nor so free of admixture, as our own. The importer of foreign corn, for the above reasons, finding his commodity lying upon his hand – and his being entirely a mercantile transaction, having to relieve his bills of three months' date, or to want the hard

Stephens, A Letter Addressed to the Landowners and Tenantry (1827)

cash which he has already paid for it, for the same length of time – would naturally content himself with a smaller profit, and get quit of his present speculation to another at a reduced price; – whereas the farmer, having his rent to pay only twice a-year, could probably have kept his grain out of the market for nearly six months. By such a transaction the circumstances of the two kinds of people are altered, and the farmer also must take the lower rate of the market; for who will give him more, in *proportion*, for his grain than the importer has received for his? Thus, at the very outset of the opening of the ports, a competition would arise which would create a sort of continually ebbing vacillation of the prices. This competition would not cease till one of the parties retired; and the probability is, the farmer would get the chances against him, as the merchant could, at the worst, dispose of his commodity wholly, at a definite and foreseen loss, if loss there were. Not only that, but the farmer could have no chance in such a competition, in which the importer, as a merchant, possessing all the requisite knowledge of different means in his exclusive power, could outwit him in many ways. A farmer is out of his sphere to enter the lists with such an antagonist; and yet, he will be obliged to do that which is foreign to his habits and experience, as the market will probably be forestalled. Let no farmer 'lay the flattering unction to his soul,' that he will have to compete with the foreign *farmer*, in our markets. With no such person, let him be assured. The foreign corn will have passed into the hands of the dealers of this country ere he see it in our markets; and this state of things I would consider a great hardship upon our farmers. Whenever it is settled, the ports will be kept constantly open for the admission of foreign grain – the dealer of this country will go over to the Continent – form connexions there – buy up the grain from the hands of the foreign farmers – take the expense of bringing it down to the shipping ports himself – and drive as hard a bargain as possible; – and, at the same time, knowing all the modes of carrying on business in our markets, he will introduce this foreign grain at the least possible expense to himself. This may be all very fair, and very legitimate in a merchant; but I maintain that it is a mode of conducting business with which our farmers could not possibly compete with success. Besides, this foreign grain, when not wanted, being ever ready to be brought into our markets, when it pleased the importer to do so, would operate as a damper upon the prices here, and it would do so continually. Nor would there be any difficulty of obtaining large supplies in the beginning of the season. The harvest on the Continent being, in general, two months earlier than here, enough time would be allowed the importer to buy corn there, at that favourable season of the year, all kiln dried, and fit to keep in vessel or granary, and which could be transported to this country as soon as we could possibly get any corn ready for the commencement of the winter markets in November. Four months could thus be employed in preparing to supply our markets with foreign grain at the very beginning of the season. Hence the question which presents itself for consideration in this part of our examination is one purely of cost, and it may be fairly stated thus: – Which of the two grains, the foreign or the home grown, can be presented, without actual loss to the party presenting it, at the lowest price in our markets? This question involves in it that which gives our whole discussion the greatest interest, and upon the decision of which depends the extent of our protection; and if we can answer it agreeably to reason, of which I have no doubt, the remaining grounds of discussion will be much narrowed. Before entering, however, upon the principal question at first, its solution will be much assisted if we make a few preliminary observations; after which, the main proposition being surmounted, its correlatives will follow almost as a matter of course. And here let me observe, that although we may not be able to apply our reasonings on such a subject as this with the same precision as that which renders a mathematical demonstration irresistible, yet we may be guided by the maxim which was laid down by the father of true philosophy, the immortal Bacon – that he who would conduct his reasonings in a *truly philosophical* spirit must found them on *facts*. Did his spirit guide the minds of some of the leading men of the present day, we would not have yet heard of that *pseudo philosophy*, which sickens the hearts of many in the land.

The countries from which we could get the greatest supply of grain, are situate on the southern shores of the Baltic Sea, and along the south eastern coast of the German Ocean. The southern provinces of Russia, in the Black Sea, abound also in corn. So does Egypt; and considerable quantities of flour may be obtained from the United States of America. Holland and Flanders are so thickly populated, that most of their grain is consumed at home. Not so, however, with the Polish, Pomeranian, and Livonian provinces. The whole country which is watered by the Vistula and its tributaries is agrarian, and so is Bohemia. In the first mentioned countries the condition of the peasantry is wretched in the extreme; and the cause ascribed by writers for this wretchedness is – our ports being shut against the importation of foreign corn, and therefore they can get no outlet for it. – This assertion bears the semblance of truth; but Sweden and Norway, the northern parts of Russia, and even Spain and Portugal, do not raise as much corn as supplies themselves. Why is the Polish grain not sent to those countries? Why wish to send it to Britain which can raise enough for itself? Why not as well wish to send it to Holland, Flanders, or France, who all have enough and to spare? The answer is obvious, Britain alone possesses the cash – the means of paying for it when bought. 'Aye, there's the rub.' The longing eyes of the Poles are fixed upon this country, because whence alone they can receive the 'rix thaler.' The Polish peasant is not free: though not his person, his labour is attached to the soil; he is obliged to work to his proprietor for food and clothing, and the little land which he occupies. He lives upon milk and rye bread – he wears the 'hodden grey,' and in winter is clothed with sheep skins turned inside out. His clothing is made at home by the females, who have little else to do. He buys no butcher meat, and as to a wheaten loaf, it never enters his lips. There is there no such person as a farmer, in our acceptation of that term; the land is farmed principally by the proprietors themselves, and the peasantry are under them as vassals, or serfs. After maintaining his serfs, and paying some taxes, the proprietor disposes of his surplus grain, which is his only income; and if he cannot get that grain disposed of his income is annihilated. Corn having lain heavy upon his hand for some years past, he has sown down some of his land to grass, and breeds Merino sheep for their wool. The present condition of the proprietors is also wretched, as their estates are heavily mortgaged to the Jews, who abound in those countries; and as the Jews are prohibited, by law, from holding land themselves, the proprietors are little else than their stewards. The peasantry receive about fivepence per day as wages, and the rent of the rent of land, on the average, is about one shilling and threepence per acre. In Bohemia the condition of the peasantry is better, but the men are idlers, as their name, 'Zigeuner,' in their own country, testifies. Field labour is mostly executed by the women. Corn is extensively cultivated; and wages and rent are low. In Saxony the peasantry are in good condition, and being Protestants they are industrious. Farmers and farms both exist in that country. Saxony, though small in extent, is populous, and is rich in grain and fruits in the valleys; and the hills, which are like undulations, are covered with herbage to the tops, and peopled with Merinos. The climate of all those countries is delightful and steady in summer; and although winter is generally severe, no frosts or unwelcome rains interfere with vegetation after field labour has commenced. Such is the condition of those countries as to possessing the means of raising corn. Take all these things into consideration, and conceive, if it be probable, that in such countries as those above described grain can cost much to raise; and the fineness of their climate makes their corn won well, and thrash out with little trouble. But, it is said, the expense of taking the corn to the shipping ports is great. In countries in which there are no navigable canals, or good roads, carriage, no doubt, is difficult and troublesome; but, on the other hand, the rivers are large and navigable for small craft – materials are cheap for the construction of barges, and the labour of men and cattle is also cheap. The distance of the country around Cracow to Dantzic is considerable; and the barks which are made to transport the grain along the rivers are never taken back again, but are sold for what they will fetch, and broken up for fuel. – This waste of timber I conceive to be the principal item of expense in transporting corn; for, as to the loss sustained by its exposure to the weather, that could be nearly removed by care. Pomerania, Mecklenburg, and Holstein, are well situate as to the vicinage of sea ports. Difficult as the transportation of grain from the interior may be, I would ask, if Britain always presented a ready market, would not our enterprising countrymen, the importers of foreign grain, find means to lessen considerably the expense of transmission through those countries? How do a few Englishmen contrive to convey the immense pine timber from the almost impenetrable and inexhaustible forests of Mount Pilatus, in Switzerland, to the Lake of Lucerne – thence down the Reuss and the Rhine as far as Holland? Let but an Englishman conceive that he will derive profit in the business, and he will soon contrive to bring corn in quantities to the sea shore, even from Bohemia. The speculation would, no doubt, be quite new to him at first, but he possesses such habits and capabilities as to pick up knowledge very quickly from experience. There is no absolute necessity, however, of penetrating so far into the heart of Europe for corn as into the valleys of Bohemia. The southern shores of the Baltic would soon yield a great deal more corn than they do at present. The grass land, which has lain for some time, will, in some degree, by this time, have recovered its fertility, and would be immediately broken up and sown with wheat – part of the barley and oats will make way for wheat – the Merinos will be disposed of (for wool will never pay like wheat in that country), and thus means may be increased for extended cultivation. It is, therefore, as clear as the sun at noon-day, that a greater extent of land will be cultivated to raise grain for this market. The very circumstance of a new and extensive market being constantly open for the admission of grain, will give a stimulus to cultivation which nothing, not even losses, for some time will prevent. Besides, the quantity raised in this country being lessened by our inferior lands being driven out of cultivation, a steady demand cannot fail to arise from this quarter; especially as the manufacturers will then, according to their present doctrines, get rich upon low wages! Take the example of the continent of South America being thrown open to our manufactures, and let those who can, deny, that that circumstance gave a stimulus to our manufacturing energy. But, of the two, the foreign farmer has an immeasurable advantage over the British manufacturer. The former will have a country abounding in wealth and active agencies, to raise his grain for; whereas the latter had a country poor, distracted, and ravaged by civil wars, and containing an idle population, to send his manufactures to, and yet he sent them in abundance. Can it then be denied that a stimulus will be given to foreign agriculture? This stimulus being allowed to exist, is it possible – is it probable, that great expense will be necessary to raise corn there in comparison with that of this country? Mr Jacob may make out any case he pleases to induce us to believe that heavy expenses attend the cultivation of corn on the Continent. He may make out a case according to circumstances as they are, but he cannot maintain that present circumstances can regulate future exertions. There are those who have visited those countries which occupied Mr Jacob's attention, and their opinions do not accord with his. M. Sismondi, I believe, has done so; and he further states, that corn can be raised at very little expense in the Crimea, and we know the climate of that part of the world is fine. From the enterprising spirit in commercial pursuits displayed by the present Pacha of Egypt, it is probable he may send wheat from that country. The United States of America may send flour, and when it is firmly packed in barrels, as they do it, it is an economical shipment, and will keep for a long time. Canadian wheat is not good; but Upper Canada possesses a fine climate, and will yet grow good wheat under the management of the new settlers. In short, with Britain for a market, what is to prevent all those countries which can raise more corn than they can use, and there are many that can, to send it to it in quantities?

If the open ports of this country bring grain from abroad, and as it raises as much as supplies it wants, it is clear that grain must be so brought in at a loss to a part of our own. We have already seen how prices must fall in our markets by a competition with foreign grain, and part of that grain will doubtless be bought. Part, therefore, of this corn will remain upon the hands of our farmer; and not only that, but the price of all that he will sell will be reduced. Corn lying upon his hand is of no use to him; and rather than raise more than he can dispose of, he will curtail his expenses as much as possible; – and the first and *only* means which he has in his *own power* to do so, is to reduce the number of his servants and horses, and lay down the inferior land upon his farm to grass. Less corn will thus be raised in this country, and, of course, more will be wanted from abroad; and the stimulus, which we spoke of before, will continue to exert its influence.

It will be here remarked, if the price of corn continue low in our markets, the period will arrive when it will not compensate any body to bring it from abroad. If such a period should arrive at all, it will not, in my opinion, arrive soon, at least not till our markets had continued low for a considerable time. Let us look to facts. When Mr Jacob was on the Continent the market price of wheat at Warsaw was fourteen shillings and ninepence per quarter; and the highest was, at Olmütz, at one pound per quarter, exclusive of the expense of transmission; and he remarks, 'if there be *no foreign demand* for wheat, the *difficulty* of selling it *at any price* is *great*.' Reverse the sentence, *create* a *foreign demand* – *open our ports* – and there will then be *no difficulty* of selling it at any price. The *difficulty of selling* thus arises from a *want of foreign demand*, and *not* from any *rate of price*. Besides, it is a well known fact, that foreign proprietors have no other sources of income than what arises from the *sale* of their grain. Whether it remunerate them or not at the prices stated above, is it probable they will keep it beside them and run the risk of starvation, when they may obtain a steady market for it here? Is it not a great deal more probable that they will, under these circumstances, not only take those prices, however small, but endeavour to raise as much more as they will be able to increase that income still farther? Had they other sources of income they would no doubt make a choice; but, situate as they are, they must sell or continue in their present miserable condition. The alternative will not be perplexing, they will be too happy to find an outlet for their grain at any price. If they did not act as I have stated, their situation would be like that of many of our mechanics at present, who will rather remain idle and starve, than work at a lower rate of wages; – although every one of them knows it would be his wiser policy to take smaller wages than to starve, for starve he must in the end, if he persist in his obstinacy. But what will be done with our own grass land, which will be greatly increased by the reduction of cultivation? The answer immediately given will be, breed more cattle and sheep, and let us have beef and mutton cheaper. Let us again look to facts. I need not state the fact to you, who all already know it from experience, that there are as many cattle and sheep in the country as there is food for. Their summer keep would no doubt be extended: but how could they be maintained during the winter, if the extent of cultivated land were contracted? And that very kind of ground, the greatest extent of which would be relinquished, is the kind which is best adapted for raising turnips for cattle and sheep. The quantity of straw, that valuable commodity in *winter*, would be much reduced. All the strongest and best wheat land would, no doubt, still be cultivated, – but that kind of land unfortunately happens to be that which is the worst suited to produce winter food for live stock. Take this season of deficiency as a guide. Will there be no difficulty this winter in fattening, and keeping in growing condition, the *usual* number of cattle and sheep? God knows, every farmer in the land must look with sorrow on the present state of his stock; no turnips, no straw, no comfort, no cleanliness, no condition, no manure for next year – nothing but misery and starvation. Our climate is so precarious at all times, but particularly in the winter season, that cattle must be kept under shelter and abandon the fields. How then could we keep more live stock with diminished means? What, too, would become of our ploughmen, who must be paid off in consequence of our decreased cultivation? The burden of maintaining them in idleness would still fall upon the landed interest. British husbandry has arrived to such a degree of perfection – it is now so systematized – that it may be compared to a fine piece of mechanism – alter but the proportions of one part of it, and you will affect the movement of the whole.

It will be remarked again, if corn be reduced in price, and some of the expense of cultivation lessened by reduction of labour, rents must be lowered so as to remunerate the farmer for his trouble. This is tantamount to saying, if any public measure deteriorate the circumstances of the farmer, the landlord must bear the burden of all that deterioration, which would be a manifest injustice. But let us again appeal to facts, and see how far this reduction can be effected. From the united testimony of many of you, in answer to queries which I lately took the liberty to ask, it appears that rent comprehends about one-third of the expenses of cultivation in this county. Allowing therefore the other portions of expense to remain unchanged, a reduction of *one-third* of the value of agricultural produce, which, I conceive, with open ports, as inevitable – would *annihilate rent altogether*. Great landlords may reduce rents considerably, and still have handsome incomes to spend, although they ought not, in justice to themselves, to reduce their rents below the proportioned allowance made by the smaller proprietors, merely because they are rich; and *their* lands, besides, are far from being rack-rented. The small proprietors, of whom there are about forty to one of the great, cannot afford to lower their rents very much – most of them having their lands partly mortgaged, or unfavourably entailed. Twenty-five per cent. would be considered a handsome reduction in rent; and yet that would comprehend only one-twelfth part of the expenses. How little would such a reduction affect expenses, being only eightpence one halfpenny per bushel of wheat, at sixty shillings per quarter; – whereas, to a proprietor, with his land mortgaged to the extent of one half of the rental, a reduction of twenty-five per cent. in the rent would reduce his income by one half; and so on in arithmetical progression to his burdens. The truth is, rents were generally raised during the war, but they were by no means raised in proportion to the value of produce, or the latter to that of labour.

Having made these preliminary remarks, and they are of the utmost importance to us in viewing the general question, we will now be prepared to consider the great point of dispute, namely, the expenses which the farmers in this county incur in raising the common produce of the soil; for it is by the establishment of this fact, and of this alone, that our remonstrances can be rendered effective. This fact would have been very difficult of attainment, had it not been for your kindness in furnishing me with data upon which I could confidently rely. No process of reasoning could possibly have arrived at a conclusion with so much certainty, as by a simple and explicit statement of your receipts and expenditures for the last ten years. The extremes of price mentioned in the value of wheat did not differ, amongst the majority of those gentlemen who returned me answers, beyond three shillings per boll, and only two exhibited a difference of five shillings. The average of the whole statements gave *sixty-four shillingr*, [*sic*] as the lowest price which it would be necessary to receive, in order that the farmers in this county may be no more than remunerated for the expense of raising a quarter of wheat, Winchester measure. I have corresponded with corn dealers on the prices which they have paid for foreign grain abroad, for the last ten years, and during that period they have been very low. But even allowing for a fair rise of price in the foreign markets, in consequence of our open ports, it is their conviction that wheat will not exceed forty-three shillings per imperial quarter, delivered free in any port in Britain on the east coast. Seven shillings per quarter for wheat, are charged for freight, insurance, and other incidents; but, it is their opinion, the expense of importation will not exceed five shillings per quarter, as foreigners are quite ready to drive a trade at low rates. Consequently, to give the farmer only a remunerating price, the duty on a quarter of wheat ought to be twenty-one shillings, at seven shillings per quarter for freight, &c.; but it ought to be twenty-three shillings, if freight, &c. are only five shillings per quarter. Allowing a reduction of twenty per cent. in rent, which would be, I conceive, as much as could be looked for as an average reduction over the island, the duty would be seventeen or nineteen shillings per quarter, according to the rate of freight, &c. It is highly probable that freight, &c. will not exceed five shillings per quarter, as foreign ship-owners have become so active since the abolition of our old navigation laws.

Although they wish our ports to be constantly open for the admission of foreign corn, it is not, I believe, the intention of the Ministry to admit it *duty free*. They will impose a duty which will be called a *protecting* one; but what will be its amount it is impossible for us at present to assert, though rumour fixes it at from ten to fifteen shillings per quarter. From what I have stated above, it cannot be less than twenty-three shillings per quarter, allowing all existing circumstances to remain unchanged – for rent cannot, in justice, be alone reduced; but I maintain that a duty of almost *any amount* would not be a *protecting* one to *us*, so long as the ports continued *always open*. This is a point on which so much difference of opinion exists, that it will be impossible for the one party to convince the minds of the other, so long as experience has not yet decided in favour of either. It is therefore unnecessary to argue upon this particular point. We can easily cede it in the mean time, as we have many arguments and analogical examples to assist us in showing the evil consequences that would ensue to our interests by the introduction of free trade into it. To me it appears as clear as that the effect follows the cause, that though twenty-three shillings per quarter of duty may appear, at first sight, ample protection to us, by placing us on a footing with the foreign farmer, *so long as our present circumstances remain unchanged*, – yet the very introduction of foreign *competition* into our markets, will *alter those circumstances*, by reducing the price of corn here, and by the necessity that will exist in foreigners to take any price rather than prevent their grain coming into the British market – the exclusion from which so long, the advocates of free trade themselves say, having already entailed so much misery upon them. Thus, the price of wheat will surely fall below sixty-four shillings per quarter – the barely remunerating price. Consequently, farming will be carried on at the expense of capital – the farmers being obliged to remain at their profession – as they know no other – as long as they possess a penny. Even *now* their capital yields them little or no profit – they get their living to be sure, as the ox which treadeth out the corn must not be muzzled; but *then* they will have no capital left. The present miserable condition of the agriculturists on the Continent, is ascribed to the extremely low prices there of late years; and what is there, in the nature of things, to prevent a similar fate overtaking ourselves under similar circumstances?

Such, Gentlemen, would be the probable effect on us, were the free trade law made to regulate our protection; and such is the evil which the commercial interest are daily praying the legislature to bring upon us. One would think they have had enough experience already, to be able to appreciate the advantages of having the agricultural population as their nearest and best customers. But they have unfortunately suffered from free trade, and have been induced by it, to throw away the fruits of their industry upon needy and *unneeding* nations. It is uncharitable in them, however, to wish our interest to be brought to the same humbled state as their own – and particularly at a time, though we were to possess all the permanent advantages which they are ever ready to assert we always enjoy, when we are suffering severely by a very deficient crop in all things, and our live stock reduced to a nominal value. The abuse, too, of our protection, upon which is lavished the odious epithets of 'Bread Tax,' 'Starvation Bill,' &c. is extremely vulgar, and may be very characteristic of 'the foul-mouthed multitude;' but such expressions are uttered in very bad taste from the lips of those who feel no shame to use them before the polished nobility, and the enlightened legislators of Britain; but with unblushing effrontery, seize every opportunity to excite the disgust of the agriculturists. Were the change entreated for to have a beneficial effect upon *every* class of the community, a sacrifice may be made by one of them, for the attainment of so desirable an object; but to pray for the passing of a measure which would probably ruin one half of the population of the country, is too serious a matter to attempt without, in the first place, meditating deeply upon its probable consequences. Of all the assertions which are constantly made by mercantile people against us, that is the most foolish, which ascribes to the present bill the power of granting us a monopoly. What sort of *monopoly* is *that* which is enjoyed by one half of the people of a country? Would merchants wish to compete with us in *raising* corn, that they seem so jealous of our 'monopoly?' If so, who hinders them from doing so, and sending their grain to our monopolizing markets, in which they may sell without a grudge from *us*? Where can they meet with more liberal monopolists? Mercantile people, however, must always have something to petition about – they are very fond of legislating – and they have been caught dictating even to Royalty itself. Let general legislation alone to the Legislators who are intrusted with it, and who are prudently jealous of their prerogatives. Let them petition by all means – state facts – and reason a case which immediately belongs to *their* own profession, but let the *Corn* Laws alone. What would they say to farmers were *they* to hold a meeting to argue about the bounty on linens, or petition for protection to our trade in the Mediterranean, against the Greek pirates? *Ne sutor ultra crepidam.* I shall conclude this paragraph by an extract from a spirited paper, one among a host, on political subjects, which appeared in Blackwood's Magazine, to the able exertions and powerful advocacy of the Editor of which, the agriculturists owe a heavy debt of gratitude. 'Agriculture,' says the writer, 'is just above distress, but it certainly is not in prosperity. When there is conclusive proof, that in average seasons we grow as much corn as we can consume, and when the prices of agricultural produce are scarcely remunerating ones, every thing that could justify a change in the Corn Law is wanting; when it is manifest that a comparatively trifling reduction of prices would plunge the agriculturists into distress; and when it is universally admitted that a free trade in corn would produce a considerable reduction, it seems to us that the establishment of such a free trade would be a matter highly deserving of impeachment.' 'We will never believe that a change of law, which is likely to have these consequences, and which, at the best, will assuredly deprive the agriculturists of a large part of their property and income, *can be an honest one*, if the rest of the community be not called upon to hazard and sacrifice in a similar manner. Instead of being thus called upon, the rest of the community is to profit from the change: it is confidently declared that the change will not only protect the manufacturers from being injured by free trade, but will benefit them very largely. What has become of English right and justice? This opinion, however, that the manufacturers will profit largely from the loss of the agriculturists, will soon receive deserved and woeful refutation. It is foolishly argued that the former would gain if they could procure the quarter of wheat for a smaller number of yards of cloth. If the manufacturer of cotton, timber, leather, wool, &c. like the agriculturist, grow his raw article upon his own land, and could grow only a certain quantity yearly, then it would benefit him if he could obtain the quarter of wheat for a smaller quantity of his manufacture. But what is the fact? He *buys* his raw article; and the *profit* of himself and his workmen arises directly or practically from a percentage on the amount of its sale when *manufactured*. If *wheat fall*, his *prices* and the *wages* of his workmen are to *fall in proportion*; this is universally admitted. If he give ten yards of cloth for the quarter of wheat, his profit per yard is at least as much as when he gives only five yards. If this profit be one shilling, in the one case he gains ten shillings, and in the other only five shillings from the bargain. His workmen receive *more* per yard for manufacturing the cloth when *ten* yards are given, than when *five* are given: if, in the one case, they receive four shillings, then profit is forty shillings: if, in the other, they receive three shillings, then profit is only fifteen shillings. The agriculturist has only a certain quantity of produce to sell: if *prices* be very *low*, they cause him to have *less* and *not more*, and he can merely consume the *goods* that his *produce* will exchange for. If his prices sink so that he can only obtain one-tenth of the cloth for the quantity of wheat, that one-tenth *must* content him. Let us separate the agriculturists entirely from the rest of the community, and let us assume that they have only wheat to buy cottons with, that they will consume all the cottons that their wheat will exchange for, and that they have ten millions of quarters of surplus wheat annually. If they sell their wheat at five pounds per quarter, they will buy fifty millions worth of cottons: if they sell it at one pound, they will buy only ten millions worth: they will consume five times more cottons, and employ five times more labourers in the one case than in the other, assuming that the price of cotton will be in both the same.

Stephens, A Letter Addressed to the Landowners and Tenantry (1827) 217

If we admit that they ought to pay fifty per cent. more for the cottons in the one case than the other on account of the difference in the cost of living, then the high price would enable them to buy above three times more cottons, and to employ three times more labour than the low one. This is not all. By employing so much more labour, they would enable the manufacturers to consume far more cottons themselves, and to export far more for the purchase of raw cotton, dyes, &c. If then consumption should be reduced from this to that allowed by the lowest price, – in the first place more than two thirds of the manufacturers would be stripped of employment: – then as many more would be deprived of bread as these had employed, and then as many more would be deprived of bread as had been employed to manufacture for the purchase of the raw articles no longer wanted. The idle hands would run down the wages and prices of those left in employment in the most ruinous manner. More than three-fourths of the manufacturers would exchange comfortable competence for starvation, and the remainder would barely earn bread and water. Let our merchants and manufacturers ponder upon this. Let them remember, that the agriculturists in one way or another, comprehend about half the population; that the latter have only their produce to buy with, and that if one-third or one-fourth be taken from the value of this produce, they will not be able to buy half the merchandise and manufactures that they buy at present. If this will not convince them, let them turn to Mr Jacob's most instructive Report, and they will perceive, that in countries where corn is exceedingly cheap, there is no bread for merchants and manufacturers. Let them be assured, that nothing more is wanted to reduce our agriculturists to the condition of the foreign ones than the reduction of wheat to forty shillings per quarter, and of other produce in proportion. A vast portion of their delusion is produced by our foreign trade. Now, when we put out of sight foreign and colonial goods, and Ireland and our colonies, our exports of British and Irish produce to foreign nations does not much exceed twenty millions annually. A large part of these exports consists of goods manufactured to a great extent by machinery; much of the raw articles are brought, and of the manufactured ones taken away, by foreign ships; and we are pretty sure that these exports do not, in all ways, give bread to more than a quarter of a million of our population. If each individual of the population should expend, on the average, sixpence per week less in manufactures, the manufacturers would lose more by this than by the total loss of the export trade to foreign countries. The chief part of the traders and manufacturers depend solely on the home trade, and the trade to our own possessions.' – 'We therefore exhort the agriculturists, landlords, farmers, and labourers, to make the most determined opposition to the proposed most unnecessary and destructive change. We exhort them to do this, not more for their own sakes than for the sake of their country.' We repeat, 'let merchants and

218   *Battles over Free Trade, Volume 1*

manufacturers ponder upon this;' and we add, let the Landed Interest also ponder well upon it.

Many arguments might be adduced against the principle of free trade, as it would affect the state of landed property – the contracts existing between landlord and tenant – the mode of living to which we have been accustomed for many years – the condition of the agricultural labourers – the future improvement of farms – and the general effect upon the state of the country. These are all important subjects; but the consideration of them, at present, would lead us far beyond the proper limits of such a communication as this. I have only touched on those points which will assist us in fixing the protecting duty which it is indispensably necessary we should possess, as it is quite evident we cannot compete with foreigners without such a protection as would amount almost to a prohibition. In establishing this I have stated many facts, the authorities for which are purposely omitted, solely from a conviction that such an appendage would be unsuitable to a letter. We have, no doubt, enjoyed a prohibitory protection for some time past; but under it our exertions have been able to prove to the whole world that we can raise as much corn as is wanted in the country. If that protection be found too high for the altered circumstances of the country, let it be made lower to meet those circumstances; but, nevertheless, it ought to be high, – and it is not necessary, in my humble opinion, to abolish, but only to amend the present law. It has been found to possess a sound principle, and therefore ought to be retained; and there is little doubt it could be so amended as to work with greater truth and precision. Indeed, how can we, burdened as we are with unavoidable expenses, occasioned by taxation being injected into the very lifeblood of the state, the ramifications of which extend into every interest – how can we, I ask, be even expected to compete with countries which are not similarly circumstanced? In France, the average taxes paid by *each* individual is *thirty-four shillings* per annum – in Russia it is *fourteen* shillings – in Prussia *ten* shillings – but in Great Britain it is *sixty-one* shillings!

Before leaving the subject finally, we can scarcely avoid directing our observations to the state of those interests which have been already subjected to the influence of free trade; and, if they afford us a happy example, we may be made inclined to follow their steps; but, alas! no ray of hope illumines the horizon in that quarter – nothing but dread and dark despair.

The Silk trade has been sadly depressed since the French silks were so liberally introduced here. There can be little doubt that foreign competition is the cause of this depression. There is such a charm in the very name of French silk, that our *haut ton*, how unpatriotically soever it may appear, cannot resist buying it; and though silks of as good quality can doubtless be manufactured in Britain, the fact of our own manufacturers selling their commodities to their customers as those of France, proves a supposed superiority in the latter. Import a new arrangement of colour, or a new pattern, from France – and the French are very inventive in this respect, indeed their chief superiority consists in this – and all the silk goods, then old, will remain till doomsday unnoticed by them; and such will always be the fate of every manufacture whose prosperity depends upon the caprice of people in fashionable life. France has always taken the lead in the *fashions* of the times, and this country seems determined to encourage her vanity in this respect.

The Cotton trade is also depressed. It has been told us over and over again, that foreigners could never compete with this country in cotton goods; and yet it is stated that there is, at present, a greater export of cotton yarn than of manufactured goods. This yarn must be manufactured abroad, else there would be no foreign demand for it. The printed cloths of Switzerland are said to outsell ours in the German markets. The United States of America are fast supplying the South American markets with cotton goods of all descriptions. Does foreign competition no harm in this case?

The Linen trade is depressed. With all our boasted superiority in machinery, our linens have but a feeble footing in the German markets; and I understand that in some kinds of linen goods, our manufacturers imitate the bear and the eagle of Russia and Germany, to pass them for foreign in the South American markets. Do we not feel foreign competition in all this?

The Wool trade is much depressed. Great quantities of merino wool are raised in Prussia, Saxony, and Spain. Now that that wool can be imported at all times, large quantities have been brought in, to the serious injury of the wool growers in this country, who cannot get theirs disposed of to the dealers at home, as their hands are full of foreign wool – nor have foreigners apparently any use for it. An increase in the number of our sheep would therefore aggravate the present evil. Does not foreign competition thus ruin our markets for home grown wool? With fine wool and superior machinery, our manufacturers cannot induce France, Saxony, or Austria, to take our fine cloths, because they make fine cloths to themselves. The United States of America would be a profitable market for our woollen cloths. Their inhabitants could obtain cheaper cloths from us than they can make for themselves; but they will rather encourage their own manufacturers, by continuing to wear their own dear cloth, than have any thing to do with our system of reciprocity.

And, last of all, the Shipping Interest is in a ruinous state. Under the old navigation laws our shipping carried all the goods to and from other countries – to and from our colonies – and to and from our colonies to other countries. In fact they were the carriers of the world. Activity and bustle were the order of the day. Now, foreign ships are allowed to trade to this country and to our colonies on the same footing as our own ships; and, as a consequence, our ships are laid up in ordinary in our harbours, and foreigners are fast occupying our former situation. The London papers mention that our ships are floating in hundreds in our wet docks in idleness, whilst foreign ones are busily employed. At Liverpool foreign vessels arrive weekly in the ratio of three to one of our ships. At Hull foreigners usurp the place of our own countrymen in the proportion of four to one. A Leeds paper mentioned lately, that an order from the Continent for woollen goods was accompanied by a strict injunction that they were to be shipped in foreign bottoms. Foreign oats arrive in our own ports in foreign vessels. It cannot be denied that foreign competition has effected this lamentable change. Indeed, considering how British ships are found in every respect, and how our sailors live and are paid, is it any wonder that foreigners, the most abject of creatures, can drive a trade at a lower rate? The wonder is why they were subjected to such a competition. The ports of Jamaica were thrown open to the United States of America, to induce them, no doubt, to trade with us; instead of which, they would not only not allow our ships to carry our colonial produce to their ports, but under heavy disabilities, but they supplied Jamaica with lumber which was formerly obtained from Canada in our ships. In short, they ran off with about thirty millions worth of our colonial produce, upon which, as formerly, we might have had our profit, and would not enter into our system of reciprocity. An Order in Council was necessary to put a stop to this business. But why was it begun? – The shipping interest partly brought upon themselves their present condition: they petitioned Parliament from all quarters to be allowed to participate in the blessings of free trade; but now, there is not a shipowner in Britain who does not heartily wish that the present law 'had never been born.' 'How fickle and short-sighted is man!'

It was not necessary to particularize so much, but with a view to show that a system of reciprocity in trade is not suited to the present circumstances of this country, and therefore to persist in it must be highly injurious to it. We thus see, that since changes were introduced into the principles of our dealing with other nations, every interest to which that change has been applied has languished, and will decay, if the progress of dissolution be not checked in good time. Notwithstanding of this the newspapers represented one of the Ministry, a few nights ago, in the House of Commons, as expressing his surprise how people out of doors will still persist in attributing any of the evils which affect the interests of the country at present to the operations of the principles of free trade! It is an old adage, 'there are none so blind as those who *will* not see.' The question which we will ask, under a tender apprehension for the fate of the interest to which we are attached, is, – Why will you subject *us* to the ruinous consequences of a measure which has been already proved, by experience in others, to be totally inapplicable to their present state and circumstances?

I must draw to a close. It is necessary for me to crave your indulgence for the hasty manner in which this letter has been composed. It was written at the spur of the moment. Better, perhaps, it had not been written at all; but I was extremely anxious that landlord and tenant should co-operate in the same measure; and, though you may differ in opinion as to the mode and extent of protection necessary, yet you must all agree that protection is indispensably necessary to your well-being as agriculturists. I have endeavoured to shew what the amount of the protecting duty ought to be; and there need be no difference of opinion on that matter, as the data from which the above results proceed have been obtained from yourselves by actual calculation and experience. There need also be no difference of opinion as to the *principle* of our protection, as, under present circumstances, it *must* be of a prohibitory nature; that is, it must make foreign corn have a difficult access to our markets. I have taken a view of our question as a practical farmer, and not as a 'political economist;' and it is in this way, I conceive, that Parliament will be best disposed to listen to us. If we lay our remonstrances fairly and firmly before the Legislature, we need not fear the result; and an opportunity to do so will be afforded us on the sixteeenth [*sic*] of January, at Brechin, of which I entreat you not to fail to take advantage. In the mean time let us be *unanimous and vigilant*, otherwise our enemies, for we *have* enemies, will probably make us one day, when it will be too late, repent of our imbecility and supineness.

I am,

Gentlemen,

With great respect and sincerity,

Your fellow in profession,

HENRY STEPHENS.

Balmadies, 20*th December*, 1826.

The Mechanic in his Own Defence; or Word About with Henry Stephens, Esq. of Balmadies being Remarks on a Letter Addressed by him to the Landholders and Tenantry of the County of Forfar, on the Corn-Law (Dundee: James Adam, W. Sime, and T. Donaldson, 1827).

TO THE PUBLIC.

THE Committee who conducted the business of preparing and forwarding the Dundee Operatives' petitions anent the corn-law, about to be presented to both Houses of Parliament, observe that the few in this county who wish to continue to fatten on the spoil of the community have been invited, by one of their number, to muster all their strength '*for a great pull, a strong pull, and a pull altogether*,' to keep 'things as they are.' The invitation is in the shape of a printed pamphlet, entitled 'A Letter addressed to the Landholders and Tenantry of the County of Forfar, – by Henry Stephens, Esq. of Balmadies.' In this *work*, the author has endeavoured, by means of all the sophistry of which *his ingenuity* is capable, to alarm the fears of his agricultural brethren for the fate of their darling corn-law.

The Committee, considering themselves to be, on the subject of the corn-law, the interim representatives of the great mass of the public of Dundee, would not feel that they had done their duty unless they had, through the medium of that powerful engine the press, endeavoured to counteract the effect which the sophistry, misrepresentation, and falsehood, contained in that Letter, is calculated to produce on the minds of those who have not directed their attention to the subject. The Committee are aware, that many will ask why they have, Don Quixotte like, come forward to grapple with such 'a straw-clad puny form,' in place of allowing his work, by silence, to sink into its merited oblivion. To them the Committee would reply, that they have other motives than the mere refutation of Stephens's *arguments* to induce them to appear before the public on this occasion.

In his Letter, Stephens speaks of two parties only who are interested in the continuance or abolition of the obnoxious corn-law, – namely, the landlords and tenants *versus* the merchants and manufactures; while he modestly keeps out of view the operative classes, 'who are the very soul and strength of our nation.' By omitting all mention of those millions of adversaries who are deeply interested in getting rid of the 'bread-tax,' Mr Stephens considerably thins the ranks of his opponents, and feels himself entitled to talk of his party, who are comparatively a mere handful, as composing one half of the population of the empire. The Committee, therefore, come forward at this time to assert and vindicate their own rights and privileges, and the rights and privileges of the great mass of the people who are neither landlords nor tenants, merchants nor manufacturers, and who are notwithstanding the consumers of nine tenths of the produce of the soil; for which, by the operation of the corn-law, they are compelled to pay to the agriculturists of Great Britain a monopoly-price.

WORD ABOUT
WITH
HENRY STEPHENS, ESQ. OF BALMADIES.

THE corn-law of this country is a subject which has long engaged the attention of almost all classes of society, and has drawn forth the merited indignation of many an intelligent mind: It has been the bane of contention betwixt the commercial and agricultural interests for some time past: In the result of this conflict between the landholder and the merchant, for the quickest mode of increasing their wealth, the one can only feel a diminution, the other an extension of their means to acquire wealth. But how does the corn-law affect those who earn their bread by the sweat of their brow? It has entailed such misery and distress on the industrious and independent-spirited artisan as to reduce him to a situation in which he feels ashamed. It has denied him not only the comforts but even the necessaries of life: It has subjected him to all the inclemency of the wintery storm, by rendering him unable to procure for himself and those who depend on him, even a covering of 'hodden-grey.'

How astonishing is it, then, to find that, amidst all this suffering among the working classes of society, our enemies (for so they term themselves) are still determined to

> 'Be to the puir like ony whunstane,
> An' haud their noses to the grundstane!'

We have now before the us [*sic*] the lucubrations of another champion of the waning cause – another asserter of the right of one part of mankind to starve or feed the other at *their pleasure*: And happy are we that they are now terror-struck for the fate of the strong fabric of their monopoly, – that they are alive to the danger of this engine of destruction to the poor – of ruin to commerce and of aggrandizement to themselves. Yes! we hail with joy the approaching conflict between its friends and foes. We hope that our senators will show, either by an *annihilation* or an *adequate modification* of this law, that *justice*, and not *self-interested motives*, is their object; and we are the more encouraged in this our gratifying anticipation, by the assurance we have already received of a liberal Ministry watching at the helm of British interests: We have a Liverpool, a Canning, a Peel, and a Huskisson, all endeavouring to mitigate our sufferings and add to our comforts, as far as their less liberal brethren in the Cabinet will allow.

We have a Hume and a Brougham eagerly aiding and advancing the march of intellect among all classes; and we have the pleasure to see how rapidly it has advanced since the close of the French war.

But we must now advert more particularly to the contents of the Letter we have already spoken of; and, in our remarks, we shall say little about its style or composition, as it may perhaps be our lot to fall into as many if not more mistakes in this respect than Mr Stephens has done. We hope, however, that, considering the advantage which education may have given him over us, our mistakes will be gently touched by the wand of Criticism, especially as we are more accustomed to handle the tools of mechanism than the pen of erudition.

Our design being to follow him in argument, should we happen to misstate, overrate, or to become abusive, we will only be treading in the path he has marked out for us – in which, it will perhaps be remembered, we are characterized as a 'foul-mouth'd multitude,' – a charge, however, which we cannot help thinking might be fairly retorted and rendered thus, – 'The foul-mouth'd few.'

Our friend begins his epistle by telling his fellows in profession that an important change is expected to take place in the present corn-law; 'and that it is but right they should examine into its probable effects on their future prospects.' No doubt; but it will require some examination to pick out the worst of their hunters, racers, dogs, gamekeepers, lackeys, cooks, and a hundred more *et ceteras*, which their future prospects of reduced rents will not perhaps afford to provide for. He next tells them he 'could have wished an abler advocate had come forward to plead their cause.' But we have to tell him, he needs not trouble himself on that score, since his cause is already so threadbare that neither the oratory of a Jeffrey nor the logic of a Moncrieff could be of the least avail.

His reasons for giving publicity to his epistle, are – 1st, 'The importance of the above examination;' 2d, 'To maintain the consistency of the proverb that he who puts his hand to the plough should not look back:' This perhaps because he has had the trouble of sitting a short time as Chairman in a nearly empty hall at Brechin. But he has a third reason for troubling them at this time, which far transcends the former: It is as follows, – 'There is a spirit of clamour and denouncement abroad against us in the land. I would therefore point out to you the sentiments of many of those petitions which are drawn up by that lynx-eyed class of the community who always look out sharply after their own interests, but who pray that you may be left without protection.' The public will judge between us here, and say which party is the more clamorous, and which has most need to look after its own interests – whether the individuals of the party who, according to their own admission, are yet above distress, or those who, by fraud and oppression, find themselves plunged into the deepest distress.

He next proceeds, – 'There have been several objections urged against this state of things; and I confess there is an apparent clumsiness in the machinery employed for this purpose; but, as far as I can learn, the system has worked well, and at no great expense,; and therefore ought to be meddled with with great caution.'

By saying that our machinery is clumsy, we suppose he means that neither Mr Hume nor Lord King can with perspicuity show the defects of his valuable system; or that neither Mr Whitmore nor Colonel Torrens are capable to write upon the subject. He says 'the system has worked well, and at no great expense,' &c. We are really at a loss to conceive whether this assertion proceeds from ignorance or duplicity: He complains that all that has been brought forward against his system is mere assertion, without a single fact to corroborate it: We really wish Mr Stephens had here given us some of his facts to prove his own assertion. These would have done more to create in us a favourable opinion of his system than all his reasoning put together. But if, as we suspect, his assertion proceeds from ignorance, we will lay before him and the public a statement of a part of those expenses which he deems so little. In the first place, we shall say, and shall afterwards prove, that 1s. per peck for oatmeal would be a fair remunerating price to the grower; and we can with safety affirm that few consumers would grudge to give that price for it: Now, we have to tell Mr Stephens, that from January 1st 1826 to December 31st same year, the average price of oatmeal has been 1s. 5d. per peck (in Dundee), Supposing the population to be 35,000 – and again, supposing each individual to consume one-half peck per week – (which may be thought by some to be too small an allowance, but when we consider that there are many among the higher classes who use little or none of this article, it may be said to be a fair estimate, and admitting it to be so) – this gives the sum of 10s. 10d. drawn from each individual, or the paltry sum of 18,958*l*. 6s. 8d. taken from the pockets of the inhabitants of Dundee to uphold Mr Stephens's darling system. This is one item of his trifling expense. Then there is the exorbitant price which we pay for potatoes, wheaten-bread, barley, pease, and the many other articles of agricultural produce which could be had at a much cheaper rate if importation were permitted: Besides, we would live comparatively more comfortable by being more fully employed in manufacturing goods to be given in exchange for foreign produce.

We will give Mr Stephens another item of those expenses (if he will permit us to class the following item among expenses) which appear to him to be so *trifling*. 'Yesterday evening an inquisition was holden, before John W. Unwin, Esq., at the Shears public-house, Chequer Alley, Whitecross Street, St Luke's, on the body of a female, Mrs Ann Barnwell, whose death was occasioned by starvation. After the examination, the room was cleared, and, after a quarter of an hour's deliberation, the Jury gave the following verdict – *'Died for want of the common necessaries of life.'* – *Mechanics' Journal*, October 1826.

226 *Battles over Free Trade, Volume 1*

We shall only give Mr Stephens another item, and then have done, – viz. 'The emaciated countenances and dejected appearance of the numerous human beings that are to be encountered in a casual walk through the streets of Glasgow, sufficiently denote what a small portion of the common necessaries of life fall to the share of the mechanic.' – *Glasgow Chronicle, August* 1826.

These appalling appearances are not peculiar to the weavers and artificers of Glasgow.

We have here presented Mr Stephens with a few specimens, from amongst thousands, which we could produce, – the greater part of which arise, either directly or indirectly, from a system which, he tells us, is carried on at no great expense. If the health and comfort and lives of his fellow creatures, be of no consequence in his eyes, we do not wonder that he is so eager to persevere in a system which has been proven to be fraught with so much mischief.

He next proceeds to tell his colleagues that 'British agriculture *must have protection.*' And why should they, and especially at the expense of the community, be protected? Is it that they who are employed in agricultural labour may live more comfortable than others? Is it because they have devoted to the service of their country 'their lives and fortunes?' Or is it because they, as the richer part of the commonwealth, exonerate the poorer from paying the taxes? – No, no! it can be none of all these: Why then should they be protected? Because they have a just and unalienable right to be delivered from the hardships which arise from a natural and free circulation of commodities between nations, and to prevent the people of Britain from purchasing their food at the cheapest market, – lest they should be obliged to reduce their hunting and racing establishments, splendid equipages, and other most *necessary* appendages of pageantry.

These, after all, are the evils which the landholders dread from the anticipated change in the corn-law, – these are the evils from which they desire legislative protection, – these are the evils from which they enjoy protection, at the expense of the other classes of the community. No wonder then that Mr Stephens should exclaim, as he has done, 'that nothing but a love of change, nothing but a spirit of innovation, could desire to abandon a system the only fault of which is fidelity to its original principle and adherence to its appointed work.' Our only wonder is that he should disgrace himself so far as to tread so unblushingly in so hacknied a path; for who does not know that these his denunciations against a love of change and his cry against innovators, has been reiterated over and over again by those who (in their day) fattened on the spoil of oppression, and were interested only in maintaining their power to do so? But, once deprive them of this power, once place them in the situation of the innovators, and we instantly find those who formerly declaimed so loudly against a love of change and innovation, themselves becoming innovators and 'fond of change;' for who would not wish to change his situation if he were uneasy? who would not wish to change a heavy burden for a lighter one? who would not wish to exchange a state of starvation for one of plenty?

Mr Stephens doubtless thinks that we have no need of change on this score; for he says, 'that the price of corn has not much exceeded its real value for these ten years past.' But, in order to show him how far he is wrong, as well as the reasonableness of our 'love of change,' we shall lay before him and the public the following statement. According, then, to our former calculation, the average price of oatmeal (in Dundee) for 1826 was 1s. 5d. a peck, and we considered 1s. its real value.[1]

By this statement, each individual pays to the landholders a weekly tax of 1s. 3½d. (a yearly tax of 3*l*. 7s. 2d); and, estimating the population of Great Britain at twenty millions, it appears that Mr Stephens and his brother-agriculturists take from us, under the existing law, the paltry sum of 67,166,666*l*. 13s. 4d. annually. This is some millions above the whole amount of the taxes levied by Government; and, were this sum made use of for Government purposes – say, for instance, to pay off the national debt, which it would soon do – we would perhaps handle it with less acrimony. It appears, however, that there exists some difference of opinion between Mr Stephens and some of his brethren on the subject of the corn-law. We fondly hope that there are many among them who have as much humanity as prevent them from going all lengths with him to enrich themselves by starving the poor. To such, Mr Stephens says he has not a shadow of a doubt but that the proposed alteration in the corn-law will be inimical to agricultural interests; and, being influenced by such a conviction, he will endeavour, by the following objections, with reasoning thereon, to impress such of their minds as maintain the negative of the above sentiment, to think well before they give their sanction with temerity to such a subverting measure. And thus he begins, – 'Britain consumes a certain quantity of corn yearly. It is an indisputable fact that she has raised as much corn as her inhabitants could consume for some years past: The simple fact of the ports having continued shut for that length of time corroborates the assertion. What use, then, is there for foreign corn? What use can we make of two watches at the same time, even though the one were made *abroad* and the other at home?'

This reasoning may chime very well in the ears of superficial readers, or those who are interested in keeping things 'as they are:' But, in our ears, who have been taught by experience to take a closer view of things, it sounds very differently, – we shall dissect our friend's logic here. We observe, then, that he lays down the following proposition, – 'That Britain grows as much corn as her inhabitants can consume;' and he takes this for granted, without more proof than the fact of the ports having been shut against foreign importation for some time; which, instead of proving his proposition, only amounts to this, – *that her inhabitants got no*

1 [Ed.: A table detailing the weekly allowance of grain per head in Britain has been omitted.]

228   *Battles over Free Trade, Volume 1*

more corn to consume than she grew. But Mr Stephens, like an artful sophist, asks the question, – 'What use, then, is there for foreign corn?' We really wish, as he delights to deal in facts, that he had been at the trouble to ascertain the quantity of corn which Britain grows yearly, at an average, and her number of inhabitants; and then by his arithmetical skill shown how much each individual had yearly to consume: By doing this, if the quotient had turned out in his favour his proposition would have been an indisputable fact: But then it might have turned out otherwise; – 'aye! there's the rub!' We know, however, that there can be nothing more certain than this – that if Britain grows as much corn as her 'inhabitants can consume,' they do not get it. What, then, becomes of it? Why, if it is grown, most undoubtedly Mr Stephens and his brethren in profession must lock it up, that it may not come into our markets till they have arisen sufficiently high to satiate his cupidity. Here, then, Mr Stephens, is the use of foreign corn: Were it permitted to be brought into our markets at all times, we might perhaps get it when you and your fellows in profession were unwilling to give us corn of your own growing, but at your own price; and thus some of those horrid scenes which we have already noticed might perhaps be prevented. We believe our friend is sufficiently aware of this; although, as if to make his point more clear, he asks, 'What use can we make of two watches at the same time, even although the one was made abroad and the other at home, – an analogy, by the by, which is surely as clumsy as it is unfavourable for the purpose it is intended: For, although we are no grammarians, our mothers have told us that the word 'WE' denotes two or more individuals. Now, supposing the 'WE,' in the case put by Mr Stephens, to consist of himself and the humble individual who is now writing for this Committee, – and again, supposing, of the two watches, that the home-made watch is finer and of better workmanship, &c., and thus may perhaps be dearer, though it may answer the end no better than the foreign-made watch – can any thing be more clear than this, – That Mr Stephens, being a landholder, and having money at his command, may purchase the home-made watch; while I, who am but a poor wight, may content myself with the foreigner; and thus *we* shall both *have watches*, which would not be the case if I could not procure for myself a foreign one? Let him now revise his analogy, and apply it as he intended, if he can. That he will be duly alive to it, we have no doubt; for, in another part of his work, after some preliminary observations regarding those countries from which we could get the greatest supplies of food, he gives the addressed a long rhapsody about Merino sheep-rearing, the amazing cheapness of carriage, labour, &c., in these countries. In short, he would make the landholders and tenantry of Forfarshire belive [*sic*] that the Egyptians, Polanders, and Americans, would feed the people of Britain for almost nothing, were it not for his blessed protective system. Every body knows, however, that he has greatly exaggerated his descriptions, that he might the more successfully alarm the fears of his friends for the

The Mechanic in his Own Defence (1827)

fate of his system. But, not content with all this exaggeration, lest he should fail in his purpose, he proceeds to shake the grimaces of poverty in their faces, by giving them a description of the Polish Serf or Peasant, which is as follows.

'The Polish Peasant is not free: Though not his person, his labour is attached to the soil; he is obliged to work to his proprietor for food and clothing, and the little land he occupies; he lives upon milk and rye-bread; he wears the 'hodden grey;' and in winter is clothed with sheep-skins turned inside out; his clothing is made at home by the females, who have little else to do; he buys no butcher-meat; and, as to a wheaten loaf, it never enters his lips.'

Such is the lamentable situation (as he would have it) of the Polish Serf. But what would many of our British mechanics give for a situation where food and clothing and a little land were their enviable lot? How happy would that part of our population in the West Country, now praying the Legislature for means to expatriot themselves from their native land – how happy, we say, would they be (at this season of the year), to be clad with the 'hodden-grey,' and how gladly would many of them, no doubt, fill their bellies with the milk and rye-bread of the Polish Serf? But how much better, we ask, is the condition of many of our own agricultural labourers? We are told that 'they are set of poor devils,' and this, too, by a knight and a landholder. And we have the authority of a Select Committee of the House of Commons for saying, that in many parts of England, more than three fourths of those employed in agricultural labour are paupers – absolute beggars, depending on legal charity for subsistence. Let Mr Stephens and his fellows in profession 'ponder upon this.' Let them contrast the condition of the Polish Peasant with our own, and candidly say which they would choose; and let them take shame to themselves, for it is from them that many of those evils spring, in depriving, by their unjust exactions, the subjects of a land of boasted intelligence and freedom, not only of the means of subsistence, but the means of acquiring knowledge, which is the true stimulus to a *spirit of independence*. But this is a picture which Mr Stephens seems no way inclined to look at. He, it appears, is blind to these few facts; or if he admits that misery exists at all among our agricultural labourers, he seems to feel confident that it will be awfully increased by any change in his system. Under the pretended impression of such a feeling, he affects to sympathize with our ploughmen, for their prospective conditition, [*sic*] in being turned out of employment as agricultural labour decreases, till he again betrays himself by showing his old *selfish principle* – and the *real truth*. The real feeling of his bosom springs forth unknown to himself; and then it is manifest that it is not the ploughmen, but himself and his fellows in profession he is sympathizing with, for the awful condition to which they will be reduced by having such a host of idle ploughmen to maintain.

But we will be his accoucheurs here, and deliver him of this intolerable load. We will take them off his hand, and teach them to make a finer and more civilized habit for the Polish Serf, while they (the Polanders) will send them and us corn and all other kinds of necessaries in return; and then, we have no doubt but our ploughmen will find themselves as well provided for as when they were *bothy-fed*.

The next bugbear he attempts to hold up, is a reduction of rents; which, he seems to think, will be an unavoidable consequence of a departure from his system; and although he admits that some of the greatest of our land-proprietors might be able to bear a small reduction of rent, yet the lesser ones could bear little, or none at all; their lands being either mortgaged or unfavourably entailed; of which latter class there are forty to one of the great ones. We really think *shame* might have suggested silence upon this point, and prevented him from exposing to the public the effects of their own or their forefathers' levities: But we are happy to see how nearly his arguments are spun out. It is truly humbling to see how far a wish to accumulate wealth will lead even the great ones of our land on the road to degradation. But he has another and a weightier reason for maintaining the present high rents: He says, 'We have the strength and power of Britain to support: Break but Britannia's right arm, with which she wields the lance, and she will soon be unable to use the shield in her own defence.' We confess we are at a loss to comprehend what the worthy gentleman here means by 'wielding the lance,' &c. Perhaps some deed of Yeoman valour had gleamed upon his mind at the time; or, pondering on the 'days of yore,' when the heroes of Chevy Chace wielded such a weapon, the thought might have struck him; for we are at a loss to know in what other way he or his fellows in profession can arrogate to themselves such a place in Britain's roll of heroes. Who (let us ask), is it that maintains the strength and power of Britain? In warlike achievements (if this be his meaning), is it not we operatives who man her fleets and compose her armies? Whose industry is it that has raised her to that eminent station she now holds in the commercial world – is it not ours? Who, then, has the best right to claim protection on the score of maintaining the strength and power of Britain? Is it not we – we who compose the strength of Britain – we whose labour is the source of Britain's wealth? Yes, it is we who have the best right to protection; for with us Britain must either stand or fall. Mr Stephens and his fellows in profession may indeed have sometimes united with us in advancing the strength and power of Britain by warlike achievements; but we cannot help thinking, that there is something so horrific in war – something so lacerating to the heart of humanity – that both of us may well be ashamed of boasting about it. Indeed, we are aware that boasting in general is strongly characteristic of the weakness of one's cause; and if we have here committed ourselves on this point, we have only to say that we were unconsciously led to it by the arrogance of our antagonist. But we have here possibly mistaken Mr Stephens's meaning. By 'maintaining the strength and power of Britain,' he may perhaps mean that he and his colleagues pay the greatest part of the taxes: But how can this be, seeing that in another part of his Letter he tells us of the poverty of about forty to one of them; and who does not know that the greatest part of the revenue arises from excise-duties on imports? With respect to the revenue drawn from luxuries that are imported, we believe they consume a goodly quantity of them; but we can hardly believe that Mr Stephens and his colleagues are such GORMANDIZERS as pay the greatest portion of the revenue by these means, considering the small proportion which they bear to the population of Britain.

Mr Stephens, however, in his zeal for maintaining high rents, affirms that they were generally raised during the war; but he adds, that they were not raised above the value of produce, nor the latter above that of labour.

With respect to the first part of his assertion, we only refer the reader to a calculation in a former part of this paper; and, with respect to the last part, that the value of produce has not risen above that of labour, we shall here insert some well-known facts, and leave the reader to judge, and him to prove his assertion, by explaining how he would distribute the price of labour so as to make it meet the price of produce. We say, then, that the principal trade of our town is weaving. It employs about one third part of its inhabitants; these are employed at two kinds of work, which we shall denominate coarse and fine. Those employed at the former kind, earn at present about 6s. a week; those at the latter about 5s. a week, – which gives an average of about 5s. 6d. a head to each individual. Now, supposing the case of a man, a wife, and three children, to be maintained by this sum, we would just ask Mr Stephens to tell us the most economical plan to spend this 5s. 6d. among these five individuals, to keep them alive – laying out of view house-rent, fuel, clothing, &c.?

The next part of the debateable landholders' monopoly which we shall take notice of, is that where he speaks of the expenses attendant on raising the crop, and avers that it is next to impossible to raise wheat at less than 64s. per quarter. As we have been furnished with sufficient information on this subject, we shall lay the substance of the same before the public, leaving the reader to judge for himself. In doing this, we shall lay down a scale of six successive crops, from 1821 to 1826, inclusive, of one acre of ground, digested accurately from the information alluded to.[1]

We have endeavoured, by laying the above before the reader, to show that agricultural produce may be raised at far less expense in this country than Mr Stephens would have us to believe; and, however widely we may differ in opinion from him, we think that wheat could be raised at 15s. or 18s. per quarter less than he states, and, at the same time, render the farmer a fair remuneration, and he and his fellows in profession all they are entitled to – a moderate

---

1 [Ed.: There follows statistics illustrative of this point.]

rent. Let him, then, ponder upon this; let the public ponder upon this; and let public opinion sound the praise of his philanthropy, in so liberally saying that 23s., or even a duty of almost any amount, would not be sufficient protection to agriculture, if the ports were allowed always to remain open.

We will now pass on to where he complains that we abuse the protection granted to him and his colleagues, by calling it 'BREAD-TAX, STARVATION BILL,' &c. He says it is extremely *vulgar* to do so, and that is is [*sic*] very characteristic of the *'foul mouth'd multitude.'*

In a former part of his Letter, he upbraided us for using clumsy machinery in advocating our cause: But we are much mistaken if he has not fallen into the same error himself, by making use of such language as the above. We, the working classes, are only twice mentioned in his lucubrations, and both times nowise to our advantage: He seems to consider us to be only a devouring machine, who must passively submit to consume these articles of his monopoly. But he must no longer consider us as such; he must remember that *we are men*, who will no longer by our silence cancel our rights, as part of the community. He should also remember that we comprise more than three fourths of the population of Great Britain; and that the clearing away of the rubbish of ignorance and superstition from our intellects, of late, has given us to see that we are trampled upon by a handful of our fellow-beings. It may perhaps be a matter of chagrin to him to think, that we, as a part of that 'foul mouth'd multitude,' should be so arrogant as lift the pen against him at this time: We have, however, to tell him, that it is not only our interest to do so, but we take a pleasure in exerting the humblest effort to destroy the props of the corn-law; because we consider it to be part of that machine whose province has been to keep the poor man in ignorance and subjection, ever since time saw one man usurp the power of tyrannizing over another.

Mr Stephens, it seems, does not like the name of a monopolizer. He would no doubt like to be viewed as a philanthropist, if he could obtain that character for nothing, – but, to be a monopolizer, ''tis an odious name;' and, to get clear of it, he asks, 'What sort of a monopoly is it that is enjoyed by one half of the people of a country?' But here again he lacks those facts for which he so unceremoniously upbraids *us for wanting* in our statements. As he has given us none, all we can do is to state a few ourselves, that the question may appear in a clearer light. We will, in the first place, give the aggregate population of the counties of Forfar in Scotland, Gloucester in England, and Cork in Ireland, – deducting therefrom the population of all the towns and villages within them whose inhabitants do not exceed four hundred. This must be considered to be much more than a fair concession, when it is kept in view that many of the country people work at mechanical professions.[1]

1 [Ed.: A table detailing the respective populations has been omitted.]

By this statement, the agricultural population does not exceed one fourth of the inhabitants of Britain. But we shall give a more unerring calculation of the proportion of numbers which the agriculturists bear to the general population of the empire.

The remainder of the farm being fallow, grass, &c.; and again, supposing that one individual will consume of wheat 1 boll, of barley 1 boll, of oats 2 bolls, of potatoes 1½ bolls, annually, which is something above our former calculation, the produce of the above farm will maintain four hundred individuals; and, as 50 is to 400, so is the agricultural population to the rest of the community. Thus, instead of half the population, Mr Stephens has only one eighth. But perhaps he had also reckoned on his side the quadrupeds (domestic and wild); in which case we doubt not but his party may even exceed a half.

But, allowing that his assertion were true, how can the agricultural labourer enjoy any part of his monopoly, when he pays as much for his food as the mechanic?

Mr Stephens complains of the officiousness of the merchants and manufacturers, for petitioning so much for an alteration of his system; and asks, what they would say were he and his friends to hold meetings to petition about the bounties on linen? We feel confident, that if they wished to protect the bounties, they would just attempt to defend them against the powerful reasonings of Mr Stephens and his brethren. But the merchants and manufactures, as well as we, would be happy to see your monoply [*sic*] making as gradual an exit from the stage of existence as the linen bounty is doing. In his endeavours to describe the odiousness of that scarecrow Free Trade, he extols, or affects to extol, the wisdom of the Americans; and he tells us, we might find a very good market with them for our woollen cloth, were it not that they are too wise for us, and will manufacture that article themselves at a much higher rate than they could obtain it from us, rather than encourage our system of reciprocity. Mr Stephens is here guilty of grossly misrepresenting the policy of the Americans. It is because Britain will not extend the system of reciprocity far enough, – because Britain will not take their corn in return for our woollen cloths, and that they have nothing else to give. Mr Stephens, farther, in his fears for innovation, attempts here again to alarm the fears of other people on the same subject, by adverting to the ruinous consequences which, he says, has arisen to our shipping interest by the late alteration in our navigation-laws. But how can it be otherwise? How can our shipowners compete with foreigners while the iniquitous corn-law keeps the price of provisions so high? It is a well-known fact, that the victualling of vessels comprises the greater part of their expenses: But Mr Stephens does not wish to look at this; he would rather have us believe that all the evil has arisen from that liberal system which has lately been adopted by the wisdom of our Government.

In his conclusion, Mr Stephens says, that it would perhaps have been better his Letter *had not been written* (printed) *at all.* In this we cannot agree with him, for more reasons than one: First, it shows the weakness of his cause – it shows that neither justice, humanity, nor shame, were inmates of the bosom who penned it. It shows also, that his fears for his monopoly are not groundless – that his monopoly is fast approaching to a dissolution. He then exhorts his brethren in profession to be unanimous – to be vigilant, 'otherwise our enemies, for we have enemies, will one day, when it will be too late, make us repent our embecility [*sic*] and supineness,' – which is an advice we hope will serve both parties.

In our conclusion, we must detain the reader a little longer. It will perhaps be thought by some that we have been advocating our side of the question on the contracted principles of party, – that is, we have been setting forth our own interest in opposition to that of the other classes of the community. Such, however, is far from our intention; and if we have said any thing in the preceding pages calculated to make such an impression on the mind of the reader, we have perhaps been led to it by following Mr Stephens too closely. He, among other calumnious insinuations, brings this charge against us, – he represents us as desiring to reduce their interests to the same miserable condition of our own; a charge (to say the least of it) which comes with very ill grace off his hand, after displaying so much selfishness and misanthropy in his pages. Mr Stephens may have paid 'too much for his whistle;' but we cannot think this a sufficient reason why he should be thus endeavouring to alarm Forfarshire by its sonorous notes of calumny and misrepresentation. We, however, are aware that no law 'can be a just one' which does not embrace the interests of the whole community so as to equalize them. We know well, that if the beam of political equity be not held fair, the one part of the community will be depressed while the other is elevated; and, impressed with such a conviction, we desire only such an alteration of the obnoxious corn-law as will promote the general interests of the whole body-politic; and, that such an alteration is loudly called for in the present state of things, both by the agricultural as well as the commercial interests, is clearly evident; For who does not see, that the existing corn-law has given rise to great fluctuations in prices? This is an effect which Mr Stephens does not attempt to gainsay. Who does not then see the embarrassments this has caused to many of our agriculturists, by leading them at times to calculate too much on the value of their produce? It is hardly necessary to say what the effects of this law have brought on the mercantile and operative classes. Let all, then, be unanimous in their prayers to the Legislature for an alteration of this law; and particularly let the latter class (to which we belong) be alive to our own interests: Let us not be lulled into a deadly apathy by the canting insinuation that we have nothing to do with legislative affairs: Let us remember that we must bear a goodly proportion of the effects of these affairs, and thus cannot be uninterested spectators: And let us remember, also, that by too much silence, we have ere this time virtually obliterated ourselves from society, and in effect become the passive 'beasts of burden' which our oppressors would have us to be.

A MOVEMENT HALTED: THE INTERNATIONAL PERSPECTIVE 1830–42

In Europe, as in the United States, protection of domestic industries remained an integral component of national commercial policy.[1] Reform was difficult, not only on account of powerful interest groups, but also because foreign states wished to emulate Britain's manufacturing success and perceived this success as resulting from protection. Despite the poor prospects for reform, there was a desire to continue Huskisson's policies in freeing international commerce but the commercial diplomacy of Whig governments achieved little in the 1830s. It was not until Robert Peel became Prime Minister in 1841 that there was a concerted effort, with coherent policy objectives, towards tariff liberalization.[2] Despite this lack of success, Anglo-French and Anglo-Zollverein negotiations reveal significantly different conceptions of commercial policy throughout Europe. The latter also indicate that the impetus for commercial reform did not emanate solely from Britain.

The French tariff was an important object of attention for commercial reformers. Prohibition rather than protection remained its defining characteristic, underpinned by atavistic notions of national self-sufficiency, and traces of physiocratic prejudice against foreign trade. The aggressive return to protection during the Revolutionary wars proved to be enduring. By 1815, France's failure to keep pace with Britain in industrial and commercial terms was apparent, and tariffs of 1816, 1820 and 1822 consolidated protection of the domestic market as a means towards further industrial development.[3]

The economic geography of France militated against extensive support for free trade, for the French economy was not export-led, and few sectors had much to gain from commercial liberalization. Whilst the prospects for reform appeared bleak, not least because protectionists dominated the Chamber of Deputies after the July Revolution, there was a readiness on both sides to arrive at a better understanding if not a formal alliance.[4] To this end, a commercial mission was dispatched to France, conducted by John Bowring and George Villiers between 1831 and 1834. The remit was to 'promote a more liberal intercourse by attempting to induce France to diminish their restrictive duties on imports of

– 237 –

foreign commodities'.[5] The British government was under no illusions as to the difficulties. In his instructions, Charles Poulett Thomson remarked on the likelihood of powerful opposition, especially amongst important protected interests such as cotton and iron.[6] Such pessimism represented a realistic appraisal of the power of French interest groups. In 1822, French ironmasters managed to raise the tariff from 15 to 25 francs per 50 kilograms on foreign iron and, by 1828, the Commission d'Enquête found French bar iron to be more than double the price of English iron.[7] Such evidence had little impact against the widespread protectionist mentality of French society. The majority of French writers attributed British prosperity to the protective system, and viewed with suspicion the attempts of 'perfidious Albion' to promote freer trade.[8] Pre-existing national prejudices, allied to the perceived pecuniary advantages of protection presented a considerable obstacle towards commercial liberalization.[9]

In surveying French commerce, the Commissioners disparagingly pointed to the incidence of prohibitions and protective duties that characterized the French tariff. Central to their argument was the damaging effect of tariffs on the entire French economy. Exclusion was perceived as the most serious abrogation of commercial enterprise. A large number and broad range of imported goods were prohibited, with irrational and wholly contradictory reasoning employed as justification.[10] Many were justified on the basis of the superior, cheaper products of foreign nations, especially Britain. The result was a huge incidence of smuggling, which damaged native industries and government revenue. Citing the report of the Budget Committee of 1832, consisting of thirty-six members of the Chamber of Deputies, the Commissioners noted the Committee's statement on imported wheat: 'Therefore let us own, that there are objects which a State ought always to produce, and with respect to which the theory of free-trade is inapplicable'. Emulation of Britain was viewed as the means towards enhancing French prosperity and manufacturing progress, with Britain providing a model for maintaining a restrictive commercial policy: 'Let us act like her ... let us not lower our Tariffs until our manufactures shall have been developed and perfected; let us beware of sacrificing the interests of our country to the pretended welfare of the world'. This argument was taken a step further with the claim that Britain's commercial liberalism was bogus, for 'far from renouncing her system, she fortifies and consolidates it'.[11] Britain's refusal to equalize wine duties lent some substance to this claim.[12]

Notions of trade liberalization did not thrive in such a politicized and suspicious atmosphere, but support for commercial liberalization came from specific export-led industries, such as Bordeaux wine merchants and silk merchants of Lyons.[13] The influence of French political economists advocating commercial reform was extremely limited at this stage, although Jean-Baptiste Say had adherents. In view of his later career, it is surprising that Louis Adolphe Thiers promoted reform. Briefly serving as Minister of Commerce in 1834, he proposed abolition of prohibitive duties and reduction of protective duties, but accepted temporary protection. Thiers argued that commercial restriction was only justifiable if 'used to protect a home industry which is likely to succeed ... but only temporarily so; it ought to come to an end when the industry has completed its education, when it has become an adult'.[14] Such justification for 'infant industries' was common in France during this period, reflecting the unequal competition represented by advanced British manufacturing industries.[15] It was not until 1836 that moderate progress was made, with reduced duties on wrought iron, coal and cotton, and removal of a number of prohibitions.[16] That so little was achieved was indicative of the strength of French protectionism, which encompassed a broad range of economic interests and was widely viewed as possessing historical legitimacy. National economic geography militated against the formation of a commercial reform movement drawing support from the mercantile and industrial classes. When the tariff was liberalized in 1860, it was significant that it resulted from the imperial dictat of Napoleon III.

The Zollverein (Confederation of German States organized into a Customs Union), formed in 1834, presented a different set of problems from France. Indeed, it has been claimed that the Anglo-Zollverein relationship dominated the commercial diplomacy of the time and was important in breaking up the mercantilist navigation system.[17] It was also one that provided ammunition for British commercial reformers as to the iniquities of the Corn Laws, and thus provides an important link with the reforms of the 1840s. The Prussian Commercial Union, formed in 1818, aimed to create a free trade customs zone amongst German states. The Prussian tariff of 1818 was the lowest tariff schedule in Europe, with imports of raw materials duty free. The liberalism of the tariff sparked discord amongst manufacturers, with Friedrich List instrumental in the formation of a protectionist movement in 1819, which became stronger with the development of German industry.[18] Many viewed Prussia's actions in terms of nation-building, in the same way as abolition of internal customs duties in Britain and France facilitated national unity through uniform administrative practices. Prussia was bold in its approach to commercial policy and, engaging Britain in commercial negotiations, sought a reduction in timber duties to reduce Canadian preference, and to place Prussian shipping on the same footing as British shipping. Determined to retain imperial preference and grant strict reciprocity, Britain rejected these proposals, considering they would constitute 'a gratuitous concession' to Prussia, and not a 'just equivalent'.[19] In rejecting these proposals, Britain acted in accordance with legislation then in force, within the complex regulations of the Navigation Acts. Undeterred, Prussia made further attempts to make a new commercial agreement in the 1820s, but these again foundered on British determination to be guided by their own interests. A diplomatic spat in 1825–6 proved to be an early example of arguments later used so effectively by British free traders. Baron Maltzahn argued that until facilities were granted for Prussian corn and timber imports, Anglo-Prussian commercial relations would not be reciprocal, accompanying this observation with a veiled threat that Prussia's geographical position made her capable of obstructing commerce.[20] The Board of Trade's response was that imperial commitments ruled out any agreement, and that Prussia wanted more than reciprocity. In demanding concessions over timber and corn, Prussia had broached the subject of the central pillars of the protective system, thus prompting an eloquent and comprehensive rejection of any proposal by a foreign government for alteration of the Corn Laws.[21] Maltzahn protested that British prohibition of corn imports accounted for the decline of British manufacturing exports to Prussian ports, and threatened retaliation.[22]

The establishment of the Zollverein was followed by the accession of many German states in the 1830s.[23] Although favourable tariff rates augured well for commercial liberalization, British suspicion that Prussia would dominate the Zollverein, and possibly exclude British products, was particularly apparent in the 1830s, exacerbated by the failure of rival customs unions in northern and southern Germany.[24] Britain concluded a commercial treaty with Frankfurt, largely to keep it out of the Zollverein, but, eventually surrounded by Zollverein territory, she joined it in 1836.[25] With the expiration of the Anglo-Prussian Convention in 1834, Prussia attempted to force a change in British commercial policy, with Prussian corn and timber imports again prominent.[26] As the 1824 Convention related only to shipping duties and had no implications for tariff rates, Viscount Palmerston correctly denied linkage of these issues and followed George Canning's view of eight years earlier that vital national considerations connected with the Corn Law question meant it must be decided by the legislature rather than the executive in negotiations with foreign countries. Finally, hinting at the Zollverein as a vehicle for Prussian aggrandizement, he posed two alternative views of the Zollverein's objectives: as a means of promoting European trade, or as a means of excluding those countries outside the limits of an 'arbitrary circle' of states.[27]

These attempts to reform the British tariff provided important practical examples and arguments for commercial reformers in Britain. The political economists at the Board of Trade regarded the Zollverein as a response to the Corn Laws, and considered Corn Law repeal would result in the Zollverein redirecting resources and investment towards agriculture. For many liberal reformers, free trade was a means of retarding Continental manufacturing.[28] Bowring's report on the Zollverein of 1840 was a classic statement of this position, in arguing that industrialization and protectionism were responses to British protectionism.

A Movement Halted 241

Similarly, the Select Committee on Import Duties argued tariff liberalization would be reciprocated by foreign nations.[29]

The evidence from European states does not appear to have supported this claim. Austria resisted further tariff reductions as she was not satisfied with the subordinate role of supplying raw materials and produce to Britain.[30] More pointedly, List attacked Bowring's presumption that Germany's predominant wish was to export corn to Britain. Whilst providing a mass of statistical and anecdotal evidence for free traders, the nature of the Anglo-Zollverein commercial relationship was not a simple free trade/protection dichotomy. In the 1840s, facing demands from German ironmasters at the influx of British iron, the Zollverein gave preferential treatment to Belgian iron. This was merely one instance of the antagonistic Anglo-German relationship, fuelled by economic rivalry just as intense as the Anglo-French relationship.[31] From 1842, the British government relinquished negotiations with foreign states, and conducted commercial policy unilaterally, thus providing the basis for the dramatic transformation of 1846.

Notes

1. J. B. Williams, *British Commercial Policy and Trade Expansion, 1750–1850* (Oxford: Clarendon Press, 1972), pp. 159–60, 181–6, 215–16.

2. L. Brown, 'The Board of Trade and the Tariff Problem, 1840–2', *English Historical Review*, 68:268 (1953), pp. 394–421; only three commercial treaties were made between 1830 and 1836: J. H. Clapham, 'The Last Years of the Navigation Acts', *Economic History Review*, 29:99 (1910), pp. 480–501, on p. 485.

3. S. B. Clough, *France: A History of National Economics, 1789–1939* (New York: C. Scribner's Sons, 1939), p. 92; E. Levasseur, 'The Recent Commercial Policy of France', *Journal of Political Economy*, 1:1 (1892), pp. 20–49, on pp. 23–4.

4. L. Brown, *The Board of Trade and the Free-Trade Movement 1830–42* (Oxford: Clarendon Press, 1958), p. 119.

5. *Times*, 2 November 1833, p. 2a.

6. See John Bowring, First Report on the Commercial Relations between France and Britain, *Parliamentary Papers* (1834), below, pp. 243–5.

7. First Report on the Commercial Relations between France and Britain, *Parliamentary Papers* (1834), xix.[64], 1, pp. 29–30.

8. Ibid., p. 26; Proudhon opposed Britain's 'insidious economic penetration', see B. F. Hoselitz, 'Socialism, Communism, and International Trade', *Journal of Political Economy*, 57:3 (1949) pp. 227–41, on pp. 230–1.

9. See 'First Report of Messrs. Villiers and Bowring', *Westminster Review* (1834), below, pp. 254–9.

10. General Statement of Prohibited Goods from Foreign Countries, *Parliamentary Papers* (1834), xix.[64], pp. 39–43, 45.

11. 26 November 1832, Report of the Committee on the Budget, *Parliamentary Papers*, xix.[64], pp. 74, 75–6.

12. See 'Divergent Paths: Britain and America, 1812–30', above, pp. 129–235.

242   *Battles over Free Trade, Volume 1*

13. See John Bowring, Second Report on the Commercial Relations between France and Britain, *Parliamentary Papers* (1835), below, pp. 246–51; *Times*, 6 February 1834, p. 5 d; 28 October 1834, p. 5 c.

14. Cited in P. Ashley, *Modern Tariff History: Germany – United States – France* (London: John Murray, 1904), p. 288; for resistance to Thiers's proposals, *Times*, 6 February 1834, p. 5d.

15. See Correspondence between Havre Chamber of Commerce and the Minister of Commerce, 14 and 18 October 1834, *Parliamentary Papers* (1835), below, pp. 252–3.

16. Commissions of 1828 and 1834 recommended modification of duties, especially the excessive protection given to iron, C. P. Kindleberger, 'The Rise of Free Trade in Western Europe, 1820–1875', *Journal of Economic History*, 35:1 (1975), pp. 20–55, on p. 37.

17. Clapham, 'The Last Years of the Navigation Acts', p. 485.

18. Williams, *British Commercial Policy*, p. 199.

19. Humboldt to Castlereagh, 9 February 1818, in 'Correspondence with Foreign Powers on Duties Levied in England on Imported Corn', *Parliamentary Papers* (1839), lxvi.[204], pp. 4–6; Castlereagh to Humboldt, 1 May 1818, in ibid., pp. 7–9.

20. Maltzahn to Canning, 25 December 1825, in 'Communications from the Prussian Minister in London, and Minute of the Board of Trade, relative to the Commercial Relations between Great Britain and Prussia, December, 1825–January, 1826', *Parliamentary Papers* (1839), lxvii.[203], p. 6.

21. See Minute of the Board of Trade, 17 January 1826, relative to the Commercial Relations between Great Britain and Prussia, *Parliamentary Papers* (1839), below, pp. 260–5; reiterated in Canning to Maltzahn, 6 February 1826, in 'Correspondence with Foreign Powers on Duties Levied in England on Imported Corn', pp. 22–3.

22. Maltzahn to Canning, 9 May 1826, in ibid., pp. 29–32.

23. W. O. Henderson, *The Zollverein*, 3rd edn (London: Cass, 1984), pp. 36–7.

24. Clapham, 'The Last Years of the Navigation Acts', pp. 488–9; Williams, *British Commercial Policy*, pp. 201–4.

25. See Lord Palmerston to the Earl of Minto, 17 January 1834, below, pp. 266–7; Williams, *British Commercial Policy*, p. 203.

26. Bulow to Palmerston, 29 May 1834, in 'Correspondence with Foreign Powers on Duties Levied in England on Imported Corn', pp. 37–40.

27. Palmerston to Bulow, 10 July 1834, in ibid., pp. 40–4; by 1847, Palmerston was convinced the Zollverein was 'formed for the purpose of excluding by high duties the importation of British manufactures into Germany', cited in A. Howe, *Free Trade and Liberal England, 1846–1946* (Oxford: Clarendon Press, 1997), p. 81.

28. Kindleberger, 'The Rise of Free Trade in Western Europe', p. 33–4.

29. Report on the Prussian Commercial Union, *Parliamentary Papers* (1840), xxi.[225], pp. 2, 13; Bowring to Palmerston, 7 August 1839, *Parliamentary Papers* (1840), xxi.[225], pp. 285–7; Select Committee Report on Import Duties, 6 August 1840, *Parliamentary Papers* (1840), v.99, [601].

30. Williams, *British Commercial Policy*, p. 211; Brown, *The Board of Trade*, p. 109.

31. N. M. Gordon, 'Britain and the Zollverein Iron Duties, 1842–5', *Economic History Review*, 22:1 (1969), pp. 75–87; Williams, *British Commercial Policy*, p. 208.

A MOVEMENT HALTED: INTERNATIONAL PERSPECTIVE 1830–42

Anglo-French Commercial Relations

John Bowring, First Report on the Commercial Relations between France and Britain, *Parliamentary Papers* (1834), xix.1, pp. 7–8, 9–11, 11–13, 26–8.

To the Right Honourable the Lords Commissioners of Trade and Plantations

MY LORDS,

In presenting to your Lordships a Report on the Commercial Relations between France and Great Britain, we have thought it desirable to divide the subject into two principal branches: the first of a general, and the second of a particular character. The early portion of our investigations will be directed to an examination of the subject as a whole, exhibiting such points, and drawing such deductions as appear most worthy of attention; while, in the concluding part, we propose to pursue our inquiries in detail through the most important articles which have been or may be profitably interchanged, for the purpose of suggesting, in every individual case, such modifications or alterations as are likely to promote the main object of our mission, namely, – the extension of the trade between the two countries.

We beg leave briefly to recall to your Lordships the circumstances in which this Commission originated, with the conduct of which, on the part of the British Government, we were entrusted.

The Commercial Legislation of France has been founded, for the most part, on the desire to make that country independent of every other, and to force within itself the production of the principal articles of consumption, in spite of natural dif-

– 243 –

244   *Battles over Free Trade, Volume 1*

ficulties, and without any reference to their cost. That legislation received its greatest encouragement under the Imperial regime, when France was excluded from many of the markets of the world, and when, in order to possess without interruption those objects of luxury which long usage had made necessaries, it appeared absolutely needful they should be created by her own industry, or grown on her own soil. And though the cost of so producing was ruinous to the consumer, and, in the long run, scarcely less so to the producer, yet the Government and the people lulled each other with the fallacy 'that the cost mattered not, as the money was spent in the nation, and the wealth of France was not expended on Foreigners.' The fact, however, cannot be denied, that many of the efforts made by France to produce the commodities she had been accustomed to import, were forced upon her by the isolation into which she was thrown by the naval superiority of Great Britain. But these efforts, however well suited to the peculiar exigencies of the time, and however creditable to the ingenuity of those who exerted them, necessarily flung the capital of France into false and unfavourable positions. When the return of the Bourbons opened to France the commerce of the world, so many interests had been created, so much labour and wealth were engaged in the production of articles which might have been more economically imported, that it was found difficult suddenly to change that legislation which gave to the French producers the benefit of a monopoly without which they would have fallen; and their fall would inevitably have brought with it much suffering and distress. A part of the arguments on which the prohibitory system was reared, namely, – that drawn from the rivalry of hostile nations, – naturally lost much of its force when France entered upon an era of tranquillity and peace. Mutual intercourse softened mutual jealousy: popular antipathies became gradually lessened by more intimate relations; and, as the severe regulations which a state of warfare introduces, become modified in a period of peace and friendly feeling, it was obvious that important commercial changes were at hand.

It is true, that many attempts had been made by the Government of England to induce that of France to attempt to consent to a revision of their commercial policy, and that these had met with little success. Formal negociations [*sic*] carried on by the higher authorities of the two Governments, presented formidable difficulties; for such negociations could scarcely be directed to the minor objects, through which alone, perhaps, those of a higher importance could be ultimately reached. The state of things produced by interference with the natural course of commerce becomes so complicated and artificial, as to render any sudden or extended alteration only less dangerous than persistence in an erroneous course; for, however desirable and imperative it may be to get rid of a vicious system of commercial legislation, yet the interests it has created and fostered become susceptible to alarm in the very ratio of their insecurity, and of the demand they make upon society. In England, it cannot be denied, that opinion had given to the Government a power of calling sound principles into action, which the Government of France did not possess. The perfection of many of our manufactures had been long considered on the Continent as pervading them all. They were represented almost universally as destined to crush all rivals by their irresistible superiority; and the manufacturing interest of France, appealing habitually to the self-esteem and apprehensions of the nation, had acquired a concentrated power, which the commercial and agricultural interests, even though supported by a considerable amount of intelligence among the people, and the favourable dispositions of some members of the Government, were unable to resist.

In the year 1830, one of your Lordships' Commissioners, being then employed by the British Government in the investigation of Financial matters, had frequent occasions of communicating with the official authorities of France, and of ascertaining the feelings that existed on the subject of the Commercial Regulations between that country and England: he found, that though the Government was unwilling to contemplate changes which should be at once extensive and immediate, yet there was a sincere desire and growing disposition to revise the Tariffs of the two countries, with a view to improve the intercourse between them, by the removal of those restrictions, impediments, and prohibitions, which had hitherto narrowed the sphere of their mutual relations. In order to accomplish this object, Baron Louis, the French Minister of Finance, proposed that a mixed Commission should be nominated by the two Governments, to hold its sittings either in Paris or London, or in both; that they should suggest, for the consideration of each Government, such changes as were likely to be beneficial and practicable, and gather together such facts as might illustrate the past or present state of the commercial relations of the two countries, or be useful with a view to their future extension. He stated that he should deem every step towards a more liberal intercourse, however seemingly unimportant, as something gained; and that it was his earnest desire to give the inquiry every possible impulse towards a system of freedom.

J. Bowring
G. Villiers

Chamber of Commerce of Boulogne-sur-Mer to the Minister of Commerce ([c. 1834]), in John Bowring, Second Report on the Commercial Relations between France and Britain, *Parliamentary Papers* (1835), xxxvi.441, pp. 661–4.

M. LE MINISTRE,

The Chamber of Commerce has read your circular of 20th September, by which, while you state your intention to institute an inquiry before the superior council of Commerce, in order to consult the different interests on the question of prohibitions, you request it will submit its observations to you, either directly or by the intervention of a delegate.

The Chamber of Commerce has thought that it would be sufficient to represent to you the opinion it has long since formed on this question, and which experience has only served to confirm.

The Chambers thanks you, in the name of that commerce of which it is the organ, for treating this question openly, and for summoning the different interests to be heard – giving publicity to their statements, in order that they may be properly judged by the country. The Chamber had felt the necessity of this publicity, and was the first to demand the printing of the proceedings of the councils-general of agriculture, manufactures, and commerce. A good cause has every thing to gain from these discussions; for impartial and enlightened men will now distinguish between the pretensions of private interest and those based on the general interests of the country.

The Chamber will not imitate some maritime towns, which, in their discouragement, have seen in the inquiry a measure which repels all improvement on our custom-house system; nor some manufacturing districts, which anticipate the ruins of our fabrics. It has too much confidence in your knowledge and patriotism to share such fears, and is persuaded that you will be able to conciliate the demands of liberality with the regard due to existing interests.

We have not at our disposal the facts necessary to furnish the details as to the cost of production of the different articles of French manufactures, toward which the inquiry directs the public attention, and to compare them with the cost of foreign articles. We shall confine ourselves to some general observations.

The question of prohibitions had appeared to us to be judged by public opinion, and we did not expect it to be defended as it has been. That is, however, to be explained when we recollect with what pertinacity the introduction of French silk goods was combated in England, as well as the exaggerated and absurd predictions which arrived from all the manufacturing districts. Our manufacturers have hitherto but too much followed this example. It is to be hoped that they will not imitate the English, who burnt in effigy the illustrious Huskisson, but

Chamber of Commerce of Boulogne-sur-Mer to the Minister of Commerce ([c. 1834]) 247

that they will submit themselves to the law that will be passed, and redouble their efforts for improving the produce of their manufacture, and reduce its price.

We have few doubts of the removal of prohibitions, but we cannot see without regret the continuance of visits in the interior for the seizure of goods, whose entrance is allowed. This inquisitorial measure produces nothing, for the customhouse has no means of interference in the interior; all those of which it can dispose being concentrated on the frontier. Why then introduce into our laws impracticable and useless measures? – measures demanding domiciliary visits, which public opinion regards as a veritable inquisition, and one of whose least inconveniencies will be to expose merchants of integrity to ever new frauds and innovations? We cannot, then, insist too strongly, that this exception to the present laws, due to the prohibitory genius of some manufacturers, should not be received and may not become, as it happened in the law of transit, an obstacle introduced into the new law in order to prevent commerce from benefiting from it.

If no system of duties subsisted already, if it were proposed to create one, we should certainly be of opinion that it should be as comprehensive as possible, and if the necessities of the State permitted it, that it should give unbounded liberty in our relations with those countries which should offer us reciprocity; for the population would have every thing to gain, in a system which would permit it to purchase the objects of its consumption, wherever they are to be found, at the lowest price, and agriculture and industry, instead of directing their efforts towards productions to which the soil and the character of the inhabitants are opposed, would employ them in producing those which offered chances of success. But we must take things in the state in which they are found, and seek that system which is most suitable to the country. This system, sir, appears to us to be that which, whilst it sufficiently protected our trades against foreign importations, should substitute, for prohibitions, duties equal to the difference of the cost prices in France and those in other countries, still leaving to French industry the amount of the expenses of transport, commission, insurances, and other expenses. But this protection should be only temporary, and should cease in a few years for all trades which, remaining stationary, should not find themselves in a condition to compete with foreign countries with a duty of 30 per cent. at most on manufactured produce, and of 5 per cent. on primary materials, independent of the expenses of transport, &c.; for a business, that with such a protection cannot support itself, would not deserve that the interest of all consumers should be any longer sacrificed to it.

We shall now answer the principal objections of our manufacturers to this system.

The English have, as they say, 150 years of experience, and we have only thirty. But is it necessary for us to make all the experiments made by them, in order to arrive at the same conclusions to which they have now advanced? Why not set up the results obtained by them as a point to start from? What prevents us from adopting their plans, which are no mystery to any body; from introducing their improvements amongst us? And is not this what we have been doing every day, and what we shall still better effect, when we shall be stimulated by rivalry? Our manufacturers are already agreed that the machines made in France are equal to the English machinery, and are not more expensive.

The English workmen are said to be ill off. It is not the inferiority of their wages which causes this misery; for these workmen are generally paid at a higher rate than ours. It depends on other causes. We have nothing to do here with the condition of the workmen, which is brought forward in very unseasonable moments. Far from wishing to diminish their gains, we should seek on the contrary to increase the mass of labour. It is important to reduce the enormous profits which are made by certain producers, and to compel others, by foreign rivalry, to make improvements which will cause a reduction of prices. The workmen will be the first to enjoy this diminution in the value of all the articles of their consumption.

Thus that would happen which has already happened in consequence of the use of machinery, which has compelled all the existing establishments to adopt it or to close their affairs. There has never been any rivalry more powerful than that. The same result will follow the rivalry with foreign countries. There will be some partial evil amongst those whom internal rivalry has already partly destroyed, but as to the general ruin with which we are threatened, it is not to be feared. What reasonable man, indeed, will believe that the English are going to employ several hundred millions of francs, in order to destroy the French manufactures? Supposing that such an absurdity were possible, that all the manufacturers of a kingdom could agree together to form such an association, and that men were to be found insane enough to risk, in such a manner, enormous sums, would Frenchmen, Americans, and Englishmen ever be wanting, sagacious enough to come to our markets to purchase back the merchandize, which would be sold in them at a loss, and to export them to foreign markets to sell them there, in rivalry with the produce of the same manufacturers? And if a league so contrary to reason were possible, would not the Government be able in an instant to reject it by the power which is entrusted to it of raising the duties by ordonnances, when the general interest of the country demanded it? There would certainly never be an idea entertained of opposing the creation of establishments, which strangers might desire to form in France, notwithstanding the rivalry which they would enter into with existing establishments. Wherefore, then, oppose the importation of foreign produce, with a sufficient protection? Would not the result be precisely the same? In short, the protecting duty being equal to the difference of the expense of production in the two countries, independent of the advantage which would still result for the French manufacturer, expenses of transport and its accessories, the position would become the same. But, it will be said, the foreign produce does not bear such burthens as ours. If you ask what advantages he derives from it to fabricate at a lower price? we reply, that he bears the burthens of his own country. If it be said that he does not contribute to the national wealth; we answer that he pays his portion into the treasury by discharging very high customs-house duties, and that he enriches his country by furnishing it with the articles of its consumption at prices which enable it to employ in other purchases the capital which it economises.

Our produce is every where prohibited, industry itself declares it to be so; it demands that government should favour its exportations. This is what we also require. But how should our produce not be prohibited when we do not admit that of other countries? How can commerce engage in exports without any means of exchange for its returns? It is not with you, sir, that we have to combat these exaggerations of some manufacturers, who accuse the merchants of the ports of disdaining labours which offer them only a moderate produce, and that in the face of a rivalry which scarcely leaves them the interest of their capitals. The exaggerated language proves one thing only, which is that they are defending a bad cause. But you will no more allow yourselves to be intimidated by the menaces of the manufacturers, who will feel, when once the law has passed, that it is their interest as well as their duty to submit to it, by instructing their workmen instead of deceiving them as to its effect.

England has begun the work. She has diminished the duties on our wines and our brandies; she has admitted our silk goods for a duty of 30 per cent., and she is disposed to concede still more to us, if we cease to prohibit her produce. For reciprocity is necessary; and we allow with our manufacturers, that in the present state of our industry we ought to make concessions only to those countries who make them to us, with some exceptions, demanded by the interest of France, for articles which we are obliged to obtain from foreign countries.

We know only one class, which has any interest in the maintenance of any prohibitions; it is that of smugglers, who, under the prohibitory system, will always brave our armies of custom-house officers. We have experience to prove it.

But in demanding, in the interest of the consumers, in that of commerce and agriculture, in that already well understood of the manufacturers themselves, the abolition of all prohibitions, and replacing them by moderate protecting duties, we cannot too strongly insist on the reduction of the duties on primary materials, necessary to their fabrication. This question cannot, according to us, be separated from that of the free entrance of coals, iron, and wool, for example. For if it is easy to abolish prohibitions, it is impossible to establish the list of duties on entry before the decision of that reduction of duties on primary materials, which it seems to us ought to precede every other. We must then begin by iron, coals, and wool – these three articles, the principals of almost all our manufactures.

250   *Battles over Free Trade, Volume 1*

We may say of agriculture what we have said of manufactures – their interest well understood is the same as that of commerce. It is necessary for all to procure at the lowest possible price the articles of their consumption; all have an interest in the greatest possible development of interior labours.

To obtain this result by reciprocal concessions, which do not sacrifice to the desire of producing every thing in France our exports to foreign countries, without which it is impossible to dispose of the excess of our produce ... But, sir, if in the foregoing considerations we have been agreed with our colleagues of the principal maritime towns, we are obliged to separate ourselves from them, when, abandoning the system of commercial liberty, they come to demand an exorbitant protection for navigation, and frequently some privilege in opposition to the principles which they have proclaimed.

Is not our navigation, in effect, protected by enormous differential duties, and must prohibitions be also added to them? What signifies that absurd measure which forbids our manufacturers from seeking in England the produce of Asia, Africa, and America, which they may import from the other countries of Europe; and which surcharges these articles with the expenses of a re-shipment at Ostend? Wherefore prohibit the importation of colonial produce by the land frontiers, and thus compel the manufacturers who are established there to be subject to the law of the great ports of Marseilles, Bordeaux, and Havre, when at a short distance from their manufactories they would find this produce at a lower price?

May not the manufacturers employ that language with regard to navigation, which has been used with respect to them? May they not say to it: – to what purpose are these privileges which augment the price of primary materials and of the articles of consumption? Why should we not receive from foreign countries that which they can furnish at a lower price than you? Is it not for the interest of the consumer that it should be thus? Why are these privileges brought forward? Is your navigation progressing? No! you have scarcely remained stationary; many complain, notwithstanding the protection of duties and prohibitions, of being unable to navigate at so low a rate as foreign countries, and you ask that a protection so unproductive of improvement shall be preserved to you. Support then, for the general interest, a foreign rivalry as you demand it for us, and if you complain, we also shall say to you, decide, imitate foreign countries, navigate as cheaply as they do, be as active and as economical, obtain from the Government your deliverance from the impediments which embarrass you, and its permission for the entrance of woods, irons, hemp, linens, and every thing you want, in order to place you on an equality with foreign countries, and you will succeed in struggling against them, and be able to do without privileges, of which we also have a right to complain.

Yes, sir, endeavour to deal justly with all exaggerated pretensions, contrary to the general interest, and to the principles of which that general interest demands

Chamber of Commerce of Boulogne-sur-Mer to the Minister of Commerce ([c. 1834]) 251

a just and impartial application, and the whole of France will applaud the truly national system to which you will have attached your name.

We resume our subject, and we demand,

1st, That all prohibitions be abolished, and the seizures in the interior suppressed, that inquisitorial measure being unproductive, and contrary to every system of internal liberty.

2dly, That the duties on raw materials and manufactured articles be immediately reduced to a rate equal to the difference between the cost prices in France and these articles delivered at Paris, the centre of consumption and of export, and the cost prices in foreign lands; still leaving to the French producer the advantage of the expenses of transport which foreign produce will have to support to arrive at the French markets.

3dly, That the duty on bar-iron be immediately reduced to 15 francs per metrical quintal, that upon cast iron in the same proportion; all duties on coal suppressed, as well as the additional tax existing on importation by sea; and, lastly, the duty on wool reduced from 20 to 10 per cent.

4thly, That after five years at the outside, from this time – a sufficient period to enable our producers to introduce the improvements already obtained from other countries – the above duties be reduced: – On raw materials to 5 per cent. On manufactured produce to 30 per cent. at the utmost, seeing that a limit will be necessary against an exorbitant protection which impedes production, makes enormous charges press upon the consumer, and is opposed to the extension of advantageous exchanges with other countries.

5thly, That the impediments which embarrass our navigation be removed, that the raw materials which are employed for the building and repairs of ships, and whose introduction would contribute to render our navigation more extensive, be admitted free of duty.

6thly, That all prohibitions, every privilege established in favour of our navigation, and principally the prohibition of importing colonial produce by the frontier, and that of receiving direct from England the produce of countries out of Europe, be abolished, and that the differential duties, having for their object to protect our navigation, should never exceed a surtax of 10 per cent.

7thly, That the removal of prohibitions and the reduction of duties, principally on manufactured articles, should take place immediately only for countries which offer us a reciprocity, except upon articles of which an indispensable necessity is felt in France, independently of the question of exchanges, which these reductions should have an object in encouraging.

8thly, That the Government occupy itself in every possible way with the improvement of our means of communication in the interior.

Correspondence between Havre Chamber of Commerce and the Minister of Commerce, 14 and 18 October 1834, *Parliamentary Papers* (1835), xxxvi.441, pp. 658–9.

HAVRE CHAMBER OF COMMERCE
Havre, 14 October 1834

We have never lost an opportunity of urging on the Government the necessity of instituting commercial inquiries; – we grieve that they have been so often attended with fruitless results.

On the late occasion the exclusion of the grave and important questions of iron and coals has much disappointed us. If we were authorized to hope that the Government had determined to propose a large reduction of duty, we should abstain from observations, – but if the unwillingness to inquire further is meant to imply that the present state of things is to be continued, we beg to state that there is much yet to be said; for there is not a single branch of industry which is not deeply interested in obtaining these articles on the most advantageous terms – no branch which has not its own facts to produce in corroboration of the demands for reduction which crowd from all sides. Whether or not the questions of iron and coals form part of the inquiry, we are sure it will furnish new reasons for a change of Tariff, as respects these important articles.

Prohibitions were established for shielding our national manufactures from foreign competition when the foreigner could offer articles of better quality or lower prices. No one can deny that they restrain commerce, and that it is the duty of Government to check them whenever they are not demanded by the interests of industry. We see with pleasure your attempt to ascertain the real wants and interests of manufacturers – but it appears to us that before the removal of prohibitions our manufacturers should be placed, as far as depends upon the Government, in a situation to compete with their rivals.

Thus, for example, in the raw materials of the cotton and woollen fabrics, the English manufacturer pays on the United States cotton only 2*s*. 11*d*. per cwt. 7 fr. 19 c. per 100 kilogrammes, while the French pays 22*s*. In England the duty on wool cannot exceed ¹⁄₁₂ of its value, *i.e.* 8½ per cent., while foreign wool pays 20 or rather 22 per cent. on its value. Let the English duties be compared with ours in all the objects employed in manufactures, and the difference will be found more or less considerable. The comparison has been made, and we refer to it again, especially with reference to matters so vitally important as coals and iron.

It may be said that, without lowering the Tariff on the articles employed on manufacture, the manufacturers may be equally protected by heavy duties on foreign articles. We do not think there is fit compensation on such a system, for heavy duties only encourage fraud, and nothing can be more opposed to the interests of our manufacturers than the clandestine import of foreign goods, as that destroys all the arrangement of regular trade.

ANSWER OF THE MINISTER OF COMMERCE (M. Duchatel)

Paris, 18 October 1834

GENTLEMEN,

I have read with care and attention your answer to my circular of 20th September, and thank you for the observations and information it contains. In recognizing the utility of the inquiry you give evidence of a discreet and wise spirit, for, living as we live under the regime of publicity, and with our constitutional usages, there would be little of propriety, or even of equity, if the Government pronounced on the grave matters which concern our commercial system, without seeking all information, and calling upon the different interests to express their wishes. If it had acted differently you may be sure it would be subject to bitter reproaches, and for once they would be well founded.

I hope the painful sentiments which you say you experienced on not seeing iron and coals among the objects of inquiry will have been dissipated by further reflection. You will have understood that their exclusion from the custom-house project need not be a consequence of their exclusion from the preliminary inquiry, since the ordinary means of information possessed may suffice without the delay which would be caused by a supplementary inquiry. But I did not intend to say that the inquiry might not throw much light on the subject of coal and iron. As raw materials they are closely connected with the cost of production of various articles. The connection is obvious, and the facts to which you refer will be duly investigated.

I shall make the same observation on what you say respecting raw materials. There is so close a connection between the matters employed by a manufacturer and the situation of that manufacturer, that any inquiry must necessarily embrace both. All is bound together, and it appears to me, that instead of seeing in an inquiry into manufactures the exclusion of raw materials, it would be perhaps more material to find there an opportunity of showing the influence which the duties upon those materials have upon industry. I shall add that it cannot escape your capacity how much the distinction between raw and manufactured materials is arbitrary and relative: the products of the soil are as much the result of labour as the products of manufactures, and there are few articles which are not of the same manufactures, if regarded with a reference to the labour which created them, and raw materials with reference to their ulterior application. Manure, pasturage, &c., are the raw materials of wool – raw wool is the raw material of woollen twist – woollen twist of woollen stuffs – and woollen stuffs are subjected to many transformations before they reach the consumer.

'First Report of Messrs. Villiers and Bowring', *Westminster Review*, 21 (July 1834), pp. 257–66.

ART. XVI. – *First Report on the Commercial Relations between France and Great Britain, addressed to the Right Honourable the Lords of the Committee of Privy Council for Trade and Plantations, by George Villiers and John Bowring, with a Supplementary Report, by John Bowring* – Presented to both Houses of Parliament by Command of His Majesty. – London: Printed by W. Clowes. fol. pp. 251. 1834.

THERE is something so novel in seeing the negociations between two leading European nations taking the course of right reason, humanity, and common interest, that the present Report may claim an elevated place among the noiseless events which enable man to bear up against the evil of those which history and folly delight to honour with their notice. Extraordinary testimony has also been borne to its importance, by the bitter scorn and earnest hate with which those employed in its construction were during its progress treated by the enemy of man. That two whole Commissioners should be employed abroad on a mission of peace and good-will, involving no interests but those of the industrious classes of two great nations, was an offence only to be surpassed by the idea of an army which should be employed abroad and not for absolutism, or a fleet which should establish the freedom of an injured people, instead of dangling, as was the olden fashion, at the heels of some despot in danger of being kicked out by an indignant nation. Had the expense of the Commission been incurred in conveying a baby frigate to furnish the toy-shop of some continental sovereign, or to transport some injurious foreigner to be the bearer of the expiring hopes and wishes of the English oligarchy to the whiskered enemies of freedom abroad, the thing would have been hailed with reverence due, and even the standing types which announce the unbroken existence of sound bills of health at Windsor, might have been displaced to make room for the announcement. But the event is at once a symptom and a cause. In spite of custom, a modicum of John Bull's money has been expended in his service; and the precedent of its happening once, will be a dangerous step towards repetition of the like.

The Commissioners, men not altogether unknown to fame, – one of them a rising young Patrician, who has the genius to see what may be accomplished in conjunction with the people, and to be among the first to strike out for the grand chances of diplomacy in their coming service, – the other a well-entered servant of the popular cause, possessed of the personal confidence of its supporters in all quarters of the globe to a greater extent than any other man in Europe, – proceed as follows, to state the origin and object of their Commission. –

'The Commercial Legislation of France has been founded, for the most part, on the desire to make that country independent of every other, and to force within itself the production of the principle articles of consumption, in spite of natural difficulties, and without any reference to their cost. That legislation received its greatest encouragement under the Imperial régime, when France was excluded from many of the markets of the world, and when, in order to possess without interruption those objects of luxury which long usage had made necessaries, it appeared absolutely needful they should be created by her own industry, or grown on her own soil. And though the cost of so producing was ruinous to the consumer, and, in the long run, scarcely less so to the producer, yet the Government and the people lulled each other with the fallacy 'that the cost mattered not, as the money was spent in the nation, and the wealth of France was not expended on Foreigners.' The fact, however, cannot be denied, that many of the efforts made by France to produce the commodities she had been accustomed to import, were forced upon her by the isolation into which she was thrown by the naval superiority of Great Britain. But these efforts, however well suited to the peculiar exigencies of the time, and however creditable to the ingenuity of those who exerted them, necessarily flung the capital of France into false and unfavourable positions. When the return of the Bourbons opened to France the commerce of the world, so many interest had been created, so much labour and wealth were engaged in the production of articles which might have been more economically imported, that it was found difficult suddenly to change that legislation which gave to the French producers the benefit of a monopoly, without which they would have fallen; and their fall would inevitably have brought with it much suffering and distress. A part of the arguments on which the prohibitory system was reared, namely, – that drawn from the rivalry of hostile nations, – naturally lost much of its force when France entered upon an era of tranquillity and peace. Mutual intercourse softened mutual jealousy: popular antipathies became gradually lessened by more intimate relations; and, as the severe regulations which a state of warfare introduces, become modified in a period of peace and friendly feeling, it was obvious that important commercial changes were at hand.'

'It is true, that many attempts had been made by the Government of England to induce that of France to consent to a revision of their commercial policy, and that these had met with little success. Formal negotiations carried on by the higher authorities of the two Governments, presented formidable difficulties; for such negociations could scarcely be directed to the minor objects, through which alone, perhaps, those of a higher importance could be ultimately reached. The state of things produced by interference with the natural course of commerce becomes so complicated and artificial, as to render any sudden or extended alteration only less dangerous than persistence in an erroneous course; for, however desirable and imperative it may be to get rid of a vicious system of commercial legislation, yet the interests it has created and fostered become susceptible to alarm in the very ratio of their insecurity, and of the demand they make upon society. In England, it cannot be denied, that opinion had given to the Government a power of calling sound principles into action, which the Government of France did not possess. The perfection of many of our manufactures had been long considered on the continent as pervading them. They were represented almost universally as destined to crush all rivals by their irresistible superiority; and the manufacturing interest of France, appealing habitually to the self-esteem and apprehensions of the nation, had acquired a concentrated power, which the commercial and agricultural interests, even though supported by a considerable amount of intelligence among the people, and the favourable dispositions of some members of the Government, were unable to resist.'

'In the year 1830, one of your Lordships Commissioners, being then employed by the British Government in the investigation of Financial matters, had frequent occasions of communicating with the official authorities of France, and of ascertaining the feelings that existed on the subject of the Commercial Regulations between that country and England: he found, that though the Government was unwilling to contemplate changes which should be at once extensive and immediate, yet there was a sincere and growing disposition to revise the Tariffs of the two countries, with a view to improve the intercourse between them, by the removal of those restrictions, impediments, and prohibitions, which had hitherto narrowed the sphere of their mutual relations. In order to accomplish this object, Baron Louis, the French Minister of Finance, proposed that a mixed Commission should be nominated by the two Governments, to hold its sittings either in Paris or London, or in both; that they should suggest, for the consideration of each Government, such changes as were likely to be beneficial and practicable, and gather together such facts as might illustrate the past or present state of the commercial relations of the two countries, or be useful with a view to their future extension. He stated, that he should deem every step towards a more liberal intercourse, however seemingly unimportant, as something gained; and that it was his earnest desire to give the inquiry every possible impulse towards a system of freedom. We feel it due to Baron Louis, who took so marked a part in the establishment of our Commission, to state, that he has always exhibited the most intelligent and unwearied zeal for the advancing of its important objects.'

'The first written communication on the part of Baron Louis was the following: –

Paris, July 28, 1831.

'Sᴵʀ,

I have read with lively interest the letter which you have had the goodness to write to me, and thank you much for the transmission which accompanies it. The opinions avowed by your Government on the subject of commerce are my own, and I shall readily repeat to you in writing what I have already said by word of mouth. If, as reason points out, the liberation of commerce is for the interest of all nations generally, France and England, the two richest in the world, cannot fail to gain on both sides by enlarging a system of exchange which a narrow policy has hitherto subjected to too many restrictions. A more liberal arrangement of the Custom Duties would increase the riches of both countries, and give new securities for the continuance of peace. It would therefore be with real satisfaction that I should see the formation of a Mixed Commission, which should prepare the work, and point out the alterations which might be made in the existing laws of the two countries in favour of free trade.'

'For my own part I should account it an honour to contribute in any way to a reform of such high importance to the progress of civilization. But you will be aware, Sir, that it is your Government that must take the initiative in any similar project. It has already entered on commercial reform; it is met by fewer obstacles, and has not to struggle against prejudices so powerful as we. It has only to express its wishes, and it will find on the part of the French Government a community of operation and of interest.'

'LOUIS.'

And it was repeated in another Letter, dated the 16th August: –

To Dr. Bowring.

'You will have received through Mr. Hamilton, Secretary to the British Embassy, the letter which I had the honour to write to you on the 28th of July last, in reply to yours of the same month. I cannot, however, allow myself to let pass the renewed opportunity of impressing on you all the importance which I attach to the measures which may be adopted in concert by our two Governments, to extend their commercial relations with each other by liberating them from the shackles which the present arrangement of the Custom Duties continues to throw about their progress.'

'LOUIS.'

The presence of the Vice President of the Board of Trade in Paris, in the autumn of 1831, and the efforts which he made to give effect to the amicable dispositions of the French Government, removed many obstacles to the appointment of the French Commissioners, and great difficulties of detail, and enabled him to lend important assistance to the initiatory proceedings of the Commission.

258   *Battles over Free Trade, Volume 1*

The Commissioners nominated by the French Government were The Baron Freville[1], Counsellor of State, and The Count Tanneguy Duchâtel[2], ditto; and to their intelligence, zeal, and aptitude, no tribute of ours can be sufficiently ample.[3]

The causes of many of the difficulties which free trade has to encounter in France, may be traced in the following paragraph. –

'In France, a very large proportion of those who are interested in the continuance of the existing commercial system, are elevated public functionaries, or are placed in immediate contact with them. It would have been idle, therefore, to have attacked great monopolies in their strongest holds. Nor can it be denied, that some of the protected manufactures are of such magnitude as to demand attention and respect. In many of them considerable numbers of workmen are engaged; and, though their employment in protected fabrics leads to the exclusion of a far more considerable number of labourers in those branches of industry whose cultivation would be the natural, instead of the forced growth of capital, yet all serious shiftings or transfer of labour, cannot but involve questions of difficulty and deep concern. In the mean time, the labouring classes, impatient of the suffering which is of necessity consequent upon the changes which every alteration of the Tariff brings with it, naturally ally themselves with their manufacturing masters, who demand the exclusion of the foreign articles which are in competition with their own. Even among these classes, however, the extension of the principles of more liberal intercourse, has produced a decided change, and so strong has been the English interest created, even among the French manufacturers, that the weavers of Lyons have lately petitioned the French Government to give all possible development to the commercial relations between England and France.' – p. 8.

The 'General Statement of Prohibited Goods from Foreign Countries,' (p. 39) with the reasons appended, forms a curious object. Some of the most remarkable items will be found stated in the last of the paragraphs that follow. –

'It is hardly necessary to remark, that if these reasons for prohibition were pushed to their necessary consequences, all commercial relations would infallibly cease. If the cheapness of a foreign article were a sufficient ground for prohibiting its importation, and the cheapness of a home article for prohibiting its exportation, no exchange at all could take place.'

'Many of the arguments which are put forward in justification of prohibitory measures are mutually destructive of each other. To keep the price of corn low in the interest of the consumer, is assigned as the reason for prohibiting exportation; and to raise the price high in the interest of the producer, as the reason for prohibiting importation: the two objects are incompatible. Again, one set of prohibitions

1   Since made a Peer of France

2   Since a Member of the Chamber of Deputies

3   [Ed.: The instructions the British Commissioners received from the government follows at this point; see above, pp. 243–5.]

'First Report of Messrs. Villiers and Bowring' (1834)

are justified because the articles are dear in France; such are the exportations of silk, rags, bark, &c. Reasonings wholly opposed to one another are, in turn, employed. There is scarcely an argument or a calculation, which if recognised as applying to some articles, is not opposed altogether to the legislation on others.'

'It requires merely to state some of the objections to importations, in order to show their narrow and anti-commercial spirit. The introduction of manufactured tin, for example, is opposed because it might benefit England, which is rich in tin mines; as if the importation into France could take place without equally benefiting her. The reasons, too, which are grounded on the superiority of other countries; as, for example, 'dangerous rivalry,' in the case of manufactured steel; 'cheapness' of foreign article, in the case of shipping; threatened 'annihilation of the French manufacture' in that of cutlery; 'extra advantages of the English' in plated ware; 'apprehension of the English' in articles of pottery; 'imprudence of admitting English sadlery, as so many persons, regardless of price, prefer it;' 'advantages of machinery' in works of iron; – all are modes of announcing the superiority of the foreign articles, and the power which foreigners possess of supplying them on cheaper terms than they can be produced at home.' – p. 45.

But, the monopolist will say, if you benefit the consumer, you injure me the monopolist. To which the answer is, that there is another person still left out, which is the French trader with whom the difference of price, saved to the consumer by the destruction of the monopolist, would have been laid out. Or put all the effects on French trade and commerce together, and the aggregate is the same with the monopoly or without; only there is this difference, that in one case the consumer gets nothing for the difference of price, and in the other he does. When will the consumers all the world over, cease to be the dupes of knavish tradesmen and more knavish legislators?

The French government is just now in a state of distress by reason of '*chiens fraudeurs*,' dogs taught to smuggle, who are stated to be carrying their operations to an extent *vraiment effrayante*, and the legislators of the *grande nation* are combining their talents for the suppression of these dogs. To such ridiculous occupations does ignorance bring the leaders of a people. As if a smuggling dog was not the best of four-legged citizens, making a saving to the public at every journey, of the difference of price in the foreign article introduced, *minus* his own diet and expenses. If the bones that are in all cathedrals in all countries were looked through, how few would have a claim on their country's gratitude to match those of a smuggling dog.

The immediate result of the efforts of the Commissioners has been the abandonment of the principle of absolute prohibition, and the substitution of duties; a step, of which the value as a movement, and as giving rise to a vast quantity of popular agitation and reflection, is independent of the positive magnitude of the opening made.

Britain and the Zollverein

Minute of the Board of Trade, 17 January 1826, relative to the Commercial Relations between Great Britain and Prussia, December 1825–January 1826, *Parliamentary Papers* (1839), xlvii.[203], pp. 269–73.

At the Council Chamber, Whitehall, January 17, 1826

READ. – Letter from Joseph Planta, Esq., transmitting by direction of Mr. Secretary Canning, the copy of a note from Baron Maltzahn, the Prussian minister at this Court, stating that he is prepared to enter into a further negotiation, with regard to the commercial relations between this Kingdom and Prussia.

Their Lordships having given their most serious and attentive consideration to the various points adverted to in the above-mentioned note, are pleased to direct that a copy of the following Minute be transmitted for the information of Mr. Secretary Canning.

The object of this note being to propose to enter into a negotiation with His Majesty's Government, for affording, if possible, a greater scope and facility to the commercial relations between the two countries, the Lords of this Committee cannot proceed to offer the observations which have occurred to them upon the contents of the Prussian note, without first doing justice to the generally enlarged principles which are professed by the Prussian Government in matters of commerce, and without acknowledging the satisfaction which their Lordships feel at the assurance that it is the wish of that Government to encourage, as much as possible, the practical application of those principles in the Prussian dominions, and in their relations with other States; convinced, as the Lords of this Committee are, that in proportion as industry and commerce are relieved from unnecessary interference and restraint, will their benefits be increased, not only for the immediate advantage of the nation acting upon that system, but, incidentally, of all other countries with which that nation may have relations of trade and friendly intercourse. The present overture is founded, as Baron Maltzahn states, upon an inference derived by the Prussian Government from the proceedings in the last Session of Parliament, that 'His Majesty's Government is disposed to favor the commerce of Foreign States, in proportion to the favors granted by those States to the commerce of Great Britain.'

– 260 –

Minute of the Board of Trade (1826) 261

That this should be assumed to be the principle, (*la maxime*) of the British Government, is not, perhaps, very surprising. It is, nevertheless, rather a deduction (in many respects erroneous and inapplicable), from the real principle of our declared commercial policy, than the principle itself.

Our general and first principle is to tender to all nations alike, and indiscriminately, equal facilities of commerce and navigation, and equal inducements to visit the ports of this country with their merchandize, either for our own consumption, or in the way of transit (*entrepôt*) to other parts of the world.

In furtherance of this principle, (with the single exception of wine from Portugal, under a specific and very ancient Treaty), we have proceeded: –

1. To abolish all discriminating duties affecting differently the like productions of foreign countries, and in lieu thereof to establish one uniform tariff for the whole.

2. To reduce that tariff to the lowest degree, consistent, in each particular article, with the legitimate objects of all duties; either the collection of the necessary public revenue, or the protection absolutely requisite for the maintenance of our own internal industry. The great reductions made, during the two last Sessions of Parliament in the duties which had been imposed for this last object, are notorious. That these reductions have been made upon no niggardly calculation, is proved by the manner in which, on the one hand, they have excited the attention, and awakened the hopes of establishments, rival to our own in foreign countries, and on the other hand, in the apprehensions under which some important branches of British industry labour, in respect to which the threatened competition of the products of other countries may interfere with their products, in our own markets.

3. The number of articles of commerce, subject either to absolute or contingent prohibition, has been very much reduced, and Government have declared their intention of recommending, at no distant period, to the legislature to substitute the protection of duties, adapted to the scale last mentioned, for that of prohibition, upon the few remaining articles which are still subject to the latter rule. In the meantime, the conditions of these prohibitions, whether absolute or contingent, are the same for all nations.

4. To abolish all discriminating duties (*droits différentiels*) upon the navigation of other nations, so that the products and merchandise of those nations, when imported in their own ships, shall be subject to the same rates only as when imported in British ships.

These are the principles which the Government of this country have professed, which have been acted upon, and which, being now by law the rule of our conduct, we have ventured to hope that other States might approve, and, after due deliberation and conviction of their advantage, might adopt. But, however desirous we may be to find other countries (even in the view of their own interest) profiting by our example, prudence required that we should not, in justice to ourselves, rely upon its efficacy altogether. The legislature, therefore, has armed the Crown with the discretionary power, under certain contingencies, of imposing higher duties than are provided by the tariff, to the extent of one-fifth, upon the produce and manufactures of such countries as refuse to us a perfect reciprocity of those facilities and advantages which we hold out alike to all. This discretionary power, in respect to the commerce, is equally applicable to the navigation of such States, so that the tonnage of their shipping may be subjected, in our ports, to any amount of duty which may be requisite fully to countervail whatever difference of charge may be levied on British ships, exceeding the charge on national ships, in the ports of such country.

This is the second general principle of our commercial system, or, perhaps, more properly it may be considered not so much another principle, as a corrective, reserved for the due maintenance of that fair and equal competition, and of that enlarged intercourse, which forms the basis of the system itself.

From this development of what the system of this country really is, the mistake in the inference laid down in the Prussian note, will be evident.

That inference supposes that, to restrain and press upon the commerce of other countries is our general rule; and to show favour, and to give facility to that commerce in particular cases, the exception. Our rule is, obviously, the reverse. Facility, extension, equality of intercourse, are what we offer to all, and what we look for in return, from all countries. We have no special favours to concede, neither have we any to demand.

It must, therefore, be manifest that the argument in the note from Baron Maltzahn, and the proposal which he has been instructed by his Court to make, in so far as it is deduced from that argument, rest in a great degree upon an unfounded supposition.

The argument, in substance, is that the Prussian system of commerce being in unison (*en harmonie*) with our own, Prussia is entitled, not only to the full benefit of our system, but to something more. Reciprocity is not denied to Prussia; at this moment it prevails between the two countries; but the Prussian doctrine appears to be that reciprocity, on her part, entitles Prussia to something more on the part of England; and it is, therefore, proposed to us, specially to favour the importation of two of the principal products of the Prussian dominions – timber and corn. The Prussian note assumes that those advantages, which Prussia proposes should be granted *immediately* in her own case, will, at some future period, be extended to other countries; but their *immediate* concession to Prussia is the proposal; and what is the return offered? why, that for a certain number of years (probably so long as the favour is limited to Prussia alone) she will engage, 'not to change her present commercial system; and not to increase the existing duties upon British merchandise.'

Minute of the Board of Trade (1826) 263

The first of these conditions is clearly of a nature so very vague and general, that it could scarcely be made the subject of a specific stipulation; and to such a stipulation which, after all, would amount to nothing more than an engagement to follow a plan conducive to her own prosperity; this country, whilst it will rejoice in the progress of that prosperity, can have no desire to bind an independent State, any more than she is prepared to be so bound herself.

The second condition would confer no special advantage upon our commerce, unless the Prussian Government were, during the period for which it is ready to stipulate not to raise the duties on British merchandise, to increase those duties on the like articles when imported from other countries. But as there is no intimation of such an intention, it is fair to assume that it is not contemplated. It may be doubtful whether it be even in the power of Prussia to establish such a difference, consistently with her existing engagements to other nations. Independently of such engagements, it could not be for her interest in her commercial relations with those Powers, to establish such a distinction in our favour, and nothing which passed between the Plenipotentiaries of this country and the Plenipotentiary of Prussia, in the discussions which terminated in the Convention of Commerce and Navigation entered into between the two Courts in 1824, could lead Prussia to suppose it to be our wish (as, in fact, it is not, or ever was) to obtain from her exclusive advantages or concessions, which might embarrass her relations with other States.

Whether Prussia has, or has not, any engagements with other Powers, either express or implied, which would make the proposed condition a merely nominal boon to this country, is best known to herself; but, be that as it may, there can be no difficulty in stating that this Government is bound to several other Powers by specific engagements which would entitle them of right to participate in all the advantages of commerce which Prussia wishes to obtain for herself, and that, among the Powers so entitled, will be found those very countries, both in the old and the new world, which are the principal competitors with Prussia in the supply of corn and timber to this country.

Independently, however, of this insuperable difficulty, it becomes His Majesty's Government, in the judgment of this Committee, when a proposal for altering our corn laws is made to us by a foreign Government, as a condition of something to be done or omitted by that Government, at once to declare that we never can entertain such a proposal. It is the decided opinion of this Committee, that upon that subject, involving, as it does, such immense interests, so closely connected with the well-being and comfort of all classes of the community, and surrounded, as it is, with so many peculiar difficulties, our legislation must, at all times, be governed entirely by considerations, originating and centering among ourselves, and that it is only to be looked at incidentally as affecting our relations with other States.

Upon the question of the introduction of Prussian corn, the Committee has only further to remark that the ports of other great countries, as well as those of England, have been shut of late years against the admission of foreign corn, and that those countries do not afford the same vent to the other productions of Prussia, or the same facility to her navigation, which are afforded by the United Kingdom. In making this remark, the Committee abstain from stating any opinion upon the general policy of these prohibitions; but it is not unfair to bring forward the fact of their existence in other countries to show that if Prussia be disposed to make it a grievance, the complaint, in the first instance, would more properly apply in other quarters, where, together with prohibition, there exist, at the same time, other difficulties thrown in the way of Prussian commerce, which it does not meet with in England.

In respect to the duties on timber, they have been imposed, and are continued, for the purpose of revenue. They are a tax upon consumption, to which all the observations of the paragraph No. 7 in the Prussian note, in vindication of the like taxes existing in Prussia strictly apply.

That these duties, considerable as they are admitted to be, do not impede the consumption of Prussian timber, by diminishing the annual demand, will be satisfactorily proved by a reference to the quantity imported during the last three years. The quantity is shown in the inclosed return, which is a complete answer to every complaint on the part of Prussia in respect to this branch of her commerce with England.

A return showing all the principal imports from that country, and the total of her trade with the United Kingdom for the same period, is likewise inclosed, in further proof that her commerce with us, taken in the aggregate, is very far from diminishing under the system which now exists.

It may fairly be asked, whether the export of British products, and British manufactures, to Prussia, has increased to an equal proportion within the like period? There is good reason to believe that is has not, and that some portion of the Prussian imports, particularly in the last year, has been paid for in bullion or British coin.

The Committee do not advert to this circumstance, as constituting, in their judgment, any valid ground of objection on our part against the system of trade now carried on between this country and Prussia; but for the purpose of inviting the Prussian Government to consider whether, upon a comparison of the facilities afforded on their side to British commerce, with those which exist here in respect to the commerce of Prussia, this fact does not give rise to a *prima facie* presumption that the next step in relaxation of still existing restraints and duties ought to be made by Prussia, before she calls upon the Government of this country to enter further upon the like course, and to do so, specially in her favour?

In conclusion, the result of the system adopted respectively by the two Governments is this: –

1st. That Prussia prohibits *absolutely* 'the trade in salt and in playing cards,' and we acquiesce in the prohibition. Great Britain has a *contingent* prohibition of corn, and Prussia complains.

2nd. That Prussia, as is admitted in Baron Maltzahn's note, levies a duty upon all British goods *in transitu* through her dominions. Upon Prussian goods deposited here for *re-exportation*, we levy none. The duty is said to be inconsiderable; but whether more or less, upon every principle of reciprocity, the knowledge of the fact that we have no such duty, should lead to the immediate removal of the transit duty upon all British goods in Prussia.

3rd. Prussia having entered into a Treaty with us for that purpose, has placed British navigation in her ports upon the same footing as her own, and reciprocally her navigation enjoys the like advantage in our ports.

And, lastly, Prussia (wisely in our estimation) acting upon the principle of giving equal facility to the commerce of all Foreign countries, will, so long as she fulfils all the conditions of that principle, which is also our principle, be entitled to claim the full benefit of its application in this country. But there are other countries from which neither in point of navigation, or duties on merchandize, does she receive the same measure of reciprocity, and towards them, as far as we know, no steps are taken by her to enforce redress.

Here is the marked difference in the systems of the two countries. The note from Baron Maltzahn, claims for that of Prussia, that 'it is as liberal, not to say more liberal than that of Great Britain.' In one respect, at least, this remark is well founded, for to those who do not grant us reciprocity, we shall apply the corrective of our 20 per cent. and our alien tonnage duties. Prussia appears to have no such defensive weapon, or if she has, not to be inclined to use it. But what is asked of us as the counterpart of this liberality of Prussia towards other Powers? Is it not that we should grant exclusive boons to her commerce, as the price of her continuing to us, for a certain number of years, those advantages which we enjoy only in common with other countries, in which Prussian commerce has not even the benefit of reciprocity?

In this state of things, whilst it appears to this Committee, that no negotiation can be undertaken on the basis proposed in the Prussian note, their Lordship's cannot but express a hope that after the explanation now given of the measures which have been recently adopted by this country, the Prussian government doing justice to those measures will be convinced of the facilities and advantages which they cannot fail to afford to her commerce. The Committee, however, do not advert to them for the purpose of repelling all negotiation. Far from it, they do so in the first place, in order to bring distinctly under the notice of Prussia, the true character and bearings of our commercial policy, and in the next place, to satisfy the Prussian Government that consistently with that policy, as well as with the engagements which, in conformity to it, we have already contracted with other Powers, we can only invite negotiation, or entertain it, when offered to us, with any prospect of a successful issue, upon the general principle of that policy, reciprocal or equivalent concession.

266   *Battles over Free Trade, Volume 1*

Lord Palmerston to the Earl of Minto, 17 January 1834, Minto Papers, National Library of Scotland, MS 12021, fols 172–5.

F. O. 17 Jany 1834

My dear Minto

I was very sorry to hear of the Severe Illness of Mons. Ancillon, but I hope that before this reaches you he will have recovered, & have been able to resume his official Duties – It is rather unlucky that he should not have been able to attend the Congress at Vienna, as he would reasonably have had more weight there than any other Person in a less prominent Situation and, it would have been desirable for the Interests of Germany & through them, for the Interests of Europe that Prussia should have been well represented at this Meeting.

The Prussian Gov^t is by general Consent admitted to be more Enlightened than that of any other German State, and might have Exercised as useful a Controul [sic] at this session, as we have Reason to believe it did during the late Meetings of the Sovereigns – I suppose Restrictions on the Press, and Encroachments on the Powers of the Chambers in the Constitutional States, together with some additions to the Powers of the diet over the smaller Independent States will be the object of the Preparations to be discussed; and it is not unlikely that the difficulties of doing anything on these Points may be too great to be overcome & that the Congress may separate [Ric Infecta?]

But there is one Matter on which in the near while I wish you would Confidentially speak to Ancillon as I did this morning to Esterhazy & shall write to Lamb to do to Metternich, and that is the Continued Military occupation of the free State of Frankfort by the Troops of the Confederation. I wish you would ask Confidentially when this occupation is likely to end. The Event which served as a Pretext for it, was a Riot in april [sic] last year a year ago, by Seventy Students & others who came into the Town unexpectedly, Surprized one guard House, killed & wounded Three or Four Soldiers, and took to their Heels as Soon as they found the Town Guard was coming down upon them. There was no Insurrection in the Town, & none of the Town-People joined the assailants. Nobody has yet been brought to Trial, & therefore it is to be presumed no very clear Evidence has been procured – The Town authorities declared themselves at the Time, perfectly capable of preserving the Peace of the Town and they protested against the Introduction of the Troops of any other Power – From that Time to this the Town has been perfectly Tranquil & no renewal of attack from without has taken Place.

Now the original occupation was an act of arbitrary & over ruling Power, not Sanctioned by any Law of the Confederation. The only Case in which the final act of 1820 authorizes the diet to Send Troops into a State being a Member of the Confederation without any Demand on the Part of the Govt of that

Palmerston to Minto (1834)

state, is a Case of open Insurrection or Revolt, when the Govt of the Revolted State may be unable to make its Demand for Help. But in this Case of Frankfort there never was any Revolt at all, and the whole of the Row was over in Half an Hour after it had begun, and many days before the Troops of the Confederation marched in. When they entered, the Town was quiet the Magistrates obeyed, and the Frankfort Gov' declaring itself perfectly competent to take Charge of the public Peace.

Now the Independence of the Free Cities of Germany has always been an object of Solicitude to the British Govt, and at no Time were They more Important & Interesting to us than they are now of all the free States & Cities Frankfort too is become one of those whose Independence it is most concerns us to see preserved Since we are connected with it by a Commercial Treaty. There are those indeed who do not seem able to say that one object to be accomplished by the occupation is to plague the People of Frankfort out of this Treaty, & to worry them into the Prussian Union, and that it was to disguise this Purpose that the Invading Troops were chiefly Austrian [.]

But be this as it may the Principle of this occupation is just as objectionable as would be that of Constantinople by the Russians; the Injurious Effect upon the Independence of the State thus occupied against its will the Same, and there is every Reason for a Speedy Evacuation.

I prefer however in the first Place making the Inquiry Confidentially, & I therefore write you a private Letter instead of a Despatch upon the Subject but we shall be very glad if you should be enabled to tell us that an Early Evacuation is intended.[1]

Yrs Sincerely
Palmerston

---

1 [Ed.: Ancillon's reply was deemed by Palmerston very satisfactory, if adhered to, see Palmerston to Minto, 4 February 1834, Minto Papers, National Library of Scotland, NLS MS 12021 fols 182–7.]

'The Prussian League', *British and Foreign Review; or, European Quarterly Journal*, 13:25 (1842), pp. 188–205.

ARTICLE VII.

Mecklenburg und der Zollverein, von H. F. RAAPE, &c. 1841.

WE have with sincere pleasure remarked that the view of our commercial relations with the Prussian Customs' League and with the States of the North-western German League, given in No. XXII. of this Review, has been productive of much good. Public attention has been called more directly to the point at issue between Great Britain and Prussia, by the simple revelation that there was a point at issue of which previously few had heard, and that this point involved principles not only of commercial policy but of international law, which could not be neglected without serious detriment to the dearest interests of this country and of the civilized world at large. The leading organs of the daily press have since conveyed a mass of useful information to the public, which has enabled the nation to decide on the commercial policy of the late ministry; and the decision has been, as we have seen in the result of the late elections, its unhesitating condemnation. The instinctive feeling of self-preservation spoke undisguisedly on this occasion; and a nation, which has a right to demand of a ministry in which it has placed confidence, a dispassionate and impartial consideration of truths which bear on such weighty interests, was roused to a simultaneous display of proper indignation at seeing the prospects of the intelligent and enterprising classes, and the sufferings of its poorer population, alike degraded to become the weapons of a scandalous party warfare.

If we appreciate the expression of public opinion in the result of the late elections correctly, it amounted to a protestation on the part of the intelligent classes of the community against a sweeping set of measures calculated to overturn our present fiscal and commercial systems. This protest, we take it, was less directed against the measures themselves, than against the manner in which they were proposed, defended and urged. No man, of whatever party, has been so blind as to view this national declaration in the light of a protestation against cheap corn, cheap sugar, and facilitation of commercial intercourse. On the contrary, it is on all hands admitted that this battle has been won. Monopoly of every kind has been proved in the struggle to be a deceptive, destructive phantom, which, like the Jew of the play, ministers to the temporary necessities of the indiscreet and pampered egoist but to secure his ultimate fall; it demands the heart's blood of its victim in payment of its inexorable claim. On this head there is no longer a doubt, except as to the amount of the concession to be made in the first instance; and this doubt is shared by many who desire the concession of every restriction, from the circumstance that its probable immediate operation is, from want of sufficient information, not very clear.

It cannot be wondered, that those who could not or would not see what progress they had made in the affray, and who even now do not seem to know how to use their vantage-ground, should show themselves absolutely insensible to the fact that there were other battles besides this to be fought, and that this triumph, although important, was but a part of a series of combats to be undertaken on different ground, some of which are accounted of even greater urgency. If monopoly were to be destroyed at home, it was equally necessary to spread this conviction abroad. If a formidable competition were to be allowed in our agriculture, was it not the more requisite to increase the preponderance of our manufactures? Did it not seem fair to say to foreigners – 'The irresistible arguments which have been brought forward to prove that we are wise in buying food where we can get it cheapest, apply with the same force to your case; it is equally advantageous to you to buy the cheapest clothing and the cheapest tools?' Was not this requisite to preserve the balance? And what has been done in this respect?

In the Number to which we have alluded we published a solemn warning of the danger the country was incurring from a neglect of our commercial interests abroad. We told the country that we had allies of a valuable description; that their commercial and political existence was threatened by the encroachments of a power whose advances had been rapid and threatened to become dangerous. We told them no unfounded tales about the flourishing state of manufactures abroad which threatened to drive our own from foreign markets, a fact which is wholly disproved by the very deeds and protestations of our supposed rivals, who dread nothing more than a reciprocity which would prove the folly of forcing industrial speculations before the resources of a country demand them, and who are now clamorous for increased protection against us. We told them, on the contrary, that manufactures were not flourishing abroad, for the plain reason which they had so often heard at home – that monopoly cannot flourish. We did more. In a work from whose nature a direction only might be expected to the labours of men endeavouring to throw light upon difficult subjects, we have devoted an unusually large space to the communication of original documents, which have placed in a comprehensive form the leading points of the grand chain of evidence, which was crying for attention to a ministry that remained deaf to all solicitations but those of party virulence and dinner-table cabal.

The selection which we made from the information collected by Dr. Bowring, and from what was withheld from that gentleman by the manufacturers and others whom he consulted abroad, made out a case, the strength of which has, we are glad to see, been appreciated by the nation. It was specially recommended to the notice

270   *Battles over Free Trade, Volume 1*

of parliament in a report[1], the object of which was to suggest means for improving the condition of the labouring classes. It has had too the effect of spreading encouragement amongst our disheartened allies abroad, and it has obliged the antagonist party in Germany to proceed cautiously in their hostility to the commercial interests of Great Britain, if it has made them not less unremitting in their toil.

The only men who were immovable in their apathy, or rather, who were so hoodwinked in the petty chase in which they had engaged, that they refused when called upon to look to the right or to the left, but who strove to keep up the 'whoop and halloo' long after the death, for purposes best known to themselves, were those of Her Majesty's late ministers in whose departments it specially lay to have guarded against the dangers which we pointed out.

We shall succinctly relate the events that have occurred since we last called attention to the proceedings of the Prussian Customs' League, from which it will appear how unwarrantable a neglect of British interests has been shown in that quarter.

Our readers will recollect that we distinctly traced the firm and protracted opposition offered by the rest of Germany to the first advances of the Prussian League. That union, which it has been thought fit to characterize as the expression of the desire of unity in Germany, and as called into life by the unanimous voice of an enlightened nation, we, by a simple reference to its history, showed to have been at every step viewed with the greatest jealousy and apprehension by the Germans, and to have called up no less than five different leagues to stop its progress, by ensuring to the states which rejected its offers the benefits which it promised without the disadvantages which it threatened to impose. After a period of twenty-two years spent in incessant open and secret negotiation, after appeals to the passions and prejudices of princes, manufacturers and peasants, we showed that a portion of Germany, for us the most important, still refused to listen to the repeated invitations of Prussia. The most powerful means of propagandism had in this emergency been resorted to by the Prussian government, which it is clear is not likely to lose in political importance by the violence of the struggle, provided it be attended with ultimate success. That portion of the press which had previously advocated liberal opinions was conciliated on the one side, whilst the means of coercion through the censorship were so vigorously set in motion on the other, that no resource was left but to take up the advocacy of the monopoly of the manufacturer, in order to escape the necessity of openly advocating despotism, and to have any subject left at all on which to express an apparently independent opinion. Like the leopard of the Indies, who when caught is trained to the chase of the antelope, the influential organs of the press were set, when thus mastered, to hunt the remaining independent states of Germany into the toils; and considering the power of this machinery, which appeared from patri-

1   Handloom-Weavers' Report, p. 76.

'The Prussian League' (1842)

otic motives to advocate what the governments proclaimed by authority, added to the fact, that in all German constitutional states the manufacturers have a powerful majority of votes amongst the deputies of the second chamber, it is truly wonderful that any opposition should have ensued. Yet was not this sufficient; a greater weight had to be thrown into the scale – the active, although indirect co-operation of British ministers in measures so hostile to British interests.

Not many months after we had distinctly pointed out the danger in which we stood of losing so valuable a commercial alliance as that of the states occupying the coast of the German Ocean and a portion of the Baltic, two treaties were brought to light, which astonished everybody except the two cabinets who had so much at stake, and who had acted from apparently opposite views of what was due to the interests of trade. We had shown the absolute necessity for requiting the little less than insulting reception and mystification of Dr. Bowring at Berlin, and the unscrupulous 'ca' me, ca' thee' alliance between agitators at home and the advocates of commercial monopoly abroad, of which he became the instrument, by a dignified abstinence from useless proffers of amity on our part towards Prussia, and by some decided mark, however trifling, of our recognition of the liberal commercial policy of the North German states. We pointed out two or three articles of pressing necessity at home on which concessions might, at no sacrifice to ourselves, be granted, and which would suffice so far to propitiate the states interested, that no attempts would be made to induce them to waver in the course they had until then pursued. A judicious use of such concessions would at the same time have settled the vexatious question of the Stade duties, which the course adopted by Lord Palmerston was only calculated to leave open in the manner in which it has been left.

The first of these treaties which was published was called a treaty of reciprocity in navigation between Great Britain and Prussia in its own name and in the name of the other states of the Zollverein. This treaty, but for the bungling manner in which it was drawn up, and which on this occasion was peculiarly serviceable, would have called a new state into existence in Europe and have cancelled the useful part of nearly all our treaties with the continental powers. This treaty would have turned a threatening phantom into a substantial and powerful enemy. The Zollverein would, by a stroke of Lord Palmerston's pen, have been placed side by side with the German confederation; and an useful defensive ally, the sense of whose own interests armed central Europe from the Adriatic to the Baltic to resist M. Thiers' new edition of the revolution of July, would have been obliged to give place to a young and aspiring pretender to conquest, which from that circumstance alone must have been the enemy of all old countries interested in maintaining order and a balance of power. The Zollverein, once recognized as an independent power in Europe, has no choice but the conquest of Holland and Denmark on the terms of a cession of Belgium of France, or of struggling with that power for the mastery. This is the power which his Lordship's uncalled for treaty of reciprocity was near starting into life.

This treaty was uncalled for, because the complaints made by Lord Palmerston himself on the repeated violations of the former treaty of reciprocity by Prussia, the correspondence respecting which has been laid before parliament, were never satisfactorily answered by the Prussian government. It was consequently a step derogatory to the dignity of the British crown to make advances to a power with whom a dispute on a question which militates against all reciprocity was pending.

It was uncalled for because it made concessions to a foreign power, whose whole commercial policy had long been one of open and avowed hostility to Great Britain, without requiring any concession on the part of that power in return. The concessions we allude to are the direct trade with our colonies, and the unprecedented clause which makes the Hanseatic and Dutch harbours the harbours of Prussia and of the states forming the Prussian League, without including the Hanse towns and Holland as parties to the treaty.

It was worse than uncalled for by the effect which it was calculated to produce on the minds of allied powers, who looked upon themselves as gratuitously abandoned on the only side to which they could resort for help against the encroachments of a dreaded rival.

It was in every respect improper on the part of a British minister, who pretended at home to rest his claim to confidence upon the opposition which his cabinet offered to monopoly, thus to throw the whole weight of British influence into the scale of Prussia against old allies of this country, on a question which solely arose upon the pretensions of Prussia to extend and perpetuate a commercial monopoly of the most dangerous kind.

But it will be said, the Hanse towns and the Dutch have not protested; that they have not publicly even remonstrated against this treaty. They have not done so publicly, because the time when a remonstrance would have been effectual was carefully allowed to slip by under the influence of a delusion too alluring to those towns not to have been grasped at by them.

The second treaty, which did not appear until a sufficient interval had elapsed after the publication of the first, was with the Hanse towns, and conceded the direct trade to our colonies; but not the article which was expected to be introduced, to correspond with the concession to Prussia contained in the other treaty to trade to and from the Hanseatic ports with England. It was confidently reported that a clause would admit of the carriage by Hanseatic vessels of all productions of all the Baltic ports or elsewhere to Great Britain and her colonies, from all ports as well as from Hamburg, Bremen and Lübeck, under whatever circumstances they might have been imported into those ports. The restriction in the treaty to goods which can *legally* be conveyed in foreign vessels from the Hanse towns, and the omission of a permission to Hanseatic vessels to import to Great Britain from the

Baltic ports direct, prove that we were bound to show a greater respect to Prussia than to the smaller states on the German Ocean. In other words, it is evident that there was a desire to sacrifice the rights of the Hanseatic towns and of Holland to Prussia when it was required, but no disposition to allow the smaller powers any advantage at which Prussia might take umbrage.

We are aware that these, with other proceedings of the late foreign minister, have been judged harshly at home, and that this sudden desire to please our Prussian allies has been ascribed to inducements of a very different kind from a desire to extend our commercial relations. It is, as our readers see, not easy to perceive how such an extension was to result from these treaties; but the serious accusation which has been founded upon their tendency is not one on which we are called upon to decide. For such charges the nation is the only fit jury, and the evidence that ought to support them has not yet been laid before it. Under these circumstances, that no protest was entered by the Hanse towns where protestations would have been useless, will excite but little surprise, and alters in no degree the responsibility of concluding one treaty which was little less than treasonable, and another which was worse than useless.

Then too, had the Hanse towns protested against the Prussian treaty, the risk must be taken into account of offending the irritable feelings of a nation like ours, with whom a moderate dose of dictation is not to be omitted in the ministerial receipt for procuring popular assent to any foreign transaction. The 'lords of human kind' are fond enough of lording it over their fellows, but they have their good sides, and one of the best is their love of fair play. The plan followed by the aggrieved powers on this occasion was one likely to result from a much more intimate knowledge of the English character than we fear that their statesmen can claim. They saw that their rights were about to be sacrificed to please a minister without the knowledge of the nation, and, as if by accord, Holland on the Rhine and Hanover on the Elbe determined to make their rights known. The Stade negotiation, which might have easily been arranged in a manner satisfactory to both parties, became on a sudden mixed up with extraneous matter, involving to the last degree the dignity of the crown and the independence of the kingdom of Hanover. We had, without asking the consent, or even soliciting the co-operation of the King of Hanover, coolly declared his ports to be ports of Prussia and of the other German states, and accorded particular privileges to strangers who should trade from his harbours, while his vessels are excluded from the Prussian ports by differential duties. Can we wonder that the negotiation did not proceed?

Holland in the same manner was alarmed at the appearance of this clause; for such clauses are usually what the strongest party chooses to call them. One application of the clause was pointed out in the treaty itself, and in order to guard against any undue interpretation of it, the Dutch government quietly published

274   *Battles over Free Trade, Volume 1*

a decree of the king in council, declaring that the steam navigation on all Dutch rivers and inland waters lay under the control of the minister of the finances, to whom application was to be made for permission, and for an approval of the hours and distances which it was intended to observe.

Thus two restrictions, one in the shape of the continuance of an old grievance and one in the imposition of a new one, resulted from this masterpiece of diplomatic policy on the part of a minister who professed to be the arch-enemy of all restrictions.

But the worst consequence of this affair was the partial breaking up of the North-western League. This league, formed between Hanover, Oldenburg and Brunswick for the purpose of securing freedom of communication to the states within it, accompanied by a moderate scale of duties on foreign merchandise, had prospered since its foundation in a manner proportioned to the resources of the lands composing it. The unceasing efforts of Prussian diplomacy were directed towards seducing or frightening one or other of the members to secede. The negotiation of the treaties before mentioned turned the scale when the chances appeared equal; and, balancing between Prussian and English commercial policy, Brunswick first listened to the voice of the former, when the English minister thus recommended her to side with a power which, even with a hostile mien, was able to command respect.

The defection of Brunswick, which has from the commencement of the present year joined the Prussian League, gave a fatal blow to the North-western League, of which, on account of the importance of the Brunswick fair, this state has been a more influential member than its diminutive territorial extent would lead a stranger to suppose.

What the reasons may have been which prevailed with the Brunswick government so far as to cause it to renounce the liberal commercial policy to which it so long adhered, we know not. Whatever they were, it is evident that they were greatly strengthened by the concessions which were thus unnecessarily made to Prussia at a moment when no word of concessions to the North-western League, which had such strong claims on our acknowledgements, was breathed. The comparative statement of the two tariffs, given in our Number XXII., shows that the duties levied by the North-western League, in some objects of great demand in trade, are from one-third to one-fifth less than the Prussian duty. Yet to the former league we were disposed to grant nothing, while to the latter we were willing to sacrifice even our alliance with the former league.

We pointed out on a former occasion the reasons why the people of an agricultural state have nothing to gain by acceding to the Prussian union. The government, it is true, gains by the immense increase of the duties on colonial produce caused by the introduction of the Prussian tariff. This is of itself a serious addition to the burthens of the people and a sad incumbrance to the trader. But the increase of taxation thus caused is as nothing when compared with that arising from the increase in price of all articles of clothing, of all tools, machinery and objects of luxury or comfort, occasioned by the protection of the Prussian tariff. There is not an implement of industry, from the knitting-needle to the steam-engine, which is not rendered less accessible to the people. Where is then the advantage to be derived from such a step for Brunswick? – we confess we cannot see it. Still less can it be to the interest of a seaport to join. The increased price of labour, the control of custom-officers, would of themselves materially detract from the present gains of merchants, who are so happy as to be exempted from such inflictions. But when Prussia comes to Hanover, Mecklenburg and the Hanse towns with the declaration that she only wishes for their accession that she may set up the long decried, and now almost abandoned, system of differential navigation dues, can it be wondered that mercantile states hesitate to adopt a proposal so fraught with ruin to their trade? The shipping of all these countries has steadily increased within the period when the shipping of Prussia, fostered by differential duties, has been decreasing. Since the commencement of our late large importation of grain from the Baltic, the Prussian shipping has somewhat recovered; but even now, if the extent and population of the two lands be compared, the shipping of Prussia bears no comparison to that of the little Duchy of Mecklenburg. According to recent statistical accounts, Prussia possesses 619 sea-ships: Mecklenburg counts 248 sea-ships, which carry 20,510 lasts. Recent statements of the trade of Bremen show likewise that the shipping of that port is in a healthy and rising condition.

Bremen will illustrate happily the arguments for and against the adhesion of the maritime states to the Zollverein. The arguments advanced on the Prussian side in favour of the union are, that Bremen, having a large trade in wines, in tobacco and in sugar-refining, the greater part of which articles are destined for the markets of the union, would find it an advantage to have no customs' line between its gates and the markets in question. This is true if the customs' line were to disappear altogether; but it appears evident that if the line be preserved, it is better for Bremen it should be there than between Bremen and the sea. Wine is an article which requires constant attention if long kept in stock. The casks must be filled and coopered from time to time; the merchant may wish to bottle in large or small quantities, and it is evident that he can do all this in his own cellar better and cheaper than in a bonded warehouse. On tobacco the duty must be paid before it can be manufactured for smoking or for snuff, and the same must take place with sugar before it can be refined. All these processes are now performed without an advance of duty by the Bremen merchant. What has he then to gain by a change of system? The Hanse towns, where no fiscal pressure is felt, will assuredly not consent to give up their present advantageous position for trade, unless forced to yield to considerations of a different kind, which we trust, for the well-being of the civilized world, will not be forced upon them, and which it clearly would be the sacred duty of a loyal British minister to the utmost to resist.

The evident advantages to the maritime states in refraining from a junction with the League, of which a few are here slightly sketched, will, we trust, prove a sufficient answer to the unseemly declarations of Prussian writers, who stigmatize all endeavours to resist the encroachments of the Zollverein as proceeding from a desire to keep Germany disunited. England, as we have repeatedly stated, has nothing to reap from disunion in Germany; on the contrary, she has but recently been a considerable gainer by the unanimity of feeling displayed by the German people on the late pretensions advanced by a French minister. But we deny that the union demanded by Prussia, accompanied with the sacrifice of local interests and long-indulged peculiarities, would be of any advantage to Germany itself. The interference which would thus be permitted to despotic governments in the dearest concerns of constitutional monarchies and republics, and which in so many is from the commencement enforced by requiring the vote and representation of small states at the periodical financial congresses to be ceded to Prussia, would clearly rob Germany of the little breathing space for freedom which is now allowed. The power of making foreign alliances, now controlled by the confederation, and of giving vent to public opinion through the press, which is fettered by a decree of the same body, were enough to sacrifice to the passion for centralization, which has been termed nationality. The control over trade and the power of regulating taxation are matters which a nation cannot abandon while it has any pretensions to freedom, or its inhabitants profess to respect themselves.

On these grounds the non-ratification of the recent treaty respecting Luxemburg, proposed between Holland and Prussia, cannot be condemned, for the king of Holland clearly only rejected the union desired on account of the arbitrary and derogatory conditions annexed to it in the details under which it was to be carried out. The proposal to a sovereign prince to cede all control over the fiscal arrangements and the trade of his states, and to resign these unconditionally to the monarch of a country with which he is willing to unite in commercial alliance, and who is thenceforth to become his representative and to legislate for him, is one of so strange a nature, that a monarch who should comply with it would have little reason to complain, if he found that with all the attributes of royalty he had resigned the very essence of his dignity. And yet these were the terms on which Luxemburg was expected to join the Prussian League, the rejection of which has formed a pretext for angry notes from the court of Berlin, and it is said, for an appeal to the diet of Frankfort to coerce the refractory member of the League. A witty German writer once described that diet as a bundle of rods tied together by the greater powers for the purpose of chastising the smaller ones. We doubt, however, very strongly whether the diet will suffer itself to be used for a purpose like this, although Austria can assuredly be outvoted on all commercial questions by the members of the Prussian League.

Opinions are thus extremely divided in Germany on the subject of this League, which is alternately put forward as the proof and as the test of unanimity of feeling, according as the one or the other best suits the views of the party declaiming. Our own opinion remains unchanged; and as our German opponents have allowed the force of one grand argument which we advanced in our review of Dr. Bowring's Report, perhaps they will allow us to express it without ascribing it to the ungenerous motive we have named. The operation of a tariff is now too well understood to admit of any misapprehension. Under the protection of high duties it is possible to raise up any branch of manufacture, or to encourage any particular manner of cultivating the soil; but this end is attained at the peril of the speculator, who invariably suffers by the loss of nearly all his investment upon so unsound a foundation. If, as in the case of most countries, the manufactures are the cause of the wealth of England instead of being the result of our prosperity, it is because we have advantages for manufacturing which are so well known as to make it idle to enumerate them. We do not consider the power of manufacturing cheaper than our neighbours a relative advantage, because in the natural course of things we should ultimately exchange objects of low value, the produce of machinery, against wares of a more refined kind, or for works of art. The power of manufacturing cheaply is, however, a positive advantage of the highest kind, and that not only for the land possessing it, but for all who choose to partake of the benefit; for the common objects of necessity must be furnished before more refined productions can be demanded. If therefore any other country could furnish these more cheaply than we can produce them for ourselves, we should recommend purchasing them with productions of a higher value. This exchange, according to the present state of the case, is against us, under the operation of a law of nature which we cannot change at present, but which may at some future time be altered; as for instance by the substitution of any other power for moving machinery than one requiring coal and iron; or by the accumulation of population on some other favoured spot; or lastly, by the transmission of a large mass of the capital of this country to some other. In such a case, if we did not prefer having a population of labourers to a population of mechanics, we ought to do what Prussia now refuses to do, purchase what we could get cheaply by selling something at a dearer rate, and it would be our business to find out something which we could so sell. Now the maritime states of Germany take this view of the matter, and are better pleased to vest their spare capital for the moment as it would seem in ships – a speculation which remunerates without protection – than in manufactures. When that branch is exhausted, they are willing to trust to the resources and ingenuity of their population for another productive line of enterprise.

The system of the Prussian League is the converse of this system, and prescribes by a large bounty, raised by a heavy tax upon the consumers, a particular line of industry, which after all only gives the consumer at a dearer rate what he could have bought with greater moral benefit at a cheaper rate. That league rejects the notion that a population has resources and ingenuity sufficient to find out lines of manufacture which would yield a more valuable return to the workman than machine-work affords.

The Prussians have a right to their own opinion, but can the maritime states be blamed for thinking for themselves? Can we as their allies, and benefited by an interchange which these states likewise hold advantageous to themselves, suffer them to be compelled, or even induced by other means than those of fair persuasion by argument, to change their system and renounce our alliance? We cannot; and the people of this country will not look tamely on at any aggression which may be attempted in the spirit of the threats with which a portion of the German press now teems. We can assure them that the proceedings on their side are strictly watched at this side, and we recommend to them to avail themselves of every possible means to give the greatest publicity to every step that may be taken.

On the grounds we have stated, our readers will find it easy to believe that Prussia has in her own hands the solution of all these difficulties. She can at a word unite all Germany under her ægis, and advance her League to the sea, while she really increases the physical and moral power of the states that join it. To effect this, she has only to leave the false basis on which her League now rests, and to adopt the sounder one of the maritime states. But it must be acknowledged that the sound basis supposes a renunciation of the principle of unnecessary centralization, and the encouragement of every local advantage for the benefit of the mechanic or the speculator. The adoption of such a system would consequently likewise afford a guarantee that free political institutions would not be meddled with. Need we ask whether, on these terms, the maritime states would hesitate to join the League; and whether the civilization of Europe under its operation would not in a few years be more advanced than through centuries of diplomatic intrigue backed by myriads of bayonets?

In advocating such a system, are we really the enemies of Germany?

But if the argument which we have advanced has any force, it follows that a careful government would show more anxiety to secure the finer kinds of manufactures than the commoner ones to its subjects. If jealousy were admissible, we should expect to find the higher productions of skill and art more highly protected than any other. But the Prussian tariff does the reverse; it imposes the highest duties on the lowest description of goods, on most of which it is wholly prohibitory, whilst it taxes lightly goods of a finer description. In cottons, for instance, the duties levied by weight equalled the following rates in 1837, and, are now higher in proportion.[1]

In the course of our argument we have made no allusion to a possible exchange of agricultural produce for manufactures, because the opinion which we put forward respecting the inability of Germany to furnish sufficient corn to supply our demand has been pronounced a correct one by the Germans themselves. The observation has been noted as novel and founded in fact by the writers in Germany who do not coincide with us in other respects.

This is an important concession, and we rejoice at having advanced the discussion so much as to have fixed this one geographical point. The bulk of the supplies required to satisfy our craving demand in a bad harvest must be drawn from Austria and Russia; and of course, if the admission of a regular trade caused an improvement of the communications with and in those distant countries, the price at which they could furnish grain would even in the cheapest years exclude the dearer German wheat from our markets. Oats and barley would stand the competition better. But this concession which the advocates of manufacturing monopoly are now endeavouring to use as an argument against all reciprocity in trade with England, fully confirms the opinion we expressed of the nature of the late mission to Berlin, at the bottom of which a desire to cater to the prejudices of a narrow-minded party evidently lay, and prevailed over the sincere desire to learn the truth.

We shall not be charged with any desire to join in the outcry raised some time back respecting the danger of not finding foreign supplies if we opened our ports too freely. Our readers will remember that we were the first to combat that supposition, and to point to the exact spots in the Russian and the Austrian empires from which those supplies could be drawn. We at the same time, in our remarks on the state of agriculture in the south of Italy, pointed out some of the trammels which prevented countries more within our reach from producing as much as they ought.

We cannot, however, deny that we regard the question of the amount of duty levied on corn as but a part (an important part no doubt) of the difficulties which now lie in the way of importation, and consequently of the procuring and securing of cheap food for the people. Hence the stress we have laid upon the urgency of studying and cultivating the means of communication with the sea from those fertile districts to which we have to look. Hence the pains we have taken to track the courses of Austrian and Russian rivers, and we have yet more to do on that score to render the information which we have given complete and convincing. Hence above all the importance we attach to the securing of more than one channel of supply for an article of such indispensable necessity as grain. Our readers will recollect that two years since we pointed out the defects of a treaty concluded with one of the most important of the countries of Europe in

---

1 [Ed.: There follows a table illustrating this point.]

this respect, heedless, as in the case of our German negotiations, of the weight of supposed authorities, under which these proceedings were sure to be sheltered against our unwelcome criticism. The time has perhaps not yet come when our arguments shall be found powerful enough to cause them to be acted upon; still we persevere, and we invite the friends of free trade, of extended commercial intercourse, to aid us in our undertaking.

We have declared that almost unbounded markets for our manufactures await our approach. We have it in our power to open the tracks along which both supplies of food must flow, and masses of manufactured goods must move in return. In Europe, in Asia, in America our commercial relations can be regulated, improved, extended – but not without care, judgement and energy in the employment of the means at our command.

These means we have already pointed out, but we must here point to them anew. The temper of the various governments, whose desire of enriching their subjects excludes our manufactures, has been sufficiently shown of late by repeated failures in the attempt to bring them to treat on the basis of reciprocity. We have it in our power to force them all to agree to our terms, by not indiscriminately allowing to all the benefits of the concessions which shall be made on the two important articles corn and sugar. If we lose this opportunity of placing our commercial relations on a sound footing, we may never regain it. We can only regain it when lost at the cost of reconstructing that odious complicated fabric, at which the first violent blow is about to be dealt. Had we the voices of a thousand warners, we would shout this warning with the might of earnest conviction in the ears of our countrymen; for we are aware that we stand alone, and that warnings which are re-echoed by no party are too apt to be disregarded. Nevertheless we persevere, and perchance our warning may not prove to be given in vain.

It has been said on all sides, you must bring forward but one subject at a time; cheap food, and nothing but cheap food; free trade, and nothing but free trade, or you will not be heard and nothing will be done. We disclaim the necessity of arguing with our countrymen as we should with fools or with children. If cheap food will buy free trade, is it not on that account the more desirable? If free trade will secure cheap food, is it not for that reason indispensable?

We repeat it then – sell your concessions and purchase plenty; sell your concessions and purchase industry, which will give you the means of purchasing enjoyment. Sell them to Russia, to Austria, to Prussia, to Holland, to Brazil, to the United States. Sell them dear to those from whom you have much to demand; sell them cheap to those who have but little to give for them. Give them away only to the Hanse towns and to those states who have no concession to make in return, because they have preceded you in adopting the system of free trade. But sell them; sell them! With all the world for buyers, it will be hard if you do not drive a profitable bargain.

THE CORN LAWS AND THE EVOLUTION OF BRITISH COMMERCIAL POLICY, 1832–46

In the history of international trade policy, repeal of the Corn Laws by Britain in 1846 occupies a distinctive place. Its implications for international commercial relations and the international state system have attracted the interest of scholars arguing that Britain acted as a hegemonic power, effectively using her economic strength to achieve commercial stability through open markets. Whilst such views have been questioned in recent years, the international concerns of free traders indicate that they possessed a vision of the world economy which, whilst embracing free commerce, also sought to shape the economic composition of nations. For example, Richard Cobden informed J. B. Smith of the potential development of Anglo-French trade in the following terms:

> Now if by opening our trade with them in wines & brandies, we can increase this dependence very greatly, we shall by & by have not only the Lyonnese but the wine growers of the South in arms for free trade, in case we threaten restrictions in default of a reciprocity[.] It will probably be by such a process as this that the French may be forced ultimately to give up their prejudices[1]

Theories of comparative advantage may have underpinned such thinking – thus giving rise to interpretations of hegemonic behaviour – but ample evidence may also be given to substantiate alternative motives and intentions.[2]

The campaign to repeal the Corn Laws illustrates how far commercial policy debate had advanced from the 1820s. William Gladstone even claimed that Sir Robert Peel's 1841 government had 'utterly forgotten' the principles of Huskissonian reciprocity, although this appears unlikely.[3] William Huskisson was certainly not forgotten by early advocates of Corn Law repeal, who saw him as one whose designs for eventual repeal were thwarted.[4] It has sometimes been argued that the importance of the Corn Laws to the British protective system was more symbolic than substantial,[5] but this view is hard to verify. First, contemporaries (on both sides of the question) viewed the Corn Laws as vitally important to the body politic of Britain. For Cobden, they were the 'key-stone of monopoly' in the protective system. For protectionists, they were an integral

– 281 –

element in the political authority of the landed classes.[6] Second, the unilateral nature of repeal, alongside significant tariff reductions on raw materials and manufactured goods, was an unprecedented and fundamentally momentous departure in the conduct of British commercial policy. These factors must then be added to the international implications of repeal. As noted above, the Corn Laws were viewed by many foreign countries as an obstacle to freer trade, a view enthusiastically propagated by political economists and the Anti-Corn Law League. Hence, repeal of the Corn Laws constituted the first step in establishing a liberal international trading system.

From its inception it was clear that the anti-Corn Law movement would be predominantly industrial and urban. In 1834, metropolitan and provincial radicals began to call for abolition of the Corn Laws, with Anti-Corn Law associations formed in Glasgow, London, Sheffield and Dundee.[7] Implicit in the critique of the Corn Laws was the injustice of 'bread taxes' raising the price of food for urban consumers for the benefit of the landed interest. The political economist David Ricardo laid the basis for repeal by arguing that it would lead to manufacturing and industrial expansion in foreign markets. Cobden extended this argument, noting that the Corn Laws contracted foreign markets for British manufacturers, and encouraged foreign manufacturing and tariff barriers. As many of these countries were agricultural, they should be exploiting their comparative advantage in supplying industrial Britain with agricultural products.[8] In this respect, evidence of industrialization in foreign countries and their willingness to trade on reciprocal terms were highly important.[9] By removing artificial interventions in the market, free traders argued that the natural economic order would be restored, food prices reduced, and the prosperity of British manufacturing industries enhanced. Nor was repeal necessarily disastrous for the agricultural sector; greater efficiency in agricultural methods and techniques promised to ensure the prosperity of British agriculture.[10]

With the formation of the Manchester Anti-Corn Law Association in 1838, the debate became more pointed, with powerful expressions of urban, provincial radicalism central to this process.[11] The identification of the League with manufacturing interests raised difficulties, most notably the suspicion, propagated by Chartists and Tory Radicals, that Corn Law repeal was sought as a means of reducing wages.[12] The emergence of Chartism meant that working-class support for the League was extremely variable, and greatly dependent on the state of local industrial relations and labour markets.[13] Well aware of the danger of identifying predominantly with a sectional interest, Cobden informed Edward Baines 'it will not have escaped your notice, that our enemies are trying hard to make the corn law a mere question between the millowners of Manchester, & the landowners'. Whilst arguing that this posed the question in the narrowest and most

The Corn Laws and the Evolution of British Commercial Policy   283

prejudicial manner, Cobden conceded Manchester had been 'too exclusively the focus of anti corn law excitement'.[14]

The League deliberately formulated its national campaign across class lines. In attempting to obtain cross-class support, the League emphasized that repeal would yield prosperity for the entire community.[15] The petitioning campaigns of 1839–42 illustrate a strategy which placed a great emphasis on public and civic participation.[16] This also extended to religion, where Evangelical economic theory lent itself to supporting the removal of artificial restrictions and belief in a natural economic order, made all the more pertinent by the conservative Church hierarchy's support for the Corn Laws.[17] The geographical range and sheer scale of submitted petitions testifies to the League's success in organizing on a national scale, but from 1842 the strategy of the League turned towards voter registration and a massive propaganda campaign involving distribution of millions of tracts.[18] The impressive diversity of petitions for commercial reform, from civic institutions of northern industrial towns to London merchants, was not without difficulties. Cobden was particularly insistent on maintaining a demarcation between the Corn Laws and free trade, and deprecated attempts to turn the League into a free-trade organization, arguing: 'We expressly limit ourselves to <u>Corn & provisions</u> – If we go beyond we do not know what to stop at'.[19] By and large, the movement was successful in its concentration on the Corn Laws, whilst supporting free trade in general.

Until 1841, protectionists had been remarkably reticent to engage in serious debate. This perhaps reflected the security they felt in the survival of protection. The Whigs' commercial proposals of 1841, including reform of timber, sugar and corn tariffs, challenged the security of protection by making commercial policy the main issue of the 1841 general election. Defenders of the Corn Laws such as Sir John Gladstone, a supporter of Huskissonian reciprocity, outlined objections to repeal, and protectionist editorials and parliamentary candidates described the nightmare scenario of dependence on foreign food supply.[20] Equally zealous were free traders such as John Bowring, whose election address described free trade as the 'Magna Charta of Labour'.[21] The League was exalted by the admission of Lord Stanley that the Corn Laws raised bread prices above their natural level and increased rentals without raising wages. This admission effectively supported the League view of the Corn Laws as a monopoly interest of the landed classes.[22]

Peel's return to power appeared an endorsement of protection, which, it was thought, was in safe hands. Yet, his tariff rationalization of 1842, including a reform of the sliding-scale of corn duties and reduced duties on raw materials and manufactured goods, facilitated by the re-establishment of income tax, indicated a bold and perhaps unpredictable approach to financial and commercial policy. Peel's reforms represented a rebalancing of direct and indirect taxation to relieve industrial and consumer interests amidst the bitter class conflict of the late 1830s and early 1840s.[23] In reducing tariffs, Peel came under criticism from protectionists concerned that whilst tariff reductions were made which encouraged imports, there was no guarantee that foreign countries would accept a greater volume of British manufactures in return. Reciprocal conceptions of commerce remained powerful.[24]

The inability of agriculture to keep pace with population growth forced Peel into conceding that Britain's economic future lay in importing a large amount of food stuffs. Two years earlier, the American 'Free Trade Missionary' John Curtis delivered an address at Manchester on America's ability to supply Britain with corn.[25] Fears were raised for the survival of protection and, although partially assuaged by the preference granted to Canadian corn in 1843, protectionists were sufficiently concerned to begin organizing in the counties. The rural–urban and industrial–agricultural divide became immediately apparent. Whereas 74,721 signatures were attached to a petition from Manchester praying for repeal in 1843, the scale of protectionist organization was much more modest.[26] The first protectionist organization, formed in Essex late in 1843, provided the impetus for further local organizations, which eventually led to the formation of a national organization in 1844.[27]

Protectionists were correct to be concerned, for Peel finally indicated that he proposed to repeal the Corn Laws late in 1845. The Irish famine occasioned the proposal but was not the cause of his conversion to repeal. Peel's resignation, followed by the Whigs inability to form a government, led to his return to power in December 1845, with Lord John Russell handing back 'with courtesy the poisoned chalice to Sir Robert'.[28] In some quarters there was relief that the Whigs would not have to deal with the question, and interestingly the view that, since Peel had effectively formed a new government, the protectionists could not complain about measures.[29] How wrong this assumption was soon became clear.

Peel's proposals unleashed a torrent of debate, which was not confined to the economic aspects of repeal, although attacks associating cheap bread with wage reductions continued to be invoked.[30] The radical political implications of repeal occupied much of the debate. The nature of the question and the interests involved lent themselves to such concerns, for repeal was a multi-faceted issue, touching issues of national self-sufficiency and security, agricultural prosperity, and the political authority of the landed classes.[31] The latter factor made Cobden fear that the Lords would reject the Bill.[32] However, the fear that rejection would provoke a political crisis and possibly hasten further constitutional reform led the Lords to pass the Bill. A number of protectionist peers issued a formal protest against the Bill, the first two points of which concerned the old themes of security during wartime, alongside an impressive critique of free trade.[33] The

The Corn Laws and the Evolution of British Commercial Policy 285

free admission of foreign corn also meant the end of imperial preference. The ramparts of the Huskissonian system, reciprocity and imperial preference, were therefore dismantled. More widely, repeal was accompanied by the completion of extensive tariff reductions begun in 1842, with duties on most raw materials and many manufactured goods abolished.[34] The unilateral nature of policymaking provoked protectionist claims that France, Prussia and America would not reciprocate, but would maintain their protective duties.[35] Peel accepted there was little prospect of immediate reciprocity but considered 'at no remote period' that France and other countries would follow Britain's example.[36]

Why protection failed in Britain when it was successfully advanced and continued to obtain support throughout Europe is a key question. Political scientists adopting a rational choice model argue that changes in the economic composition of constituencies, reflecting broader changes in the economic structure of Britain, comprising more intensive urbanization and industrialization, played an important role in facilitating repeal. One recent account argues for an amalgam of interests, ideas and institutions in explaining it.[37] Clearly, Peel's role was crucial, but political developments were underpinned by the nationwide agitation for repeal conducted by the Anti-Corn Law League, whose strategy, tactics and ideas, won the organizational and ideological battle. The failure of the protectionists to construct a broad-based movement was important. Aside from agriculture, economic interests sympathetic to protection were disparate, in contrast to the solid phalanx of urban and industrial interests supporting repeal. There is also a general sense that League ideology was consistent with the spirit of the age: progressive, optimistic, religious and moralistic, and this multi-faceted nature meant that the League possessed a wide appeal.

In terms of international commercial policy, it is almost certainly incorrect to argue that those supporting repeal viewed it as a measure that would transform the commercial policy of Europe. Most viewed it in consumerist terms as a measure that would reduce prices and promote the competitiveness of British manufacturing industry. The momentum behind repeal was not internationalist in nature – i.e., Corn Law repeal was never intended as a world-wide movement towards commercial liberty. In this sense, protectionist claims that unilateral tariff reductions would not be reciprocated by foreign nations appear vindicated.[38]

Notes

1. Richard Cobden to J. B. Smith, 1 June 1840, in A. Howe (ed.), *The Letters of Richard Cobden, Volume 1 1815–1847* (Oxford: Oxford University Press, 2007), pp. 190–3.
2. C. Schonhardt-Bailey (ed.), *The Rise of Free Trade*, 4 vols (London: Routledge, 1997), vol. 4: Free Trade Reappraised: The New Secondary Literature.

3. Cited in B. Hilton, 'Peel: A Reappraisal', *Historical Journal*, 22:3 (1979), pp. 585–614, on p. 598.
4. C. R. Fay, *Great Britain from Adam Smith to the Present Day: An Economic and Social Study* (London: Longmans, Green and Co. Ltd., 1928), p. 45.
5. J. V. C. Nye, *War, Wine, and Taxes: The Political Economy of Anglo-French Trade, 1689–1900* (Princeton, NJ, and Oxford: Princeton University Press, 2007), p. 90.
6. Cobden to Villiers, 9 November 1841, Cobden Papers, BL, Add MS 43662, fols 45–6.
7. See Ebenezer Elliott, 'An Address to the People of England, on the Corn Laws', *Tait's Edinburgh Magazine* (1834), below, pp. 289–96.
8. See Richard Cobden to John Norton, 23 August 1838, below, p. 333.
9. Cobden to John Bowring, 19 October 1839, Cobden Papers, West Sussex Record Office, CP 15, fol. 5h.
10. See Richard Cobden, 'Modern History of the Corn Laws', *Anti-Corn Law Circular* (1839); and 'The Ghost of a Dead Monopoly!', *Economist* (1846), both below, pp. 319–30, 391–4.
11. See Petition of the Chamber of Commerce and Manuractures of Manchester, 20 January 1838, in *Appendix to the Report of the Select Committee on Public Petitions* (1837–8); and 'Dilemmas on the Corn Law Question', *Blackwood's Magazine* (1839), both below, pp. 331–2, 334–43.
12. See J. Almack *The Character, Motives, and Proceedings of the Anti-Corn Law Leaguers: With a Few General Remarks on the Consequences that Would Result from a Free Trade in Corn* (London: J. Ollivier, 1843), esp. pp. 48–53.
13. See 'Support of the Anti-Corn Law League by the Working Classes', *Anti-Corn Law Circular* (1840); and 'Corn-Law Agitation Humbug', *Chartist Circular* (1840), both below, pp. 346–8, 355, for differing interpretations of the level of working-class support.
14. Cobden to Edward Baines, 12 October 1841, in Howe (ed.), *The Letters of Richard Cobden*, pp. 239–40.
15. See 'Address of the Metropolitan Anti-Corn Law Association', *Anti-Corn Law Circular* (1840), below, pp. 349–52.
16. See 'Petitions', *Anti-Corn Law Circular* (1840), and 'Our Weapons of War', *Anti-Corn Law Circular* (1840); 'Manifestations of Public Feeling on the Bread Tax', *Anti-Corn Law Circular* (1840); and 'Petition! Petition! Petition!', *Anti-Corn Law Circular* (1840), all below, pp. 344–5, 353–4, 359–60.
17. See 'The Bread-Taxing Bishops and the Bible-Reading People', *Anti-Corn Law Circular* (1840), below, pp. 356–8; cf. 'The great Author of our being created the fruits of the earth for the use and support of man', *Anti-Bread Tax Circular*, 18 November 1841.
18. *Anti-Bread Tax Circular*, 5 May, 19 May and 2 June 1842.
19. Cobden to J. B. Smith, 28 March 1841, J. B. Smith Papers, Manchester Central Library, MS 923.2 S333, III, fol. 422.
20. See Protectionist Editorial, *Chelmsford Chronicle*, 28 May 1841, and H. N. Burroughes and E. Wodehouse, Joint Election Address to the Electors of East Norfolk, *Norfolk Chronicle and Norwich Gazette*, 12 June 1841, both below, pp. 364–5, 366.
21. See John Bowring, Election Address, *Bolton Chronicle*, 26 June 1841, below, pp. 367–8.
22. See Richard Cobden to George Wilson, 25 September 1841, below, p. 369; 'Lord Stanley's Admissions', *The Anti-Bread-Tax Almanack, for the Year of our Lord 1842* (Manchester: J. Gadsby, 1842), p. 41.
23. Fay, *Great Britain from Adam Smith to the Present Day*, pp. 63–4; Hilton, 'Peel', p. 597.
24. Speech of Lord Beaumont, 18 April 1842, *Hansard* (1842), lxii, c. 623.

25. *Anti-Bread Tax Circular*, 12 August 1841.
26. See Petition of Inhabitants of Manchester, *Manchester Times, and Lancashire and Cheshire Gazette*, 11 March 1843, below, p. 375; in 1844, 3,857 petitions with 288,321 signatures were presented opposing repeal, *Reports from the Select Committee on Public Petitions* (1844), p. 877.
27. See First Annual Meeting of the Agricultural Protection Society for Great Britain and Ireland, *Morning Herald*, 14 December 1844, below, pp. 376–99; *John Bull*, 15 January 1844.
28. B. Disraeli, *Lord George Bentinck: A Political Biography*, 8th edn, revised (London: Archibald Constance & Co. 1905), p. 21.
29. See Lord Palmerston to the Earl of Minto, 27 December 1845, below, p. 380.
30. See P. Bennet, Speech to Central Suffolk Agricultural Protection Association, *Bury and Suffolk Herald*, 21 January 1846, below, pp. 381–2.
31. See 'The Corn Laws as a Buttress for the Aristocracy', *Economist* (1846), below, pp. 383–5.
32. See Richard Cobden to William Rathbone, 2 February 1846, below, p. 386.
33. See House of Lords Protest against the Corn Bill, *Hansard* (1846), below, pp. 388–9.
34. Fay, *Great Britain from Adam Smith to the Present Day*, p. 46.
35. Viscount Pollington, 24 March 1846, *Hansard* (1846), lxxxv, c. 6; Sir J. Trollope, 24 March 1846, *Hansard* (1846), lxxxv, cc. 26–7; Lord George Bentinck, 4 May 1846, *Hansard* (1846), lxxxvi, cc. 41–4; Borthwick, 8 May 1846, *Hansard* (1846), lxxxvi, cc. 261–2.
36. 4 May 1846, *Hansard* (1846), lxxxvi, cc. 67–8.
37. C. Schonhardt-Bailey, *From the Corn Laws to Free Trade: Interests, Ideas, and Institutions in Historical Perspective* (Cambridge, MA: MIT Press, 2006).
38. See French Reaction to the Reduction of British Duties on Brandy and Silk, *Kentish Gazette*, 10 February 1846, below, p. 387.

THE CORN LAWS AND THE EVOLUTION OF BRITISH COMMERCIAL POLICY, 1832–46

Elite Debate on the Corn Laws in the 1830s

Ebenezer Elliott, 'An Address to the People of England, on the Corn Laws', *Tait's Edinburgh Magazine*, 1 (May 1834), pp. 228–32.

AN ADDRESS TO THE PEOPLE OF ENGLAND, ON THE CORN LAWS. BY THE AUTHOR OF 'CORN-LAW RHYMES.'

ENGLISHMEN! you give much capital, much skill, much labour, for a little profit, a little enjoyment, a very little food steeped in bitter sweat and tears. But why do you not obtain remuneration for your capital, skill, and labour? Because your landowners will not let you. By a vast expenditure of blood and treasure, you have enabled them to decide, that society shall overbuild its base, until the edifice fall and crush them. Patient, long-suffering, and long-eared Englishmen! your ears are, at least, as long as your sufferings, or you would not have fought twenty-six years for a Bread-Tax! It is retributive upon you – the hand of God is in it – that all your miseries can be traced to your wars on French liberty. Where did you win your Bread-Tax? You won it at Waterloo. You have since been reminded of that fact – at Peterloo, and elsewhere. You will again be reminded of it, whenever it shall please the Great Unpaid – or, as it would now seem, any one of his Majesty's coroners – to shoot a dozen or so of you, at a quarter of an hour's notice, and justify a massacre by a glazier's bill, on the authority of a law made by the pensioned Parliament of Charles the Second, which sate seventeen years, and was itself an usurpation! Yes, and I fear you will again deserve to be told by your oppressors, with a sneer or a frown, that they have an instrument in the Grand Jury, (made by the same Parliament?) by which they can, at any time, secure impunity to official butchers. If these things are true, I need not ask whether the Corn-Laws were inflicted upon you by an insolent aristocracy, as a tribute on a conquered people; but I ask, why any free people should endure them? why any man of common sense, or common feeling, should support them? It seems like an insult to ask, why men who work with their hands, should support laws which at once raise the price of food, by restricting the supply, and lower that of labour by lessening the demand? Yet if there were not millions of such persons now living in this country, the Corn-Laws would not exist an hour longer. Let me, then, go through the various classes of British society, one by one, and inquire whether there really is any one class that has an interest in supporting these Corn-Laws.

Why should the proprietors of commercial land – land near towns – support them? The wealth of such persons depends upon trade alone. Yet, with inconceivable folly, some of them defend laws which are prohibiting commerce itself!

Why should the mortgagees of land or houses support Corn-Laws? By offering an accepted premium for the ruin of our trade, those laws are annihilating the only fund out of which the interest of our mortgages can be paid, and consequently destroying the securities of every mortgagee.

Why should any master manufacturer, any merchant, any shopkeeper, support Corn-Laws? By constantly lowering the rate of profit on all capital, they are depressing the wages of all labour and skill. Consequently they strike at the securities of life and property, and endanger all trading establishments. They are at the root of our strikes, and trades-unions; and seem likely to close every shop in the realm – except the potato-shop! Poor nation of shopkeepers! perhaps, your approved good masters will leave you the green-grocer after all.

Why should the owners of house property support Corn-Laws? By rendering it impossible to employ capital profitably in trade, those laws are forcing the ruinous competition of builders, and lowering rents in every street.

Why should farmers support Corn-Laws? Under our restrictive system, tenants compete for land; but, if the trade in corn were free, landowners would compete for tenants! In 1793, when the duty on imported corn was almost nominal, the price of wheat was the same at Hull as at Hamburgh; but higher than at present, though rents are now doubled! If the Corn-Laws continue, the people of England will not be able to buy wheat at any price; but the competition for farms may go on, until the whole country is covered with potato-patches – a glorious prospect for English farmers! How much longer can the landowners compete for bad tenants? The Corn-Laws are rapidly destroying the good ones! Why, then, should farmers support Corn-Laws? I trust the hour is approaching when they will rise, as one man, against them!

But why should the great landowners themselves support Corn-Laws? Because, they are, with a few exceptions, insolvent? I cannot imagine any other reason. What's got over the devil's back, sometimes goes under his belly; and a drowning man will cling to a straw. They can ultimately have no more for

Elliott, 'An Address to the People of England, on the Corn Laws' (1834) 291

their land, or its products, than a free trade would give them! If they gain by their monopoly, it must be at the expense of their heirs! They are destroying the trade which alone can pay the surplus profit called rent; that trade which, once destroyed, will leave them nothing – no, not even their lives. If they were not stone-blind, they would see that the Corn-Laws are laws for the ultimate extirpation of the vermin called landed monopolists. What is the meaning of the long argument of Sir James Grahame [*sic*], on Mr. Hume's motion? It is this, That the landowners having become bankrupt, under the Corn-Laws, therefore the Corn-Laws must continue until every body else shall become bankrupt! Bashful logician! The Corn-Laws are to be supported, because palaced paupers cannot live without Corn-Laws! Can they live *with* them? And, if they can, what right have they to live by making better men die? Oh, because, forsooth, they are the magistracy of the nation! Indeed! Their dilemma has two horns, and they may hang on which of the two they please. If they cannot live without pay, why do they not go to the workhouse for their pay, as their victims do? If they can live without pay, and yet obtain money by saying they cannot, why are they not sent to the treadmill? How often do we see a magnificent criminal near the scaffold, without a rope round his neck, and after the execution wonder at the frightful *mistake* of the executioner, or the law! It is time these worthies understood their position. I have called them mere annuitants; but I was mistaken: annuitants, if honest, are harmless, which cannot be said of men who convert the land itself into a curse! Man builds the house, and has a right either to live in it, or derive a rent from it. Man also improves the soil, and has a right to enjoy his improvements; but in this country, it is the farmer who improves the soil, not the landowner; and I beg leave to inform the latter personage, that God made the land, and intended it to be a blessing. If our landowners live on a reserved profit, what class of men could we better spare? Suppose them all in Abraham's bosom to-morrow, would not the land be as fruitful as at present? Yes, much more so. But not satisfied with living on a reserved profit, they are destroying all profit. How much longer do they suppose a fully peopled country, if Bread-Taxed, can permit the existence of proprietors who do not farm their own land? Either they must resign their land-curse, or farm the land themselves. How dignified will be their appearance in the market of Amsterdam, after annihilating both rents and markets in their own country! But they will not often appear in the market of Amsterdam. If they farm, they will fail; and so will their mortgagees after them; the acres, however, will at length find worthy owners, and England will be herself again. In the meantime, our destroyers, arraigned at the bar of public opinion, impudently plead their right to be criminal! What would Sir James Grahame say to the felons in our jails, if, instead of transportation or a halter, they demanded, as a privilege of their order, palaces, coaches, venison, and moselle? Their sole legal claims being death and a grave, he would tell them, that they had no *right* even to the honours of dissection; an alteration in the law having transferred those honours from robbers and murderers, to honest paupers. But, perhaps, Sir James is a worshipper of potatoes; ignorant that Irish potato-patches are cultivated by English bayonets; that potato-wages signify potato-profits; that potato-profits will not pay for bayonets; and that if he cover England with potato-patches, he must bid adieu both to rent and bayonets for ever!

If mortgagees, merchants, shopkeepers, manufacturers, labourers, house-owners, farmers, and landowners, great and small, have no interest in supporting Corn-Laws, why should any religious man, any man who dares to open his Bible, support them? Why have not the great religious societies of this country long ago declared war against the iniquity of iniquities? The Established Church being identified with the landed interest, I will not inquire why Churchmen support Corn-Laws. But why have not the Quakers, again and again, covered the table of the House of Commons with petitions against them? Surely they have not persuaded themselves that the follies of the wicked can be advantageous to the wise and good, or the wrongs of all a benefit to any. Why do not the enlightened and intrepid Calvinists, – the political dissenters, as they are scornfully called by the enemies of God and man, – raise their irresistible voice against the most enormous wickedness that ever outraged human forbearance? Perhaps they are satisfied with the glory of their ancestors, whose persecuted name is synonymous with all that is great and pure: 'The Pilgrim Fathers,' who planted Liberty in the wilds of America. Now, their having written one word for eternity, is the very best reason why they ought to write another. Oh, it is glorious husbandry to sow and plant immortal words, such as the Calvinists planted for immortality, when they prepared an asylum in the American forests for the oppressed of all nations; words which are things, and which ever growing, produce for ever the useful and the true! But there is a great body of religionists among us, who, how-ever meritorious they may be in other respects, have as yet earned no political honours, written no word on the page of history worthy to be reechoed from the heart of unborn ages, to the ear of the father of duration. When will they *begin* to earn on earth a good name in Heaven? During twenty-six years of anti-Christain [*sic*] warfare did they send to Parliament a single petition for peace? Was not the great measure of Catholic Emancipation carried in spite of their opposition, and the Reform Bill without their assistance? Could they be better employed than in speaking for the bread of the poor? If they do not preach for it, they preach against it, even by their guilty silence. They say, they hate slavery; and, it seems, they can see the fetters of black slaves over three thousand miles of ocean. But why did they tamely see twenty millions sterling wrung from the sweat and agony of white slaves here, to be given to the owners of black slaves, for the strengthening of the hands of whip-wielding despotism? Why do they advocate the cause of black slaves only? Perhaps, they do not meet the owners of black slaves in every street; perhaps, they wish to go to Heaven on velvet; perhaps, those who wish to go to Heaven on velvet, will not get there. If they earn no political honours, have they earned no political degradation? Are they strong only for evil, present only when Abaddon, in his worst works, is present with them? If they will take the black mote from their eyes, they will see white slavery, the Bread-Tax, and its consequences, all around them. If they do not intend to wait until God, 'shall hiss for the fly,' the sound of whose wings shall laugh them into derision from hemisphere to hemisphere, let them haste and preach words and works meet for repentance; Free Bread! Free Men! LIBERTY to every white slave in Britain! If they would cease to work iniquity, and begin to do good, they could carry the holy question of free trade in six months. Therefore it is that I wish to conciliate them. It was while hearing one of their great preachers, that I determined to write Corn-Law Hymns. That preacher, though he uttered not one noble sentiment, seemed at times (such was his power) to lift up his immense congregation, and the roof under which he preached.

'Oh,' I said to my heart, 'why does he not preach that 'The labour of the poor is his life! that he who taxeth the bread of the poor fighteth against God?' If he, and such as he, would do their Christian duty, how soon would the miseries of bread-taxed England approach their termination!' But I thought I could see, under the pulpit, his cloven feet. Greedy flames seemed to rush from his eyes, and from his mouth evil spirits, seeking what they might devour, and whom they might corrupt. I wrote Corn-Law Hymns, but wrote them in vain. To this hour they are unsung in the Zion of the sordid; for they suit not the religion of servility, expedience, and seat-rents. Only a few days ago, I wrote to a great Preacher in Lancashire, requesting him to distribute the Corn-Law Magazine among his agricultural hearers; and what do you think was his reply? 'He did not understand the subject!' He could not understand that two loaves are better than one; but his neighbour, the vicar, understands that two tithe pigs are better than one. 'He did not understand the subject!' The mystery of the bread of the poor was beyond his comprehension! I am sure it is beyond mine. I cannot understand how the poor get bread, competing, as they must under the Corn-Laws, with rivals who obtain it at half price.

Well, then, Englishmen! since they who call themselves the salt of the earth, if not too timid to be honest, are, perhaps, too cunning to be wise, and, at all events, too *discreet* to be useful, at present, in the 'cause of God's poor, and the bread that sustains them,' – allow me, a sinner, to quote a few passages from the best and oldest book in the world; a book so full of denunciations against such villanies as our Corn-Laws, that the divine author must have foreseen, thousands of years ago, the existence of those palaced paupers who are also palaced-thieves. Listen, and you shall hear better words than mine, the words that cannot lie.

'Your teachers are blind, they are *ignorant*; they are dumb dogs,' silent when they ought to bark, 'sleeping, lying down, loving to slumber: yea, they are greedy

294   *Battles over Free Trade, Volume 1*

dogs, which never can have enough: they cry, Wine, wine! to-morrow will be as to-day.'

Did you ever hear this text preached before? One would think, our holy men sometimes condescend to read the bible. Oh, what a wonderful book it is! how great, how divine, in its simplicity! But how few do we see around us who seem to have the spirit of this book in their hearts! The word is on their lips, but not its sense. Listen again, and you shall hear what the bible says of Corn-Laws: –

'The labour of the poor is his life. He who robbeth the poor is a murderer. He who taxeth the bread of the poor, fighteth against God. Wrong not the poor, for God will plead their cause. If thou oppress the poor, thy name shall become a byword; a fire not blown shall consume thee; the heavens shall reveal thine iniquity, and the earth shall rise up against thee.'

Let me now show you a picture – drawn four thousand years ago, by a pencil which cannot err – of bread-taxed England, at this moment: –

'The carpenter who laboureth night and day, the smith working at his anvil, the weaver at his loom, and the potter at his wheel, all these are wise in their work; without them, cities could not be inhabited: they maintain the state of the world.' And is not the labourer worthy of his hire? 'God gave thee a goodly land, whose stones are iron, and from whose hills thou mayst dig brass. But when thou hast built goodly houses, and when thy flocks and thy herds, and thy silver, and thy gold are multiplied, then forget not thy God; for it is he who giveth thee wealth, that he may establish his covenant. But there is a generation whose teeth are as swords to devour the poor. They have broken the everlasting covenant. They have made a covenant with death, and with hell an agreement. They devise wicked devices, to destroy the poor with lying words. They *speak* villany, they *practice* iniquity, THEY UTTER ERROR TO THE LORD! that they may make empty the soul of the hungry, and cause his drink to fail. Wo unto him that giveth to the rich! he shall surely come to want. *Wo unto them that call evil good, and good evil, that decree unrighteous decrees, to take away the bread of the poor!* Their evil deeds shall fight against them, and destroy them. Wo unto the front of pride, whose glorious beauty is a fading flower! Wo unto him that striveth with his Maker!'

I dread to quote the following awful words, because, I fear, they are too prophetic of the destiny which too many of you have deserved by their supineness, their servility, their unequalled baseness, their mean submission to a despotism unparalleled in the annals of the world; that of a few thousand beggars self-declared, and robbers self-proclaimed, who, at the bar of public opinion, with brazen modesty, plead their right to live by enormous public wrongs!

'Howl ye, inhabitants of the isles! Thou crowning city, whose merchants are princes! thy strength shall be laid waste in that day when the Lord shall punish the high ones. I will set my face against you, and break the pride of your power, and make your heaven as iron, your earth as brass. I will send the black pestilence

Elliott, 'An Address to the People of England, on the Corn Laws' (1834)   295

among you; you shall labour in vain, and eat each other, and not be satisfied; and the land shall be desolate. And into the hearts of them that are left alive I will send faintness; the sound of a falling leaf shall chase them, and they shall fly when none pursueth. Howl ye, for the day of the Lord is at hand: it shall come as a destruction from the Almighty. I will break the pride of the power of the wicked, saith the Lord. I will bring a sword upon you that shall avenge the quarrel of my covenant, – a nation from afar, from the ends of the earth, swift as the eagle flieth, because ye have broken my everlasting covenant. Now is not this the fast that I have chosen, the covenant that I have made, – that ye deal out bread to the hungry? If thou take away from the midst of thee THE YOKE, *then shall the hungry be satisfied.'*

Awake, then, England! thou hirer of iniquity! thou briber of destruction! thou persecutor of the prophets! Awake! for the Corn-Laws are compelling the stars in their courses to fight against thee. Awake, English Quakers! friends of the human race! for the spirit of Penn looks down upon you in sorrow. Awake, Calvinists, for the Pilgrim Fathers, and Hooper, Vane, and Hutchinson, behold you, blushing in heaven, and make your shame theirs. Awake, leaders of Methodism! and if your religion do not consist in supporting antichristian wars, and making base things sacred, – if it is not another consecration of Caracalla's sword, *that sword* which murdered Geta, – haste, and *begin* to preach, and do works meet for repentance. Awake, every industrious and self-sustained Englishman! every man, who is worthy to call himself a countryman of Watt, Arkwright, and Bentham! *The Corn-Laws have placed you on the verge of a volcano. If your rivals establish a system of free trade before you, you are gone for ever, as a manufacturing people! and nothing will then remain for you but potatoes; nothing for your oppressors but potatoes and salt.* Hitherto, you have been saved by a mistake of your competitors, who imagine that you have thriven in consequence of your restrictive system, while, in fact, you have only existed in spite of it! Awake, then, and put away from the midst of the THE YOKE! listen not to the miserables who believe in Owen and Sadler, Cobbett and Blackwood. Suspect every person who tells you that the Corn-Laws are *not* at the root of your miseries. Whoever tells you so, *must* be either a rogue or a fool; for as you cannot extend the surface of the island, your only hope is necessarily based on free trade, which alone could, at the same time, lower the price of food by increasing the supply, and raise the price of labour by increasing the demand. Beware of the hirelings, and the money of the Charles Street gang. Your enemies have already found their way into the Radical camp. Trust not the Regenerationists, who tell that you might, without a free-trade, honestly and easily obtain the price of twelve hours' labour for the work of eight. If their devices had originated with the masters themselves, they would still be utterly impracticable; because that which is impossible in all circumstances, is impossible in any. Discountenance those paltry and too numerous apes of the aristocracy, who, as you well know, would sacrifice the best interests of the human race for the conservation of their meanest prejudice;

or, if only half-convinced that the bargain and sale of a principle would cast the shadow of a farthing over their mahogany desks and counters. How many more sessions of your reformed Parliament can you afford to throw away? Think not, then, of his Majesty's renegade Ministers. False to themselves, can they be true to you? Trust them? What! have they not told you that your trade was never more flourishing than at present? Yes, there is one branch of your trade which does indeed flourish: I mean, the manufacture of customers into rivals! yes, and if the Corn-Laws continue but a little longer, the trade of your rivals, planted, nurtured, and matured by the madness of the landed supporters of a suicidal administration, will continue to flourish, and blossom, and bear fruit over the grave of British prosperity! Haste then, and destroy these deadly Corn-Laws, ere they subvert the empire. Let every trade, from every town, one by one, and again, and again, send petitions to Parliament. Let brave and enlightened Glasgow speak again to timid and besotted Liverpool. Let awakened Liverpool shout to cowardly and goose-ridden Manchester; Manchester to London, – and all together to England and the world. We shall then have an Union, not in name only, but in realty, – an Union that will have, and do the right, and nothing but the right. Repudiate at once, and for ever, the idea of a fixed duty. Every shilling per quarter would be a direct tax of four millions sterling, per annum, on the productive classes of Englishmen. Treat not, then, for graduated iniquity; put not in the bans for a new marriage of reptile-spawning fraud and time; but with the word Restitution, pronounced in thunder, startle your oppressors from their hideous dream of injustice and ruin made permanent. That you may do this, and, by so doing, rescue your children from want, and your country from destruction and disgrace, is the prayer of

EBENEZER ELLIOTT.

Sheffield, 28th March, 1834.

'Anti Corn Law Association', *Dundee, Perth, and Cupar Advertiser*, 16 May 1834.

Anti Corn Law Association

At a Meeting of the Inhabitants of Dundee, held in the Magdalen Yard, on Wednesday the 14th current, –

Provost KAY in the chair, –

THE following Resolutions were moved, seconded, and unanimously carried by acclamation.

1. That the enactment of corn laws, by a corrupt Parliament, entirely under the influence of the landed proprietors, was unjust, oppressive, and ought not to be submitted to, – the object of it being to prevent agricultural produce, by artificial means, from sharing the fate of other properties, which, at the close of the war, inevitably fell in value; to keep up the fictitious and unnatural war rents of the landlords, at the expense of the rest of the community.

2. That the plea of the landlords, that their property bears an undue proportion of the national burdens, is utterly unfounded. On the contrary, the whole scheme of bypast taxation, and, in particular, the stamp laws and legacy duties, have been so framed as to favour the landlords and the richer classes, and to throw the chief burden of taxation on the middle and poorer classes.

3. That this meeting declare that they are the uncompromising advocates of free trade generally; and will endeavour, to the utmost of their power, to remove the pretences on which the corn laws are partly defended, by advocating the removal of all bounties, drawbacks, and protecting duties, by means of which, trade, manufactures, and commerce, are vainly sought to be encouraged.

4. That the corn laws are as prejudicial to the actual cultivators of the soil as they are to the bulk of the community – that the landlords are the only party who can be held to have been benefited in the slightest degree by these laws; and even to them the benefit is doubtful, when their ruinous effects on the commerce and general prosperity of the country is considered; but that, in repealing them, the interests of the tenantry, who have taken farms, trusting to the operation of these destructive and delusive laws, should be carefully attended to.

5. That this meeting, deeply sensible of the fatal results which must ensue from keeping, by means of partial and unjust laws, the necessaries of life in this country at a price far above that for which they can be obtained in neighbouring countries, with the inhabitants of which we have to compete in the markets of the world, resolve to form themselves into an Association for procuring the abolition of the corn laws, and all duties imposed on the necessaries of life; and that the following individuals be appointed a Committee for organizing the Society,

298   *Battles over Free Trade, Volume 1*

with power to add to their numbers, call meetings, and transact all other business necessary for securing the object in view.[1]

6. That the Committee be directed, in the first place, to draw up and procure signatures to a petition to the House of Commons, founded on the above Resolutions, and praying the Legislature forthwith to repeal the corn laws, and all other laws and duties by means of which it has been attempted to foster and protect any particular branch of trade, commerce, or manufacture, at the expense of the general interests of the community; the petition to be forwarded to the Right Honourable Sir H. Parnell for presentation.

ALEX. KAY, Provost

1   [Ed.: There follows a list of the names of Committee members, predominantly local merchants and manufacturers.]

'The Corn Laws', *British and Foreign Review; or, European Quarterly Journal*, 2:3 (1836), pp. 270–304, extract, pp. 277–304.

ARTICLE XII.

Report of the Select Committee on Agriculture, with the Minutes of Evidence taken before them. Ordered by the House of Commons to be printed, 2nd August, 1833.

Report of the Proceedings of the Agricultural Meetings, held in London on the 14th and 15th December, 1835. London: 1835.

The committee of 1833 was of course powerless to serve the complaining parties, except with a little wholesome advice, which should have been better attended to than it has been. They apprised the landowners, that the mortgages and the family incumbrances of their estates, were matters wholly irrelevant to the subject under examination, since the question at issue was a trading question, and related to the wants of the *land*, and not to the wants of the *man*. They told them, also, that rents were contracts of a private nature, and that as, on the one hand, there existed no right in the public to call for a reduction of rent, so, on the other hand, the proprietors had no claim on the public to make any sacrifices for sustaining them. And they also told them, that having got a Corn Act, which was operating, by the magnitude of its duty, so as effectually to exclude foreign corn from their markets, they had better be quietly contented with that Act, and not seek to agitate the adoption of fresh measures.

This wholesome advice the landed interest have not taken. They are bestirring themselves from one end of the country to the other, and they seem to be determined to take the Houses of Parliament by storm. The publication of the proceedings of the landed interest, which we have placed at the head of this article, exhibits the temper they are in, and also the manner in which they will endeavour to force down any plan, which may seem to hold out the smallest advantage to themselves, at the expense of the other classes of the community. At present no sanctioned plan has appeared. Many vague suggestions of inadmissible or impracticable schemes may be drawn from the speeches at their reported meetings; but nothing appears that has received the sanction of the body, except, indeed, an intention to demand another committee of the House of Commons. The real difficulty of their situation is, that there has already been, granted to them, all they used formerly to ask for – namely, a perfect monopoly of the home market: and, although they feel no compunction in flying from the bargain they had made, when that monopoly was granted; and in seeming disposed to abuse the Government, the Parliament, and the people, in the most outrageous language, because the monopoly does not satisfy their expectations; although it fulfils those of abundant home supply, upon their promises of which, it was granted; still they are unable, however willing, to conceive any other feasible device, by the application of which they might be benefited, let the sufferers be who they may. Their rage, at the want of a weapon, with the will to strike, is venting itself in declarations, marked by recklessness of purpose and ignorance of matter.

We see in the publication before us, that under a system of delegation, a 'Central Agricultural Society of Great Britain and Ireland' has been formed in London, out of the numerous local agricultural societies which are to be found in various parts of the kingdom. At a meeting held by this Central Society, on the 15th of December last, the following resolution – which seems to be considered by them as the foundation stone of all their future proceedings – was passed. It is in these words: –

'That nothing can remove the present overwhelming distress, but the adoption of some measure, which shall either raise the price of produce to the level of the burthens imposed, or bring down the burthens to the level of the present prices.'

The hypothesis of this resolution is, 'overwhelming distress,' in consequence of certain 'burthens imposed, which the price of corn is unable to sustain;' and the two alternative propositions of it are, either to raise the price or to lower the burthens. We propose to examine the resolution under this division of it.

In the first place, we seriously question the validity of the hypothesis. We do not believe that the agriculture of these kingdoms, considered as a vast and extensive trade, is, as a whole, carried on at a loss: and we will give the grounds of our doubt.

If, for evidence of the fact, the general tenor of the statements made by the parties themselves be consulted, it will appear, that the distress is assumed from a dry unqualified comparison of the present prices of wheat with its former prices, and without any regard to the changes which may have taken place, in the art of farming, or the cost of production. The average price of wheat, reduced to the Winchester bushel, is now about 35s. the quarter, and it has been under 40s. for a considerable time. These are low prices, even if compared with those of a few years before the war: but it is by no means, thereby proved, that the present price is lower than of old, when considered with reference to the present cost of production. With the utmost readiness we admit, that no improvements in husbandry can be expected to keep pace with many of those in manufacture; but still we cannot but believe, that the labours of the farmer upon the various qualities of the soil, are far more productive than they were at the time referred to; and, unless the landowners have, for the last forty years, been indulging in mere idle boasts, great advances have, during that period, been made in the science of agriculture. The numerous agricultural societies long established in various parts of the kingdom, by the union of which their present great central association is formed, all had for their objects – the encouragement of ingenuity and skill in the devising and the bringing to perfection of new methods and new implements – and also the extensive diffusion of the knowledge of such discoveries. Are we to believe that all this was mere vapouring: and was the promise to 'make two blades of grass grow where only one grew before;' a rank delusion on the public expectation? Assuredly not, – it was sincere, and has been, in our opinion, to a very great degree fulfilled. The comparison of prices at the two periods, affords no conclusive proof of an unremunerating price at this time, unless it be also shown, that all other things remain the same; and it is known that they do not.

Before we proceed further in the examination of this resolution, we shall suggest the substitution of the more comprehensive words '*costs of production*' for the word '*burthen:*' and in speaking of the cost of production, every charge between the grower and the consumer must be taken into the account. The charge of conveyance from the one to the other is one of those which have been materially reduced; and, connected with that charge, is also the state of allocation of the people. Not only has one universal system of road-making rendered all parts of England mutually accessible to each other, but the accidents of localities, and the attraction of manufacturers, have caused the people to be far more equally distributed than it used to be. The dense, and chiefly new population of our manufacturing districts, is placed in a position, flanked on three sides, by England, Scotland, and Ireland. The mouths have met the corn half-way, and that half-way, is traversed with increased facility. The apparent lowness of the present price of corn, is in a great measure to be accounted for by an equalization of prices, thus brought about: and this proposition would be made very apparent, if we had the means of striking a present and a former average, taking in both cases, the prices *at the barn door*. Particular lands, favourably situated under the old system, must have now to contend with an enlarged domestic competition. The Middlesex hay farmers, have long felt the effects of the Paddington canal, and of the Macadamized roads round London, which have occasioned the bulky commodities of hay and straw to be brought, from a more extended circle. These are mere illustrations of trifling instances; but the great cases of improved distribution are those of Ireland and of Scotland – of steam navigation – of canals, and of railways – all of which even now may be considered, as only in an incipient state. It would take us beyond the reach of our present purpose, if we were to go largely into this branch of the subject: enough has been said to remind the reader, that a ready distribution of farming produce has led to an equalization of its prices; and that the productions of many most extensive districts, which formerly were almost without value, now partake of the average which is the result.

302   *Battles over Free Trade, Volume 1*

These are effects upon property in land, which the landowners cannot resist or control. It is madness in them to shut their eyes against such consequences. The United Kingdom will be, and must be, treated as one whole or entirety; and it is in the common nature of things to suppose, and to expect, that if, in their new predicament, all the lots of land are thrown into one general mass of equality, upon the redrawing, many, that before were prizes, will turn out blanks; and many of the old blanks, will be new prizes. For this great and still progressing change, the landed interest must prepare themselves. They may demand protection against foreigners, with what confidence they please; but protection against Ireland, and against Scotland – against bogs reclaimed and marshes drained – protection against domestic improvements – against the progress of science, and the industry of their fellow-countrymen – they can never have at the hands of a British Parliament. The price always to be considered is the price of the three kingdoms, under every possible advance in the arts of life; and we must insist, that the mere fact before us, that the average in the chief markets of England is now 5s. or 6s. lower than it was before the war, constitutes no proof, that the public of England cannot be supplied from the lands of Great Britain and Ireland, with wheat at the present price, yielding a fair trading profit to a sufficient number of producers, in the cultivation of a sufficient quantity of our national lands.

It is not, however, upon this negative proposition alone, that we formed our opinion against the hypothesis of an 'overwhelming distress,' upon which the resolution we are discussing is founded. The general appearance of the face of the country, amounts almost to positive proof, that the occupation of farming cannot be in distress. We would appeal to the observation of the tourists of last summer and autumn, whether they did not observe, in all quarters, the characters of that trim, neat, good management, which, in any calling, bespeaks thriving industry. Still, this is not positive proof; even although backed by the strong presumption, which may be drawn from the great leading fact, that the farmers of these kingdoms, have found the means of supplying the whole demand for corn, at very low prices, for four – if not five – successive years, without the aid, practically speaking, of importation. We have more proof still; for it must be remembered also, that the cry of unremunerating prices is of much longer standing. The previous five or six years, are represented to have been marked, by unfavourable seasons and short crops. The prices had ranged from 20s. to 30s. for wheat, higher than of late, and as the deficiency of quantity has been clearly proved by the extent of the imports, the argument in favour of insufficient rates of price, during that period of scarcity, is quite as strong as it now is, with reference to the late period of abundant crops, at lower prices. The distress, therefore, is of many years standing; and although there is much truth in the remark, that traders do not yield very early obedience, to the hints they receive in the falling off of their ordinary profits, it is but too true, that the practical conviction is sure

'The Corn Laws' (1836)

to come home to them, in the form of physical impossibility, if they continue guilty of a too obstinate perseverance.

We will venture to say, that there is no extensive branch of trade whatever, which could hold up a good front of apparent prosperity, at the end of ten years of continuous adversity; and therefore, we invite our readers to take, in the first instance, a general superficial view of the outward and visible condition of the three classes of persons, dependent on the lands of this kingdom – the landlords, the farmers, and the husbandry labourers. We mean nothing invidious. We delight in the splendour and affluence of our aristocracy. We ask only for information, when we say – does any one discover that the rank and station of this country is suffering any degradation, from a want of the usual display, of the splendour and affluence of the nobility, and higher gentry of the nation? Again, we ask – is there not remaining to us, an ample body of men, in the class of farmers, actually holding and farming the whole breadth of our cultivated lands; and possessing the means of producing from those lands, up to the hour in which we write, such ample crops, as to have rendered the population independent of foreign supplies, for five successive years. The case of the labourers is still more palpable, because it involves no question of capital, and is confined merely, to that of comfortable daily subsistence. Over and over again, it has been shown, that the wages of the labourers give them, in these times, a much greater command of the necessaries and comforts of subsistence, than that which they used to possess in the wages of former times – whether we make the comparison with any term of years before the war, or with any of the years in the war, remarkable for the highest scales of wages.

Thus, then, we dispute the hypothesis, of 'overwhelming distress;' founded, as it is professed to be, upon insufficiency of price, and we do so upon two grounds; – first, that a price lower in comparison with former prices, is not necessarily a low price – that is, an unremunerating price; – and, secondly, that all the parties affected by the prices, have, up to this hour, continued in a condition, in which no human power could have sustained them, if the prices had been so insufficient, in a trading point of view, as the hypothesis assumes them to have been.

We now proceed to examine the two alternative propositions, founded upon this hypothesis of 'overwhelming distress;' first, the necessity of an increased price; or secondly, in lieu of that, the necessity of a reduced cost of production. In both cases, 'the adoption of some measure,' with power to produce the intended effect, is contemplated by the propounders; and as the grand scheme of the association is to acquire a preponderance in parliament, it is clear, that the measure pointed out, is to be of a legislative character.

There are two modes by which a high price of corn may be secured. The one, by preventing a fall, – the other, by forcing a rise. Our present Act works by the first mode alone. The older Act – Mr. Pitt's Corn Act of 1791 – worked by both modes; it checked importation, when corn was falling below a certain price, and

304   *Battles over Free Trade, Volume 1*

thus attempted to arrest the fall in its progress; but if this mode failed, and the fall continued till it got downward beyond another stage, then it came forward with an active measure for forcibly raising the price; and this consisted in giving a bounty for exportation. Under both schemes of legislation, the foreign country was the fulcrum, and the foreign prices the lever, by which the home prices were to be kept at the computed necessary level. Now what we desire to know, is, whether, in plain terms, the landed interest do point to an export bounty, when they speak of a 'measure, which will raise the price' – or whether they have, behind the scenes, ready to be produced at their own proper time, some 'measure' of a different kind, the invention of which, is as yet unknown to us, and to the public. Under our total inability to imagine any such *other* mode, we shall offer a few observations upon the subject of export bounty on corn – partly in order to be prepared, lest such a proposal should be made, but still more, with the considerate object, of deterring the landed interest from attempting such a course.

Mr. Pitt's Act of 1791 had a high duty, a moderate duty, and a low or nominal duty upon foreign corn. The *first* (24s. 3d.) attached upon wheat, for instance, when the average price of British wheat was under 50s. the quarter; – the *second* (2s. 6d.) when the price was between 50s. and 54s. the quarter – the 'pivot' of that day, – and the *third* (6d.) when it was above 54s., at which time also, we may here remark, exportation of British corn was prohibited. This was the machinery which was to act upon importation. Under the head of exportation we had the three following rules: – at one price, exportation was prohibited; at another and lower, it was simply permitted; and at a lower still, it was encouraged by a bounty. Whenever the price of wheat for instance was under 44s. the quarter, the exporter was rewarded with a bounty of 5s. for every quarter, which he should take completely out of the mouths, and out of the reach of this people, and dispose of in some foreign country. We pass over the changes which were made in these import and export rates by subsequent acts, because the whole remained a dead letter during the prevalence of 'war prices,' which so far exceeded legislative calculations, as to render all trade in foreign corn legally free. At the close of the war, in the year 1814, the first step taken, was to repeal the bounties: and in this proceeding, is seen an intention of relinquishing one of the modes, before practised, for assuring a good price of corn to the British grower. That price was no longer to be forced above the level, at which it might settle, under a simple monopoly at the home market; but it was thenceforth to be left to the operation of that monopoly alone. The right of *expulsion* was relinquished; that of *exclusion* only was retained.

In the year 1792, when the price of wheat was six or seven shillings a quarter (Winchester measure) higher than it has been for some time past, our merchants were enabled to find a foreign market for about 300,000 quarters, with the aid of the five shilling bounty. If all other things remained the same, it is evident, therefore, that they could now purchase wheat for exportation to an equal advantage without the bounty. What then are the other circumstances, the change in which, since 1792, has prevented the exportation of wheat? The more abundant growth and consequent greater cheapness of corn abroad. This is the only answer, and a very portentous answer it is to the considerate farmer, who is disposed to look dispassionately into the difficulties of the question, and to try how far, by the strength of his own shoulder, he can serve himself, before he invokes the aid of Hercules, as his only resource. Now, the lower price of corn in Europe proves two very important things – first, that no export bounty short of perhaps 20s. or 30s. the quarter, could force a sale of our wheat abroad, at any thing like the prices here called remunerative; – and, secondly, that the present nominally low price, must cover more remuneration, than the higher nominal prices did before the war.

The general reduction of the open market price of corn abroad, tends to confirm our opinion, given above, that the cost of production has been lessened, by improvements in husbandry. The English and Scotch agriculturists, will hardly admit that they are behind their Polish and Prussian competitors, in the adoption of such improvements; if they do, they will only add another instance, to those already known, of the withering effects of protection. No, they will not take this ground, they will fly to their plea of 'burthens;' and, boasting rather of their superior skill, they will say, such is the weight of those *burthens*, that all their skill, and all their industry, are inadequate to support them under it. We have no objection to try the issue of this plea, because it draws the question into narrow limits. In the mean while, we establish this proposition, – that corn is now, naturally, a cheaper commodity than it used to be; and consequently, that the task of forcing up the price of it, in any particular country, by the expulsion of a supposed surplus to other countries, is a matter of far more difficulty than it formerly was.

We are free to confess – after perusing the publication we are now reviewing – that no proposal from the landed interest, can be so extravagant as to surprise us. Their associations are forming all over the kingdom, and at the same time, are concentrating and combining, under a common head, for the avowed purpose of carrying their purposes by parliamentary influence. To this end they declare, that Whig, Tory, and Radical, are as one in the great cause, and that all their political objects are to merge in that main object of promoting – their own pecuniary interest. Under such circumstances, why should we not hold ourselves prepared for the proposal of an export bounty of 20s. or 30s. the quarter upon wheat, and of proportionate sums on the other sorts of corn? Is it unreasonable to examine, beforehand, the nature and the effects of such a 'measure to raise the price of corn?' Let it be supposed, then, that, by the sheer force of bounty, the export of the various sorts of grain be equivalent to a million of quarters of wheat, and that a million, or a million and a half of money, or more, is paid to the exporters out of the exchequer. Some new specific tax, in the first place, must be imposed,

306   *Battles over Free Trade, Volume 1*

in order to raise that sum; and to this literal tax on the people, must be added another tax, less evident, though not less real, of twenty or thirty millions more, in the increased price of the agricultural produce consumed at home. If this consequence did not ensue, the scheme would be abortive: but it would ensue, although it would not last, for all such methods of hot-bed prosperity contain the seeds of their own destruction. Agriculture would receive a false stimulus, whereby the produce of the three kingdoms would be greatly increased; our manufactures would languish, consumption would, consequently, fall off, and the surplus for exportation would increase, and thus the demand of the bounty would be enlarged, by double and re-acting causes, until the means of satisfying it utterly vanished, through the failure of the revenue to keep up the supply. Or, if for argument's sake, we suppose that the bounty could be continued, at an increasing rate, with decreasing means; then the only result would be, that we should fall back to the old state of a corn exporting country, and emulate, as such, the prosperity of Poland, and of the back settlements of America. If we are now indulging in extravagant reveries, it is because we consent to suppose, that this combination of all the political parties of the country, interested in land, under the one banner and rallying point proposed by the 'Central Association,' should be able to force a 'measure to raise prices.' They say, that with union among themselves, they are strong enough to accomplish any thing. Assuming the deed to be done, we speak only the plain language of common warning, when we advise the country to prepare for its ruin.

If, however, the old nostrum of an export bounty be not resorted to, by what new machinery, hitherto unthought of, will this association *raise* the price of corn above that rate at which it settles, under a total exclusion of foreign supplies?

We now come to treat of the means of reducing the cost of production, and particularly those parts of it which may be considered in the light of 'burthens.' Under this division of the subject, the first proposition which we present to the minds of our readers, is – that there is no commodity whatever, the cost of production of which, preserves its due relation to the sale price, in any degree equal to that in which corn necessarily does; and, therefore, the complaint of unremunerating prices for *corn*, is almost a contradiction in terms. If we look at the outlay in agriculture, we find that the farmer's expenditure, consists mainly of the consumption of his own commodities. His chief engine is the horse, reared by himself: if therefore he feed his teams with oats when the price is 20s. the quarter, he ploughs his land at half the cost he would incur for that service, if oats were worth 40s. in the market. Again, the personal consumption of his labourers may be considered to consist of food, to the extent of two parts out of three; and therefore, if wheat be at 35s. a quarter, instead of 70s., there is a saving of one-third of that part of his outlay. In fact, corn reproduces corn in a greater degree by far, than any other commodity reproduces itself; and the main expenditure of the farmer is 'in kind.' For the sake of perspicuity, we will assume that the land furnishes two-thirds of the means of its cultivation; we have then to consider how the farmer stands with regard to his command of the other third. This must consist either of British manufactures or of foreign articles; and in fact it does consist of the two, in various proportions. Nothing is more notorious than the great fall in the price of British manufactures; and as they constitute, as it were, the money with which alone the landed interest buy foreign articles (for they produce nothing for exportation themselves), it must be the case; and we all know that the farmer's labourers are supplied with those necessaries and comforts, which do not consist of agricultural produce, at a most reduced, most easy rate. It is certain that the fall in manufactures is much greater than the fall in corn and meat.

If we try any other occupation by the same test, we shall clearly see how great the advantage is which agriculture has over all others. In what degree, then, does the outlay of the ironmaster, or the worker of a cotton factory, consist of his own production – how much of their expenditure is 'in kind?' If iron be at a low price, the ironmaster finds that the cost of his implements is the less on the debit side of the account; but the consumption of iron in other matters, and particularly in the support of his numerous workpeople, is so small as hardly to be traced. The owner of the cotton factory has no compensation for a low price of calicoes, except in the gowns and linen of his spinners and weavers. Let us try the case of mining for the precious metals, that is, for money itself. The silver mines of Mexico are of all degrees of productiveness, whether varying in the richness of the ores, or the depths and difficulties of the workings. Their profitableness stops when the silver raised by a man in a given time, will not be equal in quantity, to the silver he must expend for his subsistence during that time; in other words, the owner of the mine will not give a pound of that silver, which is already out of the earth, to draw eleven ounces of other silver from its bowels. Practically speaking, the cost of mining for the precious metals, may be said not to be *in kind* at all; and, therefore, such mining is a trade, the first to be stopped by reduction of the price of its produce. Farming, on the other hand, is the trade which will be the last to be stopped by such a cause; because its cost is *in kind* in a far greater degree than any other.

We now come to those costs of production which consist of burthens. – They comprise taxes, and public contributions. These may be considered to be of three sorts: – *First*, direct taxes, paid towards the general revenue of the kingdom, attaching on the processes of agriculture. – The tax on farm-horses was of this description. *Secondly*, indirect taxes, paid also to the public revenue, upon the ordinary articles of consumption, such as soap, glass, beer, &c. And, *thirdly*, direct public contributions, but of a local character, such as poor rates, highway rates, tithes, county rates, &c.

The first in this list is soon disposed of. Farmers pay no direct taxes. There is a remnant of an old land-tax, which the times, by the increase of the property charged, have reduced to an insignificant per centage amount; and it attaches so directly to the property itself, of which it is a part not belonging to the owner, that it can influence the trade of farming in no way; except that it may operate as an almost imperceptible impediment to the bringing of fresh land into cultivation, and thereby increase his home competition. Practically speaking, there is no direct tax on agriculture.

How then will stand the case of indirect taxation; and in what shape is the complaint of the landed interest against that description of charge to be discussed? Really, it presents itself in a great variety of attitudes, and those of no very fixed character. The exclusion of foreign corn, grown in 'untaxed countries,' except upon payment of import *countervailing* duties, had been thought quite as much as was necessary, to constitute a claim on the landed interest, for their proportionate contribution to the general revenue of the country. The exclusion is most complete; and we are now told that their demand for exemption from taxes, is not founded upon foreign relations alone, but also upon some relation in which they stand, domestically, towards the other interests of the country. The question of the currency, whatever may be its worth on other parts of the subject, has no bearing upon this. The domestic relations of the agricultural and the trading interests, would remain the same, whatever may be the standard, or whatever the depreciation, or appreciation of the circulating medium. If the shilling be made to pass for eighteen-pence, it will be eighteen-pence for everything. The state of the currency does not apply peculiarly to farming.

With regard to the national debt, and to the collection of the general revenue, the relations of these two great branches of industry are not equally uniform: but the difference consists in the farmer's standing in a better position, than the manufacturer or common trader. The landed interest think that they prove the existence of a quadruplicated burthen upon themselves, when they show, in figures, that the national debt is four times as large as it was before the war. We will first expose the fallacy, and consequent exaggeration, contained in an estimate, which simply compares the respective amounts of the debt at the two periods, without drawing other contemporaneous comparisons. The population of the country, is nearly double what it was, at the time, when upon a winding up of the American war, the debt was about one-fourth its present amount. Here, then, are two men instead of one to bear the burthen, speaking only numerically; but he must be a poor observer, who is not aware, that the population has so increased in quality, as well as in quantity, that the individual shoulders are broader than of old. In spite of the grumblers, we assert, that the relative strength of the country to support the burthen of the debt, is almost as equal to it now, as it was, when the debt was only one-fourth of its present amount. The sum of that amount has long remained the same, while the sum of the supporting power has been steadily increasing; and so strong is the tendency to such increase, that, if we can but be kept under rulers who will let the

'The Corn Laws' (1836) 309

energies of the country have fair play, there is ample ground for hope, that the people will not only grow up to, but actually outgrow the national debt. Let us only keep off the meddling, interfering quacks, who so ridiculously style themselves '*practical men;*' and let us act upon those really practical principles, recommended by men, sneeringly denominated '*Philosophers*' and '*Theorists*' by impertinent dunces; and we have no doubt that the day will arrive, when as heretofore, the evil of the national debt will be so lightly felt, that its utility as a fund for numerous domestic objects, will be its more prominent feature.

These remarks will not be deemed inapposite, by any person, who reflects on the character of many of the measures, which the landed interest feel justified in recommending, with an evil design on the funded property of the country. We hold out this bright prospect to the honest feelings of the people, as an inducement to oppose, with the more energy, the projects of these plunderers.

We have intimated our opinion, that the burthen of the national debt, lies more lightly on the agriculture, than on the common trade of the country – adopting the popular distinction between the two branches of industry – and we will now show why it does so. The form in which the national debt is felt by the people, is that of taxes to raise the interest. The evil of taxation is twofold; the *charge* itself is an evil; but in many instances it happens, that there lurks also in the *mode of collection*, another evil. From this second evil, the farmer, as a tradesman, is wholly exempt, except in the trifling matter of hops; in respect of which we do not remember to have heard any complaint. When speaking of farming, hop planting is hardly ever taken into the consideration; and although it be subjected to a small excise duty, it is at the same time protected by an enormous duty of customs; and, indeed, we have only alluded to the subject that we might not be accused of omission.

Since the repeal of the horse tax, which took place early in the peace; and since the subsequent repeal of every direct tax on the farmer, down to his shepherd's dog, as the only remnant that could be found in the tax tables – and since too, he is relieved from the duty on fire insurance, which is borne by every other tradesman, there can be no shape in which the second evil of taxation – namely, the evil arising out of the mode of collection – can reach him. We are aware that the barley growers take upon themselves the credit of paying the malt tax; but this pretension is wholly put down, by the over-whelming fact, that the relative price of barley is, and has long been, higher than the contemporaneous price of wheat, which is free from all tax: we shall therefore unhesitatingly assign to the case of the maltster, as a manufacturer, all the inconveniences to which, for the immense national advantage of a revenue of five millions a-year, he is subjected. The recklessness of consequences, with which some of the leading members of the landed interest, have sought to deprive the country of that great resource, for the chance of a very small, and very questionable benefit to themselves, – has fixed a stain upon their names which will not be soon or easily discharged.

Now how stands this matter – this secondary evil of taxation – in the case of the manufacturer and trader? First, there are the several excise duties on glass, soap, malt, &c., and then there are numerous custom duties, which operate very injuriously for want of modifications, which, however desirable in principle, are deemed to be unattainable in practice, in consequence of the difficulty which is found, in the framing of the legal definitions necessary for their accomplishment. Take, for instance, the high-dutied article of tea, upon which, for such reasons, it has been found necessary, at last, to impose a uniform duty – let the sort or the quality be what it may.

This difference between the case of the farmer, and that of the common trader, which we have been pointing out, might not have been worthy of all the attention we have drawn to it, if the landed interest did not constantly assert, that the national debt is chiefly borne by them. It is now clear that they contribute only by indirect taxation as general consumers, and that their business or occupation is wholly free from direct taxes, and is, therefore, also unembarrassed, by the evils attendant upon the processes of collection. And this brings us to the subject of indirect taxation, the amount of which is of course the larger, on account of the enlargement of the national debt.

It cannot be doubted that all taxes are ultimately thrown on consumption; because, if the consumer could in any case refuse to pay them, the production of the taxed articles would cease. The quantity, therefore, of the interest of the national debt, to which the farmer in his trade is subjected, must reach him almost wholly in the form of labour, the cost of which is increased, by the necessity of reimbursing to his work people, the shares which they pay in the higher prices of the goods they consume. The interest of the national debt, if computed as a capitation tax on the people, would give about 25*s.* the head, on rich and poor; but in the division between rich and poor, and particularly between skilled labourers and common labourers, it is probable that it would not amount to more than 15*s.* on the labourers in husbandry. It must be a very large farm upon which this would impose any heavy burthen, even supposing that the farmer were, from some cause wholly undiscoverable by us, to be unable, like other manufacturers, to throw it off again from himself upon the consumer of the article he produces. He has the same remedy as others have against the consumer, and it is the only remedy; he can restrain his operations till the consumer will pay; for, under our corn laws, the latter would only have the alternative of starving. During the exclusion of foreign corn from his market, the producer of British corn can have no pretence for saying, that he is burthened with taxes for which he cannot indemnify himself in the price of his goods. The greatest concession which can be made to him upon this point is, that a countervailing duty, equivalent to such taxes, should be imposed upon the importation of foreign corn; and there can be no question whether a duty exceeding the whole price, as the present duty

'The Corn Laws' (1836)

does, will not satisfy that purpose. This is beating the party with their own weapons; but far be it from our intention to admit, that they have a right to the use of such weapons. General taxation is not a ground for a countervailing duty on the foreign commodity: it is the specific tax on the home article, paid by the maker, which, and which alone, demands the countervailing charge on the same article, when brought from abroad. This, indeed, is no [*sic*] properly a protecting duty. It is demanded for the interest of the revenue in the first place; and, in the next place, it only restores the home maker to the natural equality, he is entitled to. But, if general taxation be a description of charge from which any class of society may claim exemption; or, if that be impracticable, as of course it would be – may claim indemnity or reimbursement – why may not any other and every other class claim the same? By whom, in short, are the taxes to be paid? Are the taxes of this country to be paid by the people of this country, or by the people of some other country?

Since, then, the taxes of consumption must be borne by the people of the United Kingdom as the consumers, upon what principle, we ask, is any one class of that people to be exempt from contributing their portion, according to their respective consumption, of the several dutiable articles? Upon what principle are the other classes to be called upon to bear, not only their own shares of the burthen, according to such consumption, but to take on them also the share of this privileged class? And again, what is the peculiar character by which the class, now claiming such a privilege, is distinguishable from their fellow subjects? The answer will be a curious one – it is simply, because they have got possession of all the lands of the country as their exclusive private property. The first gift to the human race, is held to have been conveyed in the words – 'the world is all before you where to choose.' And it was also said to man, 'by the sweat of thy brow shalt thou eat bread.' The people, therefore, according to the feudal notions of the landed interest, are, we presume, divided into 'Choosers' and 'Sweaters;' or, in other words, the division is between those few – very few comparatively – who, or whose predecessors for them, have seized upon every atom of the only clear gift from God to man – the land; and those many – that vast multitude of human beings – whose bread can be grown only upon the lands of others – lands, to step upon which is a trespass – of the produce of which, they cannot claim a single atom, until the holders shall be pleased to declare its price. These are the distinguishing characteristics of the two classes; and, upon the ground of such distinction alone, it is attempted to be shown that one of them, the 'Choosers,' are to pay no taxes, except as the channel of collection; and that the other class, the 'Sweaters,' after having laboured daily and duly, first for their 'bread,' and next for the means of paying their own proper share of taxes, are to labour on still more, until they have paid also the taxes of the 'Choosers.' If the Central Agricultural Association can point out any mode, through the operation of which, the incomes of the landed interest can be increased, by an amount equivalent to the taxes they are computed to pay, the effect must be, that they pay no taxes themselves, and that their share of the taxes, which must be borne by some parties, will be paid by the rest of the community in addition to their own shares.

But what is most extraordinary, the landed interest have actually effected this purpose already. They have done the very deed: for they have devised and have executed, long ago, a scheme, by the operation of which, the *landless* are compelled to pay to the *landed*, a price for the home produce, over and above its natural value in open market; which, in the aggregate, must form a sum far more than equal to the gross amount of taxes, by which the price of all the articles consumed by the landed interest is increased. Supposing that the price of wheat is sustained to the extent of 10*s.* the quarter, and that the prices of other corn, and also the prices of meat, and of other agricultural produce, are sustained in an equal proportion, by force of the Corn Laws; – it is perfectly within bounds to say, that the gross proceeds of such additional prices, must form a sum, much greater than that, at which the aggregate of taxation, falling on this class of the community, can be computed. By the laws of property, they are enabled to say – 'You shall not have that bushel of corn, except at such a price.' And by the Corn Law, they are enabled to add – 'and you shall have no other.' Having thus secured their reimbursement of taxes, upon what pretension can the landed interest demand a second payment of the same claim? We carry in our hands their receipt in full for *our* payment; couched in the language, and stamped by the restrictions, of the Corn Act; as well as by the laws, which totally prohibit all kinds of cattle, sheep, and hogs, alive, or in the shape of meat, and which impose heavy duties on butter and cheese: and yet, in disregard of this most palpable acquittance, vouched by the foreign markets, they rise upon us again, and demand a second payment. This, at least, is premature. They should certainly have waited for the levelling of the home and the foreign prices. The day, to be sure, may come, when the claim may have less injustice on the face of it than it now has, while the Corn Law secures to them a beneficial difference. Equalization seems to be in progress; and, perhaps, we shall not much longer have it in our power, to prove the *first* payment so distinctly as we now can, in the difference between the British and foreign prices of agricultural produce. When a continuation of the false stimulus of the Corn Laws, shall have increased the home productions, until their prices reassume their former level with those of the other parts of Europe, to which they are tending; – then, indeed, the landed interest will pay their own taxes. Then, too, it will require some other device – some new contrivance and machinery – for enabling them to throw off from themselves, as they now do effectually, their own share of the fiscal burthens of our common country.

We have already pointed to an extravagant export bounty, as a piece of machinery by which such an object might be effected. We can contemplate but one other for the same purpose, – and that is, to repeal all the duties on articles of use and consumption, and to commute them for a very heavy income and property tax, from which land shall be exempt. Mad and preposterous as such a proposal would be, we set it forth for deliberation, solely, because it would be a mode of doing openly and avowedly, the very thing which the landed interest would do, if they knew how, by circuitous means and hidden contrivances. If countervailing duties upon foreign articles do not afford, to the maker of the like articles at home, the protection which enables him to add the duties he pays to the price of his goods; and if, even, neither duties far beyond the countervailing point, nor the total prohibition of the foreign commodity, will arm him with the power, to throw from himself upon the consumer, the weight of his own personal taxes of consumption, – what is that plan, of a feasible aspect, which any man would propose for effecting such a purpose?

The last division of those parts of the cost of production of corn, and other agricultural produce, which we have to examine, and which can be treated as burthens, is that of the local contributions, made from the land, to the support of the church, the highways, the police, and the poor, of the parish or district, in which the land subject to the demand is situated. There is a great distinction between a rate, or charge of this nature, and a tax levied towards raising the general revenue of the empire. The difference is analagous [*sic*] to that between the various dues on shipping, payable in different ports, and the duties of tonnage, when any, collected on behalf of the crown. The first are for work performed, and services received. Harbours are constructed, lights are stationed, piers are built, and wharfs are prepared, for the use of the shipping which frequent the port where the dues are payable. So also the district charges upon land, are applied for the benefit of its owners and occupiers: and the circumstance, that those charges, instead of being voluntary, are enforced by the law, proves only, that they are the more equally levied, and more efficiently employed in the attainment of objects, which from their urgency, would otherwise be attempted, and but ill accomplished, by the desultory efforts of individuals. It is highly proper that these charges should be local: first, because the requisite amounts in various cases are governed by local peculiarities: and, next, because, as the disbursements must lie with the discretion of the respective parties, there is the greater security against improvidence.

The landed interest, when they asked only for monopoly, constantly instanced these charges as among the grounds of such a demand, and, at least, as a reason for countervailing charges on foreign corn: but it was a false plea even for that purpose; because foreign countries stand in need of churches, of highways, of police, and of funds for their poor, as well as we do. It may, no doubt be, that in some foreign countries, no regular provision is made for such objects; but then, it may be asked, will any man attempt to show by calculation, that the cultivators of districts, having none of the accommodations, for the sake of which the British districts contribute the necessary funds, are thereby enabled to raise corn, and convey it to its market the more cheaply? Such an assertion would be equivalent to a declaration, that every step in the improved methods of civilisation, was a retrogressive movement towards the savage state. In foreign countries the inhabitants either have the benefits of such local arrangements; and, if so, they have them only at the price of their cost; or, if they save the cost, then they are suffering, in the want of those benefits, a quantity of evil by no means compensated by the saving.

Desirous as we are to probe the question of the 'Corn Laws' to the bottom, we have here shown that these local charges upon land furnish no ground, even for a countervailing charge upon foreign corn. How much less, then, can they be the ground of complaint, when foreign corn is totally excluded by an enormous duty. Confined for room, and pressed for time, in consequence of the recency of the proceedings which have forced this preparatory discussion upon us, we can, here, and now, only treat these local charges with reference to their general principles. Every possible improvement, in details, ought no doubt to be made in their collection and administration; and such ameliorations are in progress. The tithes will be commuted, and the barbarism of a charge upon *gross* produce will soon become, like its rude origin, matter of history only: and we may anticipate, also, that an assimilation of some sort, will, before long, place Ireland, in respect of an unemployed pauper population, more nearly than she now is, upon a footing with England. But let not the sanguine agriculturist believe, that the pecuniary advantages of these measures, will settle themselves quietly into his pocket. When the cultivator of the soil is unrestrained in his spirited improvements, as he often now is, by the deadening calculation – that if his invested hundred pounds increase only by ten pounds, an ample return in any other case, he will close the account with no more than ninety-nine pounds in his pocket – it may be expected, that much increased capital will be expended upon our lands, and that much increase of produce, to supply our markets the more abundantly, and therefore the more cheaply, will be the result. And again, when under a system of poor laws in Ireland, human beings are no longer found to be contending for small plots of land to preserve existence; and when the estates in that country can therefore be allotted into suitable farms, and the people can be divided into masters and workmen; it may be expected, that the system of good and business-like husbandry, which then will assuredly supersede the present miserable practices, must tend to increase the productions of that naturally fertile island, in a degree, far exceeding that degree, in which its own home consumption will be at the same time enlarged. That that consumption will, to the gratification of every humane mind, be much enlarged by such changes of condition cannot be doubted. It is also to be believed that fewer starving Irish will then cross the channel for employment, in competition with English labourers. These two anticipations of our landed interest in England will be specifically realized, when, by the operation of a poor law, Ireland shall be no longer permitted to export human food, while her population are dying with famine. But the English landlords will be disappointed of those pecuniary advantages to themselves, for the sake of which they urge the adoption of the measure.

Upon rents we have at present little to say. They are private contracts in which the public has no voice, unless appealed to by the parties themselves. That the rents need not be reduced in the ratio of the reduction of the price of corn, is perfectly clear, if the other costs of production have, as we believe they have, been reduced in a still greater degree. Land is the raw material of corn, and its value computed in rent, must, like the value of other raw materials, be governed by the state of supply and demand. The improvements in husbandry and the increased facilities of conveyance which have already been noticed, are equivalent to the new acquisition of a larger surface of fertile lands, which, in proportion to their quantity and quality, tend to diminish in various degrees the ground of rent for the better parts of the older possessions, and to destroy that of the worst. It cannot now be said that we throw our inferior soils out of cultivation, by admitting the produce of the rich soils of foreign countries; the cuckoo note of this old and once constant cry is completely silenced. The operative cause is in our own richer or more tractable soils, which, under the application of greater skill, are increasing in productiveness at even a faster rate than the population increases to consume its produce. Some partial inconvenience may be suffered in such a case, but it is without remedy. What owner of a poor soil will have the front to propose, in these days, that the cultivation of certain lands, or the use of certain systems at home, shall be prohibited? We say pointedly, *in these days*, for the attempt, if made, would not be without a precedent; the owners of the old meadows in England, once petitioned for the prohibition of the artificial grasses.

While Spitalfields and Coventry were protesting, that without assistance against foreigners, they could carry on their trade no longer, Manchester stepped quietly in and took it out of their hands. While session after session it was asserted, that the shipping of England had become of no value, under its competition with foreign shipping; every year produced its abundant crop of new vessels built in the teeth of such protestations. Each of these great interests felt that they could not propose to check the spirit of domestic adventure: although, with some remnant of apparent plea against foreign interference, they have found it necessary to prepare themselves in good earnest, to contend with home competition. To the landed interest there is not a plausible particle of such a plea left; and we will tell them fairly, for their good, which has our best wishes, that the *Criers to Hercules* will be utterly lost, if they suffer themselves to be left behind in the mire, by those who adopt the laudable alternative of putting the *shoulder to the wheel*. Let them look at the map of Great Britain and Ireland – let them compute the productive powers of the lands, within the sea-girt boundaries of the British Islands – let them reflect on the quantity of growing capital in the kingdom seeking investment – and, also, on the quantity of able-bodied labourers, who will in future be *productively* employed, instead of being supported in idleness, as they have been. These will be new producers without being new consumers – a portentous consequence which has not received half the consideration it deserves. Let them also advert to the spirit of invention which is ever at work to save the consumption of food – a spirit first, and too strongly, excited by themselves. And when they have well weighed these, and similar matters, which must influence their *future* prospects – let them turn their mind to certain important facts of their *present* case. If, upon any former occasion, one of their most sanguine members had, in prophetic mood, set himself to work to describe the state of things, which would imply a condition of great agricultural prosperity, he would have drawn the picture of the present times. The great features of that picture are these. The population of the country has doubled in the last half century, and its increase is still in rapid progress. Our ports are, and have long been, shut against foreign corn. Five successive seasons have been fruitful in produce, and fortunate in harvests. We have been enabled, in the period of a few years, to repeal taxes from time to time, computed to produce in the aggregate fifteen millions – and yet, such has been the buoyant state of our general prosperity, that the measure of the revenue has, after every remission, been quickly filled again to the brink, and again has overflowed. Great reductions have been made in the national expenditure, without any diminution of the national service or the national splendour; the interest of mortgages has been lowered from five to four per cent., as a maximum; we have given twenty millions of money for the abolition of slavery, and provided for the interest of the stock created by it, out of our redundant revenue; every branch of commerce and manufactures is in full and profitable employ, furnishing millions of operatives, and their attendant population, with the ample means of commanding for their use, the products of our soil; immense sums of our surplus capital, such as, ten years ago, under apprehensions of scarcity at home, was seeking investments in foreign countries, now, under the happy prospects of plenty in our own country, are being applied to great national undertakings, finding employment and good wages for common workmen, and unskilled labourers out of number. It has often been observed, that the producers of food, measure the wants of the people, not by their physical wants, but by their pockets – by their ability to buy, and not their ability to eat – and, that when the price is not to their satisfaction, they say that there is no demand, although millions be only half fed. But of the picture we have been drawing, in the very fore ground are the strong lines of a remarkable purchasing power – the effective demand of the pocket, as well as the natural demand of the appetite.

Will the Agricultural Associations reflect on these descriptions of the past and present state, and the future prospects, of the country? Will the Grand Central Society – we beg pardon for our mistake in adding to their title the term 'grand' – it is a word in bad odour, and they have had too good taste to assume it – will then the 'Central Society' ponder over these reminiscences, and

'The Corn Laws' (1836)

carry in their minds the lessons they afford, and the guides they offer to them, when in their committees, as men of business, whose characters will be compromised by their approval of crude, absurd, and impracticable schemes, they are discussing the 'measures' they shall propose for removing the 'overwhelming distress' under which they have proclaimed that they are suffering? Say rather, will they not blush at such perversion of language? Will they not be ashamed to take their stand before the public with a cry of distress as self-dubbed paupers, and as spendthrifts confessed? Will they mix their whining complaints with the 'busy hum of men,' which would otherwise, in these piping times, consist only of sounds arising out of universal cheerfulness of voice and alacrity of movement? We put one more question – will the really great, noble, and rich of our aristocracy, by their silence, suffer it to be thought, that they hold themselves to be represented by the members of this Central Society?

In a very few days from the time while we are writing, with the impatient printer at our elbow, the High Court of Parliament will be convened. Our Constitutional Monarch will then, through his Parliament to his people, promulgate those sentiments, which, in the wisdom of His Councils, are thought fit to be so made known. May we be permitted to express a hope that, upon this occasion, the blessings of Providence will not be again spoken of as a visitation of evil. Five successive plentiful seasons have, by the bounty of the Almighty, 'filled the hungry with good things:' and shall our gracious King, because a few of the 'rich have been sent empty away,' be advised to soothe the ears of his robed and titled auditors, with lamentations over the privation of some of their superfluous and imaginary luxuries; instead of pouring forth, from the true dictates of his own kind heart, his grateful acknowledgments to Divine Providence, for so plentiful a bestowal of those gifts of nature, which constitute the blessings of the human race? Blessings – for which man is awfully responsible, if, through human institutions, they are converted into curses, or are profanely so denominated.

The subject of currency we mention, almost only to say that we are quite aware of the intentions of the landed interest, in regard to the circulating medium of the country.

It may not, however, be amiss to advert now to that particular view of the subject on their part, which is the exciting cause of their present violent movements. They treat the continuous fall in the prices of corn, since the return to cash payments, as evidence of the magnitude of the preceding depreciation. A greater mistake never was made. If a country, after having lost its precious metals, by an excessive issue of bank paper, sets about in earnest to recover them by withdrawing the necessary amount of its notes, the greatest consequent depression of prices will occur first, when they will be forced even below the proper level; and they will be kept below that level, until the quantity of gold sufficient to saturate the circulation is obtained. This end being accomplished, the prices will recover again, and take their proper station in the common markets of general commerce. It is only by offering to other countries its own goods at unusually low prices, and refraining to buy their's, that any country can suddenly draw to itself an unusual quantity of the precious metals: but when the commercial intercourse is again carried on in goods, that country is enabled to demand for her's a full equivalent; and, accordingly, getting a better price for her exports, her general prices participate in the rise. The steady and gradual fall in the price of corn, which we have been witnessing for a number of years after the restoration of our metallic currency, furnished positive evidence that the cause of that fall does not lie in the circulating medium. With respect to the general question, we hold that it has nothing to do with the particular case of the landed interest; and we may expect that the ignorance of the simplest rudiments of the science displayed by their orators, will ensure their ready discomfiture, whenever they attempt to enforce their notions upon any deliberative body of men. To that fate, then, we shall be content to leave them for this time: and we doubt not, but that we shall be early enough in the field in our next number, if, contrary to our expectations, such weak assailants be able to preserve any thing like a front in the presence of their opponents. Upon this and all other subjects, we shall honor the Central Agricultural Society with our best attentions. For the present, we take our leave of them.

Richard Cobden, 'Modern History of the Corn Laws', *Anti Corn-Law Circular*, 1 (16 April 1839), extracts.

It has been the practice with many of those public speakers and writers who have made the question of the Corn Laws the vehicle for popular declamation, to go back to remote ages for examples of selfish legislation on the part of our parliaments, whilst at the same time they have rather unfairly lost sight of the fact, that the principle of monopoly was claimed and enjoyed by the manufacturers, merchants, and shipowners of those days, to the same or even a greater extent than by the agriculturists themselves. Indeed, it may be fairly questioned, whether, down to 1820, the producers of British manufactures did not possess as large a share of legislative protection as the growers of corn.[1]

At length, however, the obvious truths which Adam Smith, Ricardo, and others had so clearly demonstrated, that these restrictions and prohibitions upon trade tended in ninety-nine out of a hundred cases to divert the national industry from its natural and profitable pursuits into artificial and less productive channels, were recognised by the statesmen of this country: and partly to stimulate industry, with the view of meeting the heavy charges of the government and debt of the nation, and partly, perhaps, from a conviction of the tardy justice of the measure to that party whose interest had been, and still is, lost sight of by the advocates of monopoly – *the consumer*, the principles of *free trade* were adopted and openly avowed by the Liverpool administration. From that time, the question of the justice or injustice of the corn laws assumes a new shape; it is no longer one of doubt to the honest inquirer, but presents itself simplified, and divested of every difficulty. All attempts to carry us back, in our discussion of the subject, beyond the period when the principle of free trade was applied to the manufactures, commerce, and shipping of Great Britain and her colonies, should therefore be sedulously avoided, as superogatory, and calculated only to mystify what has from that time been a plain and unembarrassed question. As this era in our commercial policy forms the pivot on which the arguments upon the greatest question of the present day turns, it may be well, before referring to some of the consequences of our departure in respect to the article of food from the principles then avowed, to glance at the circumstances connected with the practical adoption of the doctrines of free trade in this country.

Some preliminary steps had been taken, under the auspices of Mr. Wallace and Mr. Robinson, for the relaxation of the restrictions upon trade in 1822, when several new laws had been proposed by the government, and committees of the House of Commons had sat for inquiry into other matters connected

---

1 The following account of protective measures of the eighteenth-century has been omitted. (ed.)

with the further emancipation of our industry from the legislative trammels with which it had been beset: but it was not till Mr. Huskisson brought forward his celebrated measure for altering the laws relating to the silk trade in 1824, that the full extent of the plans of Lord Liverpool's cabinet became known to the public; and the following session, in which he made his famous exposition of the colonial, commercial, and shipping policy of the country, and brought forward and carried government bills for altering and reducing the tariff of duties upon almost every article of foreign manufacture, stamped the year 1825 as the era of a commercial revolution, more important in its effects upon society, and pregnant with far greater future consequences, than many of those *political* revolutions which have commanded so much more attention from the historian.[1]

As the measures of this period constitute, with very trifling subsequent additions of what may be termed legislative details, the modern commercial code, usually known by the term of *Free Trade*, it may be proper, for a variety of reasons, just now, to call to mind the political party and the individual statesman to whom the country is indebted for those acts, which, amongst other important changes, substituted for the renowned navigation laws of Charles II., the modern reciprocity system, – released the colonial trade from some of the trammels of the mother country, – gave the British mechanic the legal right to carry his labour to foreign markets, – repealed the combination laws, – and neutralised the laws which prohibited the exportation of machinery: – the administration which boasted of Lord Eldon for Lord Chancellor, the Duke of Wellington for Master General of the Ordinance, and Sir Robert Peel for Secretary of State, – in a word, the high-tory government, over which Lord Liverpool ruled as chief, gave to the commerce of England its present tariff of duties, and opened, to the manufactures of France and other countries, a door to the markets of Great Britain.[2] Nor did any portion of the cabinet affect to remain neuter, whilst Mr. Huskisson was prominently advocating his favourite theories. On the contrary, those principles of commercial freedom were recommended to the favourable consideration of parliament by the king in his speech, at the opening of the session of 1825, thus stamping the doctrines of *free trade* with the authority of the whole government.

The great and generous principles of commercial freedom which had been so eloquently advocated with reference to the articles of silks, woollens, &c., were now pronounced by some of the members of the House of Commons to be equally applicable to those still more necessary commodities, corn, cattle, and the like. Nay, it was even thought that the rule should have been applied to them in the first instance, and afterwards extended to those articles of manufacture, into the price of which the food of the artisan must necessarily enter. Impressed

---

1 The following account of Huskisson's reforms has been omitted. (ed.)
2 Cobden added a footnote at this point in the text listing the members of the Cabinet. (ed.)

with these views, Mr. Whitmore brought forward a motion for the revision of the corn laws, a month after the promulgation of the views of the ministry upon the subject of trade. He was, however, opposed by Mr. Huskisson, on the ground that the motion was ill-timed, but, at the same time, he stated that it would be necessary, at a future time, to revise those laws; and he added, that 'several foreign countries were in distress owing to our exclusion of their corn, and that they had in revenge shut out our manufactures.'[1]

The tendency of these observations left no doubt in the minds of the public that Mr. Huskisson would, at an early period, on behalf of the government, present to parliament a bill for reducing the duties on foreign agricultural produce. Indeed it was felt to be impossible, now that the principle of foreign competition was applied to all our manufactures, – forced indeed upon them against their wishes, and in spite of their remonstrances; – that a virtual prohibition to trade in the *corn* of other countries should be maintained in order to secure to the landlords a monopoly of the home market. Confidence was felt in the probity and genius of Mr. Huskisson, in particular; whose enlightened views, however they might arouse the hostility of the interested few, were felt to be directed towards the benefit of the public at large: and it was not supposed that he who could take into his comprehensive mind the whole of the complicated interests of this empire, would lose sight of that question which of all others involved most nearly the welfare of the great body of the people. Besides, nobody could suspect him of the design to place the English artisan in competition with the French and German weavers, whilst labouring under such heavy disadvantages in the price of food. He had already reduced such duties upon raw materials as materially interfered with our manufacturers in their competition with foreigners; and whilst removing some charges of trifling amount which were levied by the customs upon certain articles used in dyeing, he had said, that 'Even if it operated to the extent of one or two per cent, this, in the present open competition of the market, might turn the scale to our disadvantage, and ought therefore to be removed.'[2] Was it then to be supposed that he contemplated leaving a custom's [*sic*] duty of probably one hundred per cent. upon corn, the raw material which entered to so large an extent into the labour of all countries? Such a course of policy was thought to be impossible.

On the assembling of parliament, in the spring of 1826, the expectations of the public were, however, greatly disappointed at the announcement, by ministers, that they did not intend, during that session, to propose any alteration in the existing corn law. It being the last session of the parliament was the excuse pleaded for delay. On the 18th April, Mr. Whitmore again moved for a revision of the corn law. 'It was mischievous,' he said, 'to delay the decision of the ques-

---

1   Debate, 28 April, 1835.
2   Debate, 25 March, 1825.

tion a single moment, after government had applied the principle of free trade to other branches of industry, for these principles could never be applied with due effect, nor have practical justice done to them, so long as the present corn law formed part of our commercial policy.' Mr. Huskisson, towards whom, as the champion of free trade, all eyes were now turned, avoided going into the discussion of the question, urging, as a ground of postponement, that the last session of a parliament was an unfit time for agitating so important a question, and that he thought the subject ought to be reserved for the first session of the new parliament. He pledged himself, however, to take the first favourable opportunity of calling the attention of the house to the whole subject of the corn law.

The commercial distress which prevailed in 1826, and the consequent want of employment for the manufacturing population, drew public attention still more to the question of the corn law; and numerous petitions were presented, at the meeting of parliament, for a reduction of the duty on foreign grain. During the recess, Lord Liverpool and Mr. Huskisson had prepared a new corn bill, which, at the assembling of parliament, it was determined, by the cabinet, that Mr. Canning should introduce into the Commons, in the absence of Mr. Huskisson, who was confined to his house by ill health; but whether his malady was occasioned by blighted hopes, in finding himself forced, at the behest of an insatiate and powerful aristocracy, to adopt a scale of duties upon the first article of commerce, prohibitive in all but the name, his biographer does not inform us.

Nothing is more dangerous than the avowal of a great and comprehensive political principle, by a selfish and partial government. It is like a two-edged sword, which, in its recoil, sometimes wounds the unskilful hand that wields it. The administration of Lord Liverpool found themselves in this position, when, after having forced the free trade policy upon the manufacturers and merchants of the country, – after having thrown open our ports to the products of all the other manufacturing nations of the world, – and removed from our statute-books several hundred restrictive laws, affecting the interests of the capitalists and labourers of the British empire and its colonies, – they were now called upon to apply the same principle to the trade in corn. It was felt by the cabinet, which had passed those laws for withdrawing the heavy protections upon silk, linens, gloves, &c., that the cry, raised throughout the country, for a like removal of the monopoly enjoyed by the *manufacturers of corn*, could no longer be with decency disregarded.

On the 1st March, 1827, Mr. Canning introduced the government corn bill to the House of Commons; and so palpable and indisputable were the claims of justice, that the trade in corn should be placed under the same regulation as that in other commodities, that even this brilliant debater, whose whole political career had been marked by the talent for dazzling and diverting the minds of his hearers, did not, on this occasion, venture upon the attempt to mislead them from the obvious conclusions of common sense. On the contrary, he avowed, in the course of his speech, that, 'if the trade in corn was to be continued at all, it ought to be continued, as far as was practicable, under the same principles as were applied to other species of trade.' We have seen what the principles were which had been applied to the trade in gloves, silks, &c. Let us now examine the mode in which the article of corn was dealt with.

Mr. Canning proposed, on behalf of the government, that a duty of twenty shillings a quarter should be levied upon foreign wheat, when the price in the home market reached sixty shillings; that duty to diminish two shillings per quarter for every one shilling of increase in price, and to increase two shillings for every diminution of one shilling in price. The result of which would be, that, when the average price reached seventy shillings, all duty would cease, and the importation be free; and, on the other hand, when the average price fell to fifty shillings, the duty would be forty shillings.

The first and most glaring inconsistency in the rule applied to corn, in the preceding propositions, as compared with the principles already adopted, with reference to every other article of commerce, was, the laying on a graduated, instead of a fixed, duty. The next, and more enormous departure from the rule laid down by Mr. Huskisson, and adopted by the parliament, in fixing the tariff upon foreign manufactures, was, in renouncing the *ad valorem* duty, which, 'in no case should exceed thirty per cent. for the purpose of protection,' and adopting a scale of duties upon the directly opposite principle of securing to the manufacturer of corn a minimum of price, regardless of the cost at which it might be produced abroad. In the one case, the public was secured, as far as possible, against the monopoly of the home-producer, by making the duty depend upon the price at which his productions could be obtained in other countries, *whilst, on the contrary, the corn-grower was invested with a monopoly up to a certain price*, without any reference to *the cost at which his commodity might be produced abroad*. In the rule applied to our manufacturers, shipowners, &c., the avowed object was to stimulate native industry, by throwing it open to the rivalry of other nations; but the system reserved for the agriculturists, by themselves, went to the very different end of guarding their industry against the competition of foreign countries. The arguments that had been made use of by the silk manufacturers, the glovers, the glass-blowers, &c., in defence of their respective interests, that they were unable to cope with the French and other foreign competitors, were met with the sound and wholesome doctrine, that, 'if thirty per cent. duty will not sufficiently protect you, there is no wisdom in bolstering your industry by higher duties.' They were, moreover, reminded by ministers, that the public interest, and not theirs, ought to be the sole object of legislation. Very different, however, was the language held by the same ministry when legislating upon the interests of that haughty landed aristocracy which then held the cabinet, the crown, and the destinies of this empire in the hollow of its hand.

Mr. Canning's speech, a flourish of words, amongst which *'principle'* recurs with ominous frequency, was full of professions of allegiance to the landlords, by whom he was exclusively surrounded. 'Every body admitted,' he said, 'the necessity of protecting the agricultural interest, *and the only question was, the mode and degree in which that protection should be administered.'*(!)[1] The method adopted was, as we have seen, to put a prohibitory duty on foreign wheat, until the price in the home market reached fifty shillings a quarter. If, said Mr. Canning, he were asked, why, since he proposed a prohibitory duty, he did not at that point propose an absolute prohibition, he would answer, that he did not think it advisable, either for the agriculturists themselves, or for the public generally, to recognise the *'principle'* of a prohibition, on a subject which involved the main interests of the nation.[2] But, although this kind of sophistry was very well received by the great majority of the *house of landlords*, who were quite willing that the ministerial corn bill should, in theory, be viewed as emanating from the free trade system, whilst practically, and substantially, it worked for their exclusive interest, still, there was a considerable section of the agriculturists, who were too honest in their bigotry to tolerate any such rhetorical subterfuges. These zealots manfully declared for monopoly.[3] They opposed the going into committee, declaring that the agriculturists (*manufacturers*) were entitled to a prohibition of foreign corn, (*manufactures*,) that it was most unjust to expose the home grower, (*home manufacturer*,) oppressed with taxes, and obliged to purchase costly labour to a competition with the farmers (*manufacturers*) of foreign countries, where taxation was light, and the price of labour incomparably

1   For the sake of contrast, compare with this the reasoning of Mr. Huskisson, addressed to the Spitalfields and Coventry *interests*. The few additional words in italics are now inserted, to show how well the same arguments *might* have been used towards the agricultural interest: 'To this question there are three parties – the throwster, the silk manufacturer, (*the landowner, the tenant*,) and the public – certainly not the least interested or least important party in this question, but who, in the manner in which it has hitherto been argued, have been put out of view. The public are the great consumers of the article; they indulge in silk dresses (*wheaten bread*), and wear silks (*drink beer*), from which I do not wish to see them desist. I cannot see without concern – not to use a stronger expression – the appearance of pride and self-conceit, which would think it a duty to forbid the lower classes from indulging in those luxuries which he would reserve for the higher. Sir, in a country like this, not divided into castes and tribes by rigid laws, I cannot conceive that it is right to forbid any portion of his majesty's subjects those enjoyments which stimulate industry, and while they contribute to the innocent gratifications of the people, do not diminish the national resources. I for one must say, that I consider the public benefited by those facilities which place the enjoyment and luxury of a silk dress (*plum pudding*) within the reach of a greater number of persons.'

2   The frequent reference to the *principles* of free trade in Mr. Canning's speech, and the total departure from it in the terms of his resolutions, drew from Lord Milton the observation, that 'The interests of the manufacturing classes seemed to have been followed by ministers in ascertaining the principle, but the interests of the agriculturists in fixing the price.'

3   Sir E. Knatchbull, Sir Thomas Lethbridge, Lord Clive, &c. As before; the words in italics are now added, to show how admirably well the very same arguments *might* have been used in the case of the manufacturing interest.

Cobden, 'Modern History of the Corn Laws' (1839)

lower, that its effect would be to reduce prices much below what could be considered a fair remunerating price to the grower, (*manufacturer,*) and that it was a sacrifice of the landowner, (*manufacturer.*)

Nay, one[1] of this party was suddenly seized with feelings of horror at the fearful designs of the free traders, and characterised the corn bill as 'a result of the dangerous doctrines of the political economists, men who destroy whatever they touch.'

Such were the arguments now used by a party in the House of Commons, which, two years before, had assisted the same ministers in their plans of removing all those prohibitions which protected the interests of the manufacturers against the rivalry of foreigners. Nor must it be forgotten, that the free trade policy was adopted by a parliament composed exclusively of landowners, and applied to the commerce of the country, against the wishes, and in spite of the remonstrances, of the manufacturing and shipping interests. Added to which, let it be borne in mind, that Manchester, Birmingham, and Leeds enjoyed no voice in that legislature which had thus summarily disposed of the laws by which their interests were guarded. It is necessary that these facts should be remembered, that we may form a correct estimate of the morality of that body, which, composed exclusively of landowners, every one of them letting his farms to the highest bidder, now enacted a law, securing to themselves a monopoly of the trade in corn, just twenty-four months after they had applied the opposite principle of foreign competition to every other branch of the commerce of the country!

This corn bill, which passed the House of Commons without alteration, was afterwards destined to be marked in its progress by the most serious disasters. Lord Liverpool, who had given notice of the day on which, he should introduce the cabinet measure into the House of Lords, was, in the interval, visited with that malady which terminated in his death. He was, as is well known, succeeded by Mr. Canning, from whose cabinet an important section of the Liverpool ministry seceded. The Duke of Wellington, the most influential of the latter body, now opposed, in the House of Lords, the passing of the very same corn bill which he himself, as a cabinet minister, must have previously assisted in preparing. The bill was lost in the upper house, and Mr. Canning's death soon followed. During the short-lived administration of Lord Goderich, who next succeeded to the premiership, there was no attempt at legislation upon the corn question. But the Duke of Wellington, who was next called to the head of the government, lost no time in introducing the corn law under which the country still suffers, and which, whilst it partook of the principle of the bill prepared by Lord Liverpool, surpassed it in the extent of its restrictive provisions. The scale of duties by which the trade in corn is at present regulated, is given below,[2] by which it will be seen, that when the price

1   Mr. Curteis
2   [Ed.: This table has been omitted.]

of wheat in the home market is sixty-six shillings, and under sixty-seven shillings, the duty upon importation is twenty shillings and eightpence, and that, for every shilling of diminution in the price, there is an additional shilling of duty; so that, when the home price descends to fifty-two shillings, the duty reaches thirty-four shillings and eightpence. But it will be seen, that the scale of duty decreases, in an eccentric ratio, with the rise of the price in the home market, until, at seventy-four shillings, the duty falls to one shilling.

By the corn act of 1815, which, with some slight and unimportant modifications made in 1822, was in force at the time of passing the above measure, foreign wheat was prohibited till the price in the home-market rose to eighty shillings a quarter. It would, therefore, at first sight, appear as if the landowners (who then *owned* also the representation of the people in parliament) had made some restitution of booty on the score of conscience to the trading and working classes. Looking only at the facts, that the duty by the present act falls to one shilling a quarter, when the price in the home-market rises to seventy-four shillings, whereas previously wheat was virtually prohibited till the home-price reached eighty shillings, it would seem as though a considerable boon had been granted to the consumers of bread. So far, however, from being really so, when other circumstances are taken into account, it will be proved, beyond dispute, that by the present corn law, a stricter monopoly of the home-trade has been secured to the landlords of this country than had been ever enjoyed through its predecessor.

To form a correct judgment upon this point, it will be necessary to recur to the state of the currency at the time of passing the corn act of 1815. At that time, the bank restriction act was still in force, and the paper circulation of the country was at a great depreciation. By a return to specie payments, the currency became restricted, and a corresponding diminution took place in the price of all commodities; wheat, of course, included. Then followed the withdrawal of one pound notes, and the substitution of gold, which occasioned a further fall in prices, which has been variously estimated at from twenty to thirty per cent. Taking these two operations into account, we shall be quite safe in calculating the fall in the value of commodities, or in other words the rise in the value of money, to have been at least thirty per cent. between the time when the late and the present corn laws were enacted; in short, seventy shillings would purchase the same amount of commodities, wheat included, in 1828, that would in 1815 have cost one hundred. And as, by the same rule, eighty shillings in 1815 were equal in value to fifty-six shillings only in 1828, if the scale of duties had been altered with a view merely to meet this change in the value of money, without reference to any pretended enfranchisement of the trade, then, instead of throwing open the ports when the home-price reached seventy-four shillings, the trade in foreign corn ought to have been free at fifty-six shillings. But if we look at the table of duties just given, we find that at fifty-six shillings the duty on importation is thirty shillings and eightpence, which, in plain terms, is the excess of spoliation upon every quarter of wheat imported since 1828, over and above the exaction under the previous law of 1815.

This view of the question is neither original nor disputed. In the debates upon the ministerial corn bill of 1827, the altered state of the currency was one of the arguments with which the Chancellor of the Exchequer supported Mr. Canning's motion. He avowed, that 'one reason for changing the corn laws was to be found in the alterations recently introduced into the currency. How could any man, who considered the change in the value of money occasioned by those alterations, seriously propose to keep up the price to eighty shillings, at which it had been fixed by the law of 1815?' And, upon the same occasion, Sir Francis Burdett, who was opposed to a low rate of duty, consoled the landlords by telling them, that 'while the present state of the currency continued, corn was not likely to rise to high as to produce any material effect.' We shall very soon establish the truth of the eccentric Baronet's prediction, by a reference to the statistics of the foreign corn trade, before and after the law of 1828.[1]

To the above searching analysis of the preceding tabular statement, it is not necessary to add a word, unless it be to draw the reader's attention closely to the fact, that the corn law of 1828, instead of enabling the people of this country to purchase an increased supply of foreign wheat, actually caused a diminished consumption; thus affording the strongest possible proof that the duty imposed in 1828, so far from being less than that of 1815, was, taking the alteration of the currency into account, really greater; and thus, too, demonstrating by experience, what we have already endeavoured to prove by an appeal to facts and figures, that in pretending to free the trade in corn, the parliament aimed only at tightening the screw of the landlords' monopoly.

To form a correct estimate of the extent of the injustice inflicted upon the commercial and manufacturing interests by the partial and one-sided legislation of *the free-traders* of 1825–6, we must endeavour to ascertain what the average amount of *ad valorem* duty upon wheat has been during the ten years subsequent to the passing of the last corn law; and then compare it with the duty levied upon foreign manufactures during the same period. The average price of corn in the English markets, during the eleven years, from 1828 to 1838, has, according to *the Gazette* returns, been 57s. 6d, at which price the duty on importation is 29s. 8d. per quarter. During the same period the official average price of wheat in France has been 43s. 1d. But to compare the average prices of wheat in France with those in England, it is necessary to deduct twenty per cent. from the former for difference in the quality of the wheat, and the difference in the mode of taking the averages; this leaves the average price of French wheat equiv-

---

1 [Ed.: The following table, of imports of wheat, for a series of thirty-five years, copied from Porter's *The Progress of the Nation*, has been omitted.]

328   *Battles over Free Trade, Volume 1*

alent to 34s. 6d. the English quarter, during the last eleven years; and the import duty having been as an average 29s. 8d. per quarter, it follows that an *ad valorem* duty of eighty-six per cent. has been payable upon French wheat, whilst French gloves and silks have been admissible at an *ad valorem* duty of thirty per cent. But France, although celebrated for the quality of its manufactures of silks and gloves, is not famous for the cheapness of its wheat. We must glance at the prices of grain in other countries, from which our increased supplies of food ought to be drawn, in order to be able to judge correctly of the extent of the injustice to which we are alluding. In the principal markets of Russia and Prussia, the price of wheat has during the last ten years ranged at from fifteen to thirty shillings per quarter. Taking, however, the quotations at Dantzic, we find that the average price of wheat in that market, for the last eleven years, (from 1828 to 1838) has been exactly 30s. 5d. per quarter; whilst, as we have seen above, the average duty on importation has been 29s. 8d. a quarter. It follows, of course, that, taking into consideration the difference in quality, the producer of wheat in this country has enjoyed a protection of considerably upwards of one hundred per cent., against the rivalry of the Prussian corn grower, at the same time that the linens of Silesia or Moscow have been admitted into competition with the like productions of Dundee or Barnsley, at a duty of thirty per cent.

But it must be remembered that the freight upon so bulky a commodity as corn affords a species of protective tax, when compared with the small *ad valorem* rate of expense upon the transport of manufactured articles. A bale of silk goods, or a box of gloves, worth a hundred pounds, may be conveyed by sea at the same charge as a quarter of wheat, costing thirty shillings. Let us suppose the charge to be ten shillings. In the former case the expense of freight will be the half of one per cent. only, whilst in the latter instance it amounts to thirty-three per cent; – thus giving, in the item of freight alone, an additional protection of twenty-nine and a half per cent. to the landowner over the manufacturer.

Nor must it be forgotten, that whilst the principle of free trade has been applied to the cheapening of luxuries for the benefit of the few, who have enjoyed their ribbons and gloves at a reduced price, in consequence of the stimulus which French competition has given to the artisans of Coventry and Worcester, it was inconsistently abandoned in legislating upon the trade in the first necessary of life, for the mass of the people; thus debarring those very operatives who toil at reduced wages, and with increased skill to furnish cheaper clothing to the favoured rich, from the reciprocal benefit, from a principle which it was pretended should be applied to the trade of the nation at large, and not to a fraction of it exclusively. So long as this partial application of the doctrine of free trade exists, so long will the legislation of 1825 and 1826 be tainted with fraud and injustice; and instead of awarding to the lawgivers of that period the honour of having given to the world an example of generous and humane – because peace-

Cobden, 'Modern History of the Corn Laws' (1839)

ful – commercial policy, they must be regarded only as a cunning and selfish band, who sustained the mask of liberality in order the more securely to act the part of depredators.[1] So long as the corn law of 1828 remains upon our statute book, alongside of the enactments which regulate the trade in silks, woolens, and other articles of manufacture, it will be a monument of the sordid and unscrupulous character of our landed aristocracy; it presents that body with all its boasted lineage and chivalrous honour, in the lowly act of filching from the pockets of the pale mechanic the third part of his hard earnings; and it exhibits peers, baronies, and esquires, confederating against the comfort, health, and even the existence of factory children and hand loom weavers. The simple facts connected with the history of the present corn law afford the severest stricture upon the parliament and government of the country, and until those facts be disproved, or the injustice be remedied, they will affix upon both the deepest stain of corruption and tyranny.

It is impossible to leave this subject, without recurring to the conduct and views of Mr. Huskisson, both of which have been criticised by late writers, in consequence of the apparent supineness with which he regarded the question of the corn laws during the latter portion of his life. It is difficult to account for the step he took in joining the Duke of Wellington's administration, after Mr. Canning's attempt to pass the corn law, which had been concocted by Mr. Huskisson and Lord Liverpool, had suffered a defeat in the House of Lords, chiefly through the duke's opposition to the measure. The long habits of business, which made the toils of office so agreeable, – the hope of being able to carry forward some, if not all, of those views of commercial and financial policy with which his name was associated, – or the desire to cooperate with that section of the cabinet whose principles coincided with his own, – any one, or all, of these motives might have led Mr. Huskisson to join the administration of the Duke of Wellington; in doing which, he lent his great talents to the service of that haughty oligarchy which had just before destroyed his friend, Mr. Canning, and exposed himself to those ever ready imputations of venality, with which statesmen are so generally, and often so unjustly, charged.

But there are abundant proofs that Mr. Huskisson regarded the repeal of the corn law of 1828, as indispensable to the commercial prosperity of the country. It is true, that whilst still a cabinet minister, under the premiership of the Duke of Wellington, be submitted to the restraints of office, and avoided a direct

---

1   Nothing could surpass the enthusiasm which the free trade measures of Huskisson excited in the higher political circles, *whilst they referred only to the trade in silks, laces, woollens, &c.* In the biography of that distinguished statesman we are told, that his speeches, developing the views of commercial reform entertained by the government, were translated into foreign languages. Several congratulatory letters are also given, written by peers and others. Amongst them are highly flattering epistles from Lords Granville and Stafford. The latter noble correspondent conveys not only his own, but his wife's congratulations, to the advocate of free trade.

allusion to that question which the majority of his colleagues considered to be settled. But when in his speeches, both within and out of parliament, he constantly alluded to the necessity of *lightening the burdens that pressed upon the springs and sources of productive industry,* (to quote his own memorable and often repeated words) every body knew that he referred to the corn laws. Towards the close of his career, however, when no longer trammelled by the etiquette of office, and after he had probably ceased to wish for readmission to the cabinet, he often declared publicly those sentiments, upon the subject of the corn laws, which he had been known always privately to entertain. Upon one occasion, in particular, he gave the most emphatic declaration of his views, stating it to be 'his unalterable conviction that we could not uphold the corn laws, now in existence, together with the present taxation, and at the same time increase national prosperity, and preserve public contentment. That those laws might be repealed, without affecting the landed interest, whilst, at the same time, the distress of the people might be relieved, he never had any doubt whatever.'[1]

This very important evidence against the present corn law ought to be received with reverence by all parties, because all will admit, that Mr. Huskisson, from the peculiar habits of his mind, and the length of time during which he had devoted its singular powers to the study of the fiscal and commercial interests of this and other countries, was, without any exception, the greatest authority upon such matters. He was admitted, by all his contemporaries, to be, commercially, the first statesman of this commercial country: and he declared, that '*we could not uphold the corn laws and the national prosperity.*'

---

1   March 25, 1830, Mr. P. Thomson's motion for a revision of taxation.

From the Politicians to the Populace: Civil Society and Repeal of the Corn Laws, 1838–46

Petition of the President, Vice President and Directors of the Chamber of Commerce and Manufactures of Manchester, 20 January 1838, in *Appendix to the Report of the Select Committee on Public Petitions* (1837–8), App. 146, No. 1526, p. 76.

To the honourable the Commons of the United Kingdom of Great Britain and Ireland in Parliament assembled.

The Petition of the President, Vice-President, and Directors of the Chamber of Commerce and Manufactures of Manchester

Sheweth, –

That the commerce and manufactures of Great Britain are the chief causes of the wealth and power of the country, and afford an important resource for the employment of the population.

That the cotton manufacture is now the greatest of the staple manufactures of the empire, and its national importance is apparent from the fact that, besides clothing our own population, there is annually exported to foreign countries a quantity of cotton goods and yarns, nearly equal in value to the export of all other manufactures.

That this important manufacture is now carried on to a great extent in foreign countries, where it is rapidly increasing, chiefly from the advantages which the foreign manufacturer enjoys in the cheapness of food, – advantages which, with the increasing use of the newest and most approved machinery, have already enabled him to compete successfully with many British fabrics, and even in various instances to undersell, and thus to supersede British manufactures in foreign markets.

That the restrictions on the importation of foreign corn, which give the British landholder a monopoly of the supply of that article, raise the price of food in this country, and to that extent offer a bounty in favour of the foreign manufacturer; whilst at the same time they deprive the British manufacturer of all the

– 331 –

benefits he would enjoy from the demand for our manufactures in this country, which could make the most favourable returns for our exports to them in corn.

That your petitioners respectfully submit that the British landowner cannot possess a more indefeasible right to gather and dispose of the produce of his land than the British manufacturer has freely to exchange the produce of his capital and labour for the produce of foreign countries; and that, therefore, any laws which establish a distinction between the *rights* of landowners and manufacturers are unjust and oppressive, – destructive of the general interests, – and must ever be, as they ought to be, a source of strong and legitimate discontent among all classes of the manufacturing community.

That the injurious consequences of the corn laws are at present most severely felt by the hand-loom weavers, who, for past years, have had to contend, not only with improvements in machinery, but also with the constant transfer of their employment to foreign countries, where food and labour are cheap; and until those laws be repealed your petitioners can hold out no hopes of permanent improvement in the condition of that large and suffering class.

That, in addition to the evils directly felt by your petitioners, the corn laws are a further source of national impoverishment and distress, by their natural tendency to incite other countries to impose on our trade countervailing restrictions, the severity of which is constantly increasing.

That your petitioners would earnestly impress upon your honourable house the fearful consequences to the agricultural and all other interests, of endangering the prosperity of manufactures, or of strengthening motives for the transfer to other countries of the British capital and skill employed in manufactures; and they cannot, from their experience of the past, look forward without alarm to the effects of a perseverance in the present policy of the corn laws.

That, condemning as injurious all monopolies, whether agricultural or commercial, and convinced that the general good will be best promoted by an unobstructed interchange of all commodities with every nation, your petitioners, whilst they acknowledge the necessity of imposing duties upon importations, for the purpose of raising a revenue to meet the necessary expenses of the state, do not recognize the wisdom or justice of levying *restrictive duties* upon any one article for the *protection* of a particular interest; but, on the contrary, they desire to see both in manufactures and agriculture the principles of *free trade* fully established; and they therefore pray your honourable house to repeal the existing laws relating to the importation of foreign corn, and to take such measures as will gradually but steadily remove all existing impediments to the *free* employment of industry and capital. – And your petitioners will ever pray, &c.

January 20th, 1838.

Richard Cobden to John Norton, 23 August 1838, Cobden Papers, West Sussex Record Office, CP 43.

Manchester, 23 August 1838

My dear Norton

I have long deferred, ungrateful fellow that I am, to answer your kind letter: & the bountifully stored hamper which accompanied it, & which I believe emanated from the kindness of your wife might have gone even longer unacknowledged; but I am off tomorrow morning for Germany, & cannot help easing my conscience before I go, fearing that the steamer may go down with the burden instead of carrying me safely to Hamburgh – Accept then my best thanks for the substantial mode in which you have not forgotten me – I trust when I return we shall meet & then I will tell you all about the Prussians, Austrians, Dutch & Belgians – How they teach, preach, spin, plough & amuse themselves – how they live & move & have their being – I'll not remind you of Bautzen or Lutzen or Waterloo, or any of the bloody battle fields, but endeavor to tell you what progress the people of Central Europe are making in the arts of peace – Especially I shall give my attention to the operation of the starvation corn-laws upon the laborer & capitalist by tracing the growth of manufactures in countries where cheap food abounds – When I return, if nobody else will stir I'll give a lecture in Manchester to shew up the iniquitous system & excite the people here to resistance –

You would learn that we are incorporated – This will give an impetus to liberal doctrines & a rank to Manchester which are much wanted if only to operate upon the surrounding places.

My best regards to your wife & children & believe me yours very truly | R. Cobden

334   *Battles over Free Trade, Volume 1*

'Dilemmas on the Corn Law Question', *Blackwood's Magazine*, 43 (February 1839), pp. 170–6.

DILEMMAS ON THE CORN LAW QUESTION.

SINCE the Manchester demonstration, it is apparent to every body that this great question is rapidly drawing to a crisis. In this most practical of countries, when any question is once transferred from the arena of books, pamphlets, – controversy, in short, conducted by the press, – to the official arena of public institutions, 'chambers of commerce', authentic committees of any denomination, sanctioned by the presence of great leading tradesmen, we all know that such a question must very soon agitate the great council of the nation; agitate the landed aristocracy; agitate the thinking classes universally; and (in a sense peculiar to this corn question) agitate that class to frenzy, amongst whom 'Give us this day our daily bread' is the litany ascending for ever to heaven. Well it will be for us, and no thanks to some sections of the press, if this latter class do not pursue the discussion sword in hand. For they have been instructed, nay provoked to do so, in express words. And they are indirectly provoked to such a course by two separate artifices of journals far too discreet to *commit* themselves by any open exhortations to violence. But in what other result can popular fury find a natural out-break, when abused daily by the representation, that upon this question depends the comfort of their lives – that the Corn Laws are the gates which shut them out from plenty – and abused equally by the representations, that one large class of their superiors is naturally, by position, and by malignity of feeling, their deadly enemy? We, of this British land, are familiar with the violence of partisanship; we are familiar with its excesses; and it is one sign of the health and soundness belonging to those ancient institutions, which some are so bent upon overthrowing, that the public safety can bear such party violences without a tremor reaching its deep foundation. But there are limits to all things; or, if it were otherwise, and the *vis vitæ* were too profoundly lodged in our frame of polity to be affected by local storms and by transitory frenzies, even in that case it is shocking to witness a journal of ancient authority amongst ourselves – a journal to which, not Whigs only, but, from old remembrances of half a century, we Tories acknowledge a sentiment of brotherly kindness – the old familiar Morning Chronicle of London – no longer attacking *things*, and parties, and doctrines, but *persons* essential to the composition of our community: not persons only, but an entire order of persons: and this order not in the usual tone of party violence, which recognises a worth in the man while it assaults him in some public capacity; but flying at the throats, as it were, of the country gentlemen in a body, and solemnly assuring its readers, that one and all are so possessed by selfishness, and even by malignity to the lower classes, that they would rather witness the extinction of the British manufacturing superiority, or (if it must be) of the British manufactures, than abate any thing of their own pretensions. As a matter of common sense, putting candour out of the question, why should the landed aristocracy be more selfish than other orders? Or how is it possible that any one order in a state should essentially differ from the rest, among which they grow up, are educated, marry, and associate? Or, in mere consistency, what coherency is there between the assurances that our own landed interest will not suffer by the extinction of the Corn Laws, and these imputations of a merely selfish resistance to that extinction? This dilemma is obvious. Either the landlords see or they do not see the necessity of the changes which are demanded? If they do not, what becomes of their selfishness? Not being convinced of the benefits to result, they must be doing their bounden duty in resisting them. On the other hand, if they do – besides that in such a case they have credit granted to them for a clear-sightedness which elsewhere their enemies are denying them – the conclusion must be, not that they are selfish, but insane. The prosperity of manufacturing industry is, upon any theory, the *condition sine quâ non* of prosperity to the agricultural body. In the case, therefore, supposed, that the landlords are aware of a peremptory necessity in the manufacturing interest for a change in the Corn Laws, it is not selfishness, it is not 'malignity' (comprehensible or incomprehensible) in that class towards the lowest class which could stand between them and their own inalienable interest. So that upon either horn of the dilemma – seeing or not seeing the soundness of the revolution demanded – the landlords could find no principle of action, one way or other, in selfishness. Selfishness, in fact, could operate only upon the case of a *divided* interest: whereas all parties have sense enough to admit, that the interest of land and manufactures are bound up together. Or, if they were not, it would be the clear right of the landlords, and no selfishness at all, to prefer their own order. But the case is imaginary.

One other monstrous paralogism, let me notice, in this Manchester Chamber of Commerce, *subsequent* to the public meeting: they have hired a public room, and are making other arrangements for an exposure to the public eye of continental wares corresponding to our own staple manufactures, labelled with the prices here and on the Continent. Well, what is the inference which the spectator is to draw? This – that our empire, our supremacy as manufacturers is shaken. Be it so. I enter not upon the question of fact or of degree; let the point be conceded. What then? The main question, the total question, remains untouched. viz. Under the operation of what CAUSE has this change been accomplished? The Chamber will answer, That the cause lies in the different prices of bread; – but that is the very question at issue. Did ever man hear of such a *petitio principii?* Wages are but one element of price – bread is but one element of wages.

On this subject I shall remark briefly, that it is not true, as the ordinary calculation runs, that one-half, or nearly one-half of the working-man's expenditure goes in bread; potatoes, more and more in each successive year, are usurping upon bread: as an average, one-fifth part would be nearer to the truth. Then, again, bread could not, on an average of years, be had 50 per cent cheaper, as is assumed; but 20 per cent, or 25 per cent at most, all expenses allowed for. Thirdly and finally, wages cannot be assumed as, on an average, making more than 1-4th of price. The result of which three considerations is, that the difference on manufactured goods generally might, perhaps, at most turn out 1-5th of 1-5th of 1-4th on the present price; total about 1-100th part of the existing price; and this, observe, on the supposition, that the total difference went to the benefit of the consumer, and not, as in fact it would, to the benefit of profits. However, allow even his own extravagant calculations to the enemy. Then, because bread, according to him, will sink one-half, and because bread he affirms to be one-half the outlay of the workman, and because wages constitute (suppose him to say) one-third of the price generally, this would amount to one-half of one-half of one-third, or – but remember, by a most extravagant assumption as the basis – to 1-12th discount upon the present prices.

Hence – that is to say, by this last argument – it appears, that, conceding the very largest postulates, the enemy has made 1-12th – or a fraction more than 8 per cent is the total amount of difference which this enormous change in the policy of the country can effect in our manufactures.

Suppose, for example, upon 100 shillings, a sum of 33 goes on wages, 15 on profits, and 52 on raw material, (including the wear and tear of machinery). The loaf sinks from a shilling to sixpence (though the most impudent of the enemy hardly goes so far). The workman, he affirms, has hitherto spent 16s. 6d. on bread; he now spends 8s. 3d.; so far the 100 shillings sink to 91s. 9d. Upon this sum 15 per cent will amount to about eighteenpence less than before, that is, to 13s. 6d. Total discount upon 100 shillings, 9s. 9d.

Yet, again, consider that this presumes the total saving to be allowed to the purchaser. But, if that be so, how is the workman benefited? Or, if that be not so, and the total saving (which, for many reasons, is impossible) should go to the workman, then how is the manufacturer benefited?

In the first case, what motive has the working class – now under such excitement – to stir in the matter? In the second case, what motive has the Chamber of Commerce to stir? If the whole 9s. 9d. be given to the workman, how would the manufacturing interest be aided? The Continent cares nothing about the particular distribution of the 100 shillings. The Continent must have the 9s. 9d. for its own continental benefit, or else farewell to the supposed improvement of English commerce.

'*Dilemmas on the Corn Law Question*' (1839)

This, we fancy, will prove an ugly dilemma to answer; and thus far the argument applies to the *immediate* results of the change proposed.

But now for the principal argument contemplated, which applies to the *final* results of the change.

This argument requires a preliminary explanation for the majority of readers, in order to show its nerve and pressure, how you stand affected to the doctrine of Rent. Many persons think the doctrine of Rent baseless, some upon one plea, some upon another. For the present purpose, it is immaterial whether that doctrine be true or false, notwithstanding our argument is built upon it. For we offer it as an *argumentum ad hominem* – as an argument irresistible by a particular class of men, viz. the class who maintain the modern doctrine of Rent; and that class it is to a man, (the Colonel excepted) and, generally speaking, no other, who lead the agitation against the Corn Laws. Now if these men are answered, so much at least is gained, and practically all that is wanted, 'the engineers hoist upon their own petard.'

Let us say, then – with the modern economists – that the law of Rent is a fine illustration of that providential arrangement so well illustrated by Paley, under which compensations are applied to excesses in any direction, so as ultimately to restore the equilibrium. The expenditure of man's daily life lies in two great divisions – in manufactured articles and in raw products. Corn, coals, wood, for example, are entirely raw products; – other articles equally raw in their earliest form, as grapes, sugar, cotton, flax, hides, undergo processes of art so complex, that very often these processes utterly obscure the original cost of the material. These two orders of products, into which human expenditure divides itself, are pursuing constantly an opposite and counteracting course, as to cost. Manufactures are always growing cheaper – and why? Because, these, depending upon human agencies, in which the lights of experience and of discovery are for ever at work to improve, it is impossible that the motion should be retrograde. Who has ever heard of a progress from good machinery to worse? On the other hand, as to all raw products, the opposite course prevails; these are always growing dearer – and why? Partly, because land and mines, &c., are limited; partly, because, from the very beginning (unless where extreme remoteness from towns, &c., disturbs this order) men select for cultivation the best lands, &c., first. Here, therefore, the natural movement is from good to worse.

Suppose, then, the best land taken up, and that this produces a quantity of wheat [X] for one shilling. The population expanding, it becomes necessary to fall back upon a lower quality of land [No. 2], which, to produce X, must go to the expence of fifteen-pence. Another expansion of population calls into action No. 3, which produces the same X for eighteen-pence. And so on.

This basis is sufficient to reason upon. It will strike every man, as one result from this scale of descents, that the worst quality of land (No. 3) must give the price for the whole. X is the same quantity and the same quality of grain in every case; only it costs an increasing sum to produce it as the quality of land decreases. Now, in a market, the same quantity and quality, at the same time, must always command the same price. It is quite impossible for No. 3 to plead that No. 2 grows at a less cost; X; however produced, will obtain the same price; and the price of eighteenpence, as the cost of the worst land, will be the price for the whole. By the supposition, fifteenpence was sufficient to reimburse No. 2; and twelvepence was sufficient to reimburse No. 1. What then becomes of the extra threepence on No. 2? What becomes of the extra sixpence on No. 1? Answer, *that is rent*.

Now, it is evident that this scale of degradations could not take place in manufacturing industry; because here, beginning from the worst, the scale travels upwards; and, when No. 2 is discovered, No. 3 is laid aside; and so on. In land, or in mines, or fisheries, this course is impossible, for the simple reason that land and mines are limited in quantity, while machinery may be multiplied *ad infinitum*.

The next consequence which a thoughtful man will detect, perhaps, for himself, is – that always the lowest quality in cultivation (No. 3, in this case,) will pay no rent. This has furnished the main stumbling-block to the reception of the doctrine; 'there *is* no such land,' say multitudes; '*all* land pays rent.' Not so. One consideration may convince any man that there is always land which pays no rent. For it cannot be disputed that it will be a sufficient inducement to any man who combines the characters of proprietor and farmer (that is, who cultivates his own ground), to raise grain. He has the same inducement as any body else; that is, he obtains Profits and Wages; and who obtains more?

It is clear, therefore, that, however low the quality of land may be upon which population forces culture, let it be No. 25 suppose, eternally there will be a lower than the lowest of the rent-paying lands [No. 28] which will be capable of culture under the single condition of paying no rent.

However, at this moment, and for the present purpose, no matter whether there be non-rent paying land under culture or not: it is quite enough if it be granted that the *worst* quality of land, and not any average quality, or superior quality, determines the price for the whole: common sense will extort this concession from every body. The price, in other words, must always be such as to cover the worst and *least* advantageous circumstances of culture, not the best and *most* advantageous.

What follows? Why, that, as the differences of land increase by descending lower and lower, regularly these differences swell the price. The doctrine is familiar to many: for those to whom it is not, a short illustration to the eye will suffice.

The diagram below[1] represents the total price of corn, and it is divided into two sections, in order to represent to the eye the two elements of its price – wages

---

1 [Ed.: Diagrams have been omitted.]

and profits; which two are all that exist, or can exist, so long as only one quality of land is used. At any risk of tediousness, I repeat the reason: it is because, so long as a capitalist will always find a sufficient motive for employing his funds on what produces him the usual rate of profit, a moral impossibility exists that rent can be paid. The man who farms his own land has no rent to pay, and can always undersell and drive out of the market him who charges rent also in the price of his corn. And if it is not charged in the *price*, if the grower takes his outlay in rent out of his profits, then it is *not* rent in any but a verbal sense.

Soon comes the time when No. 1 is found insufficient for a growing society; No. 2 is then resorted to of necessity; that is, an inferior soil; and now the case, as to price, stands thus: No 2 pays no rent now, for the same reason as No 1 paid none, when *that* had no inferior competitor. But because No. 2 costs, by its very definition, more to produce the same result (else how is it No. 2?) – that more becomes, on No. 1, rent, which is represented in the diagram by the darker space, corresponding exactly in amount to the excess of costs on No. 2. No. 2 divides into wages and profits only; but the wages (in which is included all other expenses) are more than the corresponding section in No. 1; and precisely that 'more,' that excess, becomes rent upon No. 1.

One farther stage we will take, and have done. Population increasing, calls at length for No. 3, and then the diagram will stand thus: – That is, just as No. 2 exceeded No. 1 in cost, so does No. 3 exceed No. 2; and the excess becomes rent upon No. 2, and two rents upon No 1.

Were No. 4 called for, that would create rent upon No. 3, two rents upon No. 2, three upon No. 1, and so on for ever; the rent always expressing the exact difference in cost between any one number and that immediately below it.

ARGUMENT ON THE CORN QUESTION, FOUNDED ON THE PRECEDING EXPLANATION.

Let us apply all this to the corn question, after first pausing to notice, that even the followers of Ricardo have often failed to perceive in public questions of great moment – the extensive application of this very doctrine.

For example, twenty years ago, when the China question was at times under discussion, some eminent economists said, by way of meeting a particular argument, 'Of what consequence to this mighty. Chinese nation, of perhaps three hundred millions, is the little demand of Great Britain?' That demand is *not* little; neither in an absolute sense little, nor in relation to the domestic consumption of China. But suppose it *were* little – suppose that (instead of forty millions pounds' weight annually) it were but one million, still if this small addition to the native demand should happen so to operate as to push back the culture upon but one degree lower of soil, and that this were to make a difference of but one dollar an acre in the rent, then let it be remembered *now*, looking to the way in which rent acts, how vast might even that slight addition prove in its results? – and vast, for the very reason alleged in proof that it would be trivial; viz., in proportion to the vast population of China, and its consequent vast consumption of tea (even admitting that the majority of the people are not rich enough to taste it). For such as is the consumption of tea, such will be the scale of soils employed. The dollar additional, by the supposition, on the penultimate quality of land, would be two dollars an acre on the ante-penultimate, three on the land next above, four on the next, and so on. If the vast extent of the tea-drinking population should force the culture upon seventy grades of soil, as it might, how tremendous might be the result, even from a single additional grade being called into action! And the reason why nations are only by degrees made sensible of such changes, is, that leases or other contracts (which as to land must always be of some duration) do not suffer the total effects to appear at once: a certain proportion of the subsisting contracts falls in every year; and until then, until rents are revised and suited to the new price, the advantage flows, of necessity, into the channel of profits.

Now, apply all this to the great question before us. Multitudes of men, like Mr Jacobs, building upon accurate statistics, will dismiss the dispute in this summary way: – 'It is idle to ask what were best – corn laws or none – to import freely or to exclude – for the whole project is a chimera: it is out of our power to import in the extent proposed: so we need not lose time and temper in discussing the policy. America never was able to furnish flour for more than three days' consumption of Britain; the Baltic and all other resources never yet furnished grain for six weeks' consumption.' This answer, however, or evasion, will serve us no longer. The Philistines now meet us with this reply: – 'True; but whose fault was that? Our own. Nobody will grow what he has no prospect of selling. But let England make it fully understood in the Baltic, that she will take all the foreign grain which can support a fair market competition with her own, neither party drawing artificial helps from duties, bounties, or any fiscal imposts whatever, in that case we shall see a different scene.'

Well; *how* different? To what extent? Here comes the pinch of the inquiry. Some imagine that foreign grain, unrestricted, would drive out the English as completely as the Norway rat has driven out or exterminated the old aboriginal rat: our sheaves, as in the Scriptural dream, would bow to the Polish. Upon this basis it is that some argue this question: they contemplate the result of English agriculture being *literally* annihilated. And if you ask, what then becomes of that part of our rural population? – they answer, 'Oh! the cheapness of bread will leave money disposable for butcher's meat: there will be more extensive grazing and fattening. In that way we dispose of part: the other part will go into towns

'Dilemmas on the Corn Law Question' (1839)

and make the cotton or iron goods, by which we shall pay the Poles for manu-facturing our bread.'

But this result would not take place in this extent, even if the restrictions on foreign corn were *totally* removed. Imagine two equal vats – one full, one empty; let off the water of the one into the other, the level of subsidence will be found when each becomes half full. Invert the operation of rent, as just explained; imagine it retrograding through the very same steps by which it advanced, and it will be seen that English corn itself, after a very few steps, will have declined much nearer to continental prices. The common price at which wheat has settled of late years, is 60s. Now, a very few of the lower qualities of soil withdrawn, even on that sole change, English corn would fall to 45s. and 40s.

But now comes the ugly fact to meet the Philistines, – that, *just as rent unthreaded its steps in England, so and inevitably would rent on the Continent travel on through those very stages which, in England, have raised our corn to a higher level than elsewhere.* It is no matter where the corn is grown, so far as regards this inevitable effect, that, in Poland, as every where else, land presents us with a scale of large varieties. This monstrous deception is practised upon us at present: we see little grain (little wheat, at any rate) which has not come from the higher qualities of soil; and naturally enough, because in Poland the population, as a whole, is scanty (relatively to the extent of ground), and the population, as a wheat-consuming population, is quite trivial. Hence it is that the development of rent has but commenced. But let England transfer her agriculture to Poland, instantaneously the very same cycle of effects will be traversed which in England has been traversed since 1775; soils of every quality will be called into action; rent will arise in its graduated series upon every separated quality; a race of wealthy farmers, stout yeomen, happy labourers, aristocratic landlords, will again arise; – but unhappily, however, it cannot be added – *and no mistake,* for there will be the capital mistake that, instead of our own natural brothers, this race will be all *owshis* and *wishis.* That, however, is a collateral theme; what I now wish to notice is – simply the effect upon price. Were the plan realized which is sanctioned by the present revolutionists, the grossest delusion would be unmasked which has ever duped a people. *This delusion consists in reasoning upon the basis of Baltic prices as they are or have been, though they themselves admit (by making it our crime) that never yet has a forty days' consumption been grown on our account.* Are these men maniacs? Do they suppose that the three hundred and sixty-five days' consumption of a race like the British can be produced by the Poles without a far worse development of rent and costs than with us? Land has been often, and most conveniently for purposes of argument, treated as a corn-manufacturing machine, subject only to the condition that these machines are of various powers. Now at present, merely the best machines are used. But a permanent demand from England, eight times and a-half greater than the greatest and

342   *Battles over Free Trade, Volume 1*

most memorable ever heard of, would at once create a run upon these machines, which in one revolving year would far more than reproduce the highest prices known amongst ourselves.

But this is not all: the pressure of rent advances slowly, and only in correspondence with the population, and, at any rate, this pressure is met and, relieved by the opposite process in manufactures. But, besides this compensation, in England, where agricultural skill is great and capital overflowing, we have other compensations, *sufflamina*, or drags, which retard the motion of price upwards, in the continual application of improved machinery or improved processes to our agriculture. The full weight of declension in the soil has never been suffered with us to make itself felt; it has been checked, thwarted, kept down in every stage by growing knowledge and growing wealth. In Poland none of these *sufflamina* will be available. I need not say that every thing will have to be erected; that without our laws and institutions and national energy it cannot be created, any more than an academy of belles lettres in Caffvania. And thus the full weight, unbroken, unimpeded, will descend upon prices from the decreasing qualities of the soil ranging through all the gamut, and from the absolute defect of the vast apparatus in roads, fences, canals, &c., as well as the more intellectual parts of that apparatus, which in Scotland and eastern England has travelled through centuries to a point of perfection.

This upon the *unconditional* adoption of the new proposals. But it will be urged in reply, – Suppose it conditional, and the importation to go on until the two prices, ours and the Baltic, meet in one level. I have already said, that in that case much fewer additions will need to be made in Poland, much fewer to be laid aside in England than is commonly supposed. A very moderate change in each country, a few of the worst qualities abandoned in England, a few of the upper qualities taken up in Poland, would bring the two countries to a level. But then the evil here will be (an evil as regards the absurd expectations of the poor), that exactly in proportion as the level will be easily accomplished, and without much convulsion to existing rights, exactly in that case will the relief be small. If two or three qualities of soil cashiered in England, and two or three added in Poland, bring the two vats to a level (and possibly no greater change would be required), in such a case 50s. or 48s. might be the permanent price in both countries. Now take the difference between that and 60s. (for as to our present prices, they are mere anomalies), and consider it in the way I have suggested at page 171; then one-fifth of the price being saved in bread,[1] and one-fifth of the poor man's expenditure being on bread, he *might* receive one-fifth of a fifth, or a twenty-fifth part more on his daily expenditure. And suppose wages to enter even to the extent of a half into the elements of price (as upon some rare articles

---

1   But observe, a declension of one-fifth on wheat would not give a declension of three-tenths on bread.

they may), the result would be the half of a twenty-fifth, that is, a fiftieth part in the price of goods.

But that calculation is of less importance. The main argument upon which we take our stand, is this dilemma built on the doctrine of Rent: the *cycle* of changes to be run through in transferring our agriculture in whole or in part to the Baltic provinces, is either wide or it is narrow, either great or small. Suppose it great, suppose, in fact, our corn manufactory absolutely transferred as a whole to Poland, and a cotton, iron, &c., manufactory substituted at home, – in that case the whole ladder of descent upon inferior soils must be run down in Poland, which has caused our own prices at home; and the whole series of increments in rent be traversed, which is the very ground of our domestic murmurs, but – for this must never be overlooked – with aggravations of this evil as much less mitigated than ours as Poland is less civilized, less enlightened, less wealthy, than Great Britain. On the other form of the dilemma, the case is not so bad, simply because it is not so thoroughly carried out: but, however, though a better result, it will be one of pure disappointment. For if there should be a long series of changes before the prices of England and Poland met at the same level, then there would be an approximation made to the enormous evil just stated; and if the series should turn out small, that would be because the level of coincidence would soon be effected; and then the alteration of price would be proportionately trifling.

Such is our argument from political economy, against the proposed change; but, were the change in itself better, every body wishing well to England, must thoroughly disapprove the intemperate (in some quarters the incendiary) mode of pursuing it. That, however, is a different theme. The upshot is this: it would cause a dreadful convulsion, if we could transfer our corn manufacture to a really cheaper country; but, by the argument here applied from Rent, it appears that there is no known country which in that case would be cheaper: we add, *or nearly as cheap.*

344   *Battles over Free Trade, Volume 1*

'Petitions', *Anti Corn-Law Circular*, 23 (23 January 1840); and 'Our Weapons of War', *Anti Corn -Law Circular*, 24 (6 February 1840).

PETITIONS.

Mr. Thompson, the delegate from Settle to the banquet left with the council of the League, sixteen petitions, eight to the Lords and eight to the Commons, praying for the total and immediate repeal of the corn laws.[1]

The Manchester petition is now in course of receiving signatures. 12,000 names were attached on Monday alone! This is as it should be. The weather is against it, being wet and stormy; but the people *will* sign, rain or no rain. The *fixed duty* men have had the lead of us, and, we speak it on the authority of scores, have procured numbers of signatures under the false representation that it was for total repeal. One canvasser, who, from his professions of *piety,* ought to have known better, has actually gone so far as to declare, that he is employed by the Anti Corn-Law League! We shall not lose sight of this worthy, of Sunday school notoriety though he be.

The villages and small towns in the neighbourhood, where Anti Corn-Law Associations have not yet been formed, may have heads of Petitions and sheets on application at the Manchester Association Rooms, Newall's-Buildings.

The following is a copy of the Manchester petition, which we give, because we think our friends all over the kingdom cannot do better than adopt the same:

To the Honourable the Commons of Great Britain and Ireland, in Parliament assembled.

The humble Petition of the Inhabitants of the Borough of Manchester; assembled at a Public Meeting, duly convened by the municipal authorities of the said Borough.

HUMBLY SHOWETH,

That a free exchange of the products of industry for the corn and food of other countries is the natural and inherent right of the people of every nation, – a right clearly recognized by the Creator Himself, in awarding to various climes the different productions of the earth for the common benefit of all His creatures.

That the corn law violates the sacred principles of religion and morality, by interposing a barrier between the bounties of divine Providence and the wants of the industrious millions of the country; thus depriving them of the means of independent subsistence, and subjecting them to the evils of disease, demoralization, and premature death.

That, at the present time, the baneful influences of the corn law are exerting themselves with peculiar severity upon the middle and working classes of the

1   [Ed.: List deleted.]

community; injuring the banker by the derangement of the currency; oppressing the merchant and dealer by the excessive rate of interest; annihilating the profits of the capitalist: and reducing to pauperism the industrious artizan and labourer: and that, unless repealed, this destructive law will, by banishing our manufactures to other countries, and throwing upon the soil the entire burden of supporting a destitute and unemployed population, involve the landowners with every other class in one common ruin.

Therefore, your Petitioners most humbly pray your Honourable House that the corn laws be entirely and immediately abolished.

And your Petitioners, as is duty bound, will ever pray.

[...]

'Petition! petition!! petition!!!' – WARBURTON.

We ask you, reader, what have you done towards the success of this our great struggle for justice? Excuse us that we make it a personal question. We are looking for a MILLION of signatures; have *you* signed? We have called upon all the parishes in the country to make known their opinions on this question of questions; have *you* assisted in this organization of public opinion?

Reader, whoever you may be, you have a direct and personal interest at stake on the issue; if you care for your own welfare, give evidence to that effect. Sign a petition for the repeal of the corn law; and, having set this good example to your neighbours and friends, agitate your district, organize the more intelligent repealers, aid in every practicable demonstration, and pass the word 'Petition!' throughout the entire breadth of the land, from parish to parish, from house to house, from man to man, until full and complete success shall have crowned our efforts, and distress be driven from the hearth-stones of the children of industry.

346 *Battles over Free Trade, Volume 1*

'Support of the Anti Corn-Law League by the Working Classes', *Anti Corn-Law Circular*, 26 (5 March 1840).

SUPPORT OF THE ANTI CORN-LAW LEAGUE BY THE WORKING CLASSES.

Twelve months ago, when the repeal of the corn laws was discussed in Parliament, the bread-taxers came forward, with a great deal of swagger, and denounced repeal as a mere agitation, on the part of the selfish manufacturers, for the purpose of filling their own pockets at the expense of the working classes. 'It is a labourers' question,' quoth Mr. Cayley, triumphantly; 'the manufacturers want cheap corn that they may reduce wages.' We were quite content to make it a labourers' question, for truly it is so; and when Parliament drove us from its bar, and refused to listen to us, we forthwith appealed from the representatives of the people to the people themselves. We sent lecturers all over the country to give the bread-taxers an opportunity of proving, before their own labourers, the charge, that we wanted to rob them of their wages. We felt strong in the righteousness of our cause, and confident that truth and justice must finally triumph, spite of all opposition. One would have thought, that the landlords would have gladly availed themselves of the opportunity we afforded them of exposing the knavery with which they charged us, and have held us up to the merited scorn of our fellow-countrymen. But, no! 'Conscience makes cowards of us all.' They knew that they had neither reason nor justice on their side, and they acted like men 'wise in their generation.' They determined we should not be heard through our lecturers, and they set on their stewards, agents, butlers, bailiffs, and retainers, to annoy them, by threatening with ruin every body who should dare to let a room for a lecture; and when, driven to hold meetings in the open air, our lecturers addressed the listening crowds, then the hired bullies came to kick up all sorts of disturbances, in some cases even throwing fire-works amongst the people.

The working men, many of whom at first believed the calumnies uttered against us, began to think it strange that our accusers, instead of being foremost to support their accusations, not only ran away from all discussion, but determined every where to prevent us from being heard. Englishmen love fair play; and when they saw the conduct of the bread-taxers, they began shrewdly to suspect that there must be *reasons* why they wished to stop our mouths; and so people were the more anxious to hear what we had to say. Besides lecturers, we established the *Anti Corn-Law Circular* to carry truth into every part of the empire. What have been the results? No cause has ever made so great progress in so short a period. Our opponents dare not face us in any part of the kingdom. The wise, the learned, the good of all denominations flock to our standard, support us with their money, aid us with their counsel, and cheer us with their blessings and prayers for our success.

Whilst we gratefully acknowledge the kindness and confidence of our friends in all parts of the kingdom, we cannot avoid the expression of the especial delight we have experienced in seeing our labours appreciated by the working classes, who have proved themselves not to be such noodles as the bread-taxers desired. Where is the working man who has heard our lecturers, or read the *Circular*, who does not know, that dear bread does *not* give him higher wages, but, on the contrary, gives him *less* employment. *Every man knows, by his own experience, that so recently as 1835, when corn was only half the price it is now, he had full employment and better wages than he gets at present, although he had to pay double the price for corn.* The working men have found out their real friends. They know that the corn laws were not passed for *their* benefit, but to keep up the price of corn and to give high rents to the landlords. They are giving the best evidence of their intelligence and determination to unite in abolishing the iniquitous law which taxes 'the bread of the needy' for the benefit of the pampered idler. They are forming Operative Anti Corn-Law Associations every where to the great dismay of the bread-taxers; nay, more, they are clubbing their shillings and pence to support the Anti Corn-Law League! In our *Circular* of the 6th ult., we acknowledged the receipt of £7 7s., which was voluntarily collected by the workmen of Mr. R. Platt, of Stalybridge, and presented, through their master, to the League. Our readers will see, in our present number, another acknowledgment of £2 10s. from the workmen of Mr. T. H. Clarke, of the Shakspeare Foundry, Wolverhampton: another of £5 from the hands employed by Samuel Matley and Son, printers, Mottram: another of £5 from Langholm, Dumfriesshire, contributed in sixpences and shillings by poor people! another from Langwith and Cuckney, two villages in Nottinghamshire, which, not having the fear of the Duke of Newcastle before their eyes, sent a deputy to the Banquet, with a present of £7 to the League, and they have now sent their monthly subscription of £1, collected by subscriptions of a penny per week! These noble villagers live in what is called the Dukery, in the neighbourhood of the Dukes of Newcastle and Portland, and Earl Manvers: we hope they are placed beyond the reach of the malignity and oppression of the *ig*nobleman who dared to claim 'the right of doing what he liked with his own' (other men's consciences).

It is gratifying to receive the support of the rich; indeed, without it our labours could not be carried on: but, we doubt not, it will be as gratifying to them as it is to us to witness the testimonies of earnestness and good-will in our holy cause by the working classes; their contributions, like the widow's mite, sanctifies all the rest, and seals our triumph. 'Thanks for cheap postage,' which, though it brings us occasional anonymous bread-tax scurrilities, brings us also daily cheering evidences of the progress of our cause, particularly amongst the labouring classes;

nor is it the least pleasing privilege to receive such constant acknowledgment, from good men, of our services, and blessings on our efforts in the cause of 'the poor and needy.' We have lying before us a letter from a venerable correspondent at Greenfield, near Lancaster, who says, 'Although I am now in the 80th year of my age, I feel anxious to live to see justice done to the poor starving labourer, the mechanic, and the ignorant and misled farmer.' God, grant the good man's wish! to which, we are certain, our readers will respond a hearty AMEN!

'Address of the Metropolitan Anti Corn-Law Association', *Anti Corn-Law Circular*, 29 (26 March 1840).

ADDRESS OF THE METROPOLITAN ANTI CORN-LAW ASSOCIATION.

Fellow-Citizens,–Fellow-Countrymen,–Of whatsoever class, order, or sect, we invoke your aid and cooperation in our cause, which is neither that 'of party nor of faction, nor of any individual,' but truly and impressively 'that of every man in Britain.'

The baneful effects of the corn laws, which restrict the supply of the first and imperative necessaries of life, are daily assuming a more frightful and alarming character.

By depressing our commerce: by deranging the currency and monetary affairs of the country:

By paralysing our manufactures at home, and creating rivals abroad:

By diminishing and rendering uncertain and fluctuating the demand for labour:

By reducing wages at the time provisions are dearest, creating poverty and destitution to a frightful magnitude, increasing pauperism and crime, and lowering the physical and moral condition of the whole labouring classes:

By sowing the seeds of anarchy and discontent, which ripen in deeds of open violence against the law, rendering life and property insecure:

By exciting animosity and jealousy between the most important leading classes of the community, whose true and lasting interests are inseparable: and finally,

By exposing to frequent and violent fluctuations the whole economy of society and industry, destroying all reliance and security on the future, and thus weakening the greatest moral tie which Providence has linked to our nature.

With these views we appeal to the whole of our fellow-countrymen; we invoke the aid of all, because we are persuaded there exists no one whose true interests would not be consulted by the removal of these crying evils; but more especially we call upon our fellow-citizens of this great metropolis, energetically, to unite with us in this great cause of wisdom, justice, and benevolence, and by their efforts to give increased force and encouragement to those of the whole country.

We invoke all! We appeal to all! Without hesitation we approach the *landed interest*, and we ask their aid:

First, Because if these laws, enacted with the intention of benefitting them, were capable of fully effecting this object, it would only be greatly injuring the other interests of society, and, therefore, the advantage could not be permanent.

350   *Battles over Free Trade, Volume 1*

Second, Because these laws have not only most signally failed in their professed object, to secure high and uniform prices; but, on the contrary, have produced great and violent fluctuation, all the evils of which have been most strikingly experienced by the landed interest.[1]

Third, Because experience has shown that monopoly of every description, by creating reliance on protection, however false and ineffectual, tends, nevertheless, to paralyse and destroy the natural and healthy energy of the mind, by which alone the true and lasting interests of society are promoted, ingenuity encouraged, and improvements secured.

Fourth, Because we agree with the Parliamentary Committee of 1821, on the state of agriculture, when they say in their report, 'Your committee may entertain a doubt whether the only solid foundation of the flourishing state of agriculture is not laid in abstaining, as much as possible, from interference, either by protection or prohibition, with the application of capital in any branch of industry.' And,

Fifth, As an unemployed population must finally come upon the land for support, it follows that the landed interest can be in a prosperous condition only so long as the demand for labour expands with the increase of population. It is equally clear that this demand can arise only from an increase of manufactures, as the land cannot employ one half of the present population, much less an increasing number.[2] It is, therefore, evident, that injury to our manufacturing interest is destructive of the prosperity of the landed proprietor.

We appeal to the capitalist, the banker, and the whole money interest for co-operation. The occurrences of the past year sufficiently prove the baneful influence which these laws exercise in deranging the currency, destroying the balance of existing arrangements, producing panic and distrust, and seriously affecting the vital functions of commerce and of national credit.[3]

---

1   In 1835, when wheat was 39s. per quarter, the home growers supplied the whole consumption at this low price, except 34,000 quarters, at a cost of £76,000, paid for foreign wheat.

In 1839, when wheat reached 70s. per quarter, the enormous quantity of 2,700,131 quarters of foreign wheat was brought into competition with the landed interest; and took away from our shores upwards of seven millions sterling of gold.

2   In 1811, 895,998 families were engaged in agriculture in Great Britain. In 1831, 961,134 families were so engaged, being an increase of only 65,136 families in twenty years; or, reckoning six peasants a family, an increase of 390,816 individuals. And this is about the increase of the population every year, showing that the population increases twenty times as fast as the land has been able to employ them. In 1811, 1,129,049 families were engaged in Great Britain in trade and manufactures. In 1831, 1,434,873, being an increase of 305,824 families, or nearly two million of individuals.

3   On the 5th of October, 1838 and 1839, the bullion and deposits on the Bank of England stood thus:

	DEPOSITS	BULLION
October 5, 1838	10,012,000	9,645,000
October 5, 1839	7,781,000	2,806,000

'*Address of the Metropolitan Anti-Corn Law Association*' (1840)   351

We ask the whole mercantile world to be with us; to aid and assist us. For if the price of the first great necessary of life fluctuate so much; of that article of which a sufficient supply must first be secured at whatever price, before anything else is thought of, it follows that the fluctuating character of the price of grain must necessarily create similar fluctuations in the demand of all other articles; especially those great leading articles contributory to our manufacturing industry. It must also be obvious that any laws which tend to circumscribe and give a character of uncertainty to the demand for our manufactures, must have a similar influence on the business of our merchants, which can only be derived from the exports of those products and the imports received in exchange for them. If, therefore, by the operation of this law, there be a tendency in our manufactures to sink in competition with those of other countries, the tendency must be at the same time to renounce our commerce in favour of those countries.

The commercial interests generally are peculiarly injured by these operations; first, by the derangement of the currency, by which money is rendered scarce and dear – secondly, by reducing the demand for foreign produce, and thereby producing serious losses and embarrassment to our merchants. Consult the experience of 1839.[1]

Our merchants are, further, deeply interested in this cause. The importation of foreign grain which, because it is accidental and uncertain, is replete with these serious evils, would, if uniform and regular, though only to the same amount that it is at present, become a source of healthy and profitable trade, courted, like all other business, instead of exciting, as at present, the fears and alarms of the whole money and mercantile interests.

To traders, therefore, of every class, we appeal for support; whatever their position, from the most extensive merchant to the smallest retailer. To all it must be a most important object that the price of food should be moderate and uniform, which never can be the case under laws of prohibition and monopoly.

To the working classes we appeal with feelings of the deepest sympathy, convinced as we are of the great suffering and privation to which the operations of these laws expose them. We rely with confidence on their aid and assistance; we

---

with a debt incurred to a foreign bank of 2,500,000, to make out means of paying for foreign wheat.

1   In 1838 and 1839, the following quantities of the articles enumerated were taken into consumption, by official statements, all bearing on the industry of the country.

	1838	1839
Cotton Wool	160,756,013 lbs.	355,781,960 lbs.
Sheeps Wool	56,415,460 lbs.	53,221,231 lbs.
Raw Silk	3,683,738 lbs.	3,483,363 lbs.
Flax, &c.	1,625,080 cwt.	1,228,894 cwt.

And all the contributory articles to manufactures show a corresponding decrease, in dye stuffs, &c. &c.; and, therefore, to this extent, must have limited the demand for labour.

invite them to come and join us cordially; to come and co-operate with us, in all lawful, peaceful, but determined and persevering means, for a repeal of these laws.

Laws which abridge the market for labour, and lower its price:

Laws which limit the supply of the first necessaries of life in a rapidly increasing population, and enhance their cost:

Laws which refuse to us the bountiful gifts which Providence, in his wisdom, showers upon some parts of the earth, while there may be a deficient season in this country; until prices shall have risen so high, that the cost of provisions tends materially further to diminish the demand for labour, and to lower the rate of wages when bread is at the highest point.

Laws which tend to increase crime, and to enhance the public burthens in order to suppress it; and at the moment of the most severe pressure on the means of subsistence, to demand fresh taxation.

Such are the laws we crave your assistance to abolish; such is the misery we ask you to lend a hand to alleviate.

We have not the less confidence in your aid, because the evils which have already visited your fellow-men in the manufacturing districts, have not yet visited you in this metropolis in the same agonizing, heart-rending, appalling form, they have assumed amongst them; you have many friends amongst them for whom you feel; you read in the daily journals of all political parties the revolting details of their misery and sufferings; you have sympathy to feel for their distress; you have judgment and intelligence to know that their lot to-day may, ere long, be yours.

Above all, we invoke the warm and cordial co-operation of the whole religious and benevolent public – of the ministers of the gospel of all denominations – of the philanthropist and friend of the poor – of the members of the medical profession – we call upon all zealously to unite with us, to ameliorate the condition of our fellow working men, to put an end to those causes which ever and anon reduce this valuable portion of society to the greatest poverty, destitution, and want – which impair their physical condition, generate disease, and send thousands of suffering children to an untimely grave – which destroy and break down the great bulwark of virtue and morality – self-respect; and give rise to an immense increase of crime, depravity, and irreligion.

Finally, then, permit us, fellow-citizens, solemnly to appeal to your sympathy – to your intelligence – to invoke your aid and co-operation: – for, deeply assured as we are that our object, the *Repeal of the Corn Laws*, is for the welfare of all, it must be the imperative duty of all to assist in its accomplishment.

'Manifestation of Public Feeling on the Bread Tax', *Anti Corn-Law Circular*, 32 (23 April 1840).

MANIFESTATION OF PUBLIC FEELING ON THE BREAD TAX.

When motions for the repeal of the bread tax have been brought forward year after year, in the House of Bread-taxers, it has been usually urged that there has been no expression of public feeling against the infamous law, – 'there is no agitation in the country on the subject, say the honourable bread-taxers, and, therefore, the people do not wish for repeal.' Last year petitions signed by half a million, praying for repeal, were presented. The honourable House, calling themselves the representatives of the people, put the petitions under the table. The people, indignant at this insulting conduct, held meetings in every part of the country, passed resolutions expressive of their indignation, and again in double numbers demanded the restitution of those rights, which an unjust legislature has taken away, namely, 'The right of the people to earn their bread by the sweat of their brow.' The public voice can be no longer misunderstood, but what say the bread-taxers now? Why, 'that attempts are made to agitate the public mind by itinerant missionaries, that the house ought not to listen to agitators, that it is not consistent with its dignity to be coerced into repeal,' and so the honourable bread-taxers again excuse themselves from doing justice to the people. How long this farce is to be acted, remains with the electors to determine. Mr. Villiers's motion will be renewed on the 12th May next, when it will be seen who are for, and who against the wicked bread-tax.

The petitions for a repeal of the corn law have swelled to a number far beyond our anticipations; and the signatures will, we believe, be more numerous this session than have been attached to petitions on any subject whatever for the last twenty years. The following is the statement, according to the last published return:

CORN-LAW PETITIONS.
SESSION OF 1840 – UP TO MARCH 31, 1840.
WHOLE OF SESSION, 1839.

	Pets.	*Sigs.*	*Pets.*	*Sigs.*
For repeal	2,807	1,150,939	409	516,568
Against repeal	3,194	221,681	3,086	318,723
For alteration	22	59,638	17	10,176

It is believed that ere Mr. Villiers' motion is repeated, the number will be increased to one million four hundred thousand. Will parliament slight the prayers of so immense a proportion of the people of this country, including all the branches of that great manufacturing interest, upon the prosperity of which, by the admission of Sir Robert Peel, '*the maintenance of our position in the scale of nations depends?*' We are certain it cannot long continue to slight them. If the people remain true to themselves, and if the manufacturers and merchants of England and Scotland put forth the energy they possess, with the persevering determination which so great an object calls for, they must ere long succeed. They have on their side all the power of *Justice;* and we never knew a just cause which had obtained a proper hold on the moral sense of the people, defeated in this country. Justice to all classes, and humanity to the labouring class, demand that the tax on bread shall be removed, and that every man shall be allowed to buy his bread where he can get it cheapest.

It is worthy of remark, that whilst the number of petitioners for the *repeal* of the bread-tax this year are more than double those of last year, the petitioners in favour of the bread-tax are fewer than last year, and this, be it observed, not from any lack of zeal on the part of the landlords, nor, we regret to say, of the clergy either, to get up petitions against repeal, but because the people refuse to sign petitions in favour of the bread-tax unless *compelled* to do so. On this subject we have the most gratifying details from all parts of the country. The stewards, bailiffs, and agents of the landlords, have not been wanting in exertions, but above all the parsons have been most zealous, not in praying in the language of the liturgy for *'cheapness and plenty,'* but in going from house to house persuading and threatening people to sign petitions in favour of a law which makes the bread of the poor *'scarce and dear.'* One reverend bread-taxer employed himself in the apostolical duty of going round to all the labourers in his parish with an ink-bottle at his button-hole and a bread-tax petition in his hand, even following ploughmen into the fields; but his labourers did not meet the reward he anticipated – the majority of the labourers refused to sign, although he was not sparing in his anathemas, threatening in one instance to exclude a poor man from the communion table because he dared to say that 'he did not know what benefit dear bread was to poor folks.'

The landlords every where have been obliged to use threats to obtain signatures to bread-tax petitions. We notice in the appendix to the 21st report of printed petitions, one from the owners and occupiers of land, and others, in the parish of Goring, Durrington, and West Tarring, in the county of Sussex, in which the petitioners say, 'that they highly disapprove of the system which is now pursued by certain great landowners, of employing agents and others to procure a petition from each parish in this part of the country in favour of the corn laws, and requiring their tenants to subscribe to the same.' They go on very sensibly to say, *'that if the landlords will regulate their rents by the value of their land and by the price of corn, we are not apprehensive of any such calamitous results as are described in the several petitions which the agents and others above alluded to have laid before us for our signatures.'*

Will the landlords learn a lesson from petitions like these? If not, when the insolvent bread-taxers present themselves again at the hustings, we trust the people will teach them that 'honesty is the best policy.'

'Corn-Law Agitation Humbug', *Chartist Circular*, 59 (7 November 1840), p. 243.

CORN-LAW AGITATION HUMBUG

The Corn-law repealers are eternally dinning into the people's ears that the landlords are tyrants, and that commerce is calculated to render men '*the unflinching enemies of oppression.*' The Corn-law repealers should not flatter the commercial classes, at the expense of truth. Instead of rendering men '*the unflinching enemies of oppression,*' commerce has hitherto been the greatest destroyer of liberty ever known to man, not excepting priestcraft itself. By whom were the natives of Africa torn from friends and home, and sold to bitter bondage all their days? By commercial men. By whom is the remorseless lash wielded over the bleeding slave's back in Britain's colonies, and even in republican America? By commercial men. By whom has Hindostan been plundered and enslaved for tow hundred years? By commercial men. By whom were the simple aborigines of America and the West Indies slaughtered like sheep, and hunted down with mastiffs let loose against their naked limbs, three centuries ago? By commercial men. By whom are the liberties of the United States threatened with destruction, and her working citizens with European misery, and bondage? By her commercial men. By whom are 30,000,000 of Frenchmen at present robbed of their civil rights, and made the hopeless prey of mammon and arbitrary power? By an armed shopocracy of commercial men. By whom is England herself, the most enlightened and laborious nation of all times, ancient and modern, by whom is this magnificent country now enslaved and pauperized? By her commercial men. By whom were the Dorchester labourers and the Glasgow cotton-spinners transported – the Coercion and the New Poor-Law Acts passed – and a *gens d'armie* projected to act as spies and persecutors of our rural population? By a parliament and ministry of commercial men. Away, away, then, with the revolting cant which would unite commerce and liberty in the same breath. Heaven and hell are not more diametrically opposed to each other than is commerce to heaven-born liberty.

BRONTERRE [O'BRIEN]

356 *Battles over Free Trade, Volume 1*

'The Bread-Taxing Bishops and the Bible-Reading People', *Anti Corn-Law Circular*, 47 (19 November 1840).

THE BREAD-TAXING BISHOPS AND THE BIBLE-READING PEOPLE.

It is a curious subject for inquiry, how it is that the bishops and the people, both acknowledging the Bible to be the word of God, and taking its *precepts* for their guide, have so frequently adopted an opposite *practice*.

The people seeing it declared in Holy Writ that 'God hath made of one blood all the nations upon earth,' that 'He is no respecter of persons,' were shocked to see their brethren, who happened to have black skins, bought and sold like cattle, and, deeming such a traffic inhuman and unchristian, they earnestly set to work to abolish it. The bishops, reading and professing to teach, the same scriptures, declared the purchase and sale of immortal beings was not an ungodly practice, and *all, save one, voted for the slave trade*. The people again seeing it written, 'Train up a child in the way he should go;' 'Search the scriptures,' felt bound to carry out those injunctions, and as the best means of doing so, they established Sunday Schools, Lancasterian Schools, Bible Societies, Tract Societies, and innumerable others, for improving the moral and religious character of the community. What did the bishops? Why every effort to carry into effect these laudable designs, they discountenanced and opposed.

What a glorious conquest has Christianity achieved through the bible-reading people! Where is the bishop now who dares to outrage public decency by voting for slavery, or by *openly* opposing societies for the spread of religious truth. But there are still farther triumphs in store, for it is written, 'He that withholdeth corn the people shall curse him;' 'The bread of the needy is his life, he that defraudeth him thereof is a man of blood,' and yet, in the face of these solemn denunciations, we see the bishops, year after year, voting for the bread-tax!!!

What a delightful contrast does the conduct of the bible-reading people present to that of the bishops. – God declares those to be 'men of blood' who defraud the needy of their bread. The honest simple-minded say, 'no expediency can sanction the bread-tax; it is opposed to God's law, and therefore it is wicked; it ought to be, it must, *and it shall be abolished*;'– and so they receive our lecturers 'gladly.' In many cases, where our lecturers have been invited, a minister, or some other good man, has opened or closed the proceedings with a suitable prayer, or by singing a hymn. Some of the Anti-Corn Law Associations, before they commence their business, invoke the divine blessing on their own labours and on ours.

Prayers like these as *incense* rise

'The Bread-Taxing Bishops and the Bible-Reading People' (1840)   357

To him who dwells above the skies.

We are constantly receiving the most pleasing evidence from all quarters of the spread of religious feeling connected with our holy cause, and we have now before us an interesting letter from a place we never before heard of, and which shews that the *Anti-corn Law Circular* is penetrating to the most remote parts of the empire. We are daily receiving communications from places, which, without the aid of the Gazetteer, we should be unable to know where to find. We thank God for this manifestation of the progress of our cause.

A correspondent at Broad Winsor says –

'I am happy to inform you that we have formed an association in a neighbouring parish, which, commencing with fifteen members, now numbers thirty. We take in fifteen of the *Circulars*, meet every fortnight, when, after reading a portion of scripture and a prayer having been offered, a short address is given, and the business closes with receiving fresh members.'

We wish, when the bread tax is brought before Parliament next session, the bishops would meet together in the spirit of our poor christian friends at Broad Winsor, and then let them go to the House of Lords, and after praying for 'daily bread,' lay their hands on their hearts, and in the face of heaven, vote for the bread-tax if they dare.

Our correspondent gives us an extract from a letter written by one of the many thousands who are driven from the land of their fathers by the inhuman bread-tax. It is pleasing to see that they have a lively sympathy towards the oppressed whom they leave behind. Many a prayer daily ascends to heaven for our success, from our dear countrymen in distant lands.

'I received (says our correspondent) from a dissenting minister (Mr. A. Robinson, late of Hawkchurch, Devon) who has been obliged to leave his country from the fear of starving had he remained here, a letter, from which I send you an extract.

'My wife is engaged in teaching the children, 109 of whom are on board. There are considerably upwards of 200 emigrants on board, several amongst them truly pious, many of them truly careless. It is remarkable that, however they may differ in other peculiarities, they are all agreed to leave their native country for a foreign land, in the cheerful hope of obtaining bread for themselves and families, which the oppressions of their native land have denied them. I think I may write in the name of most on board, that though we voluntarily leave our country and all that is dear to us there, except our nearest and dearest relatives, which most of us are taking with us; yet could we have obtained bread in our own land, we should never have thought of braving the dangers of the deep, and going to the antipodes to seek it. Though we leave our country, we shall watch its interests with anxiety, and shall be glad to hear that you are delivered from one of its greatest curses, viz., the Corn Law, which has set itself insultingly in defiance of the laws of God, of justice, and of the common rights of man. 'He that withholdeth corn the people shall curse him; but it is to be feared that curse will be succeeded by a more fearful one, when the great Legislator of the universe shall appear to judge the world in equity and truth.'

We shall send a copy of the present *Circular* to each of the Bishops; peradventure the above beautiful epistle of a Christian minister, may awaken serious reflections in their minds on the wicked course they have hitherto pursued in 'defrauding the needy of their bread,' by voting for the infamous Bread-tax.

'Petition! Petition! Petition!', *Anti Corn-Law Circular*, 48 (3 December 1840).

PETITION! PETITION! PETITION!

Warburton.

The time approaches when the question of the corn laws will again be discussed in the House of Commons, and every man who thinks the bread tax an evil, should let his opinion go before parliament.

This can be done by no other means than by petitioning.

He who thinks the bread tax an evil, and who still neglects to petition, neglects his duty.

To obtain the abolition of all taxes on food, is the object of the National Anti Corn-Law League. To obtain that object, they require support and co-operation. By petitioning you afford that co-operation.

Your adversaries will endeavour to get up petitions in favour of the bread tax from every village, nay, almost from every farm-house in the country. How is this to be counteracted? By similar means, – by petitioning.

A petition may be written on a sheet of paper. Every manufactory, every warehouse, every shop, every individual, should have a petition; and the following forms will answer the purpose. The petitions may be sent to Mr. Villiers, Mr. Warburton, Mr. Hume, or any other member of parliament, or to the council of the National Anti Corn Law League, Manchester: –

GENERAL PETITION.

To the honourable the Commons of Great Britain and Ireland in Parliament assembled.

The petition of the undersigned inhabitants of (here state the name of the place.)

Humbly sheweth,

That the prohibitions and duties upon the importation of foreign corn and other provisions, impose a heavy tax upon the food of the people of this country, – a tax that has been estimated by Messrs. J. D. Hume and J. M'Gregor, individuals filling the highest offices in the Board of Trade, to amount to upwards of fifty millions sterling a year.

That the taxes and prohibitions upon food enable the owners of the soil to augment enormously their own incomes at the expense of every other class of the community.

That if the language of warning and remonstrance were permitted by the rules of your honourable house, your petitioners would speak in terms commensurate with the enormity of the evil of which they complain. They entreat your honourable house, however, to weigh well the dangers that must impend over the wealth, peace, and happiness of the empire, so long as the welfare of the great majority of the people is sacrificed by partial and unjust laws to the interests of the few.

Therefore, your petitioners most earnestly and humbly pray that your honourable house will immediately set an example of religion and morality by totally abolishing the inhuman bread tax.

And your petitioners will ever pray.

WORKMEN'S PETITION.

To the honourable the Commons of Great Britain and Ireland in Parliament assembled.

The petition of (here state the designation of the petitioners as, for instance, the workmen employed in the manufactory of Mossrs. A. and B.)

Humbly sheweth,

1. That your petitioners are working men, having no other property but in the labour of their hands.

2. That your honourable house has repeatedly acknowledged that you cannot keep up the rate of wages by act of parliament.

3. That, nevertheless, your honourable house has passed a law to raise the price of the workman's bread, by which the rent of land is kept up.

4. That your petitioners consider it very unjust to pass a law to raise the price of food, and, at the same time, to confess that you are not able to pass a law to keep up wages.

5. That your petitioners, therefore, humbly pray your honourable house to blot, at once and for ever, the bread tax from the statute book.

And your petitioners will over pray.

Societies and individuals are requested to put themselves into communication with the League.

Prepared sheets for petitions will be furnished on application at the Rooms of the League, 5, Newall's Buildings, Market-street, Manchester.

'Mr. John Gladstone's Remedy for the Distress of the Working Classes', *Liverpool Mercury*, 21 May 1841.

A short time ago Mr. John Gladstone favoured the world with his ideas on the corn laws, through the medium of a letter to the *Morning Post*. In this letter he endeavoured to show that the said corn laws are the perfection of human wisdom, and that any alteration in them must be prejudicial to all classes of the community, consumers included. This conclusion he arrived at by the aid of fallacies and assumptions a thousand times refuted, and these put together in a style which would have disgraced a schoolboy; but he evidently thought his own production a master-piece – a complete demolition of the Anti-Corn-law League, and in this idea he was flattered and confirmed by the Tory journalists generally, who quoted his letter and lauded its author to the skies. Encouraged by this reception, Mr. Gladstone has written another long letter to the *Post*, in utter condemnation of the Chancellor's Budget. In this letter he contends that any alteration in the timber duties must be most prejudicial to our North American colonists and to the shipping interest – that the introduction of foreign sugar at a protecting duty of 50 per cent. must be fatal to the West Indies, though he says that the planters would maintain the contest until they were utterly ruined; and with regard to the corn laws he contends, as before, that the substitution of a fixed for a prohibitory duty would produce not the slightest benefit to any class of the community, whilst it would be most injurious to the agricultural interest. We are too much pressed for space to examine his arguments or criticise his style, – which are worthy of each other, and we must therefore content ourselves with the concluding paragraph of his letter, which is as follows: –

'I venture to say to the manufacturer, do not delude and deceive yourselves by false hopes, or continue to persevere in requiring changes in the policy of the country, that, in my opinion, would, if adopted *as I trust they will not be* in the end, spread ruin and dismay throughout the community, from which they could not escape participating in – let them seek for the *true* causes of the distress they are now suffering under, and apply the remedy to remove it which, I believe, rests with themselves alone, before it may be too late; the cause I believe to be *over production*, supply beyond demand; whilst that demand, after making due allowances for interruptions, occasioned but temporary, yet inseparable from the nature of commerce, has, I believe, in the aggregate, undergone no diminution of a permanent character, but continues gradually to increase, whilst on the other hand, the increase of production has grown with great rapidity, stimulated by grievous success, and the application of overgrown capital, applied to the creation of new spinning mills in endless numbers, and of corresponding manufactures, which cover extensive districts of the country, and have hitherto brought up and given employment to a most extensive mass of population, dependent on these means for employment, which to afford them, has caused their rates of wages to be reduced to the lowest terms; and that are now threatened, from their increasing numbers, with still further diminished means of employment. I confess it is frightful to contemplate such a state of things, and of society, but it can no longer be concealed; and yet the only remedy seems to be, to diminish their sources of employment in order to produce future or permanent good; the love of gain, chastened by loss, will abate, and more limited, but safer undertakings will, in time, I hope, restore prosperity to all; but it is said, 'that whilst the grass grows the steed may starve' – to avoid this, increased means for emigration will, I trust, be provided, and, fortunately, we possess a field for beneficial employment in our distant colonies for the industrious and well-disposed; to emigrate may, to many, be a painful alternative, but it seems now to be the only one left to us for the excess of our population of all classes.'

This is about as rich a specimen of the bother'em style of composition as we ever met withal. It is, however, only a fair specimen of the whole; and yet, speaking of this letter, our contemporary of the *Liverpool Standard* says, –

The observations of Mr. Gladstone on political or commercial topics are always acceptable, and commend themselves to attention by the evident maturity of consideration from which they flow, and the perspicuous and pleasing manner in which they are conveyed. His letters would serve as a model of style for treating such subjects, &c., &c.

There is no accounting for taste certainly, but in our humble opinion the editor of the *Standard* must either be quizzing Mr. Gladstone, or he must have very comical notions of 'perspicuity' and models of style. A composition more contemptible in both respects could hardly have been put together. But we have to deal with more serious matters than verbal criticism. Mr. Gladstone has discovered the cause of the existing distress and its remedy. The cause is *'over production,'* in other words, too much employment for 'a most extensive mass of population,' and the only remedy less employment. There are in the manufacturing districts thousands upon thousands of people who have only three or four days work in the week; there are many who have none at all; and both classes with their families are now suffering under the most frightful distress. And what is the remedy proposed by the rich Mr. Gladstone – the pious, Church-building, Hill-Cooly trafficking Mr. Gladstone? To open new markets for our manufactures – to secure and extend the old ones – to diminish the burdens which grind the industrious classes to the dust? No, but to *'diminish their sources of employment,'* and then, says he, 'the love of gain, chastened by loss, will abate, and more limited, but safer undertakings, will, in time, restore prosperity to all.' The planter's 'love of gain,' the love of gain felt and acted upon by monopolists of every degree, must not be 'chastened by loss,' – they must still batten on their prey; and as for the starving operatives, – 'diminish their sources of employment,' exclaims good Mr. Gladstone, – 'kill them off, – or let them come to work, with the Hill-Coolies, on my sugar plantations in Demerara.' No, Mr. Gladstone, we possess 'a field for beneficial labour at home.' Our means and resources, if left unshackled by legislation for class interests, at the expense of the community at large, are amply sufficient to provide 'beneficial employment' for all. A new era is dawning upon us. The people are beginning to open their eyes to the gross fraud, injustice, and delusion which have been practised upon them. A patriotic Administration has announced the general good to be the grand object of legislation, – and the howling of the wolves, and the discordant screams of the birds of prey are good omens of the coming change. John Bull is proverbially one of the most gullible of God Almighty's creatures – but once convince him that he has been cheated and robbed, and then let the swindlers and robbers beware. He will be content with less than justice; – he now offers to accept it; but deny him that, and he may insist upon revenge as well as restitution.

Protectionist Editorial, *Chelmsford Chronicle*, 28 May 1841.

We are happy to find that our appeals in the cause of Agriculture have not been made in vain. The farmers of the county are now bestirring themselves. In addition to the public meeting at Colchester, the Committee of the East Essex Agricultural Society on Saturday last assembled, and took measures to promote petitions from every parish in the district; an influential meeting of occupiers, at Purleigh, have recorded their opinions; the Chelmsford Society, and the Hinckford Club, assemble for the same purpose this day, and the Dengie Hundred Association tomorrow, when every tenant in those districts, if true to his own and his neighbour's interest, will be present; 54 petitions have already been presented by Mr. Bramston to the Commons, and we hope the Societies at Epping, Avely, Dunmow, Braintree, Coggeshall, Halstead, and elsewhere do not intend to remain silent and inactive beneath the coming attack. In parochial petitions the plan is generally adopted of placing the amount of assessment opposite the name. This is good. It shows that the signatures have not been caught in gin palaces or bought by the score at street-corners. But let not the labourers be forgotten. They have a deeper stake in the question than even the occupiers of the soil; in general they have the sound sense to understand this, and considering their position, and the attempts which have been made to mislead them, the word 'labourer' would have as powerful an effect on upon the Legislature as the entry of a heavy mass may get. Let, then, the parochial petitions be laid before them. Let it be impressed upon their minds, in the words of a handbill which has been circulated in this county –

'That for every quarter of Foreign Corn brought into this country a quarter of home-grown Corn will be displaced, and the labour required to produce that Corn rendered useless.

'That with the fixed rates of duty proposed by the Government, Foreign Wheat can be brought into this country and sold with a profit at less than 40s. per quarter.

'That a farmer receiving only 40s. per quarter for Wheat would be obliged to pay his labourer one-third less wages than he does when he receives 60s. per quarter.

'That the wages paid to the agricultural labourers in those Countries in which Corn is cheap, and from which Great Britain must be supplied, are as follows: –

Odessa: 4d. per day

Poland & Russia: 5d. per day

Spain & Portugal: 7d. per day

Denmark & Germany: 9d per day

The average of wages in the above-named countries being only 6¼d. per day; and moreover the food of the labourers in those countries, consists *not of wheaten, but of rye bread.*

Protectionist Editorial (1841)

'That whilst the reduction of 20s. per quarter in the price of Wheat, will be the means of depriving one-half of the labourers of their employment and reducing the weekly wages of the remainder at least one-third per week, it will not enable them to buy their bread at 2d. per quartern loaf less than at present, *consequently an able-bodied labourer must give up one-third of his wages to save 2d. in the price of each loaf.*

Let them understand these facts; and let other classes, too, understand, that if agriculture should become so depressed that it would require years to restore it again to an efficient state, Prussia and Russia would probably levy a duty upon the export of corn, thus raising wheat to, perhaps, its present price; and the difference would go to enrich the foreigner instead of coming into the pockets of the landlord, the farmer, and the labourer, to be by them distributed amongst the tradesmen and shopkeepers of the country. And then farewell to the dream of Englishmen becoming the Manufacturers for the world! With the gold drained from us for food, and the riches secured by way of revenue upon it, the corn-exporting kingdoms of the continent would establish and encourage manufactures for themselves, and leave England in a state of dependence and poverty, to deplore its own short-sightedness.

H. N. Burroughes and E. Wodehouse, Joint Election Address to the Electors of East Norfolk, *Norfolk Chronicle and Norwich Gazette*, 12 June 1841.

TO THE ELECTORS OF THE EASTERN DIVISION OF THE COUNTY OF NORFOLK.

AS *an immediate Dissolution of Parliament is now openly declared, we beg leave at once to address you in the hope of being re-instated in your service. We rest our pretensions to your Support on the avowal of those Conservative Principles which a few years ago mainly recommended us to your favour, and which in the present crisis of affairs, we feel it to be our bounden duty to repeat and to maintain. With respect to the Scheme proposed by Her Majesty's Government for taking away the basis on which the Admission of Foreign Grain is now regulated, we feel convinced that you will concur with us in the opinion, that it strikes at the very root of that Protection which is essential to the Safety of Domestic Agriculture. In common with every person throughout the Empire we lament the Distress in which the great Manufacturing Districts of the Country are now placed; but we are prepared to contend that to attribute either the origin of that Distress to the Corn Laws, or to say that the Repeal of the Corn Laws alone would provide a Remedy, is a Delusion of a most mischievous Character, and one which the quiet sense of the people, unless excited and goaded into credulity by misfortune, would both reject and despise. We forbear to touch upon other topics, conceiving that those to which we have particularly referred are those in which you are more immediately interested.*

We trust that it is hardly necessary for us to assure you, that the future consideration of these subjects will have our earnest and devoted attention, and with the liveliest sense of the obligations with which we have been already honored.

We beg to subscribe ourselves, Gentlemen,
Your very faithful Servants,
EDMOND WODEHOUSE
H.N. BURROUGHES.

London, June 9th, 1841.

John Bowring, Election Address, *Bolton Chronicle*, 26 June 1841.

TO THE ELECTORS OF THE BOROUGH OF BOLTON.

GENTLEMEN, – I cannot but deem it a signal honour to have been considered worthy of your friendly notice in this important crisis of our commercial, financial, and political history.

We are engaged no longer in the petty personal strife of Whig and Tory factions struggling for place and power. Our contest now has a nobler purpose, and calls upon us for greater exertions and sacrifices. We demand FREE TRADE, the *Magna Charta of Labour*. We insist on the overthrow of those huge monopolies, by which the operative, the manufacturer, and the merchant are insulted and oppressed; monopolies which cruelly sacrifice the labouring many to the ruling few; monopolies which deprive the poor man of the hard-earned recompense of his daily toil: which narrow the markets of the world, or compel us to enter them under many disadvantages; monopolies whose fearful and mournful consequences are seen in that distress which has made such ruinous inroads among our peaceful and industrious population.

In that distress, Bolton has sadly participated. You know its cause, Gentlemen, and you must provide a remedy. To the Electors of Great Britain impoverished millions look for a relief of their sufferings. And may they not look in vain.

It is under the disguise of *protection*, that mask for fraud and pillage – that this grievous mischief has been inflicted upon us. *Protection!* But what *protection* have the multitudes who are clamouring for bread? What *protection* have the owners of the untenanted and abandoned dwellings, which tell too plainly the tale of various misery? What *protection* has the manufacturer for 'remunerating prices,' when he seeks a buyer for the produce of the loom and the spinning frame? Alas! Gentlemen! There is *protection* only for the strong and mighty, against the weak and wretched; for the small band frame and defend unjust laws against the great multitude who are called upon to obey them; for the selfish interest of a class against the great interests of society.

We are burthened with the heavy penalties of long and destructive Wars; we have to provide for costly Establishments by Land and Sea; and for an Expenditure, in my judgment, far too exorbitant for this nation after a peace which has happily endured more than a quarter of a century; but besides, and above these demands for the service of the State, an unavowed, a concealed Taxation has been levying even greater contributions upon the community. Fifty Millions are yearly taken from the people to provide for the expences of Government; but a far greater amount than fifty millions is torn from us by our Agricultural and

Colonial Monopolists. It is against this intolerable wrong that we protest; it is this master grievance that we are leagued together to redress.

My opinion on the great subjects of public interest are recorded in my Parliamentary votes while I was a Member of the House of Commons. To diffuse political rights widely and to protect them efficaciously, I have always supported a large and liberal Extension of the suffrage and its secret and unmolested exercise. To strengthen the control of the Constituency, I have advocated the Shortening the Duration of Parliaments.

In a word, Gentlemen, *the greatest happiness of the greatest number* represents the end and object of my political creed. To remove misery, to increase felicity, ought to be the purpose of benevolent and Christian legislation. Aid me to give effect to it!

With every sentiment of respectful esteem,
Believe me, Gentlemen, yours, very faithfully,
JOHN BOWRING.

Bolton, 10th June, 1841.

Cobden to Wilson (1841)

Richard Cobden to George Wilson, 25 September 1841, Cobden Papers, West Sussex Record Office, CP 59.

Leamington

25 Sepr

My dear Sir,

You & our friends including Mr Brooks will I think be very well satisfied with the use made of Stanley's confession in the House on Friday – Gibson made a capital speech. One of the best if not the best of the session. We had hoped to draw out the badger – but although he was very wroth & fidgetty he was kept down by Graham & Goulbourn, & thus we were deprived of a part of our fun. But Stanley must be quoted as our authority on all occasions. He has given up the whole case – From the best information I can get there appears to be no present intention on the part of Peel & his Buckingham cabinet to do anything. They will depend on the Chapter of accidents during the recess. If trade revives or if agitation slumbers nothing will be done. – All will depend upon what is doing out of doors during the next four months – It is absolutely a life or death struggle for the League – to get money at once – All depends on money. It is useless to wait for the Bazaar in Jany. The campaign must be opened next month & the war carried on incessantly till the next meeting of Parl^t – I expect we shall be prorogued in a week. – Can't you induce Mr Greg to come to your aid & make a must[?er] of friends to repair your finances? I go back to London tomorrow.

Yours very truly | Rich Cobden

'America and the British Corn Law. Compiled from the Work of Mr. John Curtis of Ohio', *The Anti-Bread-Tax Almanack, for the Year of our Lord 1842* (Manchester: J. Gadsby, 1842), pp. 37–9.

AMERICA AND THE BRITISH CORN LAW.

(Compiled from the work of Mr. John Curtis, of Ohio.)

The great want of England is unquestionably a market where she can exchange her goods on reasonable terms for food. She already obtains luxuries in superabundance; but these can never supply those wants of her artisans – substantial bread and meat, and a market wherein their labour can be exchanged for their necessaries. The food of tropical climates, with the exception of rice, is not calculated for export. The people of England, if they are to import food, need the production of a climate similar to their own, in which respect America is well adapted to supply them.

The two continents of America contain 15,000,000 square miles of land. Throw out one third of this as unfit for cultivation, and the remainder, at half the productive power of the lands of Great Britain, will support more than a thousand million of inhabitants.

The territory of the United States comprises one twentieth part of the habitable globe; its area being 2,300,000 square miles, or two-thirds the extent of the continent of Europe.

Let us now turn more particularly to the capability of the United States to furnish England with food in exchange for goods. All parts of the United States between thirty-seven and forty-four degrees of north latitude will produce wheat. But that part of the country best adapted to furnish an abundant foreign supply is, beyond all question, the northern part of the Mississippi valley, and the contiguous country south of the great lakes. It is called *par excellence* the wheat-growing region of America. Other parts of the country can grow sufficient for themselves, besides producing some for export, but the surplus of the newly-opened region in the north-western states already governs the market price in America. Thence foreign supplies would be chiefly drawn, and therefore it is important to direct especial attention to this region. Within its limits lie the six north-western states of the American Union, covering (exclusive of 200,000 square miles, the title to which is yet mostly in the Indian tribes) an area of 236,011 square miles. The country is unbroken by hill or mountain; the soil is fertile beyond description, and the climate is clear and salubrious; so that this vast district is as well calculated as any other on the globe to minister to the comfort and happiness of civilized man. It possesses unequalled facilities for foreign intercourse and commerce by means of its great lakes and rivers, the most distant parts of it being now within twenty days' sail of Liverpool.

The lands already sold in these six states exceed in amount the cultivated lands of the British isles by more than five million acres. At the same rate of production with British land, they are capable of feeding thirty millions of people. Include the Indian lands, which are within their border, and throw out one-third as waste, and they will sustain a population of ninety millions.

Industry, stimulated by the wants of a civilized and rapidly-progressing society, must insure a demand for all the manufactured goods, wares, and merchandise which *their agricultural produce can pay for*. The consumption of manufactures amongst such a people has no limit but their ability to purchase; and were a free trade with Great Britain given them, an immense exchange of products would instantly take place, to the unspeakably great advantage of both countries.

The cost of American flour in Liverpool, without reckoning interest or profits, would be from 26s. to 28s. per barrel, or (reckoning a barrel at 38 gallons of wheat) from 43s. to 47s. per quarter – prices which will remunerate the grower at the present rate of wages in America, and at which prices competition will always insure production to any amount which a regular market may demand; but while the present fluctuating prices occasioned by the corn law continue, the distance of the United States will prevent any large amount reaching the English market from that country, the present British corn law being more unfavourable to America than actual prohibition.

The present may justly be considered a crisis in the commercial policy of America. If it be decided that foreign markets are to continue closed against American corn – if England, which is the principal corn market of the world, refuse to exchange the produce of her mills and workshops for that of the fields of the Americans, the latter have no other alternative than to erect mills and workshops from which to supply themselves. They need no high tariff to protect them against British competition. *The English corn law is their best protection.*

The admission of American grain would unquestionably reduce the price of food, which would of course be equivalent to an increase of wages. The great enlargement of foreign trade which would result from opening the exchanges, and giving a new direction and impetus to foreign industry, would indefinitely increase employment in England, and this demand for labour would tend directly to enhance wages. There is no difficulty in perceiving the connexion between abundant employment and consequent demand for labour, and high wages; but it must require sharp optics to perceive any tendency to that result in high-priced food. Perhaps the personal experience of the writer, in paying high wages when food is cheap, may make it difficult for him to apprehend how high wages and cheap food can be opposed. He has been in the habit of employing unskilled men at common labour, and paying them 4s. 6d. per day, at the same time and place that fine flour in the village shops was a penny, bacon 2½d., and beef from 1½d. to 2d. per pound.

A statement of wages paid for labour in the United States may not be out of place. In the manufactories, the wages paid common hands are 9s. per week for females, and 20s. for males, and their board. Day labourers, in the villages, 4s. 6d. per day. Agricultural labourers, in ordinary times, 3s. per day; in harvest, 4s. 6d. to 8s. The labourer who boards himself has an additional shilling per day. In the country, one shilling per day is the ordinary price of board and bed in respectable families. Common labourers are usually employed by the month or year, at from £2 10s. to £3 sterling per month, and their board and lodgings found them. The taxes, direct and indirect, paid by an ordinary labourer, of all kinds, are usually 10s. per year. In the extreme western parts of the country, where provisions are cheapest, wages are higher, by ten per cent., than those given for the same kinds of labour in other parts of the country.

To one effect which would be produced in America by the repeal of the corn and provision laws, no party or class in England can profess indifference, and that is, *its effect on slavery in the United States*. The slave-holding states, to whose production Great Britain confines her American trade, are less populous and less wealthy then the free; yet of the produce of the former England received in 1839, according to the American estimates, £11,600,000, while of that of the latter she received less than £500,000. Thus England fosters an odious institution, which in words she loudly condemns, and spends millions to rid the world of; whilst she rejects more honourable, profitable, and wealthy customers, the fruits of whose free and active industry are in effect made contraband by British legislation.

Free trade, in destroying the odious monopoly of the American slaveholder, would give peace and plenty to England and the world, enlarge and secure trade, bind the spreading branches of the Anglo-Saxon race by natural affinity to England as their acknowledged head, and promote the liberty and civilization of the whole human family.

'Corn Laws are Potato Laws', *The Anti-Bread-Tax Almanack, for the Year of our Lord 1842* (Manchester: J. Gadsby, 1842), pp. 42–4.

CORN LAWS ARE POTATO LAWS

A third of the population of these realms are unable to procure wheaten bread or animal food. For the purpose of inquiring into the cause of this lamentable deterioration of the food of the people, it will be necessary for us to ascertain, first of all, what is the progress of population in this country, and, next, what is the provision that is made for the increasing numbers.

1821 Population of the United Kingdom 21,193,458
1831 Ditto 24,321,934
1841 Ditto 26,861,000

The above statement shows that our population is increasing at the rate of more than five thousand every week. As our land does not increase in size, and as our corn law prevents our getting a supply of corn from other countries until the price is so high that it is beyond the power of the great mass of the people to buy it, how do these rapidly increasing numbers contrive to live at all? We propose to answer this question by showing the effects of the corn law upon the habits of the most numerous portion of our population.

It may not be known to all our readers that a given surface of land, if planted with potatoes, will support more than double the number of persons that could subsist upon its produce in wheat. Mr. Newenham, who is quoted by M'Culloch as an authority, and who has taken much pains in investigating the subject, estimates that the same quantity of land requisite for the support of *one* individual who subsists on animal food and uses bread only as an additional article, will maintain *four* people who subsists wholly on bread, or *twelve* who subsist wholly on potatoes. As the rapid increase of our population has far outstripped the increased production of wheat of other grain, the poorer people have resorted to the cheaper and more abundant food of the potato. About one hundred and fifty years ago this root was grown only in the gardens of the rich. Even fifty years ago it was a rare thing to see a *field* of potatoes; they were then grown chiefly in gardens, or in the vicinity of gardens, and were wholly cultivated by the spade. We have heard an old farmer remark that there are now fifty fields of potatoes to be seen where, forty years ago, one only could be found. They are now commonly planted after the plough, furrowed, or banked up, with the plough, and even dug with the plough.

It is an undoubted fact, then, that, owing to our corn law, the great mass of the labouring poor of this country, who formerly fed upon grain, are now subsisting upon the potato; nor is it less certain that a like proportion of the working classes have been, from the same cause, reduced from meat to live upon bread. And it must be evident to every reflecting mind, that by no other means than this deterioration of food can the population of this country go on increasing upon a limited surface of land. If the corn laws are allowed to continue, more and more people must give up eating meat and bread, and resort to potatoes. There will be no check to population, for people will increase upon potatoes as fast as they do upon grain. Ireland is an example; and look at the consequence! When a people are brought to depend upon the potato, they are always at the verge of famine: it can neither be stored nor transported like wheat. The failure of one crop leaves nothing to stand between a potato-fed population and death by starvation. The people of Ireland have frequently been saved from this fate by the charity of England; but who will interpose to feed us when we shall, by the slow but sure operation of the corn law, be reduced to the same condition with the Irish?

Whilst the corn law has been gradually reducing the mass of the English people to a coarse food, it has doubled, nay, even trebled the rents of the landlords. This was foreseen by Adam Smith in his 'Wealth of Nations.' 'In Europe,' he says, writing seventy years ago, '*corn is the principal produce of land which serves immediately for human food.* Except in particular situations, therefore, the rent of corn land regulates in Europe that of all other cultivated land.' If in any country the common and favourite vegetable food of the people should be drawn from a plant of which the most common land, with the same, or nearly the same, culture, produced a much greater quantity than the most fertile does of corn, the rent of the landlord, or the surplus quantity of food which would remain to him after paying the labour and replacing the stock of the farmer, together with its ordinary profits, would necessarily be much greater. Whatever was the rate at which labour was commonly maintained in that country, this greater surplus could always maintain a greater quantity of it, and, consequently, enable the landlord to purchase or command a greater quantity of it. *The real value of his rent, his real power and authority, his command of the necessaries and conveniences of life with which the labour of other people could supply him, would necessarily be much greater.*' Book I, chapter 11.

If any proof were wanting beyond what our own experience in England affords us of the truth of this, it might be drawn from the present state of things in Ireland, where a potato-fed population are yielding a higher rent to the landlord for their potato-ground than is derived from similar soils yielding corn or cattle in England. It becomes evident then, as a consequence of what we have here stated, that it is the immediate interest of our landowners to bring us to a potato diet in this country in order to increased [*sic*] rents; and the corn law will, if submitted to long enough, enable them to accomplish their object.

Petition of Inhabitants of Manchester, *Manchester Times, and Lancashire and Cheshire Gazette*, 11 March 1843.

Petition of Inhabitants of Manchester, *Manchester Times, and Lancashire and Cheshire Gazette*, 11 March 1843[1]

To the Honourable the Commons of Great Britain and Ireland, in Parliament assembled. – The Petition of the undersigned Inhabitants of Manchester,

Humbly showeth, – That as, in the opinion of your petitioners, and as has been again and again demonstrated in your honourable house, the corn laws, in themselves and in their operations, are impolitic, injurious, partial, oppressive, cruel, and unjust; crippling to commerce, inimical to the prosperity of all classes of the community, checking the progress of morality and religion, engendering disease, multiplying the victims of premature death, promotive of discontent and disaffection among the people; and, in short, alike opposed to the laws of nature and to the word of God, and consequently afflicting the country with the direst evils; your petitioners, once more, with an opportunity increased by a greatly strengthened conviction that the corn laws constitute a fearful enormity, pray your honourable house that these laws may be immediately, unconditionally, and totally repealed.

---

1   This petition contained 74,721 signatures, *Appendix to the Report of the Select Committee on Public Petitions*, (1843), App. 200, No. 1051, p. 118

376   *Battles over Free Trade, Volume 1*

First Annual Meeting of the Agricultural Protection Society for Great Britain and Ireland, *Morning Herald*, 14 December 1844.

AGRICULTURAL PROTECTION SOCIETY FOR GREAT BRITAIN AND IRELAND.

The first annual meeting of the above society was held yesterday, at the offices of the society, 17, Old Bond-street. Among those present were the Duke of Richmond (the President), who took the chair; the Duke of Cleveland, who arrived a short time after the commencement of the proceedings; Mr. Allix, M.P.; Mr. Colville, M.P.; Mr. W. Miles, M.P.; Mr. Newdegate, M.P., Mr. Stafford O'Brien, M.P.; Mr. Pusey, M.P.; Mr. Blackstone, M.P.; Mr. W. R. Beresford, M.P.; and a number of well-known agriculturists and members of the provincial protection societies. Of these we observed, Mr. J. J. Allnutt, Mr. R. Baker, Mr. W. Bennett, Mr. T. Ellman, Mr. R. Healey, Mr. Fisher Hobbs, Mr. J. Hudson, Mr. S. Jonas, Mr. John Ellman, Mr. Hodgson Barrow, Mr. W. R. Browne, Mr. G. Emery, Mr. H. Trower, Mr. T. Umbers, Mr. T. Weale, Mr. F. Woodward, Mr. E. Wyall, and others.

The noble Chairman said, that as this was the annual meeting of the central society for the protection of agriculture, the committee of that society had been anxious to see present as many of the members of the local societies as could conveniently attend the general meeting. He was happy to see a number of those gentleman present. He thought the main business for consideration to-day would be the report of those gentleman to whom the society had confided the management of its affairs, and with the permission of the meeting he would call upon Mr. Miles to read the document.

Mr. Miles, M.P. then read the following report: –

'Your committee, is presenting their first annual report, beg to remind the society that the subject matter of such report has been in a great degree antici-pated by the communications and statements which they have from time to time put forth, and especially by the address issued at the close of last session, which has been circulated to the number of 30,000 throughout the kingdom; and, so far as your committee are enabled to judge, has been considered satisfactory by the country societies.

'It must be obvious that for the purposes of the Agricultural Protection Society the session of parliament is the most important time for action, and its close, perhaps, the most suitable period for recapitulating those things which this society has done, and those which it has been instrumental in preventing. Of measures brought forward last session the repeal of the wool duties and the renewal of the Bank charter were the only two which seemed to your committee to come within the province of this society's consideration. On the first of these

First Annual Meeting of the Agricultural Protection Society (1844) 377

your committee considered it on the whole advisable not to interfere, because while very many members of our society and many country societies expressed a strong opinion that the change would be unfelt by the home wool grower, many others were convinced that the change would be decidedly beneficial.

'With regard to the bank charter, we never contemplated interfering as a society with those parts of it which did not affect the farmer, but there were very general apprehensions entertained as to the proposed restrictions on country banks; and your committee thought it right to recommend to country societies the adoption of a petition on that subject to parliament. Your committee have now the pleasure of reminding you that the modifications obtained in that measure were all favourable, if not entirely satisfactory, to the country banks.

'A member of the House of Commons brought forward last session a motion for an address to the Queen, representing that it was desirable to obtain authentic information upon all matters connected with the agriculture of the United Kingdom. The hon. member did not press his motion to a division, as the opposition of the government and of the agricultural members was rather to the form in which the question was brought forward than to the principle involved.

'Your committee are of opinion that agriculture has everything to hope and nothing to fear from the most minute inquiries and the largest amount of statistical information; and that if in former years such information was desirable, it is much more so now, when the statistics of every other industrial resource of the empire are becoming every year more methodised and complete.

'It would be beyond the duty of your committee to enter into an explanation of the causes which led to the discontinuance of the board established by that eminent friend to agriculture, Sir J. Sinclair. Suffice it to say, that if any machinery can with accurate results, and without inquisitorial process, place more fully before the country our resources, our difficulties, and our progress, every farmer and friend to protection will consider a benefit to have been conferred upon us, and through us upon the community at large.

'Since the recess our opponents have, by their own showing, in a great degree abandoned their itinerant lecturing, and have mainly directed their exertions towards increasing the votes of their particular party; thus turning the Anti-Corn-Law League into one registration club for the whole country. The fourth rule of our society most strictly prohibits our contesting this ground with them; nor can we regret this, believing that if not the letter of the law, at any rate, that the spirit of the constitution regards the electors of every county and town fully able to choose and to control their own representatives in the House of Commons; and whenever strangers interfere, no matter with how much industry, or with how much money, we are of opinion that the constituencies of this great and enlightened country will in the vast majority of interests [*sic*] look upon such interference as an impertinence and an insult.

'The selection and revision of our publications have occupied a considerable portion of the time of your committee, and we are glad to inform you that the demand for them has fully satisfied our most sanguine expectations; this demand has been made not all at once, or only in one district, but it has been continuous and universal, so that we have the best grounds for believing that the 200,000 tracts that we have circulated, or caused to be circulated, through the country, have not been forced upon the public, but have met the desire for information upon a most important subject, or the wish to refute the false statements of the enemies to protection.

'The newspapers continue to transfer into their columns extracts from these pamphlets, as they did from those of Mr. Cayley and Mr. Alison. It must be a matter of deep regret to all of us that the ill-health of the former gentleman prevents his taking a more active part in the good cause he has so ably defended.

'During the recess two other subjects, which seem to come within the province of this society, have engaged the attention of agriculturists – we mean the frauds suspected in the returns from which the averages are struck, &c., and the very large importations from Canada. The former subject was brought under the consideration of your committee on Tuesday last, and in compliance with a unanimous resolution passed on that occasion, his Grace the Duke of Richmond has undertaken to make the fullest inquiry; a more important one could not be named, or one whose cognisance came more completely within the scope of this society; and your committee assure you that their utmost vigilance shall be used in the detection and the remedy of these frauds.

'Notice has been given that the subject of the importation of corn from Canada will be brought under the consideration of your committee at its next general meeting; it would be, therefore, premature to pronounce any opinion, except as to that in which we are all agreed – namely, its extreme importance, that we may mention that a deputation from the Wolverhampton Society attended our last meeting and has put us in possession of some very valuable information on the subject.

'We continue to maintain the best possible understanding with our country friends, as is proved not only by the tone but by the frequency of their communications with us. Nothing has happened which seemed to us to require any such appeal as was made this time last year, and it is always our wish to effect our object rather by such communication as is compatible with the routine of every day's business than by agitation. At the same time we are well aware that our opponents, who scruple not to use, and who may be said to have put in practice, all means for gaining their ends, have obtained in particular localities, and at particular periods, apparent and temporary advantages over us; but we should be sorry that our eagerness in any cause should make us forget our duties as good citizens and friends of constitutional order, or urge us ever to create without reluctance that excitement which, whatever may be its benefits, is always attended with the evil of exasperating one class against another. Meanwhile we

First Annual Meeting of the Agricultural Protection Society (1844) 379

are quite prepared to maintain our ground firmly, feeling that by moderation, as well as by our strength, we shall be enabled to maintain it the more firmly.

'That we are formed at all may be deemed a symbol of evil times. Good citizens may regret that our formation was necessary, but that our conduct since our formation has been of a nature to cause alarm or suspicion we most strenuously deny.

'We have endeavoured to be the means and centre of communication between all the friends to agricultural protection throughout the kingdom, to collect their opinions, their wishes, their apprehensions, and to do our best to make them sympathised with and responded to by the government and by the legislature. That we can realise our own wishes, or all the wishes of all our friends, is wholly impracticable. We are of opinion that no other organization or system consistent with law and order can carry out more efficaciously than we have done the ends for which we have contended. We firmly believe that our society, as at present constituted and as at present carried on, may be made not only a more and more efficacious means, not only of protecting agriculture, but also of showing how essentially connected the prosperity of agriculture is with the maintenance of that free constitution under which it is our privilege and happiness to live.

Signed 'RICHMOND, Chairman'

Lord Palmerston to the Earl of Minto, 27 December 1845, Minto Papers, National Library of Scotland, MS 11810, fols 124–7, extract, fols 125v.–127.

I do not quite agree with you in thinking our Failure a good thing though perhaps the Advantages nearly balance the Evil – on the one Hand we Escape the duty of dealing with several very unpleasant Matters, on the other Hand we are certainly damaged in public opinion, as a Party, by the Proof which has been afforded of internal Jealousies Rivalships and Discordences [*sic*]

At all Events Peel is much stronger than he was before he resigned, & if he is to be Minister, & is coming round to liberal opinions, perhaps there is no great Harm in his being Stronger.

But he has much improved the Composition of his Cabinet by the accession of Ellenborough Dalhousie & Gladstone; & having by his Resignation taken as it were the Benefit of the Insolvent he is free from his former Engagements, & sets up Business again as a new Man.

The Tories can no longer accuse him of Treachery because he will answer by pointing to his Retirement; The Whigs cannot say he ought not to be Minister because he will reply that he is so only because they could not form an administration.

P. Bennet, Speech to Central Suffolk Agricultural Protection Association, *Bury and Suffolk Herald*, 21 January 1846

CENTRAL SUFFOLK AGRICULTURAL PROTECTION ASSOCIATION.

P. BENNET, jun. Esq., M.P., who on rising was greeted with cheers, said, one of the resolutions which had been passed, confers upon me the honour of carrying into Parliament some of your addresses; and in so doing I shall be happy in having seen so numerous a party before me, composed of such respectable materials, such honourable men. In carrying your sentiments, embodied in that petition – unable as I am to advocate it eloquently – you shall have my most strenuous endeavours, when I have that opportunity. (Loud applause.) I shall little rely upon my own powers, but I think the Hon. Gentleman at the head of the ministry ought to refer to his own eloquent, and overpowering expressions and speeches, which he has made in favour of agricultural protection. His voice has been the voice of Jacob, but his hands have been the hands of Esau. (Cheers.) The very Bill that he is endeavouring now to repeal, is his own child. Is he going to turn his back upon his own offspring? Can you believe it possible? Is it in human nature? Will he shock his nature to attain the end of those who are furious in their attacks upon the aristocracy and yeomanry, and in fact upon every class? I say the labourer is more interested in the welfare of the farmer than any one can imagine. (Hear.) The very existence of such a band of persons as the League, must be looked upon as most dangerous. They are endeavouring to attack the constituency of England with money; – (hear, hear,) – dirty money! We have honour, and I hope principle. (Applause,) I say they have avowed their intentions, and their wish of driving the aristocracy to the dust; when with them, I think, all classes, will, more or less suffer. (Hear, hear.) The agricultural landlord is described as a wolf. Gentlemen, let us beware of wolves in sheep's clothing. (Loud and continued applause.) They claim credit for alleviating the condition of the labourers; they say it is their object to give them cheap bread. (Hear, hear.) The word should be 'cheap wages,' (Hear, and applause.) That is the way the manufacturers wish to increase their profit. They have made immense fortunes under the very law of protection that they are now trying to upset. It is under these laws that they have amassed their fortunes. Some of their people have set their minds upon becoming some of the wolves. They wish to come and settle where smoke would not disturb them, where they are in some degree secluded, and where they can escape from the men who have been ruined in their service. (Cheers.) Many of the manufactories are exceedingly prejudicial to the lives of the men employed in them. I think, in advocating the cause, that I can say no more than has already been done so eloquently by the Chairman and others. For myself, I think we do not come here to be persuaded that protection is necessary, but to show that we are not those apathetic people described by the League; that we are determined to stand by protection and by the laws of the land. Sir Robert Peel has told us that when he did weaken our protection, he did it as a compromise and the agricultural body received it as a compromise, with the understanding that it should be final. (Hear, hear.) Although we do not know the measure that is to be proposed, there is no doubt that there is something brewing, for we were thrown by the Premier into the hands of Lord John Russell, who proposed a fixed duty. But, gentlemen, I beg to say that the representatives of the counties more particularly, and of the towns immediately connected with the agricultural interest, are returned expressly on the principle of protection; and the persons who returned these members are the agriculturists and yeomanry of the country. Are the members that were returned under these circumstances likely to be guilty of a defalcation of duty – likely to swerve from those feelings that have hitherto guided their public conduct? Are they to throw you over? If they do, it will be a disgrace to them; it will impeach the character of Englishmen, and more particularly of representatives who are returned for the express purpose of supporting the agricultural interest. I can assure you from my own experience, that the attacks of the League as to the registration are most violent, and more particularly in Middlesex, where they have made attacks upon the Judges of the Bench, who have received letters to the effect that they should have their votes preserved by the League if they would support their interest. I think that is going a good way. Again, where a notice has been left at a door, the persons who left it said, 'you need not give it to your master,' so that in many instances, before they returned home, and learned that an objection had been laid, the time for sustaining their votes in the Registration Courts was passed. I do not think that an honourable mode of proceeding. I can only add that in every way in my power I will advocate your interests, and I am happy to see so much unanimity among those present. If the great majority of the room are as determined to act in union, as the single hand held up against the resolutions, I think we shall be able to withstand all attacks upon our rights.

'The Corn Laws as a Buttress for the Aristocracy', *Economist*, 4:126 (24 January 1846), p. 104.

Till a recent period the protectionists were accustomed to represent the Corn Laws as essential to the welfare of the labouring classes. They continually described the point at issue as a labourer's question. The laws, it was said, kept up the rate of wages. For several years the labouring classes, nettled by repeated disputes with their masters, believed the assertion, and refused to co-operate with them to obtain the repeal of the laws. They believed that the League had no other object than to beat down wages, and they preferred, as they avowed, the supremacy of the land-owner to the enrichment of the manufacturers. Latterly their own condition has impressed on them a different opinion, and they are now convinced, by experience, that dear food is another name for low wages. The protectionists are on this point no longer credited even by the agricultural labourers; their fallacies are detected; and they have changed their tactics. Having failed to delude the democracy, they now say the law must be preserved to keep down the very class for whose benefit they formerly pretended it was maintained. This important revelation was published by all the morning papers on Tuesday week.

At Willis's rooms, on the previous day, the Duke of Richmond, discarding the stale pretences that Corn Laws secure national independence, preserve equal prices, and extend the cultivation of our own soil, avowed that the Corn Laws must be maintained to prevent the extension of democratic opinions. His Grace said 'the yeomanry of England and the agricultural interest of the empire stand between the advocates of Corn Law Repeal and the democratic principle which they wish to carry out.' His Grace regards the Corn Laws, then, as the bulwark of the aristocracy, and declares that the League attacks them with the hope of gaining a triumph for the democracy. So the Corn Laws are maintained by the protectionists, according to the Duke of Richmond, to prevent democracy becoming predominant in the State.

The public cannot be wholly unprepared for this avowal. In 1827 the late Earl Grey regarded 'standing by his order' as synonymous with preserving the Corn Laws. On several occasions, statesmen of different parties and various capacities have defended these laws as essential to the predominance of the aristocracy. Sir Edward Knatchbull expressly described them as intended to maintain the station of the aristocracy and portion younger members of its families. In that passage of the Rev. Mr Leveson Harcourt's speech at Chichester, which we quoted the week before last, he also described these laws as keeping up the dignity and power of the aristocracy.[1] He said the laws added 20 per cent to the income of the tithe-owners and landowner, and that they would not be able to

---

1   [Ed.: 'Condition of Agricultural Labourers', *Economist*, 4:126 (10 January 1846), pp. 36–7.]

maintain their station if this 20 per cent were taken away by the abolition of the laws. Thus we have a succession of testimony to the fact that the aristocracy maintain these laws to preserve their power and enrich themselves. All which they have told us about benefiting the farmer and the labourer, who form part of the democracy, they now contradict, and in one emphatic sentence, declare that the people must be taxed and starved, in order to prevent them rising to an equality with the aristocracy.

Sir Robert Peel has had a difficult task to preserve the Corn Laws so long, even before the selfishness of their advocates was avowed. At the head of one of the strongest governments, in point of parliamentary support, that ever existed – a government, too, which possesses, to a very considerable extent, the confidence of all the influential classes – a government which is considered necessary for the safety of the country by the commercial as well as the landed interest, and would find support though its measures were tyrannical and absurd – this government, animated by good will and composed of staunch friends to the agriculturists, now finds, and has found, it impossible to continue the Corn Laws. It felt itself obliged, in the very high tide of its power in 1841–42, to concede a large alteration of the law, and a tariff which struck at the root of protection to agriculture. Every year since, it has, from necessity, made fresh concessions, not to clamour and faction – they were all on its own side – but to reason and conviction. Against all authority in moral and political science were the Corn Laws made and maintained, and every time that a statesman opened his mouth to discuss any other commercial question, he blurted out something directly opposed in principle to them. They are condemned, then, by statesmanship, philosophy, and justice. Hence the strong government was unable to maintain the Corn Laws unaltered. They are an attempt, as Lord Beaumont avows, to counteract the benevolence and wisdom of Nature, and only failure is possible. To conquer nation after nation, and place the whole world under the yoke of one man, may be possible; but to conquer the seasons, to subdue the desires and appetites of men, and the inevitable consequences of seasons and appetites, are beyond the power of conquerors or of parliaments. The strong government, therefore, has failed; legislation since 1815, in respect to these laws, has been nothing but a continued failure, as repeated complaints, repeated committees of inquiry, and repeated alterations of the law, explicitly prove. According to the Duke of Richmond, however, the law is to be maintained, in spite of all these warnings, to keep down the democracy. By that declaration of his Grace any minister who may wish to preserve these laws, must find all the difficulties of his task immeasurably augmented. If even Sir Robert Peel tried, in spite of experience, to preserve the law as far as he could, in compliance with the demands of his party, – if he wishes to maintain the aristocracy, – this declaration by one of that body, must strengthen the League by the fiery zeal of the bulk of the democracy, and urge

'*The Corn Laws as a Buttress for the Aristocracy*' (1846)

the whole Chartist body to aid in destroying the Corn Law as a means of overcoming the aristocracy.

We cannot expect the Duke of Richmond and men of his class to be very observant of alterations in public opinion. Let us remind the aristocracy therefore of one remarkable fact. Within the memory of many persons living, nearly the whole of our literature was embued [*sic*] with aristocratic opinions. Novels were then generally written with a view to inculcate respect and love for the aristocracy; they are now written to raise the condition of the labouring classes. The bulk of the journals, daily, weekly, monthly, and quarterly, were Church and State. The democratic literature was mostly disreputable, and only escaped prosecution by skulking and creeping, so as rather to be hidden than seen and read. It was confined to what was called penny trash. All the *respectability* of the press, nearly all its learning, nearly all its wit, were ranged on the side of the aristocracy and the hierarchy. Now, the reverse is the case. The bulk of the journals of every class is for the repeal of the Corn Laws, and adverse to the pretensions of the aristocracy. The wit, the learning, and the respectability of literature are now on the side of the democracy. It is Anti-Church-and-State. The most popular of our present novels are anti-aristocratic. A great change then has taken place in the national mind. How far that may have been brought about by the obstinate adherence of the aristocracy to the Corn Laws, or the imbecility of mind shown in their defence, we cannot say; but we can say, that it is in some measure a consequence of that dreadful poverty and degradation of the multitude, particularly of the peasantry, continued through many years of peace, and great exaction, from which the aristocracy, with its Corn Laws, made itself responsible, and which it was bound to remove.

With this change in the public mind, it seems something like madness in the aristocracy to proclaim their intention of preserving the Corn Laws as a check on democracy. The people are now told by the Duke of Richmond that the aristocracy stands between them and plenty, and that they will get political power as well as food, by abolishing the Corn Laws. Did an exclusive corporation ever more openly invite the enmity of the masses, and urge them to destroy it? The world is astounded at this moment by the almost incredible silliness of one Duke and the almost equal ignorance of another, and now comes a third Duke, who tells the people they must submit to be taxed and starved, in order to preserve the supremacy of the Dukes. The thing is impossible. The nation is full of ingenuity and skill; it is boiling over with courage and enterprise; it teems with a god like intellect, impatient even of the control of the material world; and it can no more be bound by the selfish rules of the Dukes of Norfolk, Buckingham, and Richmond, than the Niagara can be forced back by the mud-bank with which a child momentarily impedes the flow of a petty rivulet. Such a puissant nation cannot be governed by such men; and the retention of one fragment of the laws to maintain their supremacy, involves nothing less, sooner or later, than the convulsion of the empire.

Richard Cobden to William Rathbone, 2 February 1846, Paget Papers, Leicestershire Record Office, DE 1274/10.

Manchester
2 Feby 1846
Private

My dear Sir

It appears to me that the only proper course for the League to take out of doors is to stick to our principle, without opposing Peels really great measure, or even denying its merits – But we must not lose sight of the fact that his measure may be rejected in the Lords, or the government may be tripped up any moment upon some other vote, or it may go to pieces[.] In any case we shall have to fall back upon the Country, & rely upon our old watchword, & the union of <the League> principle – If we depart a hairs-breadth from our old ground we shall be a prey to all kinds of discord – Besides, the best way of helping the government to carry our <his> <its> own measure is by standing firm to our principle – If we throw up our caps for him<Peel> we shall weaken his hold upon the protectionist party – Let him be able to point to the League as wanting something more than he is offering to do – But I am not sure that we shall not get the immediate repeal even yet, at the instance of <the> protectionists themselves – for when they see that total repeal is inevitable, they will I think prefer the immediate[.] Therefore every motive impels us to stand by our principle out of doors – As respects the course to be pursued by our friends in the House, we shall of course take a vote on Villiers motion the same as last year, & failing in that we shall do our best to help Peel to carry his measure

Believe me | Yours very truly | Richd Cobden

French Reaction to the Reduction of British Duties on Brandy and Silk, *Kentish Gazette*, 10 February 1846.

THE Paris journals seem generally pleased with Sir R. Peel's commercial scheme. The reduction of the duties on brandy and on silks is especially regarded as a great boon to two important branches of French industry. But while our neighbours admit the merits and liberality of the measure, as regards England, none of them hint at any reciprocity on the part of France, or show any of that willingness to follow our example in adopting free-trade principles on which Sir R. Peel laid so much stress in his 'exposition.'

388   *Battles over Free Trade, Volume 1*

House of Lords Protest against the Corn Bill, 25 June 1846, *Hansard* (1846), lxxxvii, cc. 961–4.

The following Protests against the Third Reading of the Bill to Amend the Laws relating to the Importation of Corn were entered on the Journals:
—

(No. 1)
DISSENTIENT –

1. Because the repeal of the Corn Laws will greatly increase the dependence of this country upon foreign countries for its supply of food, and will thereby expose it to dangers against which former statesmen have thought it essential to take legislative precautions.

2. Because there is no security nor probability that other nations will take similar steps; and this country will, therefore, not only be exposed to the risks of failure of supply consequent on a state of war, but will also be exclusively subject to an unlimited influx of corn in times of abundance, and to sudden checks whenever short crops shall reduce the ordinary supply from the exporting countries, or their Governments shall deem it necessary to take precautionary measures for their own protection, thus causing rapid and disastrous fluctuations in the markets of this country.

3. Because under a system of protection the agriculture of this country has more than kept pace with the increasing demand of its increasing population; and because it is to be apprehended that the removal of protection may throw some lands out of cultivation, and check in others the progress of improvement which has led to this satisfactory result.

4. Because it is unjust to withdraw protection from the landed interest of this country, while that interest remains subject to exclusive burdens imposed for purposes of general, and not of special advantage.

5. Because the loss to be sustained by the repeal of the Corn Laws will fall most heavily on the least wealthy portion of the landed proprietors, will press immediately and severely on the tenant-farmers, and through them, with ruinous consequences, on the agricultural labourers.

6. Because indirectly, but not less certainly, injurious consequences will result to the manufacturing interest, and especially to the artisans and mechanics, from competition with the agricultural labourers thrown out of employment, but

principally from the loss of the home market, caused by the inability of the producers of grain, and those dependent on them, to consume manufactured goods to the same extent as heretofore.

7. Because the same cause will produce similar evil results to the tradesmen, retail dealers, and others in country towns, not themselves engaged in agricultural pursuits, but mainly dependent for their subsistence on their dealings with those who are so engaged.

8. Because the effect of a repeal of the Corn Laws will be especially injurious to Ireland, by lowering the value of her principal exports, and by still further reducing the demand for labour, the want of which is among the principal evils of her social condition.

9. Because a free trade in corn will cause a large and unnecessary diminution of annual income, thus impairing the revenue of the country, at the same time that it cripples the resources of those classes on whom the weight of local taxation now mainly falls.

10. Because a general reduction of prices consequent on reduction of the price of corn, will tend unduly to raise the monied interest at the expense of all others, and to aggravate the pressure of the national burdens.

11. Because the removal of differential duties in favour of Canadian corn is at variance with the legislative encouragement held out to that Colony by Parliament, on the faith of which the colonists have laid out large sums upon the improvement of their internal navigation; and because the removal of protection will divert the traffic of the interior from the St. Lawrence and the British ports of Montreal and Quebec, to the foreign port of New York; thus throwing out of employment a large amount of British shipping, severing the commercial interests of Canada from those of the parent country, and connecting those interests most intimately with the United States of America.

12. Because the adoption of a similar system with regard to other articles of commerce will tend to sever the strongest bond of union between this country and her Colonies, will deprive the British merchant of that which is now his most certain market, and sap the foundation of that colonial system, to which, commercially and politically, this country owes much of its present greatness.

(No. 2)
DISSENTIENT –

Because the Bill for repealing the Corn Laws is not accompanied, as in justice it ought to have been, by the following measures, viz.: –

1. The entire and immediate repeal of all the taxes which fall directly upon land – the land tax, the malt tax, and the hop duty.

2. The equalization of all the rates of which the occupiers of land bear at present an unfair and undue proportion – the poor rates, the highway rates, and the county rates.

3. An alteration of the Tithe Commutation Act, which can no longer be just or applicable.

4. A legislative enactment authorizing all persons who hold leases of land for unexpired terms of years to surrender them on giving six months' notice before any of the usual days of payment.

5. A legislative enactment directing the payment stipulated in every contract to be reduced according to the proportion which the average price of wheat at the time of making such payment bears to its average price at the time that such contract was formed, so that such payment may be of the same value as was originally intended and agreed to by the parties.

6. A legislative enactment authorizing the cultivation of tobacco and the preparation of sugar from beetroot and other vegetables, and exempting the said tobacco and sugar from the payment of any duty.

7. The entire and immediate repeal of those taxes which are imposed upon articles of general consumption, of the Excise duty on soap, and of the Customs duties on sugar and coffee, the produce of British Colonies, and on those sorts of tea and tobacco which are used by the labouring classes.

'The Ghost of a Dead Monopoly!', *Economist*, 4:153 (1 August 1846), pp. 989–90.

THE GHOST OF A DEAD MONOPOLY!

When we read (in romance) of some outrageous malefactor, whose crimes have been expiated on the scaffold, leaving a legacy of curses upon all whose exertions have tended to rid society of his presence, we feel pity for the unhappy criminal and contempt for his denunciations. But when such an offender attempts to perpetuate amongst a body of deluded followers, admiration for his crimes, neither pity or contempt should prevent the strongest expressions of disapproval of such posthumous iniquity.

Now, the little clique of monopolists who meet at No. 17, Bond street, and designate themselves the 'Central Society for the Protection of British Agriculture and Industry,'–British idleness would have been the right words, – speaking by the voice of their President, the Duke of Richmond, and, in the name of their condemned and executed monopoly, have put forth an address to the farmers as mischievous in purpose as it is effete and ludicrous as a political manifesto. The mischievous purpose being directed towards the farmers, is one which falls directly within our province, whilst an exposure of the silliness of the address as a political document is incident to an examination of that purpose. There can be no doubt that reliance upon some especial legislative interference in their favour has been the one main cause of the backwardness of farmers and landowners in all that concerns their instrument of production – land. They have been protected against competition for thirty years, and we have now the general admission that, taking the country through, the soil is not half cultivated. Can there be a more decisive argument against the 'protective system?'

And we must do the great body of farmers and a very considerable portion of the landholders the justice to say, that they have now made up their minds to exert themselves, and are talking about, if not setting about, improvement, with more or less of energy or skill. They have much to learn, much to forget, and more to do. But still they have got over the helpless state in which they folded their hands and cried 'God help us.' The farmers especially are regarding the subject in a very business like manner. They are beginning to calculate. They are setting off the losses sustained through protection against the profits – save the mark! – obtained by protection, and the result is not favourable to the system of restriction. When political science was an occult science, – supposed by many weak and worthy persons to have some not very remote affinity to the black art, and landlord legislators voted in solemn silence against every attempt to touch the corn laws, – the busy, and the indolent, and the ignorant, had some excuse for regarding the monopoly of the home market as somehow or other mysteriously bound up with our 'institutions.' The unknown is the magnificent; the obscure is that which startles the ignorant. But now that Adam Smith has been popularized – and one can't enter an omnibus or a railway carriage without hearing very decent discussions on economical questions – it is time for the section of landowners represented by the Bond street clique to give up the illusion that they can delude the farmers. When the Protectionists were driven to defend their monopoly *viva voce*, their game was up. The 'Protection Societies' gave the death-blow to 'Protection.' We speak advisedly when we say that more farmers have been made free-traders, or have been reconciled to the idea of free-trade in corn, by the sayings of Protection societies than by the direct teachings of the League. Bond street statistics, monopolist history, and Protectionist predictions, had a strong tendency to make men interpret them by the rule of contraries; and the dullest farmer that was ever whipped up by the steward to shout at his landlord's bidding, could not but be aware that, whatever might be the effect of the attack of its enemies, monopoly could never survive the defences of its friends.

We venture to assert that we know something more of the agricultural mind – the temper of the farmers as a class – than has ever been known by any Protectionist landlord or politician of the day; and we say that the tone adopted by the 'farmers' friends' has ever been singularly ill suited to attract the farmers. They are perhaps slow, but eminently practical men of business; and the only hold the politicians who call themselves 'Protectionists' had over the tenantry was a certain undefined fear the farmers for some time entertained that free trade would produce an enormous and sudden reduction of prices. That fear being got over, the influence of the parliamentary Protectionists will cease unless they can address themselves to the real interests of the tenantry. But that is not their object; for it is a rule with few exceptions, that a high Protectionist landowner is a liberal landlord. He seems to imagine a farmer can't be trusted out of leading strings, or that he is to be regarded as only a bettermost kind of bailiff. Than this nothing can be more adverse to the interests of agriculture.

Well, in this position of things, the 'Central Society,' having no public object, and no plan of political action, think fit to address to the farmers a sickly compound of maudlin sentiment and melodramatic bombast, from which we select a few specimens, for the purpose of warning the farmers against any diversion from the practical objects they are now generally seeking, namely, improved and secure tenures, and the abrogation of obsolete practices and burdens.

'The committee consider it their duty to address to those societies in connection with them some remarks on the present position of affairs, as well as some suggestion as to *a future course of conduct.*'

A speedy dissolution, one would have thought, the only rational 'future course' which could have been suggested to the local societies. But the address soon slides from the 'societies' to the farmers, whom it is a pure fiction to treat as identical. The protection societies were formed in 1844.

'It was rather to strengthen than to censure Sir Robert Peel that the farmers then came forward: and if they have subsequently found the man they placed in office, and strengthened in office, holding office only to betray them, they have at least the satisfaction of knowing that they have done their duty, or recollecting *that the most generous and confiding natures are ever those most easily deceived*, and of feeling that no man can be blamed for not foreseeing an event which has had no parallel, as we hope it will have none, in the history of our country.'

Now the Bond street centrals must suppose farmers don't recollect the contents of the newspapers, or that they do not read them; for no one remembering the contents of the 'Protectionist press' in 1842 can forget the denunciations of Sir Robert Peel consequent upon his corn law and tariff of that year. If any man was deceived as to the course Sir Robert would, sooner or later, take with respect to free trade in corn, he must have practised gross self-deception. We know that the farmers generally were not deceived. They saw that the end was coming, and they wished it. Their attendance at Protection societies was all a sham; they were, in a manner, compelled to do so, and it was expressly understood that the farmers were only to attend, they were not expected to subscribe ... Certainly the present government is not likely to deceive the Protectionist farmers; for the members of it are as much free traders as Sir Robert Peel, and 'something more.' But as to the Protectionists in Parliament representing the farmer, nothing can be further from the fact. The members who have most urged the farmers' interests or spoken the farmers' feelings are the free-trade members, especially Mr Cobden, Mr Bright, and Mr Villiers. At this moment, if the farmers had their own way, there is scarcely a county in England in which Mr Bright would not be the farmers' candidate, from having made the abatement of the game nuisance his peculiar question. But hear again the 'farmers' friends;' can any rational man avoid laughing at the following passage: –

'No man living can tell the effect which a free importation of corn will have on agricultural prices. But as for the *selfish and cruel maxim of 'buying in the cheapest and selling in the dearest market,' yet a little while and that maxim must be proved impracticable, or must prove itself deadly.* No private individual can carry it out without sacrificing to it all the domestic affection and all the kindly charities of life, no nation can carry it out without such horrible oppression of the poor as must inevitably be followed by national convulsion. As for the minister who has asserted this maxim, we behold him now without his office and without his party.'

A farmer sends to the fens for his seed oats where they are cheap, and sends his wheat to Mark lane where it is dear, and he is now told by his political advisors that that very ordinary operation is 'impracticable' or 'deadly!!!' How the few who have faith in 17 Bond street must stare at the announcement of such a creed. Then they are to 'wait in cautious neutrality.'

'All is not lost: many, very many, of those who believed that we must embark on this fearful venture, are yet most reluctant to see the agricultural interest lowered from the political or social position it has hitherto occupied, and those men will labour earnestly with us in the maintenance of that position. Do not let us reject their aid – we have formidable enemies; we need all our friends; meanwhile, let us support those who have proved themselves true to us; and, where we have been betrayed, let us look out for men whose hearts, to use a farmer's phrase, 'are in the right place.' Pledges we have seen shamelessly violated; and a course of action may, we know, be wise or unwise, according to time and circumstances; *but a stern hostility to a vicious and dangerous system of political economy, an earnest recognition of the rights of British agriculture, and an uncompromising assertion of these rights – these are what our yeomen must now look for.*'

How darkly grand; how sublimely obscure. It is scarcely necessary to express a hope that no rational farmer or landowner will be influenced by such trash, or induced to turn aside from the straight path of practical improvement to follow the political Will-o'-the-wisp the centrals of No. 17 have produced.

COPYRIGHTS AND PERMISSIONS

'Commerce with France. Observations on, Office' ([*c.* late 1785]), PRO, BT 6/111/4. Reproduced with permission from the National Archives (Kew, Surrey).

Minutes of the Committee of Trade, 14 March 1786, Liverpool Papers, BL, Add. MS 38389, fols 271–5. Reproduced with permission from the British Library, London.

William Eden to Robert Liston, 27 September 1786; Ralph Woodford to Robert Liston, 24 October 1786; Ralph Woodford to Robert Liston, 29 December 1786, Liston Papers, National Library of Scotland, MS 5545, fols 84–5, 118–19, 151–2. Reproduced with permission from the Trustees of the National Library of Scotland.

Daniel Hailes to the Marquis of Carmarthen, 25 October 1786, PRO, FO 27/18/20. Reproduced with permission from the National Archives (Kew, Surrey).

George Sinclair to Henry Dundas, 9 November 1796, Melville Papers, National Archives of Scotland, GD51/1/393. Reproduced with permission.

James Stephen to Spencer Perceval, 5 December 1807; James Stephen to Spencer Perceval, 23 May 1808, Perceval Papers, BL, Add. MS 49183, fols 25–8, 58–9. Reproduced with permission from the British Library, London.

Lord Palmerston to the Earl of Minto, 17 January 1834, Minto Papers, National Library of Scotland, MS 12021, fols 172–5. Reproduced with permission from the Trustees of the National Library of Scotland.

Richard Cobden to John Norton, 23 August 1838; Richard Cobden to George Wilson, 25 September 1841, Cobden Papers, West Sussex Record Office, CP 43, 59. By courtesy of the Governors of Dunford House and with acknowledgement to the County Archivist, West Sussex Record Office. By courtesy of the National Council of YMCAs, Trustees of the Cobden Estate. Copyright © Elizabeth Cobden Boyd. Reproduced with permission.

– 395 –

Lord Palmerston to the Earl of Minto, 27 December 1845, Minto Papers, National Library of Scotland, MS 11810, fols 124–7. Reproduced with permission from the Trustees of the National Library of Scotland.

Richard Cobden to William Rathbone, 2 February 1846, Paget Papers, Leicestershire Record Office, DE 1274/10. By courtesy of the National Council of YMCAs, Trustees of the Cobden Estate. Copyright © Elizabeth Cobden Boyd. Reproduced with permission.

For Product Safety Concerns and Information please contact our EU representative GPSR@taylorandfrancis.com Taylor & Francis Verlag GmbH, Kaufingerstraße 24, 80331 München, Germany

Printed and bound by CPI Group (UK) Ltd, Croydon, CR0 4YY
08/05/2025
01864526-0005